ARBITRATION INSIGHTS

International Arbitration Law Library

Series Editor Dr. Julian D.M. Lew QC

In the series *International Arbitration Law Library* this book,
*Arbitration Insights – Twenty Years of the Annual Lecture of the School of
International Arbitration, Sponsored by Freshfields Bruckhaus Deringer*,
is the sixteenth title.

The titles published in this series are listed at the end of this volume

ARBITRATION INSIGHTS

Twenty Years of the Annual Lecture
of the School of International Arbitration,
Sponsored by Freshfields Bruckhaus Deringer

Edited by Julian D.M. Lew QC and Loukas A. Mistelis

 School of International Arbitration

 FRESHFIELDS BRUCKHAUS DERINGER

KLUWER LAW
INTERNATIONAL

A C.I.P. catalogue record for this book is available from the Library of Congress.

ISBN 90 411 2606 6

Published by:
Kluwer Law International
P.O. Box 316
2400 AH Alphen aan den Rijn
The Netherlands

Sold and distributed in North, Central and South America by:
Aspen Publishers, Inc.
7201 McKinney Circle
Frederick, MD 21704
United States of America

Sold and distributed in all other countries by:
Turpin Distribution Services Ltd
Stratton Business Park
Pegasus Drive
Biggleswade
Bedfordshire SG18 8TQ
United Kingdom

Printed on acid-free paper

FOREWORD

The School of International Arbitration, Centre for Commercial Law Studies, Queen Mary University of London, established in 1986 an annual public lecture. The objective was and is to provide an eminent figure in international arbitration a platform on which to explore or raise new issues or existing problems of interest on different aspects of international arbitration and to offer his or her insights.

In 1987 Freshfields (now Freshfields Bruckhaus Deringer), endowed this annual lecture. The School's Annual Lecture is now well known as the Freshfields Arbitration Lecture. A pattern has emerged according to which lecturers alternate as coming from England or from overseas and if from overseas alternating between common and civil law backgrounds.

The lecture series is now well established on the arbitration agenda and has confirmed the interaction between theory and practice that the School has pursued since its inauguration.

Most of the twenty lectures have been published before, in *Arbitration International, International and Comparative Law Quarterly*, or in *Arbitration*. ICLQ This volume brings together the previously published lectures – with endnotes and updates, where necessary – and two of the three unpublished lectures as well an overarching introduction and a preface. The original style of the lectures and/or their publication has been maintained.

Particular thanks are due to Freshfields Bruckhaus Deringer for the continuing and generous support they have provided over the years to the lecture series and this publication. In the twenty years, Martin Hunter, Nigel Rawding and, more recently, Geoff Nicholas have coordinated the support and organization of the lectures with the assistance of Sue Harper, Bettina Horn and Julie Hudson from

Freshfields and Sandra Baird from the School of International Arbitration. Fan Yang, a research student at the School of International Arbitration, Centre for Commercial Law Studies, provided the necessary editorial assistance.

As always, it has been a pleasure to work with Kluwer Law International on the project. Our publishers, Bas Kniphorst and Vincent Verschoor, have shown patience as deadlines were drawing close. Their encouragement and support are much appreciated.

Julian D M Lew QC
Visiting Professor

Head, School of International
Arbitration

Loukas A Mistelis
Clive M Schmitthoff Professor of
Transnational Law and Arbitration
Director of Studies, School of
International Arbitration

2 September 2006

TABLE OF CONTENTS

Chapter 3
The Future of Arbitration: Flexibility or Rigidity   47
Giorgio Bernini

Chapter 4
The Problem of Delay in Arbitration   63
Lord Bingham

Chapter 5
Punitive Damages in Arbitration   81
E. Allan Farnsworth

Chapter 9
Streamlining Arbitral Proceedings: Some Techniques of the Iran-United States Claims Tribunal   153
Howard M. Holtzmann

Chapter 10
'Tell It to the Judge – But Only if You Must'   169
Arthur L. Marriott QC

Chapter 11
May the Majority of an International Arbitral Tribunal be Impeached? 201
Stephen M. Schwebel

Chapter 12
'Pastures New' (Review of Arbitration Act 1996)   213
Kenneth Rokison QC

Chapter 13
Does the World Need Additional Uniform Legislation on Arbitration   223
Gerold Herrmann

Chapter 17
Arbitration's Protean Nature: The Value of Rules and the Risk

*Jan Paulsson**

PREFACE

The floating garden of international arbitration is assuredly not as glamorous a venue as we might think it deserves to be, yet it can boast of one glittering event which has become as much a part of our little world as the Oscars have come to epitomize Hollywood. Deep in the gloom of November London, of a late afternoon within hailing distance of Guy Fawkes' Day, one can depend on the best and the brightest – past, present and future – to set aside their quotidian tasks and gather *en masse* for this lecture. Some years ago, a visiting outsider, namely the senior partner of the law firm which gives the event its name (a man who knew boardrooms better than courtrooms), attending as a symbolic host, expressed his astonishment at the number of senior judges and barristers – familiar to him only from the media – who bestirred themselves to come and listen passively to a lengthy lecture about a minor discipline of the legal profession.

A lengthy old-fashioned lecture it remains, quite out of style when compared to the Tylney Hall format which has now irresistibly spread around the arbitral planet, in tune perhaps with the prevailing ethos of cyberspace agora; and yet the crowd returns, replenished and rejuvenated each year by a phalanx of eager students very likely to pronounce the subject to be the most fascinating on their curriculum.

Scholars and practitioners may quickly accept invitations to jet off to conferences here and there to join an array of panellists and deliver one of a number of 'papers', but the most elementary instinct of self-preservation would cause even the most shining of illuminati to think twice about presenting themselves before this little army of cogniscenti and aficionados – to offer themselves not as the

* Joint Head, Public International Law Group and Head, International Arbitration Group, Freshfields Bruckhaus Deringer, Paris; President, LCIA.

Julian D.M. Lew and Loukas A Mistelis (eds), Arbitration Insights, xvii-xviii
© 2007 Kluwer Law International. Printed in the Netherlands

main event, but the *only* event, expected to hold attention and fill the better part of an hour with something meaningful.

Unsurprisingly, lecturers in this setting, having accepted the challenge, tend to rise to the challenge and produce something worth recording. And so the purpose of the present volume is to save this treasure trove of insights lest they be lost in the sands of time (which as you surely know, dear reader, are in truth *quicksands*).

The traditional pattern has been to alternate Londoners and visitors, and the podium has been occupied by a truly remarkable series of orators. True enough, some of the lectures are dated. Professor Farnsworth's delivery on punitive damages in arbitration (1990) will not suffice for someone seeking to ascertain the legal position today. But there are few better sources of understanding the contours, the context, and the antecedents of the issue. Veterans of these events will have their own favourites. But surely no one present will forget the unique performance of Gerold Herrmann (1998), then (officially) Secretary of UNCITRAL and (unofficially) the godfather of the Model Law, who performed the miracle of delivering at once the longest, the most substantive, and the most side-splittingly hilarious of all these lectures. (And perhaps the most obvious cause for regret that there will never, alas, be a DVD, since the exquisitely Hermannesque asides are not captured by the text – quite possibly censored by the author himself.) And equally unforgettable will be the prodigious scholarship of Johnny Veeder (1999), coupled with a restless and unconventional mind, leading the audience into utterly unexpected directions, seeming historical odds and ends, only to reveal grand patterns in a greater tapestry, and to bring us all to perceive a larger project, to experience a transcendent recognition that *this* is why we have chosen to labour in our demanding vineyard; *this* is why we are satisfied with the struggles of our 'minor discipline'.

Paris, May 2006

ACKNOWLEDGMENTS

The School of International Arbitration and Freshfields Bruckhaus Deringer have given their permission for the lectures to be published in leading journals. Seventeen lectures were published before. The following list acknowledges the original publication of chapters;

The second lecture (chapter 2) by Lady Fox, 'States and the Undertaking to Arbitrate', was first published in 37 *ICLQ* 1-29 (1988).

The fourth lecture (chapter 4) by Lord Bingham, 'The Problem of Delay in Arbitration', was first published in 56(3) *Arbitration* 164-175 (1990).

The fifth lecture (chapter 5) by E. Allan Farnsworth, 'Punitive Damages in Arbitration', was first published in 7(1) *Arbitration International* 3-15 (1991).

The sixth lecture (chapter 6) by Sir Roy Goode, 'The Adaptation of English Law to International Commercial Arbitration', was first published in 8(1) *Arbitration International* 1-15 (1992).

The seventh lecture (chapter 7) by Albert Jan van den Berg, 'The Efficacy of Award in International Commercial Arbitration', was first published in 58(4) *Arbitration* 267-274 (1992).

The eighth lecture (chapter 8) by Lord Steyn, 'England's Response to the UNCITRAL Model Law of Arbitration', was first published in 60(3) *Arbitration* 184-193 (1994).

The ninth lecture (chapter 9) by Howard M. Holtzmann, 'Streamlining Arbitral Proceedings: Some Techniques of the Iran-United States Claims Tribunal', was first published in 11(1) *Arbitration International* 39-50 (1995).

The tenth lecture (chapter 10), by Arthur L. Marriott QC, 'Tell It to the Judge – But Only if You Must' was first published in 12(1) *Arbitration International* 1-25 (1996).

The eleventh lecture (chapter 11) by HE Judge Stephen M. Schwebel, 'May the Majority of an International Arbitral Tribunal be Impeached?', was first published in 13(2) *Arbitration International* 145-153 (1997).

The twelfth lecture (chapter 12) by Kenneth Rokison QC, '"Pastures New" (Review of Arbitration Act 1996)', was first published in 14(4) *Arbitration International* 361-368 (1998).

The thirteenth lecture (chapter 13) by Gerold Herrmann, 'Does the World Need Additional Uniform Legislation on Arbitration?', was first published in 15(3) *Arbitration International* 211-236 (1999).

The fourteenth lecture (chapter 14) by V.V. Veeder QC. 'Lloyd George, Lenin and Cannibals: The Harriman Arbitration', was first published in 16(2) *Arbitration International* 115-139 (2000).

The fifteenth lecture (chapter 15), by Pierre Mayer, 'Reflections on the International Arbitrator's Duty to Apply the Law', was first published in 17(3) *Arbitration International* 235-247 (2001)

The seventeenth lecture (chapter 17) by William W. Park, 'Arbitration's Protean Nature: The Value of Rules and the Risk of Discretion', was first published in 19(3) *Arbitration International* 279-301 (2003).

The eighteenth lecture (chapter 18) by Alan Redfern, 'Dissenting Opinions in International Commercial Arbitration: The Good, the Bad and the Ugly', was first published in 20(3) *Arbitration International* 223-242 (2004).

The nineteenth lecture (chapter 19), by Horacio Grigera Naón, 'Arbitration and Latin America: Progress and Setbacks', was first published in 21(2) *Arbitration International* 127-176 (2005).

The twentieth lecture (chapter 20), by Julian D.M. Lew QC, 'Achieving the Dream: Autonomous Arbitration?', was first published in 22(2) *Arbitration International* 179-203 (2006).

TABLE OF ABBREVIATIONS

Julian D,M.Lew and Loukas A. Mistelis (eds), Arbitration Insights, xxi-xxvi
© *2007 Kluwer Law International. Printed in the Netherlands*

IFCAI	International Federation of Commercial Arbitration Institutions
JCAA	Japan Commercial Arbitration Association
LCIA	London Court of International Arbitration
OECD	Organisation for Economic Co-operation and Development
PCA	Permanent Court of Arbitration (The Hague)
SCC	Stockholm Chamber of Commerce Arbitration Institute
SIAC	Singapore International Arbitration Centre
UNCITRAL	United Nations Commission for International Trade Law
UNIDROIT	International Institute for the Unification of Private Law
Vienna	Austrian Federal Economic Chamber in Vienna
WIPO	World Intellectual Property Organisation

GENERAL ABBREVIATIONS

AC	Law Reports, House of Lords (Appeal Cases)
ADRLJ	Arbitration and Dispute Resolution Law Journal
ALI	American Law Institute
All ER	All England Law Reports
Am J Comp L	American Journal of Comparative Law
Am J Int'l L	American Journal of International Law
Am Rev Int'l Arb	American Review of International Arbitration
Ann IDI	Annuaire de l'Institut de droit international
Arb Int	Arbitration International
Arbitration	Arbitration, Journal of the Chartered Institute of Arbitrators
ASA Bulletin	Swiss Arbitration Association Bulletin
Asian DR	Asian Dispute Review

ATF	Arrêts du Tribunal Fédéral Suisse
BGB	Bürgerliches Gesetzbuch (German Civil Code)
BGE	Entscheidungen des schweizerischen Bundesgerichts
BGHZ	Sammlung der Entscheidungen des Bundesgerichtshofs in Zivilsachen
BIT	Bilateral Investment Treaty
Boston U Int'l L J	Boston University International Law Journal
Brooklyn J Int'l L	Brooklyn Journal of International Law
BYBIL	British Yearbook of International Law
CA	Court of Appeal of England and Wales
CC	Code civil, codice civile, civil code
CCLS	Centre for Commercial Law Studies
CCP	Code of Civil Procedure
CISG	United Nations Convention on the International Sale Goods
CLR	Commonwealth Law Reports
Clunet	Journal de droit international
Columbia J Transnat'l L	Columbia Journal of Transnational Law
Con LR	Construction Law Reports
CPR	Civil Procedure Rules (England)
Disp Res J	Dispute Resolution Journal
Duke L J	Duke Law Journal
ECHR	European Convention on Human Rights
ECJ	Court of Justice of the European Communities
ECR	Report of Cases before the Court of Justice of the European Communities
EHRR	European Human Rights Reports
EJCL	Electronic Journal of Comparative Law
ER	English Reports
EWCA Civ	Neutral citation for England and Wales Court of Appeal civil division decisions
F 2d	The Federal Reporter Second Series
F 3d	The Federal Reporter Third Series

FAA	United States Federal Arbitration Act
FS	Festschrift
F Supp	Federal Supplement
Geo Wash J Int'l L & Eco	George Washington University Journal of International Law and Economics
Hastings Int'l & Comp L Rev	Hastings International and Comparative Law Review
HKHC	Hong Kong High Court
HL	House of Lords
IBA Rules	IBA Rules on the taking of Evidence in International Commercial Arbitration, 1999
ICC Bulletin	International Chamber of Commerce International Court of Arbitration Bulletin
ICJ	International Court of Justice
ICJ Rep	International Court of Justice Reports
ICJ YB	International Court of Justice Yearbook
ICLQ	International and Comparative Law Quarterly.
ICSID Rev-FILJ	ICSID Review – Foreign Investment Law Journal
IECL	International Encyclopaedia of Comparative Law
InsO	Insolvenz Ordnung
Int ALR	International Arbitration Law Review
Int'l Bus Law	International Business Lawyer
Int'l Law	International Lawyer
ILA	International Law Association
ILM	International Legal Materials
ILR	International Law Reports
IPRax	Praxis des internationalen Privat- und Verfahrensrechts
Iran-US CTR	Iran-US Claims Tribunal Reports
JBL	Journal of Business Law
J Int'l Arb	Journal of International Arbitration.
Law & Policy in Int'l Bus	Law & Policy in International Business

Lloyd's Rep	Lloyd's Law Reports
LNTS	League of Nations Treaty Series
Louisiana L Rev	Louisiana Law Review
Loy LA Int'l & Comp LJ	Loyola Los Angeles International and Comparative Law Journal
Mealey's IAR	Mealey's International Arbitration Reports
Michigan J Int'l L	Michigan Journal of International Law
Minn L Rev	Minnesota Law Review
Model Law	UNCITRAL Model Law on International Commercial Arbitration adopted 21 June 1985
MR	Master of the Rolls
NCPC	French Code of Civil Procedure (Nouveau Code de Procedure Civile)
New York Convention	1958 New York Convention on the Recognition and Enforcement of Foreign Arbitral Awards
NY	New York
NYAD	New York Appellate Division
NYLJ	New York Law Journal
NY L Sch J Int'l & Comp L	New York Law School Journal of International and Comparative Law
OJ	Official Journal of the European Communities
OLG	Oberlandesgericht
PC	Privy Council
PECL	Principles of European Contract Law
PIL	(Swiss) Private International Law
QBD	Queen's Bench Division
RCADI	Recueil des Cours de l'Académie de Droit International de la Haye / Collected Courses of the Hague Academy of International Law
RDAI/IBLJ	Revue de droit des affaires internationales / International Business Law Journal
Rep	Report
Rev Arb	Revue de l'arbitrage

Rev crit dip	Revue critique de droit international privé
Rome Convention	EC (Rome) Convention on the Law Applicable to Contractual Obligations 1980
SchiedsVZ	Zeitschrift für Schiedsverfahren
S Ct	Supreme Court of the United States
SDNY	Southern District of New York
SIA	School of International Arbitration, Queen Mary University of London
Stanford J Int'l L	Stanford Journal of International Law
Texas Int'l LJ	Texas International Law Journal
Tulane L Rev	Tulane Law Review
U Cin L Rev	University of Cincinnati Law Review
U Ill L Rev	University of Illinois Law Review
UKPC	Neutral citation for decisions of the Privy Council
UNCITRAL Notes	UNCITRAL Notes on Organizing Arbitral Proceedings
Unif L Rev	Uniform Law Review
UNTS	United Nations Treaty Series
Vanderbilt L Rev	Vanderbilt Law Review
WAMR	World Arbitration and Mediation Report
Washington Convention	Washington Convention on the Settlement of Investment Disputes between States and Nationals of other States 1965
WIPO Expedited Rules	WIPO Expedited Rules
WL	Westlaw
WLR	The Weekly Law Reports
WTAM	World Trade and Arbitration Materials
Yale LJ	Yale Law Journal
YBCA	Yearbook of Commercial Arbitration
ZPO	German Code of Civil Procedure (ZPO)

Loukas Mistelis[*]

CHAPTER 1

ARBITRATION INSIGHTS: EVOLUTION AND THEMES

I. THE ESTABLISHMENT AND HISTORY OF THE LECTURE SERIES

1-1   The School of International Arbitration was established in 1985[1] within the Centre for Commercial Law Studies, at Queen Mary, University of London, to develop international arbitration as a self-luminous academic research subject, to promote advanced teaching and learning in the theory and practice affecting the law of international arbitration, to contribute to the development of this law and to train professionals interested and involved in the arbitration process. The School is a continually developing academic entity, centrally placed in the interface of policy, theory and practice, and is widely acknowledged as the leading academic research centre[2] on international arbitration in the world.[3]

---

[*]   Clive M Schmitthoff Professor of Transnational Commercial Law and Arbitration; Director, School of International Arbitration, Centre for Commercial Law Studies, Queen Mary University of London.

[1]   While there has been teaching of international arbitration at Queen Mary, University of London, since 1982, the School was only created in 1985 and has been headed since by Professor Julian D M Lew QC. The School was launched with a major conference, the proceedings of which were edited and published in a celebrated volume. See Julian D M Lew (ed), *Contemporary Problems in International Arbitration* (CCLS and Kluwer 1986).

[2]   The most recent empirical research conducted by the School looked into the attitudes and choices of multinational corporations towards international arbitration. The findings are published in Loukas Mistelis, 'International Arbitration – Corporate Attitudes and Practices. 12 Perceptions Tested: Myths, Data and Analysis. Empirical Research Report', 15 *American Review of International Arbitration* 525-593 (2004) [published in June 2006] and a short version is accessible at www.pwc.com/arbitrationstudy.

[3]   The 20th anniversary of the School was celebrated with a major international conference; the contributions presented to the conference were edited and published in Loukas A Mistelis and Julian D M Lew (eds), *Pervasive Problems in International Arbitration* (Kluwer Law International 2006), while the contributions (by Loukas Mistelis, Jack Coe, Emmanuel Jolivet, Doug Jones, Christopher Drahozal, Eric Bergsten and Patricia Shaughnessy) to the workshop on

1-2   The approach of the School from the outset was to recognise that arbitration is an international system of dispute resolution. Given that the disputing parties, the subject matter of their disputes, their legal representatives and the arbitrators entrusted with the settlement of disputes, invariably transcended national boundaries, arbitration is increasingly a transnational process, regulated by and following international and non-national rules and practices.[4]

1-3   In the mid 1980s most saw international arbitration as a branch of another legal discipline: arbitration was either connected with civil procedure, occasionally a subject tied to and regulated by national procedural codes and mainly taught and practiced by proceduralists;[5] or a subject associated with private international law and the so-called *droit des affaires internationales* (international business law).[6] A leading arbitration authority noted that back in 1985 there was 'lack of international and comparative outlook'.[7]

1-4   An additional problem related to the fact that arbitration was treated as an esoteric subject, practised by a few eccentric and cosmopolitan legal practitioners with an international flair (which often meant that they were fluent in a second language or that they have studied abroad). While arbitration was practiced by bigger law firms with strong international litigation practices there were hardly any specialist arbitration practice groups or departments in most major law firms.

1-5   In the last twenty years there has been a greater acceptance of and resort to arbitration for international business, disputes of all kinds and under all systems.[8] Whilst it remains difficult or even impossible to determine exact numbers the figures given by the major institutions suggest continuous growth in numbers.[9] The situation is similar with investment arbitration numbers. Although established in 1966, by 1985 only a couple arbitrations had been filed under the

---

teaching, research and training in international arbitration were published in 22(2) *Arb Int* 243-336 (2006).

[4]   See Julian D M Lew, 'Introductory Remarks', in Mistelis and Lew (eds), ibid, at para 2.

[5]   See, for example, the regulation of arbitration in the German *Zivilprozessordnung* (Law of Civil Procedure), the Greek Code of Civil Procedure and the situation in Japan. In France arbitration is regulated in the Code de Procedure Civile but is taught and practiced by both proceduralists and conflicts (private international) lawyers

[6]   See, for example, the Swiss Private International Law Act which contains provisions relating to international arbitration and the practice in Switzerland and other countries of private international lawyers specialising in the field of arbitration.

[7]   Pierre Lalive, 'International Arbitration – teaching and research', in Julian D M Lew (ed), *Contemporary Problems in International Arbitration* (CCLS and Kluwer 1986) 16, at 17.

[8]   Loukas Mistelis, supra note 2, at p 527.

[9]   Ibid, at p 528.

ICSID Rules. There were not many Bilateral Investment Treaties, and other regional multilateral dedicated investment treaties were not in the landscape.

1-6 International arbitration is nowadays well established at the junction of national, international and conflicts laws, public and private law and substantive and procedural law. The international arbitration market has been growing over the last 10 years in line with the growth in international trade, and is likely to continue to do so. Arbitration has become a more prominent area of legal practice and a distinct academic subject in many universities, typically at post-graduate level.[10] Many new academic programmes have been introduced all over the world, most of which are taught in English. A number of very good commentaries on international commercial arbitration, textbooks and practitioner handbooks have emerged in recent years.[11] However, it is difficult for a single book to address in sufficient depth the many complex, interesting and frequently evolving issues arising out of commercial and investor-state arbitrations.

1-7 In 1986 the School established an annual lectureship. The public lecture aimed at providing an opportunity to an eminent arbitration lawyer to address the arbitration community and to express views, ideas and insights on intriguing pervasive or emerging. The first lecture in 1986 was delivered by Professor Pierre Lalive on the subject of 'State Enterprise, Force Majeure and Good Faith in International Arbitration'. In 1987 Freshfields (now Freshfields Bruckhaus Deringer), endowed this annual lecture, which in that year was delivered by Lady Fox on the topic of 'States and the Undertaking to Arbitrate'. In 2005 the 20th lecture was delivered by Professor Julian D M Lew QC. The School's Annual

---

[10] For example, the School of International Arbitration, Queen Mary University of London, the oldest specialist arbitration research centre, currently has 24 PhD students and 200 students on the LLM and Diploma programmes. More than 10,000 international arbitrations take place every year and the 12 best known arbitration institutions administer over 3000 cases annually.

[11] See, for example, in the last five years, Gary Born, *International Commercial Arbitration – Commentary and Materials* (Transnational Publishers / Kluwer Law International 2nd Edition) 2001; Thomas Carbonneau, *Cases and Materials on Commercial Arbitration and Documentary Supplement,* 3rd edition (Juris Publishing) 2003; *Fouchard, Gaillard, Goldman on International Commercial Arbitration* (ed. by Emmanuel Gaillard and John Savage), Kluwer Law International 1999; Julian D M Lew, Loukas A Mistelis and Stefan Kröll, *Comparative International Commercial Arbitration*, Kluwer Law International 2003; Jean-François Poudret et Sébastien Besson, *Droit comparé de l'arbitrage international,* (Bruylant, LGDJ & Schulthess 2002); Alan Redfern & Martin Hunter with Nigel Blackaby and Constantine Partasides, *Law and Practice of International Commercial Arbitration* (Sweet & Maxwell 4th edition) 2004; Tibor Várady, John J Barceló, III, Arthur T von Mehren, *International Commercial Arbitration – A Transnational Perspective* (West Group – American Casebook Series, 3rd edition) 2006.

Lecture is now well known as the Freshfields Arbitration Lecture. Seventeen of the twenty lectures have been published, usually in *Arbitration International* but also in the *International and Comparative Law Quarterly* and in *Arbitration*. This volume brings together the published lectures – with adequate endnotes and updates, where necessary – and two of the three unpublished lectures as well this overarching introduction and a preface by Jan Paulsson. The original style of the lectures and/or their publication has been maintained.

1-8 The lecture series has confirmed the interaction between theory and practice that the School has pursued since its inauguration. In addition the series is a testament of School's policy of ensuring a comparative and international approach to the study and research of international arbitration: a pattern has been to alternate between UK and overseas based speakers (and in the cases of overseas based speakers alternating between common law and civil law), balancing out views and attitudes towards arbitration.

II. THE THEMES OF THE LECTURE SERIES

1-9 In most cases the lecturers were free to select their topic and/or theme. However, some themes have been recurring in the lectures:
- States and state enterprises in arbitration, including investment arbitration (Lalive 1986, Fox 1987, Veeder 1990, Lauterpacht 2001);
- National regulation of arbitration with particular focus on the English Arbitration Act and the UNCITRAL Model Law (Goode 1991, Steyn 1993, Rokison 1997, Herrmann 1998, Grigera Naon 2004);
- Arbitration proceedings (Bernini 1988, Holtzmann 1994, Schwebel 1996, Redfern 2003);
- Availability of remedies (Farnsworth 1990);
- Efficiency of arbitration process (Bingham 1989, van den Berg 1992, Marriott 1995);
- Impact of rules of law and national law on arbitration tribunals and the arbitration process (Mayer 2000, Park 2002, Lew 2005).

1-10 While the lectures will be presented in the chronological order in which they were delivered, it is worth while of exploring the recurring themes in this introduction. The reader of this collection can follow these threads and draw on conclusions from the insights delivered by the lecturers and contributors to this volume.

A. States and State Enterprises in Arbitration

1-11 In the last twenty years the arbitration community has witnessed a major expansion of investor-state arbitration. Hence it should come as no surprise that there have been four pioneering lectures on the topic, all of them well received by the fortunate audiences and the readership of the two of them that have been published prior to this volume.

1-12 The first lecture under this theme was delivered by Professor Pierre Lalive in 1986 (being also the first lecture in the series). Professor Lalive gave his lecture the title: 'State Enterprise, Force Majeure and Good Faith in International Arbitration'. While the lecture has never been published, the theme has been explored by the lecturer in a number of published articles.[12] The lecture explored the observance of good faith in transactions and disputes involving states and state enterprises and also assessed the impact of force majeure.

1-13 The second seminal lecture of this theme was delivered by Lady Fox in 1987 under the title 'States and the Undertaking to Arbitrate'.[13] The chapter examines the two bases of authority for arbitration (i.e. party autonomy and judicial supervision of the State) and how they apply to a State as party to interstate arbitration and to international commercial arbitration with a private party. The topic is dynamic and Lady Fox has provided an addendum to the original lecture and publication included in chapter 2.

1-14 Fourteen years later the third lecture in the same theme was delivered by Professor Sir Elihu Lauterpacht. The title was 'Arbitration between States and Investors: Retrospect and Prospect'. The lecture has never been published before, but it is included in this volume as chapter 16. Professor Lauterpacht discusses State-investor arbitration in the second half of the twentieth century with particular focus on the major changes in the number and character of the tribunals in which such arbitration can take place, the development in the law to be applied and the associated questions of review of the substance of arbitral decisions and their implementation.

---

[12] See, for example, Pierre Lalive, 'Arbitration with Foreign States and State-Controlled Entities: Some Practical Questions', in Julian D M Lew (ed), *Contemporary Problems in International Arbitration* (CCLS and Kluwer Law International 1986), 295.

[13] The lecture was first published in 37 *ICLQ* 1-29 (1988).

1-15 The fourteenth lecture looked at arbitration involving states and investors from a historical perspective and was delivered by Johnny Veeder QC. The erudite lecture explored a significant arbitration and had the intriguing title 'Lloyd George, Lenin and Cannibals'.[14] Mr Veeder conducted research on previously publicly unavailable sources and discusses the 1928 Harriman Arbitration, brought up against the USSR.

B. National Regulation of Arbitration

1-16 The decade between 1986 and 1996 saw enormous changes to national arbitration law. UNCITRAL adopted and published in 1985 the Model Law in International Commercial Arbitration. Thereafter there was much discussion about its adoption and about whether English law should be adapted to international standards set by the Model Law. Indeed many countries have enacted the Model Law[15] while interestingly enough some of the arbitration superpowers have designed different laws.[16] These issues were explored in several lectures

1-17 The first lecture on the national and international regulation of arbitration was delivered by Professor Sir Roy Goode in 1991. The title was 'The Adaptation of English law to International Commercial Arbitration'.[17] Sir Roy examined in the beginning of the 1990s whether and to what extent English law accommodated international commercial arbitration. At the same time he highlighted the principles and rules that are fit for international commercial arbitration, largely inspired by the UNCITRAL Model Law. Reception of such

---

[14] The lecture was first published in 16(2) *Arbitration International* 115-139 (2000).

[15] Almost 50 countries have enacted legislation incorporating the Model Law. These include Australia, Azerbaijan, Bahrain, Bangladesh, Belarus, Bulgaria, Canada, Chile, in China: Hong Kong Special Administrative Region, Macau Special Administrative Region; Croatia, Cyprus, Egypt, Germany, Greece, Guatemala, Hungary, India, Iran (Islamic Republic of), Ireland, Japan, Jordan, Kenya, Lithuania, Madagascar, Malta, Mexico, New Zealand, Nigeria, Norway, Oman, Paraguay, Peru, the Philippines, Republic of Korea, Russian Federation, Singapore, Spain, Sri Lanka, Thailand, Tunisia, Ukraine, within the United Kingdom of Great Britain and Northern Ireland: Scotland; in Bermuda, overseas territory of the United Kingdom of Great Britain and Northern Ireland; within the United States of America: California, Connecticut, Illinois, Oregon and Texas; Zambia, and Zimbabwe.

[16] England has adopted a new Act in 1996, France has the new Code of Civil Procedure 1981, Switzerland the new Swiss Private International Law Act 1987 and Sweden the Swedish Arbitration Act 1998. China has the 1994 Arbitration Act with some amendments while in the US the main law is the Federal Arbitration Act 1925.

[17] The lecture was first published in 8(1) *Arbitration International* 1-15 (1992).

principles and consideration for civil law thinking would strengthen English law and put England at the forefront of the development of international commercial arbitration and the evolution of transnational commercial law.

1-18 Lord Steyn delivered the eighth lecture in 1993 under the heading 'England's Response to the Model Law of Arbitration'.[18] Lord Steyn, at the time Chairman of the Departmental Advisory Committee on Arbitration Law, pointed out that the UNCITRAL Model Law should be used as a yardstick by which to judge the quality of then existing arbitration legislation and to improve it. He also illustrated that the draft arbitration bill at the time had the Model Law as its single most important influence.

1-19 The twelfth lecture was delivered by Ken Rokison QC in 1997 under the title 'Pastures New' (Review of Arbitration Act 1996). It was the first main lecture to discuss the then newly adopted 1996 Arbitration Act.[19] The Act was designed to consolidate the statutory law of arbitration and the related practice into one statute. However, the Act was not a mere restatement of the law; some modifications of substance were made: a fundamental alteration of the balance of power between arbitrators and the courts, and an unprecedented flexibility has been given to the parties and the tribunal as regards the conduct of the arbitration. Mr Rokison concluded with his assessment of the Act indicating that the Act alone cannot guarantee that arbitration in London will continue to flourish; the challenge was for the courts and the arbitration community to safeguard the objectives of the Act.

1-20 Dr Gerold Herrmann gave the thirteenth lecture. The title was 'Does the World Need Additional Legislation on Arbitration?'[20] The then Secretary General of UNCITRAL delivered a most entertaining and insightful lecture surveying various proposals for addenda to existing arbitration legislation and whether legislative treatment of some or all of the suggested issues is desirable and feasible. Issues examined include arbitration agreement and in particular the questions of writing and arbitrability, consolidation and other multiparty matters, powers and duties of arbitrators, procedural issues, court assistance, and reinforcing recognition and enforcement of arbitration awards. He concluded that the world itself would decide whether it needs additional uniform legislation.

---

[18] The lecture was first published in 60(3) *Arbitration* 184-193 (1994).
[19] The lecture was first published in 14(4) *Arbitration International* 361-368 (1998).
[20] The lecture was first published in 15(3) *Arbitration International* 211-236 (1999).

7

1-21 Finally, Dr Horacio Grigera Naón delivered in 2004 the nineteenth lecture on 'Arbitration and Latin America: Progress and Setbacks'.[21] This significant lecture examined the historical evolution of arbitration in Latin America by looking at doctrine, legislation and court practice (including a full assessment of Calvo doctrine), He analysed the expansion of international commercial arbitration in the twentieth century as well as the role of political and socio-economic developments. He then provided an account of the present situation with particular focus on the efficacy of arbitration agreements and awards in Latin America. This insightful lecture sets standards for the assessment of progress in national and regional arbitration law and practice.

1-22 In the last twenty years there has been an undisputed reform élan relating to arbitration legislation that justified the attention lecturers gave on significant developments under the UNCITRAL Model Law, the 1996 English Arbitration Act and the evolution of arbitration in Latin America. Three more lectures (by Professors Mayer, Park and Lew) dealt with the impact of law and other standards in arbitration but are discussed below under the heading Arbitration and (Soft) Law.

C. Procedural Matters and Availability of Remedies

1-23 Procedure is one of the perennial problems of international arbitration. Styles and techniques of conducting arbitration hearings, safeguard of party autonomy, flexibility and tribunal discretion are importance procedural matters. However, the only universal principle is respect of due process, equal and fair treatment of the parties. Several lecturers decided to explore matters of procedure and to make insightful recommendations.

1-24 Professor Giorgio Bernini delivered the third lecture in 1988 under the heading 'The Future of Arbitration: Flexibility or Rigidity'. This lecture has never been published before and focussed on the fact that while arbitrators may have the scales of justice they would normally never have the sword, lacking coercive power. He argued that while the human factor (and ability of arbitrators) is possibly most important to arbitration and this alone can safegaurd the process without any need for increasingly detailed regulations.

---

[21] The lecture was first published in 21(2) *Arbitration International* 127-176 (2005).

1-25 Howard Holtzmann delivered the ninth lecture with the title 'Streamlining Arbitral Proceedings: Some Techniques of the Iran - United States Claims Tribunal'.[22] He looked at the concern over the slow pace of some arbitral proceedings and the need to improve the efficiency of arbitration. In particular, he discussed techniques used by the Iran-US Claims Tribunal, including the initiative of arbitrators to state in advance what evidence would be needed to establish prima facie proof of certain complex facts; the willingness of arbitrators to establish and enforce strict schedules for presentations by the parties during oral hearings; and the use of agendas or checklists for pre-hearing conferences to plan the proceedings.

1-26 HE Judge Stephen Schwebel, delivered in 1996 the eleventh lecture under the heading, 'May the Majority Vote of an International Arbitral Tribunal be Impeached?'[23] He examined the validity of international arbitration awards from the standpoint of the two cases of the International Court of Justice passing upon the validity of international awards and drew more general conclusions, also in relation to the loopholes of international commercial arbitration. He concluded that the judicial and the arbitration process 'is an exemplar of the wise dictum that the best must not be permitted to be the enemy of the good'.

1-27 In 2003 Alan Redfern delivered the eighteenth lecture with the title 'Dissenting Opinions in International Commercial Arbitration: the Good, the Bad and the Ugly'.[24] The starting point is that such opinions are not discouraged while they risk breaching the confidentiality of the tribunal's deliberations and also risk undermining the authority of the tribunal's award while adding little or nothing to the reputation of international commercial arbitration. Against this background he examined the practice and modern trends concluding that it would be too much to demand conformity from all arbitrators; but also that the time has come to enquire whether the present leniency towards dissenting opinions has gone too far.

1-28 The late Professor Allan Farnsworth delivered in 1990 the fifth lecture under the heading 'Punitive Damages in Arbitration'.[25] He asked at the outset about the sorts of relief that arbitrators may award and pointed out, as the New York Court of Appeals has affirmed that the 'remedies available in arbitration are

---

[22] The lecture was first published in 11(1) *Arbitration International* 39-50 (1995).
[23] The lecture was first published in 13(2) *Arbitration International* 145-153 (1997).
[24] The lecture was first published in 20(3) *Arbitration International* 223-242 (2004).
[25] The lecture was first published in 7(1) *Arbitration International* 3-15 (1991).

not confined to the traditional forms of law' and it is 'for the arbitrators to fashion the remedy appropriate to the wrong'.[26] He concluded that often the availability of remedies will be a matter for the drafter of the arbitration clause and that one should not automatically jump on the bandwagon of international public policy with the consequence that punitive damages will never be granted.

D. Efficiency of Arbitration Process

1-29 The control of the arbitration proceedings by the parties, the tribunal or indeed the law is an ongoing debate as is the question of finality and efficiency of arbitration awards. These critical matters are multi-facetted and while the lectures provide food for thought they are not intended to be the definitive answers; they merely provide profound insights for informed opinion. They also indicate the concern that arbitrators provide a service and that such a service ought to meet the needs of the business community, the users of the arbitration process.

1-30 Lord Bingham examined in the fourth lecture in 1989 a pervasive issue, 'The Problem of Delay in Arbitration'.[27] He suggested that the arbitrators should be encouraged and empowered to manage the process avoiding undue delays; he also pointed out that it should be permitted for parties to exclude such power either in the arbitration agreement or in any agreed upon institutional rules.

1-31 In 1992 Professor Albert Jan van den Berg delivered the seventh lecture entitled 'The Efficacy of Awards in International Commercial Arbitration'.[28] He looked at the destiny of various awards and discussed the regime governing setting aside of arbitration awards. He concluded after looking at developments in the early 1990s that the efficacy of awards is not in danger because of the availability of an action for setting aside an award in the country of origin, mostly because of the creeping unification effected through the wide adoption of the UNCITRAL Model Law creating progressively a system similar to that of the New York Convention.[29]

---

[26] *Paver & Wildfoerster v Catholic High School Association*, 38 N.Y.2d 669, 676, 677, 345 N.E.2d 565, 569 (1976).

[27] The lecture was first published in 56(3) *Arbitration* 164-175 (1990).

[28] The lecture was first published in 58(4) *Arbitration* 267-274 (1992).

[29] 1958 United Nations Convention on Recognition and Enforcement of Foreign Arbitral Awards now adopted by more than 135 states. See www.uncitral.org.

1-32 Arthur Marriott QC delivered the tenth lecture in 1995 under the heading 'Tell it to the judge – but only if you must'.[30] Marriott used the lecture to discuss the access to justice programme spearheaded by Lord Woolf and the debate for the modernisation the civil justice system, including the introduction and promotion of ADR. The lecture was indeed at the forefront of developments at the time and provides a significant record of the emergence of modern ADR in English law.

E. Impact of Law and Rules of Law on Arbitration Tribunals and the Arbitration Process

1-33 Finally another important theme relates to the autonomy of the arbitration process and the regulatory role, if any, of law and rules of law of national, international or transnational origin. This theme does not only have theoretical and philosophical dimensions; it also affects the determination (and application) or national laws, international laws and rules of law or equitable principles relevant to arbitration tribunals and the arbitration process.

1-34 Professor Pierre Mayer was the fifteen lecturer in 2000. His topic was 'Reflections on the international arbitrator's duty to apply the law'.[31] Several questions were raised: Do arbitrators and judges have the same relation to the law? Do arbitrators enjoy more freedom? Does their sense of equity and fairness play a greater role? Are arbitrators supposed to apply a conflict of laws rule? He concluded that the relation of the arbitrators to the law is more complex than the relation of the judges to the law. In general, international arbitrators enjoy a greater freedom, as an arbitrator is 'the sole master as regards the selection of the system … whose rules he will apply'. That said the arbitrator also has a 'professional duty … to comply with the law, and even to approach the law with respect'.

1-35 In 2002 Professor William (Rusty) Park delivered a lecture under the heading 'Arbitration's Protean Nature: the Value of Rules and the Risks of Discretion'.[32] He questioned the wisdom of unfettered arbitrator discretion. He particularly examined the importance of default procedural rules (for the avoidance of an apparent 'ad hoc justice' that could damage the perceived legitimacy of arbitration) and the feasibility of including a set of more precise

---

[30] The lecture was first published in 12(1) *Arbitration International* 1-25 (1996).
[31] The lecture was first published in 17(3) *Arbitration International* 235-247 (2001)
[32] The lecture was first published in 19(3) *Arbitration International* 279-301 (2003).

procedural protocols in institutional rules to apply unless parties expressly opt out of the default provisions. Such an approach would both confirm the autonomy of the arbitration process but would also contribute to the emergence of international arbitration practice.

1-36 Finally, Professor Julian Lew QC delivered the twentieth lecture in 2005. His title was 'Achieving the Dream: Autonomous Arbitration'.[33] He examined the concept of autonomous arbitration, not controlled by national law. In this regard he discussed the relevance and binding nature of internationally accepted practices, ideal and nightmare scenarios (with undue and damaging court and law intervention). He concluded that international arbitration is today an autonomous, largely self-regulating dispute resolution mechanism. In support he provided several examples from case law in various jurisdictions as well as an insightful approach to understanding international arbitration practice.

1-37 The lecture series has matured and become widely accepted in academic and professional circles. It is the largest annual arbitration lecture in the world and the audiences are getting bigger every year. This is entirely due to the insightful and engaging approach all first twenty lecturers have taken. They provide food for thought and further debate. This volume brings the first lectures together to provide for a reference book for a set of lectures delivered by a group of experts. This is a major legacy and we can only hope that the next twenty years of lectures will be of the same calibre.

---

[33] The lecture was first published in 22(2) *Arbitration International* 179-203 (2006).

Hazel Fox * **

CHAPTER 2

STATES AND THE UNDERTAKING TO ARBITRATE

I. INTRODUCTION

2-1 The institution of arbitration, on one view, derives its force from the agreement of the parties; on another view, from the State as supervisor and enforcer of the legal process. The contractual obligation of both parties enables the settlement process to override national differences in law and procedural obstacles which exist in local courts. On the other hand, a State's jurisdiction over its territory and nationals provides an independent supervision of the settlement process and effective enforcement of decisions made according to law: usually this exercise of jurisdiction is direct through the State's own courts, but in arbitration it is carried out through the alternative process of reference to an arbitrator and recognition and execution of the arbitral award.[1]

---

* Director of the British Institute of International and Comparative Law, formerly [editors' note: currently Honorary] Fellow of Somerville College, Oxford. This paper is based on the Freshfields lecture given, at the invitation of Professor R. M. Goode, Director, Centre for Commercial Law Studies, at Queen Mary College London on 8 June 1987. I am grateful to Professor Bin Cheng and Lawrence Collins for their comments on an early draft.

** [Editors' note: Lady Hazel Fox CMG QC, 4-5 Gray's Inn Square, is a Vice President of the British Institute of International and Comparative Law].

1 René David, *Arbitrage dans le commerce international* (1982, Eng. Translation 1985), pp. 78, 81. 'Arbitration and the justice of the courts should not be regarded as competitors doomed to be enemies, but rather as two institutions whose purpose is to cooperate for the sake of better justice: a satisfactory regime for arbitration cannot be imagined without some degree of co-operation with the courts, which are called to give assistance to, and also to exercise control over arbitration ... It is not clear in the case of international disputes as to which national courts will be called to settle any dispute which may arise. This factor may well justify the desire to be free from the particular constraints of national laws and lead us to analyse the award as being a product of the free will of the parties'.

For inter-State arbitration, J. H. Ralston, *Law and Procedure of International Tribunals* (1926); K. S. Carlston, *The Process of International Arbitration* (1946); J. L. Simpson and H. Fox,

2-2 These two bases, the autonomy of the parties and the judicial supervision of the State as sources of the authority of arbitration are given varying weight in national legal systems in relation to domestic arbitrations.[2] The great expansion of international commercial arbitration in the last ten years[3] is attributable to the successful harnessing of these two bases in the relatively simple machinery provided in the New York Convention on Recognition and Enforcement of Foreign Arbitral Awards of 1958.[4] By this Convention the agreement of the parties to arbitrate is given effect and the resulting award executed in an increasing number of countries by the legal systems of the States parties to that Convention. The two bases, however, continue to create uncertainty as to the ultimate foundation and source of authority and have produced tensions which are still in process of being resolved.

2-3 The theoretical dispute as to the legal possibility of a floating supranational arbitral award, in no way dependent on any local forum or law,[5] is one area of tension; another arises from conflicts between local courts and the arbitral tribunal as to jurisdiction and the applicable law to determine the capacity of the

---

International Arbitration, Law and Practice (1959). For international commercial arbitration, A. Jan van den Berg, *The New York Arbitration Convention of 1958* (1981); Craig, Park and Paulsson, *International Chamber of Commerce Arbitration* (1984); Redfern and Hunter, *Law and Practice of International Commercial Arbitration* (1986). See also Mustill and Boyd, *The Law and Practice of Commercial Arbitration in England* (1982).

[2] The Italian *arbitrato irrituale* is an extreme example of the autonomy of the parties; it is a contractual institution not subject to any of the formalities of the Italian Code of Civil Procedure and enforcement cannot be effected by an award but only on the basis of an action on the contract to arbitrate: A. Kassis, *Problémes de Base d l'Arbitrage, Vol. I, Arbitrage juridictionnel et arbitrage contractual* (1987). The statutory arbitration which is conducted before a tribunal whose jurisdiction derives not from the consent of the parties but the statute under which the dispute has arisen is an extreme example of the process totally subject to the judicial supervision of the State: Mustill and Boyde, idem, p. 2.

[3] From its foundation in 1919 to April 1987, of the 5,930 requests for arbitration filed with the International Chamber of Commerce, half were filed in the last 11 years. The current annual rate is about 300 cases a year with 659 pending as at January 1987. The London Court of Arbitration currently has about 60 cases a year, all being of an international character with at least one party being a non-UK national.

[4] (1959) U.N.T.S. No. 4739, p. 38. As of 31 Dec. 1986 71 States are signatories to the New York Convention.

[5] F. A. Mann, 'Lex Facit Arbitrum in International Arbitration', in *Liber Amicorum for Martin Domke* (1967), p.157; W. W. Park (1983) 32 I.C.L.Q. 21; P. Lalive (1976) Rev. de l'Arbitrage 155; J. Paulsson (1981) 30 I.C.L.O. 358, (1983) 32 I.C.L.Q. 53; W. L. Craig (1985) 1 Arbitration Int. 49; K. H. Bockstiegel (1984) 1 Jo. of Int. Arb. 223. See Donaldson MR in *Deutsche Schachtbau und Tiefbohrgesellschaft mbH* v. *Ras al Khai-mah National Oil Co.* [1987] 2 All E.R. 769 upholding the arbitrators' choice of 'internationally, accepted principles of law governing contractual relations' as the proper law.

parties to agree to arbitrate and the validity of the arbitration agreement.[6] Further conflicts arise in relation to powers of revision, annulment or appeal exercised by local courts over the arbitral award.[7] The extent to which the assistance of local courts is available, prior to the making of the award, to preserve assets for the subsequent performance of the award, is a further reflection of these tensions; in this situation, on the one hand, autonomy of the parties is asserted by prohibiting any application to a local court by either party to the arbitration for pre-award attachment measures (as is the case in an arbitration conducted under the ICSID Convention rules),[8] on the other, the enforcement powers of the State are made available through its courts to back up the effectiveness of the arbitration process (as the English court did in the *Rena K*).[9]

2-4 I propose to look at the working of these two sources of authority for arbitration as they apply to a State as party to inter-State arbitration and to international commercial arbitration with a private party. These problems are frequently addressed by a definition of the State so as to exclude State-trading entities and render the latter subject to the full rigours of private law. Another method is to distinguish activities of the State in the exercise of sovereign power, *de jure imperii*, from those of a commercial nature, performed in the market place, *de jure gestionis*. I propose, however, to address the problem in a broader, different way. I want to examine what obligations are invoked in the undertaking to arbitrate and to see if the content of these obligations is the same for the State as party to international arbitration (whether inter-State or commercial) as for the

---

[6] H.M. Holtzmann, 'Arbitration in the Courts: Partners in a System of International Justice' (1978) Rev. de l'Arbitrage 253; B. Goldmann in *ICC Court of Arbitration 60th Anniversary: A Look at the Future* (1984), p.257. The power of the arbitrator to rectify the arbitration agreement is also a controversial area, *Ashville Investments Ltd.* v. *Elmer Contractors* (1987) *The Times,* 29 May 1987, distinguishing *Crane* v. *Hegemann Harris Co. Inc.* [1939] 4 All E.R. 68.

[7] Recent legislation in the UK, France and Belgium has restricted recourse to local courts from international commercial arbitrations held in those countries. Schlosser, 'L'Arbitrage et les voies de recours' (1980) Rev. de L'Arbitrage 286; Stein and Wolman, 'International Commercial Arbitration in the 1980s: A Comparison of the Major Arbitral Systems' (1983) 38 Int. Lawyer 1685.

[8] Washington Convention on the Settlement of Investment Disputes between States and Nationals of other States 1965 (ICSID Convention) 575 U.N.T.S. 160, Art.26; *Guinea v. Maritime International Nominees (MINE)* (1985) 24 I.L:M. 1639 (Belgian court held no jurisdiction, because ICSID's jurisdiction was exclusive and lifted attachment order on Guinea's assets); also (1987) 26 I.L.M. 382 (Geneva Surveillance Authority on appeal similarly lifted attachment order against Guinea's assets); but cf. *Guinea and Soguipeche v. Atlantic Tritan Co.* (1987) 26 I.L.M. 373 where French Court of Cassation reversed Court of Appeal of Rennes and allowed provisional measures in the form of attachment.

[9] [1979] Q.B. 377.

private party to commercial arbitration. For the purposes of the discussion the term State is limited to the State as a direct party and excludes separately incorporated State-trading entities. Even without them the position is complicated by the fact that today the State may itself or through its departments of State be a party to commercial arbitration and that a private party may, by means of mixed claims commissions – and the Iran-US Claims Tribunal is the latest version – have its private claims taken up by the State and presented through an inter-State arbitration.

2-5 To illustrate the difference in a State's undertaking to arbitrate from that of a private party, two specific areas of law will be examined: first, the State's attitude to enforcement of the award and the relationship of its consent to arbitration to its consent to proceedings in local courts. Second, the extent to which a State's consent to arbitrate has binding effect on claims of its nationals submitted by the State to inter-State arbitration.

2-6 First, however, it is useful to consider in a general way the expectations of States concerning arbitration based on their use of the process over the last 50 years.

2-7 It is not possible in the space available to support the argument by examination of the various types of arbitration to which a State is party.

2-8 One area relates to arbitration cases with a private party concerning settlement of oil and other concessions and investment disputes such as the *ARAMCO, BP, TOPCO* and *LIAMCO* cases against Libya, *Kuwait v. Aminoil, Framatome* and *Elf Aquitaine*[10] and arbitrations held under the ICSID Convention.[11] Another relates to *ad hoc* inter-State arbitrations on boundary disputes in cases like *The Rann of Kutch*,[12] the *Argentine-Chile Frontier Award*,[13]

---

[10] *Saudi Arabia v. Aramco* (1963) 27 I.L.R. 117; *BP Exploration Company (Libya) Ltd v. The Government of the Libyan Arab Republic* (1973) 53 I.L.R. 297; *Texaco Overseas Petroleum Co. (TOPCO) and Californian Asiatic Oil Co. v. The Government of the Libyan Arab Republic* (1977) 53 I.L.R. 389; *Libyan American Oil Company (Lliamco) v. The Government of the Libyan Arab Republic* (1977) 62 I.L.R. 146; *Government of Kuwait v. Aminoil* 66 I.L.R., 519; *Framatome et al. v. Atomic Energy Organisation of Iran* published in French in Clunet (1984) Jo. Du D.I. 58 and in English under the title *Company Z and others (Republic of Zanadu) v. State Organisation ABC (Republic of Utopia)* (1983) VIII Y.B. Comm. Arb. 94; *Elf Acquitaine v. National Iranian Oil Co.* (1986) XI Y.B. Comm. Arb. 97.
[11] For up-to-date account see (1987) 4 ICSID News.
[12] The *Rann of Kutch Arbitration* (India and Pakistan) (1976) 50 I.L.R. 1.

or under dispute settlement clauses relating to the interpretation of treaties as the *French US Air Services* Arbitrations[14] or the *Young Loans Arbitration* in respect of German external debts after the Second World War.[15] However important and distinct in legal character these arbitrations may be, they do not contradict the general point to be made. They are relatively few, always of an optional consensual character and dependent on the continuing co-operation of the State in the arbitration proceedings if an effective award is to be achieved. There are also, of course, institutionalised methods of State arbitration for specific types of disputes, as for example human rights under the European Convention. In so far as these institutionalised methods involve automatic participation of the State, they constitute an exception and thereby a contrast to the general position now to be considered.

2-9 The expectations of States differ very considerably from those of private parties who resort to commercial arbitration. Here it may be as well to remember that, unlike the situation of the private party who chooses flexibility of the arbitral processes an escape from the strict requirements of litigation, arbitration in any form is for the State a loss of liberty, an acceptance of constraints from which it is otherwise free. All international proceedings are instituted by some form of arbitration clause. There is not today and never has been any general method of compulsory adjudication at the international level. The absence of a court with international competence over States was remedied by the establishment of the Permanent Court in 1921 after the First World War, now replaced by the International Court of Justice set up after the Second World War. But as is well known the jurisdiction of that Court was and still is dependent on the consent of the parties. (The complaint of the United States in the recent judgment on the merits in the case of the *Military and Paramilitary activities against Nicaragua* brought by Nicaragua against the United States was precisely on the ground that no consent by the parties to the Court's jurisdiction had been proved to exist; Nicaragua had never completed the process of ratification necessary to its acceptance of the compulsory jurisdiction of the ICJ, it forgot to send the necessary telegram and in any event the United States had expressly revoked its acceptance of the Court's jurisdiction as it was (or so it maintained)

---

[13] Award of HM Queen Elizabeth II for the Arbitration of a Controversy between the Argentine Republic and the Republic of Chile 24 Nov. 1966, HMSO 59-162 (1969); 16 U.N.R.I.A.A. 109.

[14] Case concerning the interpretation of the Air Transport Services Agreement between USA and France (1969) 16 U.N.R.I.A.A. 5; Case concerning the Air Service Agreement of 27 March 1946 (*US v. France*) (1979) 54 I.L.R. 304.

[15] *Young Loans Arbitration* (1980) 59 I.L.R. 494; See generally A. M. Stuyt, *Survey of International Arbitrations 1794-1970*.

free to do three days before the Nicaraguan application was filed. The International Court found against the United States on both grounds; it held that there was sufficient evidence of Nicaragua's consent and the purported revocation of US consent was ineffective.)[16]

2-10 The Optional clause, Article 36(2) of the Statute of the Court, introduced a form of compromissory clause; unilaterally a State might in advance confer by declaration some general or limited jurisdiction on the International Court which, if matched with a similar undertaking of another State, generated jurisdiction. The practice of attaching reservations to a State's acceptance of the Court's jurisdiction and the requirement of reciprocity of commitment have considerably reduced the effectiveness of the Optional clause as a basis for compulsory adjudication. The construction of the terms of States' acceptance of the Court's jurisdiction has led to a great increase in preliminary objections relating to the jurisdiction of the Court. Of the 71 cases before the Court from 22 May 1947 to 31 July 1985, 46 judgments and 18 advisory opinions have been given. In 27 of those preliminary objections were taken as to jurisdiction or admissibility. Nor has the number of States willing to accept in advance the Court's jurisdiction increased. As at 31 July 1985 only 46 States out of a possible 160 or so had accepted the compulsory jurisdiction of the ICJ and many of these attached reservations as to subject matter and duration. The United States has since withdrawn its acceptance.[17]

2-11 In many respects, therefore, the Permanent Court was – and its successor, the International Court, even more so, remains – an institutionalised arbitration tribunal rather than a court. It has the attributes of court in that it is a permanent institution staffed by judges drawn from countries other than those of the parties and has a statute and rules of procedure which the parties take no part in drafting. But it resembles an arbitration in that the parties initiate the proceedings by consent, are entitled each to have a judge of their own nationality, and in the absence of international machinery – the recourse to the Security Council under Article 94 of the UN Charter is too political a measure to be of much legal assistance – the execution of the judgment very much depends on the parties' good faith. A recent revision of the rules appears to increase the control of the parties; it is now possible for a dispute to be heard in a chamber of the Court, the

---

[16] *Nicaragua/US Military* and *Paramilitary Activities* (Jurisdiction and Admissibility) [1984] I.C.J. Rep. 392.
[17] (1985-6) I.C.J.Y.B. 60.

members of which are appointed by the Court after the President has ascertained the views of the parties as to its 'composition'.[18]

II. OBLIGATIONS CONTAINED IN THE UNDERTAKING TO ARBITRATE

2-12 So much then for States' general attitude towards arbitration of inter-State disputes: let us now examine more closely the content of the undertaking to arbitrate and the extent to which it depends on the two sources of authority, the autonomy of the parties and judicial supervision of the State. The undertaking to arbitrate in arbitrations between private parties involves three major commitments:

1. an immediate irrevocable obligation to refer the dispute to arbitration;
2. an obligation to settle the dispute by means of arbitration in preference and prior to resort to any other type of legal proceedings;
3. an obligation to honour the award of the arbitrator.[19]

A. Between Private Parties

2-13 In arbitration between private parties their good faith and voluntary commitment supports these obligations but, should one party disregard them, domestic courts provide procedures of varying effectiveness to enforce these obligations. A party who cannot get the other side willingly to arbitrate may when sued on the dispute seek the court's aid to direct the parties back to the arbitration. So far as English law is concerned, where the English court is satisfied that the agreement to arbitrate is valid according to its proper law it will give effect by staying local proceedings. Such a stay is mandatory where the agreement is not a domestic arbitration agreement within the meaning of section 1 of the Arbitration Act 1975. The same remedy is available to enforce the second undertaking where a party in disregard of the arbitration agreement seeks to commence legal proceedings in relation to the arbitrable issues and the court, by declarations as to the status of the agreement to arbitrate or as to the jurisdiction of the arbitrator and by supervision of the appointment and conduct of the arbitrator, will support the arbitrator in the carrying out of the arbitration. Finally, when the award is made a limited right of appeal is available and the court will by summary procedure or by action on the third undertaking, the promise to honour the award, convert the arbitral award into a judgment so that a

---

[18]   1978 Rules of the ICJ, Art. 17(2).
[19]   David, *op. cit. supra* n.1, at p.209; Mustill and Boyd, *op, cit, supra* n.1, at p.73

party may obtain its recognition and proceed to enforce it by all measures available for execution of judgments of the English court.[20]

B. Between States

2-14 The position with regard to the three commitments in the undertaking to arbitrate is rather different in international arbitrations between States. As has been seen there is not today and never has been any general method of compulsory adjudication at the international level. A State which makes the undertaking to enter into an arbitration knows that nothing but good faith and the general principle, *pacta sunt servanda*, holds it to the arbitration. There is generally no external authority which can make an order compelling the State to submit to the arbitration. Even where a jurisdiction clause is construed by the International Court to confer jurisdiction upon it, a State which disagrees may flout the order of the Court, as the United States has done in the *Nicaragua* case. No legal sanction follows under international or municipal law. The sole deterrent is the disapproval of world opinion.[21] Similarly, there is no method by which a State can be restrained from resorting to legal methods of settling a dispute other than the agreed arbitration. Indeed the second commitment to settle the dispute exclusively by arbitration may not be one recognised in international arbitration. The International Court of Justice, anxious to encourage parties to settle their disputes by whatever means they choose, has held parties to be free, whilst engaging in proceedings before the Court, at the same time to refer the dispute to the Security Council (*US Diplomatic and Consular Staff in Tehran* case),[22] to a regional process of settlement (the Contadora process in the *Nicaragua-US Military and Paramilitary* case)[23] and to bilateral discussion (*Aegean Sea Continental Shelf* case).[24] These are bilateral solutions pursued as

---

[20] Mustill and Boyd, *idem*, as to remedies for the first undertaking p.9 and Chap. 30, for second undertaking p.21 and Chap.32 and for the third undertaking p.30 and Chap.28.

[21] Schwarzenberger, *International law as applied by International Courts and Tribunals,* Vol. IV, *International Judicial Law* (1986), pp. 724-726. Rosenne, *The International Court of Justice* (1957), p.82. The unilateral withdrawal of a State from continued participation in arbitration after consenting to the setting up of the arbitration tribunal, as in the *Hungarian Optants* case and the *Buraimi Oasis* arbitration terminates the arbitration and the arbitrator's powers; these truncated arbitrations present a serious challenge to the immutability of the arbitration and have led to a distinction between use of arbitration as a method of diplomacy and as a judicial process: 1955 U.N.Y.B. 339-340, (1953) 1 I.L.C.Y.B. 51-52; Schwebel, *International Arbitration: Three Salient Problems* (1987), Chap. 3.

[22] [1980] I.C.J. Rep. 3, 21-24.

[23] See also *Merits* [1986] I.C.J. Rep. 14.

[24] [1978] I.C.J. Rep. 3, 12.

an alternative to arbitration. But international law also countenances unilateral acts, however unfriendly, to persuade another State to yield in a dispute, always provided they do not amount to threat or use of force or illegal reprisals.[25]

2-15 Finally, the content of the third commitment to honour the award appears to differ from that in the private party's undertaking. Whenever the latter is required to comply with the award in good faith by his own efforts, a passive role is also envisaged, should he default, of subjection to local courts' powers so far as necessary to enforce the award. In an arbitration between two States there is no question of submission to a third authority; each State undertakes to exercise its own powers to execute the award and should it lose to accept the exercise of the other party's State powers for the performance of the award. Whilst the Covenant of the League of Nations imposed a general obligation 'to carry out in full good faith any award that may be rendered'[26] it is usual for most arbitration agreements to contain a specific article under which the contracting States agree to accept the award as final and binding and also undertake 'to take such measures as may be requisite to carry out the arbitral award'.[27] In mixed claims commissions it is usual to set out detailed provisions for the time, date and manner of payment of money claims. The Mexican-US Claims Commission of 1923, for instance, requires the Commissioners to determine the value of any property for which a restitution order is made and gives the respondent State an option, to be exercised within 30 days of the award, to pay the value rather than restore the property.[28] On occasions States seek a declaration of the legal

---

[25] *US French Air Services Arbitration* (1979) 54 I.L.R. 304, Zoller, *Peacetime Unilateral Remedies: An Analysis of Countermeasures* (1984).

[26] Art. 13(4).

[27] *Aguilar Amory and Royal Bank of Canada* claims, Convention between Great Britain and Costa Rica 12 Jan. 1922, 1 U.N.R.I.A.A. 371; *Trail Smelter* case (Canada/US), Convention for Settlement of Difficulties of 15 Apr. 1935, Art. XII: 'The Governments undertake to take such action as may be necessary in order to ensure due performance of the obligations undertaken hereunder, in compliance with the decision of the Tribunal' 162 L.N.T.S. 73. Indo-Pakistan Location Boundary Case (Rann of Kutch) Arbitration Agreement of 30 June 1965, Art. 3(iv): 'Both Governments undertake to implement the findings of the Tribunal in full as quickly as possible' 548 U.N.T.S. 277. See Witenberg, *L'Organisation judiciaire; la procedure et la sentence internationale* (1937).

[28] In the General Claims Commission between Mexico and USA set up by Convention signed at Washington, 8 Sept. 1923, the contracting States undertook 'to give full effect' to the decisions of the Commission, that the result of the proceedings of the Commission were to be a 'full, perfect and final settlement of any such claim upon either government', and as regards their nationals every such claim to be treated 'as fully settled, barred and henceforth inadmissible, provided the claim filed has been heard and decided' (Art. VIII). Article IX provided that a balance between the total amounts awarded to the nationals of each State having been struck, a

position in the first instance from the arbitrator, leaving the parties themselves to agree the method of carrying out the award. For instance, in boundary arbitrations it is usual for the parties to provide for a technical commission to carry out the demarcation of the boundary in accordance with the award.[29] Whilst a State is possibly under obligation to give effect through its national laws and courts to an award to which it is party, the cases to date have revealed obstacles of incorporation into national law and of political allocation of resources.[30] The practice has been to leave to the government of the State itself as a matter of discretion the decision as to the means of performing the award.[31]

2-16 In this connection the security account established at a third State's central bank under the Algiers Accords in January 1981 between Iran and the United States which effected the release of the US Iran hostages in Tehran provides possibly a unique precedent. In that case the security account was initially funded in advance of the arbitration of claims between the States by $1 billion of Iranian assets frozen in the United States: awards have been paid out of that security account which, in accordance with the provisions of the claims settlement agreement between the two States, Iran has replenished on two or three occasions when the account has fallen below $0.5 billion: to date that replenishment has been out of actual interest.[32]

---

lump sum in gold coin or its equivalent was to be paid at Washington or the City of Mexico to the government of the country in favour of whose citizens the greater amount might be awarded: A.H. Feller, *The Mexican Claims Commission 1923-1934* (1935).

[29] In the Agreement for Arbitration of 22 July 1971 between Argentina and Chile for the Beagle Channel dispute Art. XII(1) provided that when the proceedings before the Court of Arbitration have been completed, it should transmit its decision to Her Britannic Majesty's Government which should include the drawing of the boundary line on a chart, and Art. XV provided 'The Court of Arbitration shall not be *functus officio* until it has notified Her Britannic Majesty's Government that in the opinion of the Court of Arbitration the Award has been materially and fully executed': Cmnd. 4781 Misc. 23 (1971).

[30] Simpson and Fox, *op. cit. supra* n.1, at p.259; *Socobelge v. The Hellenic State* (Belgium, Tribunal Civil de Bruxelles, 1951) 18 I.L.R. 3; *Société Européenne d'Etudes et d'Enterprises v. World Bank, Republic of Yugoslavia and Republic of France* (1982) J.D.I. 931; *Waltham Press v. Union of Soviet Socialist Republics* (1982) 20 Can. Y.I.L. 282.

[31] In the debate on the State Immunity Bill Elwyn Jones LC said 'it is generally accepted that States do not take coercive action against each other or their property' 388 *Hansard*, H.L. Debs, 17 Jan. 1978, col. 76.

[32] Declaration of the Government of the Democratic and Popular Republic of Algeria of 19 Jan. 1981 (General Declaration), paras. 6-7, reprinted in (1981) 20 I.L.M. 223; Lillich (Ed.), *The Iran-US Claims Tribunal 1981-83* (1984), p.5. In January 1986 the balance in the security account fell below US$500 million due to the payment of awards in favour of US claimants. It was replenished (and again in October 1986) by transfer of interest earned by the security account and held in a separate account by the Depositary Bank (1987) XII Y.B. Com. Arb. 230.

2-17 It is, therefore, plain that an undertaking to arbitrate may have different connotations for a State when engaging in inter-State arbitration than for a private party to commercial arbitration. Which of these connotations applies when the State itself becomes a party to international commercial arbitration? This question is particularly relevant when the scope of the undertaking is considered as regards proceedings in local courts.

III. EXTENSION OF UNDERTAKING TO ARBITRATE TO COVER LOCAL COURT PROCEEDINGS

2-18 A private party's undertaking to arbitrate is an exception to the general compulsory jurisdiction which some local court is entitled to exercise over him. As demonstrated, this is not the position for the State. A State's undertaking to arbitrate is a restriction on freedom. Is the State's undertaking when given as a party to commercial arbitration confined, therefore, to consent to comply with the arbitration process or does it extend to acceptance of the jurisdiction of local courts to support the arbitration? Once again the basis of arbitration is exposed. Clearly if the undertaking to arbitrate rests solely on consent of the parties and that consent is interpreted in the same way as a State's undertaking to arbitrate in inter-State arbitrations, it deprives the proceedings, the arbitrator and the award of the support and enforcement procedures of local courts.

A. State Immunity

2-19 Do these supervisory and enforcement powers of the local court apply when a State is party to a commercial arbitration? The obstacle to an immediate answer is the doctrine of State immunity. Until recently there was widespread observance of a rule of absolute immunity.[33] There could be no local proceedings or enforcement measures against a State without its consent and that consent had to be expressed and given before and after judgment. For the adjudication stage English law required express consent by an authorised agent of the State to be given direct to the court after proceedings had begun – in other words an express submission.[34] After judgment a further express consent to execution was required.[35] Under such an absolute rule the consent to refer a dispute to commercial arbitration, even though made in writing and confined to an existing dispute, was

---

[33] *The Christina* [1938] A.C. 485; *Berizzi Bros. v S.S. Pesaro* 271 U.S. 562 (1926); Lauterpacht (1951) 28 B.Y.B.I.L. 220.
[34] *Kahan v. Federation of Pakistan* [1951] 2 K.B. 1003.
[35] *Duff Development Co. v. Kelantan Government* [1924] A.C. 797.

insufficient to constitute consent to the local court's jurisdiction or waiver of the State's immunity.

2-20 The rule of absolute immunity has been modified in the last ten years, extensively as to the adjudication stage, less dramatically for the enforcement stage.[36] The broad justification for the modification has been that a State expresses its consent to local jurisdiction by engaging in trade, entering into transactions with close connections with a particular country, and that it is artificially narrow to require the consent to be express, in the face of the court and only to be given at a time after proceedings have been commenced in respect of the particular dispute. On the basis of this philosophy legislation of the United States, Great Britain, Canada, South Africa, Singapore, Pakistan and Australia has restricted the immunity before national courts in two ways. These laws have redefined the conditions of waiver and submission sufficient to constitute consent of a foreign State in the eyes of the local courts. Second, they have identified a number of transactions in respect of which the plea of immunity may not be raised. The commercial transaction is the best known non-immune exception, but for present purposes the exception which makes commercial arbitration non-immune and subject to proceedings in local courts in respect of the arbitration is the most relevant.

B. Section 9 of the State Immunity Act 1978

2-21 Provisions relating to waiver of immunity are to be found in all of the national legislation and the extent to which they render non-immune proceedings relating to arbitration agreements depends on their wording which differs.[37] Section 9 of the United Kingdom State Immunity Act 1978, however, specifically deals with the effect a State's agreement to arbitrate may have on

---

[36] European Convention on State Immunity 16 May 1972, U.K.T.S. (1979) No 74 (Cmnd.7742), (1972) 11 I.L.M. 470 US Foreign Sovereign Immunities Act 1976, UK State Immunity Act 1978, Singapore State Immunity Act 1979, Pakistan State Immunity Ordinance 1981, South Africa Foreign States Immunity Act 1981, Australian Foreign States Immunities Act 1985. Draft articles on Jurisdictional Immunities of States and their Properties (1987) 26 I.L.M. 625; State practice is collected in Materials on Jurisdictional Immunities of States and their Property UN St. Leg. Ser B/20 as updated in the Special Rapporteur's Reports, 4th Report (1982) Y.B.I.L.C. Vol. II, pt. 1, p. 199; 5th Report (1983) Y.B.I.L.C. Vol. II, pt. 1, p.25; 6th Report (1984) Y.B.I.L.C., Vol. II, pt. 1, p.5 and 7th Report U.N.G.A. doc. A/CN4/388. See also Sinclair (1980-II) 167 Hag. Rec. 121; Badr, *State Immunity, An Analytical and Prognostic view* (1984).

[37] FSIA 1976, s.1605(a)(1) and s.1610(a)(1); UK State Immunity Act 1978, s.2; Canadian State Immunity Act 1982; s.4; Australian Foreign States Immunities Act 1985, s.10.

immunity.[38] By that section, 'where a State has agreed in writing to submit a dispute which has arisen or which has arisen or which may arise in arbitration the State is not immune as respects proceedings in the courts of the United Kingdom which relate to the arbitration'.

2-22 This section appears to effect a massive imputed extension of a State's consent to local proceedings. On the widest construction of the section the agreement to arbitrate removes State immunity from proceedings in respect not only of commercial but of non-commercial matters, in respect of foreign awards as well as English and from proceedings enforce the award. Such a construction produces the paradoxical result that a State by express consent to arbitration renders itself more subject to the adjudicative and enforcement powers of the local courts than when it expressly submits by written agreement under section 2 of the 1978 Act to the jurisdiction of the English court itself. It would further appear to defeat the function of the arbitral process as a different and alternative method of dispute settlement to litigation and to disregard the intention of the State which consents to arbitration precisely on the basis that it is not itself and does not wish the dispute in which it is involved to be subject to local courts' jurisdiction.

2-23 Such a wide construction highlights sharply the tension in the two bases of arbitration which I have been discussing. On one view, a State as party to an arbitration consents solely to the first base, the consensual obligation to comply with the award. The widely observed immunity of the State from enforcement proceedings in the local courts prevents the second base, the judicial supervision of the arbitration process, having any operation in an arbitration to which a State is a party. A State carries over into private law arbitration the characteristics of inter-State arbitration and its status as a litigant in local courts – that is, no enforcement except by the State itself or, at least, with its consent.[39]

---

[38] The Singapore State Immunity Act 1979, s.11, the South Africa Foreign States Immunities Act 1981, s.10, and the Pakistan State Immunity Ordinance 1981, s.10, have a similar provision to that in the UK Act but it is omitted in the Canadian Act; for Australia see text at *infra* n.51.

[39] This view accepts that State immunity is a relevant plea only in respect of proceedings in local courts and that it is a well-established principle that State immunity cannot be raised as a plea to jurisdiction or a defence to the merits in an arbitration to which a State is party: J. Gillis Wetter (1985) 2 Jo. Of Int. Arb. 7 and cases there cited. Where however the assistance of the local courts is required for the arbitration or to enforce the arbitral award, under the rule of absolute immunity a plea of State immunity may be raised.

2-24 On a second view, however, commercial arbitration is seen as the modern novel process; it provides a process of worldwide enforcement of commercial obligations. Just as foreign courts enforce against a private party an arbitral award more readily than a judgment obtained in his home court, so by the State's consent to arbitration foreign courts are enabled to enforce awards in circumstances where they would by reason of immunity refuse or be unable to enforce judgments obtained in their courts.[40] In the light of the tension between these two approaches it is now necessary to examine more closely the detailed arguments for and against a wide construction of section 9 of the UK Act.

2-25 First, the section contains no express limitation to proceedings relating to arbitration of commercial matters. Had section 9 followed Article 12 of the European Convention on State Immunity 1972 – and one of its purposes was to enable HMG to ratify that Convention[41] – it would have restricted the proceedings to those relating to 'commercial or civil matters'. By omitting to do so, it theoretically covers all arbitration, domestic and international, relating to non-commercial matters.[42] For States the distinction has great importance; many disputes with private parties arise by reason of the exercise of governmental power, or involve mixed issues of commercial law and public law. It is in this sensitive area that a State may consent to settlement by arbitration where it would adamantly oppose reference to a local court. To impute automatically submission to the local court by reason of the consent to the agreement to arbitrate is to endanger States' willingness to consent to any third party process of settlement. The 1958 New York Convention on Reciprocal Enforcement of Arbitral Awards recognises the significance of the distinction between commercial and non-commercial matters by allowing States to limit the

---

[40] This approach is supported by Delaume (1983) 38 Arb. Jo. 34, (1981) 75 A.J.I.L. 786; and Lord Denning in a case decided prior to the State Immunity Act 1978, *Thai Europe Tapioca Services Ltd v. Government of Pakistan* [1975] 1 W.L.R. 1485.

[41] 388 *Hansard*, H.L. Debs, cols. 52-55, 17 Jan. 1978. Article 12 of the European Convention on State Immunity provides:
(1) Where a Contracting State has agreed in writing to submit to arbitration a dispute which has arisen or may arise out of a civil or commercial matter, that State may not claim immunity from the jurisdiction of a court of another Contracting State on the territory or according to the law of which the arbitration has taken or will take place in respect of proceedings relating to
(a) the validity or interpretation of the arbitration agreement;
(b) the arbitration procedure;
(c) the setting aside of the award,
unless the arbitration agreement otherwise provides.
(2) Paragraph 1 shall not apply to an arbitration agreement between States.

[42] The section does not apply to arbitration agreement between States, s.9(2).

obligation of their courts to give effect to foreign awards 'only to differences ... which are considered as commercial under the national law of the State making the declaration'.[43]

2-26 Despite the application of section 9 to non-commercial matters, are there other inherent limitations which reduce its scope? The second omission appears to be any limitation of the section to English arbitration. Is an undertaking by a State to refer a future dispute to arbitration outside the United Kingdom, and for which the proper law is a foreign law, within the section so as to constitute consent to proceedings in the English court? Dr Mann considers the section extends to foreign awards.[44] Although, as far as I know, the point has not appeared in any English reported case, this disregards the additional requirement that the English court will require a jurisdictional connection between itself and the arbitration agreement, such as England being the place of arbitration, which would rule out such extreme situations.[45] Certainly in the United States, where, under the FSIA 1976, section 1605(a)(1) permits waiver 'either expressly or by implication', the case law after some hesitation has emphasised the need for territorial links with the US courts and refused to construe a waiver of immunity in respect of one jurisdiction as waiver to all jurisdictions.[46] On this analogy consent to arbitration in England may constitute consent to proceedings in English courts but consent to arbitration elsewhere will not. Section 9 of the UK Act should, therefore, be interpreted as removing immunity only in respect of agreements to arbitrate in England. Even if restricted to English arbitrations, it is necessary to know for what type of proceedings relating to the arbitration immunity of the State party to the arbitration agreement is removed. Does the section permit proceedings in the English court to enforce the award without the consent of the State? Had section 9 once again followed the wording of Article 12 of the European Convention there would have been no ambiguity. Article 12 expressly limits the local court proceedings to those relating to the validity or interpretation of the arbitration agreement, arbitration procedure and the setting aside of the award. When the Bill was first presented to the House of

---

[43] Art. 1(3).
[44] F.A. Mann (1979) 50 B.Y.I.L. 43, 58.
[45] RSC, Order.11; 949 *Hansard*, H.C. Debs, col. 409.
[46] *Verlinden Bv v Central Bank of Nigeria* 488 F. Supp. 1 284 (S.D.N.Y. 1980), affirmed on other grounds 647 F 2d 320 (2d Cir. 1981) reversed 103 S.Ct. 1962 (1983), *Maritime International Nominees Establishment (MINE) v Republic of Guinea* 693 F 2d 1095 (2nd Circ. 1981). See Kahale (1981) 14 N.Y.U. Jo. of In. & Pol. 29; Sullivan (1983) 18 Tex. Int. L.J. 329; Oparil (1986) 3 Jo. Int. Arb. 61.

Lord the relevant clause contained an additional sentence stating that the section did not apply to proceedings for the enforcement of the award. Such a limitation would seem to have been in conformity with the general approach which was to separate off enforcement measures and to require a separate express consent by the State to their application. The section in its final version, however, omitted the additional sentence.[47] Does this mean that section 9 removes immunity for proceedings relating to arbitration not only to matters arising before or during the arbitration but also to the recognition and enforcement of the award? On one view, the omission of the words does not alter the limitation of proceedings relating to the arbitration to the pre-award phase. The Act, it is argued, maintains the distinction between the adjudicative and enforcement stage of proceedings: section 9 and the removal of immunity by agreement to arbitrate relate to the adjudicative stage. Section 13 deals with the enforcement stage and subject to the exceptions in subsections (3) and (4) expressly prohibits the court from giving effect to the award or the property of a State being subject to any process for the enforcement of an arbitral award. Only written consent under subsection (3) is sufficient to waive the immunity from enforcement. Accordingly, on this view the implied consent of section 9 is limited in its effect to proceedings relating to matters before or during the arbitration.

2-27 On another view, a more restricted view of section 13(2)(b) is taken, namely that it is concerned with the prohibition of attachment of State property to enforce an arbitration award except by written consent or in respect of property for the time being in use or intended for use for commercial purposes. On this view, section 13 provides no bar to enforcement of arbitration awards, merely a limitation as to the property which may be attached. Certainly Lord Wilberforce, in the committee stage, argued against the inclusion of the bar: a State's entry into an arbitration clause should constitute implied waiver from execution unless express reservation to the contrary was made.[48] The net result on this view is that English courts may recognise arbitral awards and enforce them but only in respect of property of the State in commercial use. This is certainly the view of Dr Mann.[49] Professor Crawford, who advised the Australian government in the preparation of its legislation on State immunity, considered the construction of the UK section not free from doubt. He recommended that the Australian Act

---

[47] 389 *Hansard*, H.L. Debs, col. 76, 17 Jan. 1978.
[48] 389 *Hansard*, H.L. Comm., col. 1524.
[49] (1979) 50 B.Y.I.L. 43, 58.

should make the matter plain.[50] That Act accordingly contains a wide provision clarifying most of the ambiguities in the English statute – by section 17(1) a State which is party to an arbitration agreement is not immune from the recognition and enforcement of an award made pursuant to the arbitration, wherever the award was made.[51] The Australian Act also limits section 17 to non-immune matters so presumably it excludes non-commercial matters. Under this provision a State which consents to arbitration consents to proceedings being brought against it to enforce the award in local courts anywhere in the world. The second basis of arbitration is imputed from consent to the first basis, agreement of the parties to arbitrate.

2-28 It is important not to lose sight of the principle of the matter in the legislative history and points of statutory construction. Unilateral legislation of single States expanding the meaning of consent and non-immune situations, as the Australian section and the widest construction of section 9 of the 1978 Act purport to effect, cannot alone alter the international rule of immunity.[52] A foreign State may disregard such unilateral provisions if contrary to international law. There is some support for a more limited rule in the draft convention on jurisdictional immunities which the International Law Commission has been preparing for the past seven years and which had its first reading in 1986. The draft article adopted by the Commission contains the three limitations initially set

---

[50] Australian Law Commission Report No. 24 Foreign State Immunity (1984) 62. See also Triggs (1982) 9 Monash Univ. L.R. 104.

[51] Section 17 provides:
(1) Where a foreign State is a party to an agreement to submit a dispute to arbitration, then, subject to any inconsistent provision in the agreement, the foreign State is not immune in a proceeding for the exercise of the supervisory jurisdiction of a court in respect of the arbitration including a proceeding:
(a) by way of a case stated for the opinion of the court;
(b) to determine a question as to the validity and operation of the agreement or as to the arbitration procedure; or
(c) to set aside the award.
(2) Where –
 (a) apart from the operation of subpara. 11(2)(a)(ii), subsec. 12(4) or subsec. 16(2) a foreign State would not be immune in a proceeding concerning a transaction or event; and
(b) the foreign State is a party to an agreement to submit to arbitration about the transaction or event, then subject to any inconsistent provision in the agreement, the foreign State is not immune in a proceeding concerning the recognition as binding for any purpose or for the enforcement of an award made pursuant to the arbitration, wherever the award was made.

[52] 'If one State chooses to lay down by enactment certain limits, that is by itself no evidence that those limits are generally accepted by States' *I Congreso del Partido* [1983] A. C. 244, 260 *per* Lord Wilberforce.

out in Article 12 of the European Convention; immunity is removed only in respect of civil or commercial matters and only in respect of proceedings in local courts which have a sufficient jurisdictional nexus with the arbitration (the arbitration either being held on the territory within the local court's jurisdiction or subject to its law). Finally, consent to arbitration is not construed as removing immunity from the enforcement stage of the arbitral award.[53] This reinstatement by the International Law Commission of a treaty rule adopted in 1972 provides fairly strong evidence that the international law in this area is more restricted than the provisions contained in the UK and Australian legislation.

2-29 In the absence of a clear statement at international law of the rule, it will only be when a majority of States comply with national legislation such as the Australian and UK provisions that one can say with certainty that there is sufficient State practice to show that the international rule is accurately expressed in the terms of the national legislation. A moderate assumption of the supervisory function over both the adjudicative and enforcement stage of an arbitration with territorial connections with the local jurisdiction is the rule most likely to obtain the approval of States. It gives, after all, some weight to the second basis of arbitration, the judicial supervision of the arbitral process, yet preserves the widely observed immunity of the State from enforcement in local courts. It would be wrong to allow a party to a commercial arbitration, just because it is a State, to disregard that second basis altogether which, as discussed, is part of the inherent nature of the arbitral process and upon which much of the effectiveness of modern arbitration depends. A compromise solution has to be sought by which the first basis of arbitration, autonomy of the parties, is employed to identify and give independent force to a limited and agreed version of the second basis. It is here that jurisdictional links to one particular system of

---

[53] Art. 19 of the draft articles provides:
Effect of an arbitration agreement. If a State enters into an agreement in writing with a foreign natural or juridical person to submit to arbitration differences relating to a [commercial contract] [civil or commercial matter], that State cannot invoke immunity from jurisdiction before a court of another State which is otherwise competent in a proceeding which relates to:
(a) the validity or interpretation of the arbitration agreement,
(b) the arbitration procedure,
(c) the setting aside of the award
unless the arbitration agreement otherwise provides.
U.N.G.A. Official Records, 41st Session, Supp. No. 10 (A/41/10), Chap. II, pp.5-23, reprinted (1987) 26 I.L.M. 625. See also Art. III(g) of the draft Resolutions on jurisdictional immunities of the Institute of International Law, prepared by Professor I. Brownlie (1987) 62 Inst. I.L. Ann. 98, 101.

local courts and the commercial nature of the arbitration are all-important. If in the arbitration agreement the State consents to the applicable law as English law, or to the arbitration being held in England and identifies the arbitration as relating to commercial matters, it is a small extension of that express consent to hold it subject to the supervision of the English courts for the purposes of the arbitration proceedings whether before or during the award.

2-30 Such moderate assumption should not, in my view, extend to attachment of State assets before or after the award. At the present stage of the development of commercial arbitration and States' growing co-operation I would not extend that judicial supervision beyond recognition of the award. To dismantle State immunity from enforcement in respect of arbitral awards whilst preserving it for proceedings in local courts would unduly strain the legal system and forfeit States' co-operation. I would prefer courts to require an express acceptance of such liability to attachment in the arbitration agreement by the State or at any rate an acknowledgement that the arbitration relates to commercial matters. In the meantime, until the position is clarified, private parties in drafting arbitration clauses with States are well advised to include express waiver of immunity by the State both to adjudication and enforcement proceedings in the local court.

IV. MIXED CLAIMS COMMISSIONS AND ARBITRAL CLAIMS TRIBUNALS

2-31 The second illustration of the working of the two bases of arbitration is drawn from one institutional form of international settlement which has a long history and recent developments suggest it may have particular relevance for commercial arbitration. That institution is the mixed claims commissions of the nineteenth century which in time led to the mixed arbitral tribunals set up under the peace treaties of the First World War. The earliest commissions are to be found under the Jay Treaty of 1794 between Great Britain and the United States to settle the boundary and war claims outstanding after the War of Independence. Although the commissions were interrupted by disagreements between the English and American commissioners, their enquiries into the facts and elucidation of principle aided the final settlement, the United States paying £600,000 in three annual instalments for the 'confiscated debts' owed to the British, and Great Britain £2,330,000 in respect of 533 separate awards made to US nationals for loss of vessels and cargoes.[54] Further mixed commissions were

---

[54] 52 Consolidated T.S. 243; Moore, *International Adjudications*, Vols. 1-4; A. de la Pradelle and N. Politis, *Recueil des Arbitrages internationaux* (2nd ed.), Vol.1, pp.1-28.

set up by States, in particular to settle claims of their nationals for loss arising out of war or civil disturbance; this procedure was used against France after the Napoleonic wars, for US and British claims against Mexico (1838 and 1868), Chile (1883 and 1886), Venezuela (1869 and 1903), Peru (1904), in settlements involving Germany after the First World War, and again in claims of the United States against Mexico (1923 and 1924).[55] The most recent example is the Iran-US Claims Tribunal which, in addition to dealing with direct claims between the two States and disputes as to interpretation of the two declarations contained in the 1981 Accords of Algiers, confers jurisdiction on the Tribunal to decide claims (including counterclaims arising out of the same transaction) of nationals of the United States against Iran and claims of nationals of Iran against the United States.[56] Terminology is not always exact. The institution has developed over the years with the inclusion of neutral members in the composition of the commission either at a second stage or throughout; in this form the institution is usually described as an arbitral claims tribunal. There has also been an extension to individual claimants of some right of participation in the proceedings.[57]

2-32 In all these commissions and arbitral claims tribunals some common features are observable. In all proceedings the claim of injured nationals is espoused by the State which enters into a treaty to settle the dispute with another State. The treaty between the States is more in the form of a submission than a compromissory clause – the subject matter, the tribunal, the law applicable are all agreed.

2-33 The subject matter of the dispute is broadly identified, though its precise scope often remains a fruitful source of argument in cases coming before the commission. US Secretary of State Pickering complained that the Jay Treaty 'in effect made the United States the debtor for all the outstanding debts due to British subjects and contracted before the treaty of peace'.[58]

---

[55] Verzijl, *International Law in Historical Perspective Pt. VIII* (1976), Chap. IX; Simpson and Fox, op. *cit. supra* n.1, at Chaps. 1-4; Dolzer, 'Mixed Claims Commissions' 1 Encyclopaedia of Public Int. L. 146; Ralston, *op. cit. supra* n.1; Feller; *op. cit. supra* n.28; Recueil des decisions des Tribunaux arbitraux mixtes institutes par les Traites de Paris, Vols, 1-10 (1922-1930).

[56] Claims Settlement Declaration, 19 Jan. 1981, reprinted (1981) 20 I.L.M. 230.

[57] Simpson and Fox, *op. cit. supra* n.1, at pp.10-12, 34-41; Burchard (1927) 21 A.J.I.L. 472.

[58] Secretary of State Pickering to Minister of US in London, 5 Feb. 1799, Moore, *op. cit. supra* n.54, Vol.3, at p.170.

2-34 The composition and procedure of the tribunal is agreed, though again some flexibility is left to the tribunal which may by administrative decisions taken early on in the proceedings lay down general guidelines as to the disposition of the claims.[59]

2-35 The law applicable is international law supplemented in some instances by special rules on which the parties agreed – as did Great Britain and the USA in the Washington Rules on the duties of neutrality for the Alabama Claims.[60] The origin of the treaty for settlement by a mixed claims commission or arbitral tribunal is the inadequacy of local law to compensate for the loss suffered (no, or inadequate, provision for damage from war, civil disturbance, or act of State is usually to be found in local laws) and the recognition by the contracting States that a standard external to local laws is required to provide compensation. It is a well established principle that diplomatic protection of aggrieved nationals is precluded as long as the remedies available under domestic law have not been exhausted by the private party.[61]

2-36 The relationship of the jurisdiction of the commission or claims tribunal to that of local courts is a variable one.

2-37 Some treaties specifically exclude the role requiring exhaustion of local remedies, others define the circumstances in which it shall be applicable. The Algiers Accords setting up the Iran-US Claims Tribunal contain both types of provision. Claims arising under a binding contract for exclusive sole jurisdiction of the competent Iranian courts are excluded (Article II.1), whilst claims referred to the Arbitral Tribunal are treated as transferred with the consequent effect that they are 'to be considered excluded from the courts of Iran or of the United States or of any other court' (Article VII.2).

2-38 Other treaties provide a right of appeal to the arbitral tribunal (as in the London Agreement on German External Debts 1953, from the mixed

---

[59] Mixed Claims Commission US and Germany, Administrative Decisions and Opinions to 30 June 1925 (1925); Borchard (1925) 19 A.J.I.L. 133.

[60] Treaty of Washington, 8 May 1871, Art. VI, 143 Consolidated T.S. 146, 149; Moore, *op. cit. supra* n.54, Vol.1 (1898), p.550.

[61] *Panevezys v. Saldutiskis Rly.* Case P.C.I.J. Ser.A/B No 76 (1939); *Interhandel* case [1959] I.C.J., Rep. 6; 18 *Halsbury's Laws* (4th ed.), Foreign Relations Law 909, para. 1751.

commission to the arbitral tribunal)[62] or a right to obtain a ruling on the interpretation of the treaty rules from the arbitral tribunal (as domestic courts of the contracting States might do under the Austro-German Property Treaty 1957).[63]

A. The Position of the Individual Claimant

2-39 A common feature to all these procedures is that the States are the parties. Although in the commissions under the Jay Treaty the subsequent nineteenth-century mixed commissions the individual was permitted to file his claim and the sums awarded were qualified by reference to that claim, ultimate control throughout was retained by the State. Cases were conducted by agents appointed by the two States and it was rare until after the First World War for individuals to present memorials to the commission, participate in oral proceedings, appear as witnesses or be represented by counsel.[64] Claims by individuals were directly presented in the mixed arbitral tribunals set up under the peace treaties after the First World War but only after they had been subjected to a clearing system of national offices of the counties concerned. Although the Franco-German Tribunal dealt with 20,000 cases and the Anglo-Germany and German-Italian Tribunals with some 10,000 cases each, these represent only a fraction of the claims settled through the national clearing system.[65] After the Second World War the London Agreement on German External Debts set up a complicated three-tier system of appeals to which individuals had somewhat limited rights.[66] Claims of less than £250,000 in the Iran-US Claims Tribunal are to be presented by the government of the national concerned; claims in excess may be presented by individual claimants but the agents of the two States are present throughout the hearing with a right of audience.[67]

2-40 It is unwise to refer to the Iran-US Claims Tribunal as a modern illustration of claims commissions without at the same time noting its novel features which distinguish it from previous inter-State arbitrations.[68] Reference has already been

---

[62] London Agreement on German External Debts, 27 Feb. 1953, Arts. 28(4), 31(7), 333 U.N.T.S. 2. Simpson and Fox, *op. cit. supra* n.1, at pp.35-40.

[63] German Bundesgesetzblatt 1958 II 129.

[64] Simpson and Fox, *op. cit. supra* n.1, at pp.99-102.

[65] Wuhler, 'Arbitral Tribunals' 1 Encyclopaedia Public Int. L. 146

[66] See reference at *supra* n.62.

[67] Claims Settlement Declaration, *supra.* n.56, Arts.III(3), VI(2).

[68] See D. Lloyd-Jones, 'The Iran-US Claims Tribunal: Private Rights and State Responsibility', in Lillich (ed.), *op. cit. supra* n.32, at p.51.

made to the parties' establishment in advance of a security account out of which private parties' claims could be paid. The General Principles in the first declaration for the Algiers Accords of 17 January 1981 between Iran and the United States (which effected the release of the hostages) also emphasised the intention to achieve a settlement of outstanding private law claims as well as public international law claims against either State. Principle B stated that 'it was the purpose of both parties … to terminate all litigation as between the government of each party and the nationals of the other and to bring about the settlement and termination of all such claims through binding arbitration'. To this end the terms of reference of the Tribunal included claims of US nationals against Iran and of Iranian nationals against the United States for debts, contracts (including transactions which are the subject of letters of credit and bank guarantee), expropriation and other measures affecting property rights. The applicable law provision also does not disregard the private law aspect of the arbitration, the Tribunal being directed in Article V to decide 'all cases on the basis of respect for law, applying such choice of law rules and principles of commercial and international law rules as the Tribunal determines to be applicable'.

2-41 The settlement of claims through the Iran-US Claims Tribunal provides an example of the fusion of State and private party claims in one procedure. An increase in demand for such procedure is to be expected if States deliberately use their private law either by suspension of local remedies or change of substantive rules as a response to perceived illegal action on the international plane by another State. Any solution of the international dispute will then necessarily require a settlement of private claims which have been generated in the course of the dispute.

2-42 This increasing fusion of State and private party claims in one procedure before an arbitral claims tribunal leads back to a consideration of the basis of arbitration and the scope of the undertaking to arbitrate.

B. Relationship of Arbitral Claims Tribunals to Local Courts

2-43 It will be important to clarify the relationship between such claims tribunals and local courts if private law claims are increasingly to be referred to them. Is the authority of such an arbitral claims tribunal based on consent of the parties or the judicial authority of the State? Is it the agreement of the two States which gives legal force to the decisions of the tribunal or the combination of the judicial powers of two States? So far as the first base is concerned, does the consent of the State bind its national in all circumstances in respect of any claim that it may seek to bring in local courts whether within the State or a third State? As regards the second base, whilst international law permits and third States must recognise the exercise of judicial authority of a State within its territory or over its nationals, does international law require similar recognition by a third State of a settlement by bilateral treaty between two States of the claims of their nationals? If it does, in the absence of a treaty with the third State or implementing legislation, how are the courts of the third State to be satisfied of the validity of the awards and jurisdiction of the arbitral claims tribunal? Even if so satisfied, may those courts still reject the decisions of such tribunals, as they do in respect of foreign judgments, on grounds of fraud or by reason of the award being contrary to public policy or opposed to natural justice?

2-44 It may be helpful to illustrate these questions by an example. At the time of the US air strike on Libya the United States government froze Libyan assets in the United States. Suppose a US national tries in England to recover a loan owed to him by a Libyan State-owned bank and suppose, subsequently the United States and Libya agree to refer all claims to arbitration, must the English court discontinue the action?

2-45 Now I appreciate that I am posing the question in such general terms that no answer is possible. The terms of the US freezing order, whether its ambit includes the loan arrangement between the US and Libyan nationals the proper law of the transaction, whether the US national has exhausted local remedies in Libya, are all issues which require elucidation. But in broad terms you can see the underlying interests involved.[69]

2-46 There is first the situation of the individual whose claim is the subject of political settlement between States. If he refers his claim to the arbitral claims tribunal set up buy the two States, then arguably he has personally submitted to its jurisdiction and any award will bind him finally.[70] But supposing he does not do so but wishes to continue with is action in the English court? Suppose, indeed, aware of the uneasy relations between their governments, the parties expressly chose to make the contract of loan subject to the jurisdiction and law of England. To what extent is the US national affected by the treaty of settlement

---

[69] For a recent case involving some of the considerations raised in the hypothetical example in the text, *see Libyan Arab Foreign Bank v. Bankers Trust Co.*, 2 Sept. 1987, Staughton J.

[70] As the court found in respect of the plaintiff in *Dallal v Bank Mellat*, see text *infra* in 72, Dicey and Morris, *Conflict of Laws* (11th ed., 1987), p.563.

between the United States and Libya? Is the arbitration treaty anything more than an agreement *inter alios*? The private party is not a direct party to the treaty and the espousal of his claim by means of the treaty enabling it to be brought before the tribunal is a matter of discretion for the State and not of right on the part of the national claimant. Certainly English law provides no remedy to such a claimant whereby he can force the UK government to take up and present his claim against another State or any remedy to enforce the payment over to him for any sum awarded or recovered by the UK government in respect of his claim under such an arbitration agreement.[71]

2-47 Has the US national a right to exhaust local remedies in Libya or to continue with his English suit and to oppose the conversion of his claim to local proceedings into an arbitration claim?

2-48 The original claim may either be grounded in private law on the contract or, if the Libyan court can be shown also to have jurisdiction, in international law on a denial of justice from the Libyan courts for failure on Libya's part to observe minimum standards in the treatment of aliens. It is generally the latter type of claim which States refer to arbitral claims tribunals although the root cause of dissatisfaction often arises from some breach of contract due to disruption of normal business relations between the countries. From the point of view of the private litigant either type of claim derives from the laws of one or other of the States parties to the arbitration. States are free to change such laws. Is the reference to arbitration equivalent to such legislative action so as to defeat any continuance or initiation of proceedings in the local court to give effect to the national's claim? This raises a nice question whether either applicant or respondent State is free to dispense with the requirement of exhaustion of local remedies when the private party concerned still wishes to pursue them. It seems probable that provided the claim is between nationals of the States concerned and is wholly grounded in the territory of one or the other, whether based on private law or public international law, it can be terminated by the States' reference of it to arbitration. The constitutional law, however, of a particular State may require enabling legislation to direct its courts to stay or discontinue proceedings. Here, reference to the second basis of arbitration, the judicial authority of the State, seems necessary to extend the arbitration agreement beyond the direct parties to

---

[71] *Civilian War Claimants Association Ltd v. R.* [1932] A.C. 14; *Tito v Waddell (No.2)* [1977] Ch. 106; 18 *Halsbury's Laws* (4th ed.), Foreign Relations Law 728, paras. 1419, 1768; F. A. Mann, *Foreign Affairs in English Courts* (1986), p.77.

persons outside the agreement. Is this second basis, judicial authority of a State, available and sufficient to extend the jurisdiction of the arbitral claims tribunal to the courts of a third State and overclaims that may be grounded on the laws of third States? Will the second basis give primacy to the tribunal's jurisdiction? Will it bring to a halt proceedings in local courts in respect of the same claims, render null any order by such courts to attach assets in respect of the claims and require the local courts of a third State to recognise and give effect to the awards of the tribunal?

2-49 Whether such reference by treaty and legislation would effectively defeat causes of action grounded on a third State's laws with sufficient jurisdictional connection to entitle the courts of that third State to take jurisdiction is a more difficult question. It also raises the extent to which a third State and its courts are bound to give effect to a bilateral treaty to which the third State is not a party.

C. Dallal v. Bank Mellat

2-50 It was precisely these problems which Hobhouse J had to consider in the recent decision of *Dallal v. Bank Mellat*.[72] The claimant in that case had personally submitted to the jurisdiction of the Iran-US Claims Tribunal and his claim had no independent basis in English law or jurisdictional links with the English court. But the reasoning of the judgment suggests that the English court has an inherent power to give effect to an arbitration award grounded in international law even though there was no treaty between Great Britain and the States setting up the arbitration tribunal and no implementing English legislation.

2-51 A US national in that case had a claim for two cheques dishonoured by an Iranian bank. The Iran-US Claims Tribunal had dismissed the claim by a majority award, with the American arbitrator dissenting, on the ground that the applicant had failed to discharge the burden of proof that the transaction was not

---

[72] [1986] 2 W.L.R: 745. The relationship between local courts and the Iran-US Tribunal has also arisen in West German and French courts. The exercise of concurrent jurisdiction by a West, German court (Frankfurt am Main District Ct., Feb. 1980) by attachment of Iranian assets to enforce US companies' claims, suspended in US courts, led Iran to file a complaint before the Iran-US Tribunal, Case No.A/5. The French Cour de Cassation has refused to annul an award obtained in an ICC arbitration against the Iranian Air Force which the applicant is seeking to enforce by filing a claim before the Iran-US Claims Tribunal and in proceedings before West German courts: *Commandement des Forces Aeriennes de la Republique Islamique d'Iran c. Bendone – De Rossi* International, 1st Ch. Civ. Cour de Cassation, Arret No. 449, 5 May 1987, (July 1987) I.F.L.R. 44.

illegal as contrary to the Iranian foreign exchange law, and held that the US applicant should not be allowed to amend his claim to a plea of unjust enrichment. The applicant subsequently brought an action on the cheques in the English court and the defendant, relying on the award of the Iran-US Claims Tribunal, applied to strike out the action as an abuse of the process of the court. Hobhouse J, in considering the validity of the arbitration and the award, tested it by reference to the two bases of arbitration, consensual autonomy of the parties and the power of the State to enforce the legal process. He first approached the problem as one of recognition of a valid arbitration agreement either under the New York Convention or by English conflict of laws rules. By reason of the arbitration being held at The Hague it was argued the proper law of the arbitration agreement was Dutch.[73] Here a well-known obstacle, the legal requirement for a formal submission of the parties, is encountered. Article 623 of the Dutch Civil Code required such a formal submission and its absence rendered any agreement a nullity. Consequently there could be no recognition by the English court of the proceedings and award of the Claims Tribunal 'from the application of the ordinary principle applicable to consensual arbitration'.

2-52 It was suggested by the plaintiff that if Dutch law was not the proper law, international law might be. Hobhouse J was emphatic that private parties had no consensual autonomy to choose international law:

> But what I am concerned with here . . . is not an agreement between States but an agreement between private law individuals who are nationals of those States. If private law rights are to exist, they must exist as part of some municipal legal system and public international law is not such a system. If public international law is to play a role in providing the governing law which gives an agreement between private law individuals legal force it has to do so by having been absorbed into some system of municipal law.[74]

---

[73] A Bill was presented to the Netherlands Parliament which provided that awards of the Iran-US Tribunal should be arbitral awards within the meaning of Dutch law, and not subject to challenge in Dutch courts either for jurisdiction or substance except for compliance with rules of natural justice or on grounds of public policy. The Bill was not proceeded with. Bill entitled 'Applicability of Dutch Law to the Awards of the Tribunal sitting in the Hague to hear Claims before Iran and the United States', reprinted in Iranian Assets Litigation Rep. 6, 899 (15 July 1983).

[74] [1986] 2 W.L.R. 745, 759.

2-53 Unable to rely on the consensual agreement of the private parties as the source of authority, the judge turned to the second source of authority, the State's exercise of judicial powers. Describing the proceedings at The Hague as akin to a domestic 'statutory' arbitration, where the jurisdiction of the arbitral tribunal is defined not by any choice or agreement of the parties, he set himself to find the relevant 'statute' to govern the present international situation. This he does as follows:

> The jurisdiction and authority of the tribunal at The Hague was created by an international treaty between the United States and the Republic of Iran, and was within the treaty-making powers of the governments of each of those two countries. Each of the parties was respectively within the jurisdiction and subject to the law-making power of one of the parties to the treaty. Further, the *situs* of all the relevant choses in action are within the jurisdiction of one or other of the two States which are parties to the treaties. Again the municipal legal system of each of the relevant States recognises the competence of the tribunal at The Hague to decide the arbitration proceedings. Accordingly the arbitration proceedings at The Hague are recognised as competent not only by competent international agreements between the relevant States, but also by the municipal laws of those States . . . there is no reason in principle why the curial law of a tribunal cannot derive concurrently from more than one system of municipal law . . .in the present case there are two systems of municipal law with the requisite international competence which give validity to the arbitration proceedings. There is no reason in principle why that validity should not be recognised by the English courts.[75]

2-54 This is a lengthy excerpt but I have given it in full to show that the focus has shifted away from the arbitration. There is no question now of the validity of the underlying agreement between the private parties which gave rise to the dishonoured cheques, nor to the absence of any direct agreement between them to refer it to the Claims Tribunal, nor to the validity based on consent of the parties to the resulting award. The enquiry, relying as it does on case law relating to the recognition of decisions of consular courts given in respect of private nationals of States which were not in direct treaty relations with Great Britain,[76] has shifted the focus from consensual autonomy to the competence of

---

[75] *Idem*, p.761.
[76] *The Laconia* (1863) 2 Moore P.C. (N.S.) 161, *Messina v. Petrococchina* (1872) L.R. 4 P.C. 144.

the tribunal. If under international law a tribunal is competent, Hobhouse J considers its competence ought to be recognised by English courts. Such competence need not be conferred by treaty, but binds the nationals of the States parties to the treaty and any private party who voluntarily resorts to the arbitral claims tribunal to pursue his claim.

2-55 These are resounding principles and exciting news for international lawyers. The *Dallal* decision suggests a route not merely for regularising the relationship of the Iran-US Tribunal with local courts of third States but opens up the prospect of general recognition by local courts of inter-State arbitration. Equating international law with foreign municipal law, the case in effect extends the common law action to enforce a foreign judgment[77] to the decision of an international tribunal established by international law. If a bilateral agreement between two States is given such recognition, should the English court not also extend it to judgments of the International Court, which is established by a multilateral treaty to which the majority of States are parties? If it be argued that the recognition is limited to awards affecting the rights of private parties, then surely any arbitral tribunal established by treaty qualifies, whether or not Great Britain is a party to the treaty, provided it purports to decide conclusively issues which otherwise would be decided by the local courts of the contracting states.

2-56 So far as the facts of *Dallal v. Bank Mellat* are concerned, the treaty between the United States and Iran was confirmed by local legislation of both countries. In the first instance, in the United States it was done by Presidential decree.

2-57 On the setting up of the Iran-US Claims Tribunal, in a decree of 24 February 1981 the President suspended all claims for equitable or judicial relief in connection with the claims, and provided that 'during the period of suspension all such claims should have no legal effect in any action pending or to be commenced in any court of the United States'. The constitutionality of this Presidential decree was upheld by the Supreme Court in *Dames & Moore v. Regan Sec. Of Treasury*; the Supreme Court there held that Congress had implicitly approved the practice of claim settlement by executive agreement and that the suspension of claims was not an ouster of jurisdiction but effected 'a change in the substantive law governing the law suit' and the provision of an 'alternative forum, the claims tribunal which is capable of providing meaningful

[77] Dicey and Morris, *op. cit. supra* n.70, at p.561.

relief'.[78]   In the words of Justice Rehnquist who delivered the judgment of the Court, 'The frozen assets serve as a bargaining chip to be used by the President when dealing with a hostile country'.   Private law actions by individual claimants could not therefore be allowed to minimise or wholly eliminate this 'bargaining chip'.

2-58 Whilst, in pursuit of the praiseworthy goal of obtaining the release of hostages, criticism of the Presidential decree and suspension of vested rights of action was muted, it is worth pausing to ask how we in the UK would view such action.   The government would not have executive power to do so and would have to enact legislation.   As Parliament is theoretically capable of doing anything it pleases, presumably by Act of Parliament existing causes of action could be terminated in a manner similar to the American method.   It is an interesting speculation whether such interference with vested rights of property and contractual expectations would involve any infringement of the Treaty of Rome in relation to the Common Market or to human rights, particularly the right of property in the First Protocol under the European Convention of Human Rights.

2-59 But these speculations apart, is it sufficient to leave such an important extension of jurisdiction into the international field to a common law action?   It appears from the decision in the *Dallal* case that there is sufficient scope in such procedure to ensure the application of the safeguards relating to rules of natural justice and local public policy which currently apply for the enforcement of foreign judgments and awards.[79]   But what of the broader view of public policy? Should the recognition of a treaty conferring international competence be left to individual litigants' resort to a common law action?   Are all such bilateral treaties removing claims of nationals from local courts to inter-State arbitration likely to be ones which, in the words of the judge in the *Dallal* case, the English court will 'not frustrate'?   Should not the decision to endorse or frustrate a treaty arrangement made between other States be with Parliament?   Such endorsement has certainly been required in the case of foreign judgments, as the recent entry into force of the Civil Jurisdiction and Judgments Act 1982 illustrates, and also the UK legislation for foreign arbitral awards giving effect to the New York Convention 1958 and the ICSID Convention.

---

[78]   453 US 654 (1981) 673.
[79]   Dicey and Morris, *op. cit. supra* n.70, at p.571; *Dallal v. Bank Mellat* [1986] 2 W.L.R. 745, 765.

2-60 The fusion of international law with local law is an admirable goal but if it is to be done so as to avoid international conflict surely it ought to be done by observance of constitutional procedure, opportunity for parliamentary debate and taking due account of all interests involved.

V. CONCLUSION

2-61 To summarise:

1. Commercial arbitration, both domestic and international, depends on two sources of authority, the consensual autonomy of the parties and the power of the State to enforce the legal process.

2. Private litigants as a general rule are subject to compulsory adjudication of their disputes by courts. Resort to arbitration arises from the voluntary choice of a more flexible procedure. States are not generally subject to compulsory adjudication; all forms of arbitration are a restriction on their freedom of action.

3. The undertaking to arbitrate comprises three elements: an immediate irrevocable obligation to refer the dispute to arbitration; an obligation to settle the dispute by arbitration in preference and prior to resort to legal proceedings; and an obligation to honour the award of the arbitrator. In inter-State arbitration the State's undertaking to arbitrate probably does not extend to the second obligation and the first and second obligations are given effect solely by operation of the first basis, the consensual autonomy of the parties. The undertaking of the State does not contain a commitment to respect the power of a third State to enforce the award.

4. In international commercial arbitration the undertaking of the State to arbitrate cannot of itself constitute consent to the award being enforced by court proceedings. Such consent may be construed or imputed as consent to enforcement by English courts where the State in the arbitration agreement consents to the applicable law as English law or to the arbitration being held in England, and identifies the arbitration as relating to commercial matters and commercial property. Section 9 of the State Immunity Act 1978 should be so construed.

5. Reference of private party disputes by States to settlement by mixed claims commissions or arbitral claims tribunals involves no consent by the private party to arbitrate unless he subsequently submits his claim to the commission or tribunal. The second basis, the power of the two States to enforce the award of the commission or tribunal should not extend beyond their own courts. If the award of the arbitral claims

tribunal is to receive recognition and enforcement in the courts of a third State, that State must be a party to the treaty setting up the claims commission or tribunal and/or enact legislation requiring its courts to give effect as judgments to the awards of such mixed claims commission or arbitral claims tribunal.

VI. ADDENDUM [22 OCTOBER 2005]

2-62 The question whether section 9 of the State Immunity Act permits the enforcement of an arbitral award rendered outside the UK in respect of non-commercial matters would not seem to date to have been authoritatively settled by an English court. Registration of a foreign judgment given against State has been held by an English court to be an act of adjudicative jurisdiction, *AIC v. Government of Nigeria and Anor* [2003] EWHC 1357 (QB), and hence, arguably, an application to enforce an arbitral award is also an exercise of adjudicative jurisdiction, for which section 9 of the 1978 Act removes immunity 'as respects proceedings relating to the arbitration'. The then Lord Chancellor, Elwyn Jones LC, certainly intended such a result when he put forward an amendment relating to the section of the original clause in the Bill to delete the words:

This section does not apply to proceedings for the enforcement of an award.

2-63 But it is not clear whether he envisaged that removal of immunity to extend to proceedings for enforcement relating to non-UK arbitrations. Introducing the amendment he said:

This Amendment is intended to remove the immunity enjoyed by States from proceedings to enforce arbitration awards against them. Clause 10(1) [s. 9(1)] removes immunity from proceedings relating to arbitration where the State has submitted to arbitration in the UK or according to UK law, but by section (2) enforcement proceedings are excepted; if the Government's Amendments to clause 14 are accepted, the property of a State which for the time being in use or intended for use for commercial purposes will become amenable to execution to satisfy the arbitration award. However, it will not be possible to proceed to such execution without first bringing enforcement proceedings to turn the award into an order of the court on which the execution could be levied, and, unless the State had waived its immunity to enforcement, Clause 10(2) would prevent the necessary steps being taken.

This Amendment will delete the subsection. [Hansard HL, 16 March 1978, col, 1517.][80]

2-64 It is to be noted that Article 17 of the United Nations Convention on State Immunity, adopted in 2004, removes State immunity solely where a State has entered into 'an agreement in writing with a foreign national or juridical person to submit to arbitration differences relating to a commercial transaction',[81] and restricts the non-immune proceedings to the validity, interpretation or application, the arbitration procedure or the confirmation or setting aside of the award.

2-65 The English provision removing immunity may, therefore, be more to the advantage of the non-State party to the arbitration, although not in conformity with the rule of international law as now set out in the UN Convention.

---

[80] See also the Lord Chancellor at col. 1523 re amendment permitting execution against State property in commercial use:

> The power to enforce judgments and arbitral awards against the property of the State will be very wide, wider than that under the US Act.

[81] By the Understanding annexed to Article 17 of the Convention 'the expression "commercial transaction" includes investment matters'. This may possibly remove arbitrations with a State party held pursuant to a bilateral investment treaty but would not seem directly to address the issue under discussion. The term 'commercial transaction' itself is defined in Article 2(1)(b) and 2(2) of the Convention, the latter which permits the purpose of the transaction to be taken into account in determining a 'commercial transaction', 'if, in the practice of the forum, that purpose is relevant in determining its non commercial character' has particularly attracted criticism.

*Giorgio Bernini**

CHAPTER 3

THE FUTURE OF ARBITRATION: FLEXIBILITY OR RIGIDITY?**

I. Introduction: The General Theme

3-1 It is for me a great honour and a pleasure to be here today. The significance of the Freshfields Lectures is well established in the domain of arbitration. I am especially grateful to the organisers of this reunion during which I am offered the privilege of debating a theme which I deem of paramount interest.

3-2 Viewed in more general terms, the theme in question has inspired the conference which took place in Bologna, at the end of May of last year, under the joint sponsorship of ICCA and of the University of Bologna, on the occasion of the celebrations for the IX Centennial of our *Alma Mater Studiorum*.

3-3 The theme of the conference was articulated on a dual premise.

3-4 The arbitrators may have the scale of justice, seldom, if ever, the sword. Lacking powers of coercion, as they do in the light of many systems, they have to turn to persuasion in order that the parties accept their rulings and ultimately their award.

3-5 The situation is becoming more dramatic due to a verification that one can hardly challenge: in arbitration mores are deteriorating. This is due in part to the involvement in international arbitration of a growing number of countries, often

---

* GIORGIO BERNINI, LL.M., S.J.D. (Michigan), [Emeritus] Professor of Commercial Law, University of Bologna, [Former] President, International Council for Commercial Arbitration (ICCA).

** The lecture was delivered in 1988 and has never been published.

Julian D.M. Lew and Loukas A. Mistelis (eds), Arbitration Insights, 47-62
© 2007 Kluwer Law International. Printed in the Netherlands

differing to a great extent in legal and cultural background, with inevitable repercussion on the acceptability and practice of arbitration. To the extent that in some countries international arbitration is sometimes regarded with suspicion, especially when Sovereign States or Public Entities are parties to it.

3-6 The situation thus described branches out into different topics, *inter alia,* the function of the Arbitral Tribunal, the establishment of procedural rules, the compliance with the arbitrators' orders and ultimately the function and responsibility of the bodies administering arbitration. The problems that one encounters when dealing with the above subjects, should be viewed in the light of a basic feature which characterises the development of arbitration: i.e. the perennial, and yet insolved dilemma, whereby flexibility is juxtaposed to rigidity in *ad hoc* as well as in administered arbitration.

3-7 Arbitration is undoubtedly becoming more and more complicated and its traditional ideal simplicity risks being confined to the realm of past dreams. Arbitration is perhaps growing too big for its contractual vestment. If this is true, how can one cope with the trend towards detailed procedural regulation without relinquishing the classic values upon which the present acceptance of arbitration has been built?

3-8 A reasonable forecast on the future of arbitration must depend upon the answers to such questions. This is why my recent studies were concentrated on this theme which I have the honour of presenting today to such a learned audience.

II. DILEMMA: FLEXIBILITY VERSUS RIGIDITY

3-9 One can hardly dispute that procedural flexibility is a traditional feature of international arbitration. However, it is undeniable that arbitration is currently revealing a tendency towards an increased rigidity of procedural forms. The debatable ensuing issue can be best approached, and hopefully settled, through an answer to the following questions:

(i) What are the factors causing the present increased rigidity of procedural forms?

(ii) Is maintenance of reasonable flexibility deemed necessary and/or opportune in *ad hoc* as well as in administered arbitration?

(iii) In the affirmative, how can one cope with the existing trend towards detailed procedural regulations (which undoubtedly bring about rigidity) without relinquishing a tradition of flexibility upon which the present acceptance of arbitration has traditionally been built?

3-10 Flexibility has always been quoted as one of the classic features of arbitration. Especially in the domain of international arbitration, flexibility is the prerequisite to a reasonable compromise between various procedural philosophies, thus favouring the effectiveness of arbitration among parties of different socio-political extraction. Specificity of international arbitration calls for the application of a reduced number of rules, thus allowing national or regional peculiarities to remain confined to the domain of domestic arbitration. Last, but certainly not least: flexibility is traditionally cited as a praiseworthy alternative to the inevitable rigidity of court proceedings.

3-11 In the light of the above, it is understandable why students and practitioners of arbitration are increasingly worried by the finding that arbitration is undoubtedly becoming more and more complicated and its traditionally ideal simplicity (i.e. the prerequisite to flexibility) risks being confined to the realm of utopia.

3-12 The reasons why past simplicity is fading away should be analysed with reference to the different chronological steps, corresponding to the various stages characterising the institutional sequence of the proceedings through which arbitration comes into being and is carried to its physiological end. Also the ensuing award may undergo certain tests before becoming binding between the parties and, eventually, before acquiring the status of '*res judicata*'.

3-13 The first step, i.e. the initial stage of the procedural sequence, coincides with the appointment of the arbitrators. The second step, or stage, extends over the implementation of the arbitral proceedings, which culminate with the issuance of the award. The third step, or stage, comes into being whenever the award is subject to setting aside actions, or else its exequatur is opposed and possibly refused.

3-14 It is with reference to each of the above-mentioned steps, or stages, that a value judgment should be expressed concerning the widespread contention that arbitration is becoming more rigid, and, in general terms, more complicated than it used to be. May one also add that complaints are often raised against the quasi-judicial pugnacity which at present appears to have been transplanted in the domain of arbitration.

3-15 As usual, truth lies in the middle. The traditionally ideal simplicity of arbitration has probably been unconsciously magnified through the rose-tinted spectacles of wishful thinking. Furthermore, when praising the merits of arbitration, one tends to confuse, in historical perspective, arbitration viewed as a means to settle *ad hoc* disputes and arbitration viewed as the outward expression of close-knit communities of merchants characterised by standardised contractual practices and by mores and business customs convened from time immemorial. Allusion is hereby made to communities of merchants whose existence still finds its origin in the medieval guilds. Also maritime arbitration partakes of the same philosophy. In this perspective arbitration appears as one of the manifold facets of an unchallenged way of life, and its effectiveness is enhanced by the constant reference to generally accepted business and ethical canons.

3-16 Generalised compliance with arbitral awards is therefore not surprising, especially if one properly appraises the circumstance that the social sanction for non-compliance amounts, in terms of fact, to the breaking of all ties with the community. The sanctity of this rule still prevails in the field of commodities (or quality) arbitration, wherein the instances of setting aside actions brought before the judiciary are very rare indeed.

3-17 The above circumstances should be taken into due consideration when assessing the real impact of the generally accepted praise fostering simplicity and elasticity of arbitration. The background conditions greatly change when one moves out of the pattern of an arbitration deeply embedded in the basic values of a given community. When referred to a fragmented sociological background as regards the approach to litigation, arbitration cannot be taken for granted as the optimum instrument to solve disputes, nor can it be deemed standardised in terms of procedural *modus operandi*. Its ambit is vast and varied, its features may diverge, sometimes to a considerable extent. The range of its use extends over themes like construction, investments, business associations and consortia, distribution, transfer of technology, to cite but a few. Correspondingly, the structural and organisational requirements of arbitration undergo considerable change. Even the ambit of arbitrability is not uniform in the different countries, although, as a general trend, it appears to be constantly expanding. Suffice it to remind, in this connection, the fields of antitrust, patents and securities.

3-18 The source of the above changes should be mainly traced to the varying features of the contractual schemes to which the arbitration agreement is appended. Such schemes tend to become all the more complex and interdependent. In the light of contemporary reality major economic transactions are rarely comprised in one contractual scheme; they extend over a variety of contracts, linked through precise ties of manifold connections. Within a like background a clear distinction should be made between economic and legal elements. The former are to be combined to the end of completing a mosaic representing the economic (or business) transaction in its entirety; the latter, consisting of a network of different contractual relations, are to provide the overall regulation of said economic transaction, although the direct relationship among the various parties (privity of contract) may undergo considerable change from case to case.

3-19 Given its contractual foundation, arbitration is bound to be affected by this kaleidoscopic combination of sources. This is why, also in the course of arbitral proceedings, problems have emerged formerly confined to the domain of civil procedure. Allusion is made to multi-party arbitration, consolidation, connection between different proceedings, intervention of third parties, suspension of proceedings, and other similar problems which are likely to arise in the ambit of situations characterised by a plurality of parties and/or of proceedings.

3-20 The impact of this reality upon the traditional scheme of arbitration may become disruptive. This is why, after approaching the general theme of this report, I came to the preliminary conclusion that arbitration may be growing too big for its contractual vestment. The answer, in terms of principle, is probably in the affirmative; the consequence, however, is not necessarily negative, if the different situations are properly discriminated and if the opportune remedies are put into being. In other words, I personally believe that an acceptable compromise can be worked out whereby the traditional features of arbitration may be preserved to a reasonable extent without ignoring the basic data emerging from contemporary reality.

III. DIFFERENT SITUATIONS CALL FOR DIFFERENT REMEDIES

3-21 The remedies should be kept distinct if viewed in the framework of *ad hoc* as opposed to administered arbitration. The reason for this difference is intuitive. In the first hypothesis, as a rule, there exists no pre-prepared set of rules automatically applicable to the incoming proceedings; in the second, the parties are aware of the rules governing arbitral proceedings even before the occurrence of the dispute. Problems like those arising in the case of multiplicity of parties and/or of proceedings can only be solved through directions emanating, directly or indirectly, from the will of the parties. This, at least, under the systems where no overriding judicial intervention can pollute the 'purity' of a decision-making power resting solely on contractual foundations. It follows that in *ad hoc* arbitration a system designed to cope with multi-party arbitration can hardly be worked out, given its intrinsic complication, at the level of the arbitration clause. In terms of practicability, the numerous variables can effectively be settled only after the dispute has arisen. This, obviously, may not be the aptest time.

3-22 The situation is different if one turns to administered arbitration, wherein the variety of applicable rules can give rise to a detailed set of arbitration procedures. In addition, the institutional presence of an appointing authority can ensure that the arbitrators will be nominated in the proper number, irrespective of the number of the parties participating in the arbitration. When choosing this alternative, however, the parties should be fully aware that their right to designate an arbitrator may be sacrificed on the altar of multi-party arbitration. Furthermore, the increased detail of the applicable rules inevitably and irreversibly entails an increased rigidity of the proceedings. The parties, therefore, are faced with a clear choice: if they seek solution of the difficult problems arising out of situations involving multiplicity of parties and/or of proceedings, they must accept, together with the waiver of their right to appoint an arbitrator, the increased rigidity of the proceedings. Every choice entails a renunciation. As a known saying lucidly states, you cannot have your cake and eat it.

3-23 The foregoing remarks lead to the conclusion that at present, in addition to the dichotomy between *ad hoc* and administered arbitration, a further distinction should be drawn concerning the features of the respective proceedings. In the first place, one may still find a reasonably simple and flexible arbitration wherein the parties maintain their right to appoint an arbitrator of their choice. This type of arbitration, however, cannot be successfully used to settle, in the context of the same proceedings, certain sophisticated problems which one may encounter in contemporary practice. In the second place, a new arbitral paradigm has emerged more closely resembling a court proceeding administered by the local judges. Within this second type of arbitrations the problems which I have defined as more 'sophisticated', may also find an adequate solution. The parties may thus have their choice, without the possibility, however, of combining only the advantages of both systems. In particular, may I be permitted to stress it again, without being prepared to surrender, in case they choose the quasi-judicial type of arbitration, a certain number of prerogatives traditionally tied to the intrinsic notion of arbitration.

3-24 The analysis would not be complete unless exhaustive reference were made to a third factor which was merely enunciated in the foregoing comments.

3-25 I indicated that when dealing with complex situations, rigidity is bound to ensue because the multiple contractual framework in which the dispute is to be placed does not allow the use of the simpler scheme of arbitration to which we are accustomed. I have also pointed out that the complexity in question may be dealt with either through detailed regulation, more likely to be found in administered arbitration, or else through an intervention *'ex lege'* of the courts of justice. The latter may hand down the necessary measures concerning, for instance, consolidation of different arbitral proceedings. This solution, more often encountered within the common law systems, has also been adopted by the new Dutch legislation. The solution in question deserves a comment going beyond the bounds of the subject of this report. The need for a court intervention demonstrates that arbitration alone cannot cope with situations requiring the exercise of institutional powers which are external to the scope of the parties' intent as consecrated in the arbitration agreement. In terms of principle such an occurrence should not be looked upon disfavourably *per se.* However, one should also stress that this type of court intervention injects a different dimension into the traditional ambit of the relations, or 'links' to use an accepted terminology, existing between arbitrators and the courts. Such ambit diverges under the various legal latitudes: however, as a common denominator, one may possibly cite only judicial assistance concerning the appointment of the arbitrators. If one goes further, the sphere of discrepancy among different domestic laws sharply increases. This is certainly the case when dealing with the subject of consolidation of different arbitral proceedings. If consolidation or similar measures may be ordered by the courts without the parties' assent, a new element is inserted into the classic notion of arbitration. This element may be equated with the parties' prior (and blank) acceptance of the possible occurrence whereby the original arbitration pattern contractually convened may undergo radical changes as regards the number of parties in dispute, the number of arbitrators, and the ambit of the matter in dispute. Last, but certainly not least, the occurrence in question may bring about the result that after the consolidation the parties may be subjected to a decision rendered by arbitrators who were neither designated by them nor appointed by an authority indicated in their original arbitration agreement.

3-26 I refrain here from expressing any judgment on the merits of consolidation by the courts as regards the specific problem of multi-party arbitration. May I only be permitted to point out that the existence of such a power represents an element of disharmony if referred to the notion of contractual arbitration. Such notion is supported by a massive weight of authority, *inter alia* as a reaction to quasi-judicial (or jurisdictional) types of arbitration still prevailing under certain domestic legislations. Also the New York Convention gives due weight to the notion of a merely 'binding (hence contractual)' arbitration.

IV. A REALISTIC APPROACH TO THE APPRAISAL OF FLEXIBIITY AS OPPOSED TO RIGIDITY: INSTANCES IN WHICH RIGIDITY MAY BE AVOIDED

3-27 In the foregoing paragraphs I tried to define the ambit in which rigidity should be deemed, in terms of actual fact, unavoidable. The result of the analysis tends to diminish the potential danger of rigidity, as it confines it to situations where the parties are seeking a result which can only be achieved with great difficulty within the contractual bounds of arbitration. If this is the result that the parties want, they cannot pretend at the same time that the traditional features of arbitration remain unaffected. It follows that in assessing the real impact of the juxtaposition between flexibility and rigidity, one should move out of the special situations pointed out above, where rigidity may be defined as inevitable. It is certainly not so when rigidity does not occur as the necessary consequence of the widened scope of traditional arbitration. In this second instance, rigidity may be avoided if one so wishes. Personally I am of the opinion that it should be avoided to keep arbitration in its traditionally accepted tracks.

3-28 The source of this 'avoidable' rigidity can be traced to a tendency, often encountered today, favouring meticulous regulation of arbitration proceedings. This may happen, in principle, both in *ad hoc* as well as in administered arbitration. In terms of real fact, the danger is potentially more acute in administered arbitration, where one is more likely to indulge in detailed sets of arbitration procedure. Since in history nothing happens by chance, one should identify the reasons for such increased rigidity in order to prescribe the best therapy.

3-29 When arbitration was deeply embedded in the way of life of a close-knit community, there was little room, if any, for procedural problems. Arbitration was the expression of common beliefs and its administration was not hampered by misunderstandings due to differences of ideology, and hence of action coherent with it.

3-30 This original uniformity has broken down in direct proportion to the wider acceptance of arbitration. All the more so if conflicting national philosophies are not confined to the legal domain but rather touch on socio-political and religious factors deeply embedded in the respective communities, be they viewed at national or at regional level. Differences of basic understanding and lack of mutual knowledge inevitably lead to diffidence. Diffidence may best be overcome through the establishment of rules aimed at guiding future action. In my opinion, the increased trend towards rigidity is, to a considerable extent, the expression of an aggravated need for detailed regulation stemming from the above cited negative factors, inevitably accentuated when the use of arbitration is extended. This extension, however, is to be fostered if one wishes to favour the cause of arbitration. As I pointed out in proposing a set of guidelines for ICCA's future action (Yearbook, Comm. Arb. n. XII-1987, p. XVII):

> At the present stage, it is essential that attention be pragmatically focused on concrete issues touching on the effectiveness of international arbitration and awards. Furthermore, the time is more than ripe for a decided effort towards a closer collaboration between industrialised countries (be they capitalist or socialist) and developing countries regarding the promotion of international arbitration.

One is thus faced with the 'new frontier' of arbitration. To remain confined to the countries traditionally favouring arbitration would amount to an intellectual exercise bordering upon narcissism.

3-31 Although understandable in historical perspective, the trend towards exceedingly meticulous regulation is, in my opinion, a danger. The parties, faced with an off-putting set of rules, may lose faith in arbitration, in the belief that this instrument tends to become like a complicated court proceeding.

3-32 To avoid such a danger there is only one therapy: shifting the emphasis from the rules governing the proceedings to the qualification of arbitrators. This statement is not a paradox and I shall come back to it when dealing with foreseeability of results, the last topic of this report.

3-33 If the arbitrators are truly experienced they will be able to instil the necessary confidence into the parties, to prevent all possible misunderstandings and to smoothly conduct the proceedings without relying on an illusively exhaustive set of rules. It will be the arbitrators' task to set only the basic rules of the game, implementing them with intelligent firmness and through the enactment of further directions as the case may be. Together with regulatory logorrhoea, prudent arbitrators shall also avoid the opposite danger, i.e. that of letting the parties loose to play their contentious game the way they deem fit.

3-34 In between these two extremes the arbitrators shall set their course, refraining from behaving as inquisitors but also avoiding a posture like that of a Roman emperor sitting in the Colosseum to watch the gladiators massacre each other.

3-35 Rigidity in arbitration is conversely proportionate to the intelligence and experience of the arbitrators. This approach is intended to realistically overcome the trite picture of a common law arbitrator limiting his/her function to that of a qualified witness, as opposed to that of a civil law arbitrator intervening actively in the proceedings, sometimes as a *'negotiorum gestor'* for the parties. These lithographic images are nothing other than the expression of doctrinal generalisations which rarely, if ever, find a counterpart in actual practice. In international arbitration, if the relative proceedings are properly administered, a compromise is always achieved between the different procedural philosophies in such a way as to allow the parties to carry out their right of defence without limitations deriving from purely domestic principles. One should further remember that principles and rules set with reference to court proceedings cannot be transplanted as such from the judicial *milieu* (where judges have *inter alia* powers of coercion) to the arbitral *milieu* (where arbitrators as a general rule have no comparable powers). As a consequence, arbitrators can hardly afford a purely passive role, as one cannot persuade people by remaining idle. Constant vigilance may best allow the subsequent completion of the basic rules handed down at the outset. In conclusion, it rests with the arbitrators' prudent discretion to safeguard the elasticity of the proceedings without allowing confusion to arise out of disorderly exchanges between the parties.

3-36 When speaking of basic principles their explicit enumeration becomes difficult, and possibly misleading, *'in vitro'*. Only the variety of individual cases may guide the arbitrators' choice, without prejudice to the general assertion that the principles in question should, in any and all instances, be detailed enough to characterise the incoming proceedings without causing them to become sclerotic.

3-37 In the light of the above it is recommended that the arbitrators set *ab initio* only the guidelines concerning the written and oral exchanges between the parties; the logistics and the expected chronology of the proceedings; the criteria under which evidence is going to be received; the limits, if any, within which rules typical of court proceedings (statements under oath, discovery, examination of witnesses) apply to the arbitration at issue.

3-38 More detailed directions should be left to subsequent orders to be enacted by the arbitrators, as the case may be, in the light of the vicissitudes occurring, in terms of actual fact, in each individual proceeding.

3-39 The same criteria should prevail when the arbitrators, together with the parties, are called upon, after the dispute has arisen, to execute and/or detail their agreement to arbitrate.

3-40 Within the ICC practice the execution of the arbitrators' terms of reference is prescribed by the Rules (Art. 13). Without casting any value judgment on the terms of reference as such, the analysis of the techniques adopted in the preparation of this document offers a fair guidance as concerns the appraisal of trends favouring rigidity as opposed to elasticity. Here again I take the liberty of expressing my inclination towards drafting techniques which are not too analytical, i.e. which do not pretend to offer an all encompassing regulation, thus limiting the ambit of the arbitrators' future discretion. The contents of the terms of reference should be confined to basic guidelines and the arbitrators should be granted the power to later decide on a case by case approach in harmony with the implementation of the proceedings.

3-41 As regards the terms of reference, rigidity may derive, in particular, from excessive detail in the breaking down of the issues to be decided by the arbitrators. Lengthy documents, where the issues are split into fragments following the logical approach of the arbitrators preparing the draft, may bring about the additional danger of prejudicing the case.

V. FORM OF PROCEEDINGS AND FORESEEABILITY OF RESULT IN INTERNATIONAL ARBITRATION

3-42 It is not easy to crystal-gaze, in general terms, whether in the future flexibility will prevail over rigidity or vice versa.

3-43 Whenever rigidity is the direct consequence of special situations, like those characterised by a multiplicity of parties and/or of proceedings, the answer indicating rigidity as the winner is obviously necessitated. It remains to be seen, however, whether the parties will favour a new type of arbitration which differs, sometimes to a considerable extent, from the traditional arbitration to which the average user is accustomed. Without venturing any further thought, I shall simply recall that the uncertainties still surrounding the diffusion of multi-party arbitration should suggest a cautious answer.

3-44 The answer is different when dealing with 'avoidable' rigidity. Here a true value judgment is involved and I repeat my propensity for flexibility. Rigidity, as pointed out above, is a danger, in future perspective, as it departs from the traditional canons which have led to widespread acceptance of arbitration. Rigidity is not even to be recommended, in pragmatic terms, as a better instrument to conduct 'difficult' arbitrations. Quite the contrary: in international arbitration rigidity may hinder the effective implementation of the proceedings by limiting the arbitrators' discretion without the contribution of countervailing advantages. When aimed at very diversified situations (as is generally the case in international arbitration) no set of rules can be, at the same time, both harmonious and exhaustive. No enumeration at all is better than an incomplete enumeration. In international arbitration the pretence of handing down a complete set of rules can rarely succeed. No rules whatsoever may be deemed complete unless susceptible of giving rise to univocal construction and uniform interpretation in the light of well established legal systems. This is not the case for international arbitration, nor is it to be wished that the ties between international arbitration and individual domestic systems become any stronger: quite the contrary! This means, in methodological terms, that for the orderly implementation of the proceedings the parties should rely on a case-by-case approach: i.e. on arbitrator-made rules rather than on detailed and pre-prepared sets of arbitration procedure.

3-45 My plea in favour of elasticity bears on the conclusions relating to the last topic of this report: form of proceedings and foreseeability of results in international arbitration. In the domain of the judiciary this query is a classic. In arbitration, however, the dose of the various intellectual ingredients should be personalised. When facing court proceedings the parties rely, in terms of foreseeability of results, on the judicial system as such. The institution, rather than the individuals, gives the assurance or nurses the worry. The form of proceedings is a facet of the ensemble. It is governed by an exhaustive set of detailed rules, accompanied by a solid body of case law. Its structural and chronological stability, together with the availability of published precedents, allows a reasonable forecast concerning the duration of the proceedings, the form of the same and their basic features. The parties may also venture a fairly sound guess regarding the criteria of admissibility of their evidence as well as the rules under which the same is going to be received. Also in terms of basic guarantees, like due process, the right to be heard and, more generally, the exercise of the right of defence, it is the status of the system, and certainly not the person (unknown beforehand) of the individual judge, which should undergo scrutiny and appraisal by the utiliser of justice. When facing the judiciary also neutrality, like impartiality, are to be evaluated at institutional level. Only in the exceptional hypothesis justifying an abstention and/or a challenge does the judge come into play as an individual.

3-46 Also in the framework of a judicial system the form of proceedings is the object of critical appraisal, often in comparative perspective, *inter alia* to the end of bringing about all necessary improvements by way of legislative reform. Classic themes like oral versus written form, inquisitorial versus adversary system, due process and human rights, are heatedly debated. Foreseeability of results is one of the major concerns.

3-47 The different solutions, however, cannot be transplanted as such from the judicial to the arbitral context. As regards in particular the specific theme of foreseeability of results, the peculiar nature of arbitration requires a different method of inquiry. Arbitration, as a system, does not offer institutional guarantees comparable to those existing within the judiciary. The individuals, rather than the arbitration as such, are to be regarded as critical in venturing a guess on foreseeability of results. By the word 'individuals' a reference is made not only to arbitrators but also to administrators of arbitral proceedings, viewed, as the case may be, not only as bodies, but also as natural persons charged with personal responsibilities in the performance of their duties.

3-48 In arbitration the relevance of precedents, though of growing importance, still is relatively modest. Hence the understandable temptation, especially in administered arbitration, to offer quasi-institutional guarantees through detailed sets of rules aimed at covering every stage of the arbitral proceedings. This temptation, as already anticipated, should be resisted, as it favours rigidity without any appreciable improvements in terms of foreseeability of results. It is not the detail of the pre-prepared rules which affords the institutional guarantee, but rather their source, together with the incisiveness of their enforcement. Along these lines even the most exhaustive set of rules aimed at governing arbitral proceedings can ever be equated with a piece of legislation like a code of civil procedure, drawing its strength from the inner nature of a sovereign system.

3-49 The strength of arbitral justice lies elsewhere: in essence, in the choice of the best arbitrators and of the best administrators, as the case may be. The form of the proceedings should be such as to allow the fullest exploitation of the professional talents chosen *ad hoc* in the different capacities. It should favour flexibility, as a marked advantage over the institutional rigidity of any court proceedings. It should never rival the judiciary in terms of strictness in the application of procedural canons of conduct, with the potential danger of inheriting only the negative features of court procedure. Elasticity does not antagonise foreseeability of results, provided, however, that a number of fundamental principles are clearly set as imperative and punctually complied with. It is the notion, already mentioned, of 'basic rules' which the arbitrators should hand down at the inception of the arbitration, to be completed by subsequent orders as the vicissitudes of each individual case may require.

3-50 I already stated the difficulty of analytical enumerations (*retro*, para. 3-35). By way of conclusion may I be permitted to approach the problem from another angle, i.e. by taking as common denominator the safeguard of the full exercise of the right of defence. It is now generally accepted that the arbitrators should ensure the orderly progress of the proceedings, preventing and repressing dilatory tactics, whether by way of superfluous written statements, or new and last minute allegations, as well as submission of inadmissible or not relevant evidence. It was also agreed that the right to be heard is to be understood not only as the right to make submissions, whether by way of evidence or legal argument, but also as the right to be fully informed about submissions of the other party and to discuss them. Reference should also be made to obstructing techniques realised, more often than not, with the complicity of unscrupulous party appointed arbitrators. Episodes may also be reported in which the courts have lent too complacent a hand in obstructing pending arbitrations.

3-51 To conclude, I am convinced that the safeguard of the parties' right of defence should be the yardstick to be used in deciding, throughout the proceedings, *inter alia* on the admissibility of late submissions, on the refusal to hear redundant evidence, on granting of delays, on resisting to dilatory and/or obstructive tactics. This calls for a joint action to be carried out by the arbitrators and by the administering bodies. It should also be stressed that tolerance or intransigence *vis-à-vis* procedural violations should not be guided by subjective notions of fairness and justice, but by a rigorous concern over the protection of the parties' procedural and substantive rights. The parties themselves are fully entitled to expect from the arbitrators a behaviour characterised by a subjective status of good faith and by an objective competence as regards the conduct of the proceedings and the safeguard of due process. The arbitrators are under a duty to inform the parties of all factual and legal arguments upon which their decision will be grounded. In conclusion, their main concern should be that of ensuring an effective right of defence, taking into consideration the fact that this notion of 'effectiveness' is being properly defined also by domestic judiciaries. To use a generally accepted and comprehensive terminology (of common law extraction) the safeguard of due process should be insured to the fullest extent as regards all steps, or phases of the arbitral proceedings.

3-52 The above conclusions place great responsibility upon the arbitrators and fully justify the plea of quality which is always raised when touching upon international arbitration. Before experienced arbitrators flexible forms of proceedings are no bar to foreseeability of results. In addition to the fundamental qualities of neutrality, independence and impartiality, fairness and competence are to be expected from the arbitrators, and one should never forget, in addition, that the number of actions filed by a dissatisfied party with the aim of setting aside the award, with ensuing court control over the same, is constantly increasing.

3-53 Flexibility and intelligent firmness are the best tools in the hands of a competent arbitrator. Once the rules of the game are established, thus building the parties' reliance upon foreseeable results, no change should take place without informing them.

3-54 In the *milieu* of administered arbitration discussions have taken place concerning the opportunity of supplying the arbitrators with a check-list of all items on which rules should be issued in the interest of good administration of the proceedings. The initiative is laudable as compliance with the check-list would increase, to the parties' benefit, the foreseeability of results. In more general terms, quality as such appears of the essence also as regards the administration of arbitral proceedings, which can greatly help, if properly conducted, foreseeability of results. New organisations are born every day with a frantic pace. A caveat, therefore, appears opportune. As I wrote in commenting on ICCA's activity in 1987 (Yearbook, Comm. Arb., XII-1988, p. XX):

> Also the flourishing of arbitral organisations should be praised in principle, but carefully scrutinised in practice. The expansion of human endeavours and the maintenance of high standards of quality are not incompatible per se: they just are difficult to achieve.

3-55 To conclude, nothing will ever replace human competence. It has been said and written that no institution can be better than the persons administering it. Arbitration is certainly no exception. Only the quality of the arbitrators and of the administrators, and certainly not the illusory guarantee stemming from increasingly detailed regulations, will allow foreseeability of a reasonably swift and just result. Otherwise one must conclude with the Poet: *'That old common arbitrator, time, will one day end it'* (Shakespeare, Troi. and Cres., IV -5 -225).

3-56 Undoubtedly, the mere lapse of time is not the type of foreseeability that the parties are entitled to expect in international arbitration.

*Lord Bingham**

CHAPTER 4

THE PROBLEM OF DELAY IN ARBITRATION

I. INTRODUCTION

4-1 I am indebted to Sir Robert Megarry for drawing my attention to a form of arbitration which flourished in County Down during the last century. The parties agreed on an impartial chairman, who sat at the head of a long table with the parties on either hand. Down the middle of the table a line was drawn, and grains of oats were placed along it at intervals of a few inches. A foot or so from the head of the table the line stopped, and two grains of corn were placed a few inches from the middle, one in front of each party. Then, with the chairman as umpire, a hen turkey was gently placed on the table at the far end. The turkey would then delicately peck her ladylike way all up the table until, when she reached the two grains of corn at the top, she delivered her award in favour of one party or the other by taking first the grain nearer to him.

4-2 It is, however, recorded that on one occasion the loser in such an arbitrament was a litigious character who refused to accept the decision as just, and brought a civil bill in the county court against the winner. On the facts being proved, the county court judge dismissed the action, whereupon the plaintiff exercised his right to appeal to the assize judge. This was an aged and learned equity lawyer, Lefroy C.J., who unlike counsel for the defendant knew little of local customs. During cross-examination of the plaintiff the following passage occurred:

* The author is a judge of the English Court of Appeal. This article is an edited version of a lecture delivered at the School of International Arbitration on 11 May 1989 as the 1989 Freshfields Arbitration Lecture. [He moved to the House of Lords in 2000 as Lord Bingham of Cornhill and became the Senior Lord of Appeal in Ordinary.]

Julian D.M. Lew and Loukas A. Mistelis (eds), Arbitration Insights, 63-80
© 2007 Kluwer Law International. Printed in the Netherlands

Counsel: 'Tell me, wasn't the turkey for the defendant?' No answer.
Counsel: 'Tell my Lord the truth, now. Wasn't the turkey for the defendant?'
Chief Justice: 'What on earth has a turkey to do with this case?'
Counsel: 'It's a local form of arbitration, my Lord.'
Chief Justice: 'Do you mean to tell me that the plaintiff has brought this case in disregard of the award of an arbitrator?'
Counsel: 'That is so, my Lord.'
Chief Justice: 'Disgraceful! Appeal dismissed with costs here and below.'
Counsel (sotto voce): 'The Lord Chief Justice affirms the turkey.'

4-3 It will, I am sure, be at once obvious that this form of arbitration, although perhaps unattractive to professional arbitrators, has in large measure most of the merits claimed for this form of dispute resolution. It is very inexpensive, the more so since the bird can be used again. It is private. It enables the parties to select an expert tribunal. It minimises, as the story shows, the opportunities for judicial intervention. And, relevantly to my theme today, it promotes the expeditious determination of references: the opportunities for delay are so limited that, one way or another, the reference is likely to be settled once and for all very shortly after the submission of the dispute to arbitration.

4-4 This is, as all would agree, desirable. But a series of cases in England over the last decade has shown that it is a result which is by no means always achieved. The facts of these cases are all, of course, different, but the broad pattern is similar. A commercial contract contains an arbitration clause. It may also contain a short contractual limitation period. A claim, or suspected claim, arises under the contract. The claimant gives notice of claim and appoints an arbitrator. The respondent also appoints an arbitrator. A third arbitrator or umpire is probably appointed. There may or may not be some interlocutory activity, such as the exchange of pleadings. The matter then becomes dormant. The claimant, whether through pessimism as to his chances, distraction with other business, the lethargy of his advisers or for any other reason, does nothing to pursue the claim. The respondent is only too happy to do nothing, hoping that he will never hear of the matter again. He has no incentive to goad the claimant into action. The arbitrators do nothing, awaiting an indication of the parties' wishes. One of them may in due course collect his fees and close his files. Then the claimant seeks to re-awaken the reference and renew his claim for an award in his favour. This may be 6, 8, 10, 12 or more years after the dispute arose. Any relevant limitation period will have expired. Witnesses may have died or disappeared. Recollections may have dimmed. Documents may have been routinely destroyed. A fair, or as some prefer to say satisfactory, trial of the dispute may no longer be possible, and the respondent may be irretrievably prejudiced if the reference goes ahead. What is to be done? It must be very doubtful whether, over the last decade, anything has generated more commercial litigation than the answer to this seemingly straight-forward question. I calculate that it has occupied upwards of 180 judicial court days. When one takes account also of the time and expense devoted to litigating this question by the various parties and their advisers it is plain that a simple and inexpensive answer to the problem, if achievable, is much to be desired.

4-5   The problem appears to be peculiar to arbitration. That is not, of course, to say that parties to court actions do not behave in very much the same way as parties to arbitration references. They do. But when a plaintiff is guilty of gross delay after starting his action and the defendant is thereby seriously prejudiced in conducting his defence or otherwise, the defendant has the now well-established right to apply to the court for dismissal of the plaintiff's action. As one of the losing advocates in *Allen v. McAlpine*[1] and *Birkett v. James*[2] I shall forbear to criticise those decisions. But whatever their demerits, these decisions do provide in court proceedings a definitive answer to the problem which has plagued stale arbitrations. The defendant need not wake up the sleeping dog in order to kill it. But if a plaintiff after gross, inordinate and prejudicial delay seeks to revive his action the defendant can apply to the court for its instant dismissal for want of prosecution. Unless an answer is found, the arbitration process, which ought to be superior to its forensic counterpart, must in this procedural respect at least be regarded as inferior.

II. SUGGESTED SOLUTIONS TO THE PROBLEM OF DELAY

4-6   I would like at this point briefly to identify the solutions to the problem which have been discussed in the commercial arbitration cases over the last ten years, both because the scatter of judicial opinion which they display is extraordinary and because I shall venture to suggest hereafter that, even among these rejected solutions, some are a good deal more equal than others. Certain of the solutions have been expressed by different judges in different ways, and subject to certain qualifications and modifications, but looking at the judgments broadly I think it is possible to identify about eight suggested solutions.

---

[1]   [1968] 2 Q.B. 229.
[2]   [1978] A.C. 297.

4-7 (1) That parties who submit disputes to arbitration impliedly clothe the arbitrators with jurisdiction to give effect to their rights and remedies in much the same manner as a court, including jurisdiction to make an award dismissing a claim if the claimant's delay in prosecuting it is so gross as to make the dispute not fairly triable. This solution was adopted by Donaldson J. at first instance in *Bremer Vulkan Schiffbau und Maschinenfabrik v. South India Shipping Corporation*[3] and his reasoning was found convincing by Lloyd J. in *The Splendid Sun*.[4] Nicholls L. J. in *The Antclizo*[5] would, if free to do so, have favoured an implied term in the arbitration agreement itself that the arbitrators should have jurisdiction to dismiss stale claims no longer fairly triable. But a rather similar argument had been rejected by Bridge J. in *Crawford v. A.E.A. Prowting Ltd.*[6] and it was thereafter expressly rejected by all three members of the Court of Appeal and all five members of the House of Lords in *Bremer Vulkan*.

4-8 (2) That the court has an inherent jurisdiction to restrain arbitration proceedings where it is just and convenient to do so, and it may be right and just where the claimant has been guilty of such delay that a fair hearing is impossible. Donaldson J. did not think, on the authorities, that this solution was open to him in *Bremer Vulkan*, but it was accepted by Lord Denning M.R. in that case[7] and by the dissenting minority in the House of Lords, Lord Fraser[8] and Lord Scarman.[9] It was not, however, accepted by the majority, so that avenue was blocked.

4-9 (3) That a claimant's failure to prosecute an arbitration claim to the point where it is no longer fairly triable is a repudiation of the arbitration agreement between the parties, which the respondent is entitled to accept; acceptance of the Claimant's repudiation brings the arbitration agreement to an end, and the respondent can then enjoin the claimant from further pursuing the claim. This solution was adopted by Donaldson J. in *Bremer Vulkan*,[10] by Lloyd J. in *The Splendid Sun*[11] and by all three members of the Court of Appeal in *Bremer Vulkan*. But it was decisively rejected by the majority of the House of Lords in

---

[3]   [1981] A. C. 909, 919.
[4]   [1980] 1 Lloyd's Rep. 333, 336.
[5]   [1987] 2 Lloyd's Rep. 130, 147.
[6]   [1973] Q.B. 1.
[7]   [1981] A. C. 909, 939G.
[8]   *Ibid.*, at p. 993C.
[9]   *Ibid.*, at p. 997F.
[10] *Ibid.*, at p. 924.
[11] [1980] 1 Lloyd's Rep. 333, 335.

Bremer Vulkan, unless the respondent was himself guiltless of any failure to press the matter forward. The basis of this qualification was the well-known – perhaps I should say notorious – ruling that parties to an arbitration agreement are subject to a mutual obligation, binding as much on the respondent as the claimant, to press the reference to a hearing, with the result that a respondent who has himself failed to do so cannot complain of repudiation by the claimant. The consensual nature of the arbitration agreement was held to distinguish the position of a respondent in an arbitration from a defendant in an action, who is fully entitled to sit tight and do nothing. But since respondents habitually behave in practice in just the same way as defendants, the practical effect is to block this route also. This chilling blast did not deter Lord Denning M.R. from adhering to this solution in *The Splendid Sun*[12] and *The Hannah Blumenthal*,[13] but on those occasions his judicial comrades in arms left him to go over the top alone.

4-10 (4) That delay in the prosecution of a claim in arbitration may, when so gross at to make the dispute no longer fairly triable, have the effect of frustrating the arbitration agreement and so entitling the respondent to treat the agreement as at an end. This solution had a good run, being favoured by Lord Denning M.R. in *Bremer Vulkan*,[14] *The Splendid Sun*[15] and *The Hannah Blumenthal*,[16] by Staughton J.[17] and Kerr L.J.[18] also in *The Hannah Blumenthal*, and by the Court of Appeal in *The Argonaut*.[19] It was, however, rejected by Fox L.J. in *The Splendid Sun*[20] and by Griffiths L.J. in *The Hannah Blumenthal*.[21] finally falling in the House of Lords in *The Hannah Blumenthal*.[22] a claimant's failure to prosecute his claim was not an extraneous supervening event capable of founding a plea of frustration and a respondent could not complain of a frustrating delay to which he had contributed by opting to do nothing.

4-11 (5) That an arbitration reference of agreement may be abandoned by the consent of the parties. This solution was adopted by the Court of Appeal in *The*

---

[12] [1981] Q.B. 694, 704G.
[13] [1983] 1 A.C. 854, 877A.
[14] [1981] A. C. 909, 940.
[15] [1981] Q. B. 694, 703.
[16] [1983] 1 A. C. 854, 878.
[17] *Ibid.*, at p. 867.
[18] *Ibid.*, at p. 885.
[19] [1982] 2 Lloyd's Rep. 214.
[20] *Supra.*
[21] *Supra.*
[22] *Supra.*

Splendid Sun[23] and approved in principle by the House of Lords in *The Hannah Blumenthal*.[24] The problems inherent in the exercise of finding a contract when neither party has said or done anything were, however, highlighted by the Court of Appeal in *The Leonidas D*[25] and have been further explored in such cases as *MSC Mediterranean Shipping Co. v. B.R.E. Metro*,[26] The Agrabele,[27] Cie. Francaise d'Importation et de Distribution S.A. v. Deutsche Continental Handelsgesellschaft,[28] The Antclizo,[29] *The Golden Bear*[30] and *The Multitank Holsatia*.[31]

4-12 (6) That each party's right to ask the arbitration tribunal to proceed to an award should be regarded as a contractual right in the nature of a power, which will lapse if not exercised within a reasonable time. In *The Leonidas D*[32] Robert Goff L.J. expressed tentative regret that this argument had not been advanced in *Bremer Vulkan*, but accepted that this approach was difficult to reconcile with what Lord Diplock had said in that case. Following discussion of this possible approach by Mr Beatson in the Law Quarterly Review,[33] reliance was placed on it in argument in *The Golden Bear*,[34] but Staughton J. shared the opinion that it was inconsistent with the *ratio* of the House of Lords decision in *Bremer Vulkan* and did not regard the right to ask for an award as being a discretionary right to which the requirement of reasonableness could be held to apply.

4-13 (7) That where a claimant's delay in prosecuting his claim is so great as to make a fair trial of the dispute impossible, the court may give leave under section 1 of the Arbitration Act 1950 to revoke an arbitrator's authority and order under section 25 (2)(b) that the arbitration agreement shall cease to have effect with respect to the dispute referred. In *Bremer Vulkan*[35] Roskill L.J. was unimpressed by an argument based on section 1 alone, but it is not apparent that reference was

---

[23] [1981] 1 Q. B. 694.
[24] [1983] 1 A.C. 854.
[25] [1985] 2 Lloyd's Rep. 18.
[26] [1985] 2 Lloyd's Rep. 239.
[27] [1985] 2 Lloyd's Rep. 496, [1987] 2 Lloyd's Rep. 223 (C.A.).
[28] [1985] 2 Lloyd's Rep. 592.
[29] [1986] 1 Lloyd's Rep. 181, [1987] 2 Lloyd's Rep. 130 (C.A.), [1988] 2 Lloyd's Rep. 93 (H.L.).
[30] [1987] 1 Lloyd's Rep. 330.
[31] [1988] 2 Lloyd's Rep. 486.
[32] [1985] 2 Lloyd's Rep. 18, 20.
[33] 102 L. Q R. 23 (1986).
[34] [1987] 1 Lloyd's Rep. 330.
[35] [1981] A. C. 909, 955.

made to section 25. The argument was, however, deployed by Dr F. A. Mann in a note in *Arbitration International* [36] and was seen by Kerr L.J. in *The Antclizo* [37] as providing a possible solution. Fortified no doubt by this support, counsel in *The Multitank Holsatia* [38] put the argument to the test. In the result Phillips J. did not have to rule on it, but his judgment suggests that, if obliged to rule, he would have been inclined to rule against.

4-14 (8) That the court may, under section 5 of the Arbitration Act 1979, by order extend an arbitrator's powers on a claimant's failure to comply with the arbitrator's order, entitling the arbitrator 'to the extent and subject to any conditions specified in that order, to continue with the reference in default of appearance or of any other act by one of the parties in like manner as a judge of the High Court might continue with proceedings in that court where a party fails to comply with an order of that court or a requirement of rules of court'. I shall in a moment comment briefly on this and some of the other solutions.

4-15 The bonds of judicial reticence – or such of them as still remain – have not prevented forthright criticism of the law as it now stands. According to Lord Denning M.R. in *The Splendid Sun* [39] the mutual obligation upheld in *Bremer Vulkan*'comes as something of a surprise to everyone: especially to the denizens of Essex Court and St. Mary Axe ... I cannot believe that the House of Lords intended any such thing. I think that we must have misunderstood the ruling in some way or other'. Kerr L.J. in *The Hannah Blumenthal* [40] spoke from personal knowledge when saying that the decision 'has been received with the greatest concern, not only in the City and the Temple, but also abroad among practitioners and institutions who look to this country as an important venue for international commercial arbitrations'. In Dr Mann's view, the decision was universally recognised to be an aberration.[41] The current doctrine of consensual abandonment has fared no better. To Robert Goff L.J. the finding of offer and acceptance from silence and inaction was 'most surprising'.[42] To Saville J. it was 'the antithesis of agreement as a matter of English law'.[43] I expressed some

---

[36] (1986), Vol. 2, p. 240.
[37] [1987] 2 Lloyd's Rep. 130.
[38] [1988] 2 Lloyd's Rep. 486, 493.
[39] [1981] Q.B. 694, 701.
[40] [1983] 1 A.C. 854, 885.
[41] *Arbitration International* (1988), Vol. 4, p. 158.
[42] *The Leonidas D*[1985] 2 Lloyd's Re p. 18, 25.
[43] *MSC Mediterranean Shipping Co. v. B.R.E. –Metro*[1985] 2 Lloyd's Rep. 239, 241.

unease at what seemed a somewhat artificial and unreal process of reasoning and analysis.[44] Staughton J. considered a contract created by simple inactivity to be an odd creature in English law.[45] In *The Antclizo*,[46] Kerr L.J. expressed the belief that no one concerned with the state of our law of arbitration could view the present position with equanimity and believed the state of the law to be regretted by most if not all judges and practitioners.

III. OTHER JURISDICTIONS

4-16 It may at this point be worth turning our attention away from this black hole of English jurisprudence to ask how others have tackled this problem and, indeed, whether they have found there to be a problem at all. I cannot claim to have made anything approaching a comprehensive comparative survey, so what follows – largely dependent on charitable donations of information by friends whom I have approached – is a somewhat random sample of experience.[47]

4-17 In Hong Kong, New South Wales, Victoria, Singapore, Bermuda and perhaps other Commonwealth jurisdictions the nettle has been grasped by legislation. Section 29A of the Hong Kong Arbitration Ordinance is the model. By a 1982 amendment, a statutory implied term is imported into every arbitration agreement that the claimant shall exercise due diligence in prosecuting his claim. Where there has been undue delay by a claimant in instituting or prosecuting his claim an arbitrator or party may apply to the court for an order terminating the arbitration proceedings and prohibiting further proceedings. Unless the delay is intentional or contumelious the court may make an order only if the delay has been inordinate and inexcusable and gives rise to a substantial risk that it is not possible to have a fair trial or is likely to cause serious prejudice. This is an attempted codification of the rule familiar in English court proceedings.

4-18 This is a different – and, as I shall suggest, less attractive – solution from that adopted in The Securities Association Full Arbitration Scheme Rules which in Rule 12 give the arbitrator power in his discretion to strike out all or any part

---

[44] *Cie. Francaise d'Importation et de Distribution S.A. v. Deutsche Continental Handelsgesell-schaft* [1985] 2 Lloyd's Rep. 592, 599.

[45] *The Golden Bear* [1987] 1 Lloyd's Rep. 330, 340.

[46] [1987] 2 Lloyd's Rep. 130, 148, 149.

[47] The author particularly wishes to acknowledge help valuably given by Ronald Bernstein QC, David Bird, Stephen Bond, Lori E. Fox, Kerry Harding, Martin Hunter, Francis Miller, Lord Justice Mustill, Michael Nussbaum, Mr Justice Phillips and V.V. Veeder, QC.

of a claim or defence on the grounds of inordinate and/or inexcusable delay on the part of any party, where such act or omission has, in the opinion of the arbitrator, given rise to a substantial risk that a fair determination of the dispute referred to the arbitration will not be possible, or which is such as to cause or to have caused serious prejudice to the other party. That provision contrasts, for instance, with Article 14.3 of the London Court of International Arbitration World-Wide Rules which empowers the Tribunal to proceed on notice despite the default of one party, but does not tackle the problem where a claimant wishes to prosecute a claim which, because of his delay, can no longer be fairly tried. Article 23 of the Stockholm Rules is to somewhat similar effect. In these cases, it seems clear, an activist arbitrator, willing to take the initiative and act as progress-chaser, is envisaged.

4-19 The American cupboard, usually a treasure-house of curious instances, is on this occasion relatively bare. Where there has been long delay in demanding arbitration, the courts have in clear cases applied the doctrines of laches and waiver.[48] Where an award is made after the expiration of an agreed or mandatory limit, the award is treated as made without jurisdiction, although this rule has been the subject of some recent erosion.[49] There have, however, been cases of abandonment. In *Agman Managers Ltd. v. Old Republic Insurance Co.*,[50] an agreement provided for arbitration of disputes before a tripartite panel. Old Republic demanded arbitration and each party selected its arbitrator. The party appointed arbitrators then failed to select the third member. More than three years later, Old Republic sought to revive the arbitration, but Agman moved to stay, contending that the arbitration had been abandoned. The court agreed, since Old Republic had done nothing to press forward the selection of the third arbitrator. But the court also found that Old Republic had begun proceedings on the same dispute in the Illinois State Courts, and that rather lessens the interest of the case.

4-20 More interesting are two recent decisions on facts which have a familiar ring: *M/V Archangelos III* [51] and *M/V Agios Nicolaos III*.[52] These were disputes between different owners and charterers, with substantial sums at stake. The vessels were managed by the same company which initiated the arbitrations and

---

[48] 25 A.L.R. 3d. 1175.
[49] 56 A.L.R. 3d. 819.
[50] N.Y.L.J. 1 Dec. 1978, at 6, col. 1.
[51] SMA 2541.
[52] SMA 2540.

then gave up business. The claimants started off to prove their claims. In one case one hearing was held; in the other, three. But demands for discovery were never met, contemplated additional hearings were never requested and in each case a period of inactivity lasting two-three years followed. The arbitrators asked what was happening and received no answer. The delay was by the claimants, who simply failed to prosecute their claims. In the end the arbitrators set final deadlines for the claimants to proceed on pain of dismissal, and the deadlines (although extended) were not met. In both cases awards were made dismissing the claims with prejudice. The matters came before the U.S. District Court for the Southern District of New York, which upheld the awards. In one case the court said:

> '. . . This arbitration arising in 1983 was in effect dismissed for failure of the petitioner to prosecute the arbitration. That decision was eminently fair. . .'

Implicit in these decisions was an acceptance that arbitrators do not exceed their powers by dismissing claims in these circumstances, provided reasonable deadlines are set and due warnings given of the likely penalty for non-compliance.[53] These decisions are, I shall suggest, a valuable pointer towards a solution. The Commercial Arbitration Rules of the American Arbitration Association do not address this problem, and indeed provide in Rule 30 that 'An award shall not be made solely on the default of a party'.

4-21 The UNCITRAL Model Law provides, in Article 25:

> Unless otherwise agreed by the parties, if, without showing sufficient cause,
> (a) the claimant fails to communicate his statement of claim in accordance with article 23 (1), the arbitral tribunal shall terminate the proceedings. . .
> (c) any party fails to appear at a hearing or to produce documentary evidence, the arbitral tribunal may continue the proceedings and make the award on the evidence before it.

4-22 Article 23 (1) requires the claimant to state the facts supporting his claim 'within the period of time agreed by the parties or determined by the arbitral tribunal'. These provisions do not really touch our problem. Article 25 (a) applies only to a breach at the very beginning of the arbitral process, and then only if the claimant is in breach of an agreement or order. Article 25(c) could bite only if the claimant failed to appear at a hearing, which would require a hearing to have

---

[53] *The Arbitrator*, March 1989, Vol. 21.

been fixed, or to produce documentary evidence, which would assume an obligation to produce. These provisions are plainly not directed to the revival of an arbitration reference by the claimant after it has lain dormant for years. Article 28 of the UNCITRAL Arbitration Rules is to very much the same effect and is open to the same comment.

4-23 The Court of Arbitration of the International Chamber of Commerce is on the whole agreeable that an arbitration reference should remain in abeyance if both parties want it, but does not bless that course unless both parties expressly agree. The Secretary General knows of no case where arbitrators have treated a reference as closed or declared it to be abandoned for want of prosecution, nor is an arbitral tribunal in his view entitled to make an award in favour of a party simply because his opponent has not participated in the arbitration. The ICC does, however, firmly believe that it has power under its rules to control delay. This view was given in evidence by the late Secretary-General in *Gregg v. Raytheon*, which was heard with *Bremer Vulkan* in the Court of Appeal and arose out of an ICC arbitration. Both Lord Denning M.R.[54] and Roskill L.J.[55] rejected this construction of the rules. The ICC's belief nonetheless persists. But delay can occur even in an ICC arbitration, as *Gregg v. Raytheon* shows, and although the *Black-Clawson case*[56] was not one of inactivity – far from it – the arbitration proceedings did last for a very long time.

4-24 The Netherlands Arbitration Act 1986 at first sight looks more hopeful. A note to the English text of Article 1040 reads 'The first paragraph is concerned with the default of the claimant, which intends to preclude "sleeping dog arbitrations". The arbitral tribunal has a discretionary power to terminate the proceedings by means of an arbitral award. An arbitral award will be appropriate in cases where a decision is to be given as to the costs of arbitration'. So one looks with expectation at the text of Article 1040: '(1) If the claimant, without showing good cause, fails to communicate his statement of claim or duly explain the claim, in spite of having had a reasonable opportunity to do so, the arbitral tribunal may terminate the arbitral proceedings by means of an arbitral award'. Sub-articles (2) and (3) deal with default by the respondent and are not therefore germane to this discussion. It seems plain that sub-article (1) confers a power of summary dismissal where the claimant defaults in one of the specified ways, but

---

[54]   [1981] A.C. 909, 941A.
[55]   *Ibid.*, at p. 948E.
[56]   *Black Clawson International Ltd. v. Papierwerke Waldhof-Aschaffenburg A.G.*[1981], 2 Lloyd's Rep. 446.

this again applies only at the very beginning of the arbitration process and would not touch the dog which had completed the preliminaries successfully but had then fallen fast asleep.

4-25 The new Swiss law of international arbitration appears to contain nothing of even passing relevance. Perhaps dogs do not fall asleep in the land of the cuckoo clock.

4-26 In France the New Code of Civil Procedure enables the judge to declare that a case may be dropped for lack of party diligence, but such a power is nowhere given to arbitrators.

4-27 A Swedish commentator, Dr Wetter, has observed[57] that cases such as *Bremer Vulkan*

> are extremely unlikely to arise in other jurisdictions in which arbitrators certainly would not permit an arbitration proceeding to remain stalled or inactive for many years but would bring it to an end by award or dismissal; failure to do so might well expose arbitrators to liability for neglect to properly carry out their duties.

His view may be coloured by experience in Sweden where, as in France and some other countries, a statutory time limit applies for making the award unless the parties themselves agree a different period. When, in Sweden, the parties do agree an award period, it cannot be extended save by their agreement.[58] If, in this situation, one party is unreasonable the arbitrator faces a dilemma: if he makes his award out of time he will be held to have had no jurisdiction; if he hurriedly makes it in time his award may be set aside for want of natural justice in denying the respondent a fair opportunity to prepare his defence. In the context of the present discussion it is worth observing that, until 1934, English arbitrators also were subject to a statutory time limit for making their award. The limit was three months, but extendable by the arbitrator or the court. The provision was abolished on the recommendation of the Mackinnon Committee in 1927, with a view to curbing unnecessary delay.

4-28 So the civil law would appear to have produced no counterpart to *Bremer Vulkan*. Dr Wetter's explanation, based on time limits for the award and personal

---

[57] *Arbitration International* (1987), Vol. 3, p. 337.
[58] *Arbitration in Sweden* (1984).

liability of the arbitrator to the parties if he fails to deliver in time, must have much force. The civilian tradition under which the judge or arbitrator is inquisitor, with responsibility for the conduct of the case, must also play an important part. An arbitrator brought up in the civil law world would not leave progress to be determined by the adversarial appetite of the parties. I think it probably true that the most extreme cases of delay have occurred in arbitrations of a kind more often encountered in the common law world than outside it, but true it is that the problems which have vexed us do not appear to have vexed others to any comparable extent. This may of course be in part because foreign laws have generally distanced the court from the arbitration process so that the problem, if it exists, may have remained largely hidden. And it may in part be because, arbitration being a consensual process governed by the will of the parties, there has been unwillingness to interfere with the results of any delay which the parties themselves must be taken to have caused or permitted.

IV. A CRITICAL LOOK

4-29 Whatever the rest of the world may think, however, it remains pertinent to ask whether the problem is one about which the judges should have become concerned and whether the English law of arbitration, having failed to produce an answer, deserves the strictures it has received. I think so, for two associated reasons. The first, already touched on, is that arbitration is, in concept, the ideal mode of dispute resolution: the parties by agreement submit their dispute to a tribunal of their choice, the tribunal being largely freed from the formal constraints which bind most courts of law and the ultimate award deriving its force more from the agreement of the parties than from the coercive power of any state. This ideal concept is somewhat marred if, as Kerr L.J. put it in *The Antclizo*,[59] one must 'countenance an enduring state of affairs for the resolution of disputes by arbitration which has long been regarded as unjust and unacceptable for litigation'. My second reason, not depending on any comparison between arbitration and litigation, is that courts are right to chafe when presented with evidence of clear injustice which they are powerless to remedy. Such is, in my view, the position when an arbitrator is called upon to resolve a dispute too stale for him to decide with confidence and when a respondent is called upon to face a claim of which he had heard nothing for years and which his opponent's delay had prejudiced his ability to resist. So it seems worth a brief critical look at some

---

[59] [1987] 2 Lloyd's Rep. 130, 149.

of the eight solutions outlined above. I hope I shall not be thought too perverse if I take them in the reverse order.

4-30 Section 5 of the Arbitration Act 1979 is invoked about once every three weeks or so. Applications by the arbitrator are very rare, perhaps because of understandable uncertainty how the section works,[60] perhaps because of uncertainty how the costs of applying will be borne. Very few respondents apply, doubtless for fear of prodding the claimant into life. If the respondent did apply with a view to obtaining a default award in his favour, it is not clear that the claimant could properly be debarred from attending and seeking to prove his case. As Donaldson J. observed in *Bremer Vulkan*,[61] with reference to *ex parte* hearings and not section 5, 'But what if he {the claimant} does attend and wishes to present his case. Can the arbitrator refuse to allow him to do so? Unless there is power to dismiss the claim for want of prosecution I do not think he could. And if he could not, the respondent would be at a hopeless disadvantage'. The vast majority of applications under section 5 are by claimants, almost always in construction disputes and rarely in shipping or commodity arbitrations. So the section has some value where an eager claimant faces a foot-dragging respondent. But that is not the problem with which we are concerned.

4-31 It was accepted by Dr Mann in his note and by Kerr L.J. in *The Antclizo* [62] that section 1 was enacted with a clear intention far removed from the present problem. Section 25 (2)(b), however, does give the court a discretion to order that an arbitration agreement shall cease to have effect with respect to a dispute referred. Accepting, as *Mustill & Boyd* suggest,[63] that 'the remedy is. .. likely to be reserved for cases where the arbitration has gone irrevocably wrong', it is hard to resist Kerr L.J.'s comment[64] that that is precisely the position in the line of cases which have caused the most serious problems since *Bremer Vulkan*. But I am not surprised that Phillips J. was wary of accepting this ingenious solution. Section 1 was designed to prevent a party revoking his arbitrator's authority. But the court could give him leave to do so, such leave being envisaged where the arbitrator was guilty of some shortcoming. It would be a curious exercise of the court's power to give leave to revoke where the shortcoming was that of the party himself, in causing or permitting gross delay, rather than of the arbitrator.

---

[60] See Mustill & Boyd, *Commercial Arbitration* (2nd ed.), p. 539.
[61] [1981] A.C. 909, 920.
[62] [1987] 2 Lloyd's Rep. 130.
[63] *Commercial Arbitration* (2nd ed.), p. 500.
[64] *The Antclizo, supra*, at p. 150.

Furthermore, it seems plain that such an order would run counter to the prevailing philosophy of international arbitration, which is to minimise the role of the court.

4-32 The subtlety of regarding a claimant's right to ask an arbitral tribunal to proceed to an award as a contractual right in the nature of a power, liable to lapse if not exercised in a reasonable time, is incontestable. But I cannot for my part see any difference between this right and other contractual rights which do not lapse on a failure to exercise them in a reasonable time, and I share the general view that if this argument had been advanced in *Bremer Vulkan* it would not have survived the majority decision.

4-33 The distaste widely expressed for the exercise now undertaken to decide whether an agreement to abandon has been made between two dumb and inactive parties is one I fully share. To Walter Savage Landor's work *Imaginary Conversations* the cases now provide a judicial sequel which might be entitled *Imaginary Non-Conversations*. The silent communication of intentions between claimant and respondent also reminds one a little of Francis Thompson's cricket match '*At Lords*':

> 'For the field is full of shades as I near the shadowy coast,
> And a ghostly batsman plays to the bowling of a ghost,
> And I look through my tears on a soundless – clapping host ...'

4-34 It is, I suggest, high time for stumps.

4-35 It seems to me, in respectful agreement with the House of Lords, that frustration cannot be relied on to solve the present problem without inflicting very considerable violence on that doctrine as it has, at least in recent years, been understood.

4-36 The notion that a claimant in arbitration owes his opponent a contractual duty to prosecute his claim with reasonable diligence was perhaps somewhat artificial, but nothing like as unconvincing as the reciprocal obligation which the majority of the House of Lords substituted in *Bremer Vulkan*. But that doctrine is now the law, and despite opportunities to think again in *The Hannah Blumenthal* [65] and *The Antclizo* [66] the House has declined to overrule the earlier decision. If,

---

[65] [1983] 1 A.C. 854.

as was suggested in *The Antclizo*, the solution must be found in legislation, it is unlikely that repudiation has any further part to play.

4-37 The principle supported by the dissenting minority in *Bremer Vulkan*, that the court may intervene by injunction in such cases under the wide terms of section 37 of the Supreme Court Act 1981, seems to me to have much to commend it. But it is open to one serious objection, that it would be seen (particularly abroad) as unwarranted interference by the courts in the arbitration process. A solution which escapes this accusation is to be preferred.

4-38 So one comes to the first of the suggested solutions, that the arbitrator himself has the power to dismiss. The reason given by Bridge J. in *Crawford v. A. E. A. Prowting Ltd.* [67] for rejecting that theory, based on the mutual obligation theory of arbitration, does not appeal to me any more than it did to Donaldson J. in *Bremer Vulkan*. But for historical reasons convincingly deployed by Roskill L.J. in that case, it is hard to argue that an arbitrator has always been clothed with all the powers of a judicial officer. Why, if that is so, was section 12 (6) of the 1950 Act required? But it would seem to me, as to Nicholls L.J. in *The Antclizo*,[68] a small and acceptable step to imply a term into the arbitration agreement that the arbitrator should have power to dismiss stale claims no longer fairly triable. Had this simple expedient been adopted, a mountain of futile litigation might have been avoided. As it is, legislation to amend the present law has been called for by the Master of the Rolls, other commercially-experienced members of the Court of Appeal, the commercial judges, the Commercial Court Committee and now the House of Lords.

4-39 Lord Brandon suggested in *The Antclizo* [69] that section 12 (6) of the 1950 Act might be amended to confer on the court a power to strike out claims in arbitrations on grounds of delay. Lord Goff also favoured such a power, but without indicating whether it should be given to the court or the arbitrator. Lord Justice Mustill's Departmental Advisory Committee on English Arbitration had by this time unanimously resolved that the power should be conferred on the arbitrator rather than the court. Its reason was that the modern philosophy of arbitration, recognised in the 1979 Act and in many decisions of the higher courts, was to keep judicial intrusion in the arbitration process to a minimum. In

---

[66] [1988] 2 Lloyd's Rep. 93.
[67] [1973] Q.B. 1.
[68] [1987] 2 Lloyd's Rep. 130.
[69] [1988] 2 Lloyd's Rep. 93, 95.

a further paper the Committee point out that if the power to dismiss were to be vested in the court, it might prevent the United Kingdom adopting the Model Law. Even if the power were in the arbitrator, but with a right to appeal to the court, compatibility with the Model Law would have to be considered.[70]

4-40 To legislate to give the arbitrator power to dismiss might seem straightforward enough, but the Departmental Advisory Committee has valuably drawn attention to hidden reefs. Apart from the American cases I mentioned, no such power appears to exist or to have been exercised anywhere outside the Commonwealth. To many foreign lawyers the power would seem objectionable in principle. When should the power be exercisable? It is easy to answer: when the equivalent power would be exercisable in the High Court. But it would not be altogether easy for lay arbitrators or foreign lawyers to understand or discover the principles on which a High Court judge acts, and those principles do not lack critics. The requirement to find incremental prejudice has led to some extraordinary contortions, and the inability to dismiss within the limitation period (which may be very long) leads to the survival of some very hoary actions. Should there be a right of appeal and, if so, by whom, on what terms and on what basis? Should it be permissible to contract out?

4-41 These are all substantial and pertinent questions. My own preference would be for a power in the arbitrator, very much as established in the American cases I mentioned. The power could be exercisable as provided by the Securities Association rule quoted earlier. I would give a right of appeal only to an aggrieved claimant, with the leave of the arbitrator or the commercial judge; where leave was granted the judge would review the arbitrator's decision and not substitute his own. I would permit parties to exclude the power, either in their agreement or in any institutional rules by which they agreed to be governed.

4-42 But the cult of the sleeping dog may have almost had its day. The delays which habitually afflict ordinary civil litigation have led to demands that the pace of an action should not be dictated by the lethargy of the litigants' advisers and that, as in the United States, judges should monitor the conduct of actions, set schedules and chase progress. Arbitrators, much more than judges, already do this, but if such conduct became the norm a statutory power to dismiss could quickly become a dead letter. Of course the activist arbitrator must be scrupulous in giving each party a full right to present its case and in avoiding the faintest

---

[70] See Articles 5, 18 and 25 of the Model Law.

suggestion of bias. If, however, arbitrators accept it as an important part of their duty fairly and discreetly to keep arbitrations on the move, the dogs will have no chance to sleep and the judges, for a change, may doze.

*E. Allan Farnsworth**

CHAPTER 5

PUNITIVE DAMAGES IN ARBITRATION

I. INTRODUCTION

5-1 'For this relief much thanks; 'tis bitter cold'. Thus the sentinel Francisco to his fellow Bernardo at the beginning of Hamlet. Many a winning party to a protracted arbitration has echoed Francisco's sentiment – 'For this relief much thanks' – as the arbitrators have at last made their award. This article deals with the limits of 'this relief'. What sorts of relief may arbitrators award?

5-2 It is conventional wisdom, at least in the United States, that arbitrators have broad powers in granting relief. In an oft-quoted dictum, the New York Court of Appeals, the state's highest court, has affirmed that

> the remedies available in arbitration are not confined to the traditional forms at law' and that it is 'for the arbitrators to fashion the remedy appropriate to the wrong.[1]

The Uniform Arbitration Act, in force in over half of the states of the United States, provides:

> the fact that the relief was such that it could not or would not be granted by a court of law or equity is not a ground for vacating or refusing to confirm an award.[2]

---

* [The late Professor Farnsworth was until his death in 2005] Alfred McCormack Professor of Law, Columbia University. This paper is an edited version of a lecture delivered at the School of International Arbitration, Centre for Commercial Law Studies, Queen Mary and Westfield College, University of London, as the 1990 Freshfields Arbitration lecture.
[1] *Paver & Wildfoerster* v. *Catholic High School Ass'n*, 38 N.Y.2d 669, 676, 677, 345 N.E.2d 565, 569 (1976).
[2] Uniform Arbitration Act § 12(a) (5).

Julian D.M. Lew and Loukas A. Mistelis (eds), Arbitration Insights, 81-96
© 2007 Kluwer Law International. Printed in the Netherlands

The rules of the American Arbitration Association reaffirm this broad power, providing that 'the Arbitrator may grant any remedy or relief which he deems just and equitable and within the scope of the agreement of the parties).[3]

5-3 A court may, for example, uphold an award granting equitable relief – specific performance or an injunction – even though the court would not itself have granted that relief. Thus in 1960 the highest court of the State of New York upheld an award granting specific performance of a construction contract, even though a court would not have ordered specific performance because of the burden of supervising compliance with the order. 'It would be quite remarkable if, after the parties had agreed that arbitrators might award specific performance [by incorporating AAA rules so providing], and after the arbitrators had so ordered, the courts would frustrate the whole arbitration process by refusing to confirm the award'.[4]

5-4 An even more dramatic example was supplied just last year by the Minnesota Supreme Court, which held that it was within the power of arbitrators to require a building contractor to purchase from the owner real property on which the building contractor had built town houses with gross construction deficiencies. The objective of this creative relief was to place on the building contractor the obligation to remedy the defects and to bear the risk of potential warranty liability to buyers of town houses.[5]

5-5 Thus the question arises: to what extent do arbitrators have the power to grant relief that a court would refuse to grant? I shall address this question in one context only, that of the power of arbitrators to award punitive damages.

II. PUNITIVE DAMAGES

5-6 The matter of punitive damages is of considerable current interest in the United States. For one thing, the institution of punitive damages is being challenged on constitutional grounds – the United States Supreme Court having

---

[3] American Arbitration Association, Commercial Arbitration Rules, rule 43.
[4] *Grayson-Robinson Stores* v. *Iris Construction Co.*, 8 N.Y.2d 133, 137, 168 N.E.2d 377, 378–79 (1960)
[5] *David Co.* v. *Jim W. Miller*, 444 N.W.2d 836 (1989).

rejected one challenge in 1989, with another pending at the present time.[6] For another thing, in a significant minority of states, courts have expressed a willingness to grant punitive damages for aggravated breach of contract – a development to which I will return later. And for yet another thing, to which I will also return, a split of authority on the enforceability of an arbitral award of punitive damages has produced a significant quantity of writing by both scholars and practitioners.

5-7 Suppose that a contract is made by an English supplier to furnish and put into operation sophisticated machinery for an American buyer in California. Suppose that the contract contains a broad arbitration clause providing for arbitration in California and incorporating the rules of the American Arbitration Association along with a choice of law clause referring to California law. A dispute arises and the American buyer, asserting that there has been an 'aggravated' breach by the English supplier, initiates arbitral proceedings in California under the clause, and demands, not only compensatory damages of $10,000,000, but punitive damages of another $10,000,000 for the English supplier's 'bad faith breach'. The English supplier might ask four distinct questions:

    (1) Will a court in California grant a motion to stay arbitration of the punitive damage claim on the ground that arbitrators have no power to award punitive damages?

    (2) If a court will not stay arbitration of the punitive damage claim, will the arbitrators, applying California law, award punitive damages?

    (3) If the arbitrators award punitive as well as compensatory damages, will a court in California vacate the part of the award granting punitive damages?

    (4) If the court in California refuses to vacate the award and the American buyer seeks to have it enforced by a court in England, will that court refuse to enforce it on grounds of public policy?

A. Will a Court Stay Arbitration of the Punitive Damage Claim?

5-8 Even in the United States, we have little authority on this precise question. (Although it is similar to the third question, it is not identical for it is possible that a court might vacate an award of punitive damages once rendered even

---

[6] *Browning-Ferris Industries of Vermont* v. *Kelso Disposal, Inc.*, 109 S. Ct. 2909 (1989); *Pacific Mutual Life Insurance Co.* v. *Haslip*, 553 So.2d 537 (Ala. 1989), cert. granted, 110 S. Ct. 1780 (1990).

though it would decline to stay arbitration of the punitive damage claim, presuming that the arbitrators would not exceed their powers.) *Willis v. Shearson/American Express Inc.,*[7] to which I will return later, arose on a motion to stay arbitration proceedings on the ground that a demand for punitive damages was improper in an arbitration. The federal district court in that case rejected this contention and held that the demand for punitive damages could go to arbitration under the federal arbitration law.

5-9 Assuming that an American court would follow this precedent and refuse to stay arbitration of the punitive damage claim, we come to the second question.

B. Will the Arbitrators Grant Punitive Damages?

5-10 This question has two aspects. First, will the arbitrators consider the case at hand an appropriate one for punitive damages under the applicable law, in this case, California? Second, will the arbitrators assume that they – as arbitrators – have the power to award punitive damages assuming that the case is an appropriate one?

5-11 As to the first aspect – the appropriateness of punitive damages under the applicable law – there is, I take it, a marked difference between the law in England and that in the United States. While in England, as I understand it, a court may grant punitive damages in some cases of tort and for breach of a fiduciary duty, it is still the case that punitive damages are not available for what are essentially breach of contract actions. As it was put in *Addis v. Gramophone Co.;*[8] 'damages for breach of contract [are] in the nature of compensation, not punishment'. In this respect American courts have become more generous than British courts, awarding punitive damages – it often seems – not only in furtherance of the traditional goals of punishing a past wrong and deterring similar conduct in the future, but also out of a sense that 'compensatory' damages do not fully compensate an aggrieved party for all the harm that party has suffered.

5-12 Our courts generally may award punitive damages in tort actions, and a number of courts have awarded punitive damages for a breach of contract that is in some respect tortious. Some courts have gone to considerable lengths to find

[7] 569 F. Supp. 821 (M.D.N.C. 1983).
[8] [1909] A.C. 488, 494 (H.L.) (Lord Atkinson). But see *Rookes* v. *Barnard*, [1964] A.C. 73 (H.L.).

the necessary tortious conduct.[9] In this California outdid the other states by creating a new tort of 'bad faith breach' of contract.

5-13 The first sighting of this new tort came during the 1950's and involved actions against insurers that were regarded as having broken contracts with their insured's in bad faith.[10] Not until 1984, however, was there a serious suggestion that this new tort of bad faith breach might be extended beyond the insurance cases. In that year the California Supreme Court decided *Seaman's Direct Buying Service v. Standard Oil Company of California*,[11] a case involving an oil dealership contract. In remanding for a new trial, the court in dictum defined a new tort where a party to a contract 'in addition to breaching the contract ... seeks to shield itself from liability by denying, in bad faith and without probable cause, that the contract exists'. The court declined to pass on 'whether and under what circumstances, a breach of the implied covenant of good faith and fair dealing in a commercial context may give rise to an action in tort', but it said there had to be some 'special relationship like that between insurer and insured'. 'No doubt', it added, 'there are other relationships with similar characteristics and deserving of similar legal treatment'.

5-14 In 1988, however, the California Supreme Court pulled in its horns to a considerable extent by refusing, in *Foley v. Interactive Data Corp.*,[12] to find that an employer's wrongful discharge of an employee involved a bad faith breach of an employment contract under the dictum in Seaman's case. After criticizing the 'uncritical' extension by lower California courts of the insurance model 'without careful consideration of the fundamental policies underlying the development of tort and contract', the court reached this somewhat surprising conclusion: 'we are not convinced that a 'special relationship' of the kind required by *Seaman's* 'analogous to that between insurer and insured should be deemed to exist in the usual employment relationship'. (One might well ask where it would exist if not between employer and employee.)

---

[9] See generally E. Farnsworth, *Contracts*, § 12.8 (2nd ed. 1990).
[10] See, e.g., *Communale v. Traders & General Ins. Co.*, 50 Cal. 2d 654, 328 P.2d 198 (1958).
[11] 36 Cal. 3d 752, 768–769, 686 P.2d 1158, 1166–1167 (1984).
[12] 47 Cal. 3d 654, 689, 692, 765 P.2d 373, 393, 395 (1988).

5-15 Only a few states have been tempted to follow California's lead in *Seaman's* case.[13] And the moderating effect of *Foley* on the spread of the doctrine of bad faith breach remains to be seen. Nonetheless the spectre of punitive damages for bad faith breach of contract continues to stalk the corridors in the courthouses of a significant minority of American states.

5-16 This brings us to the second aspect – assuming that the arbitrators consider the case at hand an appropriate one for punitive damages under the applicable law, will they assume that they – as arbitrators – have the power to award such damages? I have found little authority on this precise question.[14] The reports of the Iran-United States tribunal at The Hague shed some light on it. In a separate opinion in one case,[15] an American arbitrator suggested that 'punitive or exemplary damages might be sought' in that tribunal for unlawful expropriation. He saw 'strong reasons' why it would be appropriate for an international tribunal to award punitive or exemplary damages 'for unlawful expropriation, for otherwise the injured party would get only what it would have gotten by lawful expropriation and would receive nothing additional for the enhanced wrong done it and the offending state would experience no disincentive for the repetition of unlawful conduct'. (Parenthetically it is worth noting that in this argument the traditional goal of deterrence is mingled with the sense that traditional 'compensatory' damages do not fully compensate.)

5-17 This second aspect – whether arbitrators will assume that they have the power – has a somewhat uncertain relation to the third and fourth questions, which go to enforceability, since – in spite of the fact that most arbitral awards are complied with voluntarily and without judicial intervention – prudent arbitrators may decline to render an award of punitive damages if it would not be enforceable. The International Chamber of Commerce Rules[16] state that 'the arbitrators ... shall make every effort to make sure that the award is enforceable at law'. The Rules are silent, however, with respect to the place where the award is to be enforceable. Is it the place of arbitration? (This raises my third question.)

---

[13] According to a footnote in *Foley*, 'In only three cases outside of California have courts held that a breach of the covenant of good faith and fair dealing gives rise to tort damages'. 47 Cal. 3d at 686 n. 26, 765 P.2d, at p. 391, n. 26.

[14] See *Wall Street Journal*, p. 1, June 11, 1990 ('Stock Investors Win More Punitive Awards in Arbitration Cases').

[15] *Sedco Inc.* v. *NIOC*, 10 Iran-U.S. C.T.R. 180, 205 (1986) (separate opinion of Brower). See also *Amoco International Fin. Corp.* v. *Iran*, 15 Iran-U.S. C.T.R. 189, 248 (1983) (Virally, Ch.).

[16] ICC Rules art. 26.

Or is it the place or places where enforcement is likely to be sought – or may possibly be sought? (This raises my fourth question.) Julian Lew has written that 'an arbitrator must ensure that his award does not offend the national public policy of the place where enforcement is sought'.[17] Putting such a responsibility on the shoulders of the arbitrators raises two practical questions. First, how is this responsibility to be discharged if the place of enforcement is uncertain, as where enforcement is likely to involve a ship that calls in many ports? And second, assuming that the arbitrators can foresee the likely place or places of enforcement, how and at what stage of the procedure are they to be informed by the parties as to possible difficulties in enforcing an award in that place or those places? A satisfactory answer must take account of the circumstance that often the question will not arise until after hearings have concluded and the arbitrators are in the process of preparing their award. One may ask whether the arbitrators' responsibility should not be limited to avoiding an award that they know or at least suspect will be unenforceable in a probable place of enforcement, with the responsibility on the claimant to inform the arbitrators as to potential problems. This brings us to the third question. Suppose now that the arbitrators have rendered an award imposing on the English respondent $10,000,000 in compensatory and $10,000,000 in punitive damages.

C. Will a Court where the Award is Rendered Refuse Enforcement?

5-18 This question, like the previous one, has two aspects – parallel to those just discussed. First, will a court vacate the award on the ground that the arbitrators have misapplied the applicable substantive law – in this case that of California – in awarding punitive damages? Second, will a court vacate the award on the ground that arbitrators have no power to award punitive damages in any case?

5-19 As to the first aspect, the answer is a resounding 'No'. Even if it should appear that the arbitrators had misapplied the applicable law and awarded punitive damages for bad faith breach where the Supreme Court of California would not have done so, the award could not be upset for this reason. In the United States, the test for vacating an award on the ground of substantive error of law is put in terms of 'manifest disregard of the law'. The United States Court of Appeals for the Second Circuit described it this way in 1986: 'The error must have been obvious and capable of being readily and instantly perceived by the average person qualified to serve as arbitrator' and 'the term 'disregard' implies

---

[17] J. Lew, *Applicable Law in International Commercial Arbitration*, p. 537 (1978).

that the arbitrator appreciates the existence of a clearly governing legal principle but decides to ignore or pay no attention to it'.[18] As a judge of New York's highest court protested in 1984 in dissent, 'there is in fact virtually no restraint on arbitral excesses ... short of a violation of public policy or totally irrational result yet to be found by this court, an award will not be set aside'.[19]

5-20 That being so, it will not be open to the English respondent to argue in an American court that the arbitrators misapplied *Seaman's* and *Foley* in awarding punitive damages. The English respondent's only hope in an American court is that arbitrators simply lack the power to award punitive damages in any case – even if a court would have the power to do so. This is the second aspect of the third question, and as to this aspect the law in the United States is both ample and in disarray.

5-21 Last year a committee of the New York State Bar Association described the 'case law on this issue' as being 'in a state of flux'.[20] Although the United States Supreme Court has, up to now, taken no position on the matter, it did hold in 1985 that a treble damage claim under the American anti-trust laws was arbitrable in Japan.[21] The committee noted that in recent years the United States Supreme Court has expanded the substantive areas that may be arbitrated, resorting to a strong 'federal policy favouring arbitration' and requiring that courts 'rigorously enforce agreements to arbitrate'.[22]

5-22 The leading contrary authority is *Garrity* v. *Lyle Stuart Inc.*,[23] a 1976 opinion of the court of last resort in New York, the New York Court of Appeals. That case arose under a publishing contract containing a broad arbitration clause. The author claimed damages for, among other things, fraudulent inducement to enter the contract. The arbitrators awarded both compensatory and punitive damages, but the Court of Appeals, in a four-to-three decision with a vigorous dissent, vacated this award of punitive damages on the ground that it involved 'a sanction reserved to the state'. On this rationale it is clear that the parties cannot,

---

[18] *Merrill Lynch, Pierce, Fenner & Smith Inc. v. Bobker*, 808 F.2d 930, 933 (2d Cir. 1986).
[19] *Silverman* v. *Benmor Coats Inc.*, 61 N.Y.2d 299, 461 N.E. 2d 1261 (1984) (Kaye, J. dissenting).
[20] New York State Bar Association (Commercial and Federal Litigation Section), Report on Punitive Damages in Commercial Arbitration, p. 1 (1989).
[21] *Mitsubishi Motors Corpn.* v. *Soler Chrysler-Plymouth Inc.*, 473 U.S. 615 (1985). See also *Shearson/American Express Inc.* v. *McMahon*, 107 S. Ct. 2332 (1987) (treble damage RICO [Racketeer Influenced and Corrupt Organisations Act] claim).
[22] Report cited in note 20, *supra*, at pp. 4–5.
[23] 40 N.Y.2d 354, 356, 353 N.E.2d 793, 794 (1976).

even by explicit provision, empower the arbitrators to grant punitive damages. A few other state courts have taken the same position as *Garrity*.

5-23 The federal courts have, however, generally taken the opposite view. Thus in *Willis* v. *Shearson/American Express Inc.*[24] a federal district court in 1983 held that a claim for punitive damages under a broad arbitration clause was arbitrable. And in 1985, in *Willoughby Roofing & Supply Co. v. Kajimia International*,[25] the United States Court of Appeals for the Eleventh Circuit upheld an award of punitive damages on a claim of 'wilful fraud'. 'In light of the federal policy favouring arbitration ..., our task is to resolve all doubt in favour of the arbitrator's authority to award a particular remedy'. In 1989, the United States Court of Appeal for the First Circuit reached a similar conclusion in *Raytheon Co.* v. *Automated Business Systems*,[26] refusing to vacate the part of an award granting punitive damages under California law for breach of the duty of good faith and fair dealing as well as for fraud. The court drew an interesting distinction between labour arbitration and commercial arbitration, characterizing labour arbitration as 'part of a continuing and ameliorating enterprise between parties who maintain an ongoing relationship', making award of punitive damages inappropriate. 'Commercial arbitration, by contrast ..., is normally considered a one-shot endeavour'. Although the court's conclusion was based in part on the respondent's failure to make clear and timely objection to the claim for punitive damages, its adherence to the principle announced in *Willoughby* is plain. Thus, although the United States Supreme Court has not yet spoken, the handwriting on the wall suggests that Garrity's days are numbered – if indeed it retains vitality at all.[27]

5-24 As to which is the better view, controversy continues. The 1989 report of the New York State Bar Association committee, mentioned earlier, found 'compelling arguments in support of both the position that punitive damages

---

[24] *Supra*, note 6.
[25] 776 F.2d 269 (11th Cir. 1985), affirming 598 F. Supp. 353 (M.D. Ala. 1984).
[26] 882 F.2d 6, 10 (1st Cir. 1989).
[27] Since this article was submitted for publication, two federal district courts have locked horns over this proposition. *Compare Fahnestock & Co V. Waltman*, (S.D.N.Y. Aug. 22, 1990) (LEXIS Genfed Dist.) (applying *Garrity*, 'the arbitration panel's award of punitive damages must be vacated'), *with Barbier v. Shearson Lehman Hutton*, (S.D.N.Y. Dec 3, 1990) (LEXIS Genfed Dist.) (declining to follow Fahnestock)

should not be allowed in arbitration and the position that punitive damages should be allowed under appropriate conditions'.[28]

5-25 The common arguments against allowing arbitrators to award punitive damages (the position in *Garrity*) are these:

1. The power to impose penalties is by its nature a power of the State and cannot be conferred on an arbitral tribunal by private agreement.
2. Arbitrators, who do not necessarily have legal training, are not qualified to impose punitive damages, and their imposition of such damages raises questions of fairness since judicial review is limited.
3. Allowing arbitrators to impose punitive damages will have an undesirable impact on the selection of arbitrators and perhaps on the willingness of persons to serve as arbitrators.
4. Allowing arbitrators to impose punitive damages will either frighten parties away from arbitration or invite closer judicial scrutiny of awards.
5. In any event, there are few situations in which the law permits punitive damages.

5-26 The common arguments in favour of allowing arbitrators to award punitive damages (the position in *Willoughby*) are these:

1. The reluctance to allow arbitrators to award punitive damages is simply a manifestation of the historical mistrust of arbitration, a mistrust that has generally been rejected.
2. The agreement of parties who use a broad arbitration clause should be respected, particularly since the parties are always free to exclude punitive damages by express provision if they choose to do so.
3. Fears of abuse by arbitrators of a power to award punitive damages have not been borne out in practice.
4. Arbitrators have traditionally been accorded broad powers as to remedies.
5. Denying the parties the power to award punitive damages where a court would do so may either result in the duplication of proceeding, (with a separate claim for punitive damages being brought in a court) or a loss of a substantive right to punitive damages (if a separate claim would be rejected by a court).

---

[28] Report cited in note 20, *supra*, at p. 2. For an extensive discussion, see Stipanowich, *Punitive Damages in Arbitration: Garrity v. Lyle Stuart, Inc. Reconsidered*, 66 B.U.L. Rev. 953 (1986).

5-27 Assume now, as we must, that an American court would not vacate an award of punitive damages, either on the ground of 'manifest disregard' of the applicable law or on the ground that arbitrators have no power to award punitive damages at all. We come to our fourth question.

D Will a Court in another Jurisdiction (than where the Award was Rendered) Refuse Enforcement?

5-28 This is a different question from the third, since the criterion is 'public policy' rather than 'manifest disregard'. As a federal district court put it in 1987, 'manifest disregard' of law, whatever the phrase may mean, does not rise to the level of contravening 'public policy' as that phrase is used in Article V of the Convention'.[29] This distinction finds support in the Mustill Report, which faulted the UNCITRAL Model Law for failing to distinguish the two questions. The Report granted that grounds for attack in a country other than that in which the award was rendered were properly narrow. 'This consideration does not at all apply to the grounds on which ... an attack can be made' in the country of the award, which will generally be broader.[30] In short, it is more difficult for a respondent to succeed in preventing enforcement in *another* jurisdiction once the respondent has failed in the place of the award.

5-29 Under Article V(2)(b) the United Nations (New York) Convention, now adhered to by some 80 countries (the United Kingdom in 1975; the United States in 1970), a court may deny recognition or enforcement to a foreign arbitral award if, under the court's own law, 'recognition or enforcement of the award would be contrary to public policy'. According to the Restatement (Third) of Foreign Relations Law, however, 'United States courts have construed the public policy exception to the enforcement of foreign arbitral awards narrowly'.[31] According to the leading case, decided by the United States Court of Appeals for the Second Circuit in 1974, 'public policy' is to be read narrowly and refers not to *national* public policy but to public policy that is in some respect international in character. 'To read the public policy defence as a parochial device protective of

---

[29] *Brandeis Intsel Ltd. v. Calabrian Chemicals Corp.*, 656 F. Supp. 160 (S.D.N.Y. 1987).
[30] Departmental Advisory Committee, Report on the UNCITRAL Model Law on International Commercial Arbitration 60–61 (Department for Enterprise 1989).
[31] Restatement (Third) of Foreign Relations Law § 488, Comment 2.

national political interests would seriously undermine the Convention's utility'.[32] The notion that courts are not to recognise '*national* political interests' suggests a kind of 'international' public policy – a limited category that (to take Julian Lew's examples) might include abhorrence of slavery, discrimination, murder, piracy, and the like[33] – perhaps also some kinds of unfair restraints on competition.

5-30 What of punitive damages? My civilian colleagues insist that punitive damages are unknown in their countries. Of the common law countries, only in the United States – to my knowledge – are punitive damages awarded in what are essentially breach of contract cases – and then only in a minority of states. Might such an award be offensive to some 'international' public policy? I am aware of only one case – an American one. In *Laminoirs – Trifileries – Cableries de Lens v. Southwire Co.*,[34] a federal district court in 1980 faced just this question. Arbitrators, applying French law, had decided that interest rates on the award should jump 5% per year if the award was not paid within two months, following a French statute providing for a 5% jump if a judgment is not paid within two months. The court characterised this as a 'penalty' (although as I have mentioned French courts do not award punitive damages as such) – 'a sum of money which the law exacts by way of punishment for doing something that is prohibited or omitting to do something that is required to be done'. The court then refused to enforce the 'penalty', applying the public policy exception. 'The law does not lightly impose penalties. ... A foreign law will not be enforced if it is penal only and relates to the punishment of public wrongs as contradistinguished from the redressing of private injuries'. This part of the opinion has since been quoted with approval by another federal district court.[35]

5-31 You may have – as I have had – difficulty in reconciling this line of cases with the 'bad faith' breach cases. How can there be a public policy against punitive damages in aggravated breach of contract cases if some courts themselves award such damages for 'bad faith' breach? One possible answer is that the public policy in question is one against allowing parties to delegate a 'public power' to punish to an essentially private forum. Another possible answer

---

[32] *Parsons & Whittemore Overseas Co. v. Société Générale de l'Industrie du Papier (RAKTA)*, 508 F.2d 969, 974 (2d Cir. 1974).

[33] J. Lew, *Applicable Law in International Commercial Arbitration*, p. 535 (1978).

[34] 484 F. Supp. 1063, 1069 (N.D. Ga. 1980). For an extensive discussion, see Note, 20 Loyola of L.A. L. Rev. 455 (1987, appearing in a later version as Note, (1988) 4 Arb. Int. 255.

[35] *Brandeis Intsel Ltd. v. Calabrian Chemicals Corpn.*, supra, note 27.

is that the wrong addressed by the French statute in *Laminoirs* was one against the state (refusal to honour a judgment of a court), not a private wrong – and so distinguishable. A third possible answer is that our law is in disarray on this point. I suspect the last of these.

5-32 In any event, our hypothetical case requires that we look to the law of England, not that of the United States. While I am no expert on the law of the United Kingdom, I can make some surmises. In the mid-1970's the United Kingdom and the United States had negotiations on a proposed Convention Providing for the Reciprocal Enforcement of Judgments in Civil Matters. Negotiations foundered, however, because of fears in the United Kingdom that British courts would, under the proposed Convention, be required to enforce extravagant 'compensatory' judgments in product liability cases involving claims for personal injuries brought against British manufacturers. One might discern in this at least a national policy against the enforcement of extravagant damage awards. More recently, the United Kingdom enacted the Protection of Trading Interests Act 1980, barring British courts from entertaining proceedings to enforce 'a judgment for multiple damages'. Although the Act does not appear to speak to judgments for punitive as distinguished from multiple damages, nor to arbitral awards of any kind, it is not difficult to discern a national policy hostile to the enforcement of arbitral awards of punitive damages.

5-33 What conclusions should one draw from this? The answer is clearly up to the United Kingdom. Colleagues from civil law systems seem to think that an award of punitive damages would not be against their international public policy – though their courts 'never' grant punitive damages. The situation in such countries differs from that in England, however. A French magistrate, for example, has in practice the power to take account of the character of the breach when assessing damages, since this part of the opinion is not motivated. Punitive damages may thus be assessed in practice if not in principle. It is otherwise in England where, since the nineteenth century the principles for the award of damages have been elaborately articulated by judges as a means of wresting control in this area from the jury.

III. LESSONS FOR DRAFTING ARBITRATION CLAUSES

5-34 What lessons are to be drawn by the drafter of an arbitration clause? Plainly the drafter has significant control over the availability of punitive damages – both in conferring on arbitrators the power to award them and in denying to arbitrators that power. I turn first to the latter – denial of the power to award punitive damages.

5-35 If the arbitration clause plainly states that the arbitrators have no power to award punitive damages, that ends the matter – in every jurisdiction, even where arbitrators would otherwise have that power. As the trial court said in Willoughby:

> If parties to an arbitration desire to exclude the issue of punitive damages from the consideration of an arbitrator and reserve it for judicial hearing, they are free to specify that in the contract.[36]

Indeed, as you will recall, one argument in favour of allowing arbitrators to award punitive damages in general is that the parties are free to strip them of that power by express agreement, if they so choose.

5-36 If the parties want to strip the arbitrators of this power, however, they should use plain language. In Willoughby, the contract provided that on its termination by the contractor, the contractor was to pay the subcontractor 'the actual damage resulting from such termination', but not for anticipated profits or work undone or materials unfinished. The contractor argued that this barred an award of punitive damages for breach of contract or fraud, but the federal Court of Appeals rejected this argument and read the clause narrowly, as limited to termination as distinguished from breach of contract or fraud.[37]

5-37 What would be the effect of a choice of law provision selecting the law of a state, such as New York, in which arbitrators do not have the power to award punitive damages? The federal Court of Appeals for the 11th Circuit – the same court that decided Willoughby in 1985 – faced this question in 1988 in *Bonar v. Dean Witter Reynolds*,[38] a case involving a claim against a securities dealer. An arbitration clause incorporated the American Arbitration Association rules. A choice of law clause provided that the 'agreement and its enforcement shall be governed by the laws of the State of New York'. The arbitrators awarded punitive damages. The respondent securities dealer sought to vacate the award arguing that, although under Willoughby the award was unassailable, the parties

---

[36] 598 F. Supp. at p. 365.
[37] 776 F.2d at p. 270.
[38] 835 F. 2d 1378, 1387 (11th Cir. 1988).

94

had contracted out of Willoughby by choosing New York law – including Garrity. The Court of Appeals rejected this argument:

a choice of law provision in a contract governed by the [federal] Arbitration Act merely designates the substantive law that the arbitrators must apply in determining whether the conduct of the parties warrants an award of punitive damages; it does not deprive the arbitrators of their authority [under Willoughby] to award punitive damages.

As in *Willoughby*, so too in *Bonar*, the court leaned against an interpretation that would have stripped the arbitrators of the power to award punitive damages.

5-38 The lesson for the drafter is obvious. If you would strip the arbitrators of the power to award punitive damages, you should – in so many words – either ban 'punitive' (or 'exemplary') damages or allow only 'compensatory' damages. The drafter who uses plain English, however, can eliminate the risk of an award of punitive damages.

5-39 The converse is not necessarily true. It does not follow that the drafter can so simply confer on arbitrators a power to award punitive damages if they would not otherwise have that power. According to the opinion in *Garrity*, awarding punitive damages is 'a sanction reserved to the state'.[39] That being so, the parties cannot – even by express language – empower arbitrators to impose that sanction. It may be worth noting, parenthetically, that even under *Garrity*, the parties have the power to provide for a penalty as distinguished from liquidated damages. At least so it was held in a case decided a year before *Garrity*– a case distinguished in *Garrity*– in which the New York Court of Appeals upheld an award of treble damages pursuant to a penalty clause in a contract.[40]

5-40 In other jurisdictions than New York, however, a provision authorizing the award of punitive damages may carry weight. Although it is unlikely that parties will include an explicit authorisation of punitive damages, a court may be influenced by both the breadth of the arbitration clause and the arbitration rules that it incorporates. In Willis, for example, the court noted that the broad arbitration clause covered 'any controversy arising out of or relating to' the brokerage account – which suggested to the court that the arbitrators were

---

[39] See text at note 23, *supra*.
[40] *Associated General Contractors* v. *Savin Bros.*, 36 N.Y.2d 957, 335 N.E.2d 859 (1975).

empowered to entertain a controversy over punitive damages.[41] And in Willoughby, for example, the trial court observed that the clause incorporated the Construction Industry Arbitration Rules, notably Rule 43 under which the arbitrators can grant any remedy 'which is just or equitable' – which suggested to the court that the arbitrators were empowered to award punitive damages.[42]

5-41 It does not appear that drafters of arbitration clauses have given much attention to the question of punitive damages – at least in the past. Stephen Bond, Secretary General of the International Chamber of Commerce's International Court of Arbitration analysed clauses in 237 arbitration cases presented to the Court in 1988 and found that none of them dealt explicitly with remedies – including punitive damages.[43] This does not, to be sure, end the inquiry since most arbitration clauses are broad clauses (recall *Willis*) and incorporate rules (recall *Willoughby*) that may influence a court. Furthermore, the possible effect of a choice of law clause cannot be excluded. What would be the effect of a clause choosing the law of a state that allowed arbitrators to award punitive damages (reversing the situation in *Bonar*)? What would an English court make of a choice of California law? Would it regard it as irrelevant on the arbitrator's power to award punitive damages?

5-42 Perhaps the impact on the drafter is the most important aspect of this topic. And you cannot draft against that which you know not of. I hope that this article will at least make readers aware of a risk that is likely to materialise in arbitration with increasing frequency in the coming years.

---

[41] 776 F.2d at 823.
[42] 598 F. Supp. at 357.
[43] Bond, *How to Draft an Arbitration Clause*, 6 J. Int. Arb. 65 (1989).

*Sir Roy Goode**

CHAPTER 6

THE ADAPTATION OF ENGLISH LAW TO INTERNATIONAL COMMERCIAL ARBITRATION

I. INTRODUCTION

6-1 The UK Department of Trade and Industry Advisory Committee on Arbitration, established some years ago under the chairmanship of Lord Justice Mustill and now chaired by Lord Justice Steyn, is currently engaged in work on a new Arbitration Act.[1] It is therefore an opportune time to examine the extent to which English law adequately accommodates international commercial arbitration.

6-2 The high regard in which English law and English courts are held in other jurisdictions is amply attested by the regularity with which parties to contracts having no significant connection with England select English law as the governing law and English courts to determine their disputes. But we must constantly guard against arrogance or complacency. We live in a highly competitive world. The City of London may at present be pre-eminent as a financial centre but we cannot take it for granted that this will continue. We may

---

* [Professor Sir Roy Goode FBA, QC is Emeritus] Norton Rose Professor of English Law in the University of Oxford, Fellow of St. John's College, Oxford. This is a revised and slightly expanded reproduction of the Freshfields Arbitration Lecture delivered at Queen Mary and Westfield College, University of London, on 5th June 1991. Though the writer is a member of the Department of Trade and Industry Advisory Committee on Arbitration the views expressed here are purely personal and should not be taken as indicating the Committee's current thinking. I should like to express my thanks to my research assistant, Miss Regina Asariotis, for all her assistance in gathering sources for the lecture here reproduced.

1 A privately financed project made possible through the initiative and labours of Mr. Arthur Marriott and his team and proceeding under the direction of a Bill Sub-Committee chaired by Mr. Martin Hunter, whose firm so generously supports the lecture series referred to above.

Julian D.M. Lew and Loukas A. Mistelis (eds), Arbitration Insights, 97-114
© 2007 Kluwer Law International. Printed in the Netherlands

feel that our laws and procedures are superior to those of other States but if we cut ourselves off from outside influence we may discover sooner than we think that our ideas have become outmoded, that they are no longer seen to be responsive to the needs of the international business community.

6-3 It is salutary to reflect that a mere seventeen years ago we were almost the only developed jurisdiction that still retained the concept of absolute sovereign immunity; that a mere twelve years ago we were still applying a procedure unique to this country, the special case stated, in international as well as domestic arbitration, and only the steady loss of business made us think again; that even to-day our law is unable to comprehend something as basic as the creation of an international organisation under international law except so far as it has become localised by English legislation; and that foreigners trading on our swap markets are expected to investigate the power of local authorities to engage in market operations.[2]

6-4 The fact is that whilst we are not impervious to foreign influence we are not very good at doing the influencing ourselves. Though we make major contributions to the preparation of international conventions we are usually the last major State rather than the first to ratify. Thus while some three dozen States, including many major jurisdictions, have ratified the Vienna Convention on Contracts for the International Sale of Goods, we remain reluctant to concede that anything could possibly be better than our century-old Sale of Goods Act[3] and we conveniently ignore the fact that for every sale contract governed by English law there are several others that are governed by foreign law available only in a foreign language to which the common law has made no contribution, leaving our nationals much more exposed than they would be under the Convention, for which there is an official English text and comprehensive commentaries in English.

6-5 So while others might look to us for leadership we are all too often followers rather than leaders, with the result that when issues of interpretation of a Convention arise our courts are late in the field and their ability to influence thinking in other jurisdictions is correspondingly reduced.

---

[2] *Hazell v. Hammersmith and Fulham London Borough Council* [1991] 2 W.L.R. 372.
[3] The current Act is, of course, the Sale of Goods Act 1979 but for the most part this re-enacts the Sale of Goods Act 1893.

II. THE NEEDS OF FOREIGN PARTIES ARBITRATING IN ENGLAND

6-6   Contracting parties carrying on business in different States not infrequently choose the law of a third State to govern their contract and the curial law of that State to control the arbitration. The principal reason is to avoid one party being given what is perceived to be the undesirable advantage of arbitrating under his own law and his own country's arbitration rules with which he and his lawyers are likely to be much more familiar than their foreign counterparts. The parties thus submit themselves to the law of and to arbitration in a country for whose law and administration they may in a general sense have the highest regard but whose history, culture, traditions, language, method of contracting, legal reasoning and rules of substantive law and procedure are quite different from their own. Indeed, their two countries may have much more in common with each other than with the selected third State.

6-7   What, then, do such parties expect when they come to arbitrate in a foreign land? One thing they may reasonably expect is that the arbitrator will have regard to the international character of the transaction. They may have chosen English law, but does that mean English law as applied in all its detail to domestic transactions? An international transaction is not the same as a domestic transaction and a dispute between two foreigners is not the same as a dispute between two Englishmen. We can reasonably suppose that when they invoke English law they envisage English law applied with a broader brush and with an eye to established international usage and the need to accommodate the particular factors that are peculiar to transactions involving a foreign element.

6-8   So also with rules of procedure and evidence. When foreigners pay us the courtesy of arbitrating in England, we like to think they have a perception of English arbitration procedure as embodying highly developed principles of fair play and natural justice; but does it follow that they also intent to submit themselves to the very same rules of procedure and evidence that are applied in all their particularity to purely domestic disputes? Again, I would suggest not. Foreign parties are entitled to assume that the arbitrator will have regard to procedures and modes of proof appropriate to the arbitration of an international commercial transaction.

6-9   It is against this background that I turn to consider English arbitration law as it affects transactions involving a foreign element.

III. THE RULES OF ENGLISH LAW GOVERNING INTERNATIONAL COMMERCIAL
ARBITRATION

6-10 The old law merchant, a diffuse and uncodified body of trade usage, was international in character, was founded on good faith and was largely free from the technicalities of national law. In England its application was not dependent on contract; in relation to dealings between merchants it was recognised by statute and by the courts as not only normative but superior to dispositive law. Its administration was informal, flexible and fast. Special privileges and protections were conferred on merchants from overseas. Eventually it was supplanted by national law, which localised international transactions through the development and application of conflict of laws rules and to a high degree subjected arbitration to the rules of evidence and procedure applicable to litigation.

6-11 To what extent does modern English law make special accommodation for international commercial arbitration? It cannot be denied that we have made some moves in the right direction. Our rules of public policy are applied somewhat less stringently to transactions with a foreign element; and in the case of non-domestic agreements to arbitrate outside the special categories of admiralty cases, insurance and commodities we make it easier to exclude appeals to the courts. Moreover, by enacting the New York Convention we have removed in the case of non-domestic arbitration agreements the discretion normally enjoyed by our courts to refuse a stay of proceedings by reason of an agreement to arbitrate.[4]

6-12 How far have we gone beyond this? Dr. Gilles Wetter, an eminent Swedish authority well disposed to this country and its institutions has observed perceptively that:

> London is the *locale* of the greatest number of international arbitrations in the world. Yet the vast majority of these are viewed by the arbitrators, counsel and the parties as wholly domestic in character in the sense that the proceedings are indistinguishable from those which take place between two English parties. In Sweden, to the contrary, arbitrations in which at least one party is non-Swedish are treated as being multi-dimensional, in recognition

---

[4] Arbitration Act 1975, s. 1.

of the particular requirements and problems inherent in transnational disputes.[5]

6-13 The force of this observation may be seen from the following propositions of English law which are believed to be tolerably accurate:

(1)   An arbitrator cannot, by ruling on his own jurisdiction, preclude a pre-award ruling by the court as to whether he has jurisdiction.

(2)   An arbitrator cannot adjudicate on the validity of the agreement containing the arbitration provision under which he was appointed.

(3)   An arbitrator is obliged to observe the rules of evidence applicable to ordinary litigation except so far as the parties otherwise agree.

(4)   An agreement purporting to confer on an arbitrator power to decide a case ex aequo et bono has no legal effect.

(5)   A party can, with leave of the High Court, appeal from an award on grounds which include an error of law on the face of the award, except where the parties have exercised their right to make an exclusion agreement.

6-14 Every single one of these propositions of law, designed for domestic arbitration, appears equally applicable to international arbitration, except that the exclusion agreement can in the latter case be made in advance of the dispute, whereas in a domestic arbitration it is valid only if made after the dispute has arisen. And on each proposition English law is quite out of line with the prevailing approach in other major jurisdictions. Of course, this does not necessarily mean that we are wrong. To the contrary, we have it on what was previously the highest political authority that in international matters the United Kingdom is the only one in step, the sole observer of the true faith! As it happens, I believe this to be true of the first proposition. But we need to look at each of them more closely. The five propositions will be considered under two broad heads, the limits of arbitral power and the availability of judicial review.

---

[5]   'Choice of Law in International Arbitration Proceedings in Sweden' (1986) 2 *Arbitration International* 294 at p. 298.

A. The Limits of Arbitral Power

i. The Arbitrator's Power to Determine his Own Jurisdiction

6-15 Much has been written about Kompetenz-Kompetenz and a brief comment will suffice. The arbitrator's power to determine his own jurisdiction is subject to judicial intervention not only after his award but before it. This is the particular characteristic of the English law rule on Kompetenz-Kompetenz, and with one qualification it is sensible, for it avoids expense and it is flexible, the court retaining a discretion to refuse to intervene where it considers it more expedient for the arbitrator to give his award first.

6-16 The qualification is that this power should be limited to direct jurisdictional issues, as opposed to those which arise indirectly through an attack on the validity of the agreement pursuant to which the arbitrator was appointed. That should be dealt with by accepting the arbitrator's power to determine questions affecting the validity of the agreement.

ii. Arbitrator's Jurisdiction to Rule on the Validity of the Agreement

6-17 Where English law is not merely particular but peculiar in the popular sense is in the situation where there is a dispute as to the very existence or validity of the agreement relied on as containing the agreement to arbitrate. This is not in truth a question of Kompetenz-Kompetenz at all, but a quite distinct question whether an arbitrator has power to adjudicate on the validity of the agreement containing the clause pursuant to which he was appointed. English law adheres to the perceived logic of the proposition that if the agreement of which the arbitration clause forms part is invalid the reference to arbitration is necessarily invalid.

6-18 In taking this stance English law is isolated. The essential question is the intention of the parties. In general, it is to be assumed that they intend to confer on the arbitrator power to determine the validity of the contract between them, so that only if the agreement to arbitrate is itself vitiated does the arbitration fall to the ground. Even without the well established doctrine of separability the logic of the English position would be arid and unhelpful. In the law of contract we find nothing inherently illogical in allowing a party to exclude the other's right to rescind for misrepresentation, even though the clause excluding rescission forms part of a contract which upon rescission would be rendered retrospectively null and void. In the conflict of laws we see no great difficulty in the proposition that the law to be applied to determine the validity of a contract is the law which would be applicable if the contract were in fact valid, a principle now embodied in the Rome Convention which we have enacted. If we can swallow the camel of these particular circularities, why should we strain at the gnat of autonomy of an arbitration clause? Of course, the assumed separate agreement is notional but there is no harm in that; the concept of separability is simply a device to give effect to the presumed intention of the parties that the arbitrator's remit is to include, where necessary, a ruling on the validity of the substantive agreement.[6]

iii. Observance of Rules of Evidence

6-19 On the need to follow rules of evidence that magisterial work, Mustill and Boyd, has the following to say:

> It is widely believed that an arbitrator, merely because he is an arbitrator, is empowered to act on evidence which would not be strictly admissible in a Court of Law. This is not so. Arbitrators are bound by the law of England, and the rules regarding admissibility of evidence are part of that law.[7]

6-20 Even for domestic arbitrations such a rule lacks merit. One of the reasons why parties opt for arbitration is informality and a commercial approach to the determination of their dispute. The notion that they intend the rules of evidence for litigation to be applied in all their rigour is surprising indeed. In the case of international arbitration such a rule has nothing in its favour. The English law of evidence possesses a most unfortunate tendency to rigidity in the formulation of rules which fly in the face of experience and are alleviated only by the robust good sense of our trial judges.

6-21 Three examples will suffice. We have a parol evidence rule, a rule greatly eroded by exceptions and so complex and circular in character that our Law Commission finally decided not to recommend its abolition because it was impossible to say what it meant![8] We have a rule against hearsay evidence, also subject to numerous exceptions, which if properly applied would exclude a good

---

[6] The most recent decision is the judgment of Steyn J. (as he then was) in *Harbour Assurance Co. (UK) Ltd.* v. *Kansa General International Insurance Co. Ltd.* [1992] 1 Lloyd's Rep. 81, in which he indicated that had he not felt constrained by prior authority he would have held that the arbitrator was entitled to rule on the question of the initial illegality of the agreement.

[7] *Commercial Arbitration* (2nd edn., London 1989), p. 352.

[8] *Law of Contract: The Parol Evidence Rule* (Law Com. No. 154, Cmnd. 9700, 1986).

deal of both oral and documentary evidence upon which ordinary businessmen rely. We have rules for the interpretation of contracts which, so the House of Lords has ruled not once but several times, render evidence of pre-contract negotiations and post-contract behaviour absolutely inadmissible for the purpose of construing a contract,[9] though we all know that such evidence regularly surfaces in agreed bundles of documents placed before the court and is often the most reliable guide to the meaning of the contract.

6-22 Now if we in England wish to tie ourselves hand and foot by rules of this kind in domestic legislation, so be it. But why, in an international arbitration, should we expect foreign parties accustomed to business evidence and to relaxed evidential rules in their own countries, to be circumscribed by our arcane jurisprudence on evidence? The mediaeval courts of common law, which were notoriously strict in their approach to evidence, were nevertheless content to tolerate and recognise the informality of the merchant courts in the reception of evidence. How ironic if we in the closing years of the 20th century, when the volume of international trade has reached unparalleled levels, should now impose a more severe regime than our predecessors of the Middle Ages!

6-23 The only requirement should be that the arbitrator acts fairly and in conformity with natural justice.

iv. Decisions Ex Aequo et Bono

6-24 English courts have always set their faces against giving legal effect to an award based on an arbitration agreement by which the arbitrator is empowered to decide the case *ex aequo et bono*. The reason ascribed to this rule is that such an agreement negates an intention to create legal relations, so that there is no contract and thus no award that the law can recognise.[10] As I have pointed out

---

[9] *James Miller & Partners v. Whitworth Street Estates (Manchester) Ltd.* [1970] A. C. 583; *Prenn v. Simmonds* [1971] 1 W.L.R. 1381; *Schuler AG v. Wickman Machine Tools Ltd.* [1974] A.C. 235.

[10] *Orion Compania Espanola de Seguros v. Belford Maatschaapij voor Algemeene Verzekringen* [1962] 2 Lloyd's Rep. 257, *per* Megaw J. at p. 264; *Deutsche Schachtbau-und-Tiefbohrgesellschaft mbH v. Ras Al Khaimah National Oil Co.* [1987] 2 Lloyd's Rep. 246, *per* Sir John Donaldson M. R., at p. 253. In the latter case the Master of the Rolls, in whose judgment the other members of the court concurred, concluded that in an arbitration under the ICC Rules, which allow the arbitrators, in default of a choice of law by the parties in their contract, to determine the proper law by the rule of conflict they consider appropriate, the arbitrators were perfectly entitled to select as the proper law 'a common denominator of

elsewhere,[11] this conclusion is based on a decided *non sequitur.* The fact that the parties wish the award to be arrived at otherwise than by recourse to rules of law does not mean that they intend to deny legal force to the undertaking to arbitrate on the resulting award, merely that the arbitrator may apply non-legal criteria in reaching his decision. Mr. Steward Boyd QC has argued powerfully that if this is what the parties want there is no reasonable basis upon which to deny it to them:

> ... there is a widespread and growing appreciation of the extent to which arbitrators in other jurisdictions are permitted to decide in accordance with principles which are not those of any one fixed system of law, but an amalgam or distillation of many systems of law, or indeed no recognised system of law at all. What principle of English public policy, it may be asked, would require the English courts to refuse to recognise and enforce a foreign award made in accordance with such principles if it is valid in accordance with the law of the country by which the arbitration is governed? And if there is no such principle of public policy precluding enforcement of such an award made abroad, should not such an award be equally enforceable if made in England under English arbitration law? [12]

B. The Availability of Judicial Review

6-25 I now turn to an issue which is both complex and controversial: the judicial review of an arbitral award.[13] Prior to the Arbitration Act 1979 the special case stated procedure and a fairly liberal post-award appeal regime provided endless opportunity for dilatory tactics, and the resultant loss of foreign business became so noticeable that legislative action had to be taken. The 1979 Act abolished the special case stated procedure and introduced provisions design to curb appeals on a point of law.

6-26 Under section 1 of the Arbitration Act 1979 an appeal on a question of law arising out of an arbitral award lies to the High Court with the consent of all the

---

principles underlying the laws of the various nations governing contractual relations' (*ibid.*, at p. 254). The decision generated much debate but is plainly in accordance with principle. The parties themselves could have selected an amalgam of the rules of different legal systems; the ICC Rules gave the arbitrators the same freedom.

[11] *Commercial Law* (London, 1982), p. 975.

[12] '"Arbitrator not to be bound by the Law" Clauses' (1990) *Arbitration International* 122, at p. 123.

[13] For an excellent comparative survey, see Adam Samuel, *Jurisdictional Problems in International Commercial Arbitration: A Study of Belgian, Dutch, English, French, Scandinavian, US and West German Law* (Zürich, 1989).

parties or, in the absence of a valid exclusion agreement, with leave of the court.[14] Leave is not to be granted by the High Court 'unless it considers that, having regard to all the circumstances, the determination of the question of law concerned could substantially affect the rights of one or more parties to the arbitration agreement'.[15] That is the sole constraint on the court's power to grant leave to appeal in non-exclusion cases, and does not by itself provide a great deal of encouragement to those who favour finality or predictability in arbitration. It has been left to the courts to give effect to the perceived will of Parliament substantially to reduce judicial review of arbitral awards.

6-27 As the result of the 'guidelines' laid down by the House of Lords in *The Nema*[16] and *The Antaios*[17] and a spate of ensuing case law the factors relevant to the issue now appear to include the following: whether the situation is 'one-off' or repeat; whether, in the former case, it is of limited interest or raises an important point of principle; whether the dispute depends upon the interpretation of contracts or clauses in general use in a particular trade; whether determination of the point of law by the court would add significantly to the clarity and certainty of English commercial law; whether the circumstances in which the reference was made suggest that the parties attached importance to the speed and finality of the decision; whether it is clear, probable or merely possible that the arbitrator has gone wrong in law, noting, however, that the degree of certainty of error required varying according to the first two factors mentioned and has been expressed in a wide variety of judicial expressions. To quote again from Mustill and Boyd:

> Thus it is said that the award must be 'obviously wrong on a mere perusal'; that it must be 'clearly wrong'; that the judge 'would need a good deal of convincing the arbitrator was right'. Leave would, however, be given if the judge received the decision 'with very considerable surprise'. It is not enough, however, to show 'very considerable doubt'. On the other hand the bare word 'wrong' has also been employed. No doubt other expressions can and will be used in the future. We suggest that it is unprofitable and indeed misleading to attempt a reconciliation. These turns of phrase reflect the reaction of the court to a particular award, in relation to a particular question

---

[14] *Ibid.*, s. 1(3).
[15] *Ibid.*, s. 1(4).
[16] [1981] 2 Lloyd's Rep. 239.
[17] [1985] A. C. 191.

of law, and they show that the principles of the exercise of the discretion are not confined to rigid categories.[18]

6-28 The learned authors continue:

... Other factors may have a powerful influence on the exercise of the discretion: more powerful, on occasion, than the judge's estimate of the general utility of a decision. Thus, if the way in which the reference was brought into existence and conducted was such as to suggest that both parties wished for a speedy resolution of the dispute, or if the parties deliberately abstained from asking for a reasoned award, it is less likely that leave will be given.... Conversely, if the arbitrator is asked to make a reasoned award, this will be some evidence that the desire for speed and finality was not paramount.[19]

6-29 Finally, we are told that:

Since the Nema did not purport to lay down exclusive criteria for the grant of leave to appeal, other factors will on occasion have to be taken into account.[20]

6-30 The analysis of the case law to the end of 1988 takes up no fewer than nine pages of commentary in the latest edition of Mustill and Boyd[21] and the flow of cases has continued unabated. Not one of the factors to which I have alluded appears anywhere in the 1979 Arbitration Act; it is pure judge-made law, a robust and sensible approach to an indeterminate statutory provision. But how far is it law at all? In the *Aden Refinery* case Mustill L. J. pointed out that the guidelines themselves were not intended to be immutable but were subject to adaptation or refinement to meet varying or unforeseen circumstances. On the other hand those passages in *The Nema* and *The Antaios* which dealt with the *spirit* in which judges should approach the discretionary power conferred on them (namely to be consistent with the intention of Parliament to secure finality) were authoritative pronouncements which judges should observe.

---

[18] *Op. cit.*, at p. 607
[19] *Ibid.*
[20] *Ibid.*, p. 608.
[21] *Op. cit.*, pp. 600–609.

6-31 This brings us to the question of appeals to the Court of Appeal which require leave of the High Court *and* a certificate that the question of law is of general public importance or is one which for some other special reason should be considered by the Court of Appeal. Subject to these conditions it was until recently generally assumed that such an appeal was governed by the *Nema* guidelines. Then it was realised that this postulated the trial judge giving leave to appeal on the ground that the decision he had rendered only moments before was almost certainly wrong! Hence the ruling in *Geogas SA v. Trammo Gas Ltd.*[22] that the relevant test was not whether there was a strong prima facie case that the judge was wrong but whether the question of law certified by the judge was worthy of consideration by the Court of Appeal, which involved an assessment whether there was sufficient doubt about the correctness of the decision to warrant such consideration, whether the decision of the Court of Appeal would add significantly to the clarity and certainty of English commercial law or whether for some other reason the Court of Appeal should consider the question of law.

6-32 If one were asked by foreign parties negotiating a contract whether if they chose English arbitration and the rules of natural justice, procedure and jurisdiction were to be followed, they could rely on the award being final, one's answer would have to be: 'God only knows!' Let me emphasise once again that this is not the fault of the judiciary. To the contrary our courts have laboured mightily to promote finality and restrict judicial review but they have been hampered by the almost total absence of meaningful criteria in the legislation and have thus had to make bricks with precious little statutory straw.

6-33 Where, then, does this leave us? The parties to a contract, who have chosen arbitration in order to secure informality, finality and confidentiality, find all their expectations frustrated because the judge considers that an issue of law in their private dispute raises questions of general importance which will help *other* parties in *future* cases and will add to the clarity and certainty of English commercial law. Now I am perfectly happy to accept the underlying premiss that English commodity associations and English arbitrating parties share a burning enthusiasm to enrich English jurisprudence – or that if they do not, then they jolly well should! But why should foreign parties be exposed to the delay, the expense and the breach of confidentiality involved in an appeal to the court? Why should such parties have to face the uncertainty of a procedure so utterly

[22] [1991] 2 W.L.R. 794.

dependent on judicial discretion? Why, in short, should parties to an international commercial arbitration be served up as cannon fodder for the English legal system? As that great lawyer Lord Devlin sardonically remarked: 'The next step would, I suppose, be a prohibition placed on the settlement of cases involving interesting points of law'.[23] If there is indeed a general interest in the authoritative determination of a particular issue there should no be difficulty in organising an agreed test case in litigation or arbitration. If no two parties can be found who are willing to initiate a test case, it suggests that the point is not of such interest after all – except, perhaps, to the academics and the judges!

6-34 It might be argued that the parties' inferred desire for finality is outweighed by the interests of the State in having authoritative rulings on points of major importance in English commercial law and in maintaining a watchful eye over arbitrators, so that they are aware of the prospect of judicial review if they overstep the mark. But even if such a standpoint were at one time tenable it has now been fatally undermined by the provisions of the 1979 Act permitting exclusion agreements - the clearest possible statutory acknowledgment that in international arbitrations, at least, there is no fundamental principle of public policy at stake which necessitates the preservation of judicial review against the wishes of the parties.

6-35 We ought not to expect foreigners to be familiar with our rules on exclusion agreements when drafting their contracts. Nor should the onus be on the parties to prove a desire for finality, when such desire is the norm rather than the exception. We should emulate the law of other countries, both those who have adopted the UNCITRAL Model Law and those who have not, in restricting judicial review to fundamental and clearly defined grounds.[24] Such an approach is not peculiar to civil law systems. It has been adopted by Australia and Canada and also by the United States, where what has to be shown is not mere error of law but 'manifest disregard for the law'. It is noteworthy that the Rules of our own London Court of International Arbitration expressly exclude judicial review.

IV. TOWARDS A TRANSNATIONAL COMMERCIAL LAW

6-36 I have earlier remarked on the way in which English law localises international commercial transactions, converting them to the status of domestic

---

[23] *The Judge* (Oxford, 1979), at p. 106.
[24] See K.P. Berger, 'The Modern Trend Towards Exclusion of Recourse Against Transnational Arbitral Awards: A European Perspective', 12 Fordham Int. L.J. 605 (1989).

transactions. This is not in itself surprising, for it is the conventional approach of the conflict of laws. You select the conflict rule and then apply the law ascertained by that rule. What tends to be overlooked is the necessary third enquiry: is that law, according to its own terms, to be applied as if it were a domestic transaction or do the foreign elements qualify its application or even exclude it entirely? Even if the spatial reach of the rule of domestic law is limited only by the conflict of laws rules of the forum – an assumption which in my view tends to be made too readily and without adequate consideration of the policy of the *lex fori*– it does not follow that it must be applied in exactly the same way to an international transaction as to a domestic one. Yet it remains the case that when English lawyers speak of international trade law they do not mean the *international* law of trade, they mean the *national law* governing international trade transactions.

6-37 In recent years there has been an increasingly strong reaction against the domestication of international contracts. It is interesting to note, for example, that even though French lawyers believe even more passionately in the quality and good sense of their law than we do in ours, yet French courts were among the first to declare that it was not appropriate to apply French conceptions of *ordre public* to international transactions. This reaction against the domestication of international contracts is one we do well to observe, for in my belief it is the motive force which impels lawyers whose vision transcends national boundaries to urge recognition of a new *lex mercatoria*.

6-38 It was my friend and colleague the late Professor Clive Schmitthoff, the doyen of international trade law scholars, who is credited with propounding the new transnational law merchant,[25] and his ideas were picked up and developed by others.[26]

---

[25] Clive M. Schmitthoff, 'The Law of International Trade, its Growth, Formulation and Operation', in *The Sources of the Law of International Trade* (ed. Schmitthoff, London, 1964).

[26] The most notable exponent being the distinguished French scholar Professor Berthold Goldman. See B. Goldman, 'Frontières du droit et *lex mercatoria*', (1964) IX Archives de philosophie du droit 177 and, for a more recent exposition, *Lex mercatoria* (1983) Forum Internationale, lecture 3. See also Aleksander Goldštajn, 'The New Law Merchant' [1961] J.B.L. 12 and 'Reflections on the Structure of the Modern Law of International Trade', in *International Contracts and Conflicts of Laws* (ed. Petar Šarčević, London, 1990), Chapter 2.

6-39 Much has been written about the *lex mercatoria*,[27] a concept of which English lawyers, in their pragmatic way, have tended to be somewhat dismissive. Indeed, they are not alone, for there is world-wide controversy not only as to the scope of the *lex mercatoria*[28] but as to its very existence. Let me say at once that I do not myself believe in a body of customary international commercial law as an independent legal norm 'floating in the transnational firmament', to use the graphic words of Sir Michael Kerr when rejecting the concept of a stateless arbitration procedure.[29] It is clear that uncodified international trade usages,[30] so far as identifiable, are capable of being given normative force by a national or supranational legal system and to that extent constitute a modern *lex mercatoria*. But the usages which are said to constitute the *lex mercatoria* do not penetrate a contract or a legal system merely by being there. They have to be triggered by a legally adoptive act – express or implied contractual incorporation, adoption by legislation or self-executing Convention or reception by the courts of a national or supranational legal system. Until so adopted they exist merely as facts, not as normative rules. No party can be required to have imposed upon him rules for

---

[27] With particular reference to international commercial arbitration and the conflict of laws. See, for example, Ole Lando, '*The Lex Mercatoria* in International Commercial Arbitration' (1985) 34 I.C.L.Q. 747; F. A. Mann, '*Lex facit arbitrum*' in *International Arbitration: Liber Amicorum for Martin Domke* (ed. P. Sanders, The Hague, 1967); M. Mustill, 'The New *Lex Mercatoria*: The First Twenty-five Years', in *Liber Amicorum for the Rt. Hon. Lord Wilberforce* (ed. Bos and Brownlie, Oxford, 1987), reprinted, with minor amendments, in 4 Arb. Int. 86 (1988).

[28] The wide view of the *lex mercatoria* equates it with transnational commercial law, by which is generally meant that set of rules, from whatever source, which governs international commercial transactions and is common to a number of legal systems. Such commonality may derive from uncodified international trade usage, from codifications of that usage exemplified by the ICC's Incoterms and Uniform Customs and Practice for Documentary Credits, from standard-term contracts which have acquired international currency, from common principles established in different jurisdictions (whether independently or by the adoption in a particular jurisdiction of a principle developed by the courts of a different jurisdiction) and by a variety of international instruments such as Conventions, model laws and model rules. There is, of course, no magic in labels; but the concept of the *lex mercatoria* as an autonomous anational body of law can have no significance in relation to judicial decisions, legislation or operative Conventions, nor to contracts effective under a national legal system. The anational corpus of law contended for must therefore be international customary law; but in identifying international custom it is legitimate to look to all sources providing evidence of practice, including Codes and Conventions.

[29] *Bank Mellat* v. *Helleniki Techniki SA* [1984] Q.B. 291, at p. 301.

[30] When customary international trade usages become codified, as in the case of the various sets of rules promulgated by the International Chamber of Commerce, their status tends to change, in that they typically take effect by express contractual incorporation or, in some countries, by legislative adoption. But even in a transaction where they have not been effectuated in one of these ways they may be referred to as the best evidence of current usage.

which he has not contracted and which neither emanate from a national or supranational legal system nor have received the imprimatur of that system. Even the normative effect of the old law merchant was dependent upon its acceptance into national legal systems, an acceptance everywhere qualified by certain preconditions grounded on public policy.

6-40 I am not unaware of the strong, though far from universal, body of opinion which holds that even without the authority of the contract an arbitrator is free to apply the conflict rules he considers appropriate and to disregard the curial conflict rules, a subject authoritatively examined by Dr. Lew in his much cited work on the applicable law in arbitration.[31] This, of course, makes it much easier to recognise the arbitrator's right to apply a floating *lex mercatoria*. But the adoption of conflict of laws Conventions, and in particular the Rome Convention on the law applicable to contractual obligations, makes it increasingly difficult to detach arbitration from national conflict of laws rules, for such Conventions require the application of a national law (unless the parties otherwise agree) and the Conventions themselves form part of transnational commercial law.

6-41 Nevertheless it is clear that the *lex mercatoria* is a source to which, so far as its rules can be identified, national judges are entitled to resort by receiving them into their own legal system. We ourselves have done it quite recently when we drew on prevailing foreign legal doctrine to abandon our theory of absolute sovereign immunity in favour of the modern theory which requires the court to distinguish *acta jure imperii* from *acta jure gestionis*.[32]

6-42 Thus we ought not to be dismissive of the *lex mercatoria*, for it is a resource which, with the huge growth in harmonising Conventions, codifications of trade terms and trade usages, and other harmonising measures, will increasingly be drawn upon by our civilian colleagues. As Redfern and Hunter rightly point out:[33] 'There *is* evidence of a unified international standard in the practice of many modern forms of commerce'.

6-43 I believe it to be important that as part of the European market we do not allow ourselves to become isolated from current thinking merely because ours is a common law tradition. When our courts decide to jettison a long hallowed

---

[31] Julian Lew, *Applicable Law in International Commercial Arbitration* (New York, 1978).

[32] *I Congreso del Partido* [1983] 1 A.C. 244.

[33] *Law and Practice of International Commercial Arbitration* (London, 1986) at p. 90. This passage has not, however, been reproduced in the second edition (London, 1991).

principle as running counter to generally modern thinking, then, while in form they merely declare what the law is now seen to be, the reality is that they are exercising a power to create a new rule. Similarly, when they reach out to the doctrine or jurisprudence of other jurisdictions to find a solution to a problem which our own case law has not had occasion to address, they are acting creatively in admitting into English law that which has become received wisdom elsewhere. In so doing they are not applying some anational norm floating in a jurisprudential vacuum; they are applying English law as reinterpreted in the light of internationally recognised principle and practice. And if it is open to a national judge to draw on external influences to interpret national law, why should it not be equally open to an arbitrator, whose function is to apply a national law as if he were a judge?

V. THE ADAPTATION OF ENGLISH COMMERCIAL LAW TO INTERNATIONAL COMMERCIAL ARBITRATION

6-44 What I have attempted to demonstrate is the importance of sensitivity to international trends in the application of domestic law to international transactions and international commercial arbitration. We take pride in the fact that English has now become the *lingua franca*. Yet perhaps we should pause to ask ourselves this question: when an English company seeks to break into the French market, to whom will the French award their contracts? To the Englishman, whose language they well understand; or to the Italian, who speaks French? So also in the field of commercial law and commercial arbitration. We in England have much to be proud of in our legal tradition, in particular, the adaptability of our substantive commercial law and the high calibre of our judicial and arbitral institutions. If we are at fault it is not, I believe, in anything fundamental but rather in a certain procedural conservatism, a failure in our arbitration law to match the sensitivity of our substantive law to the needs of the market, coupled with a degree of imperviousness to external influence which is inimical to our legal development. In the result our arbitration law is rigid where it should be flexible and uncertain where it should be predictable.

6-45 It is almost everywhere the rule that an arbitration clause is to be treated as independent of the contract of which it forms part. That is a rule we should adopt. It is widely recognised that an arbitration agreement can confer on an arbitrator power to reach a legally binding decision *ex aequo et bono*. We should do likewise. We should also refrain from imposing on arbitrators the shackles of English rules of evidence which are alien to other legal systems. All that is required is that the arbitrator should observe the agreement of the parties and the rules of natural justice. Finally, we should emulate other States in restricting judicial review to clearly defined categories – want of jurisdiction, impropriety, procedural unfairness, manifest disregard of the law, public policy requirements[34] and the like – and to cases where the parties themselves opt for judicial review. The clarification of English commercial law, whether for the enrichment of our jurisprudence in general or for the benefit of future contestants in particular, is not in my view a proper ground for destroying the privacy and finality of the dispute resolution procedure for which the parties have opted. Other countries do not find it necessary to permit judicial review in such cases; what is so special about English arbitration that we should find it necessary to act differently?

6-46 I have expressed the view that there is nothing fundamentally wrong with English arbitration law. But in restating its principles and rules in a new Arbitration Act we must draw on the inspiration of the UNCITRAL Model Law (which as Lord Justice Steyn has so rightly observed is one of the most remarkable achievements of UNCITRAL[35]) to liberate ourselves from the shackles which fetter our freedom of movement in international commercial arbitration. By showing ourselves receptive to the practices of international arbitrators and to the trends of thought of our civil law friends and colleagues we do not diminish the influence of the English common law and its tried and tested institutions; rather we strengthen it, so that instead of merely responding belatedly to approaches that have become commonplace elsewhere in Europe, instead of being a reluctant follower along trails blazed by others, we can ourselves influence not only the development of international commercial arbitration but, more fundamentally, the evolution of transnational commercial law.

---

[34] Which should be applied from a transnational rather than a domestic viewpoint. See generally, Pierre Lalive, 'Transnational (or Truly International) Public Policy and International Arbitration' in *Comparative Arbitration practice and public policy in arbitration* (ed. P. Sanders), ICCA Congress Series No. 3, VIII the International Arbitration Congress, New York 1986, 257.

[35] 'Towards A New English Arbitration Act', (1991) *Arbitration International* 17, at p. 18.

*Albert Jan Van Den Berg**

CHAPTER 7

THE EFFICACY OF AWARD IN INTERNATIONAL COMMERCIAL ARBITRATION

I. INTRODUCTION

7-1   By way of introducing the subject matter of my lecture, I would like to tell you about an experience which I had as practising lawyer in the enforcement of a foreign arbitral award some time ago. The case concerns the well-known Pyramids Oasis arbitration. The background of the case was the following.

7-2   Attracted by the Open Door Policy to foreign investors promulgated by the late President Anwar Sadat of Egypt, Southern Pacific Properties ('SPP') embarked on a prestigious project to build an exclusive tourist village near the Pyramids of Gizeh. The project included not only luxurious villas for wealthy Arabs and Europeans, but also a golf course and an artificial lake. For the project, SPP concluded an agreement with the Egyptian General Organisation for Tourism and Hotels ('EGOTH'). Beneath the signatures of SPP and EGOTH, the words appeared: 'approved, agreed and ratified by the Minister of Tourism' and the signature of the Minister. The agreement contained a clause for ICC arbitration in Paris.

7-3   When the first bulldozers appeared in the desert, the environmentalists in Egypt awoke. They asserted, amongst other things, that the artificial lake would have the effect that the pyramids would sink in the sand. The opposition became

*   The author is both Partner, Stribbe & Simont, Amsterdam and Professor of Law, Erasmus University, Rotterdam. The Freshfields Lecture 1992 was delivered at Queen Mary and Westfield College, London University, on 27 May 1992. [Professor van den Berg now practices from van den Berg and Hanotiau law firm].

Julian D.M. Lew and Loukas A. Mistelis (eds), Arbitration Insights, 115-131
© 2007 Kluwer Law International. Printed in the Netherlands

so strong that the Egyptian government stopped the project at the end of May 1978.

7-4 When an amicable settlement proved to be impossible, SPP initiated ICC arbitration against both EGOTH and the Egyptian State. It claimed approximately US$42.5 million as damages. The Egyptian State objected to the competence of the arbitrators. It argued that it was not a party to the agreement in which the arbitration clause was included.

7-5 By an award dated 16 February 1983, made in Paris, the arbitrators held that Egypt was a party to the agreement. They ordered Egypt to pay SPP US$ 12.5 million as damages plus interests and costs. Egypt fiercely resisted this and applied to the Court of Appeal of Paris to set aside the award.

7-6 In the meantime, SPP requested me to seek enforcement of the award in the Netherlands. The Netherlands was chosen because it was discovered that my country had been so generous in allocating large sums of development money that Egypt had been administratively unable to draw on them.

7-7 On 12 July 1984, I was conducting arduous negotiations for another client in Athens. Around 3 o'clock in the afternoon, my office called me informing me that I had won the enforcement proceedings. The President had overruled Egypt's argument that it was not a party to the arbitration clause on which the award was based.

7-8 My pleasure over this result, however, lasted only 2 hours. At 5 o'clock I received a call from Paris from the French lawyers who acted for SPP in the setting aside proceedings before the Court of Appeal of Paris. I was now informed that on the very same day the Court of Appeal of Paris had set aside the arbitral award. The Court of Appeal took a view which was diametrically opposed to the view of the President in Amsterdam. It found that Egypt had not become a party to the arbitration clause in the agreement.

7-9 Thereupon, I had to suspend the enforcement proceedings in the Netherlands and eventually to withdraw them when the French Court of Cassation rejected SPP's recourse. Incidentally, SPP subsequently started ICSID arbitration which, now 9 years later, have still not yielded a final result.

7-10 This frustrating experience has led me to rethink the question whether the action for setting aside the award in the country of origin should be maintained in international arbitration. And this is the subject matter which I would like to explore with you during this lecture. I will first give you an outline of the prevailing regime governing setting aside in international arbitration. Thereafter, I will review recent developments concerning the setting aside of awards in international arbitration. These developments are twofold. First, certain countries attempt to exclude the setting aside of the award. Secondly, it is said in particular in France that that a foreign enforcement court should give little no or a limited effect to a setting aside in the country of origin. Against the background of the prevailing legal regime and these developments, I will then address the question whether the action for setting aside of arbitral awards should be retained in international arbitration.

II. PREVAILING LEGAL REGIME CONCERNING ANNULMENT

7-11 Almost all national arbitration laws provide in one way or another for the setting aside of the award. It is beyond the scope of this lecture to deal with the many differences in these proceedings.

7-12 There are also differences among the arbitration laws with respect to the grounds upon which an arbitral award can be set aside. Broadly speaking, the grounds can be divided into the following categories:
1. Lack of a valid arbitration agreement;
2. Violation of the principles of due process;
3. Violation of the scope of authority of the arbitral tribunal (infra, extra or ultra petita);
4. Failure to follow rules on appointment of the arbitrators and the arbitral proceedings;
5. Formal invalidity of the award (including lack of signatures and, if applicable, reasons); and
6. Violation of public policy (including non-arbitrability).

7-13 For some countries, such as England, a seventh category can be added:
7. Error in law.

7-14 However, in most countries it is a basic principle that the merits of an arbitral award cannot be reviewed by a court.

7-15 While the above categories are to a certain extent the same, the major differences appear to be the cases brought under these categories by the legislators and courts in the various countries. Again, it would be beyond the scope of this lecture to deal with these differences.

7-16 As regards the question which country's judicial authority has jurisdiction over the setting aside of the award, it appears to be a generally accepted principle that this authority is the court in the country of origin of the award. That country is in the vast majority of cases the country in which the place of arbitration is located.

7-17 Since the courts in the country of origin have exclusive jurisdiction over the action for setting aside of the award, the question arises what is the legal effect of a decision in the country of origin setting aside an award in that country. There can be no doubt that once an award has been set aside, it has become devoid of legal force and effect in the country of origin. But the lack of legal force and effect is also extended beyond the boundaries of the country of origin. That is the case if enforcement of the award is sought in other countries under the New York Convention (by now 85 [more than 135]). Article V(1)(e) of the Convention provides, namely, that enforcement may be refused if the award has been set aside in the country of origin. This means that a setting aside in the country of origin has in principle an extraterritorial effect under the New York Convention.

7-18 The action for setting aside the award should, of course, be distinguished from the action for enforcing the award. Whilst the setting aside of an award has an extraterritorial effect, a refusal of enforcement does not have such effect. A foreign court can in principle ignore the refusal of enforcement in another country.

7-19 As regards enforcement of an award itself, a distinction should also be made between enforcement of an award in the country of origin and enforcement abroad under the New York Convention. In most countries, the enforcement of an award made in the country where enforcement is sought consists of relatively quick, summary proceedings in which the control exercised by the courts over the arbitral award is very limited (usually violation of public policy only). In contrast, enforcement abroad under the New York Convention provides for a more extensive control on the basis of the grounds of refusal for enforcement listed in Article V of the Convention.

7-20 What is interesting for the question of reassessing the setting aside of awards in international arbitration is that the grounds for refusal of enforcement under the New York Convention come close to the grounds on which an award can be set aside in an increasing number of countries. As will be discussed later, this may have the effect that judicial control over the award can effectively be exercised in two fora on more or less the same grounds (i.e., in the country of origin in setting aside proceedings and in the foreign country where enforcement is sought).

III. RECENT DEVELOPMENTS

7-21 Having given an overview of the prevailing legal regime governing setting aside of awards in the international context, I may now turn to the recent developments in legislation and case law in a number of countries with respect to the setting aside of arbitral awards.

7-22 The developments are to be distinguished between the country of origin and the foreign country in which enforcement of the award is sought.

A. Country of Origin

7-23 A first country that is to be mentioned in *Belgium*. In 1972, Belgium adopted the Uniform Law setting forth in the European Convention providing a Uniform Law on Arbitration, Strasbourg, 20 January 1966.[1] By Law of 27 March 1985, a fourth paragraph was added to Article 1717 of the Judicial Code, which provides that when both parties to an arbitration in Belgium are non-Belgian, setting aside of the arbitral award by the Belgian courts is excluded altogether.

7-24 The Belgian amendment is to the extreme. No setting aside whatsoever is possible. It is not even possible for the parties to agree that the Belgian courts will have jurisdiction to set aside the award in international arbitration (a so-called 'opting in').

7-25 The effect of the amendment is that it concentrates judicial control over the international arbitration process on the enforcement court.

---

[1] European Treaty Series 56. This Convention has not entered into force. Austria and Belgium signed the Convention. Austria has not implemented the Strasbourg Uniform Law. The Belgian implementing law dated 4 July 1972, is published in *Monitor Belge* of 8 August 1972. The law is set forth in Articles 1676 through 1723 of the Belgian Judicial Code. See, generally, L. Matray, 'National report: Belgium' in *The International Handbook on Commercial Arbitration* (Suppl. 8 December 1987).

7-26 For enforcement of Belgian awards between non-Belgians in foreign countries, there does not seem to be a problem. In most cases, enforcement abroad will be governed by the New York Convention.

7-27 But what about enforcement *in Belgium* of an arbitral award made in that country between non-Belgians? Here, the extent of control seems to be more limited than the control offered by the New York Convention in enforcement proceedings of the same award abroad. Article 1710(3) of the Belgian Judicial Code provides: 'The President [of the Court of First Instance] shall refuse the application [for setting aside] if the award of its enforcement is contrary to *ordre public* or if the dispute was not capable of settlement by arbitration'. These two grounds for refusal of enforcement correspond to article V(2)(a) and (b) of the New York Convention. It would seem to leave uncovered all grounds for refusal of enforcement listed in the first paragraph of Article V of the Convention. Even under the most generous interpretation of *ordre public* in Belgium, there seems to be an unbalanced treatment of enforcement of an award made in Belgium between non-Belgians, depending on whether enforcement is sought in Belgium (in which case article 1710(3) of the Belgian Judicial Code applies) or in a foreign country (in which case as a rule the New York Convention applies).

7-28 Another country which merits our attention is *Switzerland*. On 27 August 1969, the Swiss Federal Government approved an intercantonal agreement unifying the laws on arbitration (the 'Concordat'). Out of the 26 Cantons, 25 have now adopted the Concordat.[2] The Concordat was, however, considered too parochial and on 18 December 1987, the Swiss Parliament enacted the Swiss Private International Law Act which contains a Chapter XII (Articles 176-194) that governs 'international arbitration'.[3] By doing so, the Swiss introduced on a federal level a specific act for international arbitration in Switzerland.

7-29 Article 192 of the Act 1987 provides that the parties to an international arbitration on Switzerland may exclude the possibility of setting aside before the Swiss courts by agreement. The agreement is subject to two conditions:
  (1) none of the parties may have their domicile, their habitual residence, or business establishment in Switzerland, and

---

[2] The only dissenter is Lucerne which is in the process of joining the Concordat. See generally, R, Briner, 'National Report: Switzerland', in *The International Handbook on Commercial Arbitration* (Suppl. 12 January 1991).
[3] AS 1987, 1779-1831 SR 291.

(2)   the exclusion must result from an express statement in the arbitration agreement or by a subsequent written statement.[4]

7-30 The exclusion of setting aside of an award in international arbitration in Switzerland is less far reaching than in Belgium, since it is not achieved by statute in all cases, but requires a specific agreement of the parties (the so-called 'opting in'). Furthermore, the discrepancy between enforcement in the country of origin and abroad, which appears to exist in Belgium, does not exist in Switzerland as the second paragraph of article 192 provides that enforcement of the award in Switzerland shall take place on the basis of an analogous application of the New York Convention.

7-31 A country which seems to be in the same ranks as Switzerland, is *Sweden*. According to a decision of the Swedish Supreme Court on 18 April 1989, in the famous *Uganda* case,[5] if the parties do not have any contact with Sweden (which was the case, considering the Israeli and Ugandan nationalities involved):

'Such parties must be considered entitled to agree – even before any dispute arises between them – to limit their right to challenge the award in a Swedish court on account of formal deficiencies'.

7-32 The Supreme Court, however, considered that no such agreement had been made in the present case. The observation of the Swedish Supreme Court is *obiter dictum*. It is unclear under what conditions the exclusion agreement may be made and what the extent of the exclusion agreement is, having regard to the Supreme Court's reference to 'formal deficiencies'.

B. Foreign Enforcement Country

7-33 The development in Belgium, France and Switzerland which I just described concern the question of setting aside from the perspective of the

---

[4]   This formal requirement means that an indirect exclusion, for example, an exclusion set forth in arbitration rules, is not sufficient. See, M. Blessing. 'The New International Arbitration Law in Switzerland. A Significant Step to Liberalism', 5 *Journal of International Arbitration* (1988) p. 9 at 75.

[5]   Supreme Court, 18 April 1989, no. So 203, *Solel Boneh International Limited and Water Resources Development (International) Limited v The Republic of Uganda and the National Housing and Construction Corporation of Uganda,* reported in English in XVI Yearbook Comm. Arb. (1991) p. 606 and in French by J. Paulsson, 'Arbitrage international et voies de recours: La Cour supreme de Suede dans les sillage les solutions belge et helvetique'. 117 *Journal de Droit International* (1990) p. 589 at 598.

country of origin. I would now like to consider the developments from a foreign country's perspective. Then the question is: if and to what extent setting aside of an award by a court of origin will be given effect by the foreign courts before which enforcement of the award is sought, as a foreign award.

7-34 This question comes up in cases of enforcement of foreign awards outside the New York Convention. If the New York Convention applies, setting aside of the award by a court in the country of origin constitutes a ground for refusal of enforcement pursuant to Article V(1)(e) of the Convention. The New York Convention, however, allows one to rely on more favourable domestic law concerning the enforcement of foreign arbitral awards (Article VII(1) of the Convention). Some countries, including France, indeed have domestic law on enforcement of foreign arbitral awards which appears to be more favourable than the New York Convention.

7-35 France is, to my knowledge, the only country where the view is advocated that in cases falling outside the New York Convention, no effect need be given to a setting aside of an award in its country of origin. This view is said to be expounded by the highest French court, the Court of Cassation, in the famous case *Pabalk v Norsolor* in a decision rendered in 1984[6]. However, this decision does not clearly lay down the rule that no effect need be given to a setting aside in the country of origin.

7-36 More specific is the Court of Appeal of Paris in a recent and unpublished decision of 19 December 1991, in the case *Hilmarton Ltd. v Omnium de Traitement et de Valorsiation ('OTV')*.[7] The case concerned a contract dated 12 December 1980 between the French company OTV and the English company Hilmarton. According to the text of the contract, Hilmarton was, in exchange for payment of fees, to give advice on legal and tax matters, and to coordinate administrative matters with respect to the procurement and performance by OTV of an important public project in Algeria. When the project was awarded to OTV, a dispute arose over the balance of the fees. The contract between Hilmarton and OTV provided for ICC arbitration in Geneva.

---

[6] Cour de Cassation (First Civil Chamber), 9 October 1984, reported in *XI Yearbook Comm. Arb.* (1986) p. 484.

[7] Unpublished, docket no. 90-16 778.

7-37 By an arbitral award dated 19 August 1988, the sole arbitrator rejected Hilmarton's claim for payment of the balance of the fees. He considered that the contract was null and void since it had as its object the payment of bribes.

7-38 On 27 February 1990, OTV obtained a leave for enforcement on the award from the President of the Court of First Instance in Paris.

7-39 In the meantime, Hilmarton obtained the setting aside of the award in Switzerland before the Court of First Instance in Geneva on 21 November 1989, which judgment was confirmed by the highest Swiss court (*Tribunal Federal*) on 17 November 1990.

7-40 The Court of Appeal of Paris in turn affirmed on 19 December 1991 the leave of enforcement granted by the Court of First Instance of Paris. The Paris Court reasoned that, according to Article VII(1) of the New York Convention, the provisions of the Convention do not deprive a party of the right it may have to avail itself of an arbitral award in the manner and to the extent allowed by the law of the country where such award is sought to be relied upon. Under these circumstances, the Paris Court observed, OTV was entitled to rely on French law concerning the enforcement of awards made abroad. The Court pointed out that unlike Article V(1)(e) of the New York Convention providing for refusal of enforcement in the case of setting aside of the award in the country of origin, French law on enforcement of awards made abroad does not contain such a ground for refusal of enforcement:

> Considering that French law on international arbitration does not oblige a French judge to take into account an annulment decision on the award given with the framework of the foreign internal order (*dans l'ordre interne etranger*), and that, hence, the incorporation in the French legal order of an award which was rendered in international arbitration and which was annulled abroad on the basis of local law, is not contrary to international public policy (*ordre public*) within the meaning of Article 1502(5) of the New Code of Civil Procedure.

7-41 It is interesting to note that in 1990, as allowed by Swiss law, Hilmarton requested the ICC to reopen the case due to the setting aside by the Swiss courts of the award: rendered on 19 August 1988. According to unconfirmed reports, the sole arbitrator in the second arbitration decided that, the contract was valid and that Hilmarton was entitled to the balance of its fees. One wonders whether Hilmarton will be able to enforce the second award against OTV in France now that the French courts have already granted enforcement on the first award between the same parties on the same subject matter, since both awards flatly contradict each other.

7-42 When discussing the question whether a foreign enforcement court should give effect to a setting aside of the award in its country of origin, one cannot leave out the European Convention on International Commercial Arbitration of 1961. This Convention has been adhered to by almost all Eastern-European countries. In so far as Western Europe is concerned, the following countries have become party to the New York Convention: Austria, Belgium, Denmark, France, Germany, Italy and Spain.

7-43 The European Convention contains extensive provisions on, inter alia, the constitution of the arbitral tribunal, pleas as to the arbitral jurisdiction, the jurisdiction of the courts in relation to arbitration, the law applicable to the substance of the dispute, and the reasons for the award. The European Convention does not provide for the enforcement of the award. Enforcement is to be dealt with on the basis of the New York Convention in conjunction with the European Convention, save that the European Convention in its Article IX limits ground (e) of Article V(1) of the New York Convention.[8]

7-44 Article IX of the European Convention requires a number of conditions for the setting aside of an award in the country of origin to constitute a refusal of enforcement in another Contracting State under the New York Convention.

7-45 One of them is that the award must have been set aside on one of the four grounds enumerated in Article IX(1) (a)-(d). These grounds are virtually identical to the grounds for which an award may be refused enforcement under Article V(1) (a)-(d) of the New York Convention. Other grounds for setting aside may not be taken into account by the enforcement court under the New York Convention.

---

[8] See for the European Convention of 1961 in general, including its application by the courts and arbitral tribunals, D. Hacher, 'Commentary European Convention on International Commercial Arbitration of 1961', *XVII Yearbook Comm. Arb.* (1992).

IV. SHOULD THE ACTION FOR SETTING ASIDE ARBITRAL AWARDS BE RETAINED IN INTERNATIONAL ARBITRATION?

7-46 Having reviewed in the foregoing part recent developments concerning the setting aside of the award, I propose in this last part first to assess the motives for the above developments, second to summarise the disadvantages these developments may cause, and third, to conclude whether or not the setting aside of arbitral awards should be retained in international commercial arbitration.

A. Assessment of Motives for Above Developments

7-47 Roughly speaking, the motives given for the above developments fall into three categories: (1) inter-national arbitration should not be impeded by local arbitration laws, (2) setting aside proceedings cause unnecessary delay (see A.ii. below), and (3) setting aside proceedings amount to double judicial control (see B.iii., below).

i. International Arbitration Should Not Be Impeded by Local Arbitration Laws

7-48 The arguments for this category are twofold. The first argument is that excessive court interference in inter-national arbitral awards should be avoided and, in any case, not be exported. Thus, the setting aside of arbitral awards on the basis of some local particularities or parochial views concerning public policy should have no effect in international arbitration.

7-49 This argument does not apply in the country, of origin since the control which is considered excessive abroad is exercised anyway, either in setting aside proceedings or, if they are not available, in enforcement proceedings in that country (except Belgium). As regards enforcement abroad, it is to be noted that this argument was forceful some 20 years ago, but that nowadays court interference in the country of origin is less excessive in many countries as a result of the increasingly favourable attitude towards arbitration.

7-50 The second argument is that the choice of the place of arbitration in international arbitration is made by reasons of convenience only. Consequently, it is said, local arbitration laws should not interfere. Again, this argument was valid some 20 years ago. Nowadays, parties generally choose a place of arbitration that provides an adequate legal framework for their arbitration. Parties do inquire about this aspect and are well informed about the law and practice in many countries by a number of readily accessible publications.

7-51 Furthermore, the second argument is in fact based on the so-called 'delocalised' arbitration, i.e., an arbitration without any applicable arbitration law. No such arbitration is accepted in a vast majority of countries. Nor is doing away with setting aside the proper mechanism for arriving at delocalised arbitration. In Belgium, for example, the exclusion of setting aside does not mean that Belgian arbitration law is inapplicable to arbitration law in Belgium. In France, international arbitrations taking place in that country are subject to French international arbitration law, including the possibility of a setting aside under that law. It is therefore curious that in France this argument is advocated with respect to the setting aside of awards made abroad to which setting aside the French courts do not give effect in cases in which enforcement is not based on the New York Convention.

ii. Setting Aside Proceedings Entail Unnecessary Delay

7-52 The argument is that setting aside proceedings in the country of origin can cause considerable delays. This is indeed true for a number of countries. However, more modern arbitration laws limit the number of judicial instances before which the setting aside of an award can be brought. For example, in Switzerland setting aside of international arbitral awards is limited to one instance, i.e., the highest Swiss court (*Tribunal Fédéral*).

7-53 In addition, the commencement of setting aside proceedings in the country of origin does not foreclose the possibility of seeking enforcement of the award in other countries under the New York Convention. According to Article VI, if the setting aside of an award is requested in the country of origin, the foreign enforcement court may adjourn the decision on enforcement and may also, on the application of the petitioner, order the respondent to put up suitable security. The words 'may adjourn' and 'if it considers it proper' in Article VI indicate that the court has discretionary power to adjourn its decision on enforcement of the award and to order a respondent to provide security, pending the setting aside proceedings in the country of origin. Article VI, therefore, offers a balanced solution between the application for setting aside for reasons of delay only and the right of a bona fide party to contest the validity of the award in the country of origin.

7-54 As regards enforcement of the award in the country of origin, whether an action for setting aside has adverse effects depends on the arbitration law of that country. For example, in France, the commencement of an action for setting aside of an international award suspends by operation of law the enforcement of the award in that country.[9] On the other hand, in the Netherlands, the initiation of an action for setting aside has no suspensive effect on the enforcement proceedings; suspension of the enforcement must specifically be requested from the court, which may grant the suspension subject to suitable security by the party seeking setting aside of the award.[10] The same applies in Switzerland.[11] Consequently, delays and adverse risks can be reduced by adequate legislation.

iii. Setting Aside Proceedings Lead to Double Judicial Control

7-55 It is submitted that the arguments in support of the foregoing two categories of motives are not compelling reasons for abolishing the setting aside of the award in international arbitration. On the other hand, the third category carries more weight. The argument is that judicial control over the arbitral award is exercised twice, i.e., in setting aside proceedings in the country of origin and in enforcement proceedings in another country. Why should the same award be subject to double judicial checking?[12] From the theoretical point of view at least, it would seem an advantage for international arbitration to abolish the setting aside of the award in the country of origin. But does this advantage outweigh the disadvantages?

B. Disadvantages of the Developments Concerning Setting Aside

7-56 The following disadvantages can be said to result from the developments which I described before.

---

[9] Article 1506 of the French New Code of Civil Procedure.

[10] Article 1066 of the Netherlands Code of Civil Procedure.

[11] Article 38 of the Swiss Concordat.

[12] The judicial double checking is carried to the extreme in the UNCITRAL Model Law on International Arbitration, adopted on 21 June 1985 (UN DOC.A/40/17, Annex I, reprinted in *XI Yearbook Comm. Arb.* (1986) p. 380). An arbitral award rendered in a Model Law country can in that country be subject to annulment proceedings and enforcement proceedings but in both proceedings the same grounds (i.e., for annulment and refusal of enforcement) apply. This can be considered one of the major defects of the Model Law. As explained in section II, enforcement of an award made in the country where enforcement is sought is subject to summary control only.

i. Country of Origin

7-57 The exclusion of the action for setting aside in the country of origin, as is provided for in Belgium, Switzerland, and possibly Sweden carries three disadvantages.

7-58 First, a party whose claim has been rejected will be deprived of any remedy against the award. That party effectively has no remedy to challenge the award in the courts, as setting aside has been excluded, even if the arbitration was conducted, for example, in violation of fundamental notions of due process. The aggrieved party, therefore, will have no opportunity to have the award set aside and to have its case adjudicated in proper (new) proceedings.

7-59 Second, the exclusion of setting aside in the country of origin may lead to 'enforcement shopping' or rather an 'enforcement chase' abroad, as a losing party will not have the possibility of having the award set aside, which would mean that enforcement cannot be granted under Article V(1)(e) of the New York Convention, a winning party will attempt to enforce the award in as many countries as it can obtain jurisdiction. This disadvantage applies especially to awards that are questionable. Yet, the losing party will as a victim incur considerable costs in defending of this chase.

7-60 Third, exclusion of setting aside may create uncertainty about the status of an award for a long period of time. If an award is questionable, a party will not have the possibility of having the uncertainty adjudicated with finality in the courts. This may create a new breed of 'ghost awards'.

7-61 Apparently, the above disadvantages are conceived in the same way in practice: A proponent of the Belgian amendment described it as a 'paradise for international arbitration'.[13] Yet, it does not seem to have increased the number of international arbitrations in Belgium. Some even say that the number has decreased as parties appear to be reluctant to give up the right to challenge an award in the courts.

7-62 In Switzerland, while initially conceived as an all encompassing solution and one of the most prominent justifications of the regulation of international arbitration on the federal level, it is now believed that the possibility of excluding

---

[13] M. Storme, International Business Lawyer (1986) p. 294.

setting aside will not in practice be used frequently in Switzerland. The limited use is thought to be due, as a famous Swiss author, Professor Poudret, put it to 'the prudence of the parties, who are more concerned about certainty than about rapidity and economy, at least when significant interests are at stake'.[14] Furthermore, as another author observes, post-award litigation risk is not totally excluded since parties disappointed by an arbitral award will undoubtedly attempt to question in court the extent and effects of the exclusion agreement itself.[15]

ii. Foreign Enforcement Country

7-63 The main disadvantage of the principle that no effect need be given by a foreign enforcement court to setting aside by a court in the country of origin of an award rendered in international arbitration is that a discrepancy arises between enforcement in the country of origin and enforcement in a foreign country. Setting aside in the country of origin has as a consequence that the award cannot be enforced in that country. In contrast, the same award, notwithstanding its setting aside in the country of origin, can be enforced in a country such as France.

7-64 The limited effect to setting aside in the country of origin, as can be found in the European Convention of 1961, has the same disadvantage, albeit less forcefully, since that Convention takes into account at least a number of grounds for setting aside in the country of origin.

7-65 The disregard of setting aside of the award also involve basic legal concepts. When an award has been set aside in the country of origin, it has become nonexistent in that country. The fact that the award has been set aside implies that the award was legally rooted in the arbitration law of the country of origin. How then is it possible that courts in another country can consider the same award as still valid? Perhaps some theories of legal philosophy may provide an answer to this question, but for a legal practitioner this phenomenon is inexplicable. It seems that only an international treaty can provide a special legal status to an award notwithstanding its setting aside in the country of origin. The latter can be deemed to be the case with respect to the European Convention of 1961. However, it should be mentioned that no case has been reported in which

---

[14] J. F. Poudret, 'Les voies de recours en matiere de l'arbitrage international en Suisse selon le Concordat et la nouvelle loi federale', Revue de l'Arbitrage (1988) p. 595 at 616.
[15] Paulsson, note 5, *supra*, at 597 note 16.

the European Convention is relied upon for granting enforcement of an award that has been set aside in the country of origin on grounds other than those listed in Article IX(1) of the European Convention.

V. CONCLUSION

7-66 It is submitted that the efficacy of awards in international arbitration is not in danger because of the availability of the action for setting aside in the country of origin. During the last 20 years, notwithstanding the many different new arbitration enactments, creeping unification has occurred. The categories of grounds for setting aside are now similar in many countries. This does not mean that all cases are treated alike by the courts in the various countries in setting aside proceedings, but there is less divergence than there was 20 years ago. The harmonisation has been prompted by the increasingly favourable attitude towards international arbitration developed by the courts and legislators in many countries in the course of the last two decades. One of the main reasons for this favourable development was undoubtedly the New York Convention.

7-67 The alleged redundancy of double judicial control is rather academic. In fact, if an action for setting aside is commenced in the country of origin – which usually has to be started within a relatively short period of time – the foreign enforcement judge can, and indeed will, take appropriate measures within the framework of Article VI of the New York Convention (adjournment of the enforcement decision and provision of suitable security). If the award has been set aside in the country of origin, there will no longer be room for judicial control in the enforcement country since the setting aside constitutes a ground for refusal of enforcement under Article V(1)(e) of the Convention. And if one looks to the more than 475 court decisions reported under the New York Convention in the *Yearbook Commercial Arbitration*, a relatively minor portion (i.e., some 30 cases) involves the application of the ground for refusal of enforcement that the award has been set aside or is subject to setting aside proceedings in the country of origin. The cases in which an award has effectively been set aside in the country of origin number only three. None of them concerned the in theory much feared public policy of the country of origin.

7-68 In conclusion, there does not seem to be any need to upset the well-established principle that an arbitral award can be subject to an action for setting aside in the country of origin and that setting aside in the country of origin constitutes a ground for refusal of enforcement abroad. In the final analysis, parties can avoid many of the problems identified in this lecture by choosing a country with an adequate arbitration law and courts that are favourable to international arbitration. And that number of countries is rapidly growing.

7-69 These countries include England. But – if you allow me to express here a desire as an arbitration practitioner from overseas – please do change your Arbitration Act(s) so that foreigners will be able to understand them. You have the commercial courts which belong to the best in the world, highly supportive for international arbitration. Why then not the best Arbitration Act?

*Lord Steyn**

CHAPTER 8

ENGLAND'S RESPONSE TO THE UNCITRAL MODEL LAW OF ARBITRATION

I. INTRODUCTION

8-1 England's response to the challenge of UNCITRAL's Model Law on International Commercial Arbitration has been to use it as a yardstick by which to judge the quality of our existing arbitration legislation and to improve it. After a gestation period, which has been elephantine in its proportions, a draft Arbitration Bill has now been prepared and when a consultation paper has been completed the consultation process will start. The single most important influence in the shaping of the Bill has been the Model Law.

8-2 The genesis of the Model Law was the idea that trading nations would benefit by having available an international text as a basis for harmonising national legislation by adopting the text *en bloc* or by revising national laws in accordance with desirable features of it. It was an ambitious project, notably because arbitration is concerned with the procedure of dispute resolution and the relationship between arbitration and national courts. The divergences between national laws on arbitration are great. And it is usually more difficult to achieve harmonisation of national laws in procedural as opposed to substantive matters. That was the principal reason why the technique of a model law as opposed to a convention was adopted.

---

* Lord Justice of Appeal [elevated to Lord of Appeal in Ordinary in 1995 and stepped down in September 2005]; Chairman of the Departmental Advisory Committee on Arbitration Law (DAC) since 1990. This article reproduces the author's 1993 Freshfields Arbitration Lecture.

Julian D.M. Lew and Loukas A. Mistelis (eds), Arbitration Insights, 133-152
© *2007 Kluwer Law International. Printed in the Netherlands*

Kingdom delegation included Lord Justice Mustill (now Lord Mustill). A further 20 states sent observers. So did 14 international organisations. Lord Wilberforce represented the Chartered Institute of Arbitrators. Mr Martin Hunter was the delegate of the International Bar Association. All contributed in an active way in discussions. Inevitably, there had to be compromises between common law and civil law points of view, and the concerns of other legal cultures had to be taken into account. No international text ever satisfies everybody. But the Model Law was a remarkable achievement by UNCITRAL, ranking in importance with the New York Convention of 1958. The text is arranged in logical order, and its provisions are expressed in simple language, which will be readily comprehensible to international users of the arbitration process. Substantively, the solutions adopted by the working Group reflect a widespread consensus as to what is practical and feasible in international commercial arbitration. It is therefore not surprising that 16 states have already based new legislation on the Model Law.[1] Germany and New Zealand may follow the same route. And other states are revising their arbitration laws in the light of the Model Law.

II. THE DECISION NOT TO ADOPT THE MODEL LAW

8-4 It is pertinent to ask why the Departmental Advisory Committee on Arbitration Law (the DAC) recommended that England should not adopt the Model Law. Cynical foreign observers say that the decision is in character with Britain's role in the process of harmonisation of international trade law. Typically, they say, the United Kingdom is voluble at international congresses in promoting common law solutions in the framing of a convention and, having achieved significant success in that pursuit, it then rejects the convention as being inferior to native English law. This criticism is obviously too extravagant in its scope. But it is not entirely groundless. The Vienna Sales Convention has been ratified by 34 nations, including almost all the member countries of the European Economic Community, and most of the major trading nations of the world. My understanding is that Belgium, Japan, and New Zealand will also ratify. Yet the United Kingdom delays. I believe the reason is to be found in the deep seated antipathy of English lawyers towards multilateral conventions. The purity of the common law prevails over the needs of international commerce, and our own trading position. Moreover, as Professor Barry Nicholas, a United Kingdom delegate at the Vienna working sessions, pointed out earlier this year, it is vital

---

[1] Legislation based on the Model Law has been enacted in Australia, Bermuda, Bulgaria, Canada, Cyprus, Hong Kong, Mexico, Nigeria, Peru, Russian Federation, Scotland, Tunisia and, within the United States of America, California, Connecticut, Oregon and Texas.

that the United Kingdom should ratify the Convention quickly, so that the experience of English lawyers and of the Commercial Court can influence the way in which the Convention is interpreted and applied.[2] I would argue, however, that the decision of the DAC to recommend that England should not adopt the Model Law was justified on special grounds. And it is right to point out that the committee took this decision under the chairmanship of Lord Justice Mustill and after a most detailed and rigorous examination of the merits and demerits of the Model law as compared with English law.

8-5 Not all the reasons put forward in 1989 for not adopting the Model Law seem as compelling today as they did then. The committee stated:

> The arguments in favour of enacting the Model Law in the interests of harmonisation, or of thereby keeping in step with other nations, are of little weight. The majority of trading nations, and more notably those to which international arbitrations have tended to gravitate, have not chosen thus to keep in step. [3]

8-6 That was a judgment made four years after the publication of the Model Law. Today one would have to revise that judgment. Less than a decade after its first publication the Model Law has proved popular internationally and has become a benchmark by which the quality of national arbitration laws is judged. Nevertheless, in my view, the decision taken in 1989 was right for England. I say that for two reasons. First, although our principal statute, the Arbitration Act 1950, is of poor quality, England already has a well developed and comprehensive arbitration system which, since the watershed of the Arbitration Act 1979, has by and large proved satisfactory domestically and popular among international users of the arbitration process. In comparison the Model Law quite understandably is more skeletal in its treatment of the arbitration process. It contains many gaps which would have to be filled. Secondly, much of arbitration law is concerned with the relationship between arbitration and national court systems, and in the English system that relationship involves greater supervision of the arbitral process than is envisaged by the Model Law. Subject to two

---

[2] The United Kingdom and the Vienna Sales Convention: Another case of splendid isolation? March 1993, *Centro di studi e ricerche di diritto comparato e straniero*, No. 9. In a paper under the heading 'The Vienna Sales Convention: A kind of Esperanto?' which was presented at an All Souls seminar in April 1993 I considered the arguments for and against England ratifying the Vienna Sales Convention.

[3] 2, para. 89.

qualifications to which I will turn later, the prevailing domestic view has been that England has found the right balance between party autonomy and judicial scrutiny of the arbitral process. In combination these two factors justified the decision taken in 1989 not to adopt the Model Law.

III. THE WAY FORWARD

8-7 In its 1989 report the Mustill committee recommended that a new statute should be drafted which would 'comprise a statement in statutory form of the more important principles of the English Law of arbitration, statutory and (to the extent practicable) common law'.[4] The committee advised that:

> Consideration should be given to ensuring that any such new statute should, so far as possible, have the same structure and language as the Model law, so as to enhance its accessibility to those who are familiar with the Model Law.[5]

8-8 The government accepted this advice.

8-9 The initiative to translate the idea of a new statute into action came from Mr Arthur Marriott. It involved the privatised drafting of a new statute. It was founded by a large group of law firms, barristers' chambers and arbitration institutions. The Marriott Group engaged the services of Mr Basil Eckersley, a distinguished barrister and arbitrator. That was an inspired choice. He produced an Arbitration Bill and a Commentary. It was a *tour de force* and a convincing refutation of the notion that only a lawyer trained in the office of the Parliamentary Draftsman is capable of drafting a statute. Nevertheless the DAC resolved that the new statute should be drafted by somebody trained as a parliamentary draftsman. That decision puzzled many experienced observers. It was yet further testimony to the astonishing awe in which Whitehall holds Parliamentary Draftsmen. As Sir William Dale pointed out, legislative drafting in England is endowed with a mystique which it does not possess in civil law countries.[6] The decision of the DAC was the outcome of *realpolitik*. The DAC was advised by the Department of Trade and Industry that it was essential, in view of a crowded legislative agenda, to obtain government support for the new measure and that such support would not be forthcoming if the bill was not

---

[4] Para. 108.
[5] *Ibid.*
[6] *Legislative Drafting: A New Approach* (1977) p. 339.

drafted by a lawyer trained as a parliamentary draftstman. The DAC was motivated by one desire only: that England should have the best possible new arbitration statute as soon as possible. The committee accepted the advice it was given, as it had to.

8-10 The Marriott Working Group instructed a former parliamentary draftsman to prepare a Bill. Unfortunately, his draft failed the threshold requirement of following the structure of the Model Law. The committee rejected it as a basis for future work. The Group instructed another former parliamentary draftsman. The committee accepted her first draft as a working draft. The committee then advised on successive drafts of the Bill.

8-11 Until 1992 the project had been financed and directed by the Marriott Working Group. By April 1992 it had become clear to all concerned that it would be more sensible for the project to become a public one. The DAC recommended that the Department of Trade and Industry should take over responsibility for work on the Bill and it should be carried forward as a Government Bill. The government accepted this recommendation.[7] That is the basis on which the DAC has advised on the drafting and redrafting of the Bill. Nevertheless the work of the Marriott Group, and Mr Eckersley's draft, proved of immense value in the second and public phase of the project. Without that work we would not today have an Arbitration Bill. And the DAC has been able to draw on the very extensive experience of the Marriott Group because two leading members of the Group, Mr Arthur Marriott and Mr Anthony Bunch, generously agreed to join the committee.

IV. THE STRUCTURE OF THE BILL

8-12 The Bill looks very different from the existing arbitration legislation. The structure is different. For example, the draftsman of the 1950 statute thought it right to start the statute with a provision on the revocation of the mandate of the

---

[7] In the course of his lecture 'The Competitive Society', the 1993 Combar lecture given on 18 May 1993, the President of the Board of Trade explained the Government's approach as follows: 'We do very well in the arbitration field. But our law, built up over years, is becoming incomprehensible to the people who want to use it. Other countries have updated and clarified their law. Others are in the process of doing so. If we do not do the same, and keep abreast of them, we will lose business. I am pleased to be able to say that, having had the arguments put to me, I was able to agree to my Department taking on responsibility for preparing a new Arbitration Bill. This is being done in full cooperation with the Committee and others with direct interest'.

arbitrator, and to scatter provisions about the challenge to arbitrators across the statute. Generally the structure of the 1950 statute was illogical and confusing. The Bill has a clear and logical structure taken from the Model Law. This is an important point because it was a prime objective of the DAC that the bill should improve the accessibility of our arbitration legislation to domestic and international users alike. The 1950 statute repeatedly uses the drafting technique of deeming provisions, which provide that 'unless a contrary intention is expressed therein, every arbitration agreement shall, be deemed to include a provision that …'. Like the draftsmen of the Model Law the DAC ultimately put its faith in simplicity. The deeming provisions have been replaced by straightforward prescriptive statements, sometimes mandatory in character and sometimes not. Another new feature is that the Bill emphasises the principle of party autonomy. It also seems to me that generally the language in which the Bill has been expressed has been improved and that it is likely to be reasonably intelligible to laymen.

V. SOME MAJOR ISSUES

8-13 It will not be possible to discuss the Bill in detail. But it might be useful to consider briefly a few features of the Bill, which either involve or might arguably involve important changes in the law, as well as certain major issues which are not at present affected by the Bill but nevertheless lie at the heart of the current debate. The matters which I propose to discuss are:

    (a)   *Kompetenz/Kompetenz* and the separability of the arbitration agreement;
    (b)   Evidence;
    (c)   Procedure;
    (d)   Immunity of arbitrators;
    (e)   The relationship between the courts and arbitration:
        (i)Special categories;
        (ii)Remission
    (f)   Equity clauses.

A. Kompetenz/Kompetenz and the Separability of the Arbitration Agreement

8-14 The doctrine of *Kompetenz/Kompetenz*, that is the question whether arbitrators may decide on their own jurisdiction, causes difficulties in some countries. In England the position is straightforward. Arbitrators are entitled, and indeed required, to consider whether they will assume jurisdiction. But that decision does not alter the legal rights of the parties, and the court has the last word. The new Bill does not change the law. It merely contains a provision declaratory of the common law position. Given the fact that the Commercial Court has the capacity to decide such preliminary issues speedily, the DAC took the view that the existing practice in England is probably satisfactory. Accordingly, the Bill contains no provisions comparable to Article 16(2) of the Model Law, which requires a denial of jurisdiction to be raised not later than when the defence is served, and Article 16(3), which requires an application to a court challenging the arbitrators' decision to be made within 30 days. If the consultation process reveals strong support for corresponding provisions in our legislation, the committee will have to think again.

8-15 Until recently the doctrine of the separability of an arbitration clause contained in an integrated written agreement was not fully developed in England. Thus it was thought that a dispute whether a written agreement reflected the true intention of the parties and can be rectified always fell outside the scope of the arbitration clause in the contract. In 1987 in *Ashville Investments Ltd. v. Elmer Contractors Ltd*[8] the Court of Appeal finally laid to rest this absurd notion. The judgments in that case were a notable contribution to the development of the doctrine of the separability of the arbitration agreement. But there was still a problem. The orthodox view was that disputes as to whether a contract was invalid or illegal *ab initio* always fell outside the scope of an arbitration clause in that contract. Earlier this year *Harbour Assurance Co. (UK) Ltd v. Kansa General International Assurance Co. Ltd*[9] the Court of Appeal held that an arbitration agreement in a written contract could confer jurisdiction on an arbitrator to decide on the initial validity or illegality of the written contract provided that the arbitration clause was not directly impeached. I respectfully applaud the judgments in the Court of Appeal in *Harbour Assurance*. England has now adopted the approach of the Model Law. Article 16(1) of the Model Law reads as follows: 'An arbitration clause which forms part of a contract shall be treated as an agreement independent of the other terms of the contract. A decision by the arbitral tribunal that the contract is null and void shall not entail ipso jure the invalidity of the arbitration clause'. That provision is the most compelling evidence of the workability and desirability of a fully developed separability doctrine. Given that the relevant law has now been satisfactorily developed and settled in *Harbour Assurance*, some may think that there is no need for legislation. It is true that there will be no appeal to the House of Lords in

---

[8]   [1989] Q.B. 488.
[9]   [1993] 3 All ER 897; [1993] 3 WLR 42; [1993] 1 Lloyd's Rep. 455.

Harbour Assurance. But there is the risk that the point may come before the House of Lords in another case. And the infallibles may say that it is all far more difficult than the Court of Appeal realised, and they may reverse the beneficial development of the law. That has been known to happen. In order to guard against that risk the Bill contains in clause 3(2) a separability provision squarely based on Article 16(1) of the Model Law.

B. Evidence

8-16 In recent times it has been assumed by authors that arbitrators are bound by the technical rules of evidence unless the parties expressly or implied agree otherwise.[10] This assumption is understandable since in enacting the Civil Evidence Act 1968 Parliament assumed that the technical rules of evidence apply to arbitrations.[11] That was, however, a mere assumption and it has no prescriptive force. If there is any such rule, it must therefore be found in the case law. Here I am fortunate. In an important paper Mr Richard Buxton QC, a Law Commissioner, (now Mr Justice Buxton) examined the relevant case law with great care.[12] His conclusion was that, contrary to what was generally believed to be the position, there is no binding authority which holds that the technical rules of evidence are applicable in arbitrations. And there are *dicta* the other way. That is a view which I respectfully share.

8-17 Looking at the matter more broadly it is difficult to see why the technical rules of evidence should apply to arbitrations. A term to that effect cannot be implied in the arbitration agreement. If there is such a rule, it must therefore be a rule of positive law. But what can be the rationale for such a rule? It can only be that the rules of law governing court proceedings and arbitrations must in all respects be the same. But that is a false premise because one of the purposes of arbitration is to avoid the over-elaborate procedure of Court proceedings and the technical rules of evidence. It is also difficult to see why, in the thousands of domestic arbitrations conducted every year by architects, engineers, surveyors and other laymen, the arbitrators should have to master technical rules of evidence which sometimes baffle the House of Lords.

---

[10] Mustill and Boyd, *Commercial Arbitration*, (2nd ed.) p. 352; *Russell on Arbitration* (20th ed), p. 273.
[11] S. 18(1) (*b*).
[12] 'The Rules of Evidence as Applied to Arbitrations'. *The Journal of the Chartered Institute of Arbitrators* (1992), Volume 58. p. 229.

8-18 Moreover, in international commercial arbitrations, where the parties have selected London as the venue because of the quality of our international arbitrators and the quality of our substantive law, it is difficult to justify the application of our technical rules of evidence. And where London is imposed on the parties by the decision of the International Chamber of Commerce, or another arbitral institution, the absurdity of applying our technical rules of evidence is even greater. It is true that most institutional rules expressly exclude the rules of evidence. It is also right that the rules of evidence are usually ignored in arbitrations. These are not, however, reasons for maintaining such a rule: these are added reasons for abolishing it. Lastly, it is relevant to note that the technical rules of evidence are under siege even in the court system. The centrepiece of the technical rules of evidence is the hearsay rule. That is the rule which led the House of Lords to conclude in *Myers*[13] that the factory records containing the engine block number of cars cannot be used as evidence to identify the cars since it was hearsay evidence. The fact that such evidence was rationally superior in quality to any evidence given by employees did not help. The statutory reversal of the particular decision in *Myers* has left unaffected the impact of the hearsay rule on many classes of rationally superior evidence. Since Mr Buxton's paper was delivered, the Law Commission has convincingly demonstrated that the hearsay rule has no place in a modern court system and recommended that in civil proceedings evidence should not be excluded on the ground that it is hearsay.[14] There is, however, a risk that a court may convert the *communis error* that the technical rules of evidence apply to arbitrations into the *ratio decidendi* of a case. It is the unanimous view of the DAC that the inapplicability of technical rules of evidence to arbitrations should be made plain by legislation. Clause 11(1) of the Bill provides: 'the tribunal shall determine all procedural matters including the admissibility, relevance, materiality and weight of any evidence'. This provision is taken verbatim from Article 19(1) of the Model Law. If it becomes law it ought to remove any suspicion that in splendid isolation England insists on applying the technical rules of evidence to arbitrations.

8-19 That leaves one loose end under the heading of evidence. The losing party in an arbitration, who can identify no true question of law, frequently applies for leave to appeal under section 1 of the Arbitration Act 1979 on the ground that there was no evidence to support a finding of fact. The argument is that such a question is a question of law under section 1. To the best of my knowledge such

---

[13] [1965] AC 1001.
[14] Law Com. No. 216 (Cm. 2321).

submissions never succeed. But does the supposed rule exist? Mustill and Boyd have argued that the rule has not survived the changes introduced by the reforming measure of 1979.[15] I respectfully agree. But this relic from the last century, which was invented to control the decisions of illiterate juries, is still around and provides a convenient basis for attacking arbitrators' decisions on matters of pure fact.[16] The Bill does not expressly deal with this point. One would hope that with the final demise of the idea that arbitrators are bound by the technical rules of evidence this related rule would also perish. But one can imagine counsel arguing that the rule should be adjusted to provide that the issue whether there is relevant evidential material, as opposed to technically admissible evidence, in support of a finding of fact is a question of law. In drafting legislation one cannot, however, guard against every absurd argument. On balance I am confident that, if clause 11 (1) of the Bill is enacted, it should put an end to all arguments that it is a question of law whether there is material to support a finding of fact.

C. Procedure

8-20 It has been a conventional wisdom of English arbitration law that there is a rule of law requiring an arbitrator to conduct a reference in an adversarial as opposed to inquisitorial fashion unless the parties have agreed otherwise. In *obiter dicta* Lord Roskill[17] and Lord Donaldson of Lymington[18] have said so. Distinguished authors have also said so.[19] But there appears to be no binding precedent containing a ruling to that effect. Moreover, the powers vested in arbitrators by section 12 (1) of the Arbitration Act do not appear to be tied to the adversarial system. It contemplates that the arbitrator will examine the parties to the dispute, and presumably also their witnesses. Moreover, in sweeping terms section 12(1) provides that the parties shall 'do all other things which during the proceedings on the reference the arbitrator... may require'. That hardly looks like a legislative prescription for a rule requiring arbitrators to conform strictly to the adversarial model of the court process.

---

[15] *Commercial Arbitration*, (2nd ed) p. 596.

[16] In *The Baleares* [1993] 1 Lloyd's Rep: 215, at pp. 228 and 231–232, I explained in some detail why in my view this supposed rule should now be rejected.

[17] *Bremer Vulkcan Schiffbau und Maschenenfabrik v. South India Shipping Corpn. Ltd.* [1981] AC 909.

[18] *Chilton and Another v. Saga Holidays plc.* [1986] 1 All ER 841, at p. 844.

[19] Mustill and Boyd, *op cit.*

8-21 It seemed to me that the point should be researched. Here too I have been fortunate. I have had the advantage of meticulous historical and legal research done by Claire Blanchard.[20] A good starting point is to ask why English civil court proceedings acquired their distinctive adversarial character. Historically, the general mode of trial was by a judge and jury. The dynamics of a jury trial required one predominantly oral hearing, and involved a relatively passive judge, who left the deployment of the evidence and arguments to the lawyers.[21] There was no reason why this procedural framework should be imposed on arbitration as a matter of law. On the other hand, it is easy to see that historically the habits of the courtroom would often have been carried over into arbitration. Between 1694 and 1889 a number of textbooks were published on arbitration law. These books stated that the procedural powers of arbitrators are wider than those of judges; that arbitrators are not bound by rules of practice; and that arbitrators may in their discretion either examine the parties and their witnesses or leave it to the lawyers.[22] The contemporary case law provides an inconclusive picture. One must, of course, put to one side cases concerning court arbitrators, who were the predecessors of official referees. Clearly, it was only natural that such arbitrators would follow the same procedure as the court from which it received its authority. Subject to this qualification, and subject to the further qualification that arbitrators must always obey the principles of natural justice, there is nothing in the decided cases to show that there was an established rule requiring arbitrators to adopt an adversarial procedure. In 1889 the Arbitration Act provided by paragraph (f) of its First Schedule as follows:

> The parties to the reference. .. shall, subject to any legal objection, submit to be examined by the arbitrators. .. and shall, subject as aforesaid, produce before the arbitrators. .. documents within their possession or power respectively which may be required or called for, and do all other things which during the proceedings on the reference the arbitrators or umpire may require.

[20] A barrister practising in 4 Essex Court, Temple, London EC4 (my former chambers).
[21] Lord Wilberforce, 'Written briefs and oral advocacy', (1989) 6 *Arbitration International.*, p. 348.
[22] Cleeve, *The Law of Arbitration* (1694), p. 18; Kyd, *The Law of Awards* (2nd ed., 1799), p. 96; Caldwell, *The Law of Arbitration*, (2nd ed., 1825) p. 53; Watson, *The Law of Arbitration and Awards* (3rd ed., 1846) p. 117; Redman, *The Law of Arbitrations and Awards* (1st ed.) p. 88; Russell, *The Power and Duty of an Arbitrator and the Law of Submissions and Awards* (3rd ed., 1864) p. 183.

8-22 That provision was the forerunner of section 12(1) of the Arbitration Act 1950. It did not impose an adversarial framework on arbitrators. On the contrary, its language contradicts the notion that arbitrators are rigidly tied to adversarial procedures. Given these statutory provisions, it is not surprising that there is no binding precedent requiring arbitrators as a matter of law to follow the adversarial procedure of the White Book. It is realistic, however, to accept that throughout this century lawyers trained in civil court proceedings in fact allowed that experience to govern arbitral procedure. And it is a fact that arbitrators and lawyers generally assume that they are bound to adopt adversarial procedures.

8-23 Under the Model Law system arbitrators have wide procedural powers to proceed in accordance with adversarial or inquisitorial methods or in accordance with a mixture of both methods. Article 19 provides as follows:

(1) …, the parties are free to agree on the procedure to be followed by the arbitral tribunal in conducting the proceedings.

(2) Failing such agreement, the arbitral tribunal may, subject to the provisions of this Law, conduct the arbitration in such manner as it considers appropriate.

8-24 The DAC unanimously took the view that it would benefit English arbitration to make clear that, subject to the terms of the arbitration agreement and to the overriding principles of natural justice, arbitrators may adopt inquisitorial powers. It does not at all follow that the essentially oral character of contested hearings will be dramatically changed if our proposal is adopted. On the other hand, such a provision may be a useful weapon in the uphill fight against ever longer and costlier hearings. In order to achieve this policy objective, clause 11 (1) of the Bill in substance enacts the Model Law provision.

8-25 Before I leave the subject of procedure, there are two qualifications which ought to be mentioned. First, if an arbitrator exercises inquisitorial powers, the risk of him committing technical misconduct will become greater. After all, it is easier for an arbitrator to hold the scales fairly if matters are left to the parties. But our arbitrators would not be assuming unique burdens. After all, the adversarial system is unknown in half of the industrialised world. Secondly, my impression is that in sectors of the construction industry the idea is gaining ground that arbitrators are entitled to exercise procedural powers contrary to the wishes of the parties. That is wrong. The principle of party autonomy requires the tribunal to respect any agreement of the parties whenever it may be concluded and however informal it may be. It is enshrined in clause 11 (1) of the Bill.

D. Immunity of Arbitrators

8-26 In a collection of comparative law essays edited by Dr Julian Lew it is demonstrated how widely national laws differ on the immunity of arbitrators.[23] During the sessions of the Working Group, which led to the adoption of the Model Law, Canada proposed that the Model Law should confer immunity from liability for negligence on arbitrators.[24] It proved to be a highly controversial proposal. The draftsmen of the Model Law were seeking common ground. It is therefore not surprising that the Canadian proposal was rejected.

8-27 In England the question whether under the common law arbitrators are immune from actions in contract or tort alleging breach of a duty of reasonable care is probably still an open one.[25] The question before the DAC was whether a statutory immunity should be conferred on arbitrators. This subject was a very controversial issue in the discussions of the DAC. The opposition to such a provision took various forms, covering outright rejection of the idea as a matter of principle, difficulties of definition and the pragmatic view that in a complex area of the law the matter is best left to development by the courts. By a very narrow majority the DAC recommended that an immunity provision should be included in the draft Bill. It seems to me that the better view might be that under the common law arbitrators, because of the judicial character of their duties, already have the benefit of an immunity from liability for negligence. I would also not oppose the enactment of a statutory immunity in favour of arbitrators. On the other hand, I do not regard this aspect as one of the critically important parts of the new legislation.

E. The Relationship between the Courts and Arbitration

8-28 The supervisory jurisdiction of English courts over arbitration is more extensive than in most countries, notably because of the limited appeal on questions of law and the power to remit. It is certainly more extensive than the supervisory jurisdiction contemplated by the Model Law. Nevertheless the Sub-

---

[23] *The Immunity of Arbitrators* (1990).
[24] Holzmann and Neuhaus, *A Guide to the UNCITRAL Model Law on International Commercial Arbitration: Legislative History and Commentary* (1989) p. 1148.
[25] *Arenson v. Arenson* [1977] A.C. 405.

committee on Arbitration Law of the Commercial Court Committee, which was chaired by Mr Justice Mustill and reported in October 1985, recorded that in an extensive consultation process it received no representations for a change in the law. Similarly, the Mustill Committee, which was appointed in 1985 and reported in 1989, received no proposals for a change in the law. In its second report of May 1990 the DAC endorsed the earlier decision to maintain the *status quo*. But eventually it became clear that further thought had to be given to the so-called special categories under section 3 of the Arbitration Act 1979 and to the ambit of the power to remit under section 22(1) of the Arbitration Act 1950.

i. Special Categories

8-29 Section 3 of the Arbitration Act 1979 recognises the contractual freedom of parties under non-domestic arbitration agreements to exclude at any time appeals on questions of English law to the High Court under sections 1 and 2 of the Arbitration Act 1979. That contractual freedom is restricted by section 4(1) of the Act. It provides that an exclusion agreement made before the commencement of the arbitration shall have no effect if the question of English law arising under the award or in the course of the reference relates to any of three special categories, namely maritime, insurance and commodities disputes. Section 4(3) of the Act provides that the Secretary of State may either limit or remove these special categories by statutory instrument.

8-30 The only justification for the restriction of the freedom of contract of commercial men engaged in shipping, insurance or commodities was that it was needed to protect the standing of our commercial law. In the debates in the House of Lords, Lord Diplock made clear that the special categories were intended to apply for an 'experimental period during which it will be possible to see how the section works'.[26] After some 14 years it seemed right to review the matter. There was also considerable criticism from commentators. They argue that the standing of our commercial law is secure enough not to need the protection enshrined in the special categories provision. The DAC recently issued a consultation paper in order to invite comment on the desirability of maintaining the special categories. On this occasion that process has been specially targeted on users of the arbitration process. The DAC will want to pay the closest attention to the wishes of the markets.

---

[26] House of Lords debates, 15 February 1979, 1477.

ii. Remission

8-31 Section 22(1) of the Arbitration Act 1980 provides in sweeping terms that the court 'may from time to time remit the matters referred, or any of them, to the reconsideration of the arbitrator'. On the face of it section 22(1) creates an entirely open textured discretion permitting a court to order the re-opening of the arbitration in circumstances where an appellate court would not be empowered to order the re-opening of High Court proceedings. Since judicial intrusion in arbitration proceedings should be less extensive than the full appellate process applicable to court proceedings such an unlimited power of remission would be surprising. And the imperative of protecting the finality of awards militates strongly against it. Not surprisingly such a wide power of remission does not exist in most countries. And the draftsmen of the Model Law rejected such a wide power of remission.[27]

8-32 A jurisprudence grew up in England which in practice restricted the power of remission to four grounds: (1) error of law on the face of the award which is now of academic importance only; (2) 'misconduct' by the arbitrator: (3) the arbitrator's request to correct an admitted mistake; and (4) material fresh evidence discovered after the award.[28] In due course an ill-defined fifth category of 'procedural mishaps' justifying remission emerged; but by and large, the approach adopted kept the power of remission in tolerable bounds.

8-33 In the last four years three judgments have been given which significantly expand the power of remission. In *Indian Oil*[29] a judge of the Commercial Court remitted an award to arbitrators to consider a point which at the hearing the applicant's legal representatives consciously and deliberately had decided not to advance. In *King* v. *Thomas McKenna*[30] the Court of Appeal examined the scope of the power to remit. That case also concerned an application for remission as a result of a mistake made by the applicant's lawyer. Lord Donaldson of

---

[27] Article 34(4) of the Model Law does, however contain a narrow point of remission. It reads as follows:

> 'The court, when asked to set aside an award, may, where appropriate and so requested by a party, suspend the setting aside proceedings for a period of time determined by it in order to give the arbitral tribunal an opportunity to resume the arbitral proceedings or to take such other action as in the arbitral tribunal's opinion will eliminate the grounds for setting aside'.

[28] Mustill and Boyd, *op. cit.*, pp. 549 *et seq.*
[29] *Indian Oil Corporation* v. *Coastal (Bermuda) Ltd* [1990] 2 Lloyd's Rep 407.
[30] [1991] 2 QB 480.

Lymington gave the leading judgment. Lord Justices Ralph Gibson and Nicholls agreed. Lord Donaldson observed that the jurisdiction was unlimited. Turning to the way in which the jurisdiction is to be exercised, Lord Donaldson stated:[31]

8-34 In my judgment the remission jurisdiction extends beyond the four traditional grounds to any cases where, notwithstanding that the arbitrators have acted with complete propriety, due to mishap or misunderstanding some aspect of the dispute which has been the subject of the reference has not been considered and adjudicated upon as fully as or in a manner which the parties were entitled to expect and it would be inequitable to allow any award to take effect without some further consideration by the arbitrator. In so expressing myself I am not seeking to define or limit the jurisdiction or the way in which it should be exercised in particular cases, subject to the vital qualification that it is designed to remedy deviations from the route which the reference should have taken towards its destination (the award) and not to remedy a situation in which, despite having followed an unimpeachable route, the arbitrators have made errors of fact or law and as a result have reached a destination which was not that which the court would have reached. This essential qualification is usually underlined by saying that the jurisdiction to remit is to be invoked, if it all, in relation to procedural mishaps or misunderstandings. This is, however, too narrow a view since the traditional grounds do not necessarily involve procedural errors. The qualification is however of fundamental importance. Parties to arbitration, like parties to litigation, are entitled to expect that the arbitration will be conducted without mishap or misunderstanding and that, subject to the wide discretion enjoyed by the arbitrator, the procedure adopted will be fair and appropriate.

8-35 These two cases concerned mistakes of a party's lawyers. Given the terms of Lord Donaldson's judgment, logically the next step was to allow remission in the event of a mistake of a party. That is what happened in *Breakbulk Marine* v. *Dateline*.[32] A judge of the Commercial Court decided that he had jurisdiction to remit an award in circumstances where the applicant had failed to find a material letter before the award, although such letter was in no sense fresh evidence.

---

[31] At p. 491 C-F. It is interesting to note that the jurisdiction issue had been argued in an appeal which was settled and withdrawn before the judgments were handed down. The same issue did not arise in the only extant appeal. It seems arguable that the observations on the jurisdiction are *obiter dicta*. This may seem technical but the *stare decisis* doctrine has its technical features.

[32] 19 March 1992 (unreported).

8-36 For my part I regard this development as a retrograde step. In the field of international commercial arbitration it will be regarded as an excessive judicial intrusion in the arbitral process.[33] I would respectfully suggest that in the light of the conflicting state of the authorities a re-examination of the scope of the power to remit is not precluded. In the meantime the DAC was faced with a difficult problem. On the one hand, there was something to be said for spelling out in the Bill the circumstances in which a court may exercise a power of remission. It is however, an exceptionally difficult exercise. And the DAC did not want to enshrine the effect of *King* v. *Thomas McKenna* in a statutory provision. On balance the best course would to be to retain the language of section 22 (1) in the Bill in the hope that developing case law will confine the power to remit more narrowly.

F. Equity Clauses

8-37 Article 28(3) of the Model Law provides as follows: 'The arbitral tribunal shall decide ex aequo et bono or as amiable compositeur only if the parties have expressly authorised it to do so'. As a broad generalisation that provision mirrors a type of arbitration which is quite common in civil law countries. States in the common law family of nations are usually less comfortable with notions of good faith, and that type of arbitration is less common.

8-38 It is necessary to consider whether English law at present recognises such a form of arbitration. Equity clauses are common in reinsurance contracts made in England. On the other hand, such clauses have been given only a limited effect. If an equity clause is expressed to involve a power in arbitrators to disregard the rules of substantive law, the orthodox view is that English law does not at present recognise the concept of arbitrators acting in this way.[34] This is, however, a complex subject and it is not impossible that the courts may liberalise our arbitration law. The fact that distinguished commentators such as Sir Michael Kerr,[35] Mr Stewart Boyd QC[36] and Mr V. V. Veeder QC[37] have argued in favour

---

[33] V. V. Veeder, QC, 'Remedies Against Arbitral Awards: Setting Aside, Remission and Rehearing', *1993 Yearbook of the Arbitration Institute of the Stockholm Chamber of Commerce*, pp. 125 *et seq.*

[34] *Orion* v. *Belfort* [1962] 2 Lloyd's Rep 257; *Eagle Star Insurance Co.* v. *Yuval Insurance Co.* [1978] 1 Lloyd's Rep. 357; *Home Insurance Co.* v. *Administratia Asigurarilor de Stat* [1983] 2 Lloyd's Rep. 674; *Overseas Union Insurance Ltd.* v. *A.A. Mutual International Insurance Co.* [1988] 2 Lloyd's Rep. 63.

[35] '"Equity" Arbitration in England', 1993, 2 *American Review of International Arbitration*, p. 377.

of such a development guarantees that the prospect must be taken seriously. But in our case law the supporting planks for such a development are as yet insecure.

8-39 Protagonists of a *lex mercatoria* were encouraged by the important decision of the Court of Appeal in *Deutsche Schachtbau-und Tiefbohrgesellschaft m.b.H* v. *R'As al-Khaimah National Oil Co. ('DST v. Rakoil'*.)[38] The case concerned a Swiss arbitration and a Swiss arbitration award. The arbitrators recorded that they were applying 'internationally accepted principles of law governing contractual relations'. The issue was whether an English court should enforce the award under the New York Convention of 1958. The Court of Appeal held that the award was enforceable. The critical point is that the court held that there was no head of public policy militating against the enforcement of the award. A contrary decision would, of course, have placed England beyond the pale among the signatories of the New York Convention. But the judgments do not tell us what the position would have been if the arbitration had taken place in England and if it had been an English award. In *Home and Overseas Insurance* v. *Mentor Insurance Co (UK) Ltd*[39] the validity of an equity clause was again considered by the Court of Appeal. Lord Justice Parker made clear that he regarded an arbitration clause allowing arbitrators to decide according to good conscience as invalid. Since Lord Justice Balcombe agreed with this judgment I regard Lord Justice Parker's view as the *ratio decidendi* of the case. In a lengthy judgment Lord Justice Lloyd commented on *DST* v. *Rakoil*. He said:[40]

> [Counsel for the Plaintiffs] argued that *DST* v. *Rakoil* was concerned only with the enforcement of a foreign award, and that it has no bearing on the present case, where the contract calls for arbitration in London. But why not? If the English courts will enforce a foreign award where the contract is governed by 'a system of law which is not that of England or any other state or is a serious modification of such a law', why would it not enforce an English award in like circumstances? And if it will enforce an English award, why should it not grant a stay?

> [Counsel] argued that it would be impossible for the court to supervise an arbitration unless it is conducted in accordance with a fixed and recognisable system of law; he even went so far as to submit that the

---

[36] (1990) 6 *Arbitration International*, p. 122.
[37] British Insurance Arbitration Lecture 1992.
[38] [1990] 1 A.C. 295.
[39] [1989] 1 Lloyd's Rep 473., [1990] 1 WLR 153; [1989] 3 All ER 74.
[40] [1987] 2 Lloyd's Rep. P. 489 col. 1.

arbitration clause in the present case is not an 'arbitration agreement' at all within the meaning of the Arbitration Acts 1950-1979. It is sufficient to say that I disagree. I would only add (although it cannot effect the argument) that if [he] is right, no ICC arbitration could ever be held with confidence in this country for fear that the arbitrators might adopt the same governing law as they did in *DST* v. *Rakoil*.

8-40 I share Lord Justice Lloyd's instinctive reaction. But it seems to me that we are dealing with a complex and fundamental problem which will require further analysis. If a wide equity clause is invalid, it must be because it is subversive of a head of public policy governing arbitrations conducted in England and awards made in England. About that point *DST* v. *Rakoil* can in truth tell us very little. On the other hand, some seventy years after *Czarnikow* v. *Roth Schmidt & Co.*,[41] it may be arguable that there is no longer such a head of public policy. That issue may turn on an historical review of the swing of the pendulum from excessive judicial scrutiny to a better recognition of the imperative of party autonomy. It may be possible for a court to rule that an award made under an equity clause is nevertheless an arbitration award governed by our arbitration statutes. Conceivably, a court might also rule that such an award is not subject to the limited appellate jurisdiction under section 1 of the Arbitration Act 1979. On the other hand, even if a court regarded such a development as beneficial, the court might take the view that it is a matter for reforming legislation. Uncharacteristically, I will not express any concluded view on the point. But I am firmly of the view that the issues have not yet been comprehensively debated in a English court and that *stare decisis* ought not to preclude a re-examination of this question.

8-41 Lastly, if the consultation process shows that there is a widespread desire on the part of commercial men to be able to arbitrate in England under fully effective equity clauses that might be a factor which could conceivably weigh with a court seized with the problem. After all, while our courts do not have the advantage of Brandeis briefs, judges do like to have a window to the real world. And, if such a development is beyond the capacity of the courts, a widespread desire for such a liberalisation of our arbitration system may have to be considered by Parliament.

---

[41] [1992] 2 K.B. 478.

VI. CONCLUSION

8-42 In conclusion I would only say that, while I have sketched some of the policy objectives of the DAC, it will be essential for the DAC to examine the whole Bill in the light of the responses to the consultative process.[42] There will be ample scope for further improvements of the Bill. But something broadly like the Bill represents the best attainable arbitration legislation in England. And it would represent an enormous improvement of our arbitration legislation.

---

[42] Apart from departmental representatives from the Department of Trade and Industry, the present membership of the DAC is as follows: The Rt Hon Lord Justice Steyn; A.W.S. Bunch Esq; Stewart Boyd QC; Dr K.G. Chrystie; Clifford Clark Esq; Lord Dervaird; J. B. Garrett Esq; Professor Roy Goode QC; Martin Hunter Esq; Mrs P. Kirby-Johnson; R. A. MacCrindle QC; Arthur Marriott Esq; Oliver Parker Esq; Kenneth Rokison QC; David Sarre Esq; J.H.M. Sims Esq; Professor D. R. Thomas; Professor John Uff QC; V. V. Veeder QC; and its Secretary (Miss Maureen Dodsworth).

*Howard M. Holtzmann**

CHAPTER 9

STREAMLINING ARBITRAL PROCEEDINGS: SOME TECHNIQUES OF THE IRAN-UNITED STATES CLAIMS TRIBUNAL

I. INTRODUCTION

9-1   Almost ten years ago there was a programme in London on arbitration sponsored jointly by the Inns of Court, the Law Society and the visiting American Bar Association. In my remarks on that occasion, I expressed concern over the slow pace of some arbitral proceedings, particularly in complex international commercial disputes.[1] This year when I was kindly invited to present the Freshfields Arbitration Lecture, it occurred to me that this might be an appropriate opportunity to review the situation, to see what, if any, progress the arbitration community has made during the past decade toward achieving more efficient conduct of cases.

9-2   When discussing this subject in London ten years ago, I spoke of the sloth and the dinosaur, cautioning that we must not allow arbitration to be as slow as the sloth or as cumbersome – and therefore as obsolete – as the dinosaur.[2] Reassessing the situation today, I suggest that while all international arbitrations may have not yet developed the swiftness of the gazelle, some progress has been

---

*   [Former] Judge, Iran-United States Claims Tribunal, 1981-94; Attorney and arbitrator, New York. The author gratefully acknowledges the assistance of David D. Meyer in preparing this paper. This article reproduces (by kind permission of Freshfields and Queen Mary and Westfield College London) the author's 1994 Freshfields Arbitration Lecture, delivered at the School of International Arbitration, Centre of Commercial Studies, Queen Mary and Westfield College, University of London, 12 October 1994.

[1]   Howard M. Holtzmann, 'What an Arbitrator Can Do to Overcome Delays in International Arbitration', in *Justice for a Generation* at p. 336 (1985).

[2]   *Id.* at 337-39.

Julian D.M. Lew and Loukas A. Mistelis (eds), Arbitration Insights, 153-167
© *2007 Kluwer Law International. Printed in the Netherlands*

made toward curing the slothfulness of arbitrations and averting the fate of the dinosaur.

9-3 Perhaps the most significant development in this regard has been an increasing recognition by the arbitration community – users, practitioners and arbitrators – that there is a pressing need to improve the efficiency of arbitral proceedings. In a group as resourceful as the arbitration community, attention to problems is likely to beget solutions, and, therefore, it is encouraging that this has become a popular subject for discussion. International conferences now concern themselves not only with traditional topics such as arbitrability, enforceability and law reform, but are beginning to focus on how to achieve more efficient conduct of cases. For example, the Congress of the International Council for Commercial Arbitration (ICCA) to be held in Vienna next month will include a three-day discussion on the practical aspects of 'Planning efficient arbitration proceedings'.

9-4 Nor is it all mere talk: international organisations have taken concrete steps to increase efficiency. For example, the ICC has not only introduced the term 'fast-track arbitration' into our lexicon, but it has developed specific procedures for achieving that result when the parties seek it.[3] UNCITRAL, after having devoted its earlier attention to drafting arbitration rules and a Model Law, is now engaged in a project to provide guidelines for planning and preparing arbitral proceedings in order to achieve greater efficiency.[4] Thus, while ten years ago I could only draw attention to increasingly difficult problems, today I can report that there is widespread awareness of those problems and that concrete steps are being taken toward achieving practical solutions. The sloth is not extinct, but it is being prodded into action.

9-5 In this context, it may be helpful to consider some techniques used by the Iran-United States Claims Tribunal in efforts to streamline arbitral proceedings. It may seem anomalous to look to the Tribunal as a source of ideas for expediting arbitration proceedings in view of the very long – in my opinion, sometimes

---

[3] See Benjamin Davis, Peter J. Nickles, Hans Smit and David K. Watkiss, 'ICC Fast-Track Arbitration: Different Perspectives', (1992) 3 *The ICC International Court of Arbitration Bulletin* 4.

[4] Report on the United Nations Commission on International Trade Law on the Work of its Twenty-Seventh Session (31 May-17 June 1994), *Official Records of the General Assembly, Forty-Ninth Session, Supplement No. 17*, UN Doc. No. A/49/17 (hereinafter referred to as 'the UNCITRAL Report').

unforgivably long – proceedings in a number of its cases. Yet, the Tribunal's slow pace reflects the rather unique circumstances in which it has had to handle a very large caseload, and should not blind us to the fact that it has made some quite significant contributions to increasing the efficiency of the proceedings before it. I will discuss three of these techniques today:

- First, the initiative of arbitrators in some cases to state in advance what evidence would be needed to establish prima facie proof of certain complex facts, thereby expediting the proceeding by greatly reducing the need for voluminous evidence.
- Secondly, the willingness of arbitrators to establish and enforce strict schedules for presentations by the parties during oral hearings.
- Thirdly, use of agendas, or checklists, for pre-hearing conferences to plan the proceedings.

II. INDICATING IN ADVANCE THE EVIDENCE NEEDED TO ESTABLISH PRIMA FACIE PROOF OF COMPLEX FACTS

9-6 The opportunity for an arbitral tribunal to indicate in advance the evidence needed to establish prima facie proof of complex facts arises because arbitrators often become aware from the initial or later written submissions of the parties that they will have to decide complex issues of fact that may involve the presentation of a very large volume of evidence. In such cases, it is foreseeable that the parties will expend substantial effort, money and time unless steps are taken to streamline the proceedings. Should the arbitrators sit back and wait while the parties attempt to amass truckloads of evidence, or should they take the initiative to manage the case by indicating in advance to the parties the evidence that the arbitral tribunal considers necessary to establish prima facie proof of certain facts at issue? That was the question faced by the Iran-United States Claims Tribunal with respect to proof of the nationality of certain corporate claimants. Chamber One of the Tribunal decided to take the initiative to simplify and expedite the presentation of evidence in the Flexi-Van Case,[5] and expanded that approach a month later in the General Motors Case.[6] It will be recalled that the Tribunal in some cases sits as a Full Tribunal consisting of all nine of its members, but in most cases acts as a Chamber of three – one American, one Iranian and a chairman from a third country.

---

[5] Order of 20 December 1982 in *Flexi-Van Leasing, Inc.* and *Islamic Republic of Iran*, Case No. 36, Chamber One, *reprinted in* 1 Iran-U.S. CTR 455 (hereinafter '*Flexi-Van* Order').

[6] Order of 21 January 1983 in *General Motors Corp., et al.* and *Government of the Islamic Republic of Iran*, Case No. 94, Chamber One, *reprinted in* 3 Iran-U.S. CTR 1.

9-7 The decisions of Chamber One in Flexi-Van and General Motors established evidentiary principles that were followed by it and by the two other Chambers of the Tribunal in hundreds of cases, and were relatively early examples of its activism to streamline proceedings. Justice Neil Kaplan of the Hong Kong Supreme Court recently commented with approval on activism by triers of fact in a trenchant article entitled Role of the Judge in Civil Litigation.[7] Although Justice Kaplan was reporting on trends in court cases, his remarks are surely applicable to arbitration. He wrote:

> As we approach the end of the 20th century it is worth noting that the role of the trial judge in civil cases has undergone a remarkable transformation. Whether it is called 'case management' or 'judicial intervention' really does not matter because what is involved is a more active approach on the part of the judge. He is no longer a mere referee allowing the parties to present their cases as they wish. Not only does he take a more active role in the trial itself but in more and more cases he is actively helping to get the case into a shape that will assist him in coming to an expeditious, economic and just solution.[8]

9-8 Justice Kaplan buttresses his view by quoting a statement from Lord Donaldson's 1991 opinion in Mercer v. Chief Constable which pointed out that 'there has been a sea change in legislative and judicial attitudes towards the conduct of litigation, taking the form of increased positive case management by the judiciary'.[9]

9-9 If activism is appropriate for the judiciary, it clearly is also appropriate for arbitrators who are governed by modern arbitration rules that typically state explicitly that arbitrators shall have wide discretion in conducting cases, subject, of course, to assuring due process – or, if you will, natural justice – and having regard to any agreements of the parties and any mandatory provisions of applicable law.[10]

---

[7] Neil Kaplan, 'Role of the Judge in Civil Litigation', 2 *Judges' Forum Newsletter* 6 (March 1994).

[8] *Id.* at p. 6; *see also* McCluskey, 'The Interventionist Judge: Should the Referee Play Ball', 1 *Judges' Forum Newsletter* (May 1993).

[9] (1991) 1 WLA 367, 373.

[10] *See, e.g.,* UNCITRAL Arbitration Rules, Article 15(1); LCIA Rules, Article 5.1; ICC Rules, Article 11, AAA International Arbitration Rules, Article 16.

9-10 The decisions of the Iran-United States Claims Tribunal in the Flexi-Van and General Motors cases that I have mentioned were made under rules that empowered the Tribunal 'to conduct the arbitration in such manner as it considers appropriate',[11] a provision that you will recognise as being identical to Article 15(1) of the UNCITRAL Arbitration Rules and similar to the provision in the LCIA Rules that grants arbitrators 'widest discretion' in conducting cases.[12]

9-11 Critical factual issues arose in the Flexi-Van and General Motors cases because the arrangements establishing the Tribunal provide that it has jurisdiction over a claim by an American corporation only if the claimant was incorporated in the United States, and if, collectively, natural persons who were citizens of the United States held 50 per cent or more of its stock continuously from the date the claim arose until 19 January 1981, the date the Claims Settlement Declaration came into force.[13] These provisions posed difficult evidentiary problems in cases involving publicly owned corporations because such corporations typically have large numbers of shareholders. The extent of the problem can be appreciated when we consider that General Motors, for example, had at the relevant time 300 million shares of common stock outstanding, held by approximately 1 ½ million shareholders. The composition of this vast body of shareholders changed every day as thousands of shares were traded on various stock exchanges. Moreover, General Motors, like other companies traded on stock exchanges, does not even know the names of all persons who are beneficial owners of its shares, because many individuals choose to hold their shares in the names of their brokerage firms. In such cases, the corporation's books show only the names of the brokerage firm that is the record holder. Like most other publicly owned corporations, General Motors has the mailing addresses of its shareholders of record, but no information as to the citizenship of those persons.

9-12 The contentions of the parties in these cases are exemplified by the submissions of the parties in Flexi-Van, the first case in which Chamber One acted on these issues. On the one hand, Flexi-Van 'submitted an affidavit by its Corporate Secretary stating that more than 96 per cent of all of its outstanding common shares were held by shareholders of record who reported United States

---

[11] Tribunal Rules, Article 15(1).
[12] LCIA Rules, Article 5.2.
[13] Declaration of The Government of The Democratic and Popular Republic of Algeria Concerning the Settlement of Claims by The Government of the United States of America and The Government of The Islamic Republic of Iran (hereinafter 'the Claims Settlement Declaration'), Article III, paras. 1 and 2, *reprinted in* 1 Iran-US CTR 9, 10.

addresses'.[14] In opposition, the Iranian respondent argued that Flexi-Van could only meet its burden of proof by submitting 'detailed evidence such as either passports, birth certificates or certified copies of naturalisation documents for each of the thousands of individuals who collectively own, directly or indirectly, more than 50 per cent of the capital stock of Flexi-Van'.[15] Moreover, the Iranian position was that, because the Claims Settlement Declaration requires that claims have been owned 'continuously' from the date the claim arose until 19 January 1981, claimants should be required to produce evidence concerning the nationality of their shareholders on every day of this multiyear period in order to take account of the changing composition of the body of shareholders as shares were traded and retraded on stock exchanges.

9-13 I will not burden you with a detailed description of how the Tribunal simplified and expedited submission of evidence on these points, other than to say that, among other steps, it took the initiative to tell the parties in advance what evidence it would consider sufficient to support inferences of continuous ownership of the claim by a corporation that was a United States national. Thus, in the Flexi-Van Order, the Tribunal stated:

> With respect to evidence of continuous ownership of stock, it must be recognised that there are changes in the stockholders of a publicly-traded corporation each trading day .... Therefore, it is necessary to measure ownership on a periodic rather than a daily basis. The most practical point to find authoritative evidence with respect to ownership is the Annual Meeting of the stockholders.[16]

9-14 Accordingly, the Tribunal stated that evidence as to stock ownership would be 'sufficient prima facie, if submitted by the claimant with respect to the Annual Meeting closest to the date on which the claim arose and also the Annual Meeting closest to January 19, 1981'.[17] In other words, the Tribunal was prepared to receive evidence as of a practical date near – but not exactly on – the date the claim arose and also near – but not exactly on – 19 January 1981. If the necessary factual conditions existed on those two dates, the Tribunal indicated that it was prepared to draw the rebuttable inference that those conditions had existed continuously for the entire period between those two dates.

---

[14] *Flexi-Van* Order, *supra* note 5, at p. 456.
[15] *Id.* at p. 457.
[16] *Id.* at p. 459.
[17] *Id.* at p. 460.

9-15 To streamline presentation of proof of incorporation, the Tribunal indicated that it would accept certificates routinely issued by governmental authorities certifying when the corporation was formed and that it was still in existence.[18] Thus corporate parties were informed in advance that they did not have to submit copies of lengthy certificates of incorporation, corporate minutes and other records to prove their formation. Further, the Tribunal stated that if a corporation had been formed on a date prior to the time its claim arose and was in existence after 19 January 1981, the rebuttable inference would be drawn that the corporation had been existing continuously between those two dates – although it was theoretically possible that during the relevant period the claimant's corporate life might have been terminated and later restored by reincorporation. The Tribunal's action thus told the claimant in advance that it could make a prima facie case without submitting voluminous documentary evidence that might otherwise have been necessary to constitute strict proof of continuous existence as an entity incorporated in the United States.

9-16 As to the proof of citizenship of individual shareholders, the Tribunal informed the parties that it would not require the submission of thousands of birth certificates, passports and naturalisation certificates, but would draw inferences from information in reports that publicly traded corporations are regularly required by law to file with the United States government identifying persons holding more than 5 per cent of the corporation's stock. These reports would then be weighed in the light of information from general statistical reports regularly compiled by governmental agencies in the United States concerning foreign stock ownership.[19]

9-17 In considering the Flexi-Van Order and others that followed it, one must recognise that the Tribunal did not reach final findings of fact in those Orders; rather it stated the evidentiary parameters for establishing a prima facie case, and carefully preserved the right of the other side to submit rebuttal evidence. Thus, the Tribunal stressed that:

> The evidence described [in the Order] will prima facie be considered sufficient as to corporate nationality .... Respondent will be free to offer rebuttal evidence. From the totality of such evidence the Chamber will draw reasonable inferences and reach conclusions as to whether the Claimant

---

[18] *Id.* at pp. 458-59.
[19] *Id.* at pp.459-62.

was, or was not, a national of the United States, as defined in the [Claims Settlement] Declaration during the necessary period.[20]

9-18 It would be easy, but in my view incorrect, to dismiss the techniques used in the Flexi-Van and General Motors Orders by saying that they were devised in relation to proof of unique jurisdictional requirements arising under an international treaty, and are inapplicable to the kinds of factual problems that typically arise in commercial arbitration. As I have said elsewhere, 'The fact is that a fact is a fact. Procedures for establishing a jurisdictional fact are equally applicable to establishing a fact to prove liability or damages'.[21] Indeed, the Tribunal has in several cases taken the initiative to order the submission of documentary evidence that it considered would facilitate deciding the merits of cases involving commercial contractual issues, even when no party requested discovery of that evidence. For example, the Tribunal has ordered, sua sponte, the filing of copies of various documents not presented by either party such as (i) full texts of contracts, (ii) financial records, (iii) tax returns, (iv) promotional plans, and (v) regulations or decrees.[22]

9-19 I do not wish to leave the impression that the Tribunal has exercised such initiatives routinely in all – or even most – cases, anymore than I would suggest that other arbitration tribunals should adopt such techniques of case management in all – or most – commercial arbitration cases. But there are circumstances in which this kind of case management can be helpful, and all tribunals should consider whether and when to apply such techniques.

9-20 Arbitral tribunals may well have numerous reasons – or excuses – for not taking initiatives. There is understandable human reluctance to making a 'sea change in ... attitude', to use Lord Donaldson's apt phrase. Moreover, managing cases greatly increases the amount of work that must be done by the arbitrators in analysing written submissions and anticipating and resolving evidentiary issues in advance of the hearing. Yet, I venture to suggest that changes in attitudes are needed to achieve more efficient proceedings, and that the extra effort of the tribunal before the hearing is likely to reduce the amount of effort needed at, and after, the hearing.

---

[20] *Id.* at p. 458.
[21] Howard M. Holtzmann, 'Fact-Finding By the Iran-United States Claims Tribunal', in *Fact-Finding Before International Tribunals* at pp. 101, 104 (ed. R. Lillich, 1990).
[22] See the Tribunal Orders collected in *id.* at p. 107, n. 21.

9-21 If tribunals are to take such initiatives, at what stage of the proceedings should they do so? Obviously, a tribunal cannot 'manage' a case until it has sufficient insight into the factual issues that are posed. This insight may be provided by the initial pleadings, or may not be able to be perceived until later written submissions have been made by the parties. Discussion at a preparatory pre-hearing conference may be useful in this regard. As soon as the parameters and dimensions of the factual issues become apparent, the arbitral tribunal is in a position to consider what, if any steps, can be taken to streamline presentation of the evidence. In some cases, the nature of the factual issues whose presentation could be simplified may not be seen until the hearings have begun. At that point, the tribunal has the difficult task of deciding whether to proceed to receive masses of evidence as presented by the parties – which I suspect would be the prudent course in most cases – or whether time and money would be saved in the long run by adjourning the hearing to permit better management of the evidence along lines to be suggested by the tribunal.

9-22 Lest my comments appear theoretical, let me suggest a few relatively innovative means that arbitrators might consider in order to 'manage' presentation of evidence in commercial cases. Statistical sampling is accepted as a reliable basis for drawing inferences in a variety of contexts in modern life, as it was in Flexi-Van. Why not use it more often in commercial arbitration? I have called this an 'innovative technique'. But is it really so innovative? For a long time, generally accepted accounting principles have permitted independent auditors to determine the amount and condition of inventories – or 'stock', if you will – based on sampling, and have not required counting and inspecting each item in every warehouse. Why is that methodology not also reliable in commercial arbitration? Tribunals have the power to appoint experts. Why not, for example, appoint experts to sample thousands of invoices or production records, and to report the results of their findings? Why not apply computer technology to summarise voluminous documentary material, a technique that I understand is being used by the UN Compensation Commission in Geneva that is considering claims against Iraq? That new Commission has looked to the computer models and programs used by the insurance industry in determining masses of casualty claims arising from natural disasters. If a hurricane strikes, the insurance inspectors do not necessarily look at every damaged home in a neighbourhood, but pay claims based on extrapolations, often made by computers, after physical inspection of only a few buildings. Such methodology has proven useful in a number of fields; it is available for imaginative arbitral tribunals to adopt or adapt.

9-23 It is encouraging to note that arbitrators in England do not appear to be barred from taking such initiatives, which reflect an inquisitorial role as contrasted with the more usual common law adversarial approach. As Lord Justice Steyn instructed us in his Freshfields Lecture last year, arbitrators here are not required by law to conduct an arbitration in 'an adversarial as opposed to inquisitorial fashion unless the parties agree otherwise'.[23] He pointed out that subject to the further qualification 'that arbitrators must always obey the principles of natural justice, there is nothing in the decided cases to show that there was an established rule requiring arbitrators to adopt an adversarial procedure'.[24] This current state of English law seems likely to be strengthened even further in the future, for Lord Justice Steyn has stated that the Departmental Advisory Committee considering new legislation governing arbitration 'unanimously took the view that it would benefit English arbitration to make clear that subject to the terms of the arbitration agreement and the overriding principles of natural justice, arbitrators may adopt inquisitorial powers'.[25]

III. ESTABLISHING AND ENFORCING SCHEDULES FOR PRESENTATIONS BY PARTIES DURING HEARINGS

9-24 Arbitral tribunals can not only take initiatives to streamline the presentation of evidence, they can also establish procedures to improve the efficiency of the hearings at which evidence is considered. Thus, the Iran-United States Claims Tribunal utilises techniques to control the length of hearings in all of its cases. Tribunal hearings in The Hague operate on the basis of a timetable set in advance, and may look to some like a railway trip directed by a vigilant conductor whose eye is constantly on a stop-watch attempting to assure that every step in the journey is on schedule. While such a system makes for an efficient and cost-effective hearing, is it compatible with producing just results?

9-25 Litigators from the United States are accustomed to having appellate courts establish strict time-limits for oral argument, but expect trial courts and arbitral tribunals to allow whatever amount of time is reasonably needed by the parties to present their evidence and arguments, without regard to a pre-set timetable. Appellate courts are seen as being able to limit the length of oral argument because they have the relatively narrow task of deciding only issues of law based

---

[23] *See* Steyn, 'England's Response to the UNCITRAL Model Law of Arbitration', *reprinted in* (1994) 10 *Arbitration International* 1, at p. 8.
[24] *id.* at p. 9.
[25] *Id.* at p. 10.

on the written record of the trial in the court below. This contrasts with trial courts which are perceived as being unable to establish schedules in advance because of the difficulty of predicting the number of witnesses that may be presented, the time required for examination and cross-examination, or the strategies counsel may choose to adopt as the case proceeds.

9-26 Imagine, then, the shock experienced by an American member of the Tribunal in The Hague when first confronted by a Continental European chairman who issued a railroad-like time schedule for a hearing. To illustrate my point, let me quote from a communication to the parties by a Chairman of Chamber One, in which he described the 'normal time' allocated for one-day, two-day and three-day hearings in that Chamber. Here, for example, is the schedule for a one-day hearing:

One Day Hearing: Normal Timing
- Introduction by Chairman 9.30
- Claimant's first round presentation break 1 ½ hr. maximum
- Respondent's first round presentation lunch 1 ½ hr. maximum
- Questions by Arbitrators 15.00
- Rebuttal presentation by Claimant 45 minutes max.
- Rebuttal presentation by Respondent 45 minutes max.
- Further questions by Arbitrators, if any[26]

9-27 You will note several things about this schedule: First, the parties are free to use the time allocated to them for their presentations in any way they wish; the time allocated may be used in the proportions each counsel chooses for such purposes as opening and closing statements, arguments on facts and law, and presentation of witnesses. The other side is, in practice, allowed ten 'free' minutes for cross-examination of each witness, but if the cross-examination takes longer, the time used is to be deducted from the time allocated to the cross-examiner for his subsequent presentation. Secondly, note that each party is allocated an equal amount of time. Thirdly, observe that there is no limit on the time allowed for questions by the arbitrators; but I can tell you from personal experience that a glance, or occasional intervention, by a strong chairman serves

---

[26] Memorandum from Professor Karl-Heinz Böckstiegel to Mr M. K. Eshragh, Agent of the Government of the Islamic Republic of Iran, and Mr J. R. Crook, Agent of the Government of the United States (26 May 1987). The schedules for two-day and three-day hearings follow a similar format, differing only in that they provide longer times for the parties' first round and rebuttal presentations.

to keep his colleagues within bounds. Fourthly, note that the schedule is designated as the 'normal' timing. The word 'normal' implies that there is some flexibility. The degree to which deviations from the norm are permitted tends to vary depending on the approach of the different Chamber chairmen and the exigencies of particular cases.

9-28 The establishment and maintaining of the schedules for hearings are not as Draconian as they might appear at first glance, because hearings take place only after several rounds of written submissions by the parties. Moreover, orders setting the dates of hearings typically remind parties that documentary evidence is to be exchanged well in advance of the hearing date. As to evidence of witnesses, the Tribunal Rules, which in this respect are based on the UNCITRAL Rules, require advance submission of the names of witnesses and a statement of the subjects on which each will testify.[27]

9-29 In many Tribunal cases, parties have elected to do more than this provision of the Rules requires, and have submitted in advance not only a description of the subjects on which prospective witnesses will testify, but also signed statements by witnesses along the lines of the 'witness statements' contemplated by the IBA rules on presenting evidence.[28] Advance submission of written witness statements allows counsel to save time by eliminating the need to conduct direct examination of its witnesses, except, perhaps, to emphasise a key point or to reinforce the impression that the witness is trustworthy. Time saved in examining one's own witnesses is then available for longer cross-examination of the other side's witnesses and for more extended oral argument. When the schedule reflects that one side has more witnesses than the other, the allocation of equal time to both sides provides time for cross-examination.

9-30 By and large, the establishment of explicit schedules for hearings has worked, and counsel have generally expressed satisfaction that it is fair, particularly when conducted by a strong chairman who keeps his eye on the clock, or has an alert assistant at his elbow to assist him in doing so.

9-31 One important caveat must be noted by arbitrators who establish time schedules for hearings: it is necessary to be realistic and to set a sufficiently long

---

[27] Tribunal Rules, Article 25(2).
[28] *See* International Bar Association, Section on Business Law, Supplementary Rules Governing the Presentation and Reception of Evidence in International Commercial Arbitration, Article 5.

schedule at the outset, and the schedule must then be applied with flexibility so that each party has a fair opportunity to present its case. Failure to provide that opportunity might result in a denial of due process, or natural justice, and might thus endanger the enforceability of the award. Note that I have emphasised the word 'opportunity', for I suggest that there is no lack of fairness if a party chooses not to use wisely the opportunity given to it but, instead, squanders its time. The principles of due process and natural justice do not provide a safeguard for prolixity or imprudent planning by litigators.

IV. USE OF CHECKLISTS FOR PREPARATORY CONFERENCES TO PLAN PROCEEDINGS

9-32 The techniques for streamlining evidence and hearings that I have discussed cannot be effectively employed unless the arbitrators have a clear view of the dimensions of the case at hand. There is a growing recognition that preparatory conferences can assist in providing that view and thus in achieving more efficient arbitration proceedings. Much attention is being directed toward this procedure which also goes under various names such as 'pre-hearing conference', 'preliminary meeting', and 'administrative conference'.

9-33 Moreover, preparatory conferences are particularly useful in international cases where, as at The Hague Tribunal, the parties and the various arbitrators often come to the proceedings with widely different procedural expectations. The problem is succinctly summarised in the programme of the Working Group that will analyse this subject at the ICCA Congress to be held in Vienna next month. I can do no better than to quote from that programme:

> Most laws and rules allow arbitrators flexibility to tailor proceedings to meet the circumstances of particular cases. While that is valuable, it may leave parties uncertain as to the procedures that will be followed, particularly when the arbitrators and parties have several different legal backgrounds. In the absence of efficient planning, flexibility can lead to unpredictability and surprise in both the written and oral phases of the proceedings.[29]

---

[29] Programme, International Council for Commercial Arbitration XIIth International Arbitration Congress (Vienna, 3-6 November 1994), at p. 7.

9-34 The Hague Tribunal cannot claim to have invented the preparatory conference. Its contribution is that it was, perhaps, the first institution to publish in advance a checklist of topics that might be considered at preparatory conferences in international cases.[30] This was a precursor to the checklist for preparatory conferences now being prepared by UNCITRAL.[31]

9-35 In considering the usefulness of the checklist issued by the Tribunal for preparatory conferences, as well as the checklist now being designed by UNCITRAL, several points should be emphasised.

9-36 First, a checklist establishes no legal requirements; its purpose is only to remind the parties and the arbitrators of topics that it might be useful to discuss. All of the topics on the checklist need not be considered, and those that are chosen for discussion are subject to modification in the light of the circumstances of the particular case.

9-37 Secondly, preparatory conferences are not recommended for all cases, but are only to be held in those cases in which the tribunal considers that they would be useful. Indeed, in certain cases some, or all, of the purposes of a preparatory conference might be achieved by correspondence or telephone.

9-38 Thirdly, all of the topics on the checklist need not be considered at one preparatory conference held at a prescribed stage of the proceeding. Rather, there may be more than one preparatory conference so that various topics may be discussed at whatever stage or stages may be appropriate in the particular case.

9-39 While checklists for preparatory conferences are thus to be seen as being non-binding and are to be used flexibly, when arbitrators, in their discretion, decide to call a conference, communicating an agenda in advance to the parties is useful because it alerts everyone at an early stage to matters that may become significant as the case progresses. I understand from discussion with colleagues that a number of highly experienced arbitrators, including some here in London, have developed their own checklists for preparatory conferences that they routinely use. The advantage of standardised lists, such as the Tribunal at The Hague uses and as UNCITRAL is now considering, is that they help to

---

[30] *See*'Internal Guidelines of the Tribunal', 1 Iran-U.S. CTR 98 (1981-1982).
[31] *See* UNCITRAL Report, *supra* at note 4.

harmonise international arbitral practice and provide transparency that facilitates preparation from the very outset of a case.

V. CONCLUSION

9-40 In conclusion, I would emphasise that the various techniques for streamlining arbitral proceedings that I have been discussing have a common theme. Each of them relates to planning – planning presentation of evidence, planning conduct of hearings, and use of carefully designed preparatory conferences to facilitate planning of proceedings.

9-41 Plans, however, must be flexible. While they are indispensable in moving an arbitral proceeding forward effectively, we must always be ready to adjust plans to meet emerging circumstances. Finally, in planning and designing the total arbitral process we should always remember that each part of the proceeding must fit comfortably with the other parts and with the process as a whole. The great architect Eliel Saarinen put it well:

> Always design a thing by considering it in its next larger context – a chair in room, a room in a house, a house in an environment, an environment in a city plan.

9-42 Designing a fair and efficient arbitration requires no less.

*Arthur L. Marriott QC**

CHAPTER 10

'TELL IT TO THE JUDGE – BUT ONLY IF YOU MUST'

I. INTRODUCTION

10-1 PEEL, EVERSHED, Winn, Cantley, the Civil Justice Review, and now Woolf.[1] The problems of the civil justice system seem unending. In almost 150 years to the present day, there have been some 60 official reports on civil procedure and on the organisation of the civil and criminal courts; and a number of private reports such as those from Justice and more recently from the Heilbron Committee.[2] Some reports have been effective; others less so; and many have simply been consigned to the dustbin of history. Perhaps the most disappointing report in recent years was the Civil Justice Review in 1988,[3] well intentioned, but bland.

10-2 The significance of Lord Woolf's Report for the advocate of ADR[4] is that it is a primary and express theme of the proposed reforms to encourage and promote the settlement of disputes before litigation starts; and, if that is unsuccessful, to streamline procedures so as to facilitate the negotiation of settlements before the trial of the action. This is also the objective of ADR. It is

---

[*] Partner, LeBoeuf Lamb Greene and McRae.
[1] Lord Woolf, Access to Justice: Interim Report to the Lord Chancellor on the Civil Justice System in England and Wales, June 1995: see endnote.
[2] Heilbron QC (Chairman), *Civil Justice on Trial – The Case for Change* (June 1993).
[3] Civil Justice Review (Cm. 394 (1988)).
[4] Alternative Dispute Resolution (ADR) may be defined as a range of procedures which serve as alternatives to the adjudicatory procedures of litigation and arbitration for the resolution of disputes, generally but not necessarily involving the intercession and assistance of a neutral third party who helps to facilitate such resolution: Brown and Marriott, ADR Principles and Practice (1993), p. 9.

Julian D.M.Lew and Loukas A. Mistelis (eds), Arbitration Insights, 169-200
© 2007 Kluwer Law International. Printed in the Netherlands

the central theme of this paper to consider how and why ADR should be part of the litigation system and of arbitration as well.

10-3 The wish to promote and emphasise settlement and to streamline procedures which help bring it about, stems from the widespread and profound concern of judges, administrators, politicians, practitioners and litigants at the delays and appalling cost of civil litigation in this country. This results in a denial of access to justice. No democratic society can tolerate such a state of affairs, which the Master of the Rolls has trenchantly described as a cancer eating at the very vitals of our civil justice system.

10-4 In the Civil Justice Review, settlement of cases merited but a passing mention. Paragraph 259 referred to the possible need to introduce settlement conferences at which the judge might discuss the case with the parties and investigate the opportunity for settlement. The Review however concluded that:

> In view of the proposals for early exchange of witness statements, it is thought that opportunities for settlement will be increased and that pre-trial intervention by judges should be reserved to a pre-trial hearing in the more substantial cases.

10-5 This characteristically timid conclusion has been proved wholly wrong; and it is a salutary warning against the way procedural innovation can be abused, that the system of pre-trial exchange of statements has led to the problems in the Commercial Court so powerfully condemned by Lord Justice Staughton in the New Hampshire v. MGN case.[5]

10-6 In Chapter 18 of his report Lord Woolf indicates that he does not favour a system of court annexed ADR. He expresses general approval and support for ADR and suggests that ADR be considered at case management conferences and pre-trial reviews. This recommendation is welcome, but I would have gone further and explained how the proposed reforms will bring about greater settlement rates. I would also have examined the role of ADR in achieving settlement, because experience in the United States and elsewhere shows us, that promoting fair and just settlements and streamlining procedures more readily occurs where the courts adopt and adapt ADR methods as part of or as adjunct to the procedures of the court itself. I hope that Lord Woolf, in drafting new

---

[5] *New Hampshire Insurance Co v. MGN Limited (CA)* (unreported) 6 July 1995.

procedural rules for case-managed litigation, will propose ADR procedures which encourage litigants to negotiate, such as settlement conferences, settlement weeks, early neutral evaluation and neutral fact finding.

II. THE CASE FOR SETTLEMENT

10-7 Lord Woolf assumes (without discussion) the conceptual justification for encouraging settlement before and during litigation. But a discussion of this objective would focus our attention on precisely what we expect the courts in the civil justice system to do; would define the role of private sector dispute resolution, particularly with respect to ADR; establish what we expect by way of cost savings; clarify what we expect the state to pay for; and help us to decide how limited resources are best applied.

10-8 The assumption that settlements are preferable to adjudication is not universally shared. Some American academics, notably Professor Owen Fiss,[6] have suggested that people should be encouraged to use an adjudicatory approach rather than be deterred from it; and that they should not have their rights to obtain the decision of the court eroded by alternative means of dispute resolution. This is a minority view and widely criticised, but we should take note of it especially in public law cases. And it should lead us to concentrate on using ADR to improve the court system as well as being an alternative to it; to advocate, particularly where an element of compulsion is involved, that the court must always retain ultimate control in preventing abuse; and also to accept that some disputes are not suitable for ADR.

10-9 In my view, the primary case for the promotion of settlement rests on the broad principle that the resolution of disputes by consensus and by compromise contributes to the well-being of society as a whole. It was an old maxim of Roman law that *interest republicae ut sit finis litium*; the interest of the state should be an end to litigation. That maxim has been followed in this country. The courts as a matter of public policy encourage and enforce settlements. Paradoxically however, the role of the courts has been confined to creating an over-elaborate system of without prejudice and confidential communication in order to keep settlement discussions from going before the court at all. English judges, whilst sometimes prepared by a nod and a wink to encourage settlement have shied away from actively participating in the process.

---

[6]   Fiss, O. 'Against Settlement', (1984) 93 *Yale LJ* 1073.

A. Will the Judge Intervene?

10-10   Case management is at the heart of Lord Woolf's proposals; and, if they are to work, English judges will have to be much more interventionist than hitherto in controlling procedures, curbing delay, capping costs and encouraging settlement. Some degree of procedural obligation or compulsion may be necessary. Despite the clear and emphatic direction of Lord Templeman and Lord Roskill in Ashmore v. Lloyd's,[7] English judges at first instance have not intervened and have not exercised their powers of control.

10-11   This is contrary to the experience in many civil law countries, such as Germany and Switzerland where there is a procedural obligation on judges periodically to promote settlement. In Germany, procedural rules compel judges to do so at first instance and on appeal. The judge may make a specific proposal and will proceed to try the case if the proposal is rejected. As yet there is no power in the court to order mediation, though there is now a debate in Germany as to the desirability of mandatory arbitration in family cases. German courts, whilst less troubled by delay than we are (perhaps due to the fact that the Germans have significantly more judges per head of population than we do), are concerned by rising costs. In a recent speech of the German Minister of Justice to the 1995 Deutscher Richtertag,[8] two solutions were advocated. First, that out-of-court settlement should be further promoted[9] and, secondly, that the internal organisation of the courts should be modernised, especially by introducing service centres – shades of Lord Woolf. A feature of German fee rules which may interest the Law Society is the provision of increased fees if a case settles.

10-12   In Switzerland there is also a trend to resolve civil disputes by settlement. Some civil procedure rules expressly encourage this practice. The 'Zürcherische Zivilprozessordnung', for example, imposes in some cases a compulsory prelitigation conciliation procedure. Article 62 of the Zürcherische Zivilprozessordnung further stipulates that the judge can at any time summon the parties to attend a 'Vergleichsverhandlung' (conciliation hearing).

---

[7]   *Ashmore v. Corporation of Lloyd's (No. 1)* [1992] 2 Lloyd's Rep 1. See also the recent decision of the Court of Appeal in *Thermawear Ltd v. Linton and Another*, The Times, 20 October 1995.

[8]   (1995) 38 *Neue Juristische Wochenschrift*, p. 2441.

[9]   The statistics show that in the period 1981 to 1991 the percentage settlement rate as a consequence of judicial intervention was approximately 9 percent in the Amtsgericht; approximately 16 percent at first instance in the Landgericht; approximately 13 percent in the second instance of the Landgericht; and approximately 17 percent in the Oberlandesgericht: Federal Ministry of Justice, Bonn.

10-13 The conciliation hearing is usually ordered once the relevant issues in dispute and the applicable legal rules have been determined, after the exchange of the initial pleadings, but before any evidence has been heard.

10-14 At the conciliation hearing the judge sets out his understanding of the relevant facts, carries out a detailed legal analysis and concludes with his proposal for a settlement between the parties.

10-15 An increasing number of cases are settled by conciliation as the figures released by the Zürich Commercial Court, one of the biggest in Switzerland, demonstrate. Conciliation is not ordered in every case. However, where it is, a settlement is reached in 80 percent of all cases.[10]

B. Costs and Savings

10-16 The secondary argument in favour of compromise using ADR is not necessarily that overall cost savings in the civil justice system are achieved, but rather that there is a more efficient use of resources, thereby enabling disputes to be resolved more speedily and creating the opportunity to redirect limited resources to resolve other disputes which are of more importance to society. For example, at least one in three marriages in this country ends in divorce. The social and economic consequences are severe. We may have to decide whether to devote resources to the resolution of disputes arising from marital breakdown, in priority, for example, to consumer disputes. Use of ADR methods should provide greater flexibility in doing so.

10-17 Lord Woolf is rightly concerned at the cost of civil litigation in this country, which is out of hand. He hopes that encouraging settlement and streamlining procedures will save substantial costs. Without ADR as part of the court system, I doubt that such cost savings are possible, or that significant reallocation of resources within existing budgets will be practicable.

---

[10] No precise statistics are available with regard to the cost savings resulting from conciliation proceedings in Zürich. However, only 50 percent approximately of the normal court costs are ordered against the parties in conciliation proceedings and a further significant cost reduction results from the fact that usually one party is not ordered to pay the other side's legal costs. Significant savings also accrue to the Canton of Zürich as public expenditure on conciliation is limited to providing the services of a single judge: Zurich Commercial Court.

10-18   The cost of the court system itself is not the main issue: that could be recouped in increased fees and charges. There would (of course) have to be appropriate safeguards for litigants who could not afford the fees, but the cost of specialist courts such as the Companies Court, the Commercial Court and the Official Referees Court could be covered, as the Heilbron Report easily and convincingly demonstrated. So we must differentiate between the cost of the court system and the cost of funding legal aid, including the cost to the private purse which ultimately falls on society generally in some form or another such as higher insurance and other costs.

10-19   As Lord Woolf makes all too clear; it is therefore the funding of legal proceedings by the private and public purse which is the major problem. Whilst we know empirically that the cost of litigation is often disproportionate to the amount at stake, I confess to being shaken by Professor Hazel Genn's analysis in the Interim Report,[11] on costs awarded on taxation in 673 cases. Incidentally, it is regrettable that there is such a dearth of statistical information on such an important topic. I merely highlight one or two of the more striking figures.[12] In one half of the lowest value cases under £12,500, the costs on one side alone were close to, or exceeded, the total value of the claim. In claims of £250,000 or more, in almost 60 percent of cases the costs allowed, for one side only, were the equivalents or less than 20 percent of the claim value. Some 16 percent of bills were the equivalent of 100 percent or more of claim value, with 6 percent of these bills representing 200 percent or more of the claim value. The actual cost, even to successful litigants, is much higher, given the restrictive approach to taxation which has the effect, in practice, of reducing recoverable costs to about two-thirds of actual expenditure. When actual costs are doubled, and the cost of the court system is added, it becomes clear that the position is very serious.

C. The Green Paper

10-20   The demands on the public purse of financing civil proceedings have led the Government in the Green Paper[13] on targeting need for legal aid, to declare that two of its objectives are to make the process of resolving disputes in court

---

[11]   Woolf Report, Annex III.

[12]   Medical negligence cases had the highest average costs at £38,352, followed by commercial cases at £29,418. In 41 percent of the lowest value cases under £12,500, the costs were between £10,000 and £20,000, with a further 7 percent having costs in excess of £20,000.

[13]   'Legal Aid – Targeting Need', Consultation Paper, May 1995, Cm. 2854.

simpler, quicker and more affordable and to encourage alternative ways of resolving disputes, so that people do not always have to use lawyers and courts.

As regards ADR, the Green Paper makes two points. First, the Lord Chancellor's Department argues that mediation should be used in family matters, but although it recognises the process should be voluntary and consensual, it proposes to hold the pistol of costs to the head of the litigant who displays any reluctance or anxiety about it.[14] Secondly, the more general proposals for franchising and block contracts expressly envisage tendering for and providing ADR services by both lawyers and non-lawyers alike. I shall return to the implications of that.

D. The Labour Party's Proposals

10-21   While the Government's objectives, though not all of its methods of funding, find an echo in the Labour Party's consultation document of February 1995 entitled 'Access to Justice'[15] and in the Policy Statement[16] recently published for the Annual Conference, the Labour Party's proposals are far more radical than either the Government's or Lord Woolf's. The Policy Statement draws attention to what the Labour Party considers to be 'an imbalance between public provision for traditional litigation on the one hand and mediation services on the other'. The Labour Party proposes to transfer resources from the former to the latter through resolving disputes less by litigation and more through mediation. The Policy Statement declares emphatically that 'Comprehensive delivery of such mediation services must be built up through a nationally accredited structure'.[17]

10-22   The Labour Party intends to promote the use of ADR, believing it will offer a far wider range of options for getting access to justice and cut the cost of the court services by removing some cases from the system altogether, thereby (so it is argued) reducing the number of expensive delays. To do so the Policy Statement promises that the existing legal aid budget will be used 'to expand

---

[14]   But see the Lord Chancellor's speech to the FMA on 7 November 1995, as reported in *The Times*, 8 November 1995, for an indication that there may be a shift in emphasis on this aspect of the proposals.

[15]   'Access to Justice', a consultation paper on Labour's proposals for improving the justice system (February 1995).

[16]   'Access to Justice', Labour's proposals for reforming the civil justice system (Conference 1995).

[17]   *ibid.* p. 6.

access to alternative forms of dispute resolution such as mediation, arbitration and tribunals'.[18]

E. The Herbert Smith Report

10-23   The valuable research report prepared for Herbert Smith[19] and published in January 1995 indicates that the objective of encouraging settlement to reduce risk, delay and cost is shared in the commercial and business community. A major conclusion was that business people wanted to see more judges encouraging settlement of cases, though some thought that judges should not actually be involved in settlement discussions of cases before them, since that would compromise their objectivity. What businessmen wanted was a resolution of the case, rather than a guaranteed day in court. Apparently, businessmen viewed the outcome of civil proceedings as 'somewhat risky'. Cases settled because of 'commercial expediency and the mounting costs involved'.[20] ADR was viewed positively as an alternative to litigation, though most of those surveyed were opposed to compulsory ADR.

10-24   An example of the use of ADR in the private sector in this country is the growth of the Centre for Dispute Resolution (CEDR), started in 1990 with the active support of the CBI. CEDR has enjoyed a fair measure of success with some 800 referrals in five years. CEDR has also initiated an extensive and comprehensive training programme for mediators. Some 250 mediators have been accredited by CEDR.

10-25   And so, the momentum, on both policy and practical grounds is building up towards the introduction of ADR schemes as part of the civil justice system regardless of whether we have a change of government. Hence the title of this paper – 'Tell it to the judge. .. by only if you feel you really must' – which I took from an article in the New York Times earlier this year describing the system of mediation in some State courts in the United States. This headline essentially summarises the current debate in this country and elsewhere in the common law world on the true role of ADR.

---

[18]   *ibid.* p. 4.
[19]   'Reform of the Civil Justice System: The Views of UK Corporations', research report prepared for Herbert Smith, January 1995.
[20]   *ibid.* p. 4.

10-26 And in considering the role of ADR, I intend to focus on the consequences of ADR schemes for the financing of the civil justice system, because the principal justification for introducing ADR as a means to settlement is put in terms of likely cost savings. But given the lack of statistical information on the cost effects of procedural changes, this belief rests largely on untested and unproven assumptions.

III. THE COSTS OF LAWYERS

10-27 We must begin with the cost of lawyers for any proposals for procedural reform must grapple with the role played by lawyers and the amount and funding of their charges. Lord Woolf declares that it is a misconception that the cost of lawyers is the cause of the entire problem of delay and cost. In my view, he is being unduly kind to the legal profession. It is the level of fees which lawyers are able to command, even in the depths of the worst recession since the 1930s, combined with the inefficiencies of the civil justice system, which have been the major contributors to the financial crisis and to the breakdown of the system. Even if procedural change and market forces reduce cost, the overheads of law firms are substantial and have to be paid for, whether by hourly rates or some other fee structure. Even mediation, as some American authors remind us, takes place 'in the shadow of the law' and no matter what role we ascribe to the private sector and even to non-lawyers, civil dispute resolution will continue to require the experience, knowledge and skills which only trained lawyers can provide. The scope for radical cost savings in lawyers' fees is in my view limited, despite competition in the market place and the increasing realisation by law firms that they must improve efficiency and control costs.

10-28 The funding of the legal aid scheme and (in effect) the funding of much of the legal profession is beyond the scope of this paper, other than where it touches on ADR. However, while expenditure on the civil justice system cannot be unlimited and there is a clear need for financial and procedural discipline, a block contract franchise system for the purchase of legal services is not the way forward. I find it significant that I could not find in the Green Paper either a practical explanation of how block contracts would actually work, or a draft of a specimen contract.

10-29 The Government's proposals reveal a sense almost of despair and a misunderstanding as to the proper role of competition in profession life, particularly in the provision of dispute resolution services. I do not think that the Labour Party's proposals, which also adopt the block franchise scheme, provide the answer. In my view, there are other ways of satisfying the legitimate public concern to see public expenditure on legal services monitored, controlled and most effectively applied. Above all we must be guided by former Chief Justice Mason's admonition[21] that:

> economy is neither the sole nor the principal consideration. It is simply no use providing a legal system which, though economic, fails to maintain or win community confidence.

10-30 The second and wider assumption, made for example by the Labour Party in the Consultation Paper, though perhaps not in the Policy Statement, is also unproven and so far has little evidence to support it: and none was produced by the Labour Party. That is the assumption that:

> by encouraging dispute resolution away from the courtroom, the cost to central government of the court system, legal aid and associated expenditure can also be significantly reduced.[22]

10-31 I doubt it. First, it would be unwise, having regard, for example, to the dramatic explosion in civil legal aid expenditure since 1988 (for which incidentally the Government offers no explanation), to assume that there will be a drop in volume of business in the civil courts. On the contrary, experience in this country and elsewhere shows us, that the more readily accessible we make the courts, the more they are used, as the expansion of small claims arbitration in the County Court more than amply demonstrates. This will lead to increasing numbers of litigants in person and hopefully Lord Woolf's procedural reforms will make it easier for such litigants. Secondly, the assumption of the Labour Party Consultation Paper is inconsistent with the fact that if ADR services are introduced, they have to be paid for. For the private litigant that means an element of state funding, as the Government recognises in the Green Paper by proposing that block contracts can be entered into for the provision of mediation services by both lawyers and non-lawyers alike: the Labour Party goes even further in seeking a publicly funded shift from litigation to mediation.

10-32 We have to be wary of drawing too many conclusions from limited and incomplete statistics. I suspect that it is the clear realisation that the current system both of dispute resolution and of funding, is in grave crisis and requires change, which is a far more direct impetus to experiment with ADR.

---

[21] Sir Anthony Mason, 'The State of the Judicature', an address to the 28th Australian Legal Convention, Hobart, 30 September 1993 ((1994) 68 ALJ 125).

[22] 'Access to Justice', consultation paper, (see n. 16 above), p. 5

IV. EXPERIENCE IN THE US

10-33 We can get some guidance as to the effect of ADR on the court system from the US, where there is far more statistical and research information available than here. There are indications that the experimental arbitration schemes in the Federal Courts may be producing cost savings of up to 20 percent in the resolution of referred disputes as the Federal Judicial Center 1990 Report on arbitration in 10 District Courts suggests.[23] But, as Judge William Schwartzer, until recently Director of the Federal Judicial Center, has pointed out:

> There is still a surprising dearth of information about the process of resolving disputes, either by traditional means or by the procedures we call alternatives. We know little, for example, about the comparative cost and time effects of different forms of ADR and the traditional litigation process. We also know little about what litigants are seeking when they come to court; what prompts some litigants and not others to consent to ADR; what litigants value and what satisfies them. Much remains to be learned about assessing the effects of ADR.[24]

10-34 We should view the American experience with a healthy scepticism, though not with prejudice. We should remember that the problems of the civil justice system in the US have many causes, not all of which are found here. Thus, for example, courts in the US are swamped with drug related criminal cases and the effect of the Speedy Trial Act 1974 is to compel the American judiciary to give priority to the trial of criminal cases. The combination of the jury system, contingent fees and class actions also compound the problems which the US courts face in providing access to justice and in reducing cost and delay. These pressures caused the Americans, much earlier than any other jurisdiction, to seek other ways of civil dispute resolution.

10-35 It is therefore in the United States that we find both public sector and private sector ADR in its most advanced form, though there has been considerable and impressive work done in Australia.[25] ADR is widely used in the

---

[23] Federal Judicial Center, *Court Annexed Arbitration in Ten District Courts* (1990), p. 85. See also Federal Judicial Center, *Voluntary Arbitration in Eight Federal District Courts: An Evaluation* (1994).

[24] Schwarzer, W, 'ADR and the Federal Courts: Question and Decisions for the Future', (1994) 7 *FJC Directions* 2.

[25] In Australia private sector mediation has flourished as the example of Sir Lawrence Street's centre in Sydney demonstrates. Anecdotal evidence suggests that private sector dispute

US State and Federal courts. Statutory approval of ADR in the Federal courts is given under the 1990 Civil Justice Reform Act, but the use of ADR in the Federal courts goes back to the mid 1970s. Experiments such as the summary jury trial and early neutral evaluation were introduced. In the late 1970s three Federal district courts implemented mandatory arbitration. In the mid-1980s a group of 10 experimental arbitration courts was established and a number of courts developed mediation programmes. The Civil Justice Reform Act includes 'authorisation to refer appropriate cases to alternative dispute resolution programs'.

10-36 Judge Schwartzer has also pointed out that there are clear signs in the US that ADR is well regarded as making an increasingly significant and necessary contribution to the civil justice system. Thus, a 1992 survey of Federal Judges in the US found, that a considerable majority favoured the use of ADR in the Federal courts. Some 86 percent thought that the role of the Federal courts should be to assist parties in resolving their disputes through whatever procedure is best suited to the case. The Chief Justice of the US has noted that dramatic changes may be required in the way disputes are resolved and:

> many litigants may have a greater need for an inexpensive and prompt resolution of their disputes, however rough and ready, than an unaffordable and tardy one, however close to perfection.[26]

10-37 According to a most informative article in December 1994 by Donna Stienstra of the Federal Judicial Center,[27] at least two-thirds of the courts now authorise one or more forms of ADR. In some courts this is no more than a statement of encouragement, but in others there are detailed rules and administrative structures to promote ADR. Stienstra reveals that the most

---

resolution by mediation may be becoming more attractive than arbitration. Thus the Australians have statutory mediation in many important areas of activity, see e.g. New South Wales legislation: Legal Profession Reform Act 1993, Rules of the Industrial Court, Native Title (NSW) Act 1994; Courts Legislation (Mediation and Evaluation) Amendment Act 1994. In particular, the Commercial Arbitration Act 1984, s. 27(1) provides that parties to an arbitration agreement '(a) may seek settlement of a dispute between them by mediation, conciliation or similar means; or (b) may authorise an arbitrator or umpire to act as a mediator, conciliator or other non-arbitral intermediary between them'. See also s. 27(1) of the Commercial Arbitration Act 1984 (Vic), the Commercial Arbitration Act 1990 (QL), and the Commercial Arbitration Act 1986 (ACT). Model legislation and court rules for court annexed mediation have been endorsed in principle by the Steering Committee of Attorney General.

[26] Schwarzer, see n. 25 *supra*, p. 2.

[27] Stienstra, D, 'Evaluating and Monitoring ADR Procedures', 1994(7) *FJC Directions* 24.

common form of ADR authorised by the courts is mediation, with more than 50 courts authorising its use, some on the basis of automatic referral by case type or other objective criteria. A further 20 courts authorise individual judges to order mediation. Some 30 courts authorise the use of arbitration and there is some mandatory referral under statutory authority. Stienstra concludes that more than two-thirds of the courts authorise at least one form of ADR and at least one third authorise more than one form.

10-38   However, the debate in the US continues as to whether and to what extent the Federal courts should use ADR.[28] Legislation to expand programmes to all District courts failed last year in Congress, partly over opposition to mandatory arbitration, though some American practitioners believe that unless arbitration is both mandatory and binding the full advantages may not be realised.

10-39   The former Chief Justice of Australia has expressed similar views to those of Chief Justice Rehnquist. Great weight must be attached to these opinions, not only because the Americans and the Australians are much further advanced in the use of statutory mediation and court-attached ADR than we are, but also because in the US and in Australia case management by judges, on which Lord Woolf bases his hopes and expectations, is widely used. The American and Australian experience in case managed systems, appears to be, that if the courts are to promote settlement, ADR methods are thought to be essential. It is not my intention to debate the merits of case management as such, but rather to argue that ADR is indeed essential, if case management is to work. This is particularly so, firstly, because case management is itself expensive and secondly, because without a considerable increase in the number of judges, or the introduction of civil magistrates, I doubt that the existing system can cope with any significant increase in the work of the judges, especially of the District judges. And the question is, will the government pay for the introduction of case management? The less the government will pay, the greater the need for ADR.

V. TAKING CASES OUT OF THE COURTS

10-40   It is sometimes suggested that costs might be saved by removing certain disputes from the courts and the legal profession. This is a theme, common both

---

[28] See also Stienstra, D and Willging, TE, *Alternatives to Litigation: Do They Have a Place in the Federal District Courts?* (Federal Judicial Center 1995).

to the Labour Party's proposals and the Government's Green Paper. In my view, there are disputes which could, subject to appropriate safeguards, be removed from the court system, or handled quite differently within it. Why is it, for example, that the High Court and County Court need to be concerned with so many personal injury cases which are largely disputes between litigants financed by trade unions and insurance companies and where most of these cases settle, either before or at trial? It has long been clear that the system is not cost effective.[29]

10-41 Henry Brown and Arnold Simanowitz have made some interesting proposals for ADR in medical accident cases which merit close study;[30] and we can draw upon the experience of other jurisdictions in introducing alternative dispute resolution techniques to personal injury cases, as is the case, for example, in British Columbia where I understand that the Vancouver Centre has had over 700 mediations. There may well be scope for the development of systems of that kind and there is a clear opportunity for insurers and trade unions to collaborate to work out schemes. They might also look at the proposals for legislation in Queensland.[31] There is also justification on public expenditure grounds for compelling such schemes, if not voluntarily entered into.

10-42 I have also been struck by the description in the American literature of the use of ADR in bankruptcy cases.[32] There is a most interesting report on a trial mediation scheme in the Bankruptcy court in San Diego, California. This may be a useful precedent for us to consider here when looking at the problems of personal bankruptcy and small company insolvency.

---

[29] *Royal Commission on Civil Liability and Compensation for Personal Injury* ('Pearson Report') (Cmnd. 7054 (1978)).

[30] Brown, H and Simanowitz, A, 'Alternative Dispute Resolution and Mediation', (1995) 4 *Quality in Health Care* 151.

[31] The Queensland draft legislation concerning the pre-litigation phase of personal injuries disputes provides for greater exchange of information, for obliging exchange of settlement offers and for encouragement of early resolution: Davies, G and Leiboff, J, 'Reforming the Civil Litigation System: Streamlining the Adversarial Framework', (1995) 25 *Queensland Law Society Journal* 111, 116.

[32] Hartwell, S and Bermant, G. *Alternative Dispute Resolution in a Bankruptcy Court: The Mediation Program in the Southern District of California* (Federal Judicial Center 1988).

VI. CASES NOT SUITABLE FOR ADR

10-43 But the other side of the coin is that there are cases which are not suitable for ADR, such as those which involve the rights of the citizen against the state. This covers a wide range of administrative action, by no means confined to questions of civil liberty, but ranging across the spectrum of the exercise of state power. Thus, for example, ADR is in principle clearly inappropriate for cases involving immigration, or nationality, or taxation, or other vital administrative decisions which the courts have subjected to the powerful scrutiny of judicial review. This is not to say that ADR has no role to play in the administrative machinery of the state, but there must be careful selection of appropriate cases. In 1987, the first year of the mediation programme in the DC district of the US Court of Appeals, cases were randomly assigned. It soon became clear that there were some appeals involving the government that were simply inappropriate for mediation, such as the interpretation of a statute and questions of government jurisdiction. Selection of suitable cases was therefore introduced and there has been some measure of success.[33]

10-44 However, I think the test in this country with our system of judicial review ought to be that, whilst ADR can help in the implementation of policy and administrative decisions, it has no role to play in deciding whether those decisions are lawful.

10-45 In the commercial and private law sphere, there are cases where parties require decisions of principle to enable a market to function properly. ADR is not suitable, though it may well be appropriate to implement decisions of principle.
Attention is being focused on ombudsmen as having an important role to play in resolving civil disputes. ADR may help, though the ombudsman system is more concerned with the resolution of grievances, rather than disputes. This is in its infancy here and I hope it will develop more on the basis of grafting ADR techniques on to grievance resolution, rather than establishing a parallel or substitute system of decision making to that of the courts.

---

[33] Many Federal agencies have adopted ADR programmes in the past few years, largely due to the Administrative Dispute Resolution Act 1990: though prior to that Act, the Solicitor General had instructed all divisions of the Department of Justice to comply with the mediation programme of the US Court of Appeals. Several Federal agencies recently agreed to expand their use of ADR to resolve disputes.

10-46   Increasingly, civil justice is being dispensed in tribunals. ADR could also be used in the proceedings of various tribunals, particularly regarding an employee's rights to compensation for loss of employment. These seem to me to be ideal cases for mediation, particularly as the cost of proceedings, which sometimes last for days, is often disproportionate to the amounts at stake.

VII. ARBITRATION

10-47   As this is the Freshfields lecture, I must say something about arbitration, no longer I think regarded as part of ADR, but classed with litigation as essentially an adjudicatory process. Whereas arbitration produces a binding decision according to law, mediation does not. Its object is to produce by negotiation, a binding agreement which may or may not become an arbitral award or court judgment; and so there are vital conceptual and procedural differences.

10-48   But arbitral institutions are now more and more holding themselves out as offering ADR services. Predictably, the US is ahead in the development of ADR in the private sector. The leader in the field is the American Arbitration Association, which for many years has had mediation rules both for commercial disputes and for construction disputes. The AAA was also in the van of developing a system known by the jargon Med-Arb, which merely means the mediator can subsequently become the arbitrator if the mediation fails and (of course) only with the consent of the parties.[34]

10-49   A number of other private and independent organisations have grown up in recent years in the US, such as JAMS Endispute and the Centre for Public Resources (CPR). Yet is has taken these organisations many years since their foundation in the late 1970s to reach the position where they have full and expanding caseloads. Their start was uncertain and, despite the publicity surrounding ADR, it has taken the private institutions some time to develop.

10-50   Increasingly, 'rent a judge' services are provided by retired judges on a private and paid basis. This has given rise to the accusation of a two-tier system of civil justice, rather like the complaints in this country about the role of consultants in providing private medical treatment more rapidly than in the NHS.

---

[34]   Sometimes another neutral as arbitrator.

10-51 The AAA construction mediation rules were the basis for the mediation rules I proposed to the Hong Kong Government in the early 1980s and which, with some modification, are now in use in Hong Kong as the primary means of dispute resolution in the construction industry. The Hong Kong International Arbitration Centre which has a very large and rapidly growing number of members specialising in mediation, administers the mediation system in the Government ACP contracts, the largest infrastructure project in the world.

10-52 We sometimes overlook that the shorthand phrase 'ICC Rules' means the Rules of Conciliation and Arbitration. The ICC very sensibly amended its conciliation rules a few years ago to provide for a sole conciliator, but they are infrequently used in comparison to the number of arbitration requests.[35] So too are the mini-trial rules of the Zürich Chamber of Commerce.

10-53 Even in France, that bastion of European resistance to American influence, ADR is being seriously regarded by lawyers, both in private practice and as in-house counsel. A working party under the chairmanship of a leading Paris avocat, Me Jean Claude Goldsmith, has produced recently an excellent report advocating the use of ADR.

10-54 In Holland, a private mediation organisation, the Netherlands Mediation Institute, was established two years ago. To some extent this has provoked the Netherlands Arbitration Institute to introduce earlier this year minitrial rules under the name 'minitrage'. Although the minitrial, a concept developed by (amongst others) Jonathan Marks and Professor Eric Green in the US in the mid-1970s, is less than other forms of mediation, the NAI feels that mediation is more likely to find acceptance in the legal community in Holland, if there is a formalism about its structure and procedures which is easily recognisable to litigation lawyers. However, the NAI regards its minitrage rules as very much a stepping stone to mediation generally, if the demand is there. A measure of the interest in ADR in Holland is shown by the fact that the recent annual conference of the Dutch Bar was devoted entirely to that topic. The Dutch face essentially the same problem as we do: how to control rising expenditure on the civil justice system and improve access to justice.

---

[35] Schwartz, E, 'International Conciliation and the ICC', (1995) 10 *Foreign Investment Law Journal* 98.

10-55 The LCIA is able to organise tailor-made mediation services, relying on the UNCITRAL Rules, as it has so far thought it unnecessary to establish its own mediation rules. In my view, it will either need to do so, or develop its relationship with CEDR and thereby emphasise more its ability to provide a comprehensive dispute resolution service. The new City Disputes Panel has mediation rules. But we must not get carried away. Despite these developments it has to be said that our experience with ADR in both international and domestic commercial cases is rather limited.

A. Delay and Cost in Arbitration

10-56 The problems of delay and cost which beset the conduct of litigation in this country apply to arbitration, perhaps even more so, given the parties must pay the arbitrator's fees and expenses and the costs of accommodation and other facilities. In my view ADR has a clear role to play in facilitating settlements and streamlining procedures in arbitration as well as litigation.

10-57 Even in maritime arbitration which traditionally has been able to resolve disputes quickly and rapidly, anecdotal evidence from experienced arbitrators and practitioners suggests that cases have become more expensive to dispose of. Some consider that this is because lawyers have increasingly been involved and, apart from the expense, have a tendency to introduce a more formalistic approach. Yet, although the LMAA introduced mediation rules, they have hardly been used, perhaps because many regard shipping cases as requiring quick decisions of principle and interpretation and the existing arbitration system still manages to work.

10-58 But it is probably in the area of construction arbitration that the worst excesses have occurred. Most construction arbitrations are indistinguishable from High Court litigation, but cost more. Many arbitrators are more royalist than the king, in that they feel unable to innovate or to depart from High Court adversarial procedures. There are strong grounds for believing that standards in construction arbitration in this country have declined. The cost of engaging lawyers has driven contractors to engage claims consultants, often at lower rates and on contingent fees. There have been several disturbing accounts of a lack of ethical standards, which should give pause for thought to those who wish to weaken the rights of audience and role of the legal profession. One consequence of the decline of standards in construction industry arbitration is the apparent wish of many to establish in advance rights of appeal under the 1979 Act.

10-59   I believe that many of the procedural problems of English arbitration, particularly in the construction field, stem from the conventional wisdom in this country until comparatively recently, that, absent agreement to the contrary, arbitration had to be conducted according to High Court adversarial procedures and applying strict English rules of evidence. That view was effectively debunked in a Freshfields Lecture by Lord Steyn, to whom I would like to pay particular tribute for his firm and uncompromising leadership of the DAC in difficult circumstances.[36] Why that was the conventional wisdom I am not entirely sure, because there was more than sufficient indication from very senior and respected judges, that provided arbitrators followed the rules of natural justice, they and the parties were at liberty to conduct the arbitration as they wished. An authoritative statement of the position was given by Lord Goff, who in 1980, sitting at first instance, said in Carlisle Place Investments[37] as follows:

> However, generally speaking, an arbitrator is the master of his own procedure. The courts, in my own experience — and no authority has been cited to me otherwise — do not ordinarily attempt to control the procedure in an arbitration. They do not ordinarily give directions to arbitrators. [emphasis added]

10-60   But most practitioners in the construction industry appeared to prefer the conventional wisdom of Mustill & Boyd as endorsed by Sir William Stabb QC in Town and City Properties (Development) Ltd v. Wiltshier Southern and Gilbert Powell.[38]

B. Procedural Change

10-61   The proposed new Arbitration Bill, which all practitioners in this country should wholeheartedly support, should make for radical change. There is an overriding commitment in the Bill to the principle of party autonomy. Arbitrators and the parties will, subject to observing the rules of natural justice, be free to conduct the proceedings as they wish. Parties and arbitrators must take full advantage of this freedom if arbitration is to flourish and regain the confidence of the commercial community.

---

[36]   Steyn, J, 'England's Response to the UNCITRAL Model Law of Arbitration', (1994) 10 *Arbitration International* at p. 1.
[37]   *Carlisle Place Investments Ltd v. Wimpey Construction (UK) Limited* (1980) 15 BLR 109.
[38]   (1988) 44 BLR 114.

10-62 The procedures used in arbitration are important, not only for the health of the process itself, but because it is to arbitration that the courts have from time to time looked and by which they have been influenced, in making procedural change in litigation. It is said that the procedural reforms in the Commercial Court some years ago were influenced by the practice in international commercial arbitration with which many judges and Commercial Court practitioners had become familiar.

10-63 There are two particular matters to which I suggest arbitrators should now pay close attention. The first is the development of a proposal which I first made in Hong Kong for costing on the basis of an agreed framework and which the new Bill will clearly permit arbitrators to do. Put simply, the arbitrator and the parties should fix at a very early stage of any case, the total sum of money which the arbitrator considers should reasonably be spent on the conduct of the arbitration. It would be open to the parties to spend more if they wished, but they will not, save in very exceptional circumstances, be able to recover more than 50 percent of the amount which the arbitrator has fixed early in the proceedings.

10-64 Thus, for example, in a construction case if there was a claim for damages amounting to say £1 million, the arbitrator and the parties would together work out, and in the absence of agreement the arbitrator would decide, by what procedures and how long it would take to resolve the dispute, having regard to the amount at stake. Regard would be had to relevant documentation, not following Peruvian Guano,[39] but applying very strict tests of relevance and necessity and applying similar tests to the number of witnesses, particularly expert witnesses. A timetable would be worked out and costed. If for the sake of argument it was considered reasonable for the parties to spend a total of £100,000, the expenditure of each party, again to make the example simple, would be estimated at £50,000 and that would be the limit of recoverable costs.

10-65 The second main respect in which arbitrators may be able to innovate to the benefit not only of arbitration, but also of litigation, is in the approach to settlement. In the City Disputes Panel Arbitration rules there is a requirement on the arbitrators periodically to enquire of the parties what, if any, progress is being made towards settlement and whether the tribunal is in a position to assist parties to that end. In my view, this should become standard practice amongst arbitrators. Absent consent, they cannot of course take enquiries any further, but

---

[39] *Cie Financière v. Peruvian Guano* (1882) 11 QBD 55.

with consent anything is possible. If there are concerns that for an arbitrator to become involved in the settlement process would compromise his position as arbitrator if the attempt at settlement fails, then that can be avoided by reference to another neutral. It may be that arbitral institutions should automatically offer that service and should specifically draw the attention of the parties to it.

10-66 Experience suggests that much of the concern about Med-Arb is misplaced. We readily expect juries to forget that they have heard by mistake certain evidence or argument in criminal trials. We expect judges, who may become aware that payments into court have been made, to ignore that for the purpose of determining liability and damages. The Germans and the Swiss expect the judge to try cases if the judge's proposals for settlement are rejected. I would have thought we could trust experienced arbitrators to participate in settlement if the parties wish. The conceptual objections to the dual role are obvious, but the system appears to work and in my view merits trial in this country. I regret that the new Bill will not follow the examples of Hong Kong[40] and Australia[41] by encouraging mediation as part of the arbitral process, nor of Bermuda[42] in establishing a legislative framework for mediation. But I am sure such provisions will come in due course, perhaps as part of a mediation or civil disputes resolution statute which I think may be necessary if ADR develops much beyond the courts and arbitration.

VIII. RESISTANCE TO ADR

10-67 Despite the growing interest in ADR in this country and elsewhere, it is clear that there is substantial resistance and scepticism. It is probably more talked about than practiced. There is, for example, a general unwillingness on the part of some law firms, banks, insurance companies and other financial institutions to use ADR, or even to use arbitration, although the City Disputes Panel offers an effective alternative to litigation. To some extent this is based on ignorance and self-interest. The big battalions might well ask why they should make it easier, faster and cheaper to get redress from them, though clearly the more responsible companies and institutions recognise that it is in their wider commercial interests that disputes about their goods and services should be efficiently and fairly

---

[40] Arbitration Ordinance s. 2B.

[41] Commercial Arbitration Act 1984, s. 27 (NSW), see n. 25 above.

[42] Bermuda International Conciliation and Arbitration Act 1993. See Rawding, 'ADR: Bermuda's International Conciliation and Arbitration Act 1993', (1994) 10 *Arbitration International* 1 at p. 99.

resolved. This is seen by their participation in Ombudsmen schemes and in such consumer mediation schemes as are administered by the Chartered Institute of Arbitrators.

10-68 Many practitioners in England are concerned that ADR will reduce significantly the role and income of lawyers in dispute resolution, particularly if conventional litigation procedures are simplified and litigation becomes much faster and less expensive. Such concerns are ill-founded and short-sighted. Society changes and lawyers must change too. We cannot go on resolving disputes as we do now. There is a real, justified and profound lack of public confidence in lawyers and in the system. Lawyers who prove themselves adept and skilled in resolving disputes, whether by ADR or adjudicatory measures, will satisfy their existing clients by saving them time and money and will attract new ones.

10-69 The Government could give a lead in encouraging ADR. Despite the apparent belief that ADR will save money, so far the spending departments of Government have not insisted on ADR clauses in their forms of contract. If they were to do so, it would provide a much needed boost to the acceptability of ADR in the commercial community. In Hong Kong, it required the Government, first of all in a pilot scheme and then generally, to introduce ADR in its construction contracts, before it was generally acceptable in the private sector.

10-70 But if we are to persuade the authorities and the public to have confidence in ADR, we shall need to allay a number of legitimate concerns which are voiced even by those well disposed. There is the entirely valid point that ADR when used in conjunction with the current system merely introduces an additional layer of cost. Nevertheless, ADR, even when used in the context of existing litigation or arbitration, can result in substantial savings. The work necessary to conduct a mediation once arbitration is under way, is generally not significant in the context of the arbitration and, frequently, even if mediation fails, it can have a beneficial effect on streamlining the arbitration such as by defining the issues really in dispute and narrowing differences.

10-71 Another key concern is whether court attached ADR should be mandatory. The Herbert Smith report indicated businessmen thought not. In the US reference to court-attached arbitration and mediation is sometimes mandatory though the result is not.

10-72   Clauses requiring use of ADR in certain types of contracts, especially adhesion contracts, have been a topic of significant controversy in the US. The two main areas of interest are consumer contracts and employment agreements.[43]

10-73   Perhaps concern in this country about mandatory ADR whether private or public can be allayed by making ADR subject to the control of the courts.

IX. THE ROLE OF THE COURTS IN ADR

10-74   In any event the courts have an important and perhaps vital role to play. Mediation takes place in the shadow of the law in two distinct respects. The first is that the mediator works in the context of the parties' legal rights, though a settlement may modify or even disregard them. Secondly, the mediation, whilst not required to be conducted in accordance with the rules of natural justice, which indeed would be an impediment in that they would prevent individual and private interviews with the parties, must be conducted in a principled way, free of abuse, in order to give proper effect to the agreement to negotiate which the parties have made. And it is here that legal concepts of good faith, confidentiality, privilege and immunity come into play.

10-75   The most controversial of these, given that negotiation is at the heart of the mediation process, is the development of a principle of good faith and fair dealing in giving effect to the agreement to mediate. The high-water mark of the case against is the uncompromising reasoning of the House of Lords in Walford v. Miles,[44] distinguished in Australian in Hooper Baillie,[45] an ADR case, in which the judge also refused to follow the decision of Mr Justice Steyn in Paul Smith.[46] In his adroit judgment in Hooper Baillie, Giles J considered whether an

---

[43]   In 1994, the US General Accounting Office issued a report on arbitration of employment discrimination disputes in the securities industry. The report reached no conclusions on the fairness of arbitration of these claims. However, it did identify some weaknesses in the arbitration process, including selection of arbitrators and insufficient oversight by the Securities and Exchange Commission. Congress has considered legislation to limit the use of mandatory ADR clauses in employment contracts. In the last session of Congress, legislation was introduced but never passed. In the current session, a bill, s. 366, has been introduced, but has not been acted upon (and will likely not be acted upon). The Federal Commission on the Future of Worker-Management Relations addressed ADR in its final report. The Commission favoured expanded use of ADR to resolve workplace disputes, but expressed concern with the fairness of some ADR systems.

[44]   [1992] 1 All ER 453.

[45]   *Hooper Bailie Associated Ltd v. National Group Pty Ltd* (1992) 28 NSWLR 194.

[46]   *Paul Smith Ltd v. H+S International Holding Inc* [1991] 2 Lloyd's Rep 127.

agreement to conciliate should be given effect in law, or whether it lacked the certainty necessary for legal enforceability. After discussing the respective arguments, the judge defined what is enforced as 'not co-operation and consent, but participation in a process from which co-operation and consent might come'.[47]

10-76 The judge held that:

> an agreement to conciliate or mediate is not to be likened. ... to an agreement to agree. Nor is it an agreement to negotiate, or negotiate in good faith, perhaps necessarily lacking certainty and obliging a party to act contrary to its interest. Depending upon its express terms and any terms to be implied, it may require of the parties participation in the process by conduct of sufficient certainty for legal recognition of the agreement.[48]

10-77 I very much hope that the principles laid down by Lord Justice Kerr in Tubeworkers[49] will be followed and the emphasis in the Channel Tunnel case[50] in giving effect to the dispute resolution mechanisms agreed upon by the parties, is an encouraging sign. The provisions of the new arbitration bill are a step in the right direction.

10-78 But where mediation is not part of, or a prerequisite to, arbitration or litigation perhaps we can develop Lord Ackner's helpful reference to 'best endeavours' as mentioned in Walford v. Miles, as giving rise to enforceable obligations, and go down that road rather than the one of good faith. Yet, I believe that English law, if it is not to remain outside the mainstream of commercial and contract law elsewhere,[51] ought to develop an overriding duty of good faith and fair dealing in both the negotiation and performance of contracts and not just confined to nominate contracts such as partnerships and insurance. For myself, I am encouraged by the observations of the Master of the Rolls in the recent cases of Timeload v. BT[52] and Philips v. B Sky B.[53] We appear to be

---

[47] (1992) 28 NSWLR 194 at 206.

[48] *ibid* at 209.

[49] *Tubeworkers v. Tilbury Construction Ltd* (1985) 30 BLR 67.

[50] *Channel Tunnel Group Ltd v. Balfour Beatty Construction Ltd* [1993] 1 AC 335.

[51] For other Australian cases on good faith in the negotiation and performance of contracts, see *Coal Cliff Colleries v. Sijehama* (1991) 24 NSWLR 1; *Trawl Industries of Australia v. Effem Foods trading as 'Uncle Bens of Australia'*, 1992 Australian Contract Reports 90–011; *Renard Constructions v. Minister for Public Works* (1992) 26 NSWLR 234.

[52] *Timeload Limited v. British Telecommunications plc,* (CA), 30 November 1993, (unreported).

going in the right direction, even if we do not yet know how, when or where we will arrive.

10-79   There is, in my view, no difficulty as a matter of principle in developing the necessary concepts of confidentiality, privilege and immunity when attached to mediation though the recent High Court of Australia decision in the Esso case[54] (with which on public policy grounds I agree) has revealed a rather different approach to privacy and confidentiality in arbitration than that shown in certain decisions in England. Quite what effect that may have on the public policy issue of privacy and confidentiality of settlement discussions remains to be seen. I hope none.

10-80   I regard the more difficult problems facing us to be connected with training, accreditation and the regulation of mediators, especially where their role will be as adjunct to civil litigation and particularly if a Labour Government sought to implement proposals for accredited mediators as part of a community legal service. For the moment, I think supervision can be left to the existing institutions such as the Bar, the Law Society and the RICS and it will be interesting to see how the regulatory system develops, perhaps by direct institutional control, perhaps by delegated control to specific organisations such as CEDR and the FMA.[55] But if ADR develops as a generally accepted adjunct to litigation and particularly if it is publicly funded, then it will be necessary to create a system for the accreditation and regulation of mediators subject to ultimate control by the courts. Otherwise, standards and rights of participation will become a matter of direct bureaucratic control by the paymasters and this is constitutionally wrong.

10-81   Accordingly, I do not believe that ADR ought to develop in this country without judicial control.[56] We must define by experience the nature and limits of that control. We have had to do this in relation to arbitration. We can perhaps all too readily predict, that many practitioners in ADR will resent what they will see as unmerited court intrusion into party autonomy. But just as arbitration in this

---

[53] *Philips Electronique Grand Public SA v. British Sky Broadcasting,* (CA) 19 October 1994 (unreported).

[54] *Esso Australia Resources Ltd v. Minister for Energy and Minerals* (1995) 11 Arbitration International at p. 235; but see on mediation, the New Zealand decision in *M v. Independent Newspapers Limited* [1992] 1 ERNZ 200.

[55] Family Mediators Association.

[56] For an alternative view advocating the total independence of ADR from the court, see Professor Eric Green, 'Crisis in the Courts? Voluntary ADR: Part of the Solution', 1993 (April) *Trial* 35.

country has benefited and will continue to benefit from the exercise of limited and essential supervision and support by the courts, so too will we need to develop appropriate rules to govern the relationship between mediation and the courts.

X. ADJUDICATION AND MEDIATION IN ONE PROCEDURE

10-82   The next stage of Lord Woolf's work is the preparation of detailed rules of procedure. I advance for his consideration some ideas on the combination of adjudication and mediation in one system. I do so because I now consider ADR not necessarily as an absolute, rigid and distinct alternative to civil litigation or arbitration, but also as part of it. Many disputes require for their fair and prompt settlement, binding decisions on matters of law, construction of particular contractual terms and decisions of principle in order to indicate to the parties their legal rights. But in order to settle disputes fairly and promptly, what the parties also need is guidance towards compromise, particularly as to the implementation of a point of contract or legal principle. How often are we confronted in litigation and arbitration with trying to establish, aside from, but influence by, contractual rights, the proper commercial solution or the proper relief, particularly in long-term contracts such as joint ventures and partnerships? And we are not necessarily well served by what can be blunt instruments of orders for specific performance or rescission and awards of damages. It is often possible through mediation to fashion solutions beyond the formal powers of a judge in giving judgment or an arbitrator in rendering an award.

10-83   My ideas are in outline only. I take the common or garden commercial dispute as an example of a combined procedure. The plaintiff, when starting litigation, would be obliged to certify that an attempt to settle had been made and also to set out the result of the attempt. If, for example, the attempt had foundered on a failure to agree on the nature of a legal obligation, or liability, or the meaning of a particular contract provision, that would be pleaded in a separate document from the statement of claim. If, the difficulty in settlement was disagreement on quantum, then the nature and extent of that disagreement would be pleaded. Where formal offers had been made, these would be set out as well. The respondent would file an appropriate response.

10-84   The case would then be assigned by a court official to a particular judge, under the case management principles of Lord Woolf. The judge would consider with the parties whether the differences which had led to the collapse of the settlement negotiations before litigation, were capable of being resolved. If the obstacle to settlement had been, for example, a disagreement as to a point of legal principle or legal interpretation, then arrangements could be made for a judge (perhaps a different judge) to decide that. The decision would need to be rooted in a factual matrix, to borrow Lord Wilberforce's expressive phrase[57] or as the Master of the Rolls once put it, a sure foundation of fact.[58] The timing of the decision would be governed by the necessity to establish with confidence the necessary factual matrix. Thus, it might be that if the point was a preliminary one, it could be decided before the disclosure of substantial documentation. Any discovery required to establish the factual matrix would be the subject of very specific and very limited order.

10-85 Also the judge could consider which ADR measure might be suitable, such as early neutral evaluation, where an experienced independent third party looks at the case, its merits and the most efficient means of resolving it. I appreciate that this may involve perhaps a 'double trial' of the settlement issues and, failing settlement, of the merits, but as Lord Hoffman has pointed out,[59] nothing more concentrates the mind of the parties upon settlement, than an expression of provisional judicial opinion on the merits.

XI. OTHER STEPS

10-86 There are other steps which I think could be taken to advance the objectives of Lord Woolf. He has proposed that a senior judge should be appointed Head of Civil Justice. The judge will require administrative and advisory help. Private sector ADR practitioners and institutions should offer assistance, perhaps by membership of a committee presided over by the judge, in order properly to contribute their knowledge and experience to promote efficient dispute resolution systems as an adjunct to the courts. This would also recognise the established fact, that the private sector dispute resolution systems of arbitration and now mediation, have a vital role to play. The reality is that the courts could not cope with the disputes currently disposed of privately, without a massive increase in resources.

10-87 Secondly, the private sector should, on a pro bono or low cost basis, educate the judiciary and court administrators (who are understandably ignorant of ADR procedures and mediation techniques) and explain to them, drawing on

---

[57] *Reardon Smith Line v. Hansen-Tangen* [1976] 3 All ER 570 at 575.
[58] *Air Canada v. Secretary of State for Trade* [1983] 1 All ER 161 at 167 (QBD).
[59] Sir Leonard Hoffman, 'Changing Perspectives on Civil Litigation', (1993) 56 MLR 297 at 305.

the experience particularly in the US, how such procedural devices such as minitrial, early neutral evaluation, settlement weeks and court attached mediation and arbitration actually work. Education of judges was provided in the USA and, for example, the mediation schemes in the Local and Federal Courts in the District of Columbia began on an experimental basis with training provided free by the DC Bar.

10-88   Thirdly, I believe that it should be possible to create, using the resources of the private sector, a number of pro bono or low cost pilot schemes in various parts of the country and at various levels of the judicial system, including cases on appeal to the Court of Appeal, in order to demonstrate whether ADR schemes significantly assist the courts in the despatch of business. There are obvious criteria of savings of time and of cost, though I enter again my caveat that such schemes may not succeed in reducing the total amount of money which needs to be spent on the civil disputes system. But if the advocates of ADR are right, we should get better value for money, we should improve access to justice, we should make it easier to reach fair settlements and we should be able to direct resources to areas where, from society's point of view, there is the greatest need.

10-89   Fourthly, such pilot schemes could, if successful, be developed into a national scheme using civil magistrates which could be administered at a local level by a series of committees. We can be encouraged by US experience where mediators, often practising or retired senior lawyers, give their services free as a recognised and valued form of public service.

10-90   Fifthly, after many years of scepticism and insistence on the private sector demonstrating the efficacy of ADR, the Green Paper has opened, albeit ever so slightly, the door towards public funding of ADR systems. I think those of us who advocate ADR should force the door open a bit more. Various institutions, such as the Chartered Institute of Arbitrators, the RICS, the ICE and the Law Society, should organise ADR schemes which could participate in legal funding by block contracts.[60] But more sensibly, they might devise other schemes to the same end of financial discipline and control. I also believe that the private sector should put before a Labour Government alternatives to the proposed control by local legal aid committees; or proposals for radical restructuring of the legal aid committees. I do not believe that local legal aid

---

[60] The Law Society of Northern Ireland has given a lead in introducing an ADR scheme two years ago for the business community – an example of intelligent self-help.

committees are best suited to encourage, regulate and develop ADR as a parallel system to the courts.

XII. CONCLUSION

10-91   Lord Woolf has, yet again, rendered a signal public service. I regard his recommendations as the single most important step for many, many years towards the radical and necessary reform of the civil justice system. I particularly welcome Lord Woolf's insistence that the primary objective of his reforms is to achieve just settlements between hostile parties. I believe that is the objective and justification for ADR.

10-92   There is no doubt that there is growing support for radical change in the civil justice system. Lord Woolf's report presents an immense challenge to judges, administrators and practitioners. It must not be thrown in the dustbin of history, merely another disturbing statistic. Lawyers, judges, arbitrators and mediators are the problem solvers of our society and not, as the cynics would have us believe, mere parasites. We face a challenge which we cannot avoid, to which we must respond and which we must master.

XIII. EDITORS' ENDNOTE [FOR THE ORIGINAL PUBLICATION]

10-93   The 'Woolf Report' is Lord Woolf's Interim Report, 'Access to Justice', on the civil justice system in England and Wales, published in June 1995. Lord Woolf will publish a Final Report later this year, together with new unified rules of procedure for courts in England and Wales.

10-94   The Lord Chancellor appointed Lord Woolf in 1994 to consider the system of civil procedure in order to improve access to justice and reduce the costs of litigation; to reduce the complexity of the rules of procedure and modernise terminology; and to remove unnecessary distinctions of practice and procedure. As Lord Woolf himself recognised, many had trodden this stony path before: there have been some 60 reports since 1951 on various aspects of civil procedure and the organisation of courts in England and Wales. By 1994, however, there was widespread support for a new approach to civil litigation; Lord Woolf's freethinking reputation guaranteed a confident response; and the Woolf Inquiry Team immediately caught the imagination of judges, practitioners and users.

10-95 Many of Lord Woolf's proposals are not controversial: the single set of procedural court rules, the greater procedural flexibility for different cases, the increased small-claims jurisdiction, reduced discovery of documents and the redeployment of the judiciary etc will each help reduce unnecessary delay and expense, particularly for the individual litigant. Other proposals are contentious: for example, 'hands on' judicial case management with or, still more, without additional resources from the executive. Supporters of judicial case-management, long practised in moderation by the Commercial Court, do not easily believe in Lord Woolf's dream; and even Professor I.R. Scott concludes that without first resolving certain underlying structural issues, the implementation of this proposal is likely to prove very difficult indeed (see Scott in Zuckerman & Cranston (eds), Reform of Civil Procedure, at p. 2).

10-96 One of Lord Woolf's proposals concerned 'alternative approaches to dispensing justice' (Chapter 18). As to ADR, Lord Woolf recommended that developments on ADR in Australia, Canada and the USA should be studied further and monitored by the Judicial Studies Board; and he made the following specific proposals for ADR in the English Courts (at p. 147):

(8) Where there is a satisfactory alternative to the resolution of disputes in court, use of which would be an advantage to the litigants, then the courts should encourage the use of this alternative: for this purpose, the staff and the judiciary must be aware of the forms of ADR which exist and what can be achieved.

(9) At the case management conference and pre-trial review the parties should be required to state whether the question of ADR has been discussed and, if not, why not.

(10) In deciding on the future conduct of a case, the judge should be able to take into account the litigant's unreasonable refusal to attempt ADR.

(11) The Lord Chancellor and the court service should treat it as one of their responsibilities to make the public aware of the possibilities which ADR offers.

(12) Consideration should be given to the way in which members of the professions who are experienced in litigation and who retire at an early age, can be involved as 'civil magistrates' or otherwise, in support of the civil justice system.

10-97 To North American eyes, this theme will appear familiar; and indeed Professor R.L. Marcus has invoked Yogi Berra's attributed remark: 'it's déjà vu all over again' (Marcus, ibid, at p. 219). However, Lord Woolf does not suggest that ADR should be compulsory, either as an alternative or as a preliminary to litigation (p. 136); nor does he propose a system of court-annexed ADR, preferring the use of private ADR schemes (p. 143).

10-98 To several, Lord Woolf's interim recommendations do not go far enough. In England, there remains much to learn and understand about the practice of ADR; pragmatic caution is not always unhealthy; and hence the enormous need for Mr Marriott's grand tour d'horizon. Whatever happens next with the publication and implementation of Lord Woolf's Final Report, Lord Woolf's ideas alone must necessarily improve English civil procedure, thereby reducing cost, curbing delay and introducing flexible procedures appropriate for the particular case-in-hand. Whether ADR plays a major role in England, only time will tell.

XIV. EDITORS' ENDNOTE [2005][61]

10-99 The Lord Chancellor set up the Committee in 1994 under Lord Woolf to produce a report on *Access to Justice*. In less than a year, Lord Woolf published an interim report,[62] and his final report was published in July 1996.[63] The Government made recommendations and in February 1997 the *Civil Procedure Act 1997* received Royal Assent. Lord Woolf identified the problems of formal and inflexible proceedings, endemic delays, in short described a rather depressing picture of English civil justice system which is incomprehensible to litigants, costs significant sums of money and makes no or little use of modern technology.

10-100 Following the two Woolf Reports[64] and the *Civil Procedure Act 1997*, most recommendations were effected from 26 April 1999 through the *Civil Procedure Rules 1998*.[65] The civil justice reform had four main objectives:
- Simplification of procedure (including expediency and cost reduction through an underlying principle of proportionality);
- Judicial case management (requiring judges to actively manage the resolution process by watering down the adversarial system;

---

[61] The Endnote is based on Loukas Mistelis, 'ADR in England and Wales', 12 *American Review of International Arbitration* 167-222 (2001), at 178-182.
[62] Lord Woolf, *Access to Justice – Interim Report to the Lord Chancellor on the Civil Justice System in England and Wales*, (London: HMSO, June 1995).
[63] Lord Woolf, *Final Report – Access to Justice*, (London: HMSO, July 1996). Presented to the Lord Chancellor.
[64] http://www.lcd.gov.uk/civil/finalfr.htm.
[65] http://www.lcd.gov.uk/civil/procrules_fin/menus/rules.htm.

- Pre action protocols (aiming at encouraging contact between parties and better exchange of information; hoping that a settlement may be facilitated); and
- Alternatives to court procedure.

10-101 There are three different ways,[66] in which the Woolf Reports and the *Civil Procedure Rules* attempt to promote ADR:

- The payment system has been changed so as to enable claimants and defendants alike to make offers relating to the allocation of costs;[67]
- The settlement at the earliest possible stage is encouraged by pre action protocols[68] and an active case management;[69]
- Official encouragement is given to the avoidance of litigation through recourse to alternative dispute resolution.[70]

Lord Woolf's report contained a chapter dedicated to ADR, entitled *Alternative approaches to dispensing justice*, and most of these views found an expression in the *Civil Procedure Rules*.[71] The *Civil Procedure Rules* are undoubtedly the most fundamental change in civil litigation for more than a century. It seems that the objective of simplification of procedure in court supported by encouragement of settlement out-of-court has been successful.

---

[66] J.A. Jolowicz, 'The Woolf Reforms', in J.A. Jolowicz, *On Civil Procedure*, (Cambridge: Cambridge University Press, 2001), 386–397 at 392.

[67] CPR, rule 36 available at http://www.lcd.gov.uk/civil/procrules_fin/contents/parts/part36.htm.

[68] CPR Rule 1.4.2, at http://www.lcd.gov.uk/civil/procrules_fin/contents/parts/part01.htm# rule1_4; See also http://www.lcd.gov.uk/civil/procrules_fin/menus/protocol.htm where protocols are listed: e.g. Protocol for the Construction and Engineering Disputes, Pre-Action Protocol for Defamation; Pre-Action Protocol for Personal Injury Claims; Pre-Action Protocol for the Resolution of Clinical Disputes; Pre-Action Protocol for Professional Negligence.

[69] S. Flanders, 'Case Management: Failure in America? Success in England and Wales?' (1998) 17 *Civil Justice Quarterly* 308. See also *Cowl and Others* v. *Plymouth City Council*, Judgment 14 December 2001, reported in *The Times* 8 January 2002, (CA) *per* Lord Woolf, LCJ.

[70] See, for example, CPR rule 3.1 available at http://www.lcd.gov.uk/civil/ procrules_fin/contents /parts/part03.htm#rule3_1 and CPR rule 26.4, available at http://www.lcd.gov.uk/civil/procrules _fin/contents/parts/part26.htm#rule26_4.

[71] See, for example, CPR rules 26.4 and 1.4(2)(e) at http://www.lcd.gov.uk/civil/procrules_fin/ menus/rules.htm.

*Stephen M. Schwebel**

CHAPTER 11

MAY THE MAJORITY VOTE OF AN INTERNATIONAL ARBITRAL TRIBUNAL BE IMPEACHED?

I. INTRODUCTION

11-1 Cases of the International Court of Justice passing upon the validity of international arbitral have been few; precisely, two. The validity of an arbitral award made by the King of Spain in 1906 determining portions of the boundary between Honduras and Nicaragua was challenged by Nicaragua. Under the auspices of the Organisation of American States, Honduras and Nicaragua concluded a Special Agreement submitting the dispute to the court. In 1960, the court held that Nicaragua had in fact freely accepted the designation of the King of Spain as arbitrator, had fully participated in the arbitral proceedings, and had thereafter accepted the award. The court consequently found that the award was binding and that Nicaragua was under an obligation to give effect to it – which it did.[1]

11-2 In 1991, the court gave judgment rejecting another challenge to the validity of an arbitral award, in the case concerning the Arbitral Award of 31 July 1989.[2] It is that case on which I shall concentrate these remarks, for it has more than one aspect of high interest to the processes of international arbitration, both interstate and commercial.

---

* Judge and former President of the International Court of Justice. This is a revised version of the '1996 School of International Arbitration – Freshfields Arbitration Lecture' delivered in London on 12 November 1996. (The editors acknowledge with thanks the permission to publish this contribution by Freshfields and the School of International Arbitration Centre for Commercial Law Studies, Queen Mary and Westfield College, London University.)

[1] Arbitral Award made by the King of Spain on 23 December 1906, [1960] *ICJ Reports* 192.
[2] Arbitral Award of 31 July 1989, [1991] *ICJ Reports* 53.

Julian D.M. Lew and Loukas A. Mistelis (eds), Arbitration Insights, 201-211
© 2007 Kluwer Law International. Printed in the Netherlands

11-3 But before doing so, I may note that the predecessor of the International Court of Justice, the Permanent Court of International Justice, also dealt with a few cases of appeal of arbitral awards from mixed arbitral tribunals. Perhaps that experience was what stimulated the Government of Finland in 1929 to propose that the court be generally endowed with the authority to determine the validity of arbitral awards. While that proposal was fruitless, when Professor Georges Scelle produced his Draft Code of Arbitral Procedure for the International Law Commission some 25 years later, it provided that arbitral awards that were challenged on certain specified grounds could be referred by either party to the International Court of Justice which 'shall be competent ... to declare the nullity of the award ...'.[3]

11-4 Professor Scelle wanted to close the loopholes through which recalcitrant states had climbed in hundreds of years of inter-state arbitration. But too many States Members of the United Nations liked loopholes; they maintained that they afforded the process of international arbitration escape mechanisms which, if not desirable, were necessary for the flexibility and hence the viability of the process. So the Draft Code of Arbitral Procedure was never adopted as a treaty but, in less progressive form, as a model code of arbitral procedure. In that form, it and Professor Scelle's preparatory work have exerted a constructive influence, as more than one arbitral award has shown (e.g. *Saudi Arabia* v. *Aramco* and *Liamco* v. *Libya*).

11-5 But speaking of loopholes reminds me of the story of the late actor and humorist, W.C. Fields. He was not known for his religious devotion, so his family was surprised to see him, on his deathbed, intently studying the Bible at which he had not been seen to look for some 60 years. 'What are you doing?' they gently enquired. Fields replied, 'Looking for loopholes'.

11-6 International commercial arbitration has its loopholes, which for the most part, in most jurisdictions, have been effectively plugged through enforcement pursuant to the New York Convention. Inter-state arbitration in principle remains less secure, though in practice the very great majority of such awards are accepted and applied. An exception gave rise to the recent proceedings in the International Court of Justice to which I now turn.

---

[3] See 'Draft Convention on Arbitral Procedure adopted by the Commission at its Fifth Session' [1957] *Yearbook of the International Law Commission*, Vol. II, Arts 29 and 30, at p. 15.

II. THE ARBITRAL AWARD OF 31 JULY 1989

11-7 In 1960, the predecessor states of Senegal and Guinea-Bissau, France and Portugal, exchanged letters for the purpose of defining the maritime boundary between Senegal – then an autonomous Member of the French Community – and the then Portuguese province of Guinea-Bissau. After Senegal and Guinea-Bissau became independent, a dispute arose between them over the delimitation of their maritime claims. In 1985, they concluded an arbitration agreement which provided, inter alia, that:

- the arbitral tribunal shall consist of three members, each party appointing an arbitrator of its choice and the president being appointed by mutual agreement of the two parties;
- the tribunal shall take its decisions only in its full composition and all decisions 'including those relating to the jurisdiction of the tribunal and the interpretation of the agreement, shall be taken by a majority of its members';
- the award shall be signed by the president and registrar and shall be final and binding upon the two states which shall be under a duty to implement it.

11-8 The arbitration agreement requested the tribunal to decide 'in accordance with the norms of international law on the following questions':

1. Does the Agreement concluded ... on 26 April 1960, and which relates to the maritime boundary, have the force of law in the relations between the Republic of Guinea-Bissau and the Republic of Senegal respectively?
2. In the event of a negative answer to the first question, what is the course of the line delimiting the maritime territories appertaining to Guinea-Bissau and Senegal?[4]

11-9 Guinea-Bissau designated as arbitrator Mohammed Bedjaoui, then and now a Judge of the International Court of Justice; Senegal designated a former Judge of the Court, André Gros; and Julio Barberis, Ambassador of Argentina, was appointed president. On 31 July 1989, the tribunal handed down an award whose existence and validity came to be challenged before the court. Indeed immediately upon its being read out, the agent of Guinea-Bissau rose to

---

[4]   Arbitral Award of 31 July 1989 [1991] *ICJ Reports* 58.

challenge it, on grounds which can be understood only in the light of the following summary and quotations from the award.

11-10   The tribunal concluded that the 1960 Exchange of Letters gave rise to a valid agreement binding Guinea-Bissau and Senegal. It further held that that agreement 'does not delimit those maritime spaces which did not exist at that date, whether they be termed exclusive economic zone, fishery zone or whatever ...' but that 'the territorial sea, the contiguous zone and the continental shelf ... are expressly mentioned in the 1960 Agreement and they existed at the time of its conclusion ...'. The tribunal continued: 'Bearing in mind the above conclusions ... and the actual wording of ... the Arbitration Agreement, in the opinion of the Tribunal it is not called upon to reply to the second question.'[5]

11-11   The operative clause of the award provides:

> For the reasons stated above, the Tribunal *decides* by two votes to one: to reply as follows to the first question formulated ... in the Arbitration Agreement: The Agreement ... of 26 April 1960 ... has the force of law in the relations between ... Guinea-Bissau and ... Senegal with regard solely to the areas mentioned that Agreement, namely the territorial sea, the contiguous zone and the continental shelf ...[6]

11-12   The president of the tribunal – who together with Judge Gros had voted for the award – appended a declaration to the award stating:

> I feel that the reply given by the Tribunal to the first question put by the Arbitration Agreement could have been more precise. I would have replied to that question as follows: 'The Agreement ... of 26 April 1960 ... has the force of law in the relations between ... Guinea-Bissau and ... Senegal with respect to the territorial sea, the contiguous zone and the continental shelf, but does not have the force of law with respect to the waters of the exclusive economic zone or fishery zone ...' This partially affirmative and partially negative reply is, in my view, the exact description of the legal position between the parties... This reply would have enabled the Tribunal to deal in its Award with the second question put in the Arbitration Agreement. The *partially* negative reply to the first question would have conferred on the Tribunal a *partial* competence to reply to the second, i.e., to do so to the

---

[5]   *ibid.*, at p. 59.
[6]   *ibid.*, at p. 60.

extent that the reply to the first question would have been in the negative. In that case, the Tribunal would have been competent to delimit the waters of the exclusive economic zone or the fishery zone between the two countries. The Tribunal thus could have settled the whole of the dispute ...'[7]

11-13 In his dissenting opinion, Judge Bedjaoui referred to the declaration of President Barberis and said that it 'shows to what an extent the Award is incomplete and inconsistent with the letter and spirit of the Arbitration Agreement with regard to the single line desired by the Parties. Since it emanates from the President of the Tribunal himself, that Declaration, by its very existence as well as by its contents, justifies more fundamental doubts as to the existence of a majority and the reality of the Award'.[8]

III. CASE CONCERNING THE ARBITRAL AWARD OF 31 JULY 1989

11-14 I turn now to the court's judgment on the award. Both Guinea-Bissau and Senegal were party to the 'optional clause' conferring general jurisdiction on the court, subject to exceptions which Senegal argued debarred the court from ruling on the merits of the arbitral award. But Senegal accepted that these proceedings were not an appeal from the award or an application for revision of it, but were confined to the question of the alleged inexistence or nullity of the award. The court was confronted with sharply divergent contentions on these questions.

11-15 Guinea-Bissau argued that the award 'is inexistent, or subsidiarily that it is absolutely null and void'. As to 'inexistence', Guinea-Bissau contended that the Award was 'characterised by the total absence of a joint act of will on the part at least of two' of the three arbitrators. A decision of the tribunal required two concordant votes out of three. To be sure, 'purely formal appearances have been preserved ... the "Award" states that "The Tribunal decides by two votes to one"'. In view of Judge Bedjaoui's dissent, the two votes were those of President Barberis and Judge Gros. 'But between the "Award" and the dissenting opinion, there is the Declaration of President Barberis which, by its very presence and content, destroys appearances and indicates the obvious disagreement which had existed within the fictitious majority itself.' President Barberis would have settled the whole of the dispute, whereas the award settles only part of it; by giving what he terms the correct description of the legal position between the

---

[7]   *ibid.*, at p. 60-61.
[8]   *ibid.*, at p. 61.

parties, he implied that the position set out in the award is incorrect. On this extremely important point, the president expressed his position, irreconcilable with that of Judge Gros. In Guinea-Bissau's view, the president's declaration both demonstrated the inexistence of any award and its nullity due to an *excès de pouvoir* in failing to draw a single line delimiting the whole of the maritime interest in dispute. In the light of its content, the President's declaration was in fact a dissenting opinion. Why then did President Barberis sign the award? Guinea-Bissau asks, 'What weariness, what psychological pressure, what wear and tear (the deliberations dragged on for months on end) caused him finally to associate his name with one text, while at the same time disassociating himself from it by another one?' 'Upon analysis, the point is accordingly proved that the '"Award" is inexistent owing to the lack of a genuine majority'.[9]

11-16 Senegal rejected these arguments. It relied on a number of judgments of the International Court of Justice to show that a vote by a judge in favour of a judgment does not necessarily indicate his agreement on all points. In international arbitral practice, Senegal maintained, 'because of the majority rule applicable to the adoption of arbitral decisions, an arbitrator's vote must prevail over his separate opinion or declaration'. 'The primacy of the decision adopted by a majority vote ... is ... an expression of the very nature of the international adjudicating mechanism. The operative provisions adopted by a majority constitute in fact the sole common denominator of the majority judges, although they may not necessarily attract on all points the support of all these judges ... absolute primacy has ... been recognised for the operative provisions voted by a majority but ... all members of the adjudicating body have been authorised to express their separate views ...'. Senegal added that, if there were no rule assuring the primacy of decisions adopted by majority vote, at the end of every litigation the loser could ferret out contradictions between the vote and separate opinions with the aim of alleging that the decision is inexistent or null and void. It concluded that 'it is inherent in the nature of an international judgment or award rendered by a collegiate body that the decisions cannot have the precision which each member of the body would have separately desired. The drafting of the decision is always the result of a compromise, so that the final text reflects the agreement of the majority rather than the precise text desired by any one of the members'.[10]

---

[9] Arbitral Award of 31 July 1989, *Memorial Submitted by the Government of the Republic of Guinea-Bissau*, Volume I, at pp. 75, 76, 83.

[10] Arbitral Award of 31 July 1989, *Counter-Memorial Submitted by the Government of the Republic of Senegal*, at pp. 63, 64, 65.

IV. THE JUDGMENT OF THE COURT

11-17 In disposing of these conflicting contentions, the court, after finding that in fact there was no contradiction between the position adopted by the tribunal and that preferred by President Barberis in his declaration, held:

> Furthermore, even if there had been any contradiction ... between the view expressed by President Barberis and that stated in the Award, such contradiction could not prevail over the position which President Barberis had taken when voting the Award. In agreeing to the Award, he definitively agreed to the decisions, which it incorporated, as to the extent of the maritime areas governed by the 1960 Agreement, and as to the Tribunal not being required to answer the second question in view of its answer to the first. As the practice of international tribunals shows, it sometimes happens that a member of a tribunal votes in favour of a decision of the tribunal even though he might individually have been inclined to prefer another solution. The validity of his vote remains unaffected by the expression of any such differences in a declaration or separate opinion of the member concerned, which are therefore without consequence for the decision of the tribunal.[11]

11-18 The court accordingly held that the contention of Guinea-Bissau that the award was inexistent for lack of a real majority cannot be accepted.

11-19 It is striking that on this question the court was unanimous. That unanimity embraced the judge *ad hoc* appointed by Guinea-Bissau, Professor Hubert Thierry, this being one of the very few cases in the history of the court in which a judge *ad hoc* has voted against the position of the party appointing him – or her (the earliest example being that of Judge Suzanne Bastid). On the other issue of whether the tribunal failed to fulfil its mandate by not answering the second question, the court divided, rejecting by a majority of 11 to four the contention that the award was null and void.

11-20 In some of the separate and dissenting opinions, the court's unanimous rejection of the claim of a fictitious majority was elaborated. Judge Oda, while finding the Declaration of President Barberis consistent with the award, held that, even if the Declaration had contradicted the finding for which President Barberis had voted, it could at most be regarded 'as a *post facto* change of mind incapable

---

[11] Arbitral Award of 31 July 1989 [1991] *ICJ Reports* 64-65.

of affecting the existence of the *collective* judicial act as to which he had given not only his vote but also his signature'.[12] Judge Lachs, in referring to 'the unusual relationship between the Award and the presidential declaration', declared that the latter was 'simply an appendix added after the Award had come into being with the casting of votes ... the appended text ... cannot undo the decision itself'.[13] Judge Ni observed that, 'The vote is the most reliable indication as to whether or not' President Barberis concurred in the award. The declaration was not part of the award. It represents only the view of the author. 'It is the operative part, and in particular the voting, that counts.' He noted that Guinea-Bissau had criticised Senegal for taking refuge behind legal formalism.

11-21 'But judges or arbitrators do not vote as a mere matter of formality. They do so in order to express their precise positron. They are fully aware of the substantive implications of their vote. The vote indicates their final decision. If the Declaration, as in this case, raises an uncertainty as to whether a judge or arbitrator concurs with or dissents from a judgment or an award, it is the vote that constitutes the authentic expression of his attitude.'[14]

11-22 Judge Weeramantry, who dissented, on this issue agreed that the award must be treated as a majority award and that the plea of inexistence failed.
The court relied 'on the practice of international tribunals' as showing that the validity of a vote remains unaffected by any differences expressed by an arbitrator. But it did not specify that practice.

11-23 It did not have far to look. In 1984, the court was called upon to review a Judgment of the United Nations Administrative Tribunal, *Yakimetz* v. *The Secretary-General of the United Nations*. The critical issue was, had Yakimetz, a national of – and defector from – the USSR, received 'every reasonable consideration' for a career appointment in the United Nations Secretariat. The tribunal's majority, composed of two members one of whom was President Ustor, held that Mr Yakimetz had received such consideration, essentially because the Secretary-General said that he had. While voting for this holding, President Ustor nevertheless appended a statement maintaining that Yakimetz was not eligible for a career appointment because, having been seconded from USSR government service, he was ineligible not only for an extension of his

---

[12] *ibid.*, at p. 83.
[13] *ibid.*, at p. 94.
[14] *ibid.*, at pp. 98-99.

fixed-term appointment but for its conversion into any other type of appointment without the consent of the government concerned. Vice-President Kean took a third view, namely, that Yakimetz had not in fact received reasonable consideration for an appointment in contradiction of the terms of the governing resolution of the General Assembly. The court observed that if the remaining member of the tribunal had shared the view of President Ustor, the judgment would have been drafted to convey the view of the two-member majority that Yakimetz's secondment from USSR government service was an absolute bar to his obtaining a career appointment, so that the question of 'reasonable consideration' would not arise.[15]

11-24 The analogy between the declaration of President Barberis and the statement of President Ustor is plain. In both cases, the tribunal presidents made clear that they would have preferred a decidedly different judgment than the one rendered. In both cases, they nevertheless voted for the less preferable judgment which, only by their vote, was adopted. It may be noted that, while the *Yakimetz* judgment of the tribunal was challenged in court on multiple grounds, it was not claimed by counsel for Yakimetz nor thought by the International Court of Justice to be 'inexistent', or a nullity, on the ground that there was a lack of a genuine majority for the judgment adopted.

11-25 Other contemporaneous practice may be found in judgments of the Iran–United States Claims Tribunal. There are numerous judgments in which an arbitrator stated candidly that he voted for a judgment, not because he wholly agreed with it but because he thought it right for a majority to provide a decision. Thus, to take one of several examples, in *Granite State Machine Co. Inc.* v. *The Islamic Republic of Iran et al.*, Judge Mosk concurring stated that he did so because he thought it right to bring protracted deliberations to an end, deliberations which otherwise must continue 'until a majority, and probably a compromise solution has been reached ... I concur ... in order to form a majority so that an award can be rendered.' He quoted Professor Pieter Sanders observing that, 'If no majority can be reached, no award can be rendered, thus creating great injustice to the parties'.[16]

---

[15] 'Application for Review of Judgment No. 333 of the United Nations Administrative Tribunal, Advisory opinion' [1987] *ICJ Reports* 18.
[16] 1 *Iran–United States CTR*, at pp. 442, 450, 451.

V. Conclusions

11-26 What conclusions may be drawn from the case concerning the Arbitral Award of 31 July 1989 and the practice on which it relies?[17]

11-27 Perhaps the first is that arbitrators, especially presiding arbitrators, should exercise caution in setting out positions which are or may be seen as differing from those for which they have voted. The risk of misunderstanding may be less in a large court such as the International Court of Justice where, if one or another judge expresses views which do not sit well with his vote, in any event that vote rarely is critical to the majority. But two-to-one votes are common in international arbitration. If an arbitrator expresses views at sharp variance with his vote, while his vote will stand he may roil the parties and prejudice the execution of the award.

11-28 A second conclusion is that to demonstrate that an arbitral award is 'inexistent' may be theoretically feasible but is practically difficult. Suppose that the award in this case, while requiring a majority vote for adoption, received the favourable vote of only one arbitrator; there would be no award. Or suppose that there was a majority but a lack of genuine will because an arbitrator forming part of that majority was coerced or insane. Such a majority could not produce a valid award. One can imagine such cases but their occurrence will surely be very rare.

11-29 A third conclusion is that the more frequent and plausible claim may be that an arbitral award is a nullity. If a tribunal has exceeded its powers; if there was corruption on the part of a member of the tribunal; if there has been a failure to state the reasons for the award or a serious departure from a fundamental rule of procedure; if the undertaking to arbitrate itself is a nullity – in such cases there may be ground for declaring the nullity of an arbitral award. These cases too will be rare but presumably less difficult to carry than a claim of 'inexistence'.

---

[17] The case has attracted analysis. See in particular, Lucius Caflisch, 'Valeur et effet des declarations faites par des juges ou arbitres internationaux', in *International Law in an Evolving World, Liber Amicorum in tribute to Eduardo,Jiménez de Aréchaga* (Fundacion de Culture Universitaria, Montevideo, 1994), Vol. II, at p. 1159. This lecture has drawn with the permission of the publishers from a paper by the author, 'The Majority Vote of an International Arbitral Tribunal', first published in *Etudes de droit international en l'honneur de Pierre Lalive*, (eds C. Dominicé, C. Reymond and R. Patry) (Editions Helbing & Lichtenbahn 1993) and republished in *The American Review of International Arbitration 1991* and in Stephen M. Schwebel, *Justice in International Law* (Cambridge, CUP 1994).

Moreover, a holding of nullity – at any rate, nullity *ab initio*– will in substance encompass what a holding of inexistence would.

11-30   A final observation is this. The claim of Guinea-Bissau in the end boiled down to the complaint that the tribunal had voted for what it could muster a majority for rather than for what a majority of its members thought to be right. That complaint was well-founded. But it did not follow that the resultant award was inexistent, null and void, or even voidable. On the contrary, so much of the judicial and arbitral process is characterised by judges and arbitrators voting to form a majority rather than voting to express what each of them may see as the optimum judgment. In a collective body, there is very frequently a process of accommodation of differing views, sometimes sharply differing views. The result may be the consecration of the least common denominator. That may not be a noble result, but it is a practical result. It is better than no result. Judgments of the International Court of Justice sometimes are criticised for the brevity of their ultimate holdings, for the sparsity of the reasoning supporting the *dispositif.* Such criticism may be understandable, but it evidences a misunderstanding of the collective judicial process, which above all is directed towards the rendering of a decision. It may not be the optimum decision but it is better than no decision. So much of the process of writing a judgment is a process of eliminating points and passages on which majority agreement cannot be reached.

11-31   In short, the judicial and arbitral process is an exemplar of the wise dictum that the best must not be permitted to be the enemy of the good.

*Kenneth Rokison QC**

CHAPTER 12

'PASTURES NEW'

(REVIEW OF ARBITRATION ACT 1996)**

12-1 In England, things tend to take rather a long time to come to fruition. The members of the Departmental Advisory Committee, set up under the Chairmanship of Lord Mustill in 1985 to advise Ministers on the reforms desirable in arbitration law, were guilty at times of letting the grass grow under their feet. This too follows an English tradition. The story is told of an American tourist who asked the head gardener in Trinity College, Cambridge, how he managed to get the lawn in Great Court to look so good. 'You just mow it for 500 years', was his somewhat condescending reply. Arbitration practitioners in London have just moved to a new pasture which, if not yet mowed for 500 years, has taken some time to grow to a stage in which the animals can be let loose to graze upon it.

12-2 For the most part, it is far too soon to tell how the new Arbitration Act will work in practice. The objectives of some aspects of the Act have obviously been achieved. It was designed to consolidate the statutory law of arbitration into one statute and it has achieved this task. As a consequence, English arbitration law is easier to identify.

12-3 Coupled with this consolidation of the law, the Act was designed to re-state English arbitration law, broadly following the pattern of the UNCITRAL Model Law. But perhaps more importantly, the law has now been expressed in plain

* 20 Essex Street.
** This is a revised version of the 1997 School of International Arbitration Freshfields Arbitration Lecture delivered in London on 4 February 1998. The editors acknowledge with thanks permission to publish this contribution by Freshfields and the School of International Arbitration Centre for Commercial Law Studies, Queen Mary and Westfield College, London University.

Julian D.M. Lew and Loukas A. Mistelis(eds), Arbitration Insights, 213-222
© 2007 Kluwer Law International. Printed in the Netherlands

language, which can hopefully be understood by ordinary people possessing a reasonable degree of literacy and not merely by lawyers trained in the mysteries of statutory 'legalese'. This was the important contribution of the last of the 'head gardeners' – Lord Saville. All this has made English arbitration law more accessible.

12-4 The new Act does not purport to be comprehensive and some areas of law were, in the current climate, regarded as being too controversial or even too difficult to be the subject of legislation, one example being the vexed question of consolidation. But some modifications of substance have been made, which could, over the years, transform the practice of arbitration in London. In particular, there has been a quite fundamental alteration of the balance of power between arbitrators and the courts, and an unprecedented flexibility has been given to the parties and the tribunal as regards the conduct of arbitrations.

12-5 With regard to the relationship between the courts and arbitrators and the respective functions and powers of each, one must consider two aspects: the powers given to arbitrators and the court's power of review in relation to arbitrators' decisions. It is probably true to say that the majority of those who include arbitration clauses in their contracts, and certainly those few who refer a specific dispute to 'ad hoc' arbitration, do so because they do not wish their disputes and their commercial relationship to be referred to a national court, whether out of a desire for privacy or a fear or a suspicion of bias. Furthermore, although there are some functions which can only be effectively fulfilled by the courts – such as the stay of legal proceedings when a valid arbitration clause applies, or the filling of a vacancy when the appointment procedure breaks down – there are other functions, such as the power to order a claimant to provide security of costs, which can just as conveniently be dealt with by the arbitration tribunal. It must be right in principle that, if parties have opted to have their disputes resolved by a chosen arbitration tribunal rather than by the courts, such decisions should be taken by the arbitration tribunal and the courts should not interfere.

12-6 The House of Lords' decision in Ken Ren,[1] which maintained the courts' jurisdiction to order security for costs in relation to an arbitration, did much to damage London's reputation as an acceptable international arbitration venue, even though it was emphasised that such jurisdiction would only be exercised sparingly. London had painstakingly been seeking to rebuild its reputation since the 1979 Act abolished the 'special case' procedure and paved the way for the significant reduction in the extent of the courts' intervention by way of reviews of arbitrators' decisions on law.[2] The decision was, understandably, not well received either in England or abroad.

12-7 The 1996 Act removed the courts' power to order security for costs in relation to arbitration proceedings and gave it to arbitration tribunals.[3] In principle this can only be regarded as a move in the right direction. But arbitrators are not as yet experienced in this rather difficult exercise of discretion, consisting as it does in balancing the genuine interests of a respondent faced with a potentially expensive defence of what might turn out to be an unmeritorious claim, with those of a claimant with a potentially good claim who can ill afford to put up security for the respondent's costs as well as paying for his own. This particular clump of grass may prove for some a little indigestible!

12-8 The 1996 Act has not only specifically given arbitrators a substantial bundle of powers over interlocutory matters hitherto regarded as matters of court, but has cemented this reallocation by providing that those powers given to arbitrators cannot be exercised by the court. This change is quite fundamental. It passes to arbitrators a substantial bundle of powers, but only time will tell whether they will rise to the challenge, by being prepared in appropriate cases to exercise these powers and to do so wisely. So far very few arbitrators seem to have exercised the draconian power of dismissing a claim for want of prosecution by making an award against a dilatory claimant even though this power was first given to arbitrators in the Courts and Legal Services Act of 1990. It is now enshrined in section 41(3) of the 1996 Act.[4]

---

[1]   *Coppée-Lavalin SA/NV v. Ken Ren Chemicals and Fertilisers Ltd* [1995] 1 AC 38, [1994] 2 Lloyds Rep. 109. The case has attracted analysis. See *in particular*, B. Davenport, 'The Ken-Ren Case: Much Ado About Nothing Very Much' in (1994) 10 *Arbitration International* 3 at p. 303; D. Branson, 'The Ken-Ren Case: It is an Ado Where More Aid is Less Help' in (1994) 10 *Arbitration International* 3 at p. 313.

[2]   s. 1(1), Arbitration Act 1979, see Mustill & Boyd, *Commercial Arbitration* (1989, 2nd ed.) at p. 709.

[3]   s. 38(3), Arbitration Act 1996.

[4]   s. 41(3):

12-9 Further, it must be borne in mind that the provisions of the 1996 Act are not limited in their application to international arbitrations, but apply generally to all arbitrations whose seat is in England or Wales. These powers are therefore given to many arbitrators who are not legally qualified and not experienced in the exercise of such powers or indeed of the way in which they are exercised by others.

12-10 Regarding the question of the courts' review of arbitrators' decisions in law, the 1996 Act has not on the face of it done much to reduce potential court intervention and has not apparently given full effect to the presumed intention of the parties that all aspects of the merits of their dispute should be decided by their chosen tribunal and not by the court. In most jurisdictions, judicial review of arbitrators' decisions is unknown or has been abolished, except where the arbitration tribunal has been guilty of some procedural irregularity amounting to a denial of justice. The UNCITRAL Model Law does not provide for any general grounds of review. English law however has been slow to acknowledge and respect the autonomy of the parties in this respect. This was undoubtedly the principal reason for the comparative unpopularity of London as a venue for international arbitrations, especially those administered by the ICC in Paris, before the 1979 Act.

12-11 Anecdotal evidence suggests that some parties positively welcomed the security against potentially questionable or even perverse decisions by arbitrators, which the English courts' willingness to intervene by way of review provided. There were indeed some who mourned and no doubt still mourn the passing of the special case procedure. But they are a small minority. English law has nevertheless resisted complete and fundamental change. The 1979 Act abolished the appeal by way of 'special case' but retained the possibility of an appeal on a point of law, with leave of the Court; the House of Lords in The Nema[5] closed the door to a significant extent by interpreting the 1979 Act in a way which could hardly be justified by a mere exercise in construction.

'If the tribunal is satisfied that there has been inordinate and inexcusable delay on the part of the claimant in pursuing his claim and that the delay (a) gives rise, or is likely to give rise, to a substantial risk that it is not possible to have a fair resolution of the issues in that claim, or (b) has caused, or is likely to cause serious prejudice to the respondent, the tribunal may make an award dismissing the claim'.

[5] *BTP Tioxide Ltd v. Pioneer Shipping Ltd and Armada Marine SA, The Nema*, [1982] AC 724, [1980] 2 Lloyd's Rep. 83 at 339 and [1981] 2 Lloyd's Rep. 239.

12-12 However, the 1979 Act qualified the parties' right to exclude the possibility of an appeal to the courts (except after a dispute had arisen) within the special categories of shipping, insurance and commodity trading. These were the very categories of commercial activity in relation to which parties had tended to adopt arbitration clauses generally in their standard contract forms. The justification for the existence of these 'special categories' was that allowing unrestricted exclusion agreements would deny the courts the opportunity to develop the commercial law through the many cases which came before the court by way of appeal. It seemed to many an extraordinary exercise in chauvinism that parties should have their expressed wishes ignored, so that they could in effect pay for the development of English commercial law for the benefit of others, and at the same time have their presumed desire for confidentiality, or at least privacy, sacrificed in favour of permanent publicity through the Law Reports or other specialist reports of court decisions. Thankfully, these 'special categories' have now been abolished by the 1996 Act.[6] Commercial parties who do not wish their disputes to be susceptible of appeal to the courts and are content to abide by the arbitrators' decision, can now agree to exclude any right of appeal.

12-13 However, the 1996 Act was not designed to introduce radical or controversial change. The *Nema* 'guidelines' have therefore been given statutory force and an appeal to the courts by way of review of an arbitral tribunal's decision on a question of law is still possible. It may seem unfortunate that a statute which has gone so far down the path of recognising and giving effect to party autonomy has not taken the final step of abolishing judicial review of the merits, whether of fact or of law, especially since it will be some time before further valuable parliamentary time will be allocated to arbitration law reform. It is hoped that the gradual process which has been made since the passing of the 1979 Act will continue, and that the judges will not only apply the new statutory provisions reflecting *The Nema* guidelines strictly but will also give full effect to the additional requirement introduced by section 69(3)(d) of the 1996 Act, that 'despite the agreement of the parties to resolve the matter by arbitration it is just and proper in all circumstances for the Court to determine the question'. How this further limitation will be interpreted and applied by the courts seem to me to be of fundamental importance. Surely, in principle such cases should be rare.

---

[6] Johan Steyn, 'The "Special Categories" under the English Arbitration Act 1979. Memorandum from the Departmental Advisory Committee on Arbitration' in (1993) 9 *Arbitration International* 4 at p. 405.

12-14 Otherwise, the most important provisions of the 1996 Act are those which emphasise the very wide discretion arbitrators enjoy as to the procedure to be adopted in resolving the particular dispute before them. In the 1950s and 1960s commercial arbitration in London was still largely conducted by 'amateurs'. Most arbitrators were not professional arbitrators or even lawyers but were involved in the same trade as the disputing parties. In maritime arbitration, for example, the majority of arbitrations were handled by a few leading arbitrators who had built up their expertise within the shipping business, knew both parties and had probably done business with them. Arbitrations were informal. Where parties were represented by lawyers, they too entered into the spirit of informality. Commonly, the arbitration tribunal was made up of an umpire and two arbitrators who, if they disagreed, often acted as advocates on behalf of their respective appointing parties. The same applied to disputes arising within the commodity trades, whose standard form provided for arbitration by members of the trade, and a right of appeal to an appeal board or committee of senior members of the Trade Association concerned. In some cases the parties were represented by lawyers but often the arbitrators presented the dispute to the Appeal Board.

12-15 In my first arbitration appeal before the Appeal Committee of the General Produce Brokers Association the chairman opened the proceedings by announcing, 'This is a commercial arbitration and we are going to hold it in a commercial manner. First we will hear the parties on the facts and then the lawyers on the law'. At first I, together with all the other lawyers present, including the Association's legal adviser, was taken aback, but on reflection the proposal was full of practical common sense.

12-16 There were, I believe, few large international commercial arbitrations held in London outside the maritime and commodities trades. Only a handful of arbitrations were conducted under the auspices of the ICC, who, out of a dislike or distrust of the special case procedure, rarely if ever nominated London as the seat of arbitration if the parties themselves had not chosen it. The London Court of International Arbitration was, at that time, virtually moribund. Over the years this position has changed: London now hosts a vast number of international commercial arbitrations of all kinds.

12-17 But, far too many arbitrations in England have in recent years been conducted in all respects like proceedings in the High Court, with formal pleadings, often drafted by junior counsel, admitting, averring or even denying each and every allegation 'as if set out and traversed seriatim', with English-type discovery and with hours and sometimes days of cross-examination. Witnesses are taken painstakingly through prepared witness statements. Experts are called on both sides to tell expert arbitrators what they already know. Lengthy submissions, volumes of photostatted authorities and box upon box of documents are submitted. Arbitrators who sit outwardly patient are often inwardly grinding their teeth, for days, weeks, months and in extreme cases years. Furthermore, arbitrators are frequently copied in on all the vitriolic correspondence passing between the respective firms of solicitors in which each tries to score cheap points off the other in as offensive a way as possible. Those who indulge in this practice may regard it as a game but should realise that it is not only expensive but generally counter-productive.

12-18   The reason for all this I suspect is that in most London solicitors' firms, those conducting international arbitrations are members of the litigation department. They and the counsel they brief therefore handle a mixed case load. Only a few of the largest firms have their specialists in international arbitration and only a few counsel can claim to be arbitration specialists. Consequently arbitration, like litigation, has become too cumbersome and too expensive and has thereby failed to offer the commercial community an attractive alternative to litigation in the courts. Only a few areas, like maritime arbitrations under the auspices of the LMAA, whose members still determine a large proportion of their cases on documents alone after informal submissions, are conducted quickly and comparatively cheaply.

12-19   It is therefore not surprising that mediation or conciliation under the new label of Alternative Dispute Resolution (ADR) has taken a firm hold in the UK and increasingly elsewhere in Europe. There were many in the field of arbitration who were sceptical and tended to dismiss ADR as a nine-day wonder. But their scepticism and their complacency were misplaced as most will now admit. There is no doubt that arbitration has significant advantages over ADR, especially since the end product is a binding award widely enforceable throughout the world. But to maintain its dominant position in the resolution of international commercial disputes, arbitration has to change and has to rediscover its roots. Furthermore, those involved in arbitration in London have to change their practices if they are to maintain the important position that London still enjoys.

12-20   The 1996 Act makes it clear that, although there may be cases in which a mirror image of High Court proceedings may be appropriate, arbitrators are encouraged to adopt a wholly flexible approach and to tailor the pattern of proceedings both before and at the oral hearing according to the needs of the particular case. Arbitration is consensual and the members of the tribunal are therefore the servants of the parties. But despite section 34(1) of the Act which states that 'It shall be for the Tribunal to decide all procedural matters subject to the rights of the parties to agree in any matter', the arbitrators should not necessarily comply with the wishes of the parties' lawyers.

12-21 Section 1 of the Act states the general principles upon which the operative part of the Act is founded and according to which its provisions will be construed. According to the first of these principles, the object of arbitration is to obtain the fair resolution of disputes by an impartial tribunal 'without unnecessary delay or expense'. This general principle is clearly reflected in section 33(1)(b), one of the mandatory provisions of the Act, which states that the tribunal shall adopt procedures suitable to the circumstances of the particular case, avoiding unnecessary delay or expense, so as to provide a fair means for the resolution of the matters failing to be determined.

12-22 Further, the Act, by another mandatory provision, section 40(1), imposes on the parties an obligation to do all the things necessary for the proper and expeditious conduct of the arbitral proceedings. Consequently, if the parties' legal representatives insist on adopting procedures which the arbitral tribunal considers will result in unnecessary delay or expense, the tribunal should not hesitate to take steps to ensure that the parties themselves are made fully aware of the circumstances, including the fact that the tribunal considers that the procedure which the lawyers wish to adopt is inappropriate. However, despite section 40(1), it is probably the case that it is the parties who have the final say: as they should perhaps in what remains a consensual procedure.

12-23 True, section 65[7] gives the Tribunal the very useful sanction of directing that the recoverable cost of the arbitration or any part of the arbitral proceedings shall be limited to a specific amount. But even this power is subject to any contrary agreement by the parties. In cases where parties insist on adopting a

---

[7] s. 65:

> (1) 'Unless otherwise agreed by the parties, the tribunal may direct that the recoverable costs of the arbitration or of any part of the arbitral proceedings, shall be limited to a specified amount. (2) Any direction may be made or varied at any stage, but this must be done sufficiently in advance of the incurring of costs to which it relates, or the taking of any steps in the proceedings which may be affected by it, for the limit to be taken into account'.

wholly inappropriate procedure, the arbitrator's only and ultimate sanction is to resign. But, I suggest, this stage will rarely, if ever, be reached.

12-24 The wide discretion given to arbitrators as to the procedure to be adopted is for the most part not new. Even before the 1996 Act, arbitrators sitting in England were not obliged to comply with or follow court procedure, and, in many areas of commercial conflict such as maritime and commodity trades, generally did not do so. Furthermore, in several large ad hoc international arbitrations, experienced arbitrators have for many years been adopting a flexible approach in an attempt to minimise unnecessary delay and expense. Orders for discovery were limited to documents or classes of documents the production of which was clearly necessary in the interests of justice, and strict time limits were imposed on oral submissions as well as cross-examination. Indeed, in my limited experience sitting as a member of a true international tribunal with other members from other legal backgrounds, and in particular from civil law countries, I have been pleasantly surprised at the extent to which we have, instinctively, tended to adopt a similar approach to matters of procedure, with very little dissent. But with the threat of allegations of misconduct or 'serious procedural irregularity' hanging over them, less experienced arbitrators in London were reluctant to seek to impose what might be regarded as novel procedures on parties, preferring instead to allow the lawyers to follow the same practice they would have adopted had the matter been proceeding in the English Commercial Court.

12-25 The achievement of the 1996 Act was to emphasise that the arbitrators not only have the right but a positive duty to ensure that the procedure they adopt will avoid unnecessary delay or expense. Thus, they should no longer simply go along with a carbon copy of High Court-type procedure without considering whether it is appropriate to do so. This imposes a new obligation on arbitrators, which is not necessarily easily fulfilled. This is the new challenge to arbitrators to which they must rise.

12-26 Only time will tell whether or not the new Arbitration Act will achieve its principal objectives. It has had a flying start, not least because of the enormous public relations exercise which has been conducted to publicise it has been almost universally praised. The significant increase in referrals of new cases last year to the LCIA, the number of which almost doubled compared to the previous year (a trend which has continued in 1998), suggests that it has had considerable effect. But complacency is not yet appropriate.

12-27   The 1996 Act took a long time to come to fruition and was the product of a considerable amount of research and hard work, discussion and consultation. It owes much to the inspired leadership and guidance of its successive chairmen Sir Michael Mustill, Sir Johan Steyn and Sir Mark Saville. It is a good Act; one to be proud of. But it should not be regarded as an end in itself. Rather, it offers a new beginning. The gate is open. The fresh green grass awaits. Alone the 1996 Act will certainly not ensure that arbitration in London will continue to flourish. But it presents an opportunity and a challenge to the courts and more especially to arbitrators, who, if they adopt the bold approach which I have advocated will now at least have the comfort of knowing that they enjoy immunity under section 29(1).[8]

---

[8]   s. 29(1):

> 'An arbitrator is not liable for anything done or omitted in the discharge or purported discharge of his functions as arbitrator unless the act or omission is shown to have been in bad faith'.

*Gerold Herrmann**[*]*

CHAPTER 13

DOES THE WORLD NEED ADDITIONAL UNIFORM LEGISLATION ON ARBITRATION?[**]

I. INTRODUCTION

13-1 What an honour to be invited to the Holy Grail of Freshfields Arbitration Lecturers, and this as one of the few invitees not born on the island where the Knights of the Round Table assemble. Upon receipt of the honouring invitation, I asked some English friends for suggestions as to a suitable and interesting topic. None of them made a positive proposal; but they all agreed in the negative by telling me unanimously: 'Please, not another talk on the new English Arbitration Act! ... and certainly not by a civil lawyer!'

13-2 What a pity, since it prevents me from presenting with relish the following quotation from one of the commentaries: 'When, over 15 years ago, the United Nations Commission on International Trade Law (UNCITRAL) decided to prepare a draft uniform law on arbitration procedure, its members could hardly have imagined that their proposal would lead to a revolution in the practice of

[*] Dr jur. (Cologne); LL.M. (Berkeley, Cal.); Honorary Professor (Vienna); [former] Secretary of UNCITRAL (the views expressed in this paper are personal ones and do not necessarily reflect the views of the Organisation); [President of ICCA]; Member of ICCA, LCIA Court, Presiding Council of International Arbitration Court of Austrian Economic Chamber, Consultative Commission of WIPO Arbitration Center, and Board of ACICA.
[**] This is a slightly revised version of the 1998 School of International Arbitration Freshfields Arbitration Lecture delivered in London on 10 November 1998. The editors acknowledge with thanks permission to publish this contribution by Freshfields and the School of International Arbitration, Centre for Commercial Law Studies, Queen Mary and Westfield College, London University.

Julian D.M. Lew and Loukas A. Mistelis (eds), Arbitration Insights, 223-255
© 2007 Kluwer Law International. Printed in the Netherlands

arbitration in England. Yet such a revolution is the likely consequence of the Arbitration Act 1996'.[1]

13-3 The conclusion is obvious: England would not have that Act today without the earlier advent of the UNCITRAL Model Law. We clearly have come a long way since the mid-eighties, where an extremely influential judge warned against the theoretical or abstract French concepts sweeping over the Channel and saw the Model Law for quite some time (at least until Scotland adopted it) as being potentially useful exclusively for underdeveloped countries where arbitration was not practised anyway. As far as England is concerned, he predicted at the 1982 Annual Conference of the Chartered Institute of Arbitrators as the consequence of the Law coming into being that 'the whole of our arbitration law would have to change and that, in turn, would lead to a revolution'.[2]

13-4 I fondly remember the raging debates about the Model Law in London, with the Financial Times quoting me calling Professor Francis Mann a 'sloppy reader', in response to him inexplicably calling us 'sloppy draftsmen' – or with the Master of the Rolls John Donaldson calling me the father of the Model Law, which I had to ask him to downgrade to the status of midwife (in view of the expert input from fathers from all regions and different types of countries).

13-5 Actually there were so many discussions in England on the Model Law that a sentiment, similar to the above 1996 saturation, developed: 'Please, not another talk about the Model Law'. This Model Law saturation or fatigue may well have been one of the psychological reasons for England not to follow Jan Paulsson's advice: 'Take the Model Law, add a dash or two of London bitter and the English cocktail will be loved by the many jurisdictions traditionally guided by English law; otherwise your legal children will run away and take the Model Law as is'.

13-6 As we all know today, this is exactly what happened. These 'runaway children' of common law tradition were the first to embrace the Model Law – with, fortunately, many civil law jurisdictions following suit. We have Model Law countries in all continents, of all sizes and all stages of economic development, covering altogether more than one quarter of the world's territory. And more are likely to join in soon, such as Croatia, Greece, Honduras, Korea,

---

[1] B. Harris, R. Planterose and J. Tecks, *The Arbitration Act 1996 – A Commentary* (1996) at p. 1.
[2] As reported by Shilston, 'A View from the 1982 Annual Conference of the Chartered Institute of Arbitrators' in (1983) 49 *Arbitration* 291 at pp. 291-292.

Kyrgyzstan, Macau, Mauritania, Moldova, Mongolia, Mozambique, the Philippines, South Africa and Thailand.

13-7 As I have described elsewhere,[3] the model-law technique, as compared to the convention approach, has proven to be very successful not only in terms of numbers of jurisdictions and in terms of speed of implementation, but also in terms of the level of harmonisation: deviations from the Model Law text have, as a rule, very rarely been made, except for three countries (i.e. Bulgaria, Egypt and India), in two of which most of the deviations in fact reiterate proposals which had been advanced unsuccessfully by the representatives of those countries to the Model Law sessions of UNCITRAL. Remembering the main argument in favour of the model-law technique, namely its flexibility, which allows adjustment to local requirements, I must say that I am still waiting for the first deviation which bears a substantive connection with local conditions. Unfortunately, we do not have to wait for the first cases of real trouble caused by deviations: these have already occurred, in India with its prohibition of an even number of arbitrators and in Egypt with additional grounds for setting aside.

13-8 While deviations have been rare, most national enactments have added provisions on issues not addressed by the Model Law. Many of those issues had been discussed during the preparation of the Model Law but, for one reason or another, were not included in the final text. The disparity between national answers to those and other issues has led to suggestions to consider the preparation of uniform answers, taking into account also, of course, any answers provided by other modern arbitration laws not classified as Model Law enactments (e.g. Dutch, English, French and Swiss laws). Related suggestions have been made at the 1998 ICCA Congress in Paris[4] and UNCITRAL's New York Convention Day on 10 June 1998[5] concerning matters governed by the 1958 New York Convention and the 1961 European Convention, as well as other points possibly to be addressed in a future convention or model law.

---

[3] Herrmann, 'The UNCITRAL Arbitration Law: a Good Model of a Model Law' in (1998) *Uniform Law Review* at p. 483.

[4] *Improving the Efficiency of Arbitration Agreements and Awards: Forty Years of Application of the New York Convention* (ICCA Congress Series No. 9, XIVth International Arbitration Congress, Paris 1998, van den Berg (ed.)).

[5] *Enforcing Arbitration Awards under the New York Convention – Experience and Prospects* (United Nations, New York, Sales No. E. 99.V.2, 1999).

13-9 What I intend to do here is to survey those suggestions, various others made at yet other occasions, and add some of my own. My primary focus will be on the substance of the proposals for legislation; I will not focus on the most adequate form of legislation, i.e. a new convention or, as my current tentative hunch would indicate, a Model Law Supplement. Yet, a major question will be whether legislative treatment of any, some or all of the suggested issues is desirable and feasible. In examining this question, regard should be had to the actual impact of a problem, to the state of the current discussion and the maturity of the suggested answers and, above all, to the question whether the expected benefits of harmonisation outweigh the possible disadvantage of ossifying matters and thus impeding future development. This latter, very important concern is somewhat less strong for a model law than a convention and could be softened, as is UNCITRAL's tradition, by focusing in legislative texts on fundamental rules of principle, providing an enabling statutory framework, and leaving the detail of ever-changing practices to sets of rules at the contractual level.

13-10 Many issues need to be addressed, and I can only scratch the surface. The views expressed here are my personal ones which, moreover, are rather tentative. Also, I am presenting more questions than answers. After all, that is what the title promised, and that question will be with us for many years. By the way, after having committed myself to the topic, I remembered the title of Lord Mustill's 1996 Goff Lecture 'Too many laws'; my goose pimples only disappeared when reading his concluding remark in favour of harmonisation of national arbitration laws – even though, as he rightly says, it can never be complete – and about the UNCITRAL Model Law as a great step forward in this respect.[6]

13-11 Indeed, the success of the Model Law provides a good basis and encouragement for future uniform legislation. This lecture should help to solicit the views of as many experts as possible, triggering a worldwide discussion that would assist UNCITRAL in its deliberations in June 1999 and any future elaboration of a uniform law text. Such text could constitute yet another contribution of the United Nations to the global development of international commercial arbitration, in addition to the 1958 New York Convention, the UNCITRAL Arbitration Rules, the UNCITRAL Model Law and the UNCITRAL Notes on Organising Arbitral Proceedings.

---

[6] Lord Mustill, 'The Goff Lecture, Hong Kong 1996 – Too Many Laws' in (1997) 63 *Arbitration* 248 at p.257.

13-12   Let us now look at the first batch of issues, which all relate to the basis of arbitration: the arbitration agreement.

II. THE BASIS OF ARBITRATION

A. 'In Writing'

13-13   The proposal most often made is to adopt a more flexible or liberal definition of written form than that contained in Article II(2) of the New York Convention. The Model Law contains a more embracing formula. Yet, certain situations are arguably not covered, certainly not beyond doubt, and have led to modified formulations in enacting states.

13-14   The problem under the Model Law does not concern technical advances such as the use of electronic data messages; these are covered by the forward-looking term 'means of communication that provide a record of the agreement'. In so far as it is a problem under the New York Convention, states are offered a remedy in the form of another UNCITRAL Model Law, namely that on Electronic Commerce concluded in 1996.[7]

13-15   Rather, the problem arises from the combination of the true question of form and the way the agreement comes about (i.e. its formation), expressed by the unfortunate term 'exchange' (of letters etc.). This term, inherited by the Model Law drafters from the New York Convention, is unfortunate in lending itself to an overly literal interpretation in the sense of mutual exchange (although at the cotton exchange the commodity tends to move only in one direction).

13-16   Fact situations that have posed serious problems under the New York Convention and require at least very extensive, teleological construction of the Model Law, provided that neither estoppel or good faith nor later submission to arbitration can help, include the following: tacit or oral acceptance of written purchase order or of written sales confirmation; orally concluded contract referring to written general conditions or e.g. Lloyd's form of salvage; certain brokers' notes, bills of lading and other instruments or contracts granting rights to non-signing third parties.

---

[7]   UNCITRAL Model Law on Electronic Commerce with Guide to Enactment 1996, available – like any other UNCITRAL text – in brochure form as a United Nations publication and on the UNCITRAL website: http://www.un.or.at/uncitral.

13-17 Courts have reached rather disparate decisions in those situations, often reflective of their general attitude towards arbitration as such. In the great majority of cases, they have been able to hold the parties to their agreement, sometimes using highly creative construction.[8] Some commentators have argued that there is thus no need for a cure at the legislative level since courts are usually able to find a way by modern, updating interpretation. However, I side in this matter with Neil Kaplan QC, who has probably the richest judicial experience on this point. In his 1995 Goff Lecture he forcefully advocated a legislative solution (reminiscent of an abortive Secretariat proposal during the preparation of the Model Law).[9]

13-18 As he had suggested at an earlier Arbitration Conference in Beijing: 'A case can be made out for amending Article 7(2) by permitting an agreement to arbitrate being created by trade custom or usage or a course of dealing or conduct. If an arbitration clause is contained within an otherwise binding agreement why should it be necessary to be able to point to a signature or to a written record of the agreement? Contracts involving millions of dollars are created in this way and it is permissible to ask what is so special about the arbitration clause to require it to comply with Article 7(2)'.[10] Rusty Park has suggested in response that 'there is no reason why a business manager should not be able to accept some provisions of a contract but not others, particularly a stipulation as important as a waiver of the right to go to court'.[11] My personal reply would be: 'Yes, but then he or she should say so'. After all, in an international setting the thrust of an arbitration agreement is not the negative idea of excluding court jurisdiction (which courts, by the way, are you excluding by one arbitration clause in a contract network between a multinational consortium, with engineering and financing involving yet other countries, and a company ordering construction of a plant in yet another country?); rather, it is the positive

---

[8] *e.g.* US Court of Appeals, Fifth Circuit, 23 March 1994, No. 93-3200 (excerpted in (1995) *Y B Comm. Arb.* XX at p. 937) at p. 941, interpreting the conditions of 'signed by the parties or contained in an exchange of letters or telegrams'as relating only to an arbitration agreement (submission) but not to an arbitral clause.

[9] Kaplan, 'Is the Need for Writing as Expressed in the New York Convention and the Model Law Out of Step with Commercial Practice?' in (1996) 12 *Arbitration International* 27 at pp. 44-45.

[10] Kaplan, 'The Model Law in Hong Kong' in *CIETAC/ICCA Papers on International Commercial Arbitration* (Arbitration Research Institute China Chamber of International Commerce 1997) 495 at p. 510.

[11] W. W. Park in his draft contribution on the New York Convention (§37.03 (d)) to the upcoming third edition of W. L. Craig, W. W. Park and J. Paulsson, *International Chamber of Commerce Arbitration*.

idea of creating for an individual case something that does not currently exist, namely an international commercial court. As Yves Fortier QC once put it, international arbitration here is not an alternative, it has become, to a great extent, 'the only game in town'.

13-19 It was precisely for that reason coupled with the realisation that innumerable contracts often of high value are every day concluded over the phone or otherwise orally – that I took the liberty at the 1993 ICCA Conference in Bahrain to recommend full freedom of form (thus replacing for international commercial arbitration agreements the statute of fraud by a statute of liberty).[12]

13-20 I know that Mr Kaplan sympathises with the argument that allowing oral agreements would lead to uncertainty and litigation.[13] However, I doubt whether there would indeed be more litigation in an era of full freedom than either in the current situation of considerable uncertainty or in a possible future one with a more flexible writing requirement worldwide. After all, not to require a certain form for validity's sake does not mean that it is not advisable to use that form, and diligent business people are likely to safeguard their interests by securing and keeping a record in some form or another.

13-21 In fact, what is probably sufficient and may be recommended as a somewhat less radical solution is to allow an oral arbitration clause if the applicable law does not impose any form requirement on the main contract. Such a non-discrimination rule could operate as an exception to a future universal definition of written form which should take care of the instances of half form and third-party effects.

13-22 In order to find the ideal universal rule (short of a 'statute of liberty'), more discussion and study is needed of proposals made during the preparation of the Model Law and especially of the various formulations developed in modern national laws. For short versions one may look at the Dutch and Swiss laws, and for longer versions at the German and English laws. The English (or Hong Kong) formula, while somewhat enigmatic to foreign readers, should be high on the hit-list if Toby Landau is right in saying that it defines writing as including oral

---

[12] Herrmann, 'The Arbitration Agreement as the Foundation of Arbitration and Its Recognition by the Courts' in *ICCA Congress Series No. 6* (ICCA Bahrain Conference 1993) p. 41 at pp. 45-46.
[13] Kaplan, *supra* n. 9 at p. 29.

agreements[14] – a truly diplomatic act of a statute of liberty wrapped in formal attire (a lawyer's delight of a fiction: For the purposes of this law, Easter Bunny means Santa Claus).

13-23   To make the study more useful (and complicated), it should extend to situations of non-signing parties beyond the bill-of-lading context and cover instances of transfer to third parties who were not party to the original agreement. Examples mentioned by Jean-Louis Delvolvé at UNCITRAL's New York Convention Day on 10 June 1998 were the following: universal transfer of assets (successions, mergers, demergers and acquisitions of companies) or specific transfer of assets (transfer of contract or assignment of receivables or debts, novation, subrogation, stipulation in favour of a third party); or, in the case of multiple parties, or groups of contracts or groups of companies, implicit extension of the application of the arbitration agreement to persons who were not expressly parties thereto.[15]

13-24   There remains one important question: how to overcome the overly rigid form requirement in the New York Convention without amending or revising it? (Conventional wisdom justifiedly views tampering with that Convention as inadvisable.) A first method could be to rely on a retrospective spilling-over effect on the interpretation by courts, as advocated for provisions of the Model Law and indeed accepted by courts in Switzerland and elsewhere.[16] However, more conservative courts are less likely to do so and even others could hardly do so if the new rule would allow oral agreements. Another concern – which I do not share – could be that Article II(2) establishes a uniform rule not only for the maximum form required but also for the minimum, and thus prohibits a more liberal interpretation. Albert Jan van den Berg, who promulgated this widely held view in the first edition of his seminal treatise on the New York Convention,[17] has recently questioned that view without, however, reversing himself (yet).[18]

---

[14] Quoted as a 'somewhat sardonic' comment by Chiasson, 'A Precipice Avoided: Judicial Stays and Party Autonomy in International Arbitration' in (1996) *54 The Advocate* 63 at p. 70 (n. 35).

[15] Delvolvé, 'Third parties and the arbitration agreement', *supra* n. 5, p. 19 at p. 20.

[16] *e.g. Compagnie de Navigation et Transports S.A.* v. *MSC (Mediterranean Shipping Company) S.A.*, 16 January 1995, 1st civil division of Swiss Tribunal Fédéral, in *ATF* 121 II 38, relevant excerpts in (1995) 13 *ASA Bulletin* 503 at p. 508.

[17] A. J. van den Berg, *The New York Arbitration Convention of 1958* (Kluwer 1981) at pp. 178-180.

[18] A. J. van den Berg, 'The New York Convention: Its Intended Effects, Its Interpretation, Salient Problem Areas', in (1996) *ASA Special Series No. 9*, p. 25 at pp. 44-45.

13-25 A second method could be to rely on the more favourable law provision of Article VII of the New York Convention. I am aware that Professor van den Berg continues to see this avenue as promising only if the national law provides a full enforcement mechanism, since the Convention becomes inapplicable *in toto*.[19] I do not share this view and rather perceive the Article as an emanation of '*favor executionis*' in any relevant aspect, i.e. 'pro-enforcement bias', without getting too biased. Contemporary rules concerning formal validity tend to be liberal in providing optional references to various applicable laws. I would suggest adding the laws referenced in Article V(1)(a) for substantive validity (why should the solution for formal validity be more onerous than that for substantive validity?). Thus, effect would be given to an arbitration agreement which meets the form requirement of the law to which the parties have subjected it; if (as usual) no such choice has been made, the agreement needs to meet the form required by the law of either the place of arbitration or the place of enforcement.

13-26 If, however, one were to follow the traditional (van den Berg) view, the only effective solution would be to provide expressly for recognition and enforcement of arbitral awards based on agreements meeting the more liberal form requirement – a solution which would have to be dealt with in the wider context of a possible Model Law Supplement containing a chapter on enforcement (see below, V.A.iii).

B. Field of Application of Article II(3) New York Convention

13-27 Another candidate for uniform treatment is the field of application of Article II(3) of the New York Convention. Here, the question of Article VII or of any retrospective impact of a new rule does not arise. The issue is not addressed in the Convention, due to the last-minute inclusion of Article II. It has therefore been answered in implementing legislations and case law, and quite disparately so for agreements providing for arbitration within the state in which they are invoked and for those not specifying the place of arbitration.[20] If a uniform answer should be suggested, it could be included in model provisions of an implementing Act. Such provisions could be of practical use for any newly joining member of the New York Convention family and any other member considering revision of its implementing legislation. Moreover, they could guide

---

[19] van den Berg, *supra* n. 17 at p. 180, and 'Enforcement of Annulled Awards?' in (1998) *9 ICC International Court of Arbitration Bulletin* 15 at p. 18.
[20] van den Berg, *supra* n. 18 at pp. 33-36.

the courts of those states that have not addressed the issue either in legislation or in case law.

C. Subjective and Objective Arbitrability

13-28   In the realm of validity of the arbitration agreement we meet two more candidates for uniform treatment: subjective and objective arbitrability.

i. Subjective Arbitrability or Capacity

13-29   The first issue deals with the legal ability of a person or entity to conclude an arbitration agreement. It is of particular concern in the case of a state or a state enterprise. That practically crucial aspect was not addressed in the New York Convention – as it was in the European Convention concluded three years later. Article II accords the right to conclude valid arbitration agreements to legal persons considered by the law applicable to them as 'legal persons of public law', with the possibility for states to declare limits to that faculty. The same provision has been included in some national laws (e.g. Algerian, Bulgarian, Egyptian and Lebanese law). The Swiss Law of 1987 provides as follows: 'If a party to the arbitration is a state or an enterprise or organisation controlled by it, it cannot rely on its own law in order to contest its capacity to be a party to an arbitration or the arbitrability of a dispute covered by the arbitration agreement'.

13-30   It is submitted that a uniform rule along those lines could enhance legal certainty in the many arbitration cases where states are involved in one way or another. Such a rule could be proposed and characterised, in line with modern thinking, as a material rule of public policy of the law of international arbitration.[21]

13-31   An ancillary question possibly to be addressed in this connection is whether a state party to an arbitration agreement is prevented from invoking state immunity only as regards the arbitral proceedings or also in respect of court proceedings assisting or controlling those proceedings (while the issue of immunity from execution is clearly separate, to be dealt with later; see below, V.C.ii).

---

[21]   Thus Hanotiau, 'The Law Applicable to Arbitrability', *supra* n. 4 (sub IIb), p. 146 at p. 149.

ii. Objective Arbitrability or Domain of Arbitration

13-32   Objective arbitrability is next. Commercial subject matters reserved to the courts are in some countries determined by case law only and in others by various statutes: for instance, those dealing with anti-trust or unfair competition, securities, intellectual property, labour or company law. Various states include in their arbitration law a general formula, in modern times going beyond the traditional formula of 'what parties may compromise on or dispose of' to cover, for example, 'any dispute involving property' or 'any claim involving an economic interest' ('vermögensrechtlicher Anspruch', Switzerland and Germany).

13-33   An ambitious effort, as suggested by some commentators,[22] would be to elaborate a detailed list of non-arbitrable issues. However, I expect considerable difficulties in reaching a worldwide consensus on an exhaustive list; perhaps one could agree on three or four issues and then 'compel' states to list immediately thereafter any other issues deemed necessary by that state. Such an approach of channelled information, as used in Article 5 of the Model Law, would at least ensure certainty and easy access to information about those restrictions. Moreover, it would initially 'compel' a state to identify the non-arbitral matters and examine them as to their continuing justification.

13-34   In searching for the best approach, one faces a dilemma: the more general the formula, the greater the potential risk of divergent interpretation by courts of different states; and the more detailed the list, the greater the risk of non-acceptance by states and, to the extent accepted, the risk of ossifying matters and thus impeding further development towards limiting the realm of non-arbitrability. Nevertheless, a considered attempt should be made since the result of worldwide discussion would in itself be revealing and useful.

iii. Law Applicable to Arbitrability

13-35   The related question of the law or laws applicable to arbitrability is of equal importance, at least as long as we do not have worldwide uniformity in substance. This complex matter was discussed in some depth at the 1998 ICCA Congress in Paris where Bernard Hanotiau, in particular, surveyed the application of the law governing the arbitration agreement, the impact of the law of the seat

---

[22]   Altaro and Guiamarey, 'Who Should Determine Arbitrability? Arbitration in a Changing Economic and Political Environment' in (1996) 12 *Arbitration International* 415 at p. 427.

of arbitration, foreign policy laws ('lois de police') of the place of performance of the agreement or of the place of enforcement of the award as well as the special situation of the referral judge under Article II(3) of the New York Convention. He concluded that, while the role that public policy plays has been considerably narrowed, material rules specific to international arbitration are emerging in national legal systems. His true conclusion comes as a question: 'Should we go as far as to consider that the arbitrability of disputes is a transnational principle directly applicable without reference to any national law?' This was already many years ago the conclusion reached on this issue by the late Professor Berthold Goldman.[23]

13-36 A somewhat less futuristic but no less thought-provoking and potentially objection-provoking conclusion was presented at the recent 75th anniversary symposium of the ICC by Jan Paulsson. He recommends the following principles to direct national courts when they examine the issue in the context of the New York Convention:

1. For the purposes of Articles II and V(1)(a), an arbitration agreement shall be considered effective in casu unless the party resisting arbitration, or opposing recognition and enforcement of the award, proves to the satisfaction of the court that the agreement is invalid under both:

   (a) the law chosen by the parties to govern their agreement, and

   (b) the law of the country where the place of arbitration is located, it being understood that reference will be made only to such provisions of these laws as are applicable to arbitration of an international character. If no place of arbitration has been selected, reference shall be to the country in which is situated the authority charged with the appointment of the presiding arbitrator in the absence of party agreement thereto

2. Subparagraph V(2)(a) shall not prevent recognition and enforcement unless the non-arbitrability of the subject matter is a matter of such fundamental importance that recognition and enforcement would also violate subparagraph V(2)(b).(24)

13-37 The second proposal should, in my view, not face insurmountable difficulties. Various commentators have for a long time denied the independent

---

[23] Hanotiau, *supra* n. 21 (sub IV), at p. 167.

relevance of subparagraph (a) since it is viewed as absorbed or covered by subparagraph (b).

13-38 The first proposal, however, promises interesting and difficult discussions. Some might object to having the law of the place of arbitration play a role here since, as Mr Paulsson put it, that law 'often has no reason to apply to issues of arbitrability with respect to an international contract having no connection with the country'. Yet, I agree with him that 'in the interest of predictability it is useful to make it a law of reference' (as done by the Model Law, Articles 1(5) and 34(2)(a)).

13-39 Others might object to giving the parties full freedom to agree on a law (possibly the only one in the world that accords arbitrability to the dispute in question) without having any connection to the contract. Probably the stiffest resistance will be encountered on a point that one might overlook when first reading the proposal, namely that a judge to whom a substantive claim is brought shall disregard its own law when deciding under the referral provision of Article II(3) whether the arbitration agreement is void (for reasons of non-arbitrability). According to Mr Paulsson, 'a court faced with an Article II problem has no business applying its domestic notions of non-arbitrability; fundamental societal interests, such as the proscription of fraude à la loi, may be ensured at the stage of enforcement by virtue of Article V(2)(b)'.[24] I am not sure whether this will persuade many referral judges to disregard even those national exclusive-jurisdiction norms designed for international transactions; after all, a substantive claim tends to be brought in a jurisdiction whose courts would be competent but for the arbitration agreement. At least one conclusion is clear: exciting and possibly frustrating discussions and negotiations lie ahead.

D. Restricting or Enlarging the Scope of the Arbitration Agreement

13-40 The next batch of issues relating to the basis of arbitration concerns the restriction or enlargement of the scope of the arbitration agreement. I am thinking of consolidation and related issues as well as set-off.

---

[24] Paulsson, 'Arbitrability, Still Through a Glass Darkly', Remarks at 75th Anniversary of the ICC International Court of Arbitration, Geneva, 25 September 1998 (to be published).

i. Consolidation and Other Multiparty Issues

13-41 Consolidation, understood as a court measure forcing parties having signed separate arbitration agreements together into one arbitration, in my view has been a rather fashionable topic in the eighties, out of a burning desire to avoid inconsistent results. The world of arbitral decisions is, however, full of inconsistencies (and so are the interests of multiple parties involved). As experienced in Hong Kong and elsewhere, this has given way to a realisation that the disadvantages and procedural difficulties often outweigh the expected gain. The current legislative picture worldwide is telling and unlikely to change dramatically in the near future: to my knowledge, compulsory powers in international cases are given to the courts only in the United States and the Netherlands (where the power has been introduced into the law to suit the needs of the local construction industry and has in fact hitherto been used exclusively in domestic cases).

13-42 As pointed out by Pieter Sanders, who recommends uniform legislative treatment,[25] various other countries also have legislative provisions concerning consolidation. Yet there is a crucial difference: these provisions operate as optional rules, requiring a previous consent by all parties. Their purpose is to assist in the implementation of that general agreement of all parties. Such procedural court assistance is of practical value for arbitrations that are either ad hoc or administered by an institution which does not provide that assistance (as, however, increasingly foreseen in recently revised sets of rules). Consideration might thus be given to devising a uniform rule on court assistance if a need therefore is widely felt.

13-43 More important would be to consider a number of consolidation-related issues, drawn to our attention by Sir Michael Kerr in his seminal Keating Lecture.[26] Problems worthy of research include those raised before some US courts due to the so-called 'intertwining doctrine' which operates where court proceedings are pending concurrently with arbitral proceedings and a party asserts among several causes of action one that falls within the exclusive jurisdiction of the courts. Equally worthy of study are a variant of that doctrine applied in Canada and especially the unfortunate vestiges in some common law

---

[25] Informal proposal to ICCA Council (1998) and to be published in his upcoming *magnum opus* 'Quo vadis arbitration?'

[26] Kerr, 'Concord and Conflict in International Arbitration' in (1997) 13 *Arbitration International* 121 at pp. 135-136.

jurisdictions of a 1912 decision of the English Court of Appeal. The potential of what Sir Michael calls a 'ploy of pre-empting the institution or continuation of arbitration proceedings by an application to a local court' is a good reason for a worldwide search for similar abuse-prone devices and for elaborating an appropriate uniform answer, obviously aligned with the answer to the earlier referenced suggestion by Jan Paulsson.

13-44 In order to complicate matters or make them more fascinating for the drafters of any additional uniform legislation, I recommend to include in the research study a number of other multiparty issues which have never received the attention they deserve. I am thinking of a variety of situations where a third party is somehow involved in the arbitral proceedings, either upon its own request or upon the two other parties' request. It may be actively participating or it may be silently attending. Its participation may entail the risk of losing like any other respondent or it may lead to certain negative inferences concerning the proof of facts or even preclusions from invoking points of law. While aware of the foggy nature of the terms of reference for the suggested study, I refrain from naming any label used in procedural law since the terminology and the scope of the situations differs from country to country to a mind-boggling extent.

ii. Set-Off

13-45 Another interesting issue concerning the basis of arbitration arises from the frequent situation that a respondent invokes a certain claim not as a counterclaim, about which the arbitral tribunal would have to decide irrespective of the outcome of the claimant's demand, but as a defence by way of set-off. Let us assume that the arbitral tribunal regards the claimant's demand not as obviously unfounded and the set-off as admissible (in itself a complex issue mixing contractual and procedural law). The question then may arise whether the arbitral tribunal is competent to examine the merits of the disputed claim invoked by set-off if that claim is covered not by the arbitration agreement at hand but by either another arbitration agreement between the same parties (e.g. an arbitration clause in another contract) or a forum-selection clause. The question is extremely complex and could easily constitute the topic of a separate lecture, as shown by Klaus Peter Berger's recent survey of the current state of the discussion in the light of extreme dearth of legislative treatment.[27]

---

[27] Berger, 'Die Aufrechnung im Internationalen Schiedsverfahren', 1998 *Recht der Internationalen Wirtschaft* 426.

13-46 In short, the traditional and probably still prevailing view is that the scope of the first arbitration agreement cannot be presumed to cover any outside claim invoked by the respondent by way of set-off since the second arbitration agreement (or forum-selection clause) needs to be given equal weight. A more modern and apparently ground-gaining view is the pragmatic presumption of the arbitral tribunal's competence also for any defences ('le juge de l'action est le juge de l'exception') for the sake of procedural efficiency and peace-creating finality. Here – as in respect of earlier mentioned multiparty issues – the desired in-depth study should include the question whether an appropriate uniform rule should be elaborated for the legislative level or whether the issue can appropriately be addressed in arbitration rules (as e.g. Article 27 of the 1989 International Arbitration Rules of the Zurich Chamber of Commerce).

iii. 'Terminal' Issues

13-47 To terminate the 'basis of arbitration', let me merely mention three terminal issues addressed in some national laws and possibly warranting uniform treatment: the effect of death of a party on the arbitration agreement and on the proceedings; the effect of insolvency of a party on the agreement and on the proceedings; and the effect of a judicial setting-aside decision on the arbitration agreement.

III. POWERS AND DUTIES OF ARBITRATORS, AND OTHER PROCEDURAL ISSUES

13-48 Constraints of time and space compel me to shift gears and take you rapidly, in what may be the first fast-track approach to a Freshfields Lecture, through the next part addressing procedural issues, especially concerning the powers and duties of arbitrators.

13-49 First stop: filling of gaps, not to be confused with adaptation of contracts due to changed circumstances. The UNCITRAL view of the eighties probably still stands: no need for legislative treatment. Other procedures akin to arbitration tend to be available.

13-50 Second stop: determination of law applicable to substance of dispute failing party agreement. Model Law Article 28(2) guides via the indirect route (i.e. conflict-of-law rules deemed applicable in the sense of appropriate) to a law, not rules of law, while parties themselves may agree on rules of law. UNCITRAL was divided on whether to take the next step, i.e. the direct route towards appropriate law or rules of law. Uniformity was not ensured since not all states were expected to accept the more liberal solution. Has that changed? Does it make much difference in practice?

13-51 Third stop: truncated tribunal. Power of remaining two arbitrators to ensure integrity of arbitral process in face of obstructionistic tactics or sabotage was favoured at the 1998 ICCA Congress by Judge Schwebel[28] and Serge Lazareff.[29] Contra Tadeusz Szurski:[30] party cannot 'legally' be held responsible for misbehaviour of arbitrator, and party agreement usually provides for replacement. While proponents see a majority of developed arbitration laws granting that power, I can see only two clearly granting that power: Bermuda and Germany (both enactments of the Model Law). Case law is not generally supportive; negative decisions have been rendered even in highly developed arbitration countries (Switzerland and France). A favourable trend has emerged in respect of arbitration rules. Recent revisions of AAA, LCIA and ICC Rules envisage continuation based on reasonable exercise of discretion. Under other arbitration rules, e.g. UNCITRAL Rules, the same result has been distilled from other provisions: duty of arbitrator to carry out the mandate, majority of signatures suffices, and resignation needs to be accepted by the other two arbitrators.

13-52 Thus, should we aim for a uniform treatment in legislation, granting the power irrespective of previous party agreement therefore? Is such a rule acceptable in all parts of the world? I have my doubts, despite the reported informal sounding out of developing country representatives at The Hague who had no objection to such power in new PCA Rules[31] (which, after all, are contractual rules, not legislation). Perhaps we will have to settle for a legislative sanction or recognition of any party agreement granting such power to the rump-panel, probably with certain conditions and indicating the time-period of effectiveness.

13-53 Fourth stop: interest. During preparation of the Model Law, we saw no need for expressing the arbitrator's power to award interest. Why should he or she, authorised to award high amounts of damages, not be naturally authorised to add interest? Yet, thereafter uncertainty, stemming from an apparently obscure

---

[28] Schwebel, 'The Authority of a Truncated Tribunal', *supra* n. 4, p. 314 at p. 315.
[29] Lazareff, The Constitution of the Arbitral Tribunal, *supra* n. 4, p. 326 at p. 327.
[30] Szurski, 'The Constitution of the Arbitral Tribunal', *supra* n. 4, pp. 332-333.
[31] Jonkman, 'Regulation of Truncated Tribunals by the Permanent Court of Arbitration', *supra* n. 4, p. 319 at p. 322.

English law, spread in the common law world and led to added provisions in most enactments of the Model Law.

13-54 A recommended uniform rule should not merely grant the power to award interest from the time of birth of the debt (hopefully overcoming the judgment-dichotomy between pre- and post-decision stages) but also specify any relevant details, e.g. whether compound interest may be awarded. An additional rule on the rate of interest would seem extremely useful, if consensus could be reached. In order to avoid the vagaries of private international law with its unsettled state of affairs on this point, one should search for an acceptable substantive rule, subject to party agreement, and choose a general formula (e.g. 'reasonable commercial rate') or a more elaborate one (e.g. Article 7.4.9 UPICC: UNIDROIT Principles of International Commercial Contracts):

> '... the average bank short-term lending rate to prime borrowers prevailing for the currency of payment at the place for payment, or where no such rate exists at that place, then the same rate in the state of the currency of payment ...'.

13-55 Fifth stop: cost and fees. A considerable number of Model Law enactments have added provisions on the arbitral tribunal's power to fix and allocate cost and fees. Those provisions often differ in substance and especially as to relevant ancillary issues, e.g. request for deposits, accounting, placing a ceiling, form of decision. It would thus seem desirable to elaborate a model uniform provision for future enactments.

13-56 Sixth stop: confidentiality, another stop at which we could easily spend days of interesting discussions, and there are certainly months and years of these ahead (the topic of the late nineties). As Gavan Griffith saw it at UNCITRAL's New York Convention Day: 'There is now an appreciation that the parties' requirements for confidentiality of the proceedings are not adequately protected. This issue is not touched upon, and is as ripe for coverage in the Model Law as it is in most state laws'.[32] My own feeling is that confidentiality was regarded as natural and taken for granted, even though we were not aware of its precise scope. But four years ago an Australian decision in a case of public interest fuelled our realisation that the paradise was lost and we were all naked. We had to realise that in our cosy arbitration world of informal, confidential private

---

[32] Griffith, 'Possible issues for an annex to the UNCITRAL Model Law', *supra* n. 5, p. 46 at p. 48.

hotel-room justice a more lawyered type of proceedings, often in mega cases, had developed: 'Arbitigation', close to litigation, but in an ad hoc court created for the case, for lack of an international commercial court. The equation with litigation led to the still startling view that confidentiality may not be presumed as an essential feature, as an implied term of the arbitration agreement; if parties want it, they should so stipulate.

13-57   To stipulate such a clause (or a uniform legislative rule) is far from easy, as we realised as the 'Gang of Four' draftsmen of the WIPO Arbitration Rules. The more one tries to delimit confidentiality, the more it becomes enigmatic. Nevertheless, an effort should be made, looking at all possible situations where confidentiality would be justified and where it would hinder commercial activity (e.g. disclosure to shareholders). At least, it would be wrong to change a deeply rooted principle merely for the reason that its scope cannot be determined with precision. As Hayek thought that 'money matters', I strongly believe that 'confidentiality matters'.

13-58   Seventh stop: liability and immunity. National laws differ considerably on this point, as shown in a collection of comparative law essays edited by Julian Lew (1990)[33] and in a comparative analysis by Christian Hausmaninger of the same year.[34] Common law courts tend to equate arbitrators to judges while civil law courts traditionally focus on their contractual function as experts, with considerable disparity even within the same legal family. Partly due to the dearth of legislative treatment at the time, the Model Law drafters abstained from touching the issue (so as not to wake up sleeping dogs). However, the dogs are quite awake today. As Gavan Griffith put it in New York: 'Particularly by aggressive litigators within the North-American hemisphere, there is an emerging tactic of recalcitrant parties engaging in personal attacks on the independence of the arbitration process. It is not uncommon for arbitrators now to be threatened with proceedings and claims against them personally if they do not act in a particular manner'.[35] In order to safeguard against what I would call the 'See you later, litigator' syndrome, Gavan Griffith suggested that 'when arbitrators are honestly discharging their duties, even if one party believes imperfectly, there should be immunity from personal liability in the same manner as is usual for a judge'.

---

[33]   J. D. M. Lew (ed.) *The Immunity of Arbitrators* (Lloyd's of London Press 1990).
[34]   Hausmaninger, 'Civil Liability of Arbitrators – Comparative Analysis and Proposals for Reform' in (1990) 7 *Journal of International Arbitration* 7.
[35]   Griffith, *supra* n. 32.

13-59 In fact, a number of Model Law enactments already contain a provision along those lines, yet with considerable variations and far from uniform with other laws (e.g. Peru: 'acceptance of appointment by the arbitrators ... entitles the parties to compel them to discharge their responsibilities within the fixed period of time, under penalty of being liable for the damages caused by delay or failure to comply with their obligations', s. 16 of the 1992 Law).

13-60 The desirable search for a universally acceptable formula may start with the various formulations already adopted in national laws and should include proposals made by organisations or commentators, like the following one contained in the introductory note to the IBA's 1987 Rules of Ethics for International Arbitrators: 'International arbitrators should, in principle, be granted immunity from suit under national laws, except in extreme cases of wilful or reckless disregard of their legal obligations', or the refinement of that proposal by Christian Hausmaninger which will certainly stimulate lively discussion in the future search: 'International arbitrators should be granted immunity from civil liability suits under national laws, except in cases of intentional or grossly negligent violations of their contractual duties, if such violations have led to either the premature termination of the arbitral proceedings or the vacation of the final award. In no case shall the arbitrator be held liable for an error in the making of the award, except if such error consists in a manifest disregard of the applicable law'.[36] Any objections, your Honours or Arbitrators? Should immunity from professional liability also be legislated for witnesses, experts, arbitral institutions?

13-61 Eighth stop: foreign counsel. As brought home some years ago by the Turner case in Singapore excluding foreign counsel (of a certain famous firm which organises prestigious lectures once a year in London and Hong Kong), such a prohibition spells disaster for the local arbitration centre; and Singapore was fairly rapid in curing the defect in its enactment of the UNCITRAL Model Law. When advising legislators I have often encountered great sympathies for such prohibition, motivated, of course, by the desire to protect the interest of the local bar. What a superficial reasoning, apart from its being anathema to true international arbitration! The prohibition simply leads foreign users to take their arbitrations elsewhere unless commercial necessity requires otherwise. A rule permitting foreign representation, at least in cases involving foreign law, attracts

---

[36] Hausmaninger, *supra* n. 34 at p. 48.

international arbitrations and may well lead to retaining at least one local counsel; it thus serves local bar interests clearly better than a prohibition.

13-62 Ninth stop: conciliation, for which Professor Sanders proposes the preparation of a model law.[37] I can see transcendental glows in the eyes of converts of the ADR movement raging primarily in the common law world as understandable reaction to 'Arbitigation'. Unfortunately, the 'dawning of international commercial conciliation', which I predicted at the 1982 ICCA Congress in Hamburg,[38] shows three less desirable features which may cause disillusion in the not so distant future.

13-63 First, when listening to presentations on the many nicely distinguished ADR techniques and the roles of different participants, one gets the impression of a dangerously increasing formalisation of the process. Secondly, when law societies or other professional associations market a multitude of conciliation methods, one suspects them of recommending an 'escalation or ladder clause', as if ADR stands for 'Accumulated dispute resolution techniques': take A; if that doesn't work, take B; if that fails, try C, but don't forget to pay for all of them before depositing an advance for the final step – your arbitration. Thirdly, the obsession with novelty and uniqueness in marketing leads to overemphasising particular aspects or phases of what is one and the same natural process and to drawing artificial distinctions (e.g. between conciliation and mediation) usually crowned by acronyms that are catchy, fancy and at times misleading (like 'Mini-trial'). To name only a few other such 'alternatives': Structured CEO Negotiation, Early Neutral Evaluation, Partnering, Dispute Review Board, Lawyerless Mediation, Rent-a-Judge, Med/Arb, Medaloa, Arb/Med, Shadow Mediation and Co-Med-Arb. How could I resist the temptation of adding some new techniques the names of which I have already copyrighted?

13-64 The pacifying effect of good food is exploited by 'GOURMEDIATION©', a five-course meal in a five-star restaurant: Soup – to identify liquid proof, a fish course for discovery and other fishing expeditions, a meat course to see whether respondent meets claimant's demand, dessert to sweeten the suggested settlement terms, and cheese for the shake-hand picture

---

[37] *Supra* n. 25.
[38] Herrmann, 'Conciliation as a new method of dispute settlement' in *ICCA Congress Series No. 1* (VIIth International Arbitration Congress, Hamburg 1982) 145 at p. 165.

taking. A fast-track version is called 'TARMAC©' (not to indicate the taste of the ground beef at the ordinary locale but the speed of taking off and landing).

13-65 The human desire for travel and vacation is catered for by 'CRUISATION©' (or, if one insists on the use of ADR, 'CRUISADR©'): Proceedings take place on board of a cruise-ship that calls on a port only after settlement, usually a former warship with no space for spouses, kids or any recreational facilities. For particularly confidential cases we use submarines. Other protected names are: 'CIA©' = Conciliation integrated into Arbitration, 'INTERMEDIATION©' and, for personal injury cases, 'Doctor Med.©'.

13-66 And why not use the same marketing tools for the field of arbitration? New methods could be 'TSP' for two-stage-proceedings (e.g. liability-quantum), 'BOA contractor' as 'Best-Offer-Arbitration' for cement and other construction cases, 'BBTA' as a 24-hour-service in the form of 'Bed and Breakfast-track-arbitration©', 'ALOHA', the 'American Last Offer and Hope Arbitration©', 'ORBITRATION©' administered by 'GAC', the 'Galactic Arbitration Center', already advertised above, and influenced, as regards evidence-taking, by that blimp or space shuttle revealingly called 'US Discovery'.

13-67 Finally, the old dream of cheap arbitration is satisfied by three new techniques: 'Bud light' (for Budget Arbitration), 'CAP' (for Cost Avoidance Programme) and 'DON'T©' (Documents Only, No Travel). Unfortunately none of that will ever end up in future legislative provisions.

13-68 But what then? National enactments of the UNCITRAL Model Law, which have spurred Pieter Sanders' proposal, may provide some ideas, except where they simply reproduce the UNCITRAL Conciliation Rules. My tentative collection of studyworthy points follows.

13-69 First, a set of rules encouraging or permitting conciliation and addressing the issue of a conciliator turning arbitrator and vice-versa. Particularly in common law jurisdictions, a rule would be useful that overcomes any objection based on assertions of prejudice or even violation of natural justice (e.g. Hong Kong SAR: 'Where an arbitration agreement provides for the appointment of a conciliator, and further provides that the same person shall act as an arbitrator, then in the event of the conciliation proceedings failing, no objection can be taken to the appointment of such person solely on the ground that he has previously acted as conciliator').

13-70 However, as regards the referenced party agreement, the normal and more prudent rule, as recognised by Fali Nariman at ICC's birthday party,[39] is to provide from the outset that the conciliator will not act as an arbitrator or as counsel of a party in subsequent arbitral or judicial proceedings in respect of the same subject matter (see Article 19 of the UNCITRAL Conciliation Rules); of course, parties may later change their original position and regard the conciliator's familiarity with the dispute as an asset rather than a disadvantage. In essence, what counts is party autonomy relating even to touchy points such as caucusing next to phases of arbitration, and the law should give effect to the parties' agreement.

13-71 Secondly, regard should be had to particular concerns of keeping conciliation efforts confidential, including protection of privileged information against disclosure to the other party.

13-72 Thirdly, a useful provision, to my knowledge not found in any national law, would be to let a limitation or prescription period be interrupted by the initiation of conciliation proceedings (so as to end their discrimination if compared with arbitration or litigation). The possible alternative of starting conciliation with an agreement not to invoke expiry of such period is not always practicable, and a legislative provision would at least have the psychological effect of expressing non-discrimination.

13-73 Fourthly, settlement agreements should be accorded enforceability, either directly (as done, e.g. by Hong Kong SAR) or indirectly, by 'allowing' the parties to the settlement to commence arbitration, despite the disappearance of the dispute, and to obtain an award on agreed terms.

IV. COURT ASSISTANCE OR CONTROL (EXCLUDING ENFORCEMENT)

13-74 With this we have elegantly reached the crucial area of court involvement. On a first loop, we will see some instances of court assistance during arbitral proceedings and of court control, and on a second and final loop we will explore possible improvements in the field of recognition and enforcement of awards.

---

[39] Nariman, 'May the Same Persons Consecutively Act as Mediators/Arbitrators in Respect of the Same Dispute? Pros & Cons' and 'How Broad Should the Power of an Arbitrator to Refer the Parties to Mediation Be?' Remarks at 75th Anniversary of the ICC International Court of Arbitration, Geneva, 25 September 1998 (to be published).

13-75 First stop: assistance in getting the ball rolling. Where the agreed process of appointing arbitrators runs into difficulties, the Model Law already envisages court assistance (in Article 11, also covering later instances of e.g. challenges, Article 13). Yet, it does so only for arbitrations anchored in the country where the court is situated; the drafters did not accept a Secretariat proposal to help also in instances where the place of arbitration had not yet been determined. Germany in its enactment of the Model Law offers that assistance, provided that either the respondent or the claimant has its place of business or residence in Germany (s.1025(3)). A uniform rule along those lines seems recommendable.

13-76 Another field of initial assistance, as advocated by Werner Melis at New York Convention Day,[40] are certain pathological clauses. As provided for in Article IV of the 1961 European Convention, help could be rendered where parties have not specified the mode of arbitration (institutional or ad hoc), or where they have agreed to institutional arbitration without precisely identifying the entrusted institution, or where the parties have not stipulated the rules of the game. While the last contingency is cured by the Model Law, which provides a mini-set of arbitration rules (as a first-aid kit to get the arbitration started and proceed to an award), other possible deadlocks could be prevented by appropriate assistance. If deemed desirable, one should look for appropriate helpers: Presidents of Chambers of Commerce or a Special Committee as under the 1961 European Convention? Designated national arbitral institutions might be better. Or should we entrust international bodies, either at the universal level like the Permanent Court of Arbitration, or designated regional bodies like the Common Court of Justice and Arbitration of OHADA (Organisation pour l'harmonisation en Afrique du droit des affaires) in Abidjan?

13-77 Second stop: court assistance in taking evidence. The Model Law already provides for such assistance, yet again only for arbitrations whose seat is in the Model Law country. The drafters did not extend that assistance to foreign arbitrations; it was felt that an effective system could be established only by means of a convention, and that the availability of such assistance might induce parties to dilatory or obstructionist requests for evidence. Both concerns are no longer regarded as very forceful; besides, the Model Law itself contains a device for preventing dilatory tactics, namely the requirement of the arbitral tribunal's consent to any such request to a court (Article 27). Some recently promulgated

---

[40] Melis, 'Considering the advisability of preparing an additional Convention, complementary to the New York Convention', *supra* n. 5, p. 44 at pp. 45-46.

national laws contain the extension to foreign arbitrations and not-yet-empanelled arbitrations, such as the German Model Law enactment (ss.1025(2) and 1050) and the English Act of 1996 (ss.2(3)(a) and 43, for witnesses). A uniform rule along those lines seems recommendable.

13-78 Next stop: court assistance in giving executory force to interim measures of protection ordered by the arbitral tribunal. This is a prime candidate for uniform treatment, as advocated at New York Convention Day especially by Johnny Veeder QC[41] and Sergei Lebedev[42] (who also proposed wider court assistance by judicial interim measures of protection). The Model Law itself (in Article 17) authorises the arbitral tribunal to order certain interim measures of protection, while some other laws do not even recognise any party agreement to that effect (e.g. Austria, Greece, Italy, Sweden). The Model Law, however, does not address the issue of enforceability of such measures. National enactments, as expected by the Model Law drafters, have often answered the question. They provide either directly for enforceability or indirectly by envisaging the interim order to be made in the form of an award, triggering the applicability of the general provisions on recognition and enforcement of arbitral awards.

13-79 One should, however, recognise that the latter approach, sometimes also used in arbitration rules, faces problems where the New York Convention comes into play. It is, to say the least, far from certain whether the Convention covers interim orders that are not 'final' in the strict sense. However, in my view an interim measure is not only 'binding' (on the parties) but also 'final' in the sense of 'definite' according to its terms, which typically include a time limitation or a revision possibility.

13-80 I am not underestimating the inherent difficulties of grasping the true nature of interim measures, distinguishing between the very different types of such measures and their conditions and other procedural issues involved, as discussed, for example, by Marc Blessing at the 1997 International Arbitration Day in New York.[43] Yet, we should regard those difficulties as fascinating challenges on our way to the rewarding achievement of universally acceptable provisions. As regards a non-award approach, I recommend as a starting point the elaborate provision of the new German Law (s.1041), with possible provisions to

---

[41] Veeder, 'Provisional and conservative measures', *supra* n. 5, p. 21.
[42] Lebedev, 'Court assistance with interim measures', *supra* n. 5, p. 23.
[43] Blessing, 'The Trouble With Interim Relief in International Arbitration', AAA/ABCNY/IBA International Arbitration Day: Global Perspectives, New York, 25 September 1997.

be added in a Model Law Supplement to ensure enforceability of such measures also in countries other than where the seat of the arbitration is located.

13-81 Final assistance stop: judicial review on the merits. Before moving into the wonderland of recognition and enforcement of awards, let us take a brief stop at 'judicial review'. I am not referring to the English system of appeal on a point of law which parties may avoid by an exclusion agreement if they are aware thereof (that is why I had years ago recommended an inclusion, opting-in system for England, so as to avoid a trap to the unwary[44]). Rather, I am referring to the situation where parties agree on judicial review for arbitrations conducted under laws that do not provide for judicial review. Courts have given different answers to such party-desired 'non-finality'. One US court has given effect to the clause relying on the principle of 'ensuring enforcement of private agreements to arbitrate'.[45] Another US court felt that 'parties cannot contract for judicial review and impose on the courts burdens and functions Congress has withheld'.[46] A French court, also regarding the parties' appeal provision as invalid, went even further and held that the entire arbitration agreement therefore was flawed and invalid.[47]

13-82 The diversity of views is symptomatic of the eternal question of the limits of party autonomy and the extent to which finality is essential in international commercial arbitration. While the disparity is not particularly reassuring, the issue probably defies uniform legislative treatment, at least for the time being.

V. REINFORCING RECOGNITION AND ENFORCEMENT OF AWARDS

13-83 The views on our final loop are of a particularly tentative nature. The debate has not yet reached the stage of maturity that would allow easy consensus-building conclusions. Individual views are at times extremist and drastically changed within a few months.

---

[44] Herrmann, 'For an UNCITRAL Model Restatement of Arbitration Law in the United Kingdom' in (1988) 4 *Arbitration International* 62 at p. 66.
[45] *La Pine Technology Corporation* v. *Kyocera Corporation* 130 F. 3d 884 (9th Cir. 1997); appeal decision on case in note 45.
[46] *La Pine Technology Corporation* v. *Kyocera Corporation* 909 F. Supp. 697, 705 (N.D. Cal. 1995); similarly *Chicago Typographical Union* v. *Chicago Sun-Times* 935 F. 2d 1501 (7th Cir. 1991).
[47] *Société Diseno* v. *Société Mendes,* Cour d'Appel de Paris (27 October 1994) in 1995 *Rev. arb.* 263.

13-84   Not only the substantive side of the reinforcement effort is very tentative but also the question of form or means: do we need a convention supplementing the New York Convention? Is the appropriate vehicle a Model Law Supplement? And should that expressly interpret and complement the New York Convention, in part as a Model Implementing Act? Or should it indirectly remedy short-comings of the Convention by providing a modern enforcement system (either 'New York inclusive' or as an 'add-on') which for state members of the New York Convention would become operative via Article VII? Or is what we need (or can finally agree on) a set of UNCITRAL Guidelines, as suggested by Sir Michael Kerr?[48] Should we establish an advisory Uniform Interpretation Board whose persuasive force might be strengthened by linking it to UNCITRAL? Or should we refrain from any formal approach and leave the questions to learned judges and commentators? To make things even more interesting, the choice need not necessarily be a general one but may well vary from issue to issue.

13-85   Thus, let us turn to the issues, lumped into three groups: the concept of award; enforcement conditions and procedure; and grounds for refusal.

A. Widening/Clarifying the Definition of 'Award'

13-86   There are at least six candidates for enforceability whose coverage by the New York Convention is controversial and quite often denied or at least doubtful:

    (i)   Interim measures of protection: as mentioned earlier, for conservatory and other interim measures the executory force of a court may be desired. Yet, even if the measure is ordered by the arbitral tribunal in the form of an award or is by arbitration rules or the law of the place of arbitration accorded the status of an award, enforcement in another country is far from ensured. A uniform rule, with appropriate procedures and conditions, should grant enforceability to a measure which, even if limited in time or revisable under its terms, is definitive and binding on a party. In that context, it might be advisable to specify the various types of interim measures that would be made enforceable.

   (ii) 'Settlement agreements': as discussed earlier, these might be made enforceable even if not incorporated into an award on agreed terms; an alternative (to avoid the difficult task of precisely defining an eligible settlement agreement) could be to give effect to a clause in such agreement whereby a party subjects its assets to enforcement.

---

[48]   Kerr, *supra* n. 26 at pp. 142-143.

(iii) Certain awards not based on signed or written arbitration agreements, as discussed earlier, need to be made enforceable, too.

(iv) 'Treaty awards': various bilateral treaties (for instance, on investment) and some multilateral treaties (e.g. NAFTA and Energy Charter Treaty) suggest enforcement of awards that may not be based on a traditional arbitration agreement between the parties but, for example, on the state's offer by joining the treaty and the investor's consent by initiating arbitration. Enforcement under the New York Convention (or the Model Law) may then be a question and should be made answerable in the affirmative (with adjustments needed for the requirement to present the arbitration agreement to the enforcement judge).

(v) 'Unseated' awards, including stateless or a-national awards: While a-national (or 'free-floating') awards are more common in the imaginative world of radical de-localisers than in the real world, we may wish to anticipate future space awards, rendered in cyberspace (virtual 'CYBITRATION©' awards by seatless on-line arbitration centres) or in outer space ('ORBITRATION©' by the 'Galactic Arbitration Center', remember). As regards the probable absence of a setting-aside facility, the situation is similar to that of a country where the law or the parties have set aside that facility.

(vi) 'Award-like decisions' (in proceedings akin to arbitration): consideration might be given to ending the disparity between Italian and other courts on the qualification of the 'laudo irrituale' as well as possibly similar proceedings (e.g. 'bindend advies', 'Schiedsgutachten').

B. Enforcement Conditions and Procedure

13-87   A number of issues may be mentioned here; a number of others are likely to be added as a result of the IBA/UNCITRAL Joint Project Monitoring the Implementation of the New York Convention (about which I have reported elsewhere[49]). The last field to be covered is particularly difficult, controversial and crucial.

---

[49]   Herrmann, 'Implementing Legislation – The IBA/UNCITRAL Project' in (1996) *ASA Special Series No. 9* 135.

13-88 First, there are two issues of time: a retroactive effect of the New York Convention could be recommended to newly joining states; and a uniform time period for requests for enforcement may be commended generally, if a time-limit is regarded as justified at all (currently legislated time periods range from six months to 30 years).

13-89 Secondly, refinements to the conditions of Article IV of the New York Convention might be considered: arbitration agreement in certain cases (e.g. submission; oral agreement; treaty award) to be proven otherwise than by original or copy in writing; details of authentication or certification could be clarified (e.g. signatures on award necessary to be authenticated and, if so, how; does authentication of chairman's signature suffice); requirement of translation a matter of discretion for the court; proof of fact that a certain state is a member of the New York Convention to be established by reference to homepage of United Nations Treaty Section, thereby abolishing the current requirement in some states to have reference to a published list of the Ministry of Foreign Affairs or, much more restrictive and against the thrust of the Convention, for certification by the diplomatic or consular representative of the enforcement state in the country whose membership is to be proven; clear rule to eradicate last remnants of 'double exequatur', e.g. requirements of deposit, registration or confirmation of award to be irrelevant for foreign countries.

13-90 Thirdly, practically important questions of procedure could be examined, e.g. fees, possibly imposing a cap, in addition to the requirement of non-discrimination contained in Article III of the Convention; leave for enforcement to be granted within fixed time-limit, possibly ex parte; appeal possible against leave or against its refusal; which is the competent court.

C. Grounds for Refusal of Recognition or Enforcement

i. In General

13-91 Before looking at individual grounds, we need to look at a general matter which lies at the heart of the controversy: the relationship between the setting-aside court in the country of origin and the enforcement judge, the famous problem of 'double control', made conspicuous (but not at all created) by the Model Law with its parallel lists of grounds in Articles 34 and 36. The criticism has been especially strong in respect of domestic situations, i.e. both courts are in the same country. Albert Jan van den Berg called it the major defect of the Model

Law.[50] However, one should realise that the Model Law does not prevent any state from adding a rule concerning that relationship, including a possible preclusion effect to reduce double control, in line with its existing system of such preclusion rules. Germany, for example, addressed the issue in its enactment, s.1060(2).

13-92 Another misconception is what Lord Mustill recently presented as his memory of the UNCITRAL debates and the two philosophies in collision. The first allegedly was 'that arbitrations should be left undisturbed by the local law, complaints about procedural unfairness being addressed at the stage of enforcement in a foreign court', and the second, opposite view, which he said led to the inclusion of Article 34, was to tackle 'procedural errors and failures of justice at the earliest possible moment, on the spot, through the medium of the national court'[51] at the place of arbitration. I cannot remember a single delegation having proposed to do away with setting aside (as later legislated by one country, namely Belgium, for cases not involving Belgian interests). In fact, all delegates would probably rally around Lord Mustill's argument in favour of the second view: if complaints are reserved for the stage of enforcement there is no remedy for the claimant who, through unfairness, has seen his claim wrongfully dismissed; in the opposite case, the loser could 'be harassed by enforcement proceedings all round the world, accompanied by the blocking of credit balances and seizure of assets'. When I once expressed during an arbitration conference that same view, preserving for the loser the necessary means to attack the award at the roots rather than having to sit and wait for enforcement efforts in various countries, I was called 'award killer' by a well-known arbitrator (whose recent award had been set aside).

13-93 My view has not changed. Thus I am unable to share the view of Philippe Fouchard that setting aside should be done away with[52] or the recent view of Jan Paulsson that setting aside should be given only local effect. His main argument against any more-than-local effect of setting aside is the alleged 'international trend to attach less, rather than more, significance to the formal link between an award and the country of the arbitration', and that 'the opposite view reflects an

---

[50] van den Berg, 'The Freshfields Lecture 1992 – The Efficacy of Award in International Commercial Arbitration' in (1992) 58 *Arbitration* 267 at p. 272.

[51] Lord Mustill, *supra* n. 6 at p. 254.

[52] Fouchard, 'Suggestions to Improve the International Efficacy of Arbitral Awards', *supra* n. 4, p. 601 at p. 613.

unjustified lack of confidence in courts where enforcement is sought'.[53] But why should there be less confidence in the judges at the place of arbitration, chosen by the par-ties often because of its so-called neutrality or lack of connection with the subject matter?

13-94 Thus, my preference continues to be in favour of a global effect of setting aside, with certain reductions of the 'second' court control, at the place of enforcement. The reductions should be achieved with respect to the individual grounds for refusal set forth in Article V of the New York Convention, especially subparagraph (e) of paragraph (1). In similar vein, one should provide some kind of preclusion effect for the case where a ground has been unsuccessfully invoked at the place of arbitration – not necessarily as 'res iudicata', probably not obtainable worldwide, but as an exhortation to decline reconsideration if the court is satisfied that the respondent already had its day in court (one).

13-95 Before looking at the various grounds for refusal, I feel compelled to dispel the almost epidemic misconception that the words 'may be refused' in the English version grant discretion to the enforcement judge to enforce an award despite the existence of one of the listed grounds. The text says 'may be refused only if ...' which is identical with 'may not be refused unless' (exactly like the French version); it thus addresses exclusively the situation where none of the grounds exists, in which case the judge must or shall enforce. The Convention is silent on whether, if a ground exists, enforcement shall be refused or whether there remains discretion to enforce the award nevertheless. Based on a recent statement by Pieter Sanders, the author of the so-called Dutch proposal launched at the 1958 Conference, and the fact that even the extremely liberal and internationally minded previous draft said 'shall be refused if ...',[54] I suspect that the drafters saw no room for discretion. Yet the legislative history is sufficiently unclear to allow us today to use the Convention's silence on the point.[55]

---

[53] Paulsson, 'Towards Minimum Standards of Enforcement: Feasibility of a Model Law', *supra* n. 4, and similarly 'Enforcing Arbitral Awards Notwithstanding a Local Standard Annulment (LSA)' in (1998) 9 *ICC International Court of Arbitration Bulletin* 14; contra: van den Berg in his replique, *supra* n. 19.

[54] Preliminary Draft Convention (1953), Art. IV, reproduced in (1998) 9 *ICC International Court of Arbitration Bulletin* 35.

[55] Even Jan Paulsson's well-researched and detailed excursion into the foreign land of linguistics (*May* or *Must* Under the New York Convention: An Exercise in Syntax and Linguistics' in (1998) 14 *Arbitration International* 227) suffers from the potentially misleading imprecision of not distinguishing between the positive granting of discretion and silence on the issue. For example, his finding that the texts in four of the five official languages do not 'require refusal if

ii. Individual Grounds

13-96 Whether or not by injecting discretion or by using the window of Article VII, the following points might help to reduce court control at the enforcement stage.

13-97 Subparagraph (a): Lack of arbitration agreement irrelevant if not invoked at the latest with first substantive statement or if not referred to court according to Article 16(3) Model Law. As regards state or state agencies, the earlier considerations concerning capacity could be used to make an effort, as suggested by Hazel Fox,[56] to forge a consensus on exclusion (or waiver) of state immunity also for execution, taking into account the commercial nature of the underlying transaction. The task would be formidable, yet the effort itself might assist in clarifying matters (and possibly carving out a limited sector from the vast area currently under consideration by the General Assembly and the International Law Commission).

13-98 Subparagraphs (b) and (d): Defect in composition of arbitral tribunal or in arbitral procedure needs to be more than a minor technical flaw or oversight ('De minimis non curat praetor') and was not apparently without influence on the outcome.

13-99 Subparagraph (e): 'Not yet binding' may be narrowly defined. Suspension counts only if ordered by a court, not if it is an automatic consequence imposed by law (as in France). Setting aside should be given effect within certain limits: like Article IX European Convention, no effect to setting aside based on public policy of place of origin; the necessary filter of international public policy is provided by paragraph (2)(b) of the New York Convention. No effect to setting aside for other, peculiar and internationally unacceptable grounds, which Jan Paulsson calls 'LSAs: local standard

---

the conditions apply', based on confirmations by native speakers as to the permissive nature of the respective wording (corresponding to 'may be refused'), leads him to the conclusion that these four languages 'clearly leave room for judicial discretion'(at p. 229). But one consequence of this imprecision is his conclusion (at p. 230) 'that it is unnecessary and indeed inappropriate to resort to the Convention's *travaux préparatoires*'. In truth, however, the search for an answer to a legislative ambiguity or, as in our case, gap may not (or is it: shall not?) exclude resort to the legislative history.

[56] Fox, 'State Immunity and Enforcement of Arbitral Awards: Do We Need an UNCITRAL Model Law Mark II for Execution Against State Property?' in (1996) 12 *Arbitration International* 89.

annulments'.[57] However, the classification as an irrelevant local standard should not be left to be determined by individual Congress participants and commentators; we need more predictable and universally agreed classifications, along the lines of the Model Law, probably confined to certain basic standards set forth therein such as those in Article 18 and some other mandatory provisions.

13-100 In conclusion, I would summarise my answer to the topic as follows: let the world itself decide whether it needs additional uniform legislation. The months and years ahead promise to be interesting.

13-101 And in searching for suitable solutions, let us not only look into the future but utilise the treasure trove of ancient laws, going back to the roots of arbitration. For example, we might learn from traditional Irish laws that used 'satire, ridicule and invective to enforce the law' or 'distraint of livestock as a way of forcing arbitration between a wrongdoer and a victim' (which in today's world would mean 'distraint of car, mobile telephone or computer'). I am less sure, though, whether in the current state of ethics the following very specific rule provides a viable model: 'If a person who is of a higher rank than you refuses to repay his debt you may sit at his doorstep and fast until he submits to arbitration. If you die before he submits he shall be blamed for your death and shall suffer lifelong disgrace'.[58]

---

[57] Paulsson, 'Awards set aside at the place of arbitration', *supra* n. 5, p. 24 at p. 26 and *supra* n. 52.

[58] Dowling Dalcy, *Traditional Irish Laws* (San Francisco 1998) at pp. 4 and 23.

*V.V. Veeder QC**

CHAPTER 14

LLOYD GEORGE, LENIN AND CANNIBALS: THE HARRIMAN ARBITRATION**

I. Introduction

14-1 Over 35 years ago, on a warm summer's evening on 26 July 1963, two elderly men walked across the Kremlin Square towards the Terem Palace. The shorter man was the First Secretary of the Central Committee of the Communist Party and the Chairman of the USSR Council of Ministers, Nikita Khrushchev. The second man was tall, looking like the millionaire son of a millionaire, which was what he was. He had served as the American ambassador to Moscow and London; and he had worked as a personal adviser to Presidents Roosevelt, Truman and now, President Kennedy. He had also been elected Governor of New York and had been a candidate for his party's nomination for President. An Anglophile, he had been a supporter and friend of Winston Churchill in London during the darkest days of the Second World War, a good friend of his son Randolph; and as it proved, an even closer friend of his daughter-in-law, Pamela

* Essex Court Chambers; Visiting Professor, King's College London.
** For access to the unpublished papers of Leslie Urquhart, I am much indebted to his grandson, Neil Foster, and his biographer, Professor Kett Kennedy, Mining Tsar: The Life and Times of Leslie Urquhart (Sydney, 1986). I am also grateful for help in researching the American, British and Russian archives (and other materials) from Naomi Benson, Micheline Decker, Artemis Kassi, Nudrat Majeed, David Mortlock, Tatyana Nazarenko, Sebastian Veeder, Sam Wordsworth and Ikko Yoshida. Of course, any errors are mine alone.
   This is a revised version of the author's 1999 School of International Arbitration Freshfields Arbitration Lecture delivered on 24 November 1999. The editors acknowledge with thanks permission to publish this contribution granted by Freshfields and the School of International Arbitration, Centre for Commercial Law Studies, Queen Mary and Westfield College, London University

Julian D.M. Lew and Loukas A. Mistelis (eds), Arbitration Insights, 257-287
© 2007 Kluwer Law International. Printed in the Netherlands

(who later, much later became his wife). This man was William Averell Harriman.

14-2 No two men could have been more different in background, outlook and character than Krushchev and Harriman; or so it might have seemed. As they approached the far side of the Kremlin near the Palace of Congresses, people waiting to enter this concert-hall applauded Khrushchev; and he began to shake hands with the crowd. At some point, as recorded by journalists present, Khrushchev turned to introduce Harriman, addressing him as a friend and colleague, a fine fellow (in Russian '*molodiets*'): 'This is Mr Harriman. He has just signed a test-ban agreement with us and now I am taking him to dinner. Do you think he has earned his dinner?' And the crowd cheered both men.[1] This was the occasion of the 1963 Moscow Treaty between the United States, the USSR and the United Kingdom, banning nuclear tests in the atmosphere, space and ocean. There were several significant moments between 1945 and 1989 where the Cold War took a decisive turn away from nuclear conflict; and this occasion was certainly one of them – barely nine months after the Cuban missile crisis and only 15 months before Khrushchev's fall from power.[2]

II. THE HARRIMAN CONCESSION (1925)

14-3 Now what was the reason for this open cordiality between Khrushchev and Harriman? It did not exist with the British negotiator, Lord Hailsham. As recorded in his memoirs, Lord Hailsham regarded Khrushchev as a 'very remarkable human being whose coarseness of language and anecdote absolutely beggared description'; and as for Harriman, Lord Hailsham strongly deprecated (in his judgement) Harriman's unnecessary toughness in negotiating with the Soviet Government.[3] To Khrushchev, Harriman should have been the paradigm Soviet class and political enemy – but he was not. In his memoirs, Khrushchev warmly described Harriman as 'a highly realistic man, an experienced specialist

---

[1] 'Life', 9 August 1963, 28ff; *see also* W. Averell Harriman, *America and Russia in a Changing World* (London, 1971), p. 99; and Isaacson and Thomas, *The Wise Men* (London, 1986), p. 633.

[2] Khrushchev had long been badgered towards this partial test-ban treaty by the father of the Soviet hydrogen bomb, Dr Andrei Sakharov: *see* A. Sakharov, *Sakharov Speaks* (London, 1974), pp. 33-34; and Khrushchev (Talbott ed. and trans.). *Krushchev Remembers – The Last Testament* (London, 1974), pp. 69-71.

[3] Hailsham, *A Sparrow's Flight* (London, 1990), pp. 340-343; G.Lewis, *Lord Hailsham* (London, 1997). pp. 204-213. Somewhat unkindly, Hailsham regarded Harriman as 'already ageing'. In return, Hailsham did not endear himself to Harriman at all: *see* W.Isaaeson and E. Thomas, *supra* n. 1, at p. 631 ('the shallow and ill-prepared Lord Hailsham').

who understood us',[4] and Khrushchev based the beginning of that special understanding on Harriman's early involvement in a Russian mining concession. In a muddled form, dictating his memoirs secretly into a tape-recorder at his dacha without access to contemporary papers long after he left power, Khrushchev recalled Harriman's concession as follows:

> It was common knowledge – I think I even read about it in the newspapers – that Harriman's family used to own some manganese mines in Georgia before the Revolution. I heard confirmation of this from Stalin's own mouth after the [1941-45] war ... Stalin mentioned in passing that it might be a good idea to compensate Harriman in some way for the loss of his mines. I don't know if anything ever came of the suggestion. I know it wasn't discussed in the leadership. Nothing was discussed in the leadership. Stalin could not stand to have his ideas questioned or deliberated. He might let you talk to him if you agreed with him.[5]

14-4 In fact, the Harriman concession had been granted *after* the Bolshevik Revolution, in 1925. At a time when the United States had firmly spurned any diplomatic or other official contact with the USSR, Harriman had been one of the first American traders to take advantage of the Soviet policy on foreign concessions, with the help of American and German capital. The Harriman concession was eventually a commercial failure; and after three years, Harriman terminated his concession on agreed terms, including compensation payable by the USSR. The Soviet Government honoured that settlement; and it was still paying off the final instalments when Harriman arrived in Moscow in late 1941 as Roosevelt's personal envoy to Stalin.

14-5 It was this early, personal experience which gave Harriman his 'special' understanding of the realities of Soviet power, to which thereafter, for the next 60 years of his life, he was always adamantly opposed as a politician and diplomat. Harriman was no appeaser; but equally, he was a realist: his toughness as a negotiator in business and diplomacy was the means to an end and never an end in itself. Harriman is recognised as one of the great statesmen of the twentieth century; and he was perhaps the greatest diplomat ever to serve the United States of America, a task he performed almost to the end of his long life in 1986, aged 94.

---

[4] Krushchev, *supra* n. 2, at p. 382.
[5] *Ibid.* p. 351.

III. THE HARRIMAN ARBITRATION (1928)

14-6 All this may seem a long way from international commercial arbitration. And yet, Harriman's settlement was the direct result of arbitration proceedings brought by his company against the USSR in 1928. These proceedings secured Harriman's amicable exit from the concession with financial compensation, a feat not equally achieved by any other British or US concessionaire. Also, in taking on the Soviet Government by means of an arbitration, Harriman plainly earned its respect; or in Khrushchev's telling words: Harriman 'understood us'. The Harriman arbitration was one of the first international arbitrations to which the USSR was a party, predating even the Lena Goldfields Arbitration of 1930;[6] and it was certainly the first arbitration between the USSR and any American firm.[7] The proceedings were kept confidential by both parties, then and later; Harriman never spoke about the arbitration publicly; nor did the Soviet Government.[8] It is only the later release of archives in Moscow and Washington which allows us to know the story at all.[9]

---

[6] Under the 1921 and 1925 German-Soviet Treaties, there had been a number of non-consensual arbitrations between Soviet and German parties; but their number and extent are contested; *contrast* A. Nussbaum, 'Treaties on Commercial Arbitration – A Test of International Private-Law Legislation' (1942) 56 *Harv. L.Rev.* 219, 220 and E.S. Rashba, 'Settlement of Disputes in Commercial Dealings with the Soviet Union' (1945) 45 *Col. L.Rev.539* at p. 546 n. 82. (Underlying the English test cases surrounding the 1921 Anglo-Soviet Trade Agreement, there had been an arbitration clause in the timber sale contract agreed between Krassin and Sagor in August 1920; but that contract was probably collusive in order to test the position under English law in regard to third party claimants: *Luther* v. *Sagor (also 'Sagar')*[1921] 3 KB 532, 7 Lloyds Rep. 218, 109, 157 (Court of Appeal), reversing [1921] 1 KB 456, 5 Lloyd's Rep. 451, 287 (Roche J);*Walneff* v. *The All-Russian Co-Operative Society* (1921) 8 Lloyd's Rep. 338 (Bailhache J); and *Bragoseo* v. *Sagor* (1921) 8 Lloyd's Rep. 388 (Sankey J)).

[7] Dr Armand Hammer referred to an 'arbitration' in the summer of 1924 between Sinclair Oil and the Soviet Government, cancelling a concession over oil fields in Northern Sakhalin: *see* Hammer, *The Quest of the Romanoff Treasure* (1932), p. 141. This was a concession agreement granted in 1922 to Sinclair Exploration Company but cancelled by the Soviet Government in 1924 on the ground that the concessionaire had failed to take up its concession (because the Japanese still occupied Sakhalin and refused it entry); there was in fact no arbitration and the termination was ordered by the Moscow People's Court: see B. Landau, 'Konzessionsen in Sowjetrussland' *Ostrecht* 1926 No. 5, 478, at p. 487 (Professor Landau was a legal specialist on foreign concessions in Moscow).

[8] Harriman never referred to it in his writings or interviews; and before the Lena Goldfields Arbitration in 1930, the Soviet Government denied that any arbitration had ever taken place with any of its concessionaires.

[9] The American archives on the Harriman concession are found principally at the US National Archives, Washington DC, US State Dept Decimal File 861.637 (cited *infra* as 'US Decimal File'); and the archives of the USSR Main Concessions Committee (*Glavkoncesskom*) are kept at the State Archive of the Russian Federation in Moscow (cited *infra* as 'GARF'). I have also

IV. 'WHY' IS ARBITRATION?

14-7 The story of the Harriman arbitration addresses a question on international commercial arbitration which may need answering for the beginning of the twenty-first century, 76 years after it began with the League of Nations' Geneva Protocol on Arbitration Clauses of 1923 and 41 years after the New York Arbitration Convention of 1958. In recent Freshfields lectures, we have heard a great deal about 'what' is arbitration and 'how' is arbitration; and I can add nothing useful to those answers, so superbly given by previous Freshfields lecturers. In this lecture, I should like to address the different question, 'why'; or in short, why does international commercial arbitration exist at all?

14-8 It is now axiomatic that in the field of transnational trade all over the world, arbitration is the preferred method for resolving business disputes; but its increasing popularity cannot be explained solely by the relative enforceability of awards under the 1958 New York Convention, as compared with national court judgments. Its attraction preceded the New York Convention; and even then it did not depend upon the more limited effect of the 1923 Geneva Protocol or 1927 Geneva Convention. Nevertheless, its age is deceptive: international arbitration is still precocious and its existence less assured than it might seem. The number of international arbitrations is relatively small compared to the increasing volume of transnational trade; and its jurisprudence is surprisingly slight given that the wealth of the world is now predominantly made up of contractual promises. For example, its jurisprudence does not begin to compare historically with the weight of law made by (say) the English Commercial Court in London or the Federal and State Courts in New York. The efficacy of its procedures is even now being sorely tested by users and practitioners, in England and elsewhere; and it remains uncertain whether it can survive these tests in their more extreme form. And so 'why' is international arbitration is a big question; the complete answer remains elusive, at least to me; but my answer here is happily confined by the title of this lecture.

14-9 From 1920, the development of foreign trade with Soviet Russia and the USSR took place in political, economic and legal conditions utterly hostile to the development of international commercial arbitration; and yet it did develop. In the early months of Soviet Russia, before the Soviet policy on foreign concessions and Lenin's New Economic Policy, the Soviet leaders were legal

---

made extensive use of Leslie Urquhart's extensive private papers, an invaluable archive on microfilm (cited below as 'Urquhart Papers'), which was commissioned by Professor Kennedy for his outstanding biography, *supra* n. * *.

nihilists deeply antipathetic to commercial law and the independent adjudication of civil law disputes. Indeed there was then no civil or commercial code in Soviet Russia; the Czarist codes and courts had been swept away; and in the words of Lenin's principal specialist on legal affairs, A.G. Goikhbarg: 'Each conscious proletarian knows ... that religion is the opiate of the people. But very seldom does anybody realise that law is a still more poisonous and intoxicating opiate for the same people'.[10] The Harriman arbitration was thus a flower which sprang from poisonous and blasted ground; and moreover this was not *terra incognita* but *terra nova*. The Harriman arbitration was nonetheless no solitary plant. It blossomed against the background of the 1923 Geneva Protocol, the creation of the ICC Court of International Arbitration in 1922; and the new world-wide interest in commercial arbitration as an alternative to state courts – because the immediate origin of all these events was essentially the same.

V. PEACE THROUGH TRADE

14-10   From the beginning of the Versailles Conference, the British Prime Minister, Lloyd George, had promoted the view that the future for peace lay with transnational trade. Even after the Versailles Treaty of 1919, at a time when much of Europe lay impoverished or in famine, with many of her workers unemployed and her factories silent, Lloyd George still promoted 'Peace through Trade'. Thwarted by the malign efforts of others, Lloyd George's policy had failed in regard to Germany, with tragic results. However, that same policy now almost succeeded with Soviet Russia. His efforts to re-establish trade and diplomatic links with Soviet Russia led the British Government in January 1920 to open negotiations with the Soviet Government in the guise of the Trade Delegation from the Russian Co-Operative Societies; in March 1921 to conclude the first Anglo-Russian Trade Agreement, with *de facto* recognition; and in 1922 to convene the Genoa Economic Conference which Soviet Russia attended, along with representatives or observers from 34 countries (whether or not members of the League of Nations or even recognised by each other). From the beginning, Lloyd George also contended that essential to trade, as trade was to peace, was a system of law and a process for deciding legal rights; and from his earliest

---

[10]   See O.S. Ioffe and P.M. Maggs, *Soviet Law in Theory and Practice* (London, 1983), p. 14 (yet, Goikhbarg was also partly responsible for the 1922 RSFSR Civil Code, on which he also published a leading commentary; this code was promulgated in the autumn of 1922 as a result of the NEP and the 1922 Genoa Conference; and its terms were heavily influenced by the French and German civil codes: *see* E.H Carr, *Socialism in One Country 1924-1926* (London, 1958) p. 75ff).

meetings with the leader of the Soviet Trade Delegation (Krassin), Lloyd George secured agreement on the process of arbitration.[11] Lloyd George's policy towards Soviet Russia was bitterly opposed by France and by members of his own cabinet, including the Foreign Office (which played no significant part in the 1921 Trade Agreement or even the 1922 Genoa Conference). In the House of Commons on 7 June 1920, Lloyd George defended his negotiations with the Soviet Trade Delegation, in these terms:

> It is quite a new doctrine that you are responsible for the Government when you trade with its people. Were we responsible for the Czarist Government? Were we responsible for it, with its corruption, its misgovernment, its pogroms, its scores of thousands of innocent people massacred? We were not responsible for this, yet we continued our relations. Why, this country has opened up most of the cannibal trade of the world, whether in the South Seas or in Kumassie.[12] Have we ever declined to do it because we disapproved of the population?[13]

14-11   Later on 3 April 1922, before the Genoa Conference, Lloyd George laid out the basic principle in his new policy towards Soviet Russia: 'We have failed to restore Russia to sanity by force. I believe we can save her by trade. Commerce has a sobering influence in its operations'.[14] Again, this was 'Peace through Trade'. This double-edged reference to cannibals, however, was never popular with the Soviet Government.[15]

---

[11]   At their first meeting on 31 May 1920, both Lloyd George and Krassin raised the question as to the legal basis on which trade could be conducted (*Documents on British Foreign Policy 1919-1939*, Vol. VIII, No. 24, p. 281 at pp. 284, 290-291); and at their meeting on 16 June 1920, when Lloyd George contended that British traders had no knowledge and therefore no confidence in Soviet Russia's judicial system, Krassin replied that he was prepared to agree to the establishment of an 'arbitration court' (partly British and partly Russian) to settle such disputes (Lloyd George MSS, House of Lords Library, Folder 3, Box 107 No F/202/3/19, pp. 8 and 11). The latter meeting was also attended by the Norwegian explorer, Dr Fridjof Nansen, who countersigned the minutes as a fair summary of the proceedings. (For reasons which remain obscure, there was no reference to arbitration in the eventual 1921 Trade Agreement).

[12]   Kumasi is now in Ghana.

[13]   Hansard, Vol. 152, col. 1898 (3 April 1922).

[14]   Hansard. Vol. 152, col. 1898 (3 April 1922).

[15]   Gromyko and Ponomarev (ed.), *Soviet Foreign Policy 1917-1980*, Vol. 1 (1917-1945) (Moscow, 1981), p. 129. In the Lena Goldfields Case, the German and British arbitrators were attacked in Pravda on 9 September 1930 for making an award without the third Soviet arbitrator, on the otherwise curious ground (*inter alia*) that as 'bad jugglers of figures' unable even to amuse children, 'they ought to find their audience amongst the savages of the Pacific islands who do not know how to count up to three'.

14-12   The Genoa Conference failed in May 1922; its follow-up conference at the Hague in June-July 1922 did not succeed; there was no Marshall Plan for economic recovery; the United States remained aloof from European affairs; and Lloyd George left office in October 1922, never to hold public office again. But Lloyd George's policy of Peace through Trade is the great lesson of the twentieth century. It is the policy which at last brought permanent peace between France, Germany and Western Europe; and the rock on which the future depends for the European continent (from Cork to Khabarovsk) – and the world. Yet the same question remains today as it did for Lloyd George: even assuming that we are not listed on the menu and the cannibals are not warming the pot, how exactly do you do business with cannibals? The Anglo-American experience with Soviet concessions in the period up from 1920 to 1929[16] shows that there is an answer: you can eat with cannibals if the spoon is long enough; and if that spoon (or one of them) is international commercial arbitration.

VI. SOVIET CONCESSIONS POLICY

14-13   The Soviet policy on foreign concessions pre-dated Lenin's New Economic Policy; but by 1921, the two were related in the Soviet Government's conduct of foreign trade. From the beginning, this policy was a massive departure from all previous Soviet economic policies. First, in offering back as concessions industrial properties confiscated from their former foreign owners, the Soviet Government was virtually restoring those properties to the control and benefit of those former owners. Although title to such properties was retained by the Soviet Government, the long term of the concession was commercially similar to the leasehold estate held by the foreign owner on lands owned by the Czar (which had been common for Siberian mining properties). Second, the right freely to export and import granted to the foreign concessionaire was a major exception to the Soviet Government's foreign trade monopoly. Third, the concession delivered over to the foreign concessionaire rights over Soviet labour and Soviet trade unions, as an extraordinary exception to the general law. Fourth, the Soviet Government suspended many of its powers against the foreign concessionaire and its foreign employees: for example, the right to enter and leave Soviet Russia freely, exemption from oppressive taxation, immunity from requisition of labour and materials, and so on. Lastly, and most important for present purposes, the Soviet Government was prepared (eventually) to exempt the foreign

---

[16] In 1929, the Soviet Government's foreign concession policy effectively ended when Stalin introduced the First Five-Year Plan.

concessionaire from the Soviet courts in regard to disputes over the concession. For all these reasons, a concession agreement was much more than a private law contract under Soviet law: it was also a special higher law derogating from the general law.

14-14 In fact, there was then little Soviet law on contractual and civil obligations. The Russian Civil Code came only in late 1922, partly as a result of Lloyd George's endeavours in London and Genoa; the 1923 Russian Civil Procedural Code did not permit commercial arbitration at all; and of course Soviet Russia could not ratify the 1923 Geneva Protocol or 1927 Geneva Convention. That was a strange irony: the Geneva Protocol was conceived at the Genoa Conference which had passed on the project to the League of Nations at Geneva.[17] But whilst it was possible for Soviet Russia to support arbitration at Genoa, it remained politically hostile to the League of Nations and as a non-member, it could not accede to the 1923 Protocol or 1927 Geneva Convention; and it never did so.

VII. URQUHART AND HAMMER

14-15 The Harriman Arbitration was preceded by a number of false starts. He was preceded by two other concessionaires from the United States and the United Kingdom: Leslie Urquhart of Russo-Asiatic Consolidated Limited and Dr Armand Hammer, then of the Allied Drug and Chemical Corporation.

A. The Urquhart Negotiations (1921)[18]

14-16 The first concessionaire, British or American, was to have been Leslie Urquhart. He was a Scottish mining engineer, then the chairman of Russo-Asiatic Consolidated Limited, an English company run from London which had

---

[17] Article 14 of the Resolutions of the Genoa Conference's Economic Committee, relating to the best means of safeguarding the validity of voluntary agreements for international commercial arbitration, was referred by the League's Council at its meeting on 13 May 1922, on the British Government's initiative, to a sub-committee of six experts of its Economic Committee; the chairman of this sub-committee was F.D. MacKinnon KC (soon to become Mr Justice MacKinnon); and after a drafting session on 3-4 July 1922 at the Board of Trade in London, the eventual result was the 1923 Geneva Protocol: *League of Nations Official Journal*, June 1922 (pp. 616, 618, 620); August 1922 (pp. 987, 992, 1004); and November 1922 (p.1410).

[18] *See generally* T.S. Martin, 'The Urquhart Concession and Anglo-Soviet Relations, 1921-1922' *Jahrbücher für Geschichte Osteuropas* 20 (1972), pp. 551-559; K.H. Kennedy, *supra* n. * *, p. 162ff; Lubov Krassin, *Leonid Krassin: His Life and Work* (London, 1929) p. 184ff; and S.I. Liberman, *Building Lenin's Russia* (Chicago, 1945) p. 159ff.

controlled the largest copper, zinc, and iron mines in the Urals and Western Siberia before the October 1917 Revolution. Its mines had also produced silver and lead (60 per cent of Russia's total annual production), extending over a million hectares of land. Born in Russia in 1875, Urquhart had spent almost 25 years working in Russia before the October Revolution, dealing in liquorice to oil in the Caucasus as well as minerals in Siberia; he was well-informed on Russian affairs; he spoke good Russian; and his rotund appearance, in the later words of one Soviet official 'made him seem the reincarnation of an old-time Russian landowner, an enlightened nobleman of tsarist times'.[19] In every sense, Urquhart was a huge figure in Russia before and after October 1917, with enormous physical and financial courage. As Vice-Consul in Baku during the 1905 Revolution, he had been awarded the Victoria and Albert Medal for saving the lives of the British community, the equivalent today of the George Cross. After 1905, Urquhart built up his Siberian mines with English and American capital, which included the financial and engineering skills of Herbert Hoover, long before he became Secretary of Commerce and later President of the United States. After the nationalisation of his company's properties in 1918, Urquhart's company had registered claims for compensation against Soviet Russia in the massive sum of £56,000,000 (about one third of the total for such British claims); but the Soviet Government vehemently denied such claims, even if it had any money to pay such compensation (which it did not).

14-17   And so after the Anglo-Soviet Trade Agreement, in early June 1921, Urquhart attempted to obtain long leases over four of his former mining enterprises in negotiations with Krassin, the head of the Soviet Trade Delegation in London, in the form of a long-term concession. He and Krassin became friends; and the latter was frequently invited with his family to Urquhart's country home. Krassin was an unusual revolutionary: an electrical engineer, he had been a director of Siemens in St Petersburg before the First World War; and he was almost as much a practical businessman as Urquhart himself. After preliminary discussions, Krassin invited Urquhart to visit Moscow in August and September 1921; Lenin encouraged these negotiations (in which he took part personally); and a draft concession agreement was prepared. Given Urquhart's position as a major claimant, this draft agreement was intended by the Soviet Government to establish publicly its policy of the former foreign owner being offered back his confiscated property under a long-term concession agreement,

---

[19] S.I. Liberman, *ibid*, at p. 159. (Liberman, a Soviet foreign trade specialist in timber, worked with Krassin in London before defecting from the USSR Commissariat for Foreign Trade).

on terms which included the waiver of all claims for compensation arising from nationalisation. Accordingly, the Soviet Government was not merely negotiating a contract with Urquhart: it was also seeking to establish a public precedent.

14-18   There were, however, several grave problems, one of which concerned the arbitration clause where the Soviet Government was insisting that the chairman, or umpire, must be a Russian nominated by the Russian Academy of Science. There was a meeting of the parties' joint commission on 12 September 1921 in Moscow which recorded their very different starting-points: 'Arbitration Commission: The Soviet Government representatives insisted on the candidate for the position of arbiter being a Russian subject. This the Concessionaire categorically refused to accept and insisted on the wording of his own draft clause'.[20] Back in London, on 21 September 1921, Urquhart reported the difficulty to his board and principal shareholders; and as those minutes record:

> Clause 21: The Meeting strongly felt that an arbitrator must of necessity be a free and unprejudiced person whose actions are not controlled in any way by either of the contracting parties, and who is free from any restriction or restraint of any kind which might directly or indirectly tend to prejudice his findings in favour of either party. For this reason the Meeting emphasised that the President of the proposed Arbitration Committee should be a person of position and experience, unprejudiced in any way, and the Meeting decided that it could not withdraw the proposal that, failing mutual agreement, such President should be nominated by the American Society of Mining and Metallurgy.

14-19   And as the board and principal shareholders concluded:

> It was the unanimous feeling of the Meeting, in view of the suppression of the [Czarist] Civil Code, the suppression of Mining and Forest Regulations and of the power previously held by the local authorities in regard to schools, hospitals, roads etc, that the Company is running very great risks in signing an Agreement of this nature without the new conditions pertaining to these or any new institutions which may be established clearly set forth in the Agreement; and it was decided that until this is done, an Arbitration

---

[20] Urquhart Papers, Reel 7, p. 5985 at p. 5987 (in English; but note Urquhart's use of the Scots term 'arbiter' and not 'arbitrator').

Clause, giving an unprejudiced arbitrator the widest powers, is deemed a vital necessity.[21]

14-20   Urquhart then continued his negotiations with Krassin in London; but neither side would budge on the arbitration clause.[22] Urquhart and his board were adamantly insisting upon a neutral presiding arbitrator; and the Soviet Government insisted that he must be a Soviet citizen. This dispute over the arbitration clause was one of the principal reasons for the collapse of the negotiations in mid-October 1921; and Urquhart withdrew from further talks with the Soviet Government, with a strongly-worded announcement to his shareholders. This was a severe public blow to Soviet prestige, only six months after the Anglo-Soviet Trade Agreement which had promised so much but so far delivered little.

14-21   At a subsequent meeting of the Council of Labour and Defence chaired by Lenin, a Soviet foreign trade specialist (Liberman) recalls Lenin asking what had happened to the negotiations with Urquhart[23]: 'Whatever has become of our Comrade Urquhart? We do not hear of him or about him any more. And yet he was so polite and obliging when he was here on his visit. He was so full of flattery that we thought any minute now he might file an application for membership of the Communist party!' After a moment's silence, the answer came from the Vice-Commissar of Foreign Trade, Moisel Frumkin, Krassin's deputy and an old Bolshevik, in these terms:[24]

> Let me tell you a Jewish story: A Jewish woman was very sad because her husband had gone away and showed no sign of returning to her. Her friends finally advised her to go to a wise rabbi with the question, 'When will my husband come back?' But, as was usual in such minor cases, the rabbi's assistants would not let her in for a personal interview with the sage. She had to submit the question in writing ... An assistant brought back the rabbi's answer: 'Your husband will return in two weeks'. Two weeks passed, and two more, and still there was no husband. The woman went to

---

[21] Urquhart Papers, Reel 4, p. 3369 at pp. 3370 and 3371.

[22] The negotiations were formally terminated by Urquhart in mid-October 1921 during a visit to Krassin in London, followed by a long letter quoted in Lubov Krassin, *supra* n. 18, pp. 188-198. Urquhart did not blame Krassin personally; and his letter went through many drafts before its final version, clearly aimed at another audience in Moscow.

[23] Liberman, *supra* n. 18, at p. 162.

[24] M.I. Frumkin, shot on 29 July 1938: see R. Conquest, *The Great Terror* (Oxford, 1990), p. 120.

the rabbi again, sent in the question ... for the second time, but received the same written reply: 'Your husband will come back in two weeks'. But when a month had elapsed after that, with no result whatsoever, and then a third month, the indignant woman demanded a personal meeting with the rabbi. It was granted. The rabbi listened to the woman, then said: 'Your husband won't return at all'. Heartbroken, crushed, the woman left the rabbi's study. On her way out she encountered the assistant and she halted to berate him for deceiving her with the two previous answers, allegedly given by the rabbi. But the assistant said: 'I didn't deceive you. Those first two replies were from the rabbi'. 'But why', wailed the poor woman, 'why did he say on those first two occasions that my husband would come back to me?' 'Because the first two times he didn't see you in person!' was the assistant's explanation. 'Well, Vladimir Ilyich', Frumkin summed up, 'we should all understand why Urquhart will never return. He hadn't seen us before he came here'.

14-22 There was, however, one immediate beneficiary from the failure of Urquhart's negotiations in October 1921. After this public disappointment, the Soviet Government needed a quick propaganda victory for its foreign concession policy, preferably with an American untainted by connections with Britain. Speed and other circumstances therefore dictated a friendly co-contractor, a political pilgrim already trading in Moscow. That friendly American resident trader existed in the person of Dr Armand Hammer, then only 25 years old and still at the very beginning of his extraordinary business career, or careers.[25] Within three very short weeks, Hammer became the first American concessionaire in Soviet Russia.

B. Hammer's First Concession (1921)[26]

14-23 In his great study on Soviet concessions, the American historian Anthony Sutton places Dr Hammer and his family firmly in the group of foreign

---

[25] Hammer's special business skills are best illustrated in the case decided by the English Commercial Court in *Occidental Worldwide Investment Corp.* v. *Skibs A/S Avanti and others (The Siboen and Sibotre)* [1976] 1 Lloyd's Rep 293 (Kerr J).

[26] *See generally* Armand Hammer. *The Quest of the Romanoff Treasure* (1932), p. 149ff; A.C.Sutton, *Western Technology and Soviet Economic Development 1917-1930* (Stanford, 1968), pp. 108, 237, 268, 285; S. Weinberg, *Armand Hammer: The Untold Story* (London, 1989), p. 42ff; and E.J. Epstein, *Dossier: The Secret History of Armand Hammer* (New York, 1996).

concessionaires with non-economic links to the Bolshevik cause, their contribution being to lead the way and to instill confidence in the Soviet Government in the hope that other genuine foreign traders would follow.[27] Hammer's first concession was a concession agreement of 28 October 1921 for the Alapayesk asbestos mine near Ekaterinburg in the Urals;[28] and it was publicly announced in Moscow on 3 November 1921 as a 'victory for the concession policy of the Soviet Government'.[29] The Alapayesk mine was a small mine; it was never a successful concession; and it lost money for Hammer; but it was soon amicably terminated, in or before 1924, having served its immediate political purpose.

14-24 In fact, as legal document, this concession agreement was a sham. We can tell because it had a most peculiar arbitration clause, contained in a confidential addendum. In the concession agreement itself, article 19 provided that the Soviet Government could terminate the concession by decree if the concessionaire was in breach; article 21 provided that the concession agreement could also be cancelled 'in a [Soviet] court of law'; and article 30 provided for Soviet court jurisdiction over all disputes. However, Hammer had also secured an amendment to these draconian provisions; the addendum was drafted by Hammer, and as recorded by him in English, it read as follows:

> To avoid all red tape, delays and hindrances, the [Soviet] Government undertakes to appoint a committee of two persons, one from the Workers' and Peasants' Organisation and one from the 'Cheka' to whom in case of misunderstandings, we can refer as competent authority to settle all disputes without loss of time.[30]

---

[27] Sutton, *supra* n. 26, at pp. 283 and 285ff.

[28] Armand Hammer, *supra* n. 26, at p.84. It was signed in the Commissariat of Foreign Trade by Hammer and Boris O. Mishell for the Allied Drug and Chemical Corporation and P.A. Bogdanov (Chairman of VSNKh) and Maxim Litvinov (as Vice-Commissar of Foreign Affairs) for the RSFSR (GARF 8350/3/833, p.4 *see also* Urquhart Papers, Reel 4, p. 3684, for an English translation, without the addendum).

[29] Letter to Urquhart dated 16 February 1922 from the Department of Overseas Trade (Foreign Office and Board of Trade), relaying a despatch from the British Commercial Mission in Moscow with an English translation of Hammer's concession agreement, then still confidential (Urquhart Papers, Reel 4, p. 3682).

[30] Armand Hammer, *supra* n. 26, pp. 49 and 82. (The first organisation was RKI or Rabkrin, the Workers' and Peasants' Inspection (*Rabochaya i Krest'yanskaya Inspektsiya*).

14-25   Lenin agreed this addendum without hesitation;[31] and why not? Unlike Urquhart, Hammer was not seeking the appointment of any neutral arbitrator. And Lenin doubtless had great confidence in the Soviet worker or peasant arbitrator, particularly if he or she were guided by a Soviet co-arbitrator from the Cheka, the Soviet secret police little known for its lack of partisanship in the Soviet cause. And we should note here the absence of any third arbitrator or umpire (neutral or otherwise). With a Chekist as co-arbitrator, it would not in practice be necessary to have a third arbitrator or any other tie-breaking mechanism.

14-26   Not surprisingly, the Soviet Government never publicised Hammer's addendum containing this arbitration clause; and Lenin's *Collected Works*, as published over the years in Moscow and abroad, omitted any reference to its terms.[32] The friendly termination of this asbestos concession meant that the 'Cheka' arbitration clause was never invoked by Hammer; and indeed, how could it be? For a real arbitration clause intended to provide an effective remedy, it was necessary to await the return of Leslie Urquhart.

C. Urquhart's Concession Agreement (1922)

14-27   As Lloyd George pursued his foreign policy on Soviet Russia further into 1922 with the Genoa and Hague Conferences, the earlier breakdown in negotiations over the Urquhart concession proved only temporary. Urquhart attended both conferences, as chairman of the Association of British Creditors in Russia and as an unofficial adviser to the British Government; and so did Krassin for the Soviet Government. During the summer of 1922, shortly after the Hague Conference had dispersed, negotiations resumed between Urquhart and Krassin, on the Soviet Government's initiative. These negotiations were soon successful; and a concession agreement was signed in Berlin on 9 September 1922 by Krassin and Urquhart for a period of 99 years – subject to formal ratification by the Soviet Government within one month.

---

[31]   Hammer's version was an incomplete draft, limited to five clauses. There was a further draft (in Russian) signed in English by Hammer and Mishell on 28 October 1921; and the final version was signed by Lenin on the following day as chairman of the RSFSR Council of Peoples' Commissars, with seven clauses (GARF 8350/3/83, pp. 12 and 13; GARF 8350/1/83, p.8). Subject to a slight difference in wording, probably caused by translating Hammer's text into Russian, the 'Cheka' arbitration clause remained the same.

[32]   *See*, for example, V.I. Lenin, *Collected Works* (London, 1970), Vol. 45, pp. 362, 394, 684. Yet, Hammer published his version of the addendum in 1932; but like several statements in this book, at the time maybe no-one took it too seriously.

14-28 The arbitration clause was a compromise of the parties' previous positions. There would be five arbitrators, two appointed by each party and the fifth presiding arbitrator, if not agreed by the four arbitrators within one month, would be chosen by the concessionaire from a list of six candidates drawn up by the Soviet Government, who would be 'of world wide or European fame as learned men, lawyers, engineers or public men'. This form of wording did not necessarily exclude a Soviet citizen; but equally it did not necessarily mean that all six candidates would be Soviet citizens. It was a major compromise by the Soviet Government towards accepting a neutral presiding arbitrator. There was another compromise by Urquhart: the arbitration must sit in Moscow; but its decisions would be final and require immediate fulfilment. And if the concessionaire or the Soviet Government defaulted in the machinery for appointing any arbitrator, the other innocent party could then refer the dispute to the London High Court or the Moscow People's Court (as the case might be).[33]

14-29 The news of this concession agreement spread around the world: it was seen as an historic breakthrough. Krassin left immediately for Moscow to procure the Soviet Government's ratification; and that is when the trouble began. On 5 and 6 October 1922, at Lenin's insistence and in his presence, the Central Committee and the Council of People's Commissars refused to ratify the Urquhart concession. The true reasons remain unclear, partly because Lenin (already ill) changed his mind more than once. One reason given at the time by the Soviet Government was the continuing absence of diplomatic relations between Soviet Russia and Great Britain, with *de jure* recognition; and another reason was the British Government's then refusal to admit Soviet Russia to the Lausanne Conference on the Turkish Question. Maybe Lenin feared that the Urquhart concession would still bring no large foreign loans urgently needed for industrial recovery in Russia. And maybe, looking at the concession agreement, Lenin did not like it as a public precedent for other foreign concessionaires: whilst not offering any compensation for the loss of its property rights, the concession agreement nonetheless granted to the foreign concessionaire an advance of £150,000 in cash and 20 million roubles in Russian state bonds; and this concessionaire, as an active supporter of the former 'White' Kolchak regime in Siberia, had been severely criticised by the Soviet Government's Mikhailov

---

[33] The concession agreement was signed and sealed by Krassin and Urquhart, the former using the seal of the RSFSR (as authorised by its Council of Peoples' Commissars) and the latter (for want of the company's seal in London) his personal signet ring with the Urquhart clan's motto: 'mean, speak and do well' (PRO FO371/8162; Urquhart Papers, Reel 4, p. 3690; Lubov Krassin, *supra* n. 18, p. 199). The arbitration clause was contained in article 22 of the agreement.

Commission. However, whatever the reason or reasons, there is no evidence at all that Lenin's veto was based on the existence of an arbitration clause where the balance of decision-making could lie with a neutral non-Soviet presiding arbitrator.

14-30 This veto was Lenin's firm and final decision on the Urquhart concession, one of the last political decisions in his working life; and the Soviet Government made it public on 7 October 1922. Krassin was bitterly disappointed; and as he wrote from Moscow on the following day to his wife in London: 'Once again all my work, energy, efforts and ability have been wasted, and a small group of mules and imbeciles have undone all my work, just as a boy might destroy the thin web of a spider with one blow'.[34] Krassin then sought to resign from his post as Commissar for Foreign Trade; but his offer was bluntly refused by Lenin: 'We dismiss people from their posts; but we do not permit them to resign'.[35] Urquhart never received his concession; and Lloyd George's Government fell in the following week, on 19 October 1922. However, what was Soviet Russia's loss became Australia's gain. Urquhart then devoted the remaining years of his life to developing a new mine in Australia; and today Mount Isa Mines in Queensland remains a tribute to Urquhart's huge mining and financial skills.

VIII. THE HARRIMAN CONCESSION AGREEMENT

14-31 By 1923, the Soviet policy on foreign concessions appeared to have failed. There were a large number of small concessions mostly with German and Baltic firms; but there was nothing in the form of 'superconcessions', in Krassin's phrase, from either Britain or America. The position began to change with the United Kingdom's *de jure* recognition of the USSR on 1 February 1924; and in June 1924 in New York, negotiations began between Harriman and representatives of the Soviet Government. These negotiations were protracted, partly because Harriman was concerned to keep the support of the mines' former owners, particularly those in Germany; and the Soviet Government was co-ordinating its negotiations with other British and American interests concerned with mining concessions in Siberia, the Lena Goldfields Company[36] and the

---

[34] Lubov Krassin, *ibid*, at p. 203.

[35] Lubov Krassin, *ibid*, at p. 204, Krassin then fell ill; he recovered and eventually died in London on 24 November 1926. His family did not return to the USSR.

[36] Lena Goldfields was an English company; and under its concession agreement made in April and November 1925, in the Russian language only, it took over its own former mining

Tetihue Mining Corporation.[37] All three involved British and American capital; Lena Goldfields was to be the largest concession ever granted by the USSR; and Harriman's concession was to be the second largest.[38]

14-32 The Harriman concession agreement was eventually signed on 12 June 1925 in Moscow; and it included an elaborate arbitration clause in Russian and English. The concession concerned a large manganese deposit at Chiatura, to the west of Tbilisi in Georgia, an area which before the First World War had been the world's largest producer of manganese, producing almost half the world supply. The deposit had then been worked by a number of small private owners: Georgian, German, Belgian and French. Their mines had been confiscated by the Soviet Government (without compensation), after the Soviet invasion of independent Georgia in February 1921. (Harriman bought up their claims as a condition of the concession agreement in return for a share of the profits). Harriman undertook to work the whole deposit for 20 years, covering 7,000 acres, to build a modern concentration plant and a new broad-gauge railway and to import the technical services of US and British mining engineers. It was a vast project in difficult terrain, in every sense.

---

properties in Siberia. This agreement contained an elaborate arbitration clause; and it was negotiated by the Soviet Government in tandem with the arbitration clause in the Harriman concession (which was made in both Russian and English). The two arbitration clauses are therefore very similar (but not identical); and although the Lena Goldfields clause was agreed earlier in time, it became effective later. (The history of the Lena Arbitration in 1930, two years after the Harriman Arbitration, has already been told elsewhere: see the author's article in (1998) 17 *ICLQ* 717 appending the Lena arbitration clause, with the references there cited).

[37] The Tetihue Mining Corporation Limited was also an English company incorporated on 18 May 1925 (its London Soheitors were Freshfields, Leese and Munn). Unusually, it was formed to take over an existing concession granted by the Soviet Government on 25 July 1924 to Russian citizens who had been the previous owners of these lead, silver and zinc mines 230 miles north of Vladivostock in Eastern Siberia. If a copy exists of this 1924 concession agreement, it has not been found; but as a Soviet concession, it would probably not have contained any arbitration clause. The concession was terminated under a settlement agreement made in 1932 without recourse to arbitration.

[38] For the history of the Harriman concession, *see generally* Harriman, *supra* n. 1, at pp. 2-7; W. Averell Harriman and Elie Abel, *Special Envoy to Churchill and Stalin 1941-1946* (New York, 1975); E.J. Kahn Jr, 'W. Averell Harriman Profiles Plenipotentiary – II', The New Yorker (10 May 1952), pp. 19-51; J.E. Spurr, 'Russian Manganese Concession' *Foreign Affairs* V, No. 3 (April 1927), pp. 506-507; C. Lewis, *The United States and Foreign Investment Problems* (Washington DC, 1948), p. 178; W. Isaacson and E. Thomas, *supra* n. 1, p. 99; and E.H. Carr, *Socialism in One Country*, Vol. 3, Pt I (London, 1964), pp. 183-185. (None of these memoirs, interviews or histories records the Harriman Arbitration).

14-33 Harriman was also taking a calculated commercial risk: the world-wide demand for manganese in steel production was relatively stable; and accordingly the world price of manganese was highly sensitive to over-production. Harriman thought that he had bought control of all Soviet manganese exports; but he was to be proven wrong. In addition to competition from new manganese mines in other parts of the world, the Soviet Government (with German technical assistance), soon decided to break his *de facto* Soviet monopoly by opening itself a new manganese mine in the Ukraine; and there were to be other grave difficulties for Harriman in operating the concession. To avoid financial disaster, Harriman soon resorted to the concession agreement's arbitration clause.

IX. THE HARRIMAN ARBITRATION CLAUSE

14-34 At a time when there were no institutional arbitration rules acceptable to the Soviet Government, it is not surprising that the Harriman arbitration clause was a long clause providing detailed rules on the composition of the arbitration tribunal, the conduct of the arbitration and the enforcement of its decisions.[39] The clause consisted of 17 distinct provisions, only a few of which are here relevant: the full English version is appended below.[40]

14-35 The first paragraph was an attempt to ensure that all disputes between the Soviet Government and a concessionaire including its interpretation, execution, performance and breach should be referred to and determined by an arbitration tribunal. The second paragraph was crucial: the Soviet Government there agreed that there would be three arbitrators, two designated by the parties, but the third, the presiding arbitrator, was to be designated either by mutual agreement of the parties or by a special procedure ensuring that he would not be a Soviet arbitrator. This was a significant first step for any state at that time, but particularly for the Soviet Government. It ensured that in the event of a dispute, it would be determined not by the Soviet Government or its nominee, but by an independent neutral third arbitrator as chairman of the arbitration tribunal. This model is today standard form for international arbitration, except that all three

---

[39] As to enforcement of its decisions by (*inter alia*) a system of prescribed fines (paragraph 14), the arbitration tribunal's powers long foreshadowed the apparently innovative and controversial article 1709bis of the New Belgian Arbitration Law of 19 May 1998, which provides: 'the arbitrators may impose a fine on a party for non-compliance';*see* (1999) *Arb Int* 101 at p. 102.

[40] The concession agreement was published by the USSR in or shortly after 1927 (GARF 8350/4/105, p.1). For the Lena Goldfields arbitration clause, *see* (1998) 17 *ICLQ* 717 at p. 790.

arbitrators (not just the chairman) are required to be impartial and independent of the parties.

14-36 Paragraph 3 set out the procedure if there was to be no mutual agreement between the parties on the appointment of the presiding arbitrator. If within 30 days, there had been no agreement by the parties, then the Soviet Government was within two weeks to name six candidates from professors of the University of Paris (the Sorbonne) or from professors of the University of Oslo; and it was from those French and Norwegian professors that Harriman would be required to chose, again within a two week period, the one professor who would be the chairman and third arbitrator. Paragraphs 4 and 5 dealt with a situation where one or other party failed to comply with its obligations of nomination or choice of these several professors; and the result of these provisions is that neither party could take unfair advantage from a failure to nominate or choose. In that event the clause gave both the choice and designation of the presiding arbitrator to the non-defaulting party. This was also significant: the arbitration clause thus contained its own self-help provisions in the event of default which did not require an application to any state court for the appointment of the presiding arbitrator.

14-37 Paragraph 6 again was significant in the context of what we know today as the 'truncated tribunal'. It provided that if upon receipt of a summons from the presiding arbitrator, fixing the date and place of the first meeting, an arbitrator could not attend, or refused to participate in the arbitral award, then the disputed matter at that hearing could at the request of the other party, be decided by the chairman and the other arbitrator. It was a similar provision in the Lena Goldfields Arbitration which in 1930 allowed the German chairman and the British arbitrator to hold the hearings and make an award even though the Soviet Government had deliberately withdrawn its arbitrator in order to frustrate those proceedings. Today, where a state party can prevent an arbitrator from attending a hearing, as recent events have confirmed, this kind of provision is still needed for international commercial arbitration.[41]

14-38 Paragraph 7 protected the two arbitrators and the parties in the fixing of dates and places. Both the chairman and the arbitration tribunal as a whole were

---

[41] For example, *see* article 12(5) of the ICC Rules and article 12 of the LCIA Rules, see also *Himpurnia* v. *Indonesia*, Interim Award of 26 September 1999, Mealey's Int. Arb. Rep. 15, 1, A-1 (2000).

required to take into consideration the time reasonably necessary for each one of the parties to prepare for the journey, arrive in time at the destination, and also the accessibility to either party of the appointed place within the time fixed. By omission, it is plain here that Moscow was not fixed as the legal place (or seat) of the arbitration. That place would be fixed first by the neutral chairman and secondly by all three arbitrators (see Paragraphs 11 and 12); and it would thus be likely that a neutral place would be fixed, such as Oslo or Paris. Indeed, the Soviet Government's advisers then generally assumed that the place of the arbitration would be the place of the chairman's residence. Again, this was an important development which is now standard form. As with footballers in the European Cup, no-one likes playing in the other team's home stadium; and for arbitration users, almost invariably, a neutral place is the preferred solution.

14-39 In short, this arbitration clause (like the arbitration clause in Lena Goldfields' concession agreement) was a giant leap forward for international commercial arbitration. As regards the Soviet Government, it established, by contractual negotiation and not by treaty, the essential principle of neutral arbitration, with a neutral chairman at a neutral place.

X. THE HARRIMAN VERSUS USSR DISPUTE

14-40 At first, the Chiatura mines were successfully worked; and their exports represented a large percentage of world production. But by 1926, Harriman was experiencing difficulties with the Soviet Government, particularly over the latter's development of its large new mine at Nikopol, north of Odessa, which inevitably depressed the world price for manganese ore;[42] and unwisely in his concession agreement, Harriman had agreed to pay a minimum royalty on a guaranteed minimum production, regardless of actual sales or prices. There were also difficulties with the Soviet Georgian Government, technical difficulties in building the new broad gauge railway; labour troubles with the local miners' union; and a looming problem over the new official exchange rate required to buy roubles for local expenditure (which doubled Harriman's local costs).

14-41 In Berlin, on 4 December 1926, Harriman met Chicherin, the Soviet Commissar for Foreign Affairs; and these negotiations were sufficiently promising for Harriman to travel to Moscow to negotiate with the chairman of

---

[42] Hammer also identified the sharp fall in the world price for manganese as the cause of the Harriman's concession's failure: see Hammer, *supra* n. 7, at p. 121.

the Main Concession Committee, Trotsky. This was Trotsky's last official post within the Soviet Government, from which he was to dismissed less than a year later, shortly before his internal exile to Alma Ata. With Chicherin's assurance that an adjustment satisfactory to all parties could be found, Harriman (as he records in his memoirs) spent four hours in detailed discussions with Trotsky on 28 December 1926:[43]

> We went over the concession agreement in detail, paragraph by paragraph. His mind was like a steel trap; he understood rapidly what I was talking about but in no way revealed his own attitude on what I had said ... At the end of each point he asked me politely whether I had anything to say, and when I replied in the negative he proceeded to the next one. After we had concluded the analysis of our concession he asked me if I had anything further to add. When I indicated I had concluded, he got up and shook hands with me ... turned on his heels and walked toward the door through which he had entered.[44]

14-42 Harriman believed that Trotsky's conduct was caused by a justifiable concern that their conversation was being recorded and its possible effect on his precarious political position; and this impression was later confirmed by Trotsky's own interpreter whom Harriman met again during the war, in Moscow.[45] In the Moscow archives, there is indeed an apparently verbatim account of the meeting between Harriman and Trotsky. It records a short meeting, lasting less than 30 minutes and far short of the four hours recalled by Harriman in his memoirs. Moreover, Trotsky intervened on numerous occasions; and many of his points were extremely sharp. This document concludes with the following exchange:[46]

---

[43] Trotsky was dismissed on 17 November 1927; and he was exiled to Alma Ata on 16 January 1928; *see* D. Volkogonov, *Trotsky* (London, 1996), pp. 303 and 306. (He was succeeded as head of the Concessions Committee by V.N. Ksandrov, and later, L.B. Kamenev, both of whom were to deal with Harriman).

[44] Harriman, *supra* n. 1, at pp. 3 and 4.

[45] Trotsky's interpreter was George Andreychin, a Bulgarian and former American resident who was arrested in 1935 during the Great Terror but later released, meeting Harriman again in Moscow and Paris during and after the war (*see* Harriman and Abel, *supra* n. 38, at pp. 49 and 556). In Maxim Litvinov's (assumed) *Notes for a Journal* (New York, 1955), Trotsky is recorded as complaining to Litvinov about his post in 1926, suspecting that Stalin appointed him head of the Concessions Committee 'purposely to compromise him in the eyes of young communists ... It's already being said that I'm on Averell Harriman's pay-roll' (p. 23).

[46] GARF 8350/1/802, p. 198ff (translated into English).

Trotsky: What should I advise the Government? During the last year and a half production has frozen and the number of workers reduced. At the same time the concessionaire demands: first, instead of a wide-gauge railway, construction of which would cost not less than 6-7 million dollars and which was the concessionaire's obligation to build, according to the concession agreement, – to spend 2 million dollars for improving the narrow-gauge railway; second, to lower the minimum quantity for export; and third, to lower the royalty per ton. We have no right to interfere with the production and technical operations of the concession, but at the same time a sliding scale puts us in a position of risk, connected with the concession's trading operations. And finally, nothing gives us a warranty that the concessionaire will not one day turn from an ally into an enemy.

Harriman: We do not do things like that.

Trotsky: But in history we have many examples of that. Italy prior to 1914 was an ally with Germany and Austro-Hungary, but that did not prevent it during the war from going over to the Entente [the Allies]. And the United States did not consider that a crime. I raise such sensitive questions because I am being asked the same questions. I believe that openness should be the basis of business relations, as well as personal relations.

14-43 And on that sour note, the meeting apparently ended. After Moscow, Harriman visited Georgia and the Chiatura mines, where he concluded that there was no future in the concession. His discussions with Trotsky had not succeeded; there were still problems with 'the government and railroad bureaucracies'; and Harriman had also now gathered that Stalin was opposed to foreign concessions. More significantly, Harriman had become convinced that the Bolshevik Revolution was, in his words, a 'reactionary revolution' and a 'tragic step backward in human development'.[47] There was nonetheless, on 7 July 1927, an amendment agreed to the concession agreement; but it only postponed the inevitable rupture.[48]

---

[47] Harriman, *supra* n. 1, at p. 7. (Harriman only returned to Russia in late 1941 as President Roosevelt's special envoy; and again in 1943 as the US Ambassador to the USSR).

[48] The 1927 amendment also confirmed a novation between W.A.Harriman & Co Inc and the Georgian Manganese Company Lunited, both of Delaware, USA and controlled by Harriman (as permitted by article 66 of the concession agreement).

14-44   On 6 March 1928, Harriman commenced arbitration proceedings under the concession agreement. He appointed James Richardson Glass as his arbitrator. Glass lived in London; but he may have been an American. By telegram of 17 March 1928, the USSR appointed as its arbitrator, Dr S.B. Chlenov, a lawyer working at the Soviet Trade Delegation in Paris, a friend of Ilya Erenburg and a schoolfriend of Nikolai Bukharin. (This same Dr Chlenov was later to be appointed arbitrator in the 1930 Lena Goldfields Arbitration). It also gave notice of a defence and counterclaim in the same telegram, followed by letter of 23 March 1928. By consent, the parties extended the time for the appointment of the third presiding arbitrator; and the USSR began to draw up its list of six names as required by the arbitration clause, which included the Norwegian explorer and representative of the International Red Cross, Dr Nansen.[49] Significantly, each of the Soviet Government's six nominees was a serious candidate as a neutral presiding arbitrator.

14-45   Before the Soviet Government was required to submit its list to Harriman for his choice under the arbitration clause, the parties' negotiations in Berlin and Paris were successful in resolving their disputes; and a settlement agreement was signed in Moscow on 28 August 1928. Both sides took a realistic view of their respective prospects of success in the arbitration; and indeed neither claim nor counterclaim could succeed in full. The Soviet Government was advised that requiring Harriman to conduct all foreign exchange through the USSR State Bank (at highly disadvantageous exchange rates) could be seen as a measure amounting to partial expropriation;[50] but in so far as Harriman's case rested on a

---

[49]   Article 65(3) of the concession agreement: *see* Appendix *infra*. The six were Professor Halvdan Koot (Vice-President of the Norwegian Academy of Sciences and a member of the Nobel Committee), Av. Professor Edv Bull (former Norwegian Foreign Affairs Minister, Vice-President of the Norwegian Labour Party and a historian on Marxism and the October Revolution); Dr Nansen (who had attended one of the meetings between Lloyd George and Krassin in 1920: *see supra* n. 11), Professor Stand (former rector of Oslo University and member of the Nobel Committee), Professor Killnau (an economist) and Professor Knoph (a professor of jurisprudence) (GARF 8350/1/811, p. 103 and GARF 8350/1/823, p. 11). These names had been selected by the Soviet Ambassador to Norway and Sweden, Mme Alexandra Kollontai. (In the 1930 Lena Goldfields Arbitration, the USSR's first choice as presiding arbitrator was to be Professor Albert Einstein of Berlin, another serious candidate regrettably rejected by the English company).

[50]   This advice came privately from the Soviet arbitrator, Chlenov, who was 'generally pessimistic' regarding the Soviet Government's case, although he did not agree with all Harriman's arguments (GARF 8350/1/823, p. 118). Other Soviet officials expressed the view that by virtue of circumstances over which neither party had any control (the development of world manganese production), Harriman was guilty of a breach of the concession agreement; and the

monopoly of Soviet manganese exports, it would fail on the terms of the concession agreement itself (which granted no such monopoly). He had taken a commercial risk; and things had just not worked out for him on the world market for manganese ore.

14-46   There was therefore no arbitration award in the Harriman Arbitration; and the settlement was recorded in a formal order terminating the arbitration proceedings, signed by the two arbitrators in Paris on 14 September 1928.[51] The compensation agreed by the USSR was US$ 3.45 million, to be paid over 15 years by interest-bearing state notes with a face value of US$ 4.45 million. The compensation was not sufficient to recover Harriman's investment; but certainly he left the Soviet Union without the heavy losses suffered later by other foreign concessionaires, including Lena Goldfields and Tetihue Mining. As Harriman also recognised, his concession's withdrawal from Chiatura left their local employees, particularly the young women interpreters and secretaries of educated or 'bourgeois' background, exposed to recriminations from the Soviet Government. As he recalled in his memoirs: 'We tried to keep in touch with them and their families and assist them financially, but one of the tragedies of the operation was the unhappiness that came to these intelligent and decent people'.[52] It was more than unhappiness; and the Soviet employees of Lena Goldfields were also to suffer savage treatment in 1930.

14-47   The figures immediately troubled the US State Department when it learnt of the settlement: if the Soviet Government agreed to settle at US$3.45 million, why did it agree to pay US$ 4.45 million, with interest? The answer came soon from the Chase National Bank, which under the USSR state notes was the paying agent in New York for the USSR State Bank.[53] It transpired that the greater sum also included a separate loan of US$1 million at 7 per cent interest made by

---

compensation paid to him was 'a matter of pure expediency; not as the payment of anything that is legally due' – attributed to a high Soviet metallurgical authority from Moscow by the US Embassy in Berlin, possibly V.I. Mezhlank, vice-president of VSNKh and responsible for the Soviet iron ore and manganese industry (US Decimal File 861.637-Harriman/14: D.C. Poole's letter of 19 November 1928).

[51]   GARF 8350/1/815, pp. 145 and 140.

[52]   Harriman, *supra* n. 1, at p. 6. The US Commercial Attache in Prague later reported that a number of Harriman's Soviet employees had been imprisoned without trial after the settlement and that two stenographers had been sent to Siberia on 10-year sentences (US Decimal File 861.637-Harriman/27: K.L. Rankin's letter dated 17 July 1929 to the Department of Commerce based upon an interview with B. Rascovitch, one of Harriman's former consulting engineers in Georgia).

[53]   Letter dated 24 October 1928 from the Chase National Bank, New York (Reeve Schley) to the US State Department (US Decimal File 861/637-Harriman/18).

another Harriman company to the USSR as an inducement to agree the settlement.[54] This was the first commercial loan ever granted by any American financial institution to the Soviet Government, an important precedent then and now.[55]

14-48 Significantly, the settlement agreement also contained an arbitration clause, almost identical to the arbitration clause in the original concession agreement. It dropped the reference to Oslo University as a choice for the presiding arbitrator, limiting that choice to the Sorbonne in Paris. It was needed. In 1930, there were minor difficulties over the implementation of the settlement; and this time the arbitration clause was invoked by the Soviet Government, again appointing Dr Chlenov as its arbitrator. Harriman responded with a defence and counterclaim, appointing as arbitrator Professor Nolde and proposing a list of three candidates as neutral chairman.[56] All three were rejected by the Soviet Government; and Harriman in return rejected its proposed candidate as chairman (significantly, again a serious candidate as a neutral presiding arbitrator).[57] As before, however, it appears the parties amicably resolved their disputes without ever appointing a chairman or proceeding to an award.

14-49 Notwithstanding these disputes over the settlement agreement, the USSR eventually paid in full its state notes, principal and interest.[58] So Harriman was

---

[54] The lender was the Russian Finance and Construction Corporation, a Harriman company formed in Delaware, USA (GARF 8350/1/814, p. 236).

[55] As well as sweetening the Soviet Government's financial obligations under the settlement, the loan also secured for Harriman the release of a guaranty bond in the sum of US$1 million, which had been issued on his behalf by the National Surety Company of New York in favour of the Soviet Government under article 67 of the concession agreement.

[56] Harriman proposed Professor Max Huber (of Switzerland), Professor Walter Shuking (of Kiel University), or Marcel Plezan (a French Senator from Paris). The Soviet Government was compiling its list of six Sorbonne professors (none lawyers because, as it complained, the Sorbonne then had no law school); but it was looking at other candidates for agreement with Harriman, including Professor Nussbaum, then of Berlin University, (GARF 8350/1/823). Its eventual nominee (but rejected by Harriman) was Dr Kringe, formerly head of the legal department of the German Ministry of Foreign Affairs.

[57] In his later commentary on the practice of international arbitration in Soviet foreign trade, Dr Chlenov stressed the need for Soviet draftsmen to formulate an arbitration clause in such a way that it guaranteed for the Soviet party unbiassed arbitrators: 'The Arbitration Clause in Contracts with Foreign Firms' *Vneshnyaya Torgoviya* 1935. No. 13, p. 3. (It is often important to remember that both sides can have legitimate concerns over the impartiality and independence of an arbitrator).

[58] For the form of USSR state note denominated in US$1,000, see GARF 8350/1/814, p. 232. (Full payment was not the case with the later modest settlements agreed between the USSR, Lena

lucky; but he was a lucky man with two effective arbitration clauses. Without those remedies, luck might not have been sufficient for Harriman. In 1928 and 1930, Harriman was merely a private investor without any home state protection: the United States was not to recognise the USSR until 1933.

XI. CONCLUSION

14-50 If we answer the question honestly: 'is international commercial arbitration important?', the answer is obvious. By itself, the answer is plainly 'no'. There is no Nobel Prize for International Commercial Arbitrators; and whilst we may recall that in 1977, Lord Clark was much criticised for not discussing at all the rule of law in his famous BBC lectures on 'Civilisation', no-one thought to complain that he omitted any reference to international commercial arbitration. But if we change the question: 'is arbitration completely unimportant?', the answer is also plainly 'no'; and the Harriman Arbitration suggests two reasons why this is so.

14-51 First, arbitration has much to do with the rule of law; and the rule of law has everything to do with confidence in transnational trade. When rights and remedies can be frustrated with complete impunity, then trade inevitably suffers. And today, for transnational trade there is no equivalent and effective alternative remedy to international commercial arbitration. The existence of an arbitration clause with (at least) a neutral presiding arbitrator in a neutral place provides elements of fairness, certainty and predictability which are all essential to transnational trade. In 1922, two former practising lawyers, albeit very different and who never met each other, understood just that for Anglo-Russian trade; the former Welsh Solicitor, Lloyd George and the former St Petersburg Attorney, Lenin. Since 1922, we have seen how countries which have attacked international arbitration have soon lost foreign investment, like India and Pakistan. Whilst India appears now to have abandoned its aversion to international arbitration, other countries in Asia have sadly taken her place.

14-52 Second, Lloyd George was right: commerce does have a sobering influence in its operations; and so does international commercial arbitration. Commerce imposes its own discipline; and as for arbitration, it is part of the human instinct, in the depths of the darkest dispute, to find a means to resolve

---

Goldfields and Tetihue, in 1932 and 1934. But these were British companies; and in 1928, after the diplomatic breach in relations with the United Kingdom following the Arcos affair in 1927, the USSR was and remained concerned to obtain diplomatic recognition from the United States).

that dispute. With happily few exceptions, if there is a way, most human beings prefer to avoid disputes and not to exacerbate them, or to find reconciliation rather than enmity. Traders generally prefer to trade; and statesmen generally prefer peace to war. Increasingly, transnational trade and peace are linked; both are now indispensable to global prosperity and freedom; and international commercial arbitration is inextricably intertwined with transnational trade.[59]

14-53 And so returning to that summer's evening in the Kremlin in July 1963, it is perhaps not surprising that it was Harriman who brought those negotiations to a successful conclusion. The skills of the trader in 1928 who settled his arbitration were the same skills of the diplomat 35 years later. The world is a safer place where such skills can be deployed successfully; and as we live still through our own uneasy Genoa Conference since 1989 (for Europe and elsewhere), we should remember those who laboured successfully in much more troubled, dangerous and difficult times, as manifested by the Harriman Arbitration: namely, Lloyd George, Lenin and (of course) the Cannibals.

XII. APPENDIX:

The Harriman Arbitration Clause (Section 65 of The Concession Agreement Dated 12 June 1925, English Version)

Board of Arbitration – Section 65

1. Should the Government and the Concessionaire differ with respect to the proper interpretation of, or the proper execution and performance of, or breach of any provisions of this agreement, or of any annex or supplementary agreement thereto, such difference shall on notice from either party, be referred to and determined by an Arbitral Board.

2. The Arbitration Board shall be composed of three members, one to be designated by the Government, one by the Concessionaire and the third, the Super-Arbiter, shall be designated by the parties by mutual agreement.

3. Should such an agreement not be attained within thirty days from the day on which the defending party receives a summons in writing to appear before the

---

[59] As Professor Pipes contends, property is an indispensable ingredient of freedom; and arbitration has of course much to do with property (see Pipes, *Property and Freedom* (London, 1999)).

Arbitral Board, accompanied by a statement concerning the matter in dispute and designating the plaintiff's member of the Board, the Government shall within two weeks time name six candidates from among professors of the University of Paris (Sorbonne), or from among professors of the University of Oslo (det Kongelige Frederiks Universitet i Oslo), of whom the Concessionaire shall choose within the following two weeks, one who shall be the Super-Arbiter.

4. Should the Concessionaire, unless prevented from doing so by insurmountable obstacles, fail to select a Super-Arbiter, within said two weeks time the Government shall have the right to request the Governing Body of any one of the said educational institutions to appoint a Super-Arbiter from amongst six candidates chosen by the Government as above.

5. Should the Government, unless prevented from doing so by insurmountable obstacles, fall to select six candidates for Super-Arbiter within the above mentioned two weeks, then the Concessionaire shall have the right to request the Governing Body of any one of the above mentioned educational institutions to designate such six candidates, and thereupon the Concessionaire shall select from amongst them, the Super-Arbiter as above indicated.

6. If, on receipt of a summons from the Super-Arbiter fixing the date and place of the first meeting, either party shall fail to send its arbiter, or refuses to participate in the Arbitral Board, then the disputed matter, at the request of the other part shall be decided by the Super-Arbiter and the other member of the Board, provided that the decision is rendered unanimously.

7. The Super-Arbiter, as well as the Arbitral Board, when fixing the date and place of the meeting of the Board shall take into consideration: (1) the time reasonably necessary for each one of the parties to prepare for the journey and arrive in time at the place of destination, and (2) the accessibility to either party of the appointed place within the time fixed.

8. At the same time, the party which might encounter an insurmountable obstacle in despatching, for the appointed place, its member of the Board or its representative must take all measures to advise in time the Super-Arbiter and the Arbitral Board accordingly.

9. In all events, the Super-Arbiter or the Arbitral Board when deciding on the opening of the sitting in the absence of one of the parties must pass a ruling to such effect and give its reasons therefor.

10. The Board of Arbitration shall appoint a permanent Secretary who shall keep a record of all its proceedings. The compensation of the Chairman and the Secretary of the Board and the expenses therefor shall be borne equally by the parties, and each of the parties shall bear the compensation and expense of its member of the Board of Arbitration, as well as all expenses incurred by it in connection with any Arbitration proceeding.

11. Questions for determination by the Board of Arbitration shall be submitted in writing to the Chairman of the Board of Arbitration, and the party submitting any question for determination shall furnish the other party with a copy thereof. The Super-Arbiter shall fix the place and time of the first sitting of the Arbitral Board.

12. Thereafter the Board of Arbitration shall have full power to determine the places and times of its sittings, as well as its methods and order of procedure. Each party shall furnish the Board, in the manner and within the time prescribed by the latter, all information necessary in the case which they are able to produce, with due regard, however, to considerations of State importance.

13. The decisions of the Board shall in all cases be in writing, and a copy of each decision shall be promptly furnished to the parties. Every decision of the Board concurred in by a majority of the members therefor shall be final and binding upon the parties, and shall be promptly complied with.

14. When rendering a decision requiring one of the parties to perform a certain act, or to refrain therefrom, the Arbitral Board shall, at the same time, determine and communicate to the interested party the consequences of non-compliance with such decision, namely, it shall prescribe in such contingency the payment to the other party of a certain fine, or it shall grant to the other party the right to repair the omission of the party at fault for the latter's account, or it shall prescribe the cancellation of the agreement.

15. In the event of failure of either party to comply with any decision of the Board of Arbitration, the other party shall have the right to bring suit for the enforcement of said decision in courts of any country. Notice of suit in such case shall be served on the representative of the other party then resident in that country, and the parties hereby declare that they will not question the jurisdiction of the court of said country to try and to execute a decision of the Board of Arbitration, provided said court shall recognise that the Arbitral decision had been rendered in due form.

16. In case of necessity, as provided in the preceding paragraph, of bringing suit for the enforcement of an Arbitral Board decision, the parties agree that either party shall have the right, to assign claims arising from such decision of the Arbitral Board to any third party, in whom shall be vested all right as to the enforcement of claims granted to the parties under this Section.

17. The parties agree that the time of limitation for the bringing of disputes before the Arbitral Board provided or under this agreement shall be one and one half years.

Pierre Mayer[*]

CHAPTER 15

REFLECTIONS ON THE INTERNATIONAL ARBITRATOR'S DUTY TO APPLY THE LAW[**]

I. Introduction

15-1 I have for a long time been troubled by the question of the relationship between the arbitrator, particularly the international arbitrator, and the law that he applies – or is supposed to apply – to the merits of the case. Is it of the same nature as the relationship between the judge and the law? Does the arbitrator enjoy more freedom than the judge? Does his sense of equity and fairness play a greater role? When, in the case of an international arbitrator, he has to resolve a conflict of laws, is he supposed to apply a conflict of laws rule? If the parties have chosen the law, is he bound by that choice?

15-2 All these questions only arise, of course, when the arbitrator is required to decide 'in law', as opposed to the situation in which he is required to decide *ex aequo et bono*.

15-3 This means that these questions could not arise in antiquity, because the early conception of arbitration considered it as going hand in hand with equity. Aristotle considered that 'the arbitrator aims at achieving equity, the judge at applying the law'.[1] But this has ceased to be true. A new kind of arbitration, based on law, has emerged, as part of which the arbitrator is supposed to apply

[*]   Professor at the University of Paris I (Panthéon-Sorbonne).
[**] This is a revised version of the author's 2000 School of International Arbitration Freshfields Bruckhaus Desinger Arbitration Lecture delivered on 16 November 2000. The editors acknowledge with thanks the permission to publish this contribution granted by Freshfields Bruckhaus Desinger and the School of International Arbitration, Centre for Commercial Law Studies, Queen Mary and Westfield College, London University
[1]   L. Gernet, *Droit et société dans la Grèce ancienne* (1955), pp. 103-119.

Julian D.M. Lew and Loukas A. Mistelis (eds), Arbitration Insights, 289-305
© 2007 Kluwer Law International. Printed in the Netherlands

the rules of law laid down by the legislator. 'Amiable composition' (i.e. arbitration based on equity) has become the exception and arbitration statutes treat it as such, sometimes even ignoring it.

15-4 There could nevertheless remain something of the ancient conception, which would entail equity being mixed with law, even when the power of acting as '*amiable compositeur*' has not been conferred on the arbitrator. This is indeed the unqualified opinion of the great French comparatist René David, who once stated:

> We reject as foreign to arbitral practice and baseless as a matter of principle the distinction drawn between arbitration in law and arbitration in equity ... The concern of arbitrators, in accordance with the parties' wishes, is to arrive at a just solution, rather than the strict application of the law of a given national State.[2]

15-5 In a recent book, Dr. Marc Blessing, the well-known Swiss arbitrator, expressed more or less the same view, which he reserves, however, to international arbitration:

> An arbitral Tribunal would not fulfill its important mission properly if it only satisfied itself that it was correctly applying a given paragraph of a particular national law [i.e. the law chosen by the parties], unless it also satisfied itself that that particular paragraph indeed deserves to be applied in the relevant circumstances, and having regard to the parties and their objectively fair and subjectively reasonable expectations.[3]

15-6 Whether it is desirable that an arbitrator should tailor his application of the law to his own sense of reasonableness and fairness, and whether such attitude corresponds to the parties' expectations, is a question that deserves careful examination. But the question does not even arise if the arbitrator is deprived, both by law and as a practical matter, of the liberty that these authors demand. The first point which has to be examined is therefore that of the power, or the right, for an arbitrator to ignore, or wilfully to misinterpret the law even when the powers of an *amiable compositeur* have not been conferred on him, which is the situation on which I will focus.

[2] R. David, *L'arbitrage dans le commerce international* (Paris, 1982), no. 453.
[3] *Introduction to Arbitration: Swiss and International Perspectives* (Helbing & Lichtenhahn, 1999), p. 212.

II. THE STATUS OF LAW IN THE INTERNATIONAL ARBITRAL PROCESS

15-7 To answer the question properly, it is important to realise that what the law represents to the arbitrator is very different from what it represents to the judge. This is true in domestic matters; it is even more obvious in international matters.

A. Domestic Arbitration

15-8 There is an intimate link between the state judge and his own law, which he has to apply in domestic cases. Contrary to what has been contended by the American Movement of sociological jurisprudence, a judge, when rendering justice, does not regard the rules of law as mere guidance, among other sources of inspiration such as morals, 'people's conscience', 'political intuition' and the like.[4] The duty of a judge is also to uphold the law.

15-9 I am not referring here to the law-making power that the courts, and particularly Supreme Courts, enjoy in *common law* countries. I am referring to the more modest task of the lower courts, in *civil law* as well as in common law countries, to apply the law as it is. To apply the law is also a legislative task, in the broad sense, inasmuch as a law that is not applied in a systematic way simply ceases to exist. The organs to which the state entrusts the task of rendering justice – the courts – are necessarily bound to maintain the law by applying it, rather than allowed to destroy it by ignoring it.

15-10 Various mechanisms ensure that this is the case in reality. One is of a legal nature: the decisions of the lower courts are controlled by the higher courts, which exercise a supervisory role. Only the highest court, in each country, enjoys total freedom. Moreover, all the courts, including the highest one, are under the influence of factors of a psychological nature. All judges know that they are organs of the state, they are aware of their duties, they wish to avoid being blamed for misconduct, they are mindful of their career, etc. The entire system rests on these pillars.

15-11 The position of the arbitrator is totally different. An arbitrator does not sit as a result of his appointment by the state; he does so as a result of the parties' wishes. He is not a component of the legal system. If he ignores the law, that may

---

[4] On the American Movement of sociological jurisprudence, see F. Michaut, thesis (University of Paris X, 1984), published (Atelier national de reproduction des thèses, 1985) entitled L'Ecole de la 'sociological jurisprudence' et le mouvement réaliste américain.

well be (contrary to what Professor David and Dr Blessing contend) in violation of the parties' expectations, but that will not put in peril the very existence of the law.

15-12   At the same time, there is no efficient mechanism, either of a legal or psychological nature, which would ensure a correct, or even honest, application of the law by the arbitrator. The modern trend, followed by recent statutes, is to restrict, and sometimes even suppress, the control exercised by the courts over the interpretation given to the law by arbitrators. The only related requirement that has unanimously been retained is the obligation that the award comply with public policy.

15-13   As for psychological incentives, they are dependent on the arbitrator's own conception of his mission. If he believes, as some do, that justice is always to be preferred to a strict application of the law, he will feel perfectly free to decide in accordance with his own conviction. Even if the award violates public policy, or is otherwise subject to appeal, e.g. because, as provided under section 69 of the English Arbitration Act 1979, the decision is 'obviously wrong' on a question of law, some arbitrators will not be deterred by the risk of having their award set aside. Pride leads them to consider their award as a self-standing piece of work that has to be perfect and correct by reference to their own standards and criteria, even if this should expose it to the risk of nullification (and of wasting the time and money invested by the parties) by an unsympathetic judge.

15-14   For such arbitrators, the law ceases to be the mandatory basis for the award; it becomes a model, a reference, a privileged one no doubt, but one that can nonetheless be disregarded, should there be good reasons to do so.

B. International Arbitration

15-15   If we now turn more specifically to international arbitration, the status of the law as a non-mandatory model for the arbitrator stands out even more clearly.

15-16   First, in a good number of cases, the international arbitrator, sitting in a neutral country, will have to apply a law other than that of the legal system in which he himself is qualified. To the arbitrator, such law will represent a model with which he is hardly familiar, which stands in competition with the model by reference to which he was trained. When faced with any uncertainty as regards the interpretation of the law, he is bound to revert – as a result of a subconscious process – to what his own law provides. Also, when required to apply a rule of law that differs significantly from what he is used to considering as reasonable, the arbitrator will endeavour either to moderate or to neutralise its effects. I shall borrow an example from Sir Michael Kerr: the English rule according to which it is not permissible, when construing the provisions of a contract, to take into account either the circumstances in which such contract was concluded or those pertaining to its performance. A French arbitrator required to apply English law would find it very difficult to give effect to an interpretation contrary to that which he has reached in his own mind, based on all the facts established during the proceedings. Contrary to an English judge, he would not feel bound by any particular duty towards England strictly to apply the laws of England as the House of Lords would apply them.

15-17 Secondly, and most importantly, the status of the law in international arbitration is affected by the fact that it is up to the arbitrator to select the applicable law among the various competing laws.

15-18 In an international situation, a judge would apply his own conflict of laws rule. That rule would direct him to apply the law chosen by the parties, provided that the parties' choice meets certain conditions, expressed in the conflict of laws rule. In the absence of a choice by the parties, the conflict of laws rule would itself designate the applicable law by reference to a connecting factor. In both cases, the process is entirely mandatory: the judge is first under a duty to apply the conflict of laws rule, and then he is under a duty to apply the law determined in accordance with that rule.

15-19 For a long time, arbitrators adopted the same approach. They applied the rule of conflict of laws of the seat of the arbitration, thus more or less assimilating such law to the *lex fori*. They did so because of their apprehension, now recognised as misconceived, that they were under a duty to do so.

15-20 Thereafter, arbitrators imagined several other methods. One of the most frequently implemented – and probably one of the best – methods consists in taking into account the existence of converging conflict of laws rules in the parties' respective countries. Of course such converging result will have to be shown to exist: i.e. it will have to be shown that both sets of rules designate the same law as governing the contract.

15-21 It has also been suggested that a 'common core' identified among the substantive rules (as opposed to the earlier discussed conflict of laws rules) of both countries could be used.

15-22 Eventually, arbitrators have formed the view that they are entitled to ascertain the proper law of the contract directly, i.e. without reference to a national rule of conflict of laws. This 'direct method' allows the arbitrator complete freedom. It is frequently used, and is validated by many modern laws on international arbitration. Thus, Swiss law provides for the application by the arbitrator of 'the rules of law with which the case at hand is most closely connected'. French law and Dutch law go one step further and provide for the arbitrator to apply 'such rules as he deems appropriate'. English law is different, since it provides that the arbitrator shall apply the law determined 'by the conflict of laws rules which it considers applicable'. However, since the arbitrator can freely choose any conflict of laws rule among those existing in the world, the result is not so different.

15-23 One might think that such absolute freedom of choice for the arbitrator only exists when the parties have failed to make a choice of law, since it would be strange, if the parties have expressly chosen law X, that the arbitrator should find law Y or Z more appropriate. However, even faced with a choice-of-law clause, the arbitrator retains a certain degree of freedom since he has the power to settle in accordance with his own views any dispute between the parties concerning the validity or the scope of the choice-of-law clause itself.

15-24 For instance, one party might argue that there was no reasonable or legitimate interest behind the choice of law. Although modern conflict of laws rules do not heed such considerations, they are still considered relevant in some countries, notably in the United States. The arbitrator is free to prefer to the modern view, the view expressed in the Second Restatement of Conflict of Laws of the United States.

15-25 Similarly, a party might object that, on a certain disputed point, the law chosen by the parties must be disregarded in favour of the public policy rule ('*loi de police*') of another country. It is up to the arbitrator to decide whether such is the case.

15-26 Similarly again, a party might claim that the chosen law is contrary to certain fundamental values. Many authors consider that a national law that violates transnational public policy should not be applied. It is for the arbitrator to determine the requirements of transnational public policy.

15-27 It then appears that, in the context of international arbitration, the relationship between the law and the arbitrator is inverted, by reference to what would instinctively seem normal. The arbitrator is above the law, since he is the one who renders it applicable. He can choose freely between all the laws of the world, or at least – if he sits in England – he can choose between all the conflict of laws rules of the world. His free will is the starting point of the entire legal reasoning.

15-28   In many countries, the arbitrator's freedom extends even beyond this. It is not only a freedom to choose between the laws of the various states. It is a freedom to choose any body of legal rules, whatever their origin. An arbitrator sitting in France or in Switzerland can decide, at least if the parties have expressed no opposite view, to apply the so-called *lex mercatoria* to the case at hand. It does not matter whether the *lex mercatoria* deserves to be called 'law'. It does not even matter whether it contains pre-existing rules: the arbitrator will invent the rule he needs if he does not find a ready-made one that resolves the legal issue.

15-29   The famous *Valenciana* case, which gave the French Cour de Cassation the opportunity to proclaim that arbitrators are allowed to choose *lex mercatoria* even if it has not been chosen by the parties,[5] is an example of this. It concerned the validity of a sale agreement that did not specify the price of the goods sold. The arbitrator, for the sole purpose of escaping the nullification which would have resulted from the application of French law, held that *lex mercatoria* applied; he then went on to say that no rule of the *lex mercatoria* provides for the nullity of a sale agreement on the ground that no price has been fixed and that, as a consequence, the sale was valid.[6] Such reasoning amounts to saying that, since the *lex mercatoria* is silent about almost every issue, it allows the arbitrator to give it any meaning he wishes.

15-30   The most extreme expression of the arbitrator's freedom is the possibility for him to apply the UNIDROIT Principles relating to international trade contracts.

15-31   Such Principles represent a genuine attempt, undertaken by a group of experts acting under the auspices of UNIDROIT (the international body dedicated to achieving the progressive unification of private law), to codify the general law of contract on a comparative basis. The Principles do not have, nor

---

[5]   Civ. lère, 22 October 1991, Valenciana, *Rev. arb.* 1992, 457, commentary by P. Lagarde.
[6]   ICC Award rendered in 1988, *Rev. arb.* 1990, 701.

indeed pretend to have, binding authority. They simply represent a model; but since they have been very intelligently elaborated, they are quickly becoming very popular among arbitrators.[7]

15-32   Reduced to the mere status of a model that arbitrators are not compelled to apply, in the field of international arbitration the law loses most of its authority. On the other hand its humble condition generates equality: a law enacted by a Parliament does not carry more weight than the UNIDROIT Principles adopted by a body of experts and deprived of any official status.

15-33   In these circumstances, it is to be expected, although not necessarily approved, that an arbitrator, having decided to conform with one of these models, should nonetheless consider that his hands are not tied when it comes to applying the rules composing such model.

III. THE INTERNATIONAL ARBITRATOR'S APPLICATION OF THE LAW

15-34   Once again, the situation of the arbitrator can be compared with that of a judge.

15-35   A judge's mission and obligations are clear: they consist in rendering justice, i.e. in defining the respective rights of the parties as they result from the applicable law. This is all that the parties themselves expect of the judge. They do not expect him to upset the established order so as to impose, in breach of the law, what he subjectively considers as fair.

15-36   The position of an international arbitrator is very different. As discussed above, he owes no duty of obedience. His only obligations arise from what can be considered as the mission of an arbitrator. However such mission itself remains rather vague, since it is not associated with specific obligations as is the case for a judge.

15-37   The first uncertainty concerns the standpoint that the arbitrator should adopt. He was not appointed by the state but by the parties. This could lead one to conclude that an arbitrator's mission is to do what the parties expect of him. However, an arbitrator has his own conception of his responsibility, his own

---

[7]   Numerous awards applying the UNIDROIT Principles have already been published in (1999) 10/2 *ICC International Court of Arbitration Bulletin* and in the *Uniform Law Review*.

moral standards, and they may lead him to consider as part of his mission other considerations, e.g. considerations related to public interest.

15-38 Even if the arbitrator were to take solely into account the parties' expectations, he would have to assess what they are. Do parties expect a strict application of the law, since they have not conferred upon the arbitrator the powers of *amiable compositeur*? Do they expect a more practical and tailored assessment of the fair solution, as this may characterise, in their mind, the arbitral process? Do they expect from the arbitrator a more careful consideration of the contract, of which they could consider him to be a component, a regulating mechanism?

15-39 The mission of an arbitrator is thus much more ambiguous than that of a judge. Conflicting considerations may play a role. More specifically, there may be a conflict between on the one hand the method consisting in implementing the legal syllogism on the basis of the applicable rule of law, and on the other hand two different concerns: the search for the most equitable solution, and the endeavour to favour the solution that conforms most closely with the true will of the parties.

15-40 In other words, we have two pairs of potentially conflicting notions: law and equity on the one hand, law and contract on the other.

A. Law and Equity

15-41 The expression 'equity' has two meanings, one narrow and substantive, the other broad and technical. Taken in its narrow meaning, equity may be defined as the opposite of rigidity: it moderates, softens, lessens the burden which the rule of law imposes on a party. Taken in its broad meaning, that adopted by Aristotle to defend its merits, equity refers to any modification implemented by a judge to too general a rule of law, in order to arrive at a reasonable solution in the specific circumstances of the case.

i. Equity in its Substantive Meaning

15-42 Substantive equity is not entirely absent from statute or case law. The law sometimes leaves scope for adjustments: thus a respite will be granted to the debtor who cannot meet his financial commitments; the notion of abuse of right or that of bad faith may be invoked to resist a party's attempt to enforce his rights in too strict a manner.

15-43   Is an international arbitrator entitled to go beyond the role which the law attributes to equity?

15-44   His position, one may submit, is not very different from that of a judge. On the one hand, the parties expect of him primarily that he applies the applicable law, especially if it has been chosen by common agreement. On the other hand, an arbitrator, like a judge, will feel a legitimate repugnance in sanctioning a serious injustice to the detriment of one party.

15-45   There is a widespread belief that an arbitrator will be more inclined to moderate the strictness of the law or of the contract than a judge. Yet this fact is not scientifically established and my own experience (obviously insufficient to build statistics on) does not confirm it.

15-46   It is also frequently said (Cicero shared that view) that arbitrators would be more inclined than judges to go halfway, to find a compromise which would not entirely dissatisfy any party. Three-member arbitral tribunals would be particularly prone to adopt such an attitude. There is certainly an element of truth in this remark, particularly as regards cases involving relationships between states, thus necessarily introducing a diplomatic perspective. However, outside this field, I have never witnessed a situation where the chairman of the tribunal, having reached definite views as to what the solution of the dispute should be, was forced to moderate them in order to be able to issue an award. In most cases, the third arbitrator will surrender to the majority view. It does not matter if he does not: the award, rendered by a majority decision, will be equally enforceable. Only in relation to the allocation of the costs of the arbitration have I sometimes seen that the arbitrator appointed by the losing party succeeded in obtaining a charitable treatment, particularly when the decision rendered against that party on the merits was severe. This leads to decisions on costs that are sometimes difficult for the winning party to understand.

ii. Equity in its Technical Meaning

15-47   If pro-leniency equity, based on the arbitrator's sympathy for the parties or on a fear to displease a party, does not find a particularly fertile field in which to prosper within the framework of arbitration, the situation is different as regards equity understood as a corrective to the too general wording of a rule.
To have recourse to equity is tempting, both for a judge and for an arbitrator, because it allows them to make their own sense of reasonableness prevail over the constraints which the law would impose.

15-48   However, an objective factor sets the arbitrator apart from the judge: a number of benefits attaching to the rule of law flow from its general and permanent nature, which the judge has a duty to preserve, whereas the arbitrator focuses on a case which is unique, and which has already produced its effects. This can easily be demonstrated with a few examples:

(1)   In order to prevent fraud in respect of registration tax, the French General Tax Code specifies a 10-day time-limit for the registration of a seller's undertaking to sell land; once this period has lapsed and the agreement has not been registered, it is considered null and void. This rule is designed as an incentive for people to register the agreement and pay the corresponding tax. However, an arbitrator faced with a dispute where the agreement was not registered, and with the task of considering solely the relationship between the two parties before him, will only see the irrational aspect and unfair consequences of such a ground for annulment.

(2)   Under American law, treble damages are designed to act as a deterrent in respect of types of conduct that are considered particularly dangerous. An arbitrator will be more sensitive to the specific circumstances of the case upon which he is asked to rule, and will be reluctant to render an award whereby the victim will be unduly enriched. He will not be concerned with the deterrence of future conduct.

(3)   Until recently, French law declared void any sale agreement enabling the seller to fix the price unilaterally, or to exert a unilateral influence on the determination of the price. Admittedly, French law may permit such agreements to stand subject to judicial control to sanction any abuse, which is, according to some authors, the current position. However, the previous stance, owing to its general application, had the merit of deterring the parties from having recourse to dangerous practices and thereby of limiting litigation flowing from such abuses, which today is threatening to overload the judicial process. Arbitrators, however, had little sympathy for such general policy: since they were in a position to ascertain, by means of an expert investigation, whether the price fixed or influenced by the seller was excessive, they attempted to rescue contracts which a judge would have been bound to annul.

15-49   It is thus natural for an arbitrator to lean towards equity, more than does a judge. However, while he understandably concentrates on the case at hand, the arbitrator should not, in his quest for justice, forget to take into account the parties' expectations. To know what such expectations are in the real world, one simply has to listen to what in-house counsel, whose firms are the users of arbitration, unanimously say. What they want is certainty, which can only be achieved by applying the rules of law. They do not expect justice, since that can only mean what the arbitrator finds just, and they are not certain that they can trust his sense of justice. They do not like the *lex mercatoria* because it is not clearly defined. It is increasingly rare for them to provide for the arbitrator to rule *ex aequo et bono*.

15-50 Even if one considers that the rule of law owes its rational merits solely to its general nature, a characteristic to which the parties to the dispute submitted to arbitration are both indifferent, such rule has an undeniable virtue: by its very existence, it creates predictability.

15-51 Another of the parties' expectations is to obtain an award based on objectively valid grounds. The arbitrator who departs from applicable rules in an obvious manner, even for good reasons, exposes himself to a claim of arbitrariness. He is in fact the victim of an illusion. He pleases himself, he pleases one of the parties, but he fails to see that he is discrediting himself in the eyes of both parties, and at the same time discrediting the arbitral process.

15-52 Equity should therefore be attributed a very modest role. That does not mean, however, that it should necessarily be eliminated altogether. There are circumstances in which recourse to equity is acceptable:
   (1) Equity can guide the choice of the arbitrator as between the laws of two countries, which have links of a similar importance with the contract, and between which the parties did not make a choice.
   (2) It can help the arbitrator to choose between two equally supported interpretations of a rule.
   (3) It can possibly pioneer an evolution in the law that is unanimously advocated by doctrinal writers, or for which the Supreme Court has paved the way.
   (4) Finally the arbitrator's sense of equity can suggest to him that the rule expressed in the applicable law only deals with domestic situations, which allows him to formulate himself the rule that is supposed to apply to international situations. This last device has been used to set aside provisions, which can be found in many national laws, which fix the rate of interest at a certain percentage, regardless of the place of payment and of the currency in which the debt was expressed; indeed, such provisions lead to absurd results when applied to international

contracts. I would not personally disapprove of such a manner of reasoning.

15-53 It nevertheless remains the case that the objective and impartial nature of the rule militates in favour of a strict circumscription of the role of equity, independently of any legal obligation the arbitrator may have to apply the law.

15-54 However, another conflict may arise, opposing the will of the parties, as expressed in the contract, to the law which the contract infringed. Once again, for reasons specific to the arbitrator, but of a different nature, the law is sometimes disregarded.

B. Law and Contract

15-55 There is a definite reluctance on the part of arbitrators to declare null and void contracts concluded by the parties on a free and fully informed basis. This is so even when the contract, owing either to its purpose or to its subject-matter, appears illegal: i.e. an agreement aiming at securing a contract through corruption or an agreement whereby competitors share markets between themselves with a view to increasing prices.

15-56 One reason for such reluctance is probably related to the fact that the arbitral process rests on an agreement between the parties. An arbitrator derives his powers from the bare will of the parties. It is thus understandable that he should pay the greatest attention thereto. It may be conceived that, from a legal point of view, nothing prevents him from declaring the contract null and void, whatever the reason for such nullity; and in light of the autonomy of the agreement to arbitrate, the fact of declaring the contract void will not affect the arbitrator's jurisdiction. Nevertheless, from a psychological standpoint, the arbitrator forms part of the contractual process. His intervention (in the event of dispute) constitutes one of the terms of the parties' agreement. When accepting his mission, the arbitrator can be said to 'board the contractual ship'. He is thus reluctant to see the ship founder. For example, entrusted with the duty to rule upon such disputes as may arise during the term of a Shareholders' Agreement, he will tend to limit his mission thereto, without paying much attention to possible violations of the mandatory rules governing the transfer of shares or voting rights.

15-57 In addition, it is a fact that an arbitrator will always feel less sympathetic towards the party seeking to rely upon the nullity of the contract. Let us consider the contractor who, thanks to the payment of bribes to carefully selected persons via an intermediary, is granted a highly profitable contract. He then comes to the arbitrator arguing that the contract for the payment of a commission to the intermediary is unlawful and immoral and thus that he is released from his obligations to pay the agreed-upon 8 per cent of the main contract value.

15-58 The arbitrator will hesitate between adopting the normal attitude, which is to apply the law and to declare the contract void, and yielding to his desire to force the party that denounces the contract in bad faith to perform its obligations. His decision will not necessarily be guided by the fact that the award will be liable to judicial control, since although it will be held unenforceable in the country whose law will have been held applicable, it will be likely to be recognised as enforceable in other countries.

15-59 In most cases, cautious parties will previously have taken care to pave the road to annulment with hurdles in case one of them changes its mind. They will have provided for a neutral governing law that does not expose the contract to any ground of nullity, and at the same time chosen a neutral arbitration seat. Is it still proper to talk about illegality when the law from which such illegality stems is not applicable?

15-60 Two well-known cases illustrate the point:
  (1) In the *Mitsubishi* case, the Japanese manufacturer had entrusted the distribution of its vehicles in Puerto-Rico to Soler pursuant to an agreement prohibiting re-exportation to continental America. The prohibition was in violation of the anti-trust laws of the United States. In order, probably, to ensure that Soler abided by the clause, the distributorship agreement contained another clause providing for arbitration in Japan and submitting the contract to Swiss law.[8]
  (2) In *Hilmarton*, a French company, O.T.V., had entrusted the English company Hilmarton with the mission to act as its legal and tax adviser and to 'be responsible for coordination as regards administrative matters'. This agreement was entered into in contemplation of a public works contract to be performed in Algiers, for which tenders were requested. Algerian law, as a measure against corruption, prohibits any agency agreement for this type of contract. However, the agreement

---

[8] *Mitsubishi v. Soler* 105 S. Ct. 3346.

between O.T.V. and Hilmarton provided for arbitration in Switzerland and specified Swiss law as the governing law.[9]

15-61   Whereas even an arbitrator can easily accept that an international contract is null when its governing law declares it illegal, it is by contrast far more difficult to render applicable a law that the parties have expressly rejected. There is nevertheless a way to do so, namely via the implementation of the *'méthode des lois de police'*. Pursuant to that method, which is for instance recognised and described in Article 7 of the Rome Convention on the Law Applicable to Contractual Obligations, a judge is empowered to set aside, under certain conditions, the law that would normally be applicable, in order for a certain rule of another law to apply, a rule that has a legitimate and overriding interest in being applied, and which claims to be applied to the case at hand: a *'loi de police'*, or public policy rule. It should not be difficult to admit that what a judge can do, an arbitrator can also do.

15-62   However, does he want to do it and should he do it?

15-63   As regards the first part of the question, the conclusion at this stage must remain extremely cautious. There is yet no agreement as to the beneficial role of the method, which is a relatively recent invention in the field of conflict of laws. The application of Article 7 of the Rome Convention is not mandatory for an arbitrator, and many arbitrators are reluctant to depart from the rules of the law chosen by the parties. One can nevertheless note that in certain fields there is less hesitation in setting aside the law designated as applicable on the basis of party autonomy. Thus, if an agreement results in restrictions on competition within the European Union, an arbitrator sitting in Switzerland will not hesitate to set aside the chosen law in order to apply European Community law.

15-64   Is this nonconformity with the arbitrator's mission? In other words, should he apply a law other than the one chosen by the parties? One could argue – and it has indeed been argued – that an arbitrator is not the guardian of public policy, that his duties are towards the parties only, and that he must confine himself to the determination of disputes involving private interests. In addition, considerations as regards predictability and objectivity are irrelevant in this

---

[9]   The award rendered by the first arbitral tribunal in the *Hilmarton* case has been reproduced in part in *Rev. arb.* 1993, 327. Although the award was set aside by Swiss courts, it was granted *exequatur* by French courts. The appeal against the judgment granting *exequatur* was dismissed by the Cour de Cassation (decision of 23 March 1994, (1995) XX *Yearbook Com. Arb.* 663).

context since the majority view is that a refusal to have recourse to the '*méthode des lois de police*' does not amount to surprising or suspicious conduct on his part.

15-65 However, this seems to me too short-sighted an approach. The starting point is correct: no one conferred upon the arbitrator the duty to act as guardian of public policy. His only mission is that conferred upon him by the parties. However, he enjoys a broad freedom in the performance of that mission. One of the parties asks him to apply the *lex contractus*. The other asks him to apply a rule of public policy, having a legitimate interest in imposing its terms. Whether he follows one course or the other, he decides a disputed point, which is his role. Why should he refrain from taking into account interests that admittedly exceed those of the parties but whose legitimate nature can be universally perceived?

15-66 Corruption is a plague; this should in and of itself justify the application of the law of the state which is concerned and which has implemented deterrent measures; and it should be so, I submit, even if, as in the *Hilmarton* case, corruption has not been proven on the facts.

15-67 It would be most unsound for international arbitrators to adopt a stance of general indifference as regards general interests protected by states. The very survival of arbitration as a means of dispute resolution could be undermined as a result. The *Mitsubishi* case is enlightening in this respect. The distributor had filed proceedings before the US Supreme Court, seeking a declaration that the violation or otherwise of the Sherman Act was not an arbitrable issue since an arbitral tribunal would inevitably disregard American law and apply Swiss law in accordance with the choice made by the parties. The Supreme Court, by a majority of one only, rejected the argument. It expressed its conviction – in terms that did convey an implicit threat – that arbitrators, even if ruling under the auspices of a Japanese arbitral institution, could not fail to apply American antitrust rules. The lesson to be learnt is plain: the arbitral process, substitute for judicial justice, may thrive but only subject to the condition that arbitrators, like judges, take responsibility for the general interests identified by the law.

IV. CONCLUSION

15-68 The relationship linking an arbitrator to the law is much more complex than the relationship that ties judges to it. Extraneous to all national legal systems, the international arbitrator enjoys a high degree of freedom: he is the sole master as regards the selection of the system – not necessarily a specific national legal system – whose rules he will apply. He is faced with the temptation to rule in equity, or to give excessive priority to the upholding of an illegal contract.

15-69 Yet the law has many positive aspects of which he is not always sufficiently aware: it is neutral and predictable; it guards against arbitrariness and is reassuring for the parties; it takes into account the general interests of the community.

15-70 This leads me to conclude this article with the expression of the following conviction: an arbitrator should consider that it is his duty, not a legal one but a professional one, to comply with the law, and even to approach the law with respect. This is precisely what parties providing for arbitration, and individual national states, expect of him.

*Sir Elihu Lauterpacht QC**

CHAPTER 16

ARBITRATION BETWEEN STATES AND FOREIGN INVESTORS: RETROSPECT AND PROSPECT[1]

I. INTRODUCTION

16-1 The choice of the subject of this lecture – 'Arbitration between States and foreign investors: retrospect and prospect' – needs little justification. Foreign investment, though fundamental in world economic activity, not infrequently gives rise to some contention between the parties. Anticipation of this risk underlies the inclusion in most investment agreements of some provision for recourse to arbitration. But the value of effective dispute settlement machinery is to be judged less by the number of cases in which it is used than by the number of cases in which its use is avoided. There can be no greater inducement to the negotiated settlement of disagreements between States and investors than the knowledge, no doubt dear to all here, that the principal beneficiaries of continuing discord are the members of the legal profession. Yet, despite the layman's understanding that it is usually better to settle than to fight, there still remains a significant margin of cases that require legal intervention. It is in this context that arbitration matters. So how the process works and whether it can be made to work more effectively is a proper subject for our consideration.

16-2 Why 'retrospect' and 'prospect', you may ask? So far as 'retrospect' is concerned, who is interested in the history of arbitration? The answer is simple.

---

[*] 20 Essex Street and Honorary Professor, Cambridge.
[1] This is a lightly edited version of the Freshfields lecture as delivered on 27 November 2001. Since then there have been some important developments, especially in the field of state immunity and in relation to the willingness of domestic courts to review essentially international decision. It has not been possible to take account of all these changes in the present edited version.

Julian D.M. Lew and Loukas A. Mistelis (eds), Arbitration Insights, 307-329
© 2007 Kluwer Law International. Printed in the Netherlands

During the past half-century there have been developments in the field of arbitration between States and investors that could hardly have been conceived of at the beginning of that period. That such advances have been made shows that such advances *can* be made – a consideration of importance for the 'prospect' part of this lecture.

16-3 The developments of the past 50 years are spread over the whole spectrum of State-investor arbitration. In this lecture, however, I will focus principally on three topics: the fundamental changes in the number and character of the tribunals in which such arbitration can take place; the developments in the law to be applied; and the associated questions of review of the substance of arbitral decisions and their implementation.

II. THE FUNDAMENTAL CHANGES IN THE NUMBER AND CHARACTER OF THE TRIBUNALS

16-4 I will begin with the number and character of the tribunals in which arbitration has taken place and the sources of their jurisdiction.

16-5 In the pre-World War II period, arbitration, particularly in resource development agreements in the British colonies, was usually envisaged as a normal domestic arbitration with local law being the applicable law. The Middle East oil concessions of the 1920s and 1930s provided for *ad hoc* arbitration, usually outside the territory of the host State; though their governing law was often the local law. The Anglo-Iranian Concession of 1933 provided that the President of the Permanent Court of International Justice would be the appointing authority if the parties failed to constitute the tribunal. It was this reference to the PCIJ which proved the downfall of this clause when, in 1951, the President of the ICJ declined to regard himself for this purpose as the successor of the President of the PCIJ.

16-6 Recourse to arbitration of an *ad hoc* kind has continued to be a significant feature of development agreements since World War II. Many of these provisions have been reflected in a number of important arbitral awards: the *Aramco* case,[2] the three *Libyan Oil* cases, involving respectively BP,[3] Texaco[4] and Liamco[5] as

---

[2] *Saudi Arabia v Arabian American Oil Company (ARAMCO)*, 27 ILR 117.
[3] *BP Exploration Company (Libya) Limited v Government of the Libyan Arab Republic*, 53 ILR 297.

well as the *Sapphire*[6] and *Aminoil*[7] cases – all of them too well known to require rehearsal here.

16-7 However, the feeling developed in the middle of the fifties, to some extent encouraged by the outcome of the Iranian-Consortium negotiations of 1954, that something more was required to improve investor confidence. Initially, the thinking was in terms of a treaty establishing standards of treatment coupled with an obligation to arbitrate.

16-8 The idea of direct access by private parties to international tribunals for the protection of their investments was actively promoted by an industry body called 'APPI', the Association for the Protection and Promotion of Investment. This flowed over into the so-called 'Abs-Shawcross Draft' of 1959 which was reflected more officially at the inter-governmental level in OECD in 1967 in the form of a Draft Convention on the Protection of Foreign Property.[8] This text contained not only substantive investment protection provisions but also a dispute settlement article permitting the commencement by an investor of arbitration proceedings directly against a host State if the latter had made a declaration accepting the jurisdiction of an Arbitral Tribunal (detailed in an Annex[9]) and the investor's own State did not itself take up the case. Though the draft only appeared within a resolution of the Council of OECD and was never opened for signature, its very emergence reflected a significant forward step in the thinking of the OECD countries. The OECD Resolution reaffirmed the adherence of its Members to the principles of international law embodied in the draft and commended it as a basis for further extending and rendering more effective the application of these principles.

16-9 It may be observed in passing that the Arbitration Annex attached to the Draft Convention contained some new thoughts on the arbitration process which have still to be fully absorbed into the system. It permitted intervention by a State Party which considered that it had an interest of a legal nature which might be affected by the decision in the case. It also empowered the Tribunal to consolidate pending proceedings, with the agreement where necessary of any

---

[4] *Texaco Overseas Petroleum and California Asiatic Oil Company (TOPCO) v Libya*, 53 ILR 389.
[5] *Libyan American Oil Company (LIAMCO) v Libyan Arab Republic*, 62 ILR 225.
[6] *Sapphire International Petroleum v National Iranian Oil Company*, 35 ILR 136.
[7] *Government of Kuwait v American Independent Oil Company (AMINOIL)*, 66 ILR 518.
[8] 7 ILM 117.
[9] Ibid. at 142.

other arbitral tribunals, and, if no objection was made by any party to such proceedings, to stay proceedings if other proceedings arising out of the same facts and raising substantially the same issues were pending before any other international tribunal.

16-10   The reason, however, why the text was never opened for signature was that at that time and for more than a decade afterwards it was clear that no multilateral agreement could be reached on the standard of treatment to be accorded to foreign investors and, in particular, on the level of compensation to be paid in the case of nationalisation or expropriation.

16-11   In the meantime, however, in parallel with the continued use of *ad hoc* procedures, we begin to see in 1962 the movement towards significant institutional arbitral procedures divorced from any attempt to restate the substantive law. That the substantive law was at that time the subject of considerable controversy is reflected, for example, in the debates associated with the UN General Assembly resolution on Permanent Sovereignty over Natural Resources[10] of that same year. Of these procedural initiatives, the most important has proved to be ICSID – the World Bank Centre for the Settlement of Investment Disputes. The ICSID structure comprises two separate systems. One is the original ICSID system established by the 1966 Convention.[11] This operates only between, on the one hand, States Parties to the Convention and, on the other, nationals of States that are also Parties to the Convention. It is a watertight system. That is to say, its operation cannot be defeated by non-cooperation by the Respondent State, whether in the establishment of the tribunal or in the pursuit of its mission. The system is entirely outside the control of any national system of law, except in relation to enforcement. As regards this, the Convention provides that each Party shall recognise and enforce the pecuniary obligations imposed by an award as if it were a final judgment of a court of that State[12] – subject only to the law in force in that State relating to State immunity from execution.[13] Awards may only be challenged by way of an application for annulment by an *ad hoc* committee within the system.[14] I will return to this later.

---

[10]   UN General Assembly Resolution 1803 (XVII), Dec 14, 1962, 2:223, Jan 63.
[11]   *Convention on the Settlement of Investment Disputes between States and Nationals of Other States*, 4 ILM 532.
[12]   Article 54, ibid. at 541.
[13]   Article 55, ibid. at 542. This exception has proved to be a significant limitation on the effectiveness of ICSID awards.
[14]   Article 52, ibid. at 541.

16-12   The other ICSID system is that of the Additional Facility. This was established in 1978 to provide for cases in which either the investment receiving State or the national State of the investor is not a party to the ICSID Convention but in which the parties to the transaction nonetheless wish to use procedures similar to those of ICSID. The Additional Facility differs from the original ICSID system principally in that it contains no procedure for review like that of the original system. Nor does it create an obligation for States to recognise and enforce awards. These matters depend upon the general arbitration law of the country where the tribunal has its seat or enforcement is sought.

16-13   Both branches of the ICSID system have commended themselves to States and investors alike. So far as ICSID proper is concerned, by the end of 2005, there have been approximately 79 decisions of tribunals and 8 decisions of *ad hoc* committees. There are 96 cases pending. As to the Additional Facility, there have been 11 decisions and there are 8 cases pending.

16-14   In addition to the very fact that these systems exist, demonstrative of the greater willingness of States to contemplate effective arbitration with investors, their great importance lies in the expansion in the number and range of provisions which have endowed them with jurisdiction.

16-15   When ICSID was first established, it was contemplated that its jurisdiction would be derived from specific provisions in contracts between States and investors. This source remains in common use.[15]

16-16   It has now been supplemented by the appearance in both bilateral and multilateral investment arrangements of provisions giving the investor the right to bring proceedings either in ICSID, if both the receiving State and the national State of the investor are parties to the Convention, or in the Additional Facility, if only one of those States is a party to the Convention.

16-17   There are now some 2265[16] bilateral investment treaties which provide substantively for the promotion and protection of investment by private parties and, procedurally for arbitration at two levels. One is at the State to State level which, though obviously to be welcomed, does not require comment here. The

---

[15]   As may be seen from the awards printed in the *ICSID Reports* and from the terms of current exploration or production sharing agreements such as that of 1997 between Kazakhstan and a group of major foreign oil companies.

[16]   UNCTAD 2003, http://www.unctadxi.org/templates/Page____1007.aspx.

other is at the level of the relationship between the receiving State and the investor. These agreements may provide either for *ad hoc* arbitration at the instance of the investor, often specifying the application of the ICSID Arbitration Rules or the UNCITRAL Rules, or they may provide directly for arbitration within ICSID or the Additional Facility.

16-18 Another institutional mode of settlement, also established by bilateral agreement, is the Iran-US Claims Settlement Tribunal. This has provided US nationals with direct access to an international tribunal for the resolution of claims directly by reference to international law. It has been the most case-prolific of the post-war tribunals, basing its procedures on the United Nations Commission on International Trade Law ('UNCITRAL') Arbitration Rules ('UNCITRAL Rules').[17] Its Reports now run to 34 volumes and contain a massive jurisprudence on such matters as nationality of claims, expropriation and compensation.[18]

16-19 The wider geographical acceptance of the idea of direct individual access to arbitration is further demonstrated, as between 20 members of the Arab League, by the Unified Agreement for the Investment of Arab Capital in Arab States of 1980.

16-20 On the substantive level it provides, amongst other matters, for the protection of Arab investors from measures of seizure or nationalisation, save for the public benefit and in return for fair compensation. Procedurally, it provides that disputes arising from an investment agreement, evidently including also claims by private parties, shall be settled by way of arbitration under an annex on arbitration. This lays down a watertight procedure for establishing the tribunal, directs that the tribunal shall determine its own procedures and provides that decisions of the tribunal shall be final and binding.

16-21 Although it appears that no use has yet been made of the system, again its very existence demonstrates the acceptability outside the limited circle of traditional G7 and OECD capital-exporting countries of direct recourse by private parties to arbitration against States in respect of matters that in earlier days would have been regarded as falling solely within the domain of inter-State litigation.

---

[17] 15 *ILM* 701.
[18] See Iran-US Claims Tribunal Reports volumes 1-34.

16-22 The same is true of the Agreement for Promotion, Protection and Guarantee of Investment among Member States of the Organisation of the Islamic Conference, concluded in 1981, which entered into force in 1986 on ratification by 10 members. There are 57 members of that Organisation.[19] Here, oncemore, there is protection on the substantive level for investment. Additionally, on the procedural level, the Agreement provides that disputes may be settled by arbitration.[20] A watertight procedure is laid down for the establishment of the tribunal.[21] More recently, the most prominent reflection of the same advance is to be found in the 1992 North American Free Trade Agreement ('NAFTA')[22] which has been in force between Canada, Mexico and the United States since 1994. Chapter Eleven, in its first section, provides for the substantive protection of investments and, in its second section, elaborates a system for the settlement of disputes between an investor and the host State. In particular, it envisages the submission of a claim by the investor to arbitration under either ICSID or *ad hoc* under the Additional Facility or the UNCITRAL Rules.

16-23 The further extension of the geographical range of these developments in Latin-America is to be perceived also in the Mercosur Protocols for the Protection of Investments, both in those relating to intra-zonal arrangements (1993)[23] and in those relating to investments originating from States not parties to Mercosur (1994).[24] The Parties to the Mercosur treaty are presently Argentina, Brazil, Paraguay and Uruguay.[25] The second of these Protocols, like NAFTA, gives the investor the choice of recourse to ICSID, the Additional Facility or an *ad hoc* arbitration tribunal established in accordance with UNCITRAL Rules.

---

[19] Organisation of Islamic Conference: http://www.oic-oci.org/index.asp
[20] Article 2.
[21] UNCTAD, *International Investment Instruments: A Compendium*, vol. II, 241.
[22] 32 *ILM* 289 and 605.
[23] *Protocol of Colonia for the Promotion and Reciprocal Protection of Investments* (Mercosur, January 17, 1994). This protocol was concluded under the *Asunción Treaty Establishing a Common Market Between Argentina, Brazil, Paraguay and Uruguay* (Mercosur, March 26, 1991).
[24] *Protocol for the Promotion and Protection of Investment of Third States* 5 (Mercosur, August 1994). This protocol was concluded under the *Asunción Treaty Establishing a Common Market Between Argentina, Brazil, Paraguay and Uruguay* (Mercosur, March 26, 1991).
[25] Chile and Bolivia became Associated Members in 1996.

16-24   The Energy Charter Treaty of 1994[26] follows a similar pattern, though in relation to a more restricted subject matter. However, it embraces an entirely different set of parties – including notably the East European States, the new States that form the Commonwealth of Independent States as well as, Australia[27] and Japan.

16-25   Nor should we overlook the earlier, but near universal, acknowledgement of the possibility of direct individual action[28] under the 1982 UN Convention on the Law of the Sea[29] in matters governed by international law. There, in the context of activities in the Area of the Deep Sea-Bed, the Sea-Bed Disputes Chamber is given jurisdiction over, *inter alia*, disputes between parties to contracts relating to the Area including national or juridical persons.[30]

16-26   In short, the developments just described demonstrate the remarkable expansion and crystallisation in a period of less than 50 years of the possibility of the direct participation of investors in litigation against States. There is, of course, nothing unique in this particular feature of the growing acknowledgement of the status of non-State actors in the international legal sphere. Another, and no less important, facet of the same phenomenon is the manner in which the individual has emerged during the same period both as the subject of human rights protection and as a direct participant in international litigation connected therewith. The erosion by these advances, as also by advances in the law of the sea and international environmental law, of the Nineteenth and early Twentieth century positivist approach to international law, in which States alone were considered subjects of international law, is manifestly to be welcomed and will, in due course, no doubt be taken further.[31]

---

[26]   33 *ILM* 360. So far there have been two decisions pursuant to the arbitral procedures under this Treaty, see *Nykomb Synergetics Technology Holding AB v. Republic of Latvia*, 16 December 2003 (Arbitration Institute of Stockholm Chamber of Commerce) http://ita.law.uvic.ca/documents/Nykomb-Finalaward.doc; and *Petrobart Limited v. Kyrgyz Republic* (SCC 126/2003) 29 March 2005, (Arbitration Institute of Stockholm Chamber of Commerce), http://www.investmentclaims.com/decisions/Petrobart-kyrgyz-rep-Award.pdf.

[27]   Australia has signed the Treaty but ratification is still pending.

[28]   Part XI (Article 187).

[29]   21 *ILM* 1261.

[30]   Ibid. at 1307 (Article 187 and 189) and 1323 (Article 288).

[31]   Whether in due course such advances will actually occur is, necessarily, matter of speculation. One major inhibiting factor would be that of the volume of work and the limitations on the number of judicial or arbitral personnel available to deal with it. Unless some suitable filtering mechanism can be developed, it could be that the sheer number of cases would be more than existing international tribunals or *ad hoc* tribunals could cope with.

16-27 Accompanying these *procedural* advances and no less significant in furthering arbitrations between States and investors, has been the growing acceptance of *the direct applicability of substantive international law* to relations between State and non-State actors in the field of investment.

16-28 As just stated, it was for long basic doctrine that as States alone are subjects of international law, so international law itself can be applicable only to relations between States and, correspondingly, cannot be directly applicable to relations between States and non-State investors. In particular it was argued that as oil concessions and other similar investment agreements were not treaties governed by international law, they could only be governed by the domestic law of some particular State.

16-29 The real problem that required solution was how to exclude the applicability of the law of the host State to the investment other than for regulatory purposes. Why? Because in terms of traditional private international law if the agreement were governed by the host State law, that State had the power unilaterally to change the terms of the agreement in a manner possibly detrimental to the investor.

16-30 The solution has taken various forms. The most direct has been that of 'delocalising' the contract, that is to say, of subjecting the contract to some law other than that of the host State. This has been achieved in two ways.

16-31 One has been expressly to subject the contract to a system of national law other than that of the host State. Even in these days one can occasionally find in some agreements in the Middle East or in some of the Commonwealth of Independent States provisions for the application of the law of Texas or of Alberta. Taken by itself, however, this device would do little to preserve the contract as a whole from the impact of host State law since the national law chosen may, by its rules of private international law, accept the possibility that the law of the host State may govern matters occurring within the latter's territory.

16-32 Nonetheless, mention may here be made of one case which demonstrates the possibility that even the selection of a national system of law as the governing system of law can still involve the application of international law. In 1998 a very strong arbitral tribunal consisting of a former New Zealand appeal judge (Sir Edward Somers), a former English Court of Appeal judge (Sir Michael Kerr) and a former judge of the Australian High Court (Sir Daryl Dawson) considered a case between Sandline[32] and the Government of Papua New Guinea, then attempting to quell an insurrection in the island of Bougainville.[33] The pertinent agreement was a service agreement rather than an investment agreement, but in so far as it was between a government and a foreign contractor it had significant features in common with investment contracts. The agreement contained an UNCITRAL arbitration clause and provided expressly that it should be 'construed and governed in accordance with the laws of England'. The Government contended that the agreement that it had itself concluded was illegal under its own law and that English law would not lend its aid to the enforcement of a contract illegal in the place of performance. The Tribunal acknowledged that this proposition would apply as a matter of public policy where the contract in question is between private parties.[34] However, it then distinguished the case where the contract was concluded between a State and a private party (the clear, though not stated, assumption being that the private party was foreign) saying that one then 'enters the realm of public international law'.[35] The Tribunal observed that 'it is part of the public policy of England that its courts should give effect to clearly established rules of international law'.[36] It rejected the Papua New Guinea contention that as the agreement was with a private party it did not attract international law.[37] The Tribunal said:

> 'an agreement between a private party and a State is an international, not a domestic, contract. This Tribunal is an international, not a domestic, arbitral tribunal and is bound to apply the rules of international law. Those rules are not excluded from, but form part of, English law, which is the law chosen by the parties to govern their contract'.[38]

16-33 The Tribunal then applied the rule of international law that a State cannot rely upon its own internal laws to support a plea that a contract concluded by it is illegal.[39] Thus, we have here a valuable precedent for the direct application of

---

[32] A British company specialising in rendering military and security services to recognised foreign governments in situations of internal conflict.

[33] *In the Matter of an International Arbitration under the UNCITRAL Rules Between Sandline International Inc. and the Independent State of Papua New Guinea* (Interim Award), 117 ILR 552.

[34] Ibid. at 560.

[35] Ibid.

[36] Ibid.

[37] Ibid.

[38] Ibid.

[39] Ibid. at 561.

international law to a contract with a foreign private party – introduced on the basis that international law is part of the national law that the parties selected to govern the contract.[40]

16-34 Another technique for excluding the law of the host State which has come to be quite widely used, develops the lead given as long ago as 1933 in Article 22 (F) of the Anglo-Iranian concession. This provided that any arbitration award under it 'shall be based on the juridical principles contained in Article 38 of the Statute of the Permanent Court of International Justice'. That article prescribed that the Court should apply treaties, international custom, general principles of law, judicial decisions and the teachings of the most highly qualified publicists. When in 1954 an agreement was concluded between a consortium of the eight major oil companies and Iran, it included the following provision, the recognisable parent of many similar provisions in later petroleum legislation and investment agreements:

> 'In view of the diverse nationalities of the parties to this Agreement, it shall be governed by and interpreted and applied in accordance with the principles of law common to Iran and the several nations in which the other parties to this Agreement are incorporated, and in the absence of such common principles, then by and in accordance with the principles of law recognised by civilised nations in general, including such of those principles as may have been applied by international tribunals'.

16-35 There was in due course to be some discussion as to whether this provision, as its words suggested, made the contract exclusively subject to general principles, which some, such as Dr Mann, argued was no system and therefore could not be applied as such, or, instead, as Dr Mann insisted, made it subject to what he saw as a system, namely, public international law. Although there was some arbitral reluctance to express a firm view on this doctrinal controversy one way or the other, the approach was one that came to be accepted by arbitral tribunals as excluding the ability of the host State unilaterally to change or end the agreement. One need only mention in this connection the well-known trio of Libyan oil arbitrations as well as *Sapphire*[41] and *Aminoil*.[42]

---

[40] In this respect, *Sandline* can be seen as following in the footsteps of the *Aminoil* case where the Tribunal attached importance to the fact that 'established public international law is necessarily a part of the law of Kuwait'. 66 ILR 518 at 560.

[41] Above n 6.

[42] Above n 7.

Doctrinally, the development was to form the basis of what has come to be known as the modern *lex mercatoria*.

16-36 The argument against the direct applicability of international law reflected in part the absence of specifically detailed rules of international law to resolve disputes as to, say, validity, interpretation, the effects of breach and damages that might arise in connection with investment agreements. But as can be seen from even the most cursory scrutiny of the growing number of cases in which this kind of provision has figured, the application of international law or of the concept of general principles, no matter how expressed, has never led a tribunal to declare itself unable to decide a case by reason of the absence of sufficiently clear rules of law. Indeed, even the English courts, whose approach to such matters might be thought likely to be quite strict, have accepted (as shown in 1987 in the *Deutsche Schachtbau* case[43]) the validity of an arbitrator's determination that the proper law of a particular oil exploration agreement was 'internationally accepted principles of law governing contractual relations'.[44]

16-37 Yet whatever may have been the theoretical objections to the application of international law, by the time of the *Aramco* case, 1958[45] the Arbitrator was able to hold that that particular arbitration could only be governed by international law. The acceptability to States more generally, including investment-receiving States, of the role of international law became evident in 1966 and the years following when specific reference was made to this possibility in a growing number of treaties. Thus, Article 42 of the ICSID Convention, though stating that a Tribunal should decide in accordance with such rules of law as might be agreed by the Parties, provided that in the absence of such agreement, the Tribunal should 'apply the law of the Contracting State party to the dispute . . . *and such rules of international law as may be applicable*'.[46] Of course, this does not say that international law as it now stands is able to prescribe in detail how to resolve technical questions such as, the problem arising when a party entitled to share equally in production from a given field fails to lift its due share of the resource. But it does serve to release from the possible stranglehold of the receiving State's law a contract which might, by virtue of

---

[43] *Deutsche Schachtbau-und Tiefbohrgesellscahft mbH v R'As al-Khaimah National Oil Co,* [1990] 1 AC 295.
[44] Ibid. at 312.
[45] Above n 2.
[46] Above n 11 at 539.

being subject to that law, be declared null and void and the investor disentitled to damages or compensation.

16-38 This provision was subsequently echoed in the Additional Facility Rules,[47] and with even less qualification in NAFTA[48] and the 1994 Mercosur Protocol.[49]

16-39 The exclusion of the worst effects of local law is also to be found in the many so-called 'no change' clauses that had earlier begun to appear in the investment contracts. As early as the 1933 Anglo-Iranian Oil Company ('AIOC') Concession, to which I have already referred, Article 21 was couched in the following terms:

> 'The . . . parties declare that they base the performance of the present Agreement on principles of mutual good will and good faith as well as on a reasonable interpretation of this Agreement. . . .
>
> The Concession shall not be annulled by the Government and the terms therein contained shall not be altered either by general or special legislation in the future, or by administrative measures or any other acts whatever of the executive authorities'.

16-40 A very similar provision appeared in Article 41 of the 1954 Consortium Agreement and likewise in many subsequent arrangements.

16-41 In addition, it came to be recognised in the late 1980s that a particular risk to which investment arrangements were exposed was not that of outright expropriation or termination of the agreement, but that of a gradual erosion of the anticipated profitability of the arrangement by the host State's introduction of burdensome regulatory measures or crippling taxation. The latter could be at so high a rate as actually to place the investor in a loss position while effectively locking him into the operation. To limit this risk, some contracts began to include a provision for the maintenance of the economic equilibrium between the parties – a further restriction upon the applicability of local law. One example is the following provision in the Qatar Model Exploration and Production Sharing Agreement of 1997:

[47] Article 35.
[48] Article 1131, above n 22 at 645.
[49] Article 2(H)4, above n 24.

'The Parties acknowledge that their fiscal position has been based on this Agreement and the laws which are in force in the State of Qatar as of the Effective Date. The Parties agree that in the event that the Government shall enact any new law or decree which demonstrably has a material adverse effect on the Contractor's fiscal position with respect to the Petroleum Operations, the Government shall take all steps as may be necessary to restore the fiscal benefit contemplated to be enjoyed by the Parties under this Agreement'.

16-42   Similarly, in the agreement of 18 November 1997 between Kazakhstan and a group of major foreign oil companies including AGIP, BP, Mobil and Shell, section 40(2) provided that if any change in the law

'. . . has a materially adverse effect on the economic benefits accruing to the Contractor . . . the Parties shall amend this Agreement or take such other action as is necessary or appropriate so as to restore the overall economic benefit . . . to the Contractor'.

16-43   It is a question for consideration as to the degree to which these provisions are arbitrable. Suppose that the parties cannot reach agreement on the amendment or the action required to restore the economic position of the Contractor, is an arbitral tribunal that is empowered only to decide according to law capable of producing a solution? Would not its task appear to be less the application of the law and more the reconstruction of the Agreement? It would be regrettable if these questions were answered in a way that could deprive these important provisions of their efficacy. Such an approach would manifestly betray the apparent expectation of the Parties that their whole relationship could be resolved within the framework of the Agreement. It is not beyond the competence of arbitrators to make an objective assessment of the needs of the situation and of the measures required to put it to rights. The problem was considered in the *Aminoil* case[50] where the Tribunal, though not acknowledging the possibility that the parties had conferred upon it the power to modify the contract, found that it could meet the intentions of the parties by investigating whether a liability could be ascribed to Aminoil on account of the operation of the so-called Abu Dhabi Formula and determining the amount due to the Company thereunder.[51]

---

[50]   Above n 7.
[51]   Ibid. see generally 603 – 613.

16-44   Two other developments may be selected from the many that warrant mention in this retrospect of the development of State/investor arbitration during the past 50 years. One is not limited in its scope to this class of arbitration but extends to all international arbitration, whoever may be the parties to them. This is the New York Convention of 1958 on the Enforcement of International Arbitral Awards ('New York Convention').[52] Its paramount importance is self-evident. I shall return to this when I turn to 'Prospect'.

16-45   The other development is the erosion of the plea of State immunity as a jurisdictional objection in arbitrations to which States are parties. At the beginning of our period, a State could plead immunity in arbitration, despite its having consented to the arbitral process, and still think that it might thus bring the proceedings to a halt. But several awards have made it clear that this plea will now not succeed and that consent to arbitration is a waiver of immunity for the purpose of the proceedings.[53] It is less certain, however, whether such a waiver extends to measures of execution. To this we shall also return presently.

16-46   At this point we may draw a line under our review of the past and turn to a consideration of the future. We move from retrospect to prospect, justifying our speculation about the future by our recollection of how much has been achieved over the past half century. If we can identify the remaining problems with sufficient clarity, a constructive approach may lead to further improvements. Obviously, it is impossible to cover all such matters now. I shall limit myself to a small group of inter-connected points related to the effect and implementation of awards.

16-47   We can conveniently take as our starting point the decision in the *Metalclad* case.[54] It was a case that arose within the framework of NAFTA. I should preface what I have to say about it by declaring an interest. I was privileged to be the chairman of the three-member tribunal of which the other members were Mr Ben Civiletti, a former Attorney-General of the United States, and Mr José-Luis Siqueiros, a Mexican law professor and highly experienced commercial arbitrator. As the case before the Tribunal is now over and the

---

[52] *United Nations Convention on the Recognition and Enforcement of Foreign Arbitral Awards* (New York, 10 June 1958), 330 UNTS 38.
[53] See also Schreuer, *The ICSID Convention: A Commentary,* at 1149, para 21.
[54] *Metalclad Corporation v United Mexican States,* 119 *ILR* 615.

subsequent challenge proceedings in Canada[55] have been ended, what I have to say does not pass beyond the bounds of judicial propriety. I am not going to comment on the substance of the review decision of the British Columbia Court[56] despite the fact that it involved points of international law. I shall limit myself to examining what the procedural possibility of such a review may mean for the application of international law in State/investor arbitrations.

16-48   The case arose out of an investment made in Mexico by a United States company. The legal basis of the claim was NAFTA of which Chapter Eleven deals with 'Investment'.[57] In Section A two articles lay down the applicable substantive law.

16-49   Article 1105(1) prescribes that 'Each Party shall accord to investments of investors of another Party treatment in accordance with international law, including fair and equitable treatment and full protection and security'.[58] Article 1110 prescribes that a Party may only expropriate an investment upon, amongst other conditions, payment of the fair market value.[59]

16-50   Section B of the same Chapter,[60] as I have already said, establishes a mechanism for the settlement of investment disputes by arbitration either under the original ICSID Convention itself, or under the ICSID Additional Facility Rules, or under the UNCITRAL Rules.

16-51   *Metalclad* was not what we may call a 'full' ICSID case, brought under the Convention itself, because Mexico is not a party to ICSID. The Claimant had to choose between the Additional Facility and an *ad hoc* tribunal established under the UNCITRAL Rules. It chose the Additional Facility. However, what we must note is that the issues to be decided by the Additional Facility Tribunal were identical with those that would have been before a regular ICSID Tribunal if that option had been open to, and pursued by, the Claimant. The issues were quite simply ones of public international law involved in the interpretation and

---

[55] *The United Mexican States v Metalclad Corporation,* 119 *ILR* 645; 5 *ICSID Rep.* 238. Supreme Court of British Columbia's Supplementary Reasons for Judgment *The United Mexican States v Metalclad Corporation,* 6 *ICSID Rep.* 53.

[56] Ibid.

[57] Above n 22 at 639.

[58] Ibid.

[59] Ibid. at 641.

[60] Ibid. at 642.

application of the two NAFTA provisions referred to above. If the award had been a regular ICSID award, it would only have been open to challenge by way of proceedings for annulment under Article 52 of the ICSID Convention. Such proceedings would have involved a consideration of the decision of one international tribunal, the original tribunal, by another international tribunal, the *ad hoc* Committee, appointed by the Chairman of ICSID from the standing Panel of Arbitrators. Though not expressly required to consist of international lawyers, such Committees are almost invariably so composed. Thus, review of regular ICSID decisions is carried out by persons whose legal formation is in the field of international law – an entirely proper course, just as appeals within any national legal system are heard by other lawyers formed in the same system as the judge of first instance.

16-52   Yet, when we come to the review of an Additional Facility decision we find that it is in the hands not of an appeal body with an international legal background, but of a court of national formation whose normal judicial activity is in the field of domestic law and is rarely, if ever, involved in matters of public international law. This is not to suggest that such a court is in any way not an excellent court, but only to point out the obvious fact (though one that the draftsmen overlooked or chose to disregard) that its discipline is not that of public international law and is, therefore, not one that commends itself as a basis for the decision of questions in that area. There is a real possibility in such circumstances that the review judge before whom the matter comes may approach matters in a manner that a public international lawyer would not – for example in relation to the technique for the interpretation of treaties or the determination of the content of customary international law. This is so even though the review tribunal is concerned only with questions of jurisdiction, not of merits. In *Metalclad* the consideration of the issue of jurisdiction involved considerable discussion of international law.

16-53   The situation is, I suggest, unsatisfactory, involving as it does a confusion of international and domestic proceedings that is unlikely, if it had been fully thought out, to have commended itself to those who originally conceived the Additional Facility. Mixing within the treatment of one case both a public international law approach at first instance and a domestic law approach on review is an anomaly that should be avoided.

16-54   There is, of course, another side to the matter. A justification for the present situation can be presented along the following lines: it is better that the Additional Facility should exist than that it should not, for only thus can one partly fill the gap when the ordinary ICSID procedures cannot be invoked. As the Additional Facility falls outside the scope of the ICSID Convention, its operation is really dependent upon contract between the parties. It is therefore to be likened to a domestic arbitration, the only differences between it and, say, one conducted under UNCITRAL Rules being that the Additional Facility provides an institutional framework for the arbitration whereas the UNCITRAL Rules merely provide rules for the establishment and operation of an *ad hoc* tribunal. Once an arbitration under a contract is held in a State, then it is subject to the arbitration law of that State, including the power of its Courts to consider whether the tribunal has exceeded its jurisdiction.

16-55 True though this is, it prompts at least two thoughts which may deserve further consideration.

16-56 The first (and simpler) relates specifically to the ICSID Additional Facility. There does not appear to be any legal reason preventing the amendment of the contractual structure between the parties established by the Additional Facility Rules so as to include the idea of recourse to an *ad hoc* committee within the framework of those Rules. Such a committee could review the initial award on the same grounds as those laid down for the regular ICSID system in Article 52 of the Convention.[61] The introduction of this second tier of consideration within the contractual system is not in principle (though it is in scope) different from the scrutiny conducted by the International Chamber of Commerce ('ICC') Court of Arbitration of the draft Award of an Arbitral Tribunal that actually hears a case within that system.[62]

16-57 The necessary amendment to the Additional Facility Rules could be made quite simply by the same body that initially authorised the ICSID Secretariat to administer the Additional Facility, that is, the Administrative Council of the Centre, a body composed of one representative from each of the ICSID Contracting States. No additional treaty would be required.

16-58 There might be a question as to whether references to the Additional Facility in existing agreements should be read as referring to the Additional Facility as it was at the time those agreements were made or as it might become from time to time in the light of amendments. As regards ICSID itself, Article 44

---

[61] Above n 11 at 541.
[62] See ICC Rules, Article 27.

of the Convention provides that any arbitration proceeding shall be conducted in accordance with the Arbitration Rules in effect on the date on which the parties consented to arbitration.[63] Assuming that the ICSID approach may be applied by way of analogy to the Additional Facility, it will be a matter for closer scrutiny in each case to determine whether the date on which the parties consented to arbitrate is the date of the relevant BIT or multilateral treaty or the date on which the investor instituted the proceedings.

16-59   Even so, the change proposed would not by itself completely eliminate the exposure to review by the courts of the country in which the arbitration is deemed to have its seat. Subject to the possibility of waiver by the Parties of recourse to these national tribunals, of which I will speak in a moment, those courts would still possess the power to review the validity of awards in challenge proceedings or in proceedings for their enforcement. The *Metalclad* situation could still arise. But the likelihood of its doing so would be reduced by the possibility of prior review by an *ad hoc* committee within the Additional Facility system and the likely disposal of challenges in that way.

16-60   We may go on to ask next why should arbitrations – or at any rate, arbitrations between States and foreign investors involving the direct application of international law – be tied to the legal system of a particular State? Why should they not be completely delocalised, denationalised or floating in the same way as are arbitrations between States?

16-61   There are two reasons why ordinary arbitrations are linked to a national system. One is to safeguard the arbitral process; that is, to ensure the validity of the composition of the tribunal and its operation within the scope of its jurisdiction as well as to provide certain ancillary services such as interim protective measures. But in relation to arbitrations administered by so experienced and efficient an institution as the ICSID Secretariat, this consideration would not appear controlling.

16-62   The other reason is to aid in the enforcement of the award. This is now largely dependent upon the New York Convention, a crucially important instrument in encouraging compliance with and, if necessary, securing enforcement of, international arbitral awards whether involving States or not. The Convention appears to be founded principally upon the idea that an award, to be

---

[63]   Above n 11 at 539.

enforceable, shall have been made in the territory of a State other than the State where its recognition and enforcement are sought. It is this requirement, that there must be a territorial connection with a Convention State, that perpetuates the need for a link between an arbitration and a State. If it did not exist, if all that was required of an award to be recognised and enforceable under the Convention was appropriate proof of its existence regardless of a territorial link, the enforcement of arbitral awards would be simpler.

16-63   Article 1 of the New York Convention itself clearly states an alternative basis for recognition and enforcement. It is that the award be one that is 'not considered as a domestic award in the State where its recognition or enforcement is sought'. Unfortunately, this provision is regarded by some commentators of the highest standing as being effectively a dead letter. Nonetheless, there is much that is appealing in the idea that a denationalised or internationalised State/investor award should be regarded as non-domestic by the Courts of the State where recognition is sought and should accordingly be enforced.

16-64   We should not feel reluctant about shedding national links. After all, it has to be acknowledged that there is a distinct measure of arbitrariness and artificiality in the concept of the 'seat' of an arbitration – particularly in State/investor arbitrations.

16-65   The parties or the tribunal are free to choose the seat. The choice is not necessarily that of the country with which the contract has the closest connection, nor of the place where the hearings are actually held, nor where the arbitrators meet, nor where the award is delivered. Not infrequently the seat is chosen without reference to any of these factors.

16-66   The New York Convention refers to 'awards made in the territory of a State'. What does 'made' mean? Is it where the tribunal deliberated or where the award was signed? As is well known, awards may actually be drafted and signed in different places and the stated place of signature may well be fictional when the arbitrators are scattered, each is in a different place when he signs the award, and the text merely states that it is signed 'as at' a particular location.

16-67   If we were starting with a clean slate to compose a system for State/investor or comparable arbitrations would we feel it essential to provide for a 'seat' of the arbitration? Would it not be sufficient for the arbitrators to decide on a purely pragmatic basis where it best suits them to meet, without that choice of location introducing into the case an extraneous element that might affect either the substance or the effect of the award?

16-68   In asking this question I do little more than echo the views expressed by a leading authority in this field, Professor van den Berg. Despite his rejection of an interpretation of Article 1 of the New York Convention that would read the reference to 'awards not considered as domestic awards' as providing for enforcement of awards not made in the territory of a contracting State, he stated: 'the concept of a "de-nationalised" arbitration and the ensuing "a-national award" it is attractive and deserves more support than it has received so far. However, the insufficient legal basis and the absence of recognition by most national courts make the agreement for "de-nationalised" arbitration a hazardous undertaking full of legal pitfalls. It is therefore not surprising that only in very exceptional cases such an agreement is made . . . The sole realistic approach to providing the "de-nationalised" arbitration and hence the "a-national" award with a sufficient legal basis seems to be international conventions'.[64] He also observes that this type of arbitration may be especially appropriate for the settlement of disputes between States and foreign enterprises.[65]

16-69   There is, of course, very good sense in what Professor Van den Berg is saying and we should do more to bring about the desirable objective that he describes. But is a treaty the only way to achieve the desired end? Ought we not to reflect more on the possibility that the parties to the relevant contract might so word their arbitration clause as to preclude either of them from raising in any national proceedings any plea of lack of jurisdiction of the arbitral tribunal or of error of law in its award? Could they not undertake that in any proceedings brought in national courts for enforcement under the New York Convention they would raise no objection to the exercise by the national court of its powers on the basis that the award in question fell within the second alternative of Article 1 of the Convention, as being one that was not considered a domestic award? Or, if that undertaking were likely to be confronted by the declarations that Parties to the Convention are entitled to make, and so many have made, that they will apply the Convention only to awards 'made' in the territory of another Contracting Party, could not the parties to the arbitration agree that the award will be deemed

---

[64]   *The New York Arbitration Convention of 1958: Towards a Uniform Judicial Interpretation*, 33-34.
[65]   Ibid. at 29-30.

to have been made in the territory of another Contracting State and that neither party will argue otherwise? The power of estoppel is not to be overlooked.

16-70   This consideration of the points that could benefit from clarification or improvement over the coming years could of course be extended considerably. But the time available to us for this purpose is now fast disappearing. I shall, therefore, conclude with mention of only two.

16-71   The first relates closely to what I have just been speaking of, namely, the ability, if any, of the parties to agree that the award of the tribunal shall bring the dispute to an end, without recourse to any other court or tribunal not contemplated, expressly or impliedly, in the arbitration agreement. What is the meaning of clauses that say that 'the award shall be final, binding and without appeal' or some variant of this? Evidently, when an arbitration is conducted within a legal framework that makes no provision for recourse to any other court or tribunal, the meaning of 'final and binding' is quite clear. The proceedings end with the award. That is the position in inter-State arbitrations, save of course for the possibility of applications for interpretation or revision in the light of new facts. These are standard and fully acceptable exceptions to finality and are necessary for the proper functioning of the arbitral system. But the position is different when the same words are used in relation to awards reached within the framework of national legal systems or of institutional arrangements. There the words 'final and binding' mean 'final and binding to the extent permitted by the system'. Thus if the system allows of a challenge to validity, then the award is final and binding only if a party does not challenge the award within the prescribed time limit. For us here the question is whether, even within national legal systems or institutional frameworks, parties can effectively exclude the initiation of further recourse by either. While the concept of party autonomy in arbitration suggests a positive answer, the possibility cannot be excluded that the court to which resort is had by the party that wishes to disregard the self-imposed prohibition will take a negative view of such an attempt to exclude its competence. That is, of course, a matter of national law and such laws may vary.

16-72   But that is not a reason why, for the future, we should not seek to enhance party autonomy in two ways. One would be to elaborate a model comprehensive exclusionary clause for use in arbitration agreements. That is relatively easy. Such a clause could run along the following lines: 'The Parties agree that the tribunal's award shall be final and binding. Neither side will challenge the validity or content of the award in any other court or tribunal. In particular neither party will use any such challenge to prevent, hinder or delay the full and complete execution of the award through legal proceedings in any jurisdiction'. The impact of local public policy upon such a provision seems so unlikely that for present purposes we may disregard it.

16-73   The other approach to the same objective would be for the idea to be incorporated in due course as part of some further multilateral convention, comparable to the New York Convention, but devoted to State/investor arbitrations. And if such a convention were ever contemplated, that would be a suitable place in which to deal with the last remaining point for which I dare to seize a moment more of your time. It relates to the plea of State immunity in relation to the execution of awards. Although there is now little, if any, prospect of a plea of immunity being successful in relation to the merits of a case, there is still some uncertainty and variant practice as regards immunity from execution. This is a matter which the ICSID Convention, for example, left to the laws of the various States in which enforcement might be sought. This is unsatisfactory. With the exception, perhaps, of the protection of funds directly and exclusively committed to the use of an embassy, there appears to be no good reason why the general assets of the State should be immune from execution. While the matter could be taken care of by treaty – and perhaps should be in future BITS or a multilateral convention – an approach to its solution could be attempted by the inclusion of an extended waiver clause in the pertinent instrument of agreement – as has indeed been suggested by Mr Delaume.[66]

16-74   And so I come to my conclusion. It has been the theme of this lecture that great changes have taken place in State/investor arbitrations over the past half century. It has been a gradual process starting with private initiatives and accumulating momentum as it came to be increasingly accepted and reflected in arbitral decisions and treaties. But the fact that so much has been done does not mean that there is not much still to be done. This lecture has, I hope, identified some possibilities. There are, of course, others. In the capable hands of constructive, imaginative and vigorous lawyers, I have no doubt that over time the desirable progress will be further identified and made.

---

[66]   ICSID Review, vol. 7, 194 (1992).

William W. Park*

CHAPTER 17

ARBITRATION'S PROTEAN NATURE: THE VALUE OF RULES AND THE RISK OF DISCRETION

'In most matters it is more important that the applicable rule of law be settled than that it be settled right'. Louis Brandeis.[1]

I. SYNOPSIS

17-1 The Freshfields Lecture for 2002 questions the wisdom of unfettered arbitrator discretion. The author suggests that the absence of procedural constraint on the arbitral tribunal can create more problems than it solves, often giving the impression of an 'ad hoc justice' that damages the perceived legitimacy of the dispute resolution process. Challenging the prevailing orthodoxy about the costs and benefits of discretion, the Lecture explores the feasibility of including; in international arbitration provisions, a set of more precise procedural protocols in institutional provisions, to apply unless the litigants explicitly opt out of the default norms.

* Professor of Law, Boston University. Delivered on 4 December 2002 as the Annual Freshfields Bruckhaus Deringer Lecture, University of London Centre for Commercial Law Studies, School of International Arbitration. Copyright © 2003 William W. Park. Special thanks are due to Bob Bone, Ron Cass, Jack Coe, Adam Samuel and Tony Weir for thoughtful comments and to Pelagia Ivanova; Barbara Lauriat and Erica Smith for helpful research assistance.
[1] Louis Brandeis, J. in *Burnet* v. *Coronado Oil and Gas Co.*, 285 U.S. 393, 447 (1932) (holding non-taxable a lessee's oil income pursuant to government lease).

II. INTRODUCTION: THE WHY AND HOW OF ARBITRATION

A. Diversity of Motive and Method

17-2 Let us go back three-quarters of a century. In June 1927, the *National Geographic Magazine* published an article describing law reform under a Manchu emperor who reigned in the early eighteenth century. Emperor Kang-hsi decided that courts should be as bad as possible so his subjects would settle disputes by arbitration. Responding to a petition about judicial corruption, he decreed as follows:

> Lawsuits would tend to increase to a frightful extent if people were not afraid of the tribunals. … I desire therefore that those who have recourse to the courts should be treated without any pity and in such a manner that they shall be disgusted with the law and tremble to appear before a magistrate. In this manner … good citizens who may have difficulties among themselves will settle them like brothers by referring to the arbitration of some old man or the mayor of the commune. As for those who are troublesome, obstinate and quarrelsome, let them be ruined in the law courts.[2]

17-3 So here is one reason to arbitrate: the hope of avoiding a grossly mismanaged judicial system. But there are other motives. For international transactions, arbitration offers the hope of reducing bias and the prospect of parallel lawsuits in different countries. There may also be the expectation (whether warranted or not) of confidentiality and expertise. In some countries, such as the United States, arbitration has been fuelled by a hope of keeping consumer and employment cases away from sympathetic civil juries inclined to award high punitive damages.

17-4 Arbitrations also show enormous variation in the mechanisms used to establish the facts and the law. A letter of credit dispute might be arbitrated in a few hours on the basis of documents only. At the other extreme, a large construction case could involve years of proceedings, with pre-trial discovery,

---

[2] Frank Johnson Goodnow, 'The Geography of China: The Influence of Physical Environment on the History and Character of the Chinese People' in (1927) 51 *National Geographic Magazine* (June) 651, at 661–662. Professor Goodnow adds an editorial note to the effect that under these conditions law reform was 'naturally difficult'. Thanks are due to my friend Jim Groton for bringing this chestnut to my attention.

depositions, motions on applicable law and jurisdiction, as well as witness statements and extensive cross-examination.

17-5 This variety should not be surprising, since arbitration (like dispute resolution in general) runs the gamut from large investment controversies to small credit card debt collection. The spectrum of subject matter includes construction, baseball salaries, biotech licences, expropriation, joint ventures, auto franchises, distribution and agency contracts, employment discrimination, insurance, collective bargaining agreements and Internet domain name disputes.

17-6 The moral flavour of arbitration differs dramatically from context to context. The values of fairness and efficiency that commend arbitration to sophisticated business managers often serve to condemn the process in consumer cases, where an arbitration clause might require an ill-informed individual to seek uncertain remedies at an inaccessible venue.

17-7 Finally, the public image and aura of arbitration will vary depending on perspective. In Western Europe, arbitration traditionally took the moral high ground, portrayed as an exercise in self-governance by the commercial community involving co-operation between the private sector (which conducted the arbitration) and the state (which enforced the award). In cross-border commerce, arbitration also was seen as providing a way for companies from different parts of the world to level the procedural playing field.

17-8 In developing nations, however, arbitration has often been perceived in a much less glorious light, as a process whereby secret tribunals undermine national sovereignty and legitimate governmental regulations. Ironically, the latter view has recently gained currency among certain segments of the US population disturbed about NAFTA investment claims brought by Canadians.[3]

B. Common Themes

17-9 Yet, notwithstanding its chameleon-like character, arbitration maintains a core essence. Litigants renounce the jurisdiction of otherwise competent courts in favour of a private and binding dispute resolution mechanism. Arbitration institutions usually purport to promote equal treatment and basic notions of

---

[3] *See generally* Guillermo Aguilar Alvarez and William W. Park, 'The New Face of Investment Arbitration' in 28 *Yale J. Int'l Law* (2003).

fairness. Arbitrators are expected to possess integrity, experience, and the ability to be both a good listener and a careful reader. In most cases, litigants also want their arbitrator to be intelligent, although at least one case comes to mind in which a lawyer sought to disqualify an arbitrator whose strong intellect made it unlikely that the lawyer's client would succeed with its clever but spurious arguments.

17-10 The interaction of arbitration's diversity of form and unity of essence brings to mind the elusive Greek sea-god Proteus, who had the gift of altering shape while his substance remained the same. Similarly, arbitration is constantly reinventing itself to adapt to each particular case and legal culture, while retaining a vital core which aims at final and impartial resolution of controversies outside national judicial systems.

III. ARBITRAL DISCRETION

A. The Benefits of Procedural Autonomy

17-11 One reaction to arbitration's protean nature has been an emphasis on broad grants of procedural discretion to the arbitrators. Arbitrators can conduct proceedings in almost any manner they deem best, as long as they respect the arbitral mission and accord the type of fundamental fairness usually called 'due process' in the United States and 'natural justice' in Britain, which includes both freedom from bias and allowing each side an equal right to be heard. Consulting the entrails of a disembowelled chicken might perhaps be off limits. Negative attitudes about augury aside, however, very few constraints limit the manner in which arbitrators go about their jobs.[4]

17-12 The absence of precise procedural rules is said to constitute arbitration's strength, by allowing creation of norms appropriate to the contours of each dispute. Established dogma teaches that much of arbitration's genius lies in giving carefully chosen individuals the freedom to apply just the right touch of this or that procedural principle – the *je ne sais quoi* of justice that leads to

---

[4] For a theoretical discussion of the authority of arbitrators to create procedural rules, *see generally* Adam Samuel, *Jurisdictional Problems in International Commercial Arbitration* (1989). *See also* Julian Critchlow, 'The Authority of Arbitrators to Make Rules' in (2002) 68 *Arbitration* 4.

innovative and clever compromises.[5] Like a bespoke tailor, the creative arbitrator cuts the procedural cloth to fit the particularities of each contest, rather than forcing all cases into the type of ill-fitting off-the-rack litigation garment found in national courts. While not totally false, this view is incomplete, as we shall see in a moment.

B. Two Meanings of 'Rules'

17-13 This discretionary power exists not only in ad hoc proceedings, but also when the parties agree to a set of prefabricated institutional provisions, such as those of the International Chamber of Commerce or the American Arbitration Association. Here we encounter a slight linguistic challenge. In arbitration, the term 'rules' can bear at least two different meanings. First, there are stipulated frameworks of pre-set provisions (like the ICC or the AAA arbitration rules) that address matters related to the appointment of arbitrators and basic requirements of initial filings.[6] Secondly, specific directives for conduct of the proceedings (in both fact-finding and legal argument) govern matters such as privilege and document production.

17-14 For better or for worse, rules in the first sense (prefabricated provisions) contain few rules in the second sense (canons for conduct of the proceedings), but leave the latter questions to the arbitrators. For example, the ICC Rules provide simply that the arbitrator may establish the facts by 'all appropriate means'.[7] Both the UNCITRAL and the AAA International Rules say that the tribunal may conduct the arbitration in 'whatever manner it considers appropriate'.[8] Even the LCIA Rules (which do a better job than most in

---

[5]   In reality, of course, arbitrators rarely innovate with new-minted procedures, but instead usually draw their decisions from practice in other cases and modified analogies to national legal systems. Thus arbitration remains derivative of the procedural norms established in court litigation.

[6]   This basic framework for an arbitration might also cover timetables for early filings, the presence of party representatives at hearings, procedures for challenging arbitrators, ways to address problematic situations such as multiple parties that cannot agree on an arbitrator; the treatment of new claims that arise during the proceedings; scrutiny (or lack thereof) of the award, correction of mathematical mistakes and financial matters such as how arbitrators get paid and whether attorneys' fees may be recovered.

[7]   ICC Arbitration Rules, art. 20. This applies as long as the arbitrators 'act fairly and impartially' so as to ensure that each party has a 'reasonable opportunity to present its case'. *See* ICC Arbitration Rules, art. 15.

[8]   UNCITRAL Rules, art. 18; AAA International Rules, art. 16. In art. 16(3) the Rules go further and state that the tribunal 'may in its discretion direct the order of proof, bifurcate proceedings,

transforming litigation practice into precise directives)[9] are explicit in giving the arbitral tribunal the 'widest discretion to discharge its duties'.[10]

17-15 The same grant of discretion is found in modern arbitration statutes.[11] Enlightened arbitration statutes today usually limit mandatory judicial review to matters such as bias, excess of authority and gross procedural irregularity.[12] In some cases they may also admonish the arbitrator to act with fairness and to adopt procedures suitable to the circumstances of the particular case.[13]

IV. THE DOWN SIDE OF DISCRETION

A. The Need for Default Procedural Protocols

17-16 The time has come to present this article's tentative thesis, which with some simplification might be presented as follows: the benefits of arbitrator discretion are overrated; flexibility is not an unalloyed good; and arbitration's malleability often comes at an unjustifiable cost.[14] Therefore arbitral institutions

---

exclude cumulative or irrelevant testimony or other evidence and direct the parties to focus their presentations on issues the decision of which could dispose of all or part of the case'. By contrast, the AAA Commercial Arbitration Rules (used in domestic cases) provide that the parties shall produce evidence 'as the arbitrator may deem necessary'. *See* Rule 33, which continues that arbitrators may dispense with 'conformity to the legal rules of evidence'. Rule 34 adds that evidence by affidavit is to be given 'only such weight as the arbitrator deems it entitled'.

9   For example, the LCIA Arbitration Rules explicitly address witness preparation (art. 20.6), cross-examination (art. 20.5) and orders for the production of documents (art. 22.1(e)).

10 LCIA Arbitration Rules, art. 14.2.

11 For a magisterial survey of modern arbitration law, *see* Jean-François Poudret and Sébastien Besson, *Droit comparé de l'arbitrage international* (2002).

12 *See* William W. Park, 'Why Courts Review Arbitral Awards' in R. Briner, L. Y. Fortier, K.-P. Berger and J. Bredow (eds), *Recht der Internationalen Wirtschaft und Streiterledigung im 21. Jahrhundert: Liber Amicorum Karl-Heinz Böckstiegel* (2001), p. 595; reprinted in (2001) 16 *Int'l Arb. Rep.* (November) 27.

13 Section 33 of England's Arbitration Act 1996 admonishes the arbitrator to 'adopt procedures suitable to the circumstances of the particular case' and requires the tribunal to 'act fairly and impartially as between the parties, giving each party a reasonable opportunity of putting his case and dealing with that of his opponent', as well as to 'adopt procedures suitable to the circumstances of the particular case, avoiding unnecessary delay or expense, so as to provide a fair means for the resolution of the matters falling to be determined'.

14 The arbitration world seems to have at least one other skeptic who challenges the benefits of discretion. *See* John Uff, 'Predictability in International Arbitration' in *International Commercial Arbitration: Practical Perspectives* (2001), p. 151. After noting that arbitrator discretion results in uncertainties of both cost and proceeding length, Prof. Uff suggests (perhaps with a bit of dramatic hyperbole?) that 'in most cases it is a matter of pure chance whether the

should give serious consideration to adopting provisions with more precise procedural protocols to serve as default settings for the way arbitrations should actually be conducted. These directives would explicitly address questions such as documentary discovery, privilege, witness statements, order of memorials, allocation of hearing time, burden of proof and the extent of oral testimony.

17-17   Unrealistic expectations are resentments waiting to happen.[15] Arbitration is no exception. When an arbitrator adopts a model of procedural fairness different from what was anticipated by one of the parties, the arbitrator may well believe that his or her approach is 'the usual way things are done'. In an international context, however, competing experiences will almost always be available to indicate that other approaches are not uncommon. While a page of history is certainly worth a volume of logic,[16] arbitration's enormous variety means that even the best and the brightest may be reading from quite different pages – or may read from one page one day and another the next. An arbitrator might say, 'In my experience it is common to allow two rounds of briefs, with the respondent having the last word'. Yet on another day, with a slight adjustment in phraseology, the same arbitrator could assert the contrary, that it is 'not uncommon' to give the claimant the last word – and both statements would be correct.

17-18   The issue is not whether a model exists for a particular decision, but why one paradigm rather than another should prevail. While it seems almost axiomatic that parties themselves should be free to fashion their arbitration as they see fit, it is less evident that arbitrators ought to be in the business of setting norms for specific procedural questions on an ad hoc basis. For they may already have seen which side will be advantaged by one rule or the other.

---

parties to an international arbitration end up with what might objectively be called a "good" resolution of their dispute': *ibid.* p. 152. Stressing that predictability trumps flexibility, Prof. Uff urges that fundamental procedural decisions should be made at the time the contract is concluded.

[15]   In considering parties' expectations, the relevant time is contract signature, when neither side is informed about any specific litigation strategy. These expectations are quite different from post-dispute inclinations to see virtue in whatever rules serve their strategic ends. In the latter case, during arbitration, lawyers' procedural preferences will depend on what might be called the 'ouch test' in which a particular rule is objectionable if it hurts the client's case.

[16]   Frankfurter J. suggested this in *New York Trust Company* v. *Eisner*, 256 U.S. 345, 349 (1921) (upholding federal estate tax against constitutional attack).

17-19   This may not matter when all parties share or have adopted a common legal culture,[17] or belong to a relatively homogeneous community that shares confidence in the individuals chosen to decide the case. Two Boston law firms arbitrating before a well-known Boston arbitrator would normally be expected to behave professionally and accept rulings that comport with their common range of expectations on matters such as witness sequestration and document production.

17-20   However, if backgrounds and experiences differ materially, the ad hoc imposition of procedures uncustomary to one side and not announced in advance, risks reducing the perception of arbitration's legitimacy.[18] The aggrieved party may then feel justified attempting to disrupt and derail the proceedings with charges of procedural unfairness.

B. Arbitral Orthodoxy

17-21   To many in the arbitration community, any suggestion that arbitral discretion should be curtailed may be as welcome as ants at a picnic.[19] The flexibility inherent in arbitrator discretion not only constitutes a pillar of orthodoxy,[20] but rests on deeply entrenched practical considerations. Arbitral

---

[17]   For example, shipping arbitration in London is certainly international, but proceeds under an accepted common legal culture. A quite different sociology attaches to arbitration of cross-border contracts related to joint ventures, sales, distribution agreements, licences and agency contracts.

[18]   For a discussion of some of the tensions resulting from the heterogeneous nature of the world's legal cultures, *see* William W. Park, 'Arbitration's Discontents: Of Elephants and Pornography' in Ian Fletcher, Loukas Mistelis and Marise Cremona (eds), *Foundations and Perspectives of International Trade Law* (2001), p. 258; reprinted in (2001) 17 *Arb. Int'l* 263 and (2002) 17 *Int'l Arb. Rep.* (February) 20.

[19]   In this connection, much of the history of English arbitration during the past three decades has involved a move toward flexibility, which is all right and good. But the starting point was a hyper-legalised arbitration culture. Prior to 1979 any award might well end up being retried in court under the 'case stated' procedure. In the United States now, there is a trend to allow appeal on the merits of the dispute – on the assumption that an unappealable award presents too great a risk because of arbitrator error. The problem, of course, is that appealable awards also present a risk: that of having to try the same case twice. The question is not whether to have rules, but how many and what kind.

[20]   For some, the suggestion of diminishing arbitrators' procedural liberty might bring to mind Dostoyevsky's story of the Grand Inquisitor. Ivan recounts a dream about a sixteenth century Inquisitor who tells Jesus that it was folly for him to have offered humankind freedom. 'Nothing has ever been more insupportable for a man and human society than freedom', says the Grand Inquisitor. *See* Fyodor Dostoyevsky, *The Brothers Karamazov*, Bk V ch. 5.

institutions that aspire to market their services globally are understandably shy about taking sides in long-standing debates between different national legal systems, particularly on those controversies that divide continental and Anglo-American civil litigation.[21] By leaving procedural matters to the arbitrators' discretion, institutions side-step the hard choices about what exactly it means to conduct a fair and efficient proceeding.

17-22 Consequently, one must recognise the enormous conceptual and practical problems attached to any suggestion of reduced arbitral discretion. More than once, the dilemmas of this topic have brought to mind the notice hanging at the entrance to Dante's Inferno: *Lasciate ogni speranza, voi che entrate* – 'Abandon all hope, you who enter here'.[22] Better minds than mine have sunk beneath the waves trying to resolve the tension between rules and discretion. As our French colleagues say, *Je m'interroge*. Thus, this article remains very much a work in progress, and invites the audience's merciless critique.

V. ARBITRATION'S ARCHITECTURE

A. Institutional Provisions

17-23 Let us return briefly to the architecture of arbitration. The American Arbitration Association lists over 30 different sets of arbitration provisions, with special procedures for securities transactions, finance, construction, collective bargaining, patents and employment disputes, as well as real estate transactions in Hawaii and Michigan and auto accidents in New York. On this side of the Atlantic, a visit to the Internet yields websites for at least a dozen London-based organisations devoted primarily to arbitration, and no less than 25 professional academies and trade associations that purport to sponsor arbitration as part of a more general mission. And there is no dearth of provisions developed by

---

[21] Significant differences exist in at least five areas: (i) the familiar problems with discovery, discussed *infra*; (ii) the way documents are used at hearings (civil law practitioners may be less likely to expect that documents will be authenticated and explained by live witnesses); (iii) witness testimony (judges rather than lawyers ask most of the questions in civil law jurisdictions); (iv) experts (continentals tend to expect that the arbitral tribunal will appoint experts, while Americans usually insist on each side presenting its own experts); and (v) legal argument (the common law tradition relies more on cases while the continental practice has been to cite leading professorial commentaries). *See* Siegfried H. Elsing and John M. Townsend, 'Bridging the Common Law–Civil Law Divide in Arbitration' in (2002) 18 *Arb. Int'l* 59.

[22] Dante Alighieri, *Divine Comedy*, 'Inferno', III, 9.

continental-based institutions and by Chambers of Commerce throughout the world.

17-24 In some cases these provisions do differ. For example, the AAA International Rules restrict punitive damages, while the domestic rules do not; and the LCIA Rules give the tribunal a clear right to join consenting third parties, which is not present in most other procedural frameworks.[23]

17-25 More often than not, however, these provisions are remarkably similar. Assuming that each side gets an opportunity to be heard, conduct of the proceedings is left to the arbitrators, permitting arbitral institutions to avoid the nitty-gritty procedural questions where the real demons lurk. Few pre-set arbitration provisions tell us whether pre-trial depositions are allowed, whether a party has a right to exclude one fact witness when another is testifying, or whether a log must be created to identify allegedly privileged documents withheld during discovery. Attempts at procedural precision usually involve not rules but 'guidelines' (such as the UNCITRAL Notes for Organizing Hearings)[24] which the arbitrators are free to ignore – and often do.

B. Illustrative Questions: Privilege and Discovery

17-26 The dark side of all this discretion lies in the discomfort that a litigant may feel when arbitrators make up the rules as they go along, divorced from any precise procedural canons set in advance. Discretion may not be objectionable within a close-knit community (for example, among the diamond dealers in Amsterdam) or when everyone shares or accepts a common legal culture (as might happen in a construction arbitration where the lawyers and arbitrators share long-standing professional relationships).[25] However, in a heterogeneous transaction with parties, lawyers and arbitrators from disparate places, anxiety rather than comfort may result from a level of arbitrator discretion that permits an

---

[23] Under art. 22.1(h) of the LCIA Rules, joinder may be ordered provided there is consent of the third person.

[24] UNCITRAL Notes on Organising Arbitral Proceedings (1996). The ICC Report on Construction Arbitrations provides another example. *See* ICC Commission on International Arbitration, *Final Report on Construction Industry Arbitrations*, 9 April 2001 (Doc 420/414).

[25] In high stakes international construction arbitration in the United States, one often sees all lead counsel drawn from the active members of the American College of Construction Lawyers.

arbitrator to make critical procedural decisions after he or she has sized up the parties and the controversy.[26]

17-27   To illustrate, imagine an arbitration between a Swiss company and a US corporation. One side requests pre-trial production of a memo created by in-house counsel. The other objects on the basis that the document is protected by privilege. What is the arbitrator to do?

17-28   In the United States, the attorney-client privilege generally applies equally to all lawyers, whether independent or employed by the client.[27] By contrast, in Switzerland and many other countries, only communications to outside counsel are protected by professional secrecy.[28]

17-29   Equally troublesome is the very notion of pre-trial document production. In many parts of the world, including most of continental Europe, litigants do no more than give each other advance copies of the documents to be relied upon during the hearings, so as to avoid undue surprise. By contrast, in the United States a practice has developed by which the parties must produce to each other broad categories of dispute-related material, including documents that might help prove the adversary's case. Discovery serves as a vacuum cleaner to hoover up even marginally relevant pieces of paper that might lead to admissible evidence.[29]

---

[26]   No single appointing institution or set of litigation norms yet commands international confidence. Moreover, notwithstanding the growing corps of world class international arbitrators, tribunals still include individuals whose cultural backgrounds and predispositions may be quite different from that of a party.

[27]   *See e.g.*, *NCK Organisation Ltd* v. *Bregman*, 542 F.2d 128, 133 (2d Cir. 1976).

[28]   Swiss professional secrecy attaches to Bar membership (the qualification of *avocat*), which in turn requires 'independence'. Lawyers with the status of employee are not usually registered with the cantonal Bar. *See generally* art. 231 of the Code Pénal, art. 13 of the Loi fédérale sur la libre circulation des avocats (Loi sur les avocats), 23 June 2000 (establishing the obligation of professional secrecy) and art. 29 of the Loi fédérale d'organisation judiciaire (limiting the right to represent clients to practising lawyers and university professors). *See generally*, Bernard Corboz, 'Le secret professionnel de l'avocat selon l'article 321 CP' in (1993) *Semaine Judiciaire* 77; Albert Stefan Trechsel, *Schweizerisches Strafgesetzbuch–Kurzkommentar* (2nd edn., Zürich, 1997). For helpful conversations on professional secrecy in Switzerland, thanks are due to my friends Philippe Neyroud, Anne-Véronique Schläpfer and Olivier Wehrli.

[29]   *See* Federal Rules of Civil Procedure, Rule 26(b)(1). Sanctions for non-compliance, set forth in Rule 37, include preclusion of introduction of the evidence, striking certain pleadings and even fines for contempt of court. *See generally* Thomas Mauet, *Pretrial* (4th edn., 1999); John Beckerman, 'Confronting Civil Discovery's Fatal Flaws' in (2000) 84 *Minn. L. Rev.* 505; Irwin J. Hausman and Michael C. Harrington, 'Discovery in Arbitration: Have It Your Way' in (2002) 7 *ADR Currents* (March–May) 20. The alleged benefits of such discovery include a better

17-30 How should the arbitrator choose between these divergent models of privilege and discovery? One approach would be to apply rules in a discriminatory manner, looking to the parties' national practice and expectations. Accordingly, only communications to the US in-house lawyer would be privileged, and only the US side would be required to produce broad categories of documents.[30]

17-31 Instinctively, good arbitrators shrink from assigning procedural benefits and burdens according to the parties' national practices. Giving one side a stark procedural handicap is an excellent way to invite challenge to an award.[31] However, it can be perilous to decide which principles to follow after the proceedings have revealed the parties' positions, indicating who will get the awkward side of a rule.

C. Consensus and Legal Culture

17-32 Some questions, of course, will in practice be resolved by a race to the lowest common denominator. For example, in international arbitration it is now generally expected that lawyers will prepare witnesses by discussing the case in pre-hearing interviews,[32] even though many countries forbid this practice.[33]

---

perspective of the strengths and weaknesses in one's case, leading to settlement, or sharper definition of issues and greater ability to identify an adversary's misleading evidence.

[30] Under this approach email exchanges between in-house counsel in a large multinational (a US bank with a subsidiary) would be privileged from New York to Geneva but not in the other direction.

[31] While it might be argued that the Swiss party had no pre-dispute expectation of secrecy for in-house communications, and the Americans knew that they might have to produce documents, both sides' expectations would likely presume an equal basis for whatever privilege and document production might be granted.

[32] *See generally* George von Segesser, 'Witness Preparation' in (2002) 20 *ASA Bull.* 222.

[33] *See e.g.*, art. 13 of Geneva's Us et coutumes de l'ordres des avocats ('L'avocat doit s'interdire de discuter avec un témoin de sa déposition future et de l'influencer de quelque manière que ce soit' ('The attorney must abstain from discussing with a witness his future testimony and from influencing him in any way'.) German lawyers are likewise prohibited from interviewing witnesses out of court except in special circumstances. *See* John H. Langbein, 'The German Advantage in Civil Procedure' in (1985) 52 *Chicago L. Rev.* 823, at 834; John H. Langbein, 'Trashing "The German Advantage"' in (1988) 82 *Nw. L. Rev.* 763. By contrast, US lawyers would be considered lacking in diligence if they failed to rehearse their witnesses about the type of questions to be asked. Getting witnesses ready for testimony is seen as a way to keep the witness from being misled or surprised, arguably making the testimony more accurate. *See e.g.*, *Hamdi & Ibrahim Mango Co.* v. *Fire Ass'n of Phila.*, 20 F.R.D. 181, 182 (S.D.N.Y. 1957); *In re Stratosphere Corp. Sec. Litig.*, 182 F.R.D. 614, 621 (D. Nev. 1998). *See Wigmore on Evidence* (3rd edn.), § 788; Thomas A. Mauet, *Pretrial* (4th edn., 1999), pp. 40–48 describing techniques for interviewing witnesses.

17-33 On other questions, however, no consensus exists. For documentary discovery, continental lawyers generally feel deeply about what they perceive as the abusive US 'fishing expeditions' and scatter-gun tactics. Conversely, many lawyers in the United States believe that the bargain for arbitration never included renunciation of what for them is a basic right to shoot first and aim later.

17-34 In addressing such questions, we are all laden with baseline baggage that pushes us to presume our own conclusion, according to culturally-influenced assumptions built into our backgrounds.[34] For example, two arbitrators might agree that there must be a reasonable 'proportionality' between the burden of producing a document and the document's potential for enlightening the tribunal. Yet, in applying such a proportionality principle, a Paris *avocat* would normally start with assumptions quite different from those of a New York litigator.

17-35 The matter of costs presents another illustration of cultural blinders. European arbitrators often assume that in international arbitration, automatically the loser will pay some portion of the winner's legal costs. In fact, major institutional rules stipulate simply that arbitrators have discretion to allocate attorneys' fees, but do not suggest how that power should be exercised.[35] In at least one significant part of the world commercial community (the United States), costs do not normally follow the event.

17-36 If such procedural questions are subject to recognised norms, a litigant that did not like a particular ruling could still recognise that either side might have got the short end of the stick. But in a mixed legal culture lacking a common procedural roadmap, the loser may feel not only the sting of defeat, but also a sense of injustice.[36]

---

[34] The emotion attached to procedural expectations and baselines was brought home to me several years ago when I received a call from a former student at a large New York firm, who was about to file a request in his first ICC arbitration. With the fullest sincerity, he asked if it was true that the ICC Rules did not provide what he called 'even the most basic guarantee of pre-trial fairness'. By this oblique reference he meant the right to full US-style discovery. 'How can we prove our claim', he asked, 'without knowing what documents the other side has?' Of course, my student's continental counterpart might have had quite different expectations, anticipating that no claimant would commence arbitration without first having evidence.

[35] *See* LCIA Arbitration Rules, art. 28.2; ICC Arbitration Rules, art. 31(3); AAA International Rules, art. 31(d).

[36] A recent study by the affiliate of the American Arbitration Association found that parties to arbitration rate a 'fair and just' result as the most important element in arbitration, above all other considerations, including cost, finality, speed and privacy. *See* Richard W. Naimark and

VI. ALTERNATIVE PROCEDURAL MENUS

A. 'Rules Light' and 'Rules Rich'

17-37 Of course, the arbitral tribunal can always set forth a systematic set of rules in an initial procedural order, issued at the outset of the arbitration. Frequently, however, arbitrators may be tempted to keep the first order relatively simple, precisely to reduce the prospect of unnecessary wrangling among tribunal members, as well as litigants.

17-38 The more radical approach suggested today reverses the situation. Rather than a blank page to be completed by arbitrators, institutional provisions could contain specific protocols that the arbitrator would be required to apply unless modified by agreement of all parties.[37] Under the current regime of arbitrator discretion, the litigants are like diners in a fancy restaurant with a menu that we might call 'procedure light', which allows the chef to feed them whatever he wants, as long as each gets the same meal. To force the chef to add or subtract a dish, the diners must do so by a common accord.

17-39 By contrast, a better approach would make the litigants like a couple who are served a fixed meal that includes soup, fish, meat, vegetables, potatoes, salad, pudding and savories – which is to say, rules on privilege, discovery, time allocation and the like. One might call this a 'procedure heavy' or 'rules rich' menu. To change the menu the diners would have to indicate jointly what they did *not* wish to order, or what they wanted to add.

17-40 The reason for reversing the way dinner is served derives from the fact that once the arbitration begins, litigants almost by definition are more like a bickering old couple than an amorous twosome, and thus may not agree on much. The consequence that one side may receive procedure never expected and never really bargained for.

Stephanie E. Keer, 'International Private Commercial Arbitration: Expectations and Perceptions of Attorneys and Business People' in (2002) 30 *Int'l Bus. Lawyer* 203 (May).

[37] The relevant institutional provisions would likely list those rules that are to be non-waivable. To a limited degree, the ICC currently makes a distinction between mandatory and optional rules, providing in art. 7(6) that by the litigants' agreement ('insofar as the parties have not provided otherwise') the process for constituting the arbitral tribunal contained in arts 8–10 may be modified.

17-41 The problematic aspects of drafting such 'procedure heavy' protocols are obvious. It would be hard work, representing a tricky arbitrator is left to make up rules as he or she goes along, with the potential compromise between different norms.

17-42 But is difficulty the same as impossibility? Perhaps the drafters of more specific rules will end up like Don Quixote, tilting at windmills. But then again, they might get lucky, and be able to emulate international co-operation in other areas of commercial law.

17-43 The International Bar Association Rules of Evidence provide a notable illustration of such successful cross-border compromise.[38] In suggesting more precise norms than those contained in most institutional arbitration provisions, the IBA Evidence Rules enhance what might be called the 'objectivisation' of arbitration.[39] For example, the Rules require that a request for document production must identify either particular documents or 'a narrow and specific category of documents' and describe how requested documents are 'relevant and material'.[40]

---

[38] Often incorporated into initial procedural orders on a 'for guidance' basis, the IBA Rules on the Taking of Evidence in International Commercial Arbitration were adopted in June 1999. *See* IBA Working Party, 'Commentary on the New IBA Rules of Evidence in International Commercial Arbitration' [2000] *Bus. Law Int'l.* (Issue 2) 14. *See also* Michael Bühler and Carroll Dorgan, 'Witness Testimony Pursuant to the IBA Rules of Evidence in International Commercial Arbitration' in (2000) 17(1) *J. Int'l Arb.* 3. The rules are available at www.ibanet.org.

[39] In the United States, the Draft Principles and Rules on Transnational Civil Procedure, prepared under the auspices of the American Law Institute (ALI), represent another effort to achieve procedural compromise. Drafted by the ALI in co-operation with the Rome-based UNIDROIT (International Institute for the Unification of Private Law), Discussion Draft No. 3 was issued on 8 April 2002.

[40] IBA Evidence Rules, art. 3. On the matter of whether a document request aims at a 'narrow and specific' class of documents, *see* IBA Rules of Evidence, art. 3. *See generally*, Nadia Darwazeh, 'Document Discovery and the IBA Rules of Evidence: A Practitioner's View' [2002] *Int. A.L.R.* (Issue 4) 101. No provision is made for depositions or for documents 'reasonably calculated' to lead to evidence as in FRCP, Rule 26(b)(1). Enumerated defences to document production or admission include lack of sufficient relevance, legal impediment or privilege, unreasonable burden, loss or destruction, commercial or technical confidentiality, political sensitivity and 'considerations of fairness or equality of the Parties': IBA Evidence Rules, art. 9(2).

B. Supplementary 'Opt-In' Rules

17-44 If precise 'procedure heavy' provisions seem too radical, there are other precision-enhancing possibilities. Institutions might supplement their basic procedural framework with stand-alone procedural supplements, which the parties could adopt on an 'opt-in' basis, or the arbitrators might select at the beginning of the proceedings. At the least, arbitral institutions could explicitly affirm the arbitrators' power with respect to some of the more common procedural problems.

17-45 To maximise the value of such stand-alone procedures, basic institutional provisions (*e.g.*, the ICC or LCIA Rules) would confirm the arbitrators' power to apply the supplement even if the parties failed to do so. Such an 'override' by arbitrators would be important as a practical matter, since corporate lawyers often pay little attention to arbitration details when contracts are drafted; and once a dispute erupts, the litigants' tactical preferences crystallise to the point where agreement on procedural matters becomes difficult if not impossible. Agreement of all parties would be required to pre-empt the arbitrators' election of the supplementary rules.

17-46 Over time, such stand-alone supplements (assuming they represent reasonable compromises) might create generally accepted norms.[41] A litigant objecting to their application would then bear the burden of showing why they should not apply.

C. Gamesmanship, Over-Specificity and Escape Hatches

17-47 Rules, of course, bring their own unfortunate gamesmanship, and in some instances can impede efficient decision-making. Few would disagree that arbitrators should not be put into a straightjacket that requires strict rules of evidence or routine authentication of documents. Some things should be left to the arbitrator, while others should not. The trick is to know the difference.

17-48 In this connection, increased precision need not foreclose the proper exercise of discretion in the face of exceptional circumstances. Properly drafted institutional provisions would include appropriate safety valves and escape

---

[41] The IBA Rules of Evidence represent a shift in legal culture precisely because they are perceived as a relatively neutral and fair compromise.

hatches to allow arbitrators to override the default rules for good cause shown. The starting point, however, would be the specific rules, not a blank page.

17-49 The so-called 'Holocaust Accounts' arbitration illustrates the risks of well-meaning but misguided *over*-specificity. In 1997 the Zürich-based Claims Resolution Tribunal (CRT) was established to decide claims related to dormant Swiss bank accounts belonging to victims of Nazi persecution. To maximize the credibility of this politically sensitive process, the CRT Rules initially imposed strict procedural mandates on how the arbitrators were to proceed in establishing ownership of the contested assets. For example, inheritance was subject to 'the law with which the matter in dispute has the closest connection'.[42] This otherwise reasonable principle often invited time-consuming squabbling among relatives of a deceased account holder,[43] and yielded particularly unfortunate results when accounts were small. In such instances arbitrator discretion to divide the funds would have been one reasonable alternative to the 'closest connection' test.[44]

VII. LORE, LITERATURE AND FAIRNESS

A. Generally Accepted Norms

17-50 To some extent international practice has created consensus on arbitral norms on matters such as witness statements and the right to cross-examination.

---

[42] Rules of Procedure for the Claims Resolution Process, 15 October 1997, art. 16. The so-called 'CRT I' process terminated at the end of 2001 with the distribution of funds for all of the accounts originally published by the Swiss Bankers Association. Subsequent stages of the process ('CRT II') went forward under the direct control of a Special Master appointed by a federal court in New York, making distributions from a settlement fund without any substantial input from the original arbitrators, whose functions were terminated during the spring of 2002. CRT Rules are available at www.crt-ii.org.

[43] If a husband and wife both perished along with their children, disposition of assets might well depend on the order of death. If the father died after the others, funds passed to his cousins in New Jersey; if the mother was the last to go, the account went to her relatives in London; and if the children survived both parents, then property was divided equally among the two sides of the family. Since the order of death was rarely evident, arbitrators might have to consult presumptions contained in the inheritance laws of 1943 Hungary or France (assuming these could be ascertained), to determine which deported family member was considered to have died last.

[44] Another option would have been for accounts to be distributed simply according to a hierarchy among family relationships. For example, in the absence of a will, the money would go to specified classes of account holder relatives in designated order and shares. Children and their heirs would take before siblings, who in turn would inherit before cousins.

17-51 These norms, however, generally get picked up not in institutional provisions,[45] but in articles and books representing the experience of arbitration specialists which in turn constitute the folklore that future arbitration connoisseurs learn in training.[46]

17-52 There are several problems, however, with lore and literature that remain only hortatory and permissive. Above all, the folklore may not impress someone with little international arbitration experience, who is not yet (and may never be) a member of the club. A considerable disjunction exists between the arbitration aficionado and the newcomer. For the latter, there exists no arbiter of proper procedure. A US engineer serving as arbitrator in her first ICC proceedings might understandably see no reason to accept the authority of erudite articles written by clever Europeans who, notwithstanding their brilliance, were apparently unable

---

[45] On some other issues, arbitration rules are becoming more norm-specific. As mentioned elsewhere, art. 28(5) of the AAA International Rules restricts awards of punitive damages and art. L(d) of the AAA Optional Procedures for Large Complex Commercial Disputes permits depositions and interrogatories.

[46] *See e.g.,* Lucy Reed and Jonathan Sutcliffe, 'The "Americanisation" of International Arbitration' (2001) 16 *Int'l Arb. Rep.* 37; *see e.g.,* Julian Lew and Larry Shore, 'Harmonising Cultural Differences in International Commercial Arbitration' in (1999) 54 *Dispute Resolution J.* (August) 32; Larry Shore, 'What Lawyers Need to Know About International Arbitration', 20(1) *J. International Arbitration* 67 (2003); Karl-Heinz Bockstiegel, 'Major Criteria for International Arbitrators in Shaping an Efficient Procedure' in *Arbitration in the Next Decade* (ICC Int'l Ct. Bull. Supp. 1999); Jack J. Coe, 'Pre-Hearing Techniques to Promote Speed and Cost-Effectiveness: Some Thoughts Concerning Arbitral Process Design' in (2002) 17 *Int'l Arb. Rep.* 22; Benjamin Davis, 'Laying Down a Gauntlet: The Thirty-Six Hour Chairman' in (1992) 3 *Amer. Rev. Int'l Arb.* 170; Lee M. Finkel and Robert F. Oberstein, 'Ten Commandments of Arbitration' in (2000) 5 *ADR Currents* (March) 19; Paul Friedland, 'Combining Civil Law and Common Law Elements in the Presentation of Evidence in International Commercial Arbitration: Novel or Tested Standards?' in (2000) 17 *J. Int'l Arb.* 3; Howard M. Holzmann, 'Balancing the Need for Certainty and Flexibility in International Arbitration Procedure' in R. Lillich and C. Brower (eds), *International Arbitration in the 21st Century* (1993), p. 12; Mark Huleatt-James and Robert Hunter, 'The Laws and Rules Applicable to Evidence in International Arbitration Procedure' in *ibid*; Martin Hunter, 'Modern Trends in the Presentation of Evidence in International Commercial Arbitration' in (1992) 3 *Amer. Rev.* 204 ; Andreas F. Lowenfeld, 'The Two-Way Mirror: International Arbitration as Comparative Procedure' in (1995) *Mich. Y.B. Int'l Studies* 163; James J. Myers, 'Ten Techniques for Managing Arbitration Hearings' in (1996) 51 *Disp. Resol. J.* 28; Hilmar Raeschke-Kessler, 'Making Arbitration More Efficient: Settlement Initiatives by the Arbitral Tribunal' in (2002) 30 *Int'l Bus. Law.* 158; Alan Scott Rau and Edward F. Sherman, 'Tradition and Innovation in International Arbitration Procedure' in (1995) 30 *Tex. Int'l L.J.* 89; Arthur W. Rovine, 'Fast-Track Arbitration: A Step Away from Judicialisation of International Arbitration' in Lillich and Brower (eds), *supra*; John Uff, 'The Bill Tompkins Memorial Lecture 1994' in (1995) 61 *Arbitration* 18.

to convince the ICC to incarnate these ideas into specific rules.[47] Moreover, on matters where much has been written but little settled, even the best of us remain prisoners of our idiosyncratic experiences, tempted to see our last case as the normal way to do things.[48]

17-53 Arguments drawn from the purpose of arbitration are not always of much value. The side that wants to discourage broad document production will emphasise the goals of speed and economy. The party seeking the documents will stress that arbitration is not a flip of the coin or a roll of the dice, but requires decisions based on the facts, which can best be ascertained when all relevant documents are available to both sides.[49]

17-54 In any event, if lore and literature have indeed led to the emergence of common norms (for example, a presumption against oral depositions), it is hard to see what would be so wrong with reducing procedural strife by setting forth the consensus in a clear rule, subject always to the parties' right to opt out jointly. Either the norms are in fact widely accepted, and worthy of inclusion in a set of institutional provisions, or they are not commonly followed, and a litigant has an understandable concern about an arbitrator's ad hoc invention.

---

[47] For example, if one side to an arbitration requests the arbitral tribunal to order the opposing party to provide guarantees as security for legal costs, arbitration specialists may take guidance from the discussion and standards elaborated in the House of Lords decision in the well-known (to specialists) *Ken-Ren* case. Why, however, should the House of Lords approach constitute authority to an arbitrator in New York appointed under the AAA, UNCITRAL or ICC Rules? *See Coppée Lavalin S.A.* v. *Ken-Ren Chemicals* [1995] 1 AC 38, in which a bankrupt claimant was able to fund an arbitral proceeding through a related entity, but not necessarily to pay the expenses that might be awarded against it in case of loss. *See generally* Claude Reymond, 'Security for Costs in International Arbitration' in (1994) 110 *Law Q. Rev.* 501.

[48] Over the years, it has been my good fortune to sit with some of the best arbitrators in the world (and you know who you are). Many of these eminent individuals have strong preferences for one set of procedures or another. Ironically, they often support their desired *modus operandi* with the confident assertion that 'we should do things the usual way'. Yet what is usual for one may seem odd or impractical to another, leading careful observers to wonder, 'If the best and the brightest do not agree, how can one expect arbitration newcomers to know what's right?'.

[49] Even in non-international arbitration there may be disagreements about how arbitral objectives should play out in practice. For example, in domestic commercial arbitration, the AAA has no rule on whether pre-trial oral depositions are allowed, often giving rise to considerable acrimony and uncertainty.

B. Perceptions of Fairness

17-55 Specific pre-set rules would normally increase each side's sense that procedural decisions were made in a principled fashion. The jagged side of a rule would not appear to be assigned *ad personam*, in what the French might call *justice à la tête du client* – justice according to the face of the customer. Moreover, enhanced arbitrator concentration would be a side benefit of fixed protocols, in that tribunal energy and attention would not be diverted from the merits of the case to procedural squabbling.

17-56 The existence of reasonably ascertainable standards lies at the heart of what Western civilization has considered to be the foundation for rational economic planning. In this context, one remembers the description of 'rule of law' presented by the economist von Hayek:

> Stripped of all technicalities, this means that government in all its actions is bound by rules fixed and announced beforehand – rules which make it possible to foresee with fair certainty how the authority will use its coercive powers in given circumstances and to plan one's individual affairs on the basis of this knowledge.[50]

17-57 One might also recall the work of the late Harvard philosopher John Rawls, who proposed that those who create law should remain behind what he called a 'veil of ignorance' about the exact contingencies to which a rule might apply.[51] To be just, rules should be uninformed by any existing litigation strategy.[52] In other words, they should not be created in function of what might be called the 'ouch test', which looks to see who gets hurt by a particular rule.[53]

---

[50] Friedrich von Hayek, The Road to Serfdom (1944), p.72 . *See generally* Max Weber, *General Economic History* (F. Knight trans. 1966); Detlev F. Vagts, *Dispute Resolution Mechanism in International Business*, 203 Recueil des Cours (Hague Academy) (1987), p. 19.

[51] *See* John Rawls, *A Theory of Justice* (1971), § 24, p. 136. Rawls affirmed *inter alia* that 'justice is the first virtue of social institution'.

[52] Rawls's notion of pure justice, of course, goes further, and suggests that those agreeing to particular principles should also be ignorant of their place in society, intelligence and strength.

[53] On some matters the 'veil of ignorance' already finds limited recognition in arbitration. For example, although different methods exist to calculate arbitrators' fees (ICC looks to the amount in dispute, while AAA and LCIA base fees on time spent), no institution gives an arbitrator discretion to opt for one approach or the other (*ad valorem* or hourly) after seeing how the case develops.

17-58 The image of this 'veil of ignorance' helps explain the difference between an arbitrator who aspires to interpret pre-existing norms, and one who establishes procedures after receiving indications of how one model or another will likely affect the outcome of the case.[54]

VIII. COSTS AND BENEFITS OF INNOVATION

A. Ex Ante and Ex Post Rule-Making

17-59 Of course, none of these questions about the tension between discretion and rules is unique to arbitration. Most of what we call law involves a continuum between generality and precision. To prevent dangerous driving, one might either (i) set defined speed limits, such as a prohibition on travel above 65 miles per hour, or in the alternative (ii) declare it unlawful to drive at 'unreasonable' speeds.[55] The first approach (which might be called *ex ante* rule-making) establishes precise rules of conduct before the controverted event, while under the second approach (*ex post* rule-making) a judge or arbitrator fixes the precise contours of behaviour only after the relevant incident. At present, most arbitration frameworks follow the latter approach, mandating only 'reasonable' and 'appropriate' procedures.

17-60 In order to warrant a change from the reasonableness standard to more precise *ex ante* rules, some hope must exist that an *ex ante* approach would meet a perceived need among litigants.[56] In economic terms, the argument might be

---

[54] Similar principles obtain with respect to the substantive law applied to the merits of the dispute, where most business managers seek predictability in normal commercial relations. As the late Dr. Francis Mann noted, 'No merchant of any experience would ever be prepared to submit to the unforeseeable consequences which arise from application of undefined and undefinable standards described as rules of a lex of unknown origin': F.A. Mann, 'Introduction' in T. Carbonneau (ed.), *Lex Mercatoria and Arbitration* (1990), p. xxi.

[55] And of course, both methods implicate an authoritative adjudicatory process connected to stories: narratives of problems that law addresses, and the 'for instance' of how rules and standards should be applied.

[56] An argument might also be made that specific rules can be justified by their effect on third parties affected by a case. For example, better arbitration rules might create more attractive options for neutral dispute resolution, which in turn would facilitate wealth-creating economic co-operation in cross-border commerce and investment. On the third party effects of predictable dispute resolution, *see* William W. Park, 'Neutrality, Predictability and Economic Cooperation' in (1995) 12 *J. Int'l Arb.* 99.

made that if a need for more specific rules did exist, the market by now would have reacted. So if it ain't broke, don't fix it.[57]

17-61 To some extent this is true. Parties to arbitration have long muddled through with the sketchiest of procedural structures.[58] So why change things now?

17-62 In a way, however, this 'not needed' argument is a bit like saying that Thomas Edison need not have invented the gramophone in 1876, since people had enjoyed live music for millennia. Analogously, the fact that modern arbitration is based on arbitrator discretion does not mean that precise protocols have been tried and found wanting, but simply that they have not been tried in earnest.[59] Unless Voltaire's Dr. Pangloss was correct in asserting that all is for the best in the best of all possible worlds,[60] the present system of arbitrator discretion derives more from institutional fear of alienating one constituency or another than from any reliable indication of what the business community really wants.

17-63 Until a major service-provider adopts 'rules-rich procedure' (or at least a stand-alone option for procedure-rich rules), it is hard to know how the market will respond. No empirical studies exist to permit falsification of one position or the other concerning rule specificity.[61] Only if and when an experiment is tried

---

[57] In this connection, it is worth noting that three of the largest arbitral institutions recently overhauled their rules (AAA in 1997, ICC and LCIA in 1998) without feeling compelled to take the path to specificity.

[58] The argument that, in most cases, the parties and the arbitrators 'work things out' gives a strange echo of the approach of some transactional lawyers in failing to pay attention to contractual dispute resolution clauses. The problem, of course, is that the purpose of a dispute resolution clause is to address situations in which the parties can*not* achieve a suitable *modus operandi.*

[59] Careful readers will note the rhetorical borrowing from G. K. Chesterton, who in quite another context observed that 'The Christian ideal has not been tried and found wanting; it has been found difficult and left untried': *see* Gilbert K. Chesterton, *What's Wrong With the World* (1910), ch. V 'The Unfinished Temple', p. 48.

[60] Voltaire's *Candide* (1759) presents Dr. Pangloss as an incarnation of the ultra-optimistic theory of German philosopher Gottfried Wilhelm Leibniz, satirically summarised as *Tout est pour le mieux dans le meilleur des mondes possible. ibid.* ch. 30.

[61] The confidentiality expected in most arbitration makes it highly unlikely that any meaningful survey could be conducted on how often arbitration clauses are left out of contracts because the parties wanted rules with greater precision. Thus, no theory about aggregate costs and benefits can be falsified in any scientifically meaningful way. The arbitration community is likely to remain in the land of anecdote concerning whether it is more costly to impose attention to rules when the contract is signed or when the dispute arises. Alternative conclusions can be reached by plugging in hypothetical numbers for billable hours at contract signature and during

will we have any indication of whether greater *ex ante* precision is attractive to the enlightened.

B. Market Forces

17-64 A more serious debater might suggest that the decision to arbitrate itself indicates that market forces favour minimal procedural complexities. But the question is not whether arbitration means fewer rules, but rather which rules should be left out. Many reasons to arbitrate have nothing to do with simplicity, but derive from other concerns, such as fear of bias, a search for expertise and concern over crowded dockets.[62]

17-65 Of course, if the parties really want more detail, they can bargain for it. Unfortunately, when contracts are about to be signed, most business managers have no inclination toward arguments about what they might call the 'technicalities' of dispute resolution.[63] Usually arbitration clauses will be 'cut and paste' jobs by transactional lawyers who have little relish for questions about evidence and briefing schedules. The corporate lawyers who write contracts are often out of touch with the procedural mishaps that occur during arbitration, and generally remain in the dark about how their arbitration clauses play out during litigation.[64] This absence of any well-informed reflection about the consequences of the arbitration clause[65] inhibits rational decision-making, which creates a market failure.

17-66 Only after the dispute arises, when the transaction has gone sour, does the importance of rules hit home. But at that stage of the business relationship

---

litigation, with hypothetical percentages of contracts ending in arbitration. Like discussions on the existence of God, doctrinal underpinning in the procedural specificity debate seems to be influenced as much by what people *want* to believe as by what evidence might indicate.

[62] Concerns over due process almost inevitably end up with what one might call 'juridification' of arbitration, as the price of its procedural legitimacy.

[63] Evaluations of procedural complexity in arbitration bring to mind the old saw about one side's delay being the other's due process.

[64] For example, the ICC Arbitration Rules are procedurally complex in at least two significant ways: (i) a requirement of Terms of Reference to clarify administrative matters and claims, and (ii) a provision for award review by the ICC 'Court' in Paris. Other arbitral institutions use shorter documents to begin the proceedings and subject awards to no institutional scrutiny.

[65] The illogical fashion in which many decisions are made was recently given great public exposure by the award of the 2002 Nobel Prize in Economics to Daniel Kahneman (along with Vernon Smith), whose work with the late Amos Tversky illustrated cognitive errors involving probability.

each side will be seeking tactical advantage for its position, and thus, the litigants may not be able to agree on very much at all.

C. Risks of Reform

17-67 There are costs to any innovation, of course. To return to the gramophone analogy, even Edison's great invention had negative consequences, such as a decline in family togetherness around the old piano, and the arrival of annoying boom-boxes.

17-68 Clearly there will be drawbacks to a switch from 'procedure light' to 'procedure heavy'. At least four come to mind.

17-69 First, a shift to more specific rules would mean that lawyers and arbitrators must learn something new. Secondly, bargaining about the rules will add costs at contract signature. Thirdly, annulment motions would be more complicated, as losing parties cite non-observance of the rules as a ground for vacatur.

17-70 Finally, specific rules might cause some lawyers to counsel against arbitration, from fear of losing their margin to manoeuvre once the dispute arises.[66] Prior to the arbitration, parties do not necessarily know what rules will benefit them on matters such as discovery and punitive damages.[67] Litigation preferences become known only *after* the proverbial you-know-what hits the fan.[68]

17-71 The real question, however, is not whether there will be costs, but when costs will be incurred, and whether the potential payback from more specific rules outweighs possible drawbacks. At present, creation of specific procedures

---

[66] For example, art. 19 of the ICC Arbitration Rules restricts presentation of new claims and counterclaims after establishment of the Terms of Reference. Only after a proceeding begins will a party know whether this rule constitutes a burden (because it prevents the party from bringing a new claim) or a benefit (because it prevents new claims by an opponent).

[67] On occasion, a company or an industry may have a regular problem that could be affected by rules. For example, repeat issues might be identified in claims brought by distributors against manufacturers or by borrowers against financial institutions.

[68] This inability to foresee a rule's future effect on litigation outcomes applies equally well to court proceedings, which is precisely why most legal systems contain codes of civil litigation norms established in advance of particular controversies.

takes place after the dispute arises. By contrast, with more detailed rules lawyers would have to be alert to the default norms and negotiate around them.

17-72   Business managers will be unhappy about expenses in either case. If at contract signature the lawyers spend too much time discussing arbitration rules, there may be an extra two or three billable hours. The alternative might be a hundred billable hours to fight procedural battles during the litigation – albeit hours spent only in cases where the relationship breaks down.

17-73   Right now, it is easy to agree to arbitrate under most institutional provisions, precisely because they allow parties to remain ignorant about how their case may ultimately be arbitrated, rather than to bite the bullet at contract signature. Yet, for every instance in which a contract might omit an arbitration clause because default rules are too specific, there will be other cases in which arbitration clauses will be left out of contracts because risk-averse business managers reject a lottery of uncertain results,[69] having grown tired of how descriptions of the expected arbitral procedure usually end with the caveat: 'It all depends on whom we get as an arbitrator'.[70]

IX. THE DEVIL IN THE DETAILS

A. Triage and Drafting

17-74   Deciding when 'enough is enough' in rule-making will not be easy, either in the triage necessary to determine what questions should be subject to rules or the drafting of the substantive rules themselves.[71] The goal would be to

---

[69]   Disagreeable encounters with establishment of procedures after the arbitrators learn who gets the rough side of the rule may lead some managers simply to say 'never again' – at least until presented with an even less appealing forum proposal in a new and attractive deal. A set of more detailed procedural protocols would serve to rub the lawyers' noses in the problem, thus giving consumers of arbitral services more informed choices.

[70]   Few business managers want to negotiate each aspect of the arbitral process *de novo* although ad hoc procedures may be more acceptable in some areas (such as insurance) than in others (such as distribution agreements), perhaps due to a relative degree of homogeneity in the prevailing business culture. Of course, one also sees ad hoc arbitration in investment and development concessions with developing countries, *perhaps* for the opposite reason: that at contract signing no one can agree on the arbitration framework.

[71]   The quest for balance brings to mind the Swedish word *lagom*, meaning 'not too much and not too little', which some of my Swedish friends proudly claim is unique to their language, somehow being superior to 'enough' and 'just right'. A British judge articulated the contrast between arbitral discretion and rules as follows: 'There is a choice: on the one hand [arbitrators]

give arbitrators the tools to find out what happened in an efficient manner, while giving litigants the impression (and the reality) of fair and equal treatment.[72]

17-75   There is no reason that compromises should not be possible, since most procedural issues raise questions of degree rather than either/or propositions.[73] In questions of procedure, the way decisions are made matters less if the process is known in advance. Rather than looking for the ideal structure (what surfers call 'the perfect wave'), the drafters of procedural protocols must keep in mind the admonition of Brandeis J. that in most matters it is more important that 'the applicable rule be settled than that it be settled right'.

B. Surprise and Sequestration

17-76   Admittedly, drafting specific rules will be a slippery job. For example, it may be quite difficult to hit upon a rule that reconciles the different approaches to surprise during hearings. Most good arbitrators reject trial by ambush, requiring that each side give reasonable pre-hearing notice of exhibits and arguments. Beyond that, however, there are dramatic differences in the measure of information that must be shared with opponents in advance of the hearings.

17-77   There are those who see spontaneity in presentation of documents, as a positive element in encouraging candour, on the assumption that a witness caught off guard is less likely to give calculated responses that hide part of the truth. By contrast, others believe that giving advance notice of a document provides time for reflection that permits the witness and the law to understand the document's significance, and thus, (in theory) to arrive at a more informative presentation, which helps the slow-witted arbitrators to grasp what has happened.[74]

---

will go their own way and invent their own practices as to the way they will exercise their discretion; on the other hand they will individually decide that while the arbitrator should not slavishly follow court procedures it is in the interest of justice that there should be a measure of predictability and certainty': Peter Bowsher, 'Security for Costs' in (1997) *Arbitration* (February) 36, at 38.

[72] The Appendix *infra* lists some illustrative questions which frequently must be addressed in international arbitral proceedings.

[73] It will, of course, be tricky to involve the right individuals in the drafting process. Those with experience may not have the time, and those with the time may not have the experience.

[74] In some arbitrations there are advance exchanges not only of documents on a general basis, but also delivery of specific exhibits intended for use in cross-examination, in order to permit opposing counsel to prepare a witness on what he or she can expect. For example, there may be a protocol to the effect that 48 hours before a party-controlled witness testifies, the lawyer from the other side will deliver to opposing counsel a binder of documents to be used in the cross-examination.

17-78 To take another example, there is much debate on whether one fact witness may be present when another is testifying. In some countries (such as the United States) a litigant may have a witness excluded from hearings when not presenting evidence (a process called sequestration), as a way to reduce the prospect that the testimony of one witness will influence that of another.[75]

17-79 Yet many argue against sequestration (invoking the very same goal of enhancing the search for truth), saying that the presence of one witness with knowledge of the facts will embarrass into greater truthfulness a witness otherwise inclined to stretch or embellish reality.[76]

17-80 As a parenthesis, in doing research on the question, I learned that the practice of separating witnesses goes back to Biblical times, and is recorded in the *Book of Susanna*, written during the Maccabean period.[77] The story tells how a virtuous woman rebuffs an immoral proposal from two scoundrels who take revenge by accusing her of committing adultery under a tree in her garden. As the honourable Susanna is about to be found guilty of what was then a capital crime, the prophet Daniel arrives, just in time, and says 'not so fast'. He orders the accusers separated. Questioning each in turn, he receives divergent descriptions of the tree under which the amorous adventure allegedly occurred. One scoundrel says 'acacia' tree and the other says 'aspen' tree, thus revealing perjury and permitting Susanna to be reunited with her family, and the two villains to be sent away for execution.

17-81 Even when a consensus has emerged on a particular practice, critical details may remain open to debate. For example, international arbitrators have developed a general practice of requiring witness statements to cover oral direct testimony.[78] Yet significant differences of opinion exist on whether direct oral

---

[75] *See* s. 615 of the Federal Rules of Evidence.

[76] The question is raised in the current discussion of so-called 'witness conferencing'. *See* Wolfgang Peter, 'Witness Conferencing' in (2002) 18 *Arb. Int'l* 3. The IBA Rules of Evidence provide in art. 8(2) that witnesses may 'be questioned at the same time and in confrontation with each other'.

[77] This story derives from a Greek translation of the Hebrew Scriptures occasioned by the Hellenistic influence in the ancient Mediterranean world. Legend put the number of translators at 72 (six from each tribe of Israel), thus giving the name 'Septuagint' (from *septuaginta*, or 70). The collection ultimately included some books (such as *Susanna*) outside the Hebrew canon, called the Apocrypha in some traditions.

[78] Sometimes justified as a way to save time, pre-filed direct testimony can serve the deeper purpose of allowing counsel sufficient time to consider the other side's arguments and evidence,

testimony should be entirely replaced, or simply limited in scope, by such witness statements. Some arbitrators argue for elimination of all direct oral evidence as a way to reduce hearing time. By contrast, others fear such an extreme approach as unacceptably diminishing an arbitrator's ability to comprehend facts and evaluate witness credibility. Since most of us gain understanding by a combination of both reading and hearing, many arbitrators prefer a combination of written and oral testimony as the better approach to enlightening the tribunal. Moreover, the putative time savings are often illusory when counsel demand additional hours for cross-examination.

X. Conclusion

17-82 An American folk hero named Yogi Berra, once a catcher for the New York Yankees baseball team, is known for his colourful expressions, which simultaneously might mean everything and mean nothing. Giving directions to his house in New Jersey, Yogi once advised a friend, 'And when you come to a fork in the road, take it'.

17-83 Modern arbitrators face challenges not unlike the one presented to Yogi Berra's guest. We know some decision is necessary, but the relevant rules provide little concrete guidance.

17-84 In cross-cultural business arbitration, the widespread assumptions about the benefits of arbitrator discretion may well turn out to be incorrect, regardless of a contrary conclusion for dispute resolution within close-knit communities that share a high level of trust in their arbitrators. Ironically, the ever-changing variety in the contours of disputes and the nationalities of the litigants may call for firmer procedural protocols established in advance of the arbitration. Arbitration's legitimacy is diminished when a litigant feels that procedures were invented as a way for the arbitrator to affect the outcome of the case.

17-85 My intent is not to urge radical reform. Some great Frenchman (Talleyrand usually receives credit) remarked that anything excessive becomes

---

serving as *de facto* discovery. Each side sees in advance what sort of evidence the other has. Witness statements can have a down-side, however. If oral testimony goes beyond the scope of the statement, there might be motions to exclude otherwise useful evidence, file supplemental affidavits or recall witnesses for rebuttal. A party that ignored a requirement of advance written testimony would have an edge, since the other side would have unequal time to consider its adversary's evidence and thus (at least in theory) better inform the arbitrators on the merits of the case.

insignificant: '*tout ce qui est excessif est insignificant*'. My hope is simply to stimulate a deeper dialogue on fine tuning the balance between *ex ante* and *ex post* rule-making, with the aim of arriving at an optimal counterpoise between rules and discretion. The completion of this task, of course, may well give us another article for another day.

XI. APPENDIX

17-86 Twenty-five Illustrative Procedural Issues Arising in International Commercial Arbitration

1. May a party require fact witnesses to be excluded from the hearings when others are presenting testimony?
2. When may one side take pre-hearing oral depositions of the other side's witnesses?
3. May a party be ordered to turn over documents to its adversary that might hurt the producing party's case? If so, what showing is necessary to justify such an order?
4. May counsel prepare a witness for testimony before the hearings?
5. Are the communications of an in-house lawyer privileged?
6. Should a party invoking privilege as the basis for refusing to turn over documents be required to supply a log providing a description of the document and an explanation of the claimed privilege?
7. Should direct testimony be provided in the form of pre-filed written witness statements?
8. If witness statements are used, do they replace or simply supplement oral testimony? In this connection, may a party require that one of its witnesses be heard orally even if the other side does not request cross-examination?
9. If one side alleges fraud, may it be required to provide, at an early stage in the proceedings, a statement of particulars, indicating who said what to whom, when and where?
10. How are burdens of proof to be determined?
11. Which side has the 'last word', claimant or respondent?
12. When should arbitrators order documents to be kept confidential if both parties are unwilling to so stipulate?
13. When should a tribunal appoint experts?
14. On what questions should interim decisions take the form of awards rather than procedural orders?
15. At what stage should exhibits and witness statements be exchanged?

16. When is it appropriate to order security for costs?

17. When should pre-hearing and post-hearing memorials be simultaneous, and when should they be sequential?

18. When can issues be decided on a documents only basis? What types of questions lend themselves to such dispositive treatment without evidentiary hearings?

19. How far should the parties' counsel (rather than arbitrators) shoulder the principal responsibility for interrogating witnesses?

20. What rules of evidence apply when one side objects to a question, answer or document?

21. Should time be allocated on a 'chess clock' basis (each side is allotted the same number of hours) or an open-ended approach?

22. What grounds justify postponement of hearings?

23. What degree of familiarity between an arbitrator and a witness might require arbitrator disqualification?

24. Should witnesses testifying on the same subject present their evidence together? In this connection, should a distinction be made between fact witnesses and experts?

25. May witnesses testify by video conferencing to save the cost of long-distance travel even though one party requests their physical presence?

ADDENDUM: PROCEDURAL DEFAULT RULES (2005)

I. INTRODUCTION

17-87 To enhance fairness in arbitral proceedings, the 2002 Freshfields Lecture suggested that institutional rules might provide greater specificity in case management protocols, subject always to the parties' agreement otherwise. The modest thesis of those remarks was that litigants often feel cheated when rules applicable to matters such as document production and evidence are adopted only *after* the birth of a particular quarrel.

17-88 The problem with default rules, of course, is that they limit arbitrator discretion, flexibility and freedom, a trinity that still triggers genuflection at arbitration conferences. At dinner following the lecture, several friends made clear that they greeted its proposal with the same enthusiasm normally reserved for ants at a Sunday school picnic.

17-89 Not all reactions were negative, however. Several lawyers spoke of clients who found it frustratingly unsatisfactory that detective work about a presiding arbitrator should remain the principal gauge for predicting procedural rulings. Some letters told stories of 'imperial arbitrators' whose disregard of due process was facilitated by the absence of fixed procedural rules. One in-house counsel said that his company had come to consider arbitration an unacceptable lottery of unpredictable results.[79]

17-90 Since the lecture's publication, three factors have emerged as vital to discussions about the specific content of arbitration rules: (i) use of professional guidelines; (ii) resort to national law to fill procedural gaps; and (iii) increased awareness of the need for ground rules at the start of arbitration. Each concern provides an intellectual wrinkle to the analysis of how to achieve optimum counterpoise between flexibility and predictability.[80]

II. PROFESSIONAL GUIDELINES: THE SOFT LAW OF ARBITRATION

17-91 Increasingly, arbitral proceedings see the influence of professional guidelines that address case management questions such as evidence, ethics and organization of proceedings. The International Bar Association has issued conflicts-of-interest guidelines[81] and revised its rules on evidence.[82] The

---

[79] Other scholars and practitioners explored the Lecture's proposal of a smörgåsbord approach to procedure, offering a menu selection of rules with British, Continental or American flavor. See Lawrence E. Newman & David Zaslowsky, *Cultural Predictability in International Arbitration*, NEW YORK LAW JOURNAL, 25 May 2004, at 3.

[80] On balancing these somewhat contradictory objectives, see DOMINIQUE HASCHER, COLLECTION OF PROCEDURAL DECISIONS IN ICC ARBITRATIONS (1997) at 135. Judge Hascher commented on a procedural order in ICC Case 7314/1996, where the tribunal said it 'does not intend' to allow extensions of time, thus giving itself an exit if its perspective changed. Approving an 'aspirational model' for rule-making, he observed: 'It is a matter of knowing how to reconcile firmness and flexibility, promptness and due process'. (*Il s'agira donc de savoir concilier la rigueur avec la souplesse, la nécessité d'être à l'heure avec celle des droits de la défense.*) See also Jan Paulsson, *The Timely Arbitrator*, in LIBER AMICORUM KARL-HEINZ BÖCKSTIEGEL 607 (2001).

[81] IBA Guidelines on Conflicts of Interest in International Commercial Arbitration, approved by the IBA Council on 22 May 2004, published in 9 (No. 2) ARBITRATION & ADR (IBA) 7 (October 2004); See Markham Ball, *Probity Deconstructed – How Helpful, Really are the New IBA Guidelines on Conflicts of Interest in International Arbitration*, 15 WORLD ARB. & MEDIATION REP. 333 (Nov. 2004); Jan Paulsson, *Ethics and Codes of Conduct for a Multi-Disciplinary Institute*, 70 ARBITRATION 193 (2004), at 198-99.

[82] See IBA Working Party, Commentary on the New IBA Rules of Evidence in International Commercial Arbitration, [2000] BUS. LAW INT'L. (Issue 2) 14. See also Michael Bühler &

American Arbitration Association modified its code of ethics for arbitrators.[83] The American College of Commercial Arbitrators published a compendium of 'Best Practices' for business arbitration.[84]

17-92 Built on arbitral lore memorialized in articles, treatises and learned papers, these guidelines represent what might be called the 'soft law' of arbitral procedure, in distinction to the firmer norms imposed by statutes and treaties.[85] Nothing prevents parties from agreeing to override the guidelines, which enter the arbitration only when such agreement proves impossible.

17-93 The wisdom of such guidelines remains subject to continued discussion. Beyond cavil, however, their rules produce far-reaching effects, for the simple reason that they get cited, *faute de mieux*, to fill the gaps left by overly vague institutional rules. For example, the IBA Guidelines on Conflicts of Interest present 'red', 'orange' and 'green' lists enumerating elements that create varied levels of arbitrator disqualification.[86] Rightly or wrongly, this list has entered the canon of sacred documents cited when an arbitrator's independence is contested.

Carroll Dorgan, *Witness Testimony Pursuant to the IBA Rules of Evidence in International Commercial Arbitration*, 17 J. INT'L ARB. 3 (No. 1) 2000. The rules are available at www.ibanet.org.

[83] See generally Ben Sheppard, *A New Era of Arbitrator Ethics in the United States*, 21 ARB. INT'L (2005) (forthcoming in Issue 1); Paul D. Friedland & John M. Townsend, *Commentary on Changes to the Commercial Arbitration Rules of the American Arbitration Association*, 58 DISPUTE RESOLUTION J. 8 (Nov. 2003-Jan. 2004). The new Ethics Code, adopted jointly by the AAA and the ABA, permit a party-nominated arbitrator to be non-neutral only if so provided by the parties' agreement, the arbitration rules or applicable law. Similar changes were made in the AAA domestic commercial arbitration rules, which now establish a presumption of neutrality for all arbitrators.

[84] COLLEGE OF COMMERCIAL ARBITRATORS, *Guide to Best Practices in Commercial Arbitration* (October 2005). These build on a previous draft, presented to the CCA Meeting on 30 October 2004.

[85] For a recent survey of these non-governmental initiatives, William W. Park, *Three Studies in Change*, in ARBITRATION OF INTERNATIONAL BUFSINESS DISPUTES at 45-65 (W. W. Park, Oxford University Press, 2006).

[86] A 'red list' describes situations that give rise to justifiable doubts about an arbitrator's impartiality. Some are non-waivable (such as a financial interest in the outcome of the case), while others (such as a relationship with counsel) may be ignored by mutual consent. An 'orange list' covers scenarios (such as past service as counsel for a party) which the parties are deemed to have accepted if no objection is made after timely disclosure. Finally, a 'green list' enumerates cases (such as membership in the same professional organisation) that require no disclosure.

III. CASE MANAGEMENT AND PROCEDURAL DELOCALIZATION

17-94   The second development related to the use and misuse of rules concerns 'delocalization', a term that describes efforts to make arbitral procedure less dependent on the idiosyncrasies of national procedure.[87] At first blush, one might imagine that precise rules increase the risk of protocols that unduly favor a particular national outlook. Ironically, however, experience demonstrates that just the opposite may be true. Excessive flexibility often creates a procedural vacuum that permits arbitrators to impose their own peculiarities, which may endorse one party's parochial perspective. Even when adopted with the best of intentions, such local rules usually run counter to the parties' joint expectations at the time they initially agreed to arbitrate.

17-95   In a recent *ad hoc* proceeding in London, an American claimant and a British respondent had concluded an agreement that specified no rules for case management. The chairman, an Englishman of great distinction, announced that England's Civil Procedure Rules would apply on matters related to evidence and document production,[88] even though English arbitration law imposed no such requirement.[89]

17-96   The British side was delighted. The American party, however, felt profoundly misled by the much-touted procedural neutrality of international arbitration. In such a situation, procedural default rules might have restrained the arbitrator's *excès de zèle* for his hometown form of justice, permitting the tribunal to ascertain facts according to more neutral procedural protocols.

---

[87]   See e.g., PHILIPPE FOUCHARD, EMMANUEL GAILLARD & BERTHOLD GOLDMAN, TRAITÉ DE L'ARBITRAGE COMMERCIAL INTERNATIONAL (1996), Sections 1172-92 at 650-662.36; GEORGIOS PETROCHILOS, PROCEDURAL LAW IN INTERNATIONAL ARBITRATION (2004), Sections 2.05-2.07, at 20-22.

[88]   Some English barristers will take a more nuanced view, suggesting that for London arbitrations English procedure should be 'the starting point' for creating procedural rules. In practice, this often creates a *de facto* acceptance of English procedure, reminiscent of the T.S. Eliot poem, 'Little Gidding', which concluded that 'the end of all our exploring will be to arrive where we started'.

[89]   The 1996 English Arbitration Act establishes no mandatory norms on evidence or discovery. To the contrary, Section 34 grants the tribunal discretion on such procedural and evidential matters, subject only to the parties' right to agree otherwise.

IV. DUE PROCESS, RULES AND FLEXIBILITY

17-97 In large measure, arbitral due process requires that the parties know in advance what sort of case management to expect. Divergent views exist on questions such as document production, witness statements, experts, privilege and the scope of cross-examination. Good arguments can be mustered for more than one position. Whatever rule is adopted, however, parties should be able to anticipate its application in advance.

17-98 The problem with invocations of 'flexibility' lies in the term's chameleon-like quality. As it changes colour depending on context, flexibility can detract from orderly case management. The losing side may see itself as the victim of unprincipled decision-making, feeling that procedures were adopted to favor one side after the arbitrator saw who would receive the rough edge of the rules. Conflicts may be less when both sides' lawyers come from the same legal culture. Such is not always the case, however, in disputes arising from cross-border transactions.

17-99 By contrast, default rules can serve as constructive tools in promoting foreseeable proceedings, thereby fostering a perception that procedure is 'regular' and the parties are being treated equally. Law would hardly be law without an aspiration to grant similar treatment to those in similar situations.[90] Fidelity to pre-established standards reduces the prospect that a losing party will perceive the arbitrators' *ex post facto* rule-making as simply an exercise in choosing norms to fit the desired outcome on the merits of the case.

17-100 Default rules implicate the principles of proportionality and balance between the general and the specific in legal process. Few argue that arbitration should have no flexibility at all. The question is how much. Today is that so

---

[90] H.L.A. Hart once observed,

'We may say that [justice] consists of two parts: a uniform or constant feature, summarised in the precept 'Treat like cases alike' and a shifting or varying criterion used in determining when, for any given purpose, cases are alike or different. In this respect, justice is like the notion of what is genuine, tall, or warm, which contain an implicit reference to a standard which varies with the classification of the thing to which they are applied. A tall child may be the same height as a short man [and] a warm winter the same temperature as a cold summer'.

H.L.A. HART, THE CONCEPT OF LAW 156 (1961). Hart also refers to this as 'justice in the administration of law', not justice of the law itself. H.L.A. Hart, *Positivism and the Separation of Law and Morals*, 71 HARV. L. REV. 593 599 (1958).

many institutional rules lack substantive directions even on the most basic and vital questions, resulting in an unnecessary potential for mischief and discontent.[91]

17-101 In some cases, marriage of fairness and flexibility proves possible, giving everyone the best off all worlds.[92] Not always, however. Like the man who hoped to get his girlfriend drunk while still keeping the wine bottle full, arbitrators seeking to provide fairness without rules may find their efforts sorely disappointed.

17-102 The benefits and burdens of flexibility were impressed on me during dinner at the home of a former student, a young woman of great intellect and charm who now practices trade law in Washington. The conversation turned to the plight of an absent female friend, who was dating a man whose frequent business trips took him to Chicago, where he was suspected of having a relationship with another woman. As one might expect, the dinner guests expressed disapproval. And rightly so.

17-103 Our hostess referred to the allegedly unfaithful boyfriend as a 'cad', an old-fashioned term for men who behave discourteously toward women. Curiosity led me to ask about the term's female equivalent. What word applies to a lady who encourages romantic overtures from more than one gentleman caller? 'How', I asked, 'would you describe a woman with two boyfriends?' With hardly a moment's reflection, my former student replied, 'Well, we would call her "flexible"'.

---

[91] One example can be found in the way the International Chamber of Commerce Rules fail to address an arbitrator's contact with a single litigant. Although such *ex parte* communications are now subject to general disapproval, the ICC Rules contain no prohibition of the practice. One might make arguments about the 'spirit' of the rules, which in Article 15 say arbitrators should act 'fairly and impartially'. However, fairness and impartiality are notoriously malleable notions, as illustrated by the American practice which until 2004 allowed *ex parte* communication.

[92] For a discussion of flexibility in a choice-of-law context, see Russell J. Weintraub, *Rome II and the Tension Between Predictability and Flexibility*, in 41 RIVISTA DI DIRITTO INTERNAZIONALE PRIVATE E PROCESSUALE 561 (2005), commenting on the European Commission proposal for a regulation on law applicable to non-contractual obligations, called 'Rome II' to distinguish it from the earlier Rome Convention (1980) on applicable law in matters of contract. See European Commission Proposal for a Regulation of the European Parliament and the Council on the Law Applicable to Non-Contractual Obligations, EUR. PARL. DOC. (COM 427 final) (2003).

17-104 In a social context, such elastic standards might not matter. The merits of flexibility may be less evident, however, when substantial assets are at stake in an arbitration whose integrity depends on even-handed and predictable procedure.

Alan Redfern[*]

CHAPTER 18

DISSENTING OPINIONS IN INTERNATIONAL COMMERCIAL ARBITRATION: THE GOOD, THE BAD AND THE UGLY[**]

18-1 The Freshfields/Queen Mary College Lecture for 2003 looks at dissenting opinions in international commercial arbitration. Such opinions are not discouraged. Indeed, under some rules of arbitration they are expressly permitted. Yet they risk breaching the confidentiality of the tribunal's deliberations. They also risk undermining the authority of the tribunal's award and in the process add little or nothing to the reputation of international commercial arbitration.

18-2 An increasing number of international commercial disputes are being referred to arbitration;[1] and they are likely to be referred not to a sole arbitrator, but instead to a tribunal of three arbitrators – unless the sums involved are not sufficient to justify this.[2] Accordingly, there will generally be a link between the parties and the members of the tribunal: the parties themselves will each

---

[*] Member of the English Bar. Arbitrator and former senior litigation partner at Freshfields. This article is based on the lecture delivered on 5 November 2003 as the Annual Freshfields Bruckhaus Deringer Lecture, School of International Arbitration, Centre for Commercial Law Studies, Queen Mary College, University of London.

[**] Special thanks are due to Emilie Hertzfeld, in Paris, and James Goldsmith in London for their very helpful research assistance; to Lord Mustill for his thoughtful comments on an earlier draft; and also to Ms Anne Marie Whitesell, Secretary General of the ICC in Paris. The views expressed in this article are those of the author and may perhaps give rise to some dissent.

[1] The International Chamber of Commerce in Paris (ICC), for example, records year by year an increase in the number of disputes referred to arbitration under the ICC Rules of Arbitration; and, again by way of example, the International Centre for the Settlement of Investment Disputes (ICSID) faces an ever-increasing caseload, particularly with disputes arising from bilateral investment treaties.

[2] Parties are free to choose for themselves the number of arbitrators to be appointed to the tribunal, but the usual choice is between a sole arbitrator and a tribunal of three arbitrators.

Julian D.M. Lew and Loukas A. Mistelis (eds), Arbitration Insights, 367-392
© 2007 Kluwer Law International. Printed in the Netherlands

nominate or appoint one of the members of the tribunal as 'their' arbitrator[3] and only the third arbitrator will be appointed 'independently'. In addition, all three arbitrators will have their fees and expenses paid by the parties, either directly or through an arbitral institution.

18-3 Arbitrators in international arbitrations are expected to behave like judges, in the sense that they are expected to be impartial and independent of the parties.[4] But there is a sharp distinction between arbitrators and judges, both in the way in which they are appointed and in the way in which they are paid. It may be said (hopefully as a joke) 'Why pay a lawyer, when you can buy a judge?' – but the essence of a reputable judicial system is that judges are not appointed by the parties and are not dependent upon those parties for payment.

18-4 At the end of an arbitration, the arbitrators are required to give their decision in the form of a written award which sets out the reasons on which it is based and which is decisive of the dispute.[5] The expectation is that this award will be unanimous. If not, a majority decision, and sometimes the decision of the presiding arbitrator alone, will generally suffice.[6]

---

[3] The ICC Rules of Arbitration provide, in art. 8(4), that where the parties have agreed upon a tribunal of three arbitrators, each party shall nominate one arbitrator for confirmation by the ICC; and the third arbitrator, who will act as chairman of the tribunal, will be appointed by the ICC itself, unless the parties agree otherwise. Other Rules adopt similar provisions, allowing each party to nominate an arbitrator.

[4] This requirement is to be found in the rules of the major arbitral institutions, in the UNCITRAL Arbitration Rules and in the UNCITRAL Model Law, ('the Model Law') which is the baseline for all modern laws of arbitration and which provides, in art. 12, for the challenge of an arbitrator if there are circumstances that give rise to doubts as to the 'impartiality or independence' of that arbitrator.

[5] There is no express requirement for a written award in the ICC Rules of Arbitration, but it is clear that this is required, for instance, from the provisions for signature of the award; and, under art. 25(2) of the Rules, the award must state the reasons on which it is based. The LCIA Arbitration Rules, in art. 26, expressly require an award to be made in writing and to state the reasons on which it is based, unless the parties agree in writing to dispense with reasons. The UNCITRAL Arbitration Rules contain, in art. 32, a similar rule to that of the LCIA, as does the Model Law.

[6] The ICC Rules of Arbitration provide, in art. 25, that where the tribunal is composed of more than one arbitrator, the award may be made by a majority of the arbitrators and if there is no majority, by the chairman alone. The LCIA Arbitration Rules contain a similar provision, in art. 26. The UNCITRAL Arbitration Rules provide, in art. 31, that the award may be made by a majority of the arbitrators, but contain no 'fall-back' provision for the case in which no majority is formed. (As will be seen, this has led to problems in the Iran–US Claims Tribunal, whose rules are based on the UNCITRAL Rules.) The Model Law contains similar provisions to the UNCITRAL Rules.

18-5 An arbitrator who disagrees with the award will normally be expected to sign it, but at the same time he or she will generally be free to write a dissenting opinion, which may run to many pages and which may be highly critical of the award.[7] Do such dissenting opinions serve any useful purpose in the context of an international commercial arbitration? Or should they in fact be strongly discouraged, as being at best unhelpful and at worst evidence of bias, which does not fit well with a very real and necessary concern for independence and impartiality on the part of international arbitrators?[8]

18-6 There is no tradition of dissenting opinions in the civil law.[9] It was thought that a court's decision should appear as the decision of the court as a whole, rather than as a mathematical process by which one party emerged as the winner, having gained more votes than his or her adversary.[10] Dissenting opinions have come to international commercial arbitration as a gift of the common law. Many may rejoice at the way in which different legal procedures and traditions are mixed together to build what Sir Michael Kerr called 'the emerging common procedural pattern in international arbitration'.[11] It is doubtful, however, whether the dissenting opinion has added much, if anything, of value to the arbitral process.

18-7 It may be said, of course, that disagreement – or dissent, as lawyers like to call it – is part of the fabric of life. Indeed, life would be dull without it. If all men thought alike, they would all fall in love with the same woman. A dull dinner party may be enlivened by asking people to name their favourite painting or piece of jewellery, their favourite book or their favourite film. It is unlikely that they will all come spontaneously to the same conclusion. Or ask a football

---

[7] The ICSID Rules expressly state, in rule 47(3), that any member of the tribunal 'may attach his individual opinion to the award, whether he dissents from the majority or not, or a statement of his dissent'. Other arbitral rules, such as those of the ICC, the LCIA and UNCITRAL, make no provision for the expression of a dissenting opinion, but nevertheless, as will be seen, it is a practice which has been widely adopted in international commercial arbitration.

[8] As arbitration becomes the established method of resolving international commercial disputes, it becomes increasingly important that the parties are able to rely upon the independence and impartiality of arbitrators. A Working Group of the International Bar Association has drawn up detailed guidelines on 'impartiality, independence and disclosure in international commercial arbitration',

[9] Levy, 'Dissenting Opinions in International Arbitration in Switzerland' in (1989) 5 *Arbitration International* 35.

[10] *Ibid,*

[11] Kerr, 'Concord and Conflict in International Arbitration' in (1997) 13(2) *Arbitration International* 121.

fan for his considered view of a rival team – and then stand back and wait for a stream of expletives or a blow to the head!

18-9 Because, of course, there are different degrees of dissent, ranging from polite but measured disagreement to violence, actual or threatened. In the early days of the Iran–US Claims Tribunal, two arbitrators had an argument which ended with one threatening to throw the other down the steps of The Peace Palace.[12] There is an evident irony in that situation: the threat of physical violence at what was intended to be a haven for the peaceful settlement of disputes. And later this evening, all across England, bonfires will be lit and fireworks will be exploded, to mark an unsuccessful attempt to blow up the Houses of Parliament, by what might now be called a group of dissidents, or perhaps, more contemporaneously, a group of religious fanatics.[13]

18-10 In life, dissent or disagreement may take many forms, from the studiously polite to the dangerously violent. In law, the extremes are no doubt less extreme, but if an arbitrator or a judge simply cannot agree with his or her colleagues, there are different ways of expressing dissent, ways which here are classified, borrowing from Clint Eastwood rather than from Halsbury's *Laws of England*, as 'the good, the bad and the ugly'.[14]

18-11 The 'good' dissent may be short, polite and above all restrained, so that the dissenter says: 'It is with regret that I must dissent from the views of my

---

[12] *The Times*, 8 September 1984, p. 5. *See also e.g.* the comment by Dominique Hascher, the former General Counsel and Deputy Secretary-General of the ICC International Court of Arbitration, stating that arbitrators had to be replaced by the ICC 'where dissension between them became so great that they threatened one another with criminal proceedings, making the future of the arbitral proceeding and the possibility of deliberations amongst the arbitrators appear far too uncertain': (1995) 6(2) *ICC Bulletin* (November) 17.

[13] The lecture on which this article is based was given on 5 November 2003. Almost 400 years ago, during the early years of the reign of King James I, a group of Catholic gentlemen planned to blow up the Houses of Parliament and the King, in the hope of returning England to the Catholic faith. This 'gun-powder plot' was discovered on 5 November 1605 and the conspirators were captured and executed. The plot is commemorated by the traditional search of the vaults of Parliament by the Yeomen of the Guard, before the opening of each session of Parliament, and by bonfires and fireworks, on each 5 November: *see* Antonia Fraser, *King James VI of Scotland and I of England* (Weidenfeld and Nicolson, London, 1974), p. 105 *et seq.*

[14] Film buffs have pointed out to the author that Clint Eastwood was only one of the well-known actors in the so-called 'spaghetti western' which went under the English title of 'The Good, the Bad and the Ugly'; and that the attribution should perhaps be to Sergio Leone, who directed the film.

learned colleagues', followed perhaps by a few short, sharp sentences. Or there may be a partial dissent or dissents woven neatly into the fabric of the judgment or award, so that it is said (for example) that Judge or Arbitrator 'A' disagrees with his or her colleagues on this issue or set of issues and Judge or Arbitrator 'B' disagrees on some other issue or issues but nevertheless all the members of the tribunal find themselves able to agree upon the final decision. In the process, one or all of the members of the tribunal may have had to moderate his or her views, in deference to the other members of the tribunal, but this is the essence of a collegiate decision.

18-12 There may even be an almost total dissent, in which the judge or arbitrator makes clear his or her disagreement with much of the reasoning of the majority, but is nevertheless prepared to concur in their conclusion[15] as a matter of good sense. The *Aminoil* arbitration provides an excellent example of dissent of this kind.

18-13 Aminoil, an American company which operated an oil concession in the Kuwait sector of the divided zone between Kuwait and Saudi Arabia, had its concession terminated and its assets taken over by a decree of the Kuwait government. The subsequent dispute, which was concerned principally with the legitimacy of the government's action and the appropriate amount of compensation, was referred to arbitration in Paris. The arbitral tribunal consisted of three arbitrators, under the chairmanship of Professor Reuter, a distinguished Professor of Public International Law at the University of Paris.

18-14 In its award,[16] the arbitral tribunal upheld the legitimacy of the government's action and at the same time ordered the payment of a very substantial sum of money by way of compensation to Aminoil. Sir Gerald Fitzmaurice, a former judge of the International Court of Justice, who has been

---

[15] This type of dissent, generally expressed in a 'separate opinion', is also know as a 'concurring opinion'.

[16] The award, and the separate opinion of Sir Gerald Fitzmaurice QC, may be found in *Aminoil* v. *Government of Kuwait* (1982) XXI *International Legal Materials* 976. For a detailed account of the case, *see* Redfern, 'The Arbitration between the Government of Kuwait and Aminoil' in [1985] *BYIL* 65. For a critical comment on the award, *see* Mann, 'The Aminoil Arbitration' in [1983] *BYIL* 213; and for a supportive comment, *see* Philippe Kahn in *Clunet* 1982, 844 at p. 868. The *Aminoil* award marked the end of the so-called 'internationalisation' of state contracts, with its cavalier disregard for the law of the state concerned.

described as 'one of the greatest public international lawyers of his generation'[17] attached what he called a 'separate opinion' to the tribunal's award. He said, with old-fashioned courtesy, that whilst he naturally hesitated to differ from a view 'so skilfully constructed and persuasive as that contained in this Award', he was compelled 'by good faith and my professional conscience' to dissent on one basic issue, namely, the legitimacy of the government's act of nationalisation in the face of so-called 'stabilisation clauses' in the concession.[18] The majority of the tribunal took the view that the governmental decree was a necessary measure, and should be regarded as legitimate, particularly since the government was ready to submit to international arbitration over the issue of compensation. Sir Gerald was dismissive of this approach. He said:

> It is an illusion to suppose that monetary compensation alone, even on a generous scale, necessarily removes the confiscatory element from a take-over, whether called nationalisation or something else. It is like paying compensation to a man who has lost his leg. Unfortunately it does not restore the leg.[19]

18-15   Nevertheless, Sir Gerald concluded, there were other elements to be taken into account, 'as well as questions of realism' so that, in the result, he found himself 'in entire agreement with the operative part (*dispositif*) of the Award which is unanimous and [except on that one basic issue] I am in substantial agreement with much of the reasoning on which the award is based'.[20]

18-16   Sir Gerald referred to 'questions of realism'. What he meant, and what he had the good sense to recognise, was that it is sometimes necessary to set aside some legal arguments, however persuasive they might be, and instead to

---

[17]   By Sir Robert Jennings, himself a former Judge of the International Court of Justice, in [1984] *BYIL* 1.

[18]   *Supra* n. 16 at 1053.

[19]   *ibid.* at 1052.

[20]   *ibid.* at 1043. In an interesting comment on the *Aminoil* award in 'The Taking of Property by the State: Recent Developments in International Law', Professor Higgins wrote: 'The Award, which touches on many questions of the greatest interest, purports to be unanimous. Sir Gerald Fitzmaurice wrote a Separate Opinion. But it is very hard to see, upon reading the arguments advanced in that Separate Opinion, that he was really in agreement with the *dispositif* of the Award': (1982-III) 176 *Recueil des Cours* 305. (It is likely that Sir Gerald, as a former government adviser, realised that an award which was unanimous in its conclusion would carry more weight with the parties, and particularly the government party, than a majority award would do.)

recognise the realities of the situation. The parties themselves had agreed, in their reference to arbitration, that there was no intention of trying to reverse the government's decree. The issue before the arbitrators was principally one of compensation. On that issue, Sir Gerald was able to agree with his colleagues as to the amount awarded; and the result was that Aminoil received a substantial monetary award, which the government paid without protest or delay.

18-17 Similar 'questions of realism' have influenced other would-be dissenters, as can be seen from various decisions in the Iran–US Claims Tribunal. For example, in *Ultrasystems Inc.* v. *Islamic Republic of Iran*,[21] Judge Mosk said: 'I concur in the Tribunal's Partial Award. I do so in order to form a majority, so that an award can be rendered'. He also added a footnote: 'As Professor Pieter Sanders has written, "arbitrators are forced to continue their deliberations until a majority, and probably a compromise solution, has been reached"'.[22]

18-18 In *Economy Forms Corp.* v. *Islamic Republic of Iran*,[23] Judge Howard Holtzman, although believing that the damages awarded were half what they should have been, said: 'Why then do I concur in this inadequate award, rather than dissenting from it? The answer is based on the realistic old saying that there are circumstances in which "something is better than nothing"'.

18-19 The advantage of these 'good' dissents is that they permit an arbitrator to express disagreement, without what may be seen as a show of conceit, or petulance. And without imperilling the authority of the award. But if these are 'good' dissents, what are the 'bad' ones? Judge Stanley Fuld wrote about dissents of this kind in a learned (and amusing) article in the *Columbia Law Review*.[24] He referred to a judge in the Appellate Court who said:

> In essence, what these four judges have done here is to blindly announce a
> ... rule which not only finds no support in history, precedent, experience,

---

[21] 2 Iran–US CTR 100.

[22] Sanders, 'Commentary on UNCITRAL Arbitration Rules' in (1977) *Yearbook Commercial Arbitration* 172 at p. 208. As stated *supra* n. 6, there is no 'fall-back' provision for the case in which there is no majority.

[23] For a discussion of these and other cases, including the important decision of the International Court of Justice in the 'Case Concerning the Arbitral Award of 31 July 1989' *see* Schwebel, 'The Majority Vote of an International Arbitral Tribunal' in (1991) 2(4) *American Review of International Arbitration* 402.

[24] Fuld, 'The Voices of Dissent' in 62(6) *Columbia Law Review* 923 (1962).

custom, practice, logic, reason, common sense or natural justice, but is in utter defiance of each and all of these standards.[25]

18-20 Judge Fuld comments:

I do not know the reactions of this dissenter's colleagues, for I never spoke to them, but I am fairly confident that they did not pat him on the back and say 'well done, old fellow'.[26]

18-21 Later in the same article, Judge Fuld referred to another US judge, in a case in which the claimant had sued a railway company for injuries allegedly caused through its negligence. The jury had given a verdict in favour of the claimant but on appeal, the High Court reversed the judgment and dismissed the complaint. One judge dissented and said:

The majority opinion sweeps over the evidence in this case like an express train shooting across a trestle, ignoring signals, semaphores and swinging lanterns … Because of his experience with the train, the plaintiff will undoubtedly never park an automobile in the vicinity of a railroad track again, but from his experience with this lawsuit, he will undoubtedly also feel that he should remain far away from the courts because, from his point of view, a collision with Court-inspired law can be as devastating as a collision with a railroad locomotive.[27]

18-22 As Judge Fuld observes, it is not necessary for the dissenter to use a sledge-hammer to drive home the point that the majority do not know what they are talking about. A rapier will do just as well, as with the English jurist who is reported to have said: 'I am dissenting for the reasons so ably expressed in the majority opinion'.[28]

18-23 Finally, what are the 'ugly' dissents? These, it is suggested, are the dissents in which the dissenting arbitrator – and it is almost always an arbitrator, not a judge – does not merely disagree with his or her colleagues on issues of fact

---

[25] *ibid.* p. 924.

[26] *Ibid.*

[27] *ibid.* p. 925.

[28] *ibid.* The same (possibly apocryphal) dissent, is mentioned in Alder, 'Dissents in Courts of Last Resort: Tragic Choices?' in 20(2) *Oxford Journal of Legal Studies* 221, a scholarly review and analysis of judicial dissent.

or law, or on their reasoning, but takes the opportunity of issuing a dissenting opinion to attack the way in which the arbitration itself was conducted. The dissenting arbitrator complains, unrestrainedly and in print, that his or her views were ignored, that he or she was never properly consulted, that the majority arbitrators were ignorant of the law and biased from the outset, and so forth. In short, the dissenting arbitrator complains that the proper procedures were not followed and that the majority arbitrators have failed to behave as they should have behaved.

18-24   This is dangerous, because one of the few grounds on which an arbitral award may be annulled, or refused recognition and enforcement, is failure to observe the requirements of due process.[29]

18-25   The danger is illustrated by a recent case in the Swedish Court of Appeal.[30] An arbitral tribunal sitting in Sweden gave a majority award against the Czech Republic. The minority arbitrator, who was dismayed by the award, entered a strong dissenting opinion. He attacked the conduct of the arbitration, alleging amongst other matters that he had been deliberately excluded from the deliberations of the other two arbitrators. They, in turn, commented in their award that he had failed to discharge his duty as an arbitrator and that his failure was 'matched by the intemperance and inaccuracy of his dissent'.[31]

18-26   It seems that the dissenting arbitrator, no doubt enraged by what he perceived as lack of justice towards the party that had appointed him, encouraged the Czech Republic to challenge the award in the Swedish courts. In consequence, all three arbitrators ended up giving evidence in the Swedish court

---

[29]   The international recognition and enforcement of arbitral awards usually takes place under the provisions of the New York Convention on the Recognition and Enforcement of Foreign Arbitral Awards made on 10 June 1958 ('the New York Convention'). Under Art. V of the New York Convention, recognition and enforcement may be refused if there were procedural irregularities in the conduct of the arbitration: for further discussion of this topic, *see* Redfern and Hunter, *Law and Practice of International Commercial Arbitration* (3rd edn., Sweet and Maxwell, London, 1999), chs 9 and 10.

[30]   The text of the Partial Award of 13 September 2001 and the Dissenting Opinion in this case, *CMF* v. *Czech Republic* is available at www.cetv-net.com/ne/articlefiles/439-cme-cv_eng.pdf

[31]   Partial Award on Liability at para. 625. In a Final Award dated 14 March 2003, the Czech Republic was ordered to pay US$354 million. Following the Swedish Court of Appeal's rejection of the challenge to the Partial Award, payment was made. (On the same facts, an arbitration tribunal in London had reached a different decision which not unexpectedly has caused criticism of the arbitral process: *see e.g.* Brower, Brower II and Sharpe, 'The Coming Crisis in the Global Adjudication System' in (2003) 19(4) *Arbitration International* 424.)

proceedings, which is not something that a judge or arbitrator would normally wish to do. (In the event, the Swedish court dismissed the challenge to the arbitral award. In the course of doing so, the court had some sensible points to make about the deliberations of an arbitral tribunal, to which reference will be made later.)

18-27 It may well happen that an arbitrator is frustrated by the way in which the arbitral proceedings are conducted. Nevertheless, there are other ways than a dissenting opinion of expressing this dissatisfaction, including resigning from the tribunal if necessary.

18-29 In the courts of law, and particularly, of course, in courts which follow the common-law tradition, there is something to be said for dissenting opinions. In a comprehensive article in *the Oxford Journal of Legal Studies*, John Alder comes to the conclusion[32] that:

> The advantages of the dissenting speech lie mainly in the accountability that it helps to ensure for the judicial process by virtue of its openness and its appeal to the integrity of the panel.

18-30 He finishes by stating[33] 'This paper has tried to make a case for treating the dissent as an integral part of the judicial process'.

18-31 Senior judges have told the author[34] that they welcome the opportunity to express a dissenting judgment because, with the best will in the world, they do not always agree with the reasoning of their fellow judges and are pleased to have the opportunity to say so. They are glad that they are not always obliged to behave like a troop of soldiers, marching in step to the beat of a drum. They add that a dissenting judgment will serve to show the parties, and particularly the losing party, that their arguments have been carefully considered. They say, finally, that occasionally – and this is a perhaps rare moment of personal triumph – their dissenting judgment may be vindicated when it is adopted by a higher court, or in a later case, and so contributes to the development of the law.

18-32 It is true. This may happen.

---

[32] Alder, *supra* n. 28 at p. 245.
[33] *ibid.* p. 246.
[34] In conversations with the author.

18-33   Every student of English law knows of Lord Denning's famous dissent in *Candler* v. *Crane Christmas*.[35] Mr Candler, who had invested money in a company on the basis of accounts that had been negligently prepared, lost his investment and sued the accountants. The majority of the Court of Appeal held that, in the absence of a contractual or fiduciary relationship, the accountants owed no duty of care to that investor. Lord Denning, dissenting, disagreed. He said:

> In my opinion, accountants owe a duty of care not only to their own clients, but also to all those whom they know will rely on their accounts in the transactions for which those accounts are prepared.[36]

18-34   Twelve years later, in *Hedley Byrne*,[37] the House of Lords held unanimously that as a matter of law, the making of a statement upon which reliance is placed *could* give rise to a duty of care, even if there was no contractual or fiduciary relationship. Lord Hudson expressly referred to the judgment of Lord Denning in *Candler* v. *Crane Christmas* saying that he agreed with it 'so far as it dealt with the facts of that case'[38] and that he was therefore of the opinion that Lord Denning's judgment 'is to be preferred to that of the majority'. Lord Devlin too said[39] that he was prepared to adopt Lord Denning's statement 'as to the circumstances in which he says a duty to use care in making a statement exists'.

18-35   In the well-known *Ken Ren* case,[40] the issue that confronted the House of Lords was whether or not to make an order for security for costs in an ICC arbitration. Their Lordships agreed that the English court had the power to make such an order, but the exercise of that power was discretionary. It was argued that the court in exercising its discretion should refuse to make the order sought, because the issue would be much better dealt with in the arbitration itself. Lord Mustill, in a dissenting judgment with which Lord Browne-Wilkinson agreed, said that in his judgment an order for security for costs did not conform with the

---

[35] *Candler* v. *Crane Christmas & Co* [1951] 1 All ER 426.
[36] *ibid.* at 436.
[37] *Hedley Byrne & Co. Ltd* v. *Heller & Partners Ltd* [1963] 2 All ER 575.
[38] *ibid.* at 597.
[39] *ibid.* at 611.
[40] *Coppée Levalin NV* v. *Ken-Ren Chemicals and Fertilisers Ltd* [1995] 1 AC 38. (For a vigorous criticism of this decision, *see* Paulsson, 'The Unwelcome Atavism of *Ken Ren*: the House of Lords Shows its Meddle' (1994) 12(314) *ASA Bulletin* 439.)

type of procedure that the parties had chosen and accordingly the application should be refused, 'notwithstanding that on a narrower view it appears to answer the justice of the case'.[41]

18-36 It is perhaps significant that only a year later, when the English Arbitration Act 1996 was enacted, the power to order security for costs in an arbitration was taken away from the English court and vested in the arbitrators themselves.[42]

18-37 Finally, there is the dissenting judgment which strikes a blow for freedom, even in the midst of war, and which echoes still in the memory. During the Second World War, at a time when England was facing the threat of invasion, the Home Secretary (the relevant Minister) ordered the imprisonment of Mr Liversidge (as he was known) on the basis that he had reasonable grounds to believe that Mr Liversidge (like others imprisoned under the same Defence Regulations) was a person of hostile associations. The question that came before the House of Lords was whether the court could investigate whether or not the Minister had reasonable grounds for his belief.[43] The majority held that the courts could not review an executive decision in this way. Lord Atkin disagreed. He said:

> In this country, amidst the clash of arms, the laws are not silent. They may be changed, but they speak the same language in war as in peace. It has always been one of the pillars of freedom, one of the principles of liberty for which we are now fighting, that the judges are no respecters of persons and stand between the subject and any attempted encroachments on his liberty by the executive, alert to see that any coercive action is justified by law. In this case, I have listened to arguments which might have been addressed acceptably to the Court of King's Bench in the time of Charles I. I protest, even if I do it alone, against a strained construction put on words with the effect of giving an uncontrolled power of imprisonment to the minister.[44]

---

[41] *Coppée Levalin NV* v. *Ken-Ren Chemicals and Fertilisers Ltd* [1995] 1 AC 38 at 65.

[42] English Arbitration Act 1996, ss. 38 and 44.

[43] The case is *Liversidge* v. *Anderson* [1941] 3 All ER 338. Mr Liversidge was arrested in May 1940 and released in early January 1942: for a full account of the case, see Lord Bingham's lecture, cited *infra* n. 46.

[44] *ibid.* at 244.

18-38   Lord Atkin went on to say that he knew of only one authority which might justify the majority's view of the law. It came from Lewis Carroll:

'When I use a word', Humpty Dumpty said in a rather scornful tone, 'it means just what I choose it to mean, neither more nor less'. 'The question is' said Alice 'whether you can make words mean so many different things'. 'The question is' said Humpty Dumpty 'who is to be the master – that's all'.[45]

18-39   As might be imagined, this dissenting speech was not well received by Lord Atkin's fellow judges. They certainly did not pat him on the back and say 'well done, old fellow'![46] It was left to another eminent Law Lord to say, years later, that the time had come to acknowledge openly that the majority of the House of Lords were 'expediently and, at that time, perhaps, excusably, wrong and the dissenting speech of Lord Atkin was right'.[47]

18-40   It might well be said, particularly by common lawyers, that if judges are allowed to dissent, and to do so in terms which sometimes infuriate their fellow judges, why should arbitrators not enjoy the same freedom? There are at least three reasons.

18-41   First, the authority of a judgment rests not only on the reputation of the judges concerned but also on the reputation of the judicial system of which they form part, including the appellate courts. This judicial system should be strong enough to tolerate dissent, and even occasionally perhaps to profit by it. Even so, not all courts permit dissent. The European Court of Justice is a notable example of a court in which the secrecy of the deliberations is maintained and no dissent

---

[45] *ibid.* at 245. Amongst many others interned at this time was a young Cambridge law student of German origin who later, as Sir Michael Kerr, became an outstanding Judge of the English Court of Appeal and amongst other distinctions, President of the LCIA (and of Queen Mary College): *see* Kerr, *As Far as I Remember* (Hart Publishing, Oxford, 2002). For an account of the family's move to England, *see* the children's book for adults by Sir Michael's sister, Judith Kerr, entitled *When Hitler Stole Pink Rabbit* (Harper Collins Publishers Ltd, New York, 1971).

[46] In a lecture at the Reform Club, October 1997, entitled 'Mr. Perlzweig, Mr. Liversidge and Lord Atkin', Lord Bingham related that, in an unprecedented move, the Lord Chancellor asked Lord Atkin to take out the reference to Humpty Dumpty. Lord Atkin refused and, after delivery of his speech, he was cold-shouldered by his colleagues: *see* Bingham, *The Business of Judging* (Oxford University Press, Oxford, 2000), p. 216.

[47] Lord Diplock in *Inland Revenue Commissioners* v. *Rossminster* [1980] AC 952 at 1008.

is allowed. This rule is defended on the grounds that it builds up the authority of the court.[48] As an American judge said, more than a hundred years ago:

the only purpose which an elaborate dissent can accomplish, if any, is to weaken the effect of the opinion of the majority, and thus engender want of confidence in the conclusion of courts of last resort.[49]

18-42 Since in most cases there is no appeal from the award of an international arbitral tribunal, that tribunal is in effect a court of last resort. Even the famous US judge Oliver Wendell Holmes, who was often described as 'the great dissenter', said that he thought it 'useless and undesirable, as a rule, to express dissent'.[50]

18-43 By contrast with the courts of law, the authority of an arbitral tribunal rests on that tribunal alone; and it is a tribunal, it must be remembered, which is brought together only to determine a particular dispute, which may never have met before and which may never meet again. This is a fragile base on which to build a decision on a claim that may be worth millions of dollars. A dissenting opinion may be sufficient to overturn this fragile base and with it, an award which, for better or for worse, the parties have undertaken to honour. In other words, a dissenting opinion may lay an award open to attack. Indeed, in a recent case[51] relating to an arbitration award made by three English arbitrators, one of whom gave a dissenting opinion, the Court of Appeal said:

The difference of view between the experienced arbitrators in this case provides, of itself, ground for contending that the decision of the majority is 'at least open to serious doubt'.[52]

---

[48] *See e.g.* the comment by Alder, *supra* n. 28 at p. 234: 'dissents are not permitted in the European Court of Justice, the deliberations of which are subject to a strong requirement of secrecy and all must sign the opinion of the court. This has been defended on the ground of the need to build up the court's authority by "presenting a united front and as a defence against political pressure"'. Alder suggests that such a role is 'anti-democratic' (*ibid.* at n. 59).

[49] *Per* White J in *Pollock* v. *Farmers Loan and Trust Co.* 157 U.S. 429 at 608 (1895).

[50] In *Northern Securities Co.* v. *United States* 193 U.S. 197 at 400 (1904).

[51] *The Northern Pioneer*, Court of Appeal, Civil Division (unreported, 2002).

[52] *Per* Phillips MR at para. 64. Under English law, parties may waive their right of appeal either expressly or by implication (under Rules such as those of the ICC or the LCIA which contain such a waiver). If the parties have kept open the right of appeal, the applicant must still apply to the English court for leave to appeal, which will not be given unless it appears that the tribunal's decision on the point of law is 'obviously wrong' or if the question is one of general public

18-44 The second reason is a more sensitive one and needs to be expressed with some care. It arises from the point made at the outset of this article, concerning the different position of a judge, as opposed to that of an arbitrator. Judges are appointed by the state. They do not depend in any way on the parties who appear before them. In an international commercial arbitration, by contrast, two of the three members of the tribunal will usually have been appointed (or nominated) by the parties; and it is those parties who will pay the fees and expenses of the arbitrators. Does this create a degree of dependence?

18-45 It should not do so. The members of the arbitral tribunal, including the party-nominated members, are not the advocates or representatives of the parties. The modern insistence is upon the independence and impartiality of arbitrators. They are appointed to exercise a judicial function and they should do so, impartially and independently. Yet, when a dissenting arbitrator disagrees with the majority, and does so in terms which are likely to find favour with the party which appointed him or her, does not that cause some concern? Does the dissent arise from a genuine difference of opinion or is it influenced by other, less creditable considerations?

18-46 The ICC in Paris publishes annual statistics which show, amongst other things, the number of awards that it sends out each year which are accompanied by, or include, dissenting opinions. In 2001, there were 24 dissenting opinions. In 22 of these, where it was possible to identify the dissenting arbitrator, the dissent was made in favour of the party that had appointed him or her. There is perhaps nothing strange about this; in selecting an arbitrator, the parties will naturally look for someone likely to be sympathetic to their point of view.[53] But it would have been comforting if one or two of the dissenting opinions had gone against the appointing party![54]

---

importance and the decision is 'at least open to serious doubt': English Arbitration Act, 1996, ss. 69(1) and 82(1).

[53] As stated by Judge Richard Mosk and Tom Ginsberg, 'Dissenting Opinions in International Arbitration' in *Liber Amicorum Bengt Broms* (Finnish Branch of the International Law Association, Helsinki, 1999), p. 275: 'It should not be surprising if party appointed arbitrators tend to view the facts and law in a light similar to their appointing parties. After all, the parties are careful to select arbitrators with views similar to theirs. But this does not mean that arbitrators will violate their duties of impartiality and independence'.

[54] In fairness, it should of course be said that the two dissenting arbitrators whose identity was not clear from the award may not have dissented in favour of their appointing party.

18-47   For Maître Boisséson, to accept the principle of a dissenting opinion is to diminish the independent role of the arbitrator. 'In effect', he says:[55]

> certain arbitrators, so as not to lose the confidence of the company or the state which appointed them, will be tempted, if they have not put their point of view successfully in the course of the tribunal's deliberation, systematically to draw up a dissenting opinion and to insist that it be communicated to the parties.

18-48   A similar point is made by Judge Richard Mosk and Mr Tom Ginsburg. They say:

> Although party-appointed arbitrators are supposed to be impartial and independent in international arbitrations, some believe that with the availability of dissent, arbitrators may feel pressure to support the party that appointed them and to disclose that support.[56]

18-49   The expression of a detailed dissenting opinion may well give rise to doubts as to whether or not the arbitrator concerned is truly independent and impartial. This possibility is illustrated by the case in which the US government sought the removal of Judge Bengt Broms as an arbitrator of the US–Iran Claims Tribunal. It was asserted that there were justifiable doubts as to his independence and impartiality, based on his alleged breach of the secrecy of the Tribunal's deliberations in his concurring and dissenting opinion of 19 December 2000. Sir Robert Jennings QC, a former Judge of the International Court of Justice, was appointed to consider this challenge. In his decision,[57] Sir Robert referred to his initial puzzlement at 'some of the seeming contradictions'[58] in Judge Broms' opinion and then said:

> And there are other touches that seem to an outside observer to be a strange way of expressing a separate opinion. Eventually, however, one realises after many readings – something that has probably been tolerably obvious all along to the insiders – that it seems a strange and unusual opinion for the

---

[55] De Boisséson, *Le Droit Français de l'Arbitrage National et International* (1998), p. 802 (translation by the author).

[56] Mosk and Ginsberg, *supra* n. 53 at p. 275.

[57] Decision of 7 May 2001. A summary of this decision was published in (2001) 16(5) *Mealey's Int'l Arb. Rep.* (May 2001). The full text is available for purchase from Mealey's electronic database.

[58] Decision, *supra* n. 57 at p. 5.

reason that it is a continuation in the form of an Opinion of Judge Brom's stance and arguments made by him during the deliberations. He has been unable to resist the temptation to continue arguing with his colleagues, or at any rate with the 'smallest possible majority' of them who were not able to accept these views of his. Once that fact is realised then one has, from reading his Opinion, a quite vivid picture of what took place in the deliberation and how it eventually emerged.[59]

18-50   Sir Robert went on to say:

A rule of the confidentiality of the deliberations must, if it is to be effective, apply generally to the deliberation stage of a tribunal's proceedings and cannot realistically be confined to what is said in a formal meeting of all the members in the deliberation room. The form or forms the deliberation takes varies greatly from one tribunal to another. Anybody who has had experience of courts and tribunals knows perfectly well that much of the deliberation work, even in courts like the ICJ which have formal rules governing the deliberation, is done less formally. In particular the task of drafting is better done in small groups rather than by the whole court attempting to draft round the table. Revelations of such informal discussion and of suggestions made, could be very damaging and seriously threaten the whole deliberation process.

18-51   After concluding that this breach of confidentiality had been correctly dealt with by the President of the Tribunal, Sir Robert said:

My only concern, as the Appointing Authority, is what is the effect of the terms of Judge Brom's 'concurring and dissenting Opinion' on the question of his impartiality and his independence. A judge may be strictly and correctly impartial and independent though massively indiscreet and forgetful of the rules.[60]

18-52   On the issue of whether or not the Opinion of Judge Broms revealed a lack of impartiality and independence, Sir Robert said:

---

[59] *ibid.* p. 4.
[60] *ibid.* p. 7.

This Opinion of the Judge suggests a man who not only has very strong views but who also does not find it easy to let go of them and for whom opposition, especially successful opposition, probably only signals a need to restate his own point of view. He was not alone in his views of course. It is clear – indeed altogether too clear, as we have seen above – from Judge Broms' revelations of the deliberations that there had been, during the deliberation and probably even earlier, a sharp difference of opinion between Iran and the United States about what may be called the practicalities resulting, or not resulting depending upon the point of view, from what at first sight looks like a simple task of interpreting a few plain words.[61]

18-53   Sir Robert concluded:

I do not see how one can infer, from the evidence of this single Opinion, that the United States' suspicions of partiality are justified …

On the other hand I also feel that the present unhappy atmosphere is a damaging one for the Tribunal, and even more importantly, for the relationship between the Parties. And this is a matter in respect of which, especially after his ill-judged breaches of the secrecy of the deliberations, Judge Broms surely has some responsibility. This was a most serious error, and the apprehension of its repetition in a future case could do great harm to the usefulness of the Tribunal's deliberations, and to its efforts to find a consensus. It seems right to make it clear to Judge Broms that he should now resolve on no account to fall into this error again and to reflect that any sign of a repetition might change the balance of a decision in respect of any further challenge.[62]

18-54   Finally, there is a simple, practical argument against dissenting opinions, which would seem to carry the most weight of all.

18-55   The purpose of an arbitration is to arrive at a decision. It is the *decision* which matters; and it matters *not* as a guide to the opinions of a particular arbitrator, or as an indication of the future development of the law, but because it resolves the particular dispute that divides the parties; and it resolves that dispute

---

[61] *ibid.* p. 9.
[62] *ibid.* p. 11.

as part of a private, not public, dispute resolution process that the parties themselves have chosen.

18-56 When an award is issued, the first action that the parties and their lawyers will usually take is to turn to the end of the document, to find out whether they have won or lost. For the parties and their lawyers, it is the decision that is important. Yet, in all that is written or said about arbitration – and nowadays a great deal is written or said – there is very little about how a tribunal of arbitrators goes about reaching its decision.

18-57 The task which faces a judicial body is not easy. In his book on 'the business of Judging', Lord Bingham has described[63] the special features of judicial decision-making:

> The judge's role in determining what happened at some time in the past is not of course peculiar to him. Historians, auditors, accident investigators of all kinds, loss adjusters and doctors are among those who, to a greater or lesser extent, may be called upon to perform a similar function. But there are three features of the judge's role which will not apply to all these other investigations. First, he is always presented with conflicting versions of the events in question: if there is no effective dispute, there is nothing for him to decide. Secondly, his determination necessarily takes place subject to formality and restraints (evidential or otherwise) attendant upon proceedings in court. Thirdly, his determination has a direct practical effect upon people's lives in terms of their pockets, activities or reputations.

18-58 The same task faces an arbitral tribunal, but with this difference. In a tribunal of judges – a Court of Appeal, for instance – the judges are likely to have a shared legal background and for the most part to be of the same nationality. This is not usually so in international commercial disputes, before a tribunal of three arbitrators.

18-59 First, such an arbitral tribunal is not a permanent court or tribunal, except in special cases such as the Iran–US Claims Tribunal. Secondly, the tribunal may be composed of arbitrators of different professions: accountants, engineers or whatever the case may require. Thirdly, even if all the members of the tribunal are lawyers, they will often be of different nationalities, with different languages

---

[63] Lord Bingham, *supra* n. 46, p. 4.

and different legal backgrounds: the common law, the civil law, the *Shari'ah* and so forth. They may know each other personally or professionally, or they may, as often happens, meet for the first time when they come together as a tribunal, chosen to resolve a dispute which the parties themselves have tried but failed to resolve.

18-60   How will this disparate, *ad hoc* group of people set about trying to reach their decision? They will read (patiently or impatiently) the parties' submissions, the witness statements and the Lever-Arch files full of photocopied documents. They will listen to evidence and argument and after this, although, as the saying goes, they may not be any wiser, they should certainly be better informed!

18-61   As the case proceeds, each arbitrator will no doubt begin to form his or her own view as to how the various issues that have arisen ought to be determined; but this should not be a solitary process. The tribunal consists of three arbitrators. There must obviously be some exchange of views, some dialogue between them, if they are to try to arrive at a unanimous decision.[64] In this situation, no man – or woman – is an island. It would seem to be a matter of plain common sense that there has to be an interchange of views between the arbitrators, however it takes place, until, like a jigsaw puzzle, the pieces of the award are put together.[65]

18-62   In French law, such an interchange of views is formalised as a 'deliberation'. The Civil Code which governs French internal (or domestic) arbitrations requires the arbitrators to fix the date at which their deliberations will start (*la mise en délibéré*).[66] After that, no further submissions by the parties are allowed. Under French law too, as in other civil law countries, the deliberations

---

[64] *See* Redfern and Hunter, *supra.* n. 29 at para. 8–29: 'Where an arbitral tribunal is composed of more than one arbitrator, it is self-evident that there should be discussion between the arbitrators before the award is drawn up. Some systems of law contain mandatory provisions to this effect but, whether this is so or not, the principle that arbitrators must consult before issuing their award is well recognised'.

[65] *See* Fouchard, Gaillard, Goldman, *International Commercial Arbitration* (Kluwer Law International, The Hague 1999), para. 1374: 'Although again most laws do not explicitly require deliberations in international arbitrations to be secret, such secrecy is generally considered to be the rule. This means that views exchanged during the deliberations cannot be communicated to the parties'.

[66] Article 1468 of the French Civil Code states 'L'arbitre fixe la date à laquelle l'affaire sera mise en délibéré'.

of the arbitrators are 'secret'.[67] The emphasis is significant: the deliberations are not merely confidential, but 'secret'.

18-63 For Professor Bredin, the distinguished French Academician and author, the rule that there must be a 'deliberation' before there is any award by the tribunal, is a rule of international public order.[68] For Maître Boisséson, the rule that such a 'deliberation' should be, and should remain secret, is a 'fundamental principle, which constitutes one of the mainsprings of arbitration, as it does of all judicial decisions'.[69]

18-64 In adopting this approach, these distinguished French lawyers have the support of the rules of the International Centre for the Settlement of Investment Disputes (ICSID) which stipulates, in Rule 15, that:
(1) The deliberations of the Tribunal shall take place in private and remain secret.
(2) Only members of the Tribunal shall take part in its deliberations. No other person shall be admitted unless the Tribunal decides otherwise.

18-65 In the case in the Swedish Court of Appeal which was referred to earlier, the Czech Republic tried, as already stated, to set aside the arbitral award. One of the grounds put forward was that the arbitrator nominated by the Czech Republic had, as he proclaimed in his dissenting Opinion, been deliberately excluded by his fellow arbitrators from the deliberations of the Tribunal. In considering this argument, the Swedish Court of Appeal considered what was necessary for a proper deliberation. The court referred to two principles which might appear to come into conflict: the principle of equality amongst the arbitrators, but also the need for the tribunal to reach a conclusion without undue delay. The court said, in summary, that the arbitrators should be treated equally, but that the procedures adopted should also be cost-effective and flexible. There were no formal rules and so the deliberations might be oral or written, or both; deadlines could be set, but could also be changed as required and so forth.

---

[67] Article 1469 of the French Civil Code states 'Les délibérations des arbitres seront secrètes'.
[68] Professor J.D. Bredin, 'Le Secret du Délibéré Arbitral' in *Etudes Offertes à Pierre Bellet* (LITEC), 1991.
[69] De Boisséson, *supra* n. 55 at p. 296. *See also* the comment in Robert, *L'Arbitrage: Droit Interne, Droit International Privé* (5th edn., Dalloz), 1983, para. 360: 'Although it is practised according to a certain number of foreign laws, notably anglo-saxon, the dissenting opinion is prohibited in French domestic law since it violates the secrecy of the tribunal's deliberation' (author's translation).

18-66   The court added that whilst due process must be guaranteed:

> An arbitrator cannot prolong the deliberations by demanding continued discussions in an attempt to persuade the others as to the correctness of his opinion. The dissenting arbitrator is thus not afforded any opportunity to delay the writing of the award.[70]

18-67   It will not have escaped notice that, in this Swedish case, the secrecy of the arbitrators' deliberations was not maintained. Indeed, it could not have been when the arbitrators themselves were called upon to testify as to the meetings and discussions that were held, as they moved towards the writing of their award.

18-68   This highlights one of the problems caused by the dissenting opinion. Once an arbitrator has expressed such an opinion, the secrecy of the tribunal's deliberations may have been breached and the curtain has been lifted, if only to give a brief but tantalising glimpse of dissension within the tribunal.

18-69   It would be difficult, if not impossible, for arbitrators to have a frank and open exchange of views, to advance ideas and proposals, to change their mind and then perhaps to change it back again, if what they had said and what they had not said, what they had thought and what they had not thought, was to become known to the parties – particularly in a situation in which two of the three members of the tribunal are chosen by the parties themselves.

18-70   This in essence is the justification for keeping secret the deliberations of the tribunal. But does this secrecy need to be maintained once the award has been issued? Indeed, can it be maintained, if separate or dissenting opinions are permitted?

18-71   French law, with impeccable logic, takes the view that even to state that a judgment was made unanimously may be a breach of the secrecy of the judges' deliberation.[71] But in the context of the present discussion the point, put shortly, is this: arbitrators should be able to discuss freely and openly the case that they have to decide. Yet it is difficult for arbitrators to do this if there is a risk, real or imaginary, that one of their number will break the confidence of their

---

[70]   *See supra* n. 31, Judgment of the Swedish Court of Appeal at pp. 86 and 87.
[71]   Cass. Soc. 9 November 1945 Gaz. Pal. 1946 1. 22. Note, however, Professor Bredin's comment that legal opinion on this point seems divided: Bredin, *supra* n. 68.

discussions, whether by communication with his or her appointing party, or by means of a dissenting opinion.

18-72   There may be circumstances in which an arbitrator is compelled by his or her professional conscience to dissent from the conclusions of the majority. If so, this can be done by a 'good' dissent – short, polite and restrained. To go further, and to continue to express arguments and opinions that were *not* accepted during the tribunal's deliberations, would seem to serve little or no purpose, except that of self-justification.

18-73   It is true, as stated earlier in this article, that a dissenting opinion may point the way to a change in the law. As was said in somewhat poetic terms, it may constitute 'an appeal to the brooding spirit of the law, to the intelligence of a future day'.[72] But for this to happen, the dissent would need to be on some point of legal principle; and in addition, the dissent would need to be published as part of an award that was itself made public.

18-74   In an article that is generally favourable to the expression of dissenting opinions in international arbitration, the authors suggest that such opinions may affect decisions in the future, but they add:

> While this rationale for dissents makes sense in the context of arbitration between states, it is more problematic in the context of international commercial arbitration, which is, after all, a mainly private system of dispute resolution, although it is governed by statutes and treaties and often relies on public courts to enforce arbitration agreements and awards. The private qualities of arbitration, especially the principle of confidentiality, are usually thought to weigh against publication of awards and dissenting opinions. Arbitration, of course, has no system of *stare decisis* or precedent. Arbitrators are not bound to consider the decisions of earlier tribunals or panels. Nor is there any formal review of the law applied in arbitral awards, so there is less need to provide a source for consideration by appellate bodies. Indeed, errors of law are generally not a basis for vacating awards under domestic law or for failing to enforce them under the New York Convention.[73]

---

[72]   Hughes CJ, quoted in Alder, *supra* n. 28 at n. 108.
[73]   Mosk and Ginsberg, *supra* n. 53 at pp. 267 and 268 (references omitted).

18-75   The authors conclude that 'Arguments in favour of dissenting opinions are thus related to, although not dependent on, the issue of whether arbitral awards should be published at all'.[74]

18-76   What, in summary, is the case against dissenting opinions in international commercial arbitration? It is, first, that they may inhibit that open discussion which ought to take place secretly and within the confines of the arbitral tribunal. Secondly, that they may cast doubts on the correctness or validity of the award made by the majority. Thirdly, that they do not serve to advance the development of the law, since there is no doctrine of precedence in arbitrations and, in general no appeal against the award of an arbitral tribunal and no open publication of that tribunal's award.

18-77   It may be thought that these are weighty arguments against encouraging – and perhaps even against allowing – dissenting opinions in international commercial arbitrations. Yet we have to face reality. As Sir Gerald Fitzmaurice appreciated: 'there are questions of realism'. The reality is that, so far as international commercial arbitration is concerned, the dissenting opinion is here to stay. But then, may we not distinguish between dissenting opinions which are 'good', in the sense that they are unobjectionable in their tone and content, and the rest?

18-78   In 1985, the ICC Commission on International Arbitration set up a working group to consider dissenting opinions. From the report in the ICC Bulletin, it seems that when the working group published an interim report in 1987, it provoked an outcry from the French National Committee. First, they believed that dissenting opinions should be prohibited or at least declared to be outside the ICC system. Secondly, they complained that they had no representative on the working group.

18-79   War was averted by co-opting a member of the French National Committee onto the working group; and the group's Final Report was adopted by the ICC Commission. As might be expected, the Report[75] made a series of sensible suggestions. It did not try to rule out dissenting opinions; and it suggested that the only circumstances in which a dissenting opinion should *not*

---

[74]   *ibid.* p. 269.

[75]   *Final Report of the Working Party on Dissenting Opinions* in (1991) 2(1) *ICC International Court of Arbitration Bulletin* 32. The Chairman of the Working Party was Professor (as he now is) J. M. H. Hunter.

be sent to the parties with the award was where such opinions were prohibited by law or where the validity of the award might be imperilled, either in the place of arbitration or, to the extent that this could be foreseen, in the country of enforcement.

18-80   At a Working Session in September 2000, the International Court of the ICC reviewed its procedure in relation to dissenting opinions and came to the following conclusions:

> In the presence of a separate document submitted by one arbitrator (or by two arbitrators upholding different views in the rare case of Article 25(1) of the Rules)[76] the dissenting arbitrator should be invited to indicate if his document constitutes a dissenting opinion which he wants to have communicated to the parties or just comments for the benefit of the Secretariat and the Court. The majority should then be invited to consider whether in view of the dissenting opinion, they want to change anything in their award. At the same time the arbitral tribunal shall be informed that the dissenting opinion will be communicated to the parties when notifying the signed award. They should not be asked whether they agree or disagree with the communication of the dissenting opinion. If the arbitrators take the initiative and request that the dissenting opinion not be communicated by the Secretariat, they are to be invited to state good reasons why the communication could endanger the validity and execution of the majority award.... All comments, etc. will be submitted to the Court Session when approving the award. In the absence of valid reasons the opinion will be sent to the parties.

18-81   It may be that the communication of dissenting opinions by the ICC, and by other institutions, such as the LCIA, not only encourages arbitrators to enter a dissenting opinion but also gives an air of respectability, or even authority, to that opinion. If so, this would be unfortunate.

18-82   Why do arbitrators dissent? Some, no doubt, do so out of a sense of duty or loyalty to their appointing party, which weighs more heavily than their duty to be and to remain independent and impartial. Others, having seen the majority opinion move away from the view that they themselves have formed, will be

---

[76]   This is a reference to the case in which there is no majority on the tribunal, so the decision is made by the chairman alone.

'unable to resist the temptation to continue arguing'[77] with their colleagues. By expressing a detailed dissenting opinion, they are in effect saying to anyone who is interested: 'this is how I would have decided the dispute, if I had been the sole arbitrator'.

18-83 But, of course, a dissenting arbitrator is *not* the sole arbitrator. By putting forward a detailed dissent which continues the argument and leads to a different conclusion[78] or worse, by putting forward a detailed dissent which attacks the majority arbitrators and the way in which matters were conducted,[79] the dissenting arbitrator risks bringing the arbitral process itself into disrepute. It is difficult enough, as has already been said, for a disparate group of arbitrators, brought together perhaps for the first time and often of different nationalities and backgrounds, to reach a unanimous decision on matters on which the parties themselves and their experienced advisers have been unable to agree. It does not help if, for whatever reason, one of the members of the tribunal decides to rock the boat.

18-84 At present, a generally relaxed attitude towards dissenting opinions seems to be taken not only by the arbitral institutions, but also by arbitrators themselves. We are told by the historians that when, at the Hampton Court conference of 1604, King James I was humbly asked by the Puritan clergy for some relaxation in the church ritual which would regulate their position, he replied: 'I shall make them conform themselves or I will harry them out of the land!'[80] It would be too much to demand conformity from all arbitrators, but the time has perhaps come to enquire whether the present leniency towards dissenting opinions, however offensive they may be,[81] has gone too far.

---

[77] *cf.* the decision of Sir Robert Jennings, *supra* n. 57.

[78] In the context of this article, a 'bad' dissent.

[79] In the context of this article, an 'ugly' dissent.

[80] Trevelyan, *History of England* (Longman, 1997), p. 454; *see also* Fraser, *supra* n. 13 at p. 105.

[81] It seems that the author's idea of dividing dissenting opinions into three different categories (in this case, the good, the bad and the ugly) is not a new one. According to one US Judge, quoted in Fuld, *supra* n. 24 at p. 928): 'Dissents, like homicide, fall into three categories: excusable, justifiable and reprehensible'.

Horacio A. Grigera Naón[*]

CHAPTER 19

ARBITRATION AND LATIN AMERICA:
PROGRESS AND SETBACKS

I. INTRODUCTION

19-1 In the field of arbitration – as in many other fields, legal or not – the idea of progress is associated with the idea of growth, in its turn defined and measured in terms of the ends pursued and advances made to attain them. The teleological exercise of choosing ends and objectives defining the role of a legal institution is then of paramount importance for evaluating its growth and the instruments favouring or disfavouring it; and has been characterised as a philosophical, value-charged, exercise based on the consideration of policies and principles.[1] It thus also decisively contributes to determining the social function to be played by the institution being considered. Indeed, its growth – as well as its setbacks – may be judged by measuring the degree to which the institution fulfils the function assigned to it in light of such ends, objectives, policies and principles. In the process of selecting the latter, extra-juridical values and considerations – necessarily fashioned by sociological, economic and political or ideological factors – exert their influence and are inescapably, consciously or subconsciously, taken into account. One such factor is undoubtedly the degree of education in the institution's role and operation by those fashioning or called to

[*]   International Arbitrator. Former Secretary General of the International Court of Arbitration of the International Chamber of Commerce. Lecture delivered as the 2004 Freshfields Bruckhaus Deringer Arbitration Lecture for the School of International Arbitration, Queen Mary, London University.
[1]   B. Cardozo, *The Nature of the Judicial Process* (Yale University Press, 1921), p. 102: 'Not the origin, but the goal, is the main thing. There can be no wisdom in the choice of a path unless we know where it will lead'. *See also* B. Cardozo, *The Paradoxes of Legal Science* (Columbia University Press, New York, 1928), pp. 1–30.

Julian D.M. Lew and Loukas A. Mistelis (eds), Arbitration Insights, 393-454
© 2007 Kluwer Law International. Printed in the Netherlands

implement policies relating to it, or expected to mould their conduct in accordance with such policies. At times, political or ideological factors interfere in the normal operation of the institution, often in ways adverse to the attainment of its expected aims, and for that reason such factors may be disruptive of legitimate expectations and give rise to insecurity or uncertainty. Finally, since extra-juridical values and factors may vary over time, the aims of the institution and its function may undergo parallel change as well, and reclaim consideration from a historical perspective.

II. HISTORICAL EVOLUTION OF ARBITRATION IN LATIN AMERICA

19-2 The historical evolution of arbitration in Latin America – since its incipient steps – confirms the influence of exogenous political and socio-economic factors on the shaping of ideas and attitudes affecting the growth of international arbitration in the region. It is submitted that a proper understanding of such factors may throw light on past and ongoing or future developments of arbitration in Latin America.

19-3 A vivid illustration of the above is the case of Argentina. Historical and political factors dating back to the 1838–1840 blockade of Buenos Aires by the French fleet and the naval war of 1843–1850 between the Argentine Confederation and the Anglo-French fleet gave rise to some of the earliest examples of the utilisation of international arbitration in Latin America, and are at the root of the formation of international law doctrines which have long influenced Latin American ideas on arbitration.

19-4 The 1838–1840 French intervention had the actual purpose of distracting local French public opinion from domestic political problems[2] as well as from opposition voices in the National Assembly blaming the French government of Louis-Philippe for its inefficacy in leading French foreign policy.[3] However, its ostensible objective was to force the province of Buenos Aires to grant the French citizens residing there the same exemptions from service in the national guard enjoyed by English residents under an 1825 treaty with Great Britain. The Argentine authorities had denied the same privilege to French citizens on the basis of a statute of 1821 applicable to all foreigners residing in the province of

---

[2] Carlos Calvo, *Derecho Internacional Teórico y Práctico de Europa y América* (1868), vol. I, § 87, p. 160.
[3] J.F. Cady, *La Intervención Extranjera en el Río de la Plata (1838–1850)* (Buenos Aires, 1943), pp. 47–48.

Buenos Aires not exempted by treaty.[4] The French government's reaction was to order its navy to blockade the port of Buenos Aires, which brought about as its direct and immediate consequence the destruction of Argentine merchant ships, and the serious disruption of Argentine maritime and fluvial commerce.[5]

19-5 As an additional complication, the then Argentine ruler, controlling for all practical purposes the Argentine Confederation government and the conduct of its foreign affairs, was a backward and ruthless tyrant, Juan Manuel de Rosas. Taking advantage of such circumstance, the French government attempted to disguise its acts of aggression by presenting itself to the international community as standing 'for the principles of civilization and justice against a government totally ignorant of the iures gentium and the laws of humanity'.[6] The hostilities were put to an end through the Arana-Mackau Treaty, Article 1 of which provided for arbitration to fix the indemnity corresponding to grievances of French residents essentially relating to episodes of social unrest or disturbances in Buenos Aires, albeit totally unrelated to the issue of whether such residents had been properly summoned or not to serve in the national guard, the blockade by the French fleet or hostile acts on the Argentine side in connection therewith.[7] The arbitral tribunal was composed of six members, three chosen by Argentina

---

[4] A. Saldías, *Historia de la Confederación Argentina* (Editorial Universitaria de Buenos Aires, 1973). vol. 2, pp. 58–59.

[5] Calvo, *supra* n. 2 at § 87, pp. 160–163.

[6] Calvo, *supra* n. 2 at p. 162: Buchet-Martigny (the then French *chargé d'affaires* in Buenos Aires) stated that France

> 'representaba en esta ocasión los principios de la civilización y de la justicia en contra de un gobierno que desconocía por completo el derecho de gentes y las leyes de la humanidad'.

[7] The claims concerning the interests of French nationals arose out of episodes that predated or where unrelated to the blockade or its causes and were few in number and comparatively insignificant in economic terms. The most important was the claim of the widow of a Swiss citizen by the name of Bacle, who died during domiciliary arrest imposed on him because of accusations that he had conspired against the Rosas regime. Although a Swiss national, Mr Bacle was under the protection of the French government. Another significant claim – already accepted in principle by the Argentine government, which questioned, however, the amount of the indemnity claimed – concerned damages resulting from civil unrest in 1821 (well before Rosas came to power) inflicted to the commercial activity of a certain Despouy, a French citizen: Cady, *supra* n. 3 at pp. 49, 65. In fact, Despouy's claims originated in the closing by the authorities, for sanitary reasons, and also in response to a neighbour's complaints, of Mr Despouy's establishment for the treatment of hides and the manufacturing of colt oil. It is relevant to point out that Mr Despouy also served as go-between between the French agents and Rosas's opponents: Saldías, *supra* n. 4, at pp. 82, 98.

and three chosen by France. In case of disagreement on the name of the chairman, he would be appointed by a country selected by France.[8]

19-6 Article 1 of the Arana-Mackau Treaty has been criticised as a Rosas concession to gain stability and international legitimacy for his regime,[9] since the Argentine Confederation automatically assumed international responsibility for damages largely resulting from social perturbations or unrest beyond the control of local authorities caused to certain foreigners subject to local law and the jurisdiction of local courts without any treaty obligation to do so or pursuing full compensation for the damages inflicted to Argentine interests by the French blockade, although the Treaty (Article 2) did provide for the return of two Argentine men-o'war captured by the French fleet. The Argentine authorities had thus departed from their previous position to indemnify the French citizens in question only against compensation for all the damages to Argentine interests caused by the hostilities initiated by France,[10] despite the general consensus that French actions against the Argentine Confederation were irrational and a violation of international law.[11]

19-7 Notwithstanding these circumstances, by accepting Article 1 of the Arana-Mackau Treaty, the Argentine Confederation endorsed international arbitration as a peaceful means of resolving international disputes originated in injuries to aliens. This episode also carries elements that may help to understand and explain Latin American countries' mixed feelings vis-à-vis international arbitration. On the one hand, it confirms that, already at an early stage, international arbitration was perceived as a useful mechanism to deal with the grievances of foreign aliens for avoiding or putting an end to warfare between nations. On the other, it may account for a negative attitude towards international arbitration whenever it is perceived that resorting to arbitration or submitting to

---

[8]   Saldías, *supra* n. 4 at p. 188.

[9]   Calvo, *supra* n. 2 at p. 162.

[10] Cady, *supra* n. 3 at p. 81.

[11] References in the 1942 preface of Luis A. Podestá Costa (a then leading Argentine public international law professor and specialist, as well as a diplomat) to J.F. Cady's book *supra* n. 3 at pp. 19–20. Even Domingo F. Sarmiento, one of the founding fathers of modern Argentina, its second President, the friend of Abraham Lincoln and Horace Mann, and a staunch opponent of Rosas and everything Rosas stood for, wrote in 1845 that by opposing the French aggression, Rosas had helped to make Europe understand that European interests in Latin America could not be advanced at the cost of the independence of Latin American countries: D.F. Sarmiento, *Obras Completas (Juan Facundo Quiroga)* (Universidad Nacional de la Matanza, 2001), vol. VII, p. 183.

the jurisdiction of international arbitrators situations or disputes clearly subject to the laws and court jurisdiction of the host country, absent any pre-existing treaty obligation of such country to do so, directly or indirectly results from military or diplomatic coercion exercised by a stronger foreign power.

19-8 This incipient Argentine attitude favourable to international arbitration further manifested itself in connection with claims arising out of the joint naval action against the Argentine Confederation undertaken by the Anglo-French fleet during the 1843–1850 conflict originated in the blockade by the Confederation's fleet of the Montevideo port, also during Rosas's rule. One episode of the conflict was the 1845 closure by the Argentine Confederation authorities of the Buenos Aires port to vessels communicating with Montevideo, Uruguay. Great Britain claimed compensation for the closure of the port to English shipping and, in particular, for the losses caused to six British merchantmen prevented from entering the port because of the blockade. In 1864, Argentina and Great Britain decided to submit to arbitration the ensuing British claims, and appointed the President of Chile as sole arbitrator. Both countries had signed in 1858 and 1859 two treaties concerning the payment of monies owed by Argentina to Great Britain for damages suffered by British citizens because of the Argentine civil war between Rosas and his opponents. The sole arbitrator had to decide if the claims of the British citizens whose ships could not enter the Buenos Aires port were covered by the aforementioned treaties and, if such were not the case, if the Argentine government was or was not bound to pay compensation for the damages suffered. In an award rendered on 1 August 1870, the arbitrator found that the British claims were not covered by the 1858 and 1859 Treaties, since those claims did not originate in civil war disturbances, but in a foreign war waged by the Argentine Confederation against the authorities of Montevideo; i.e., between two independent nations. The arbitrator further reasoned that a nation in war is free to decide on the closing of its ports to foreign commerce and is the sole judge of the conditions under which it will admit foreign vessels. The arbitrator finally rejected the British claims.[12]

19-9 Events such as this reveal the absence of an anti-arbitration prejudice in the early history of the Latin American countries as independent nations and also vindicate the importance assigned to arbitration in Latin America when serving

---

[12] C. Calvo, *Le droit international théorique et pratique* (4th edn, 1870–1872), vol. III, paras 1741–1742, pp. 452–455; H. Lauterpacht, *The Function of Law in the International Community* (Oxford, 1933), para. 19, pp. 96–97.

the purpose of maintaining or restoring peace by upholding the rule of law; i.e., one of the main functions of arbitration in any of its manifestations at the international and domestic levels.

19-10   Such historical background, already considered by the alert eye of Carlos Calvo in the first (1868) edition of his treatise, also set the stage for the unfolding of the Calvo and Drago Doctrines in the years to come, and explains the role assigned to international arbitration by such doctrines. Indeed, the Calvo Doctrine is a response to the menace of foreign European intervention in South America, epitomised by the utterances of Thiers, the minister of Napoleon III, who considered Latin American countries as imperfect, bankrupted republics, which because of social and political instability and unrest, their failure to honour their debts, ensure personal security and provide proper police protection, and their inefficient and slow court system, were not to be considered equal to the countries of Europe. For these reasons, Mr Thiers advocated using force against such republics in order to advance the rights and interests of aliens and their home countries.[13]

19-11   Already before the formulation of these doctrines, concerns about the possible military intervention of foreign powers in Latin America, and the comparative weaknesses of Latin American countries because of their scarce population, inferior navy and armies, led Domingo F. Sarmiento,[14] when he was Argentine ambassador in Washington in 1866, to be the first to propose to the USA the signature of a treaty submitting to arbitration disputes arising between both countries, including those originating in injuries to aliens.[15] The clear objective of Mr Sarmiento's proposal was to improve the image of Argentina vis-à-vis world public opinion by presenting it as a staunch supporter of the rule of law based on the peaceful settlement of disputes and, in view of Argentina's comparative inferiority of forces so long as its 'embryonic state' would last, to forestall the use of force and military intervention to advance claims against Argentina by submitting disputes between both countries to a neutral arbitral tribunal, thus discrediting before world opinion any attempt to use military force

---

[13]   Calvo, *supra* n. 2 § 294, pp. 394–397.

[14]   On Domingo F. Sarmiento, *see supra* n. 11 and corresponding text.

[15]   Letter of Mr Sarmiento to the Argentine Minister of Foreign Affairs dated 29 January 1866, New York, *Obras Completas*, *supra* n. 11 vol. XXXIV at pp. 150–152..

against Argentina in order to advance claims of foreign aliens by sidestepping the arbitral resolution of the dispute imposed as a treaty obligation.[16]

19-12 As noticed by another founding father of modern Argentina, Juan Bautista Alberdi, the improvement of communications through the steamer, the train, the telegraph and submarine cable contributed to the formation of world opinion by disseminating ideas and information, in large part reflected by the press. It is in the formation and influence of such world opinion that Mr Alberdi found one of the most powerful defences against the use of force in international relations and a moral force for upholding the rule of law.[17] Carlos Calvo was to see in such public opinion the most important factor compelling states to arbitrate their disputes and enforce any ensuing arbitral awards. In his view, the recourse to arbitration and the effectiveness of arbitral determinations depend on the pressure exercised by world public opinion on states and their governments.[18]

19-13 Mr Sarmiento believed that the then recent proposal of the USA to submit to arbitration its differences with Great Britain arising out of the 'Alabama'[19] created a propitious terrain for furthering such initiative before the US government. It is clear that Mr Sarmiento had already a very realistic perception of the future evolution and expansion of interests of the USA, that he expressed more transparently in one of his later writings.[20]

---

[16] Letter of Mr Sarmiento to the Argentine Minister of Foreign Affairs dated 29 May 1866, New York, *Obras Completas*, *supra* n. 11 vol. XXXIV at pp. 158–161.

[17] J.B. Alberdi, *II Escritos Póstumos (El Crimen de la Guerra)* (Universidad Nacional de Quilmes, 2002), pp. 31–32, 48, 104.

[18] Calvo, *supra* n. 12 vol. III at para. 1806, pp. 514–515:

> 'le jour où l'opinion par sa pression croissante sera parvenue à imposer aux nations le recours à l'arbitrage, ce jour-là l'opinion, par la même pression, sera en mesure d'imposer également aux parties contestantes le respect des décisions arbitrales, comme cela du reste a eu constamment lieu, car il n'est point de cas qu'on puisse citer où des Etats, ayant remis leur différend au jugement des arbitres, aient tenté même de se soustraire aux effets de la sentence prononcée contre eux'.

[19] Claim from the USA against Great Britain for the failure of the latter to honour its duties as a neutral in the Secession War, by permitting the construction of ships in British yards used by the Southern states for bellic purposes against the Northern states. It was settled through an arbitral award in favour of the USA dated 14 September 1872, reproduced in G. Wetter, *The International Arbitral Process* (1979), vol. I pp. 48–56.

[20] 'Our persuasion is that the non-intervention policies recommended by Washington will come to an end as soon as the United States will become such a powerful nation that it will be necessarily forced to accept its high position in world affairs. A first idea … is to create a U.S. navy, which evidences the intention to make feel the presence of its flag in all the seas'. Article

19-14   Another reason also presiding over Mr Sarmiento's[21] and others'[22] advocacy of arbitration to determine state claims based on injuries to aliens was the low level of assimilation of immigrants in Argentine society, who maintained their nationality although enjoying all the rights offered to Argentine nationals (Argentine Constitution, Article 20); and who not infrequently abusively sought the protection of their home countries to advance their grievances or gave rise to situations that foreign powers seized upon to interfere in Argentine internal affairs.[23]

19-15   Mr Sarmiento's arbitration treaty proposal entrusted to the Supreme Court of the respondent country – and even of the claimant country if so 'advisable by good and sincere political considerations'[24] – the arbitration of covered disputes, and he emphasised, in further support of his proposal, the fairness of the decisions of the US Supreme Court even in respect of claims against the US government[25]. Although this aspect of the proposal – sometimes looked upon with disfavour[26] – may be regarded today as unrealistic, incompatible with present views on who should arbitrate these kinds of disputes, and not deprived of a certain naiveté,[27] it nonetheless testifies to the appeal of

---

of Mr Sarmiento on the Monroe Doctrine published in 1882 in *El Nacional, Obras Completas, supra* n. 11 vol. XXXIV at pp. 261–262 (author's free translation from the original in Spanish).

[21]   Mr Sarmiento's letter of 29 May 1866, *supra* n. 11 at p. 160.

[22]   A. Saldías, *La politique Italienne au Rio de la Plata – Les étrangers résidents devant le droit international* (Paris, 1889), pp. 10–27. Mr Saldías expressly transcribes his correspondence with Mr Sarmiento on international arbitration in connection with the problems relating to the insufficient assimilation of foreign immigrants in Argentine society.

[23]   On examples concerning the Kingdom of Italy, *see* Saldías, *supra* n. 22 at p. 42 *et seq.*

[24]   Mr Sarmiento's letter of 29 January 1866, *supra* n. 11 at 152: 'esto se conseguiría estipulando que el demandante sometiera la demanda a la Corte Suprema Federal del país demandado, *o quizá lo contrario si así lo aconsejase una buena y sincera política*'. (Emphasis added, author's free English translation).

[25]   Mr Sarmiento's letter of 29 January 1866, *supra* n. 11 at 151–152; his letter of 26 May 1866, *supra* n. 11 at p. 160. Mr Sarmiento's ideas were probably influenced by the constitutional powers vested in the US Supreme Court to decide disputes between the states of the Union. The Argentine Supreme Court was vested with similar powers under the US Constitution-inspired Argentine 1853 Constitution, in connection with disputes between the provinces of Argentina. It is interesting to point out that Carlos Calvo assimilated such powers to those of international tribunals arbitrating disputes between sovereign and independent states: Calvo , *supra* n. 12 vol. III, paras 1780–1781, at pp. 494–495.

[26]   R. Rojas, *El Profeta de la Pampa* (2nd edn. 1945), p. 477 (classic book by one of Sarmiento's leading biographers).

[27]   However, Carlos Calvo shared the same respect for the even-handedness of the US Supreme Court in arbitrating disputes, although from a somewhat more cautious perspective: 'Bien qu'elle ne soit pas absolument indépendante des influences politiques, cette Cour suprême a un

international arbitration to leading statesmen in Latin America and the importance attributed to arbitration for advancing the rule of law in international matters.

19-16 Indeed, Mr Sarmiento took justified pride in vindicating his role as precursor on this question by having parented, 17 years in advance, the idea furthered by Switzerland in 1883 to enter into a permanent arbitration treaty with the USA.[28] His enthusiasm for the future of arbitration and recognition of its importance made him become a member of the Swiss Arbitration League[29] and welcome the submission to arbitration of the Alabama dispute between the USA and Great Britain, despite the latter's initial reluctance to do so,[30] as a significant step towards the peaceful resolution of international disputes by upholding and advancing the rule of law,[31] which was hailed worldwide – even by poets and writers[32] – as a triumph of the cause of peace among nations.

19-17 The very concerns of Mr Sarmiento relating to the creation of a world order based on the rule of law and the peaceful settlement of disputes through international arbitration that would exclude the threat or use of force in international relations as an instrument to advance private or public claims are at the core of the Calvo and Drago Doctrines set forth by distinguished Argentine jurists.

19-18 Carlos Calvo propounded that foreign aliens – like nationals – are subject to the laws and jurisdiction of the state where they do business or reside, including when they suffer harm or damage as a result of local disorder, political

---

caractère auguste d'autorité qui s'impose à la considération et au respect aussi bien de l'ancien monde que du nouveau': Calvo, *supra* n. 12 vol. III, para. 1780, at p. 494.

[28] Mr Sarmiento's letter of 4 September 1884 to Adolfo Saldías, *Obras Completas, supra* n. 11 vol. XXXIV at pp. 268–270. On the Swiss proposal, approved by the Swiss Federal Council on 24 July 1883, *see* Calvo *supra* n. 12 vol. III, para. 1788 at pp. 498–499.

[29] Mr Sarmiento's letter to Adolfo Saldías of 1 September 1887, *Obras Completas, supra* n. 11 vol. XXXIV at pp. 274–275.

[30] This reluctance is reflected, for instance, in the letter of 25 September 1869 from the US Secretary of State Fish to the US Minister Motley at the English Court, reproduced at Wetter, *supra* n. 19 vol. I at pp. 28–35.

[31] Mr Sarmiento's article in *El Censor* of 9 May 1886, *Obras Completas, supra* n. 11 vol. XXXIV at pp. 270–273. Indeed, if the Alabama dispute had not been submitted to arbitration; i.e., if the British argument that only immaterial international wrongs may be subject to international arbitration had been accepted, the remaining option would have been war between the USA and Great Britain: letter from Mr Fish to Mr Motley, *supra* n. 30 at p. 33.

[32] *See* passages of August Strindberg's *The Story of the French Lieutenant*, in Wetter, *supra* n. 19 vol. I at pp. 172–173.

disturbances or civil war. The general principle postulated by Carlos Calvo is that foreign aliens may not claim or enjoy rights, treatment or protection superior to or different from those afforded to nationals.[33] A central and complementary part of the Calvo Doctrine is that, together with asserting the submission of foreign aliens to the laws and jurisdiction of the host country where they reside, it excludes the threat or use of force by their home country in support of their claims or grievances against the host country.[34] However, Carlos Calvo's main focus – certainly because he had fresh in his mind the French blockade of Buenos Aires of 1838–1840 and its outcome – was to exclude the use of military force and foreign intervention by the home country whose nationals or their interests are injured in situations of civil disturbance, that Calvo assimilates to force majeure situations beyond the control – and thus the responsibility – of the country where the disturbance takes place.[35] Calvo clearly manifests that, save such exceptional situations, he does not thereby intend to reject the general legal principle that all persons (public or private) have to pay compensation for the damages they cause.[36]

19-19 It is also clear that Calvo did not take a position adverse to submitting disputes originating in claims from foreign aliens to international arbitration. His Doctrine focused on the rejection of armed force as a means to advance private claims, but does not exclude the possibility of resolving such claims – to the extent endorsed by the home state of the claimant – by resorting to international arbitration.[37] Indeed, Carlos Calvo consecrates 83 pages of his treatise to

---

[33] Calvo, *supra* n. 2 para. 291 at pp. 387–391.

[34] Calvo, *supra* n. 2 para. 294 at pp. 392–393.

[35] Calvo, *supra* n. 12 vol. III, para. 1297 at p. 1556.

[36] Calvo, *supra* n. 12 vol. III, para. 1290 at p. 148:

  'Loin de nous la pensée de méconnaitre les titres des réclamants qui fondent leurs demandes sur cette règle de droit commun que toute personne est tenue de réparer le dommage qu'elle cause; mais ce principe applicable en temps normal et dans des circonstances ordinaires, peut on logiquement songer à l'étendre à des cas si graves et de force majeure qui renversent tout un ordre de choses établi, conduisant souvent un pays au bord de l'abîme? Les situations nous semblent essentiellement différentes, et cette différence justifie de tout point les règles consacrées par la pratique'.

[37] Calvo, *supra* n. 12 vol. I, para. 205 at pp. 350–351:

  'A côté des mobiles politiques, les interventions ont presque toujours eu pour prétexte apparent des lésions des intérêts privés, des réclamations et des demandes d'indemnités pécuniaires en faveur de sujets ou même d'etrangers dont la protection n'était la plupart du temps nullement justifiée en droit strict … La question de principe ou de droit qu'impliquent les affaires d'indemnités pécuniaires se rattachant à l'examen des devoirs mutuels des Etats … nous nous contenterons de faire remarquer ici qu'en droit

international arbitration and the analysis of arbitral decisions.[38] Some of the cases he considers in those pages are international arbitrations involving states, but which originated in claims of private citizens of the claimant state because of conduct attributed to the respondent state.[39] The opinion of Calvo in connection with such awards is invariably positive. Not only does Calvo analyse in detail the different aspects of arbitration, but also expresses his firm adhesion to this means of peaceful resolution of disputes – including those originated in private claims – to avert foreign intervention and the utilisation of force or diplomatic coercion, although he also expresses his concerns as to the difficulties in obtaining the enforcement of awards, which in his opinion largely depends on the pressure of public opinion.[40]

19-20 The Argentine diplomat and jurist Luis María Drago was chiefly concerned with banning the use of force to compel the payment of foreign public debt. As is widely known, the Drago Doctrine was directly triggered by naval action of Italy, Germany and Great Britain against Venezuelan ships and the blockade of Venezuelan ports in support of different claims of the three powers against Venezuela including, but not limited to, its failure to honour its public foreign debt.[41]

19-21 According to Drago, unlike conduct attributable to the state in matters of contract or tort, a state decision not to pay public debt is an act of state, or act *iure imperii*, that is neither justiciable before nor subject to the jurisdiction of the local courts, nor may it give rise to a denial of justice or legitimise the diplomatic protection of the home state of the foreign claimant.[42] Mr Drago contended that

---

international strict le recouvrement des créances et la poursuite des réclamations privées ne justifient pas *de plano* l'intervention armée des gouvernements, et que, comme les Etats européens suivent invariablement cetter règle dans leurs relations réciproques, il n'y a nul motif pour qu'ils ne se l'imposent pas aussi dans leurs rapports avec les Nations du Nouveau Monde'.

[38] Calvo, *supra* n. 12 vol. III, paras 1706–1806 at pp. 432–515.

[39] In addition to the arbitration by the President of Chile of the Argentine-British dispute mentioned *supra* n. 12 and corresponding text, one may mention the 1863 award of the King of Belgium of a dispute between Chile and the USA arising out of the seizure by the Vice-Admiral of the Chilean fleet of moneys obtained by the sale of goods imported by the *Macedonian*, a merchant ship sailing under the US flag, as a result of which Chile had to pay certain sums to the USA (Calvo, *supra* n. 12 vol. III, para. 1726, at pp. 442–443).

[40] *See supra* n. 18.

[41] A. N. Vivot, *La Doctrina Drago* (1911) (reprinted in *Homenaje al Doctor Luis M. Drago* (Oficina Central de Información, Caracas, 1976), pp. 91–106.

[42] Luis M. Drago, 'Los Empréstitos de Estado y la Política Internacional' (published in Spanish on 3 March 1907 in *La Nación of Buenos Aires*, in French in the *Revue Générale de Droit*

because of the sovereign nature of such decision, made on the basis of essential powers concerning the self-government of the state making it, such home state is not entitled either to resort to the use of force to compel the payment of foreign public debt or the enforcement of an arbitral award against the debtor country having defaulted on it.[43] However, Drago[44] did not reject the right of a sovereign state to agree – for example through an international treaty – to international arbitration for resolving such disputes.

19-22 Drago was also of the view that according to international law, the road to diplomatic protection of the claimant's home country in connection with foreign alien grievances arising out of host state conduct or interference in matters of tort or contract becomes expedite only after the prior exhaustion of local remedies and in case of a denial of justice either because no tribunal is made available to hear the claim or if, when hearing the claim, the local courts violate the law through manifest or flagrant injustice.[45] Thus, Drago shared Calvo's position regarding the submission of foreigners and their contractual transactions or tortious conduct to the courts and laws of the host state.

19-23 Nevertheless, like Calvo, Drago also does not exclude the possible direct submission to international arbitration of those disputes. In this latter respect, it must be borne in mind, however, that both from Calvo's and Drago's perspective, and in agreement with ideas generally accepted at the time according to which private persons lacked personality in public international law or direct standing before international tribunals in international disputes, the only form of international arbitration envisaged in connection with such disputes was state-to-state, rather than injured alien-state; ideas, in fact, that married well with the position of both jurists that international claims from foreign aliens are to be decided pursuant to the local laws and by resorting to the local courts of the host state; and that only a denial of justice[46] permitted the elevation of the ensuing

---

International Public, and in English in the *American Journal of International Law*), reprinted in *Homenaje al Doctor Luis María Drago* (Oficina de Información, Caracas, 1976), pp. 53–54, 83–84.

[43] Drago, *supra* n. 42 at pp. 55, 84. Note of Minister Drago to Minister García Merou of 29 December 1902, reprinted in Luis M. Drago, *La República Argentina y el Caso de Venezuela* (Oficina Central de Información, Caracas, 1976), pp. 17–23.

[44] Note of Mr Drago of 29 December 1902, reproduced in *La República Argentina y el Caso de Venezuela* (Oficina Central de Información, Caracas, 1976), p. 19.

[45] Drago, *supra* n. 42 at pp. 49–53, 83.

[46] A notion subject to varying interpretations, that may mean a violation attributable to the state or any of its organs, agencies or instrumentalities of the rights of foreign aliens as defined by international law, or the violation of such rights by the judiciary branch of a state either by

dispute to the international plane, in which case it could become a matter to be dealt with at the inter-state level, including through international arbitration mutually agreed by the parties, but without justifying resorting to armed intervention or other forms of coercion of the home state to seek or obtain redress for the private claim or impose its submission to international arbitration. According to such ideas, international arbitration in connection with such claims does not apply automatically but must be freely agreed upon by the states involved. For this reason the Latin American states did not accept the Porter formula received through the 1907 Hague Convention or ratified it with reservations. This Convention permits the home state of the foreign private claimant to resort to the use of force against a host state which refuses to arbitrate claims arising out of its public debt or contractual obligations, since it imposes on such state a direct obligation to entrust to international arbitration each and every dispute arising out of the interpretation or application of state contracts with a foreign private party and removes such disputes from the jurisdiction of local courts without any previous specific undertaking of such state to do so.[47]

19-24 The Calvo Clause inserted in state contracts with foreign parties – inspired in the Calvo Doctrine – deserves separate and special consideration. Its appearance as a reaction to imperialistic ambitions of the European powers in Latin America[48] may be also considered part of the response of Latin American countries to so-called 'gun boat diplomacy', too often present in their relations with the USA. Clearly, the homeward trend incarnated in the Clause, including its rejection of international arbitration as a means to resolving such claims, usually attributed to the Calvo Clause,[49] goes hand in hand with political events affecting the evolution of international arbitration in the region.

---

making an unjust decision, unjustifiedly delaying a decision on the foreigner's claims, or by denying the foreign alien access to the judicial system of the host state: L.A. Podestá Costa, *La Responsabilidad Internacional del Estado* (Academia Interamericana de Derecho Comparado e Internacional, La Habana, Cuba, 1948), pp. 163–223 at p. 198.

[47] Podestá Costa, *supra* n. 46 at pp. 201–202. E. Borchard, *Diplomatic Protection of Citizens Abroad* (1915), paras 122–123 at pp. 318–322.

[48] Borchard, *supra* n. 47 para. 382 at pp. 820–821.

[49] C. Frutos Peterson, *L'Emergence de l'Arbitrage Commercial International en Amérique Latine: L'Efficacité de son Droit* (2003), p. 26:

'en réalité, c'est sur la base de la Clause Calvo, et non pas sur la base de la Doctrine Calvo, comme certains auteurs l'affirment, que l'arbitrage fut interdit ou rejeté indirectement dans les contrats d'investissement entre des étrangers et des gouvernements (ou des organismes publics) d'Amérique latine ou dans des accords internationaux'.

19-25 The Calvo Clause normally requires the submission of all claims originated in injuries caused to a foreign alien subject to the Clause to local courts and laws and a waiver from resorting to international means for the resolution of disputes concerning injuries to such aliens, at least so long as local remedies have not been exhausted, and if exhausted, if a denial of justice has not been incurred. Such clause is normally seen as embodying strong Latin American distrust regarding international means of dispute resolution, including international arbitration, to hear and resolve such kinds of claims.

19-26 However, rather than a total exclusion of international arbitration for resolving such disputes, the Calvo Clause may be seen as a denial to grant direct standing to a private claimant before an international instance to seek redress of its grievances, and as a confirmation of the public international law principle that the resolution of the ensuing disputes may not be raised to the international plane if no denial of justice has been incurred after exhaustion of local remedies, unless an international agreement or treaty provides otherwise.[50] If the Clause is read in the light of the thoughts of Calvo as expressed in his Doctrine, it should be understood as precluding – even after the exhaustion of local remedies – the foreign alien from directly accessing, as a subject of public international law, international means to advance his claims against the host state, but not as impeding his home state and the host state from agreeing on or resorting to international arbitration to deal with such grievances, i.e., precisely the kind of dispute resolution mechanism that should be substituted for diplomatic protection

---

[50] However, it is disputed whether the Calvo Clause, and the correlative obligation it usually imposes not to resort to international means of redress, only applies to disputes relating to the contract between the host state and the foreign alien, or also extends to breaches of international law, including when any such breach is a denial of justice. It has been contended that the renunciation of diplomatic protection it entails only covers disputes arising out of the contract at stake but not other activities unrelated to such contract undertaken by the foreign private party in the host state (Podestá Costa, *supra* n. 46 at p. 216). Also, as far as a denial of justice is concerned, a distinction has been made between a denial of justice incurred in redressing a breach of international law, and a denial of justice suffered by the foreign alien in its efforts before local courts and authorities of the host state to obtain redress for the contractual breaches suffered by it: nevertheless, in neither of such instances would seeking international redress for the grievances of the foreign alien be impeded by the Calvo Clause: *North American Dredging Company of Texas(USA)* v. *United Mexican States,* 31 March 1926, at (1926) 20 A.J.I.L 800; John Dugard, Special Rapporteur, *Third Report on Diplomatic Protection,* Addendum (International Law Commission, 16 April 2002); United Nations General Assembly, UN Doc. A/CN.4/523/Add.1, pp. 13–15. For a less favourable consideration of the validity and efficacy of the Calvo Clause in international law, *see* K. Lipstein, 'The Place of the Calvo Clause in International Law' in (1945) 22 *Brit. YB Int'l L* 130.

and other forms of coercion, according to Calvo's ideas, to advance the peaceful resolution of disputes and the predominance of the rule of law.

19-27 Indeed, the mere fact that the Clause is generally presented as a contractual undertaking means that the opposite path of agreeing on arbitration for the resolution of disputes originated in such grievances – even by the host state accepting that the foreign alien directly take its claims against the host state to an international arbitral tribunal agreed or consented to by both parties – is not incompatible with Calvo's ideas as expressed through his Doctrine. In this respect, it should be pointed out that when the Clause has found its way into provisions of the Constitutions of Latin American states and thus gone beyond a merely contractual status, it has been normally limited to excluding the foreign alien's direct access to the diplomatic protection of its home state absent the prior exhaustion of local remedies, without however limiting the possibility of submitting to international arbitration disputes arising between foreign aliens and host states, even without going through the prior exhaustion of local remedies.[51] Thus, those constitutional provisions are expressions of the Calvo Doctrine to the extent it condemns the use of diplomatic protection as a disguised means of utilising force to advance international claims without necessarily excluding the possibility freely to agree on international arbitration for resolving disputes originated in claims of foreign aliens by asserting the exclusive jurisdiction of the host state courts, as the Calvo Clause purports to do. For this reason, it seems difficult to read into such provisions a constitutional law prohibition to agree on international arbitration in connection with those disputes. This is confirmed by the ratification of bilateral investment treaties and the World Bank 1965 Washington Convention on the Settlement of Investment Disputes (the 'Washington Convention') by practically all Latin American countries, including

---

[51] *See* provisions of the Constitutions of El Salvador, Guatemala, Honduras, Nicaragua, Bolivia, Costa Rica, Ecuador, Mexico in F. Oschmann, 'Calvo-Doktrin und Calvo-Klauseln' in (1993) 30 *Abhandlungen zum Recht der Internationalen Wirtschaft* 382. Article 127 of the Venezuelan Constitution (Art. 151 of the present Constitution of 17 November 1999) is the only one that clearly commands the exclusive jurisdiction of Venezuelan courts in respect of 'public interest contracts'. However, not only does there not seem to be a clear definition of 'public interest contracts' in the Venezuelan literature, but also, this very provision indicates that the exclusive jurisdiction of Venezuelan courts in respect of such contracts shall proceed unless 'that would not be appropriate in view of their nature', a matter remaining equally unclear. Consequently, this provision is far from constituting an absolute prohibition of foreign arbitration in respect of state contracts under Venezuelan law, and much less, an exclusion of the possibility of directly submitting claims from foreign aliens to international arbitration involving the alien and the host state.

many of those showing such provisions in their Constitutions. Article 27(1) of the Washington Convention permits the submission of investment disputes to international arbitration and limits diplomatic protection to instances where the host state fails to abide by the ensuing award.

19-28 The Doctrines of Calvo and Drago – and particularly the Calvo Clause – have been subject to different criticism. Unexpectedly, one of the first, regarding the Calvo Doctrine, came precisely from Mr Alberdi, a distinguished countryman and contemporary of Mr Calvo, the father of the Argentine 1853 National Constitution,[52] who wrote on the first edition of Mr Calvo's treatise. Mr Alberdi's comments were not devoid of personal animosity against Mr Calvo, whom Mr. Alberdi considered an ambitious opportunist, a plagiarist, and influenced by Rosas' chauvinistic ideas.[53] Besides this, Mr Alberdi had more in mind the status of the foreign immigrant in Argentina seeking the protection of his home country than the modern foreign investor doing transnational business. Nevertheless, some of Mr Alberdi's remarks were to be echoed later by those favouring investment protection under international law. Mr Alberdi emphasised the obligations of the host country to provide protection and security to aliens, to protect them and their interests on the basis of the aliens' justified expectations originated in their reliance on the legal framework offered by the host country, and the right of aliens, should harm result from the frustration of those expectations, to be indemnified. Mr Alberdi was of the view that respecting the rights of aliens and ensuring that they would be indemnified should such rights suffer from conduct of the host country was in the interest of such country, eager to attract foreign resources, and would also contribute to improving the standards of protection and treatment of its own citizens.[54]

---

[52] *See* P. Groussac, 'Las Bases de Alberdi y el Desarrollo Constitucional' in *Estudios de Historia Argentina* (Buenos Aires, 1918), pp. 261–371.

[53] J.B. Alberdi, 'Notas Para el Juicio Crítico del Derecho Internacional Teórico y Práctico de Europa y América de Carlos Calvo' (1868) in *Escritos Póstumos* (Universidad Nacional de Quilmes, 2002), vol. III, pp. 117, 121–125, 157–158. *See also*, J. Mayer, *Alberdi y su Tiempo* (2nd edn., Academia Nacional de Derecho y Ciencias Sociales de Buenos Aires, 1973), vol. II, pp. 942–943.

[54] Alberdi, *supra* n. 53 at pp. 139–140:

'es un mal que el derecho del hombre se haga respetar aunque ese hombre sea un extranjero? Puede el derecho del extranjero ser respetado, sin que acabe por serlo igualmente el del nacional? La violación de esa seguridad prometida por las leyes como condición de su inmigración, da lugar a una de dos cosas: o el extranjero se va del país que lo arruina, o el país le indemniza la ruina que su inseguridad le ha ocasionado, si quiere retenerlo ... No podéis darle la seguridad cuya promesa le habéis hecho venir? Reparadle el perjuicio que no habéis podido evitarle, conforme a la promesa de vuestras

19-29   However, on the main political and legal points addressed by the Calvo and Drago Doctrines – to exclude the threat or use of force and armed intervention or diplomatic coercion in support of the claims of private persons exerted by their home countries, to further the peaceful resolution of disputes, including by resorting to arbitration freely agreed by the host state, to buttress the general public international law principle that, absent a treaty obligation providing otherwise, foreign alien claims relating to economic matters are only elevated to the international plane after exhaustion of local remedies and a denial of justice, without which the home state is not entitled to resort to diplomatic protection, to affirm the principle of equality of states – their contribution to the formation of modern public international law is indisputable.[55] It should be noted that when these Doctrines came to life, the world had not yet recognised the principle of equality among sovereign nations, the condemnation of the use of force and the principle of non-intervention through multilateral instruments such as the Charter of the United Nations.[56]

19-30   Thus, the ideas and efforts of Sarmiento, Calvo and Drago belong to the same political scheme – Kampf ums Recht[57] – aimed at combatting the state of lawlessness, too often characterising the relations between strong powers and weak nations, by promoting a world order based on rules of law upholding equal sovereign rights for all states and the exclusion of foreign intervention and the unilateral use of force. If such scheme may be considered homeward oriented insofar as it exalts the recourse to local remedies, it nonetheless also favours international ones since it upholds international arbitration as a mechanism

---

leyes. Le debéis esa reparación en buen derecho; y felizmente vuestra conveniencia coincide con vuestro deber'.

[55]   In connection with the Drago doctrine *see* J. Fisher Williams, 'International Law and International Financial Obligations Arising from Contract' in (1924) *Bibliotheca Visseriana, Tomus Secundus* 34. For example, Mr Drago considered his doctrine as a political defence of the rights of South American countries, *supra* n. 42 at p. 63; J. Vanossi, 'Luis María Drago y la Deuda Pública Externa Latinoamericana' in *El Derecho*, advanced sheet of 30 April 1987, p. 4; Podestá Costa, *supra* n. 46 at p. 201.

[56]   Articles 1(1), 2(3), (4) and (7) of the United Nations Charter clearly exclude foreign intervention and the threat or use of force, even to the purpose of forcing a state to accept international arbitration or enforce ensuing arbitral awards.

[57]   In his classic work, Rüdolf von Ihering considered the struggle for rights as an element inherent in the idea of law having peace as its final objective. For Ihering, the attainment of peace depends on the recognition of the rights fought for, which is assimilated to the achievement of justice based on the balance established by the rule of law between the competing interests it reconciles. He expressly included international law as one of the legal arenas where the struggle for rights, i.e., for peace through the attainment of justice, takes place. *See* his *La Lucha por el Derecho* (1872) (Adolfo Posada (trans.) (Spanish), Perrot, Buenos Aires (1977)), pp. 122–123.

permitting avoidance of the recourse to brute force and advancing the triumph of the rule of law in international relations. Although, depending on varying political circumstances, those paths may not have always converged, the objective was always the same – to have the rule of public international law prevail in international transactions – and so, even the homeward trend facets of the Calvo Doctrine and its cousin the Calvo Clause, should be seen in that light as well, and not as an expression of chauvinism and savage isolationism, that would have been incompatible with the Argentine highly Europeanised administrations, and with the intellectual elites nurturing and advancing the Calvo and Drago Doctrines, which were clearly inspired by and implemented liberal ideas aimed at developing international free trade and economic exchanges, and according to which international arbitration is and was called to play such a paramount role. Consequently, even in their homeward connotations, those doctrines should be seen as pursuing the objective, not of a priori-stically rejecting the formation of public international law rules on those matters or excluding them from the ambit of international dispute resolution, but of advancing a state of affairs conducive to the formation of such rules, and the international adjudication of such disputes, based on a fair and just treatment of the state interests involved.

19-31 Promoting and firming up international arbitration played a central role in such scheme, the end objective of which was to apply to relationships between 'First-Class Powers' and 'Second Class Powers' the same rules expressly or tacitly applied in the relationships between 'First-Class Powers' only.[58] This explains why it has been stated that 'in the matter of referring national disputes to arbitration, the course of Latin America has been of a remarkably advanced character', a circumstance not found surprising, since 'it is to be noted that smaller nations have been much more willing to rely upon law for their vindication than have larger ones who have very generally preferred to rest their supposed rights on their ability to maintain them'.[59]

---

[58] As graphically expressed in connection with the Calvo Doctrine as far as it furthers the principle of exhaustion of local remedies: G. Winfield Scott, 'International Law and the Drago Doctrine' in (1906) CLXXXIII *North American Review* 602 at p. 603.
[59] J. Ralston, *International Arbitration from Athens to Locarno* (1929), pp. 148–149.

III. Expansion of International Commercial Arbitration in Latin America

19-32   That the political factors, and doctrines responsive to them, existing or developed by Argentine jurists in the late second half of the nineteenth century and the early years of the twentieth century, evidencing a certain Latin American homeward trend aimed at counteracting diplomatic protection and foreign intervention, did not reveal a deep-seated hostility against arbitration is shown by the fact that the first three decades of the latter century witnessed a surge in and growing prosperity of arbitration for the resolution of commercial disputes, particularly after the end of the First World War. Although such a phenomenon first manifested itself at the domestic level, it was soon accompanied by an incipient expansion of international commercial arbitration involving Latin American parties or interests.

19-33   A sign revealing this trend is the multiplication of court decisions regarding arbitration cases in this period and the matters dealt with in such cases. Thus, adverse feelings to the submission to international arbitration of matters involving state sovereign interests and their political expression could not conceal the enormous usefulness of arbitration as an instrument of peace or for the peaceful settlement of international disputes in the area of both private and semi-public transactions, particularly during and in the aftermath of the First World War. It is the Latin American merchant community that deserves praise for inaugurating this new – albeit of then limited duration – and promising stage in the history of Latin American arbitration. Unlike the recent arbitration boom in Latin America of the last two decades, this initial flourishing of arbitration in the region originated in the commercial and trade sectors, and not in government circles; i.e., from bottom to top.

19-34   An example of these developments is the 1916 bilateral agreement between the Buenos Aires Stock Exchange and the US Chamber of Commerce setting up a system of institutional commercial arbitration based on two five-member arbitration committees or panels composed of nominees of both the Buenos Aires Stock Exchange and US Chamber of Comerce – one sitting in Argentina and the other in the USA – to resolve trade disputes arising out of transactions between commercial operators of both countries.[60] This system is a direct precedent of the creation of the Court of Arbitration of the International

---

[60]   Article VI of the Agreement, published in *Boletín Oficial de la Bolsa de Comercio de Buenos Aires* (17 April 1916), p. 531.

Chamber of Commerce and the first version of its Arbitration Rules, which saw the light in 1923.[61] Already at this incipient stage, international arbitration was perceived as going beyond the strict area of private commercial transactions. In the inaugural speech launching this system, given in Buenos Aires in 1916, the Honorary Vice-President of the US Chamber of Commerce, John R. Fahey, said:

> After all, arbitration of commercial disputes between businessmen of different countries is but a modest step. It must be followed by setting up a project for the resolution through similar means of disputes involving governments and corporations of individuals from different countries. There have been situations of this sort that have often given rise to serious perturbations in several parts of the world. In many of these situations, years of endless discussions, unnecessary irritation, which often were on the point of triggering wars, would have been avoided if the disputed issues would have been submitted to disinterested experts.[62]

19-35 Economic and political events were not, of course, indifferent to such developments in the arbitration field. Argentina's economic progress was premised on capitalistic free trade ideas, and the resulting trade expansion was necessarily accompanied by initiatives to set up private dispute resolution mechanisms to deal with ensuing international disputes. The support of such trend by the USA, essentially the consequence of the difficulties in accessing European markets because of the First World War, that created the need for US industries to find alternative markets, was matched by the Argentine need to obtain manufactured goods which, had it not been because of the war, would have normally come from Europe. An additional reason may have been the need already perceived by US business to guarantee the uninterrupted flow of commodities from other nations should the USA eventually get involved in the war, as finally happened by the end of 1916. This may explain in part why the elaborate arbitration institutional mechanism agreed upon by the Buenos Aires Stock Exchange and US Chamber of Commerce granted Argentine importers the distinct concession of permitting them to resort to the arbitral tribunal placed in the country where the goods imported would likely be at the moment of checking their physical condition, which could give rise to claims as to their quality or

---

[61] Rules of the Court of Arbitration of the International Chamber of Commerce (1923). E. Schwartz, 'The Practices and Experiences of the ICC Court' in *Conservatory and Provisional Measures in ICC Arbitration* (Publication No. 519, ICC Publishing, 1993), p. 45 (note 1).

[62] Address published in Spanish in *Boletín Oficial de la Bolsa de Comercio de Buenos Aires* (17 April 1916), p. 527 (author's translation from the Spanish original).

quantity (Argentina as to manufactured goods), for the resolution of disputes arising with their US counterparts.[63]

19-36 However, it is not by chance that, as from 1919, a leading Argentine jurist, Nicolás Matienzo, in parallel developed a doctrine – based on public and constitutional law principles – asserting the exclusive jurisdiction of national courts and the rejection of arbitration to hear disputes concerning the validity, exercise and scope of sovereign state rights or the decision of certain matters governed by the Argentine Constitution.[64] There is a certain correspondence between such doctrine and the incipient presence of Argentine trade interests in the international markets. For example, 20 years later, by resorting to it, the Argentine Supreme Court of Justice invalidated choice-of-forum clauses providing for the jurisdiction of foreign courts found in a contract of affreightment for the carriage of goods by sea from or to Argentine ports, on the basis that matters relating to foreign maritime commerce concern the superior interests of the Argentine Republic, are directly governed by the Argentine Constitution and federal laws, and are thus subject to the exclusive jurisdiction of the Argentine federal courts.[65] It should be pointed out that also in this respect a similar evolution was then present in comparative law. In any case, such doctrine did not purport to extend to the broad range of private and commercial transactions not involving sovereign state interests, that remain arbitrable, nor exclude state parties from arbitral adjudication in their commercial dealings, or activity *iure gestionis*.[66]

---

[63] As highlighted by Ricardo Aldao, the Argentine negotiator of the agreement finally reached by the Argentine Stock Exchange and the US Chamber of Commerce, in his speech rendered on the occasion of executing the agreement, *see Boletín Oficial de la Bolsa de Comercio de Buenos Aires*, p. 543.

[64] N. Matienzo, *Cuestiones de Derecho Público Argentino* (1925), vol. I, pp. 5–8, 473–484. For a general description of this doctrine and its ulterior developments with multiple doctrinal and case law references, *see* H. Grigera Naón, 'El Estado y el Arbitraje Internacional con Particulares' in (1989) II/III *Revista Jurídica de Buenos Aires* 127 at pp. 143–163; from the same author and on the same topic, 'Arbitration in Latin America: Overcoming Traditional Hostility (an Update)' in (1991) 22 *Inter-American Law Review* 203, esp. at pp. 213–217.

[65] Argentine Supreme Court, *Fallos* 176–218. This principle is today embodied in art. 614 of the Argentine Navigation Law, Law-Decree 20094/73 imposing the jurisdiction of Argentine courts in connection with contracts of affreightment or of carriage of goods by sea according to which the goods are delivered in the port of destination. However, its art. 621 permits submitting disputes arising out of such contracts to foreign courts or arbitration after the dispute has arisen, which means that the exclusion of arbitration outside of Argentina – even in a case involving constitutional principles and federal laws – is not always absolute.

[66] Matienzo, *supra* n. 64 at p. 7.

19-37 The ideas of Mr Matienzo introduced a distinct innovation as far as the arbitrability of sovereign interest matters is concerned, which was not present in the Calvo Doctrine. The Calvo Doctrine is a public international law doctrine aimed at fashioning certain principles at the level of public international law, without thereby a priori-stically excluding from the realm of international arbitration any particular type of dispute ripe, according to the principles of such doctrine, for adjudication on the international plane. The ideas of Mr Matienzo are based on domestic constitutional and public law principles totally excluding foreign court or arbitral adjudication of certain disputes abstracted from the public international law sphere where the Calvo Doctrine situates itself. For that reason, the ideas of Mr Matienzo and their legal consequences, including the exclusion of foreign adjudication or international arbitration in connection with certain disputes, should necessarily see their scope limited to the national jurisdiction receiving them and do not transcend per se to the public international law dimension.

19-38 Admittedly, the above historical overview is partial and relatively far removed in time. However, despite an ever-changing political and social scenario, many of the questions, private and public interests, emotions and ideas raised, at stake or formulated at this early stage, are still lingering in varying degrees behind the scene of present matters and issues regarding the growth of international arbitration in Latin America.

IV. POLITICAL AND SOCIO-ECONOMIC DEVELOPMENTS

19-39 Ensuing Latin American political and socio-economic developments accentuated a general homeward trend relating to the resolution of international disputes that distanced itself from the internationalist ideals underlying such trends from the Calvo or Drago perspective.

19-40 One of such developments was the 1930 economic crisis and its causes, that had a devastating impact on international trade and were accompanied or followed by protectionist economic policies that brought about political and economic isolationism and the weakening of the rule of law in the international arena.

19-41 Besides, the then parallel upsurge of extreme right-wing ideologies nurtured from Italy and Germany, that translated into legal doctrines magnifying the powers of the state to the detriment of individual freedom, led to considering with a suspect eye any development of private means of dispute resolution challenging the monopoly of state courts on the administration of justice, or to the outright exclusion of such means. Such ideologies too often did find their way to legislators and governments and the minds of judges and members of the legal profession in Latin America.

19-42 Among the long-lasting consequences of this state of affairs one should mention a tendency to limit arbitrable matters and the stagnation of legislative initiatives for updating obsolete provisions regarding arbitration, mostly found in codes of civil procedure dating back to the end of the nineteenth century or the early years of the twentieth century, or responding to legal ideas and doctrines going back to that time.

19-43 Other reasons led this state of affairs to perpetuate itself, with scattered exceptions, until the early 1980s. During the 1970s the Calvo Clause gained new notoriety as a result of the formation of the Andean Pact and the issuance of Decision 24 and its progeny banning international arbitration from the resolution of foreign investment and technological disputes. In parallel, around that time, different resolutions of the United Nations regarding the treatment of expropriation of the property of foreign aliens were indisputably inspired in homeward ideas underlying the Calvo Doctrine and Clause. Nevertheless – consistently with the ideals of Calvo and Drago – those ideas were pursued at the international level by supporting an international consensus aimed at shaping the rule of public international law without excluding international arbitration and other international means of dispute resolution for resolving disputes relating to compensation for the expropriation of alien property.[67]

19-44 Despite this latter circumstance, also at that time, Latin American academic, judicial and governmental sectors opposing the submission to international arbitration of matters relating to the national public interest or the exercise of state sovereign powers, including, but not limited to, foreign investment matters, revived arguments drawn from such countries' domestic

---

[67] UN General Assembly Resolution 3281 (XXIX), 12 December 1974 (Charter of Economic Rights and Duties of States), Chapter II, Article 2, para. 2(c) provides that disputes over compensation for expropriation of foreign property will be governed by the laws and decided by the courts of the host state unless the states concerned have freely and mutually agreed to resort to other peaceful means of dispute resolution 'on the basis of the sovereign equality of States and in accordance with the principle of free choice of means'; its predecessor, UN General Assembly Resolution 1803 (XVII), para. 4, had already asserted the need to exhaust local remedies prior to elevating a dispute on compensation in case of expropriation to the international plane.

public and constitutional laws, to affirm that those matters are non-arbitrable or non-justiciable before international arbitral tribunals.[68] We have already referred to early manifestations of this trend in Argentina.

19-45 As indicated when analysing the Argentine precedent to this trend, the rejection of international arbitration as a means for resolving disputes arising out of foreign investment, administrative, public interest or public law matters and of the possibility of entering into international agreements submitting such disputes to international arbitration embodied in this trend depends on arguments based on domestic public law principles and provisions not necessarily premised upon the presence or absence of constitutional clauses modelled after the ideas of Carlos Calvo or of public international law theories inspired by them.

19-46 As will be seen later, such trend recently acquired proportions not always easy to reconcile with its historical origins and legal rationale. One of the questionable aspects of this development is an expansive definition of administrative acts, the validity and sometimes also the effects of which are considered removed from the jurisdiction of arbitral tribunals. In some instances, the scope assigned to the notion of administrative act is so vast that it covers state activity or conduct not easily categorised as state sovereign action in the pursuit of vital state interests or as constituting a legitimate exercise of exorbitant sovereign powers to safeguard such interests.[69] In any case, different manifestations of this homeward trend underlie today debates and court decisions regarding the international arbitrability of public interest matters concerning Latin American states.

19-47 This state of affairs only started to change by the late 1970s and early 1980s, also for political and economic reasons. By then, many Latin American countries, including the Andean Pact countries,[70] were abandoning or had abandoned, or were substantially tempering, their positions adverse to international arbitration in this respect because of their general economic and financial weaknesses and the decided stance adopted by the US Reagan administration against the Calvo Clause as well as in response to President

---

[68] Oschmann, *supra* n. 51 at pp. 313–323.

[69] On this matter with particular emphasis on the Latin American situation, *see* E. Silva Romero, 'ICC Arbitration and State Contracts' in (2002) 13 ICC *International Court of Arbitration Bulletin* 34; H. Grigera Naón, 'Les Contrats d'Etat: Quelques Réflexions' in (2003) 3 *Revue de l'Arbitrage* 667 at pp. 671–672.

[70] *See* Grigera Naón, 'Overcoming Traditional Hostility', *supra* n. 64 at pp. 217–218.

George Bush's Enterprise for the Americas Initiative aimed at creating a free trade zone in the Americas. This change in policy – also attuned to the prevalence of neo-liberal economic theories, the accelerated globalisation of the world economy and the endorsement by the administrations of many Latin American countries of economic policies compatible with such ideas and realities – was later reflected during the last two decades of the twentieth century by the proliferation of bilateral investment protection treaties ('BITs') and the incorporation of Mexico – traditionally a firm upholder of the Calvo Doctrine – into NAFTA, which includes a Chaper XI for the protection of foreign investment allowing the foreign investor to resort to international arbitration to advance its claims against the host state.[71] Naturally, BITs usually restrain and limit the matters that may be rendered non-justiciable or non-arbitrable under the national laws of the host state to those falling outside the scope of the BIT's provisions or the jurisdiction of arbitration tribunals set up according to such provisions. On the other hand, in connection with disputes subject to arbitration under a BIT, the exhaustion of local remedies prior to resorting to international arbitration is not required unless the applicable BIT provisions provide or permit otherwise. Argentina, the country of origin of Carlos Calvo and Luis María Drago, despite the vocal opposition of its press in the early 1980s to US policies contrary to the Calvo Doctrine or Clause,[72] has ratified dozens of such Treaties and is presently involved in not less than 30 international arbitrations arising therefrom.

---

[71] On this shift in Latin American policies, *see ibid.* pp. 221–223.

[72] An Editorial entitled 'Ataque a la Doctrina Calvo' in *La Nación* (the leading Argentine newspaper), 19 June 1981 criticizes US policies aimed at conditioning US economic aid plans to an abandonment of the Calvo Doctrine by the recipient country. The Editorial says among other things that the Calvo Doctrine is a pillar of the public international law of the Americas and that US policies are exactly the opposite of the good neighbour policies under the Franklin D. Roosevelt administration, as proclaimed by Summer Welles in 1937. An Editorial of another leading Argentine newspaper, the English language *Buenos Aires Herald*, 22 June 1981, entitled 'Reagan vs. Calvo', shares similar views and ends up on the following suggestive note:

> 'The Calvo Doctrine represents an insurance policy for Latin American countries against outside intervention in largely internal affairs and should, if judiciously applied, be respected by foreign firms investing in that region. These firms have little to fear of the doctrine as such if their contracts are tightly written in accordance with local law. The great fear would be brusque changes in the legal structure of a Latin American country due to political upheaval and insurance against being caught out in that sort of situation is a matter for industrial intelligence and not for government action against broad Latin American policies that help protect local interests'.

19-48   That following this trend did not depend on the adherence or not to any particular ideology, but on political reasons determined by discrete economic realities and the perception by each country of the conditions better adapted to attracting foreign investment and furthering economic development is proved by the fact that Cuba is party to numerous international agreements following the general pattern presented by BITs that permit the private investor to submit its claims against the host state to international arbitration.[73] In fact, different political and economic needs or priorities may give rise to different outcomes as to the degree of acceptance of international arbitration regarding investment disputes.

19-49   For example, Venezuela is probably the only Latin American country having incorporated, in its internal legislation on the Promotion and Protection of Foreign Investment, provisions regarding the application of international law and on the submission to arbitration of investment disputes. This legislation provides that foreign investment in Venezuela is entitled to just and equitable treatment in accordance with the 'rules and criteria' of international law, and that foreign investors are not subject to expropriation or confiscation, or equivalent measures in violation of international law. It also allows the Venezuelan state and the foreign investor to enter into stabilisation agreements, requiring the approval of the Venezuelan Congress, freezing tax, export promotion and other specific benefits applicable to the investor and investment covered by their provisions on the date the stabilisation agreement was entered into. Nevertheless, submission of investment disputes to arbitration, national or international, is not free from qualifications or ambiguities and not so straightforward. Any claims arising out of the application of this legislation, once the administrative means of recourse under Venezuelan law have been exhausted, may be submitted to the jurisdiction of either the Venezuelan courts or 'Venezuelan arbitral tribunals'. In the case of claims arising out of stabilisation agreements, only submission to institutional arbitration in accordance with the Venezuelan Arbitration Act is permitted; thus, the question whether, in this specific case, a submission to international

---

[73] Among many others, agreements between Cuba and (1) Argentina of 30 November 1995 (art. 9, UNCITRAL Arbitration); (2) People's Republic of China of 24 April 1995 (art. 9, UNCITRAL Arbitration; arbitration only applies to resolve disputes regarding the amount of compensation); (3) Kingdom of Spain of 27 May 1994 (art. XI: the private investor may choose between UNCITRAL and ICC arbitration); (4) Germany of 30 April 1996 (art. 11, ad hoc arbitration, with the Chairman of the ICC International Court of Arbitration as appointing authority); (5) Great Britain of 30 January 1995 (art. 8, the parties may agree on either UNCITRAL or ICC arbitration); (6) Italy of 7 May 1993 (art. 9, ad hoc arbitration with the President of the Permanent Court of Arbitration at The Hague acting as appointing authority).

arbitration of the foreign investor's claim is possible or not under the terms of such Act, is left without a clear answer. However, if the investment dispute (including under any stabilisation agreement entered into according to this legislation's provisions) is covered by a BIT to which Venezuela is a party or by the Washington Convention, or by the Multilateral Investment Guarantee Agency (MIGA) Convention, international arbitration is allowed.[74] Finally, it is worth pointing out that this legislation permits the direct submission to an international arbitration tribunal (without prior exhaustion of local remedies) of the resolution of any dispute between the Venezuelan state and the home state of the foreign investor (in absence of a BIT entered into by both states) arising out of the interpretation or application of such legislation not resolved through diplomatic means after a period of 12 months. The ensuing arbitral decision will be binding and final.[75]

19-50 It cannot be concluded, however, that the widespread ratification of such treaties, which have not met with acceptance by all Latin American countries – Brazil remains a distinct and important example – or the isolated Venezuelan legislation example just mentioned necessarily means that these countries have abandoned their position that the Calvo Doctrine is a part of public international law from the Latin American perspective as to the submission of foreign investors to local laws and the jurisdiction of local courts and the rejection of diplomatic protection or the elevation to the international plane of foreign investment claims before local remedies have been exhausted and a denial of justice has been incurred.[76] Indeed, the very existence of such treaties, and the fact that their signing with their Latin American counterparts has been strongly

---

[74] Venezuela, Ley de Promoción y Protección de Inversiones (Gaceta Extraordinaria No. 5390 of 22 October 1999), arts 6, 11, 17–18, 21–23. Venezuela has ratified several BITs and a free trade agreement having Mexico and Colombia also as parties that includes a chapter on foreign investment protection modelled after NAFTA's Chapter 11: T.B. de Maekelt and C. Madrid M., 'Al Rescate del Arbitraje en Venezuela' in *El Derecho Privado y Procesal en Venezuela (Homenaje a Gustavo Planchart Manrique)*, vol. II, pp. 719, 724–726.

[75] Venezuela, Ley de Promoción y Protección de Inversiones, art. 21.

[76] As has been recently stated:

'Latin American States still cling to the Clause as an important feature of their regional approach to international law. While they have demonstrated some flexibility in their attitude to new institutions creating dispute settlement procedures for foreign investors, there is no doubt that many of these institutions are still judged by their adherence to the Calvo Clause. Moreover, key resolutions of the General Assembly on international economic law show the strong influence of Calvo':

Dugard, *supra* n. 50 at 15.

supported by the central nations, may be an indication that, except for the matters covered by them, the Calvo Doctrine maintains its claims of legitimacy under public international law. On the other hand, there are noticeable differences from BIT to BIT as to the matters subject to BIT provisions and thus to international arbitration; there is also a new generation of BITs, in part inspired in NAFTA Chapter 11, reducing the areas falling within the scope of treaty provisions or directly subject to international law, thus concomitantly reducing the matters excluded from domestic law or subject to international arbitration under the treaty at stake, both circumstances underlying the fact that BITs constitute an exception to the general international law rule subjecting foreign investors and investments to the laws and courts of the host country and requiring the prior exhaustion of local remedies or a denial of justice as a precondition to accessing remedies available on the international plane. The recent Chapter 10 on Foreign Investment of the Chile-United States Free Trade Agreement is an example of this development.[77] However, the mushrooming of these treaties unequivocally denotes a radical shift in the attitude of Latin American countries vis-à-vis international arbitration, not only in respect of state–party arbitrations within a public international law context, but also in regard to commercial arbitration at large, that is in tune with the general attitude favourable to arbitration underlying the ideas of Calvo and Drago. Nevertheless, as more recent developments considered below seem to indicate, the ratification of such treaties is not always a reliable indication that the views of governments and courts in favour of international commercial arbitration are firmly stabilised in all Latin American countries.

---

[77] For example, its provision on national treatment (art. 10.2) and its most favoured nation clause (article 10.3) do not apply to public contracts (art. 10.7(5)(a)) or to already existing measures adopted within sectors listed in Annex I of the Treaty (art. 10.7(1)(a)), their continuation or renewal, or their modification provided such modification does not aggravate the non-conformity of the measure with arts 10.2 or 10.3. These latter articles do not apply to new measures taken within sectors listed in Annex II of the Treaty. Investment authorisations or agreements are governed by the laws stipulated in such authorisations or agreements. In absence of choice, they will be governed by the laws of the host state including its conflict of laws rules, the provisions of the authorisation or agreement, international law to the extent applicable, and the Treaty provisions. For a more recent and perhaps revolutionary example, *see* the Treaty Between the United States of America and the Republic of Uruguay Concerning the Encouragement and Reciprocal Protection of Investment, 25 October 2004.

V. PRESENT SITUATION OF LATIN AMERICAN ARBITRATION

19-51   To assess the present situation of Latin American arbitration and its future growth, it is necessary to look at recent or contemporaneous legislative changes and case law regarding arbitration, without losing sight, however, of the impact of exogenous socio-political and economic factors and the influence of historical precedent.

19-52   Undoubtedly, the attitude of Latin American legislators and courts in respect of technical instruments having a direct bearing on the functioning, recognition and binding effects of the arbitration agreement is revealing of the way such factors and precedent influence legal reasoning apparently premised on more strictly technical or juristic notions.

19-53   Indeed, an analysis of how technical instruments such as the autonomy of the arbitral procedure from national laws, the extra-territorial recognition and enforcement of arbitral awards, the Kompetenz-Kompetenz powers of arbitrators, the progressive limitation of non-arbitrable or non-justiciable matters, or the specific performance of the arbitration agreement have fared before Latin American legislators and courts becomes a sort of litmus test revealing the degree of influence of such exogenous elements on the evolution of arbitration in the different Latin American jurisdictions. At the end of the day, it all boils down to the degree of efficacy of the arbitration agreement – and its ultimate manifestation, the arbitral award – accorded by Latin American laws and courts. It is to this question that we now turn our eyes.

VI. EFFICACY OF ARBITRATION AGREEMENTS AND AWARDS IN LATIN AMERICA

19-54   The wave of modernisation of legislation on arbitration in Latin America combined with the ratification of the Panama and New York Conventions observed in the last two decades has led to the removal of many of the legal obstacles to ensuring the efficacy of arbitration agreements and awards in accordance with modern international comparative arbitration law trends. The great majority of Latin American laws on arbitration recognise today the autonomy of the arbitration agreement from the underlying transaction,[78] the

---

[78]   Venezuela, Ley de Arbitraje Comercial, art. 7; México, Commercial Code, art. 1432; Paraguay, Ley de Arbitraje y Mediación 1879/02, art. 19; Bolivia, Ley de Arbitraje y Conciliación No. 1770, art. 11; Perú, Ley General de Arbitraje No. 26572, art. 106; Ecuador, Ley de Arbitraje y Mediación, art. 5; El Salvador, Ley de Mediación, Conciliación y Arbitraje Decree No. 914, art.

authority of the arbitrators to decide on their own jurisdiction,[79] and limit the means of recourse available against arbitral awards essentially to those based on the violation of basic due process principles.[80] By ratifying the Panama and New York Conventions, the Latin American countries have endorsed policies favouring the recognition of full effects to the arbitration agreement and limiting the grounds to deny recognition and enforcement to foreign arbitral awards by, inter alia, eliminating the antiquated double exequatur requirement.

19-55 The most obvious and last remaining throwback to the old Latin American legal framework governing arbitration – certain obsolete Brazilian law provisions denying the specific performance of the arbitration agreement and only permitting the seeking of damage compensation against the recalcitrant party refusing to arbitrate, and basing the recognition and enforcement of arbitral awards on the double exequatur system – were eliminated in 1996 through the introduction of the present Brazilian Arbitration Act. Although one of the last Latin American countries to ratify the New York Convention, Brazil had already broadly endorsed its principles regarding the recognition of the validity of arbitration agreements and the recognition and enforcement of foreign arbitral awards by ratifying the Panama Convention and including in the 1996 Brazilian Arbitration Act provisions on the specific performance of the arbitral agreement and on the recognition and enforcement of foreign arbitral awards, the latter closely modelled after the UNCITRAL Model Law on Commercial Arbitration and the New York Convention itself.

19-56 However, despite the rosy landscape generally presented by the black letter law on arbitration in Latin America after its recent modernisation, its substance or spirit has not always been properly understood or applied. In certain cases, the Latin American courts have ignored express legal provisions aimed at

---

30. On Costa Rica, S. Artavia B., *El Arbitraje en el Derecho Costarricense* (2000), pp. 167–168; Chile, Law 19971 on International Comercial Arbitration, art. 16(1).

[79] Venezuela, Ley de Arbitraje Comercial, arts 7 and 254; México, Commercial Code, art. 1432; Paraguay, Ley de Arbitraje y Mediación 1879/02, art. 19; Bolivia, Ley de Arbitraje y Conciliacion No. 1770, art. 32; Perú, Ley General de Arbitraje No. 26572, art. 106; El Salvador, Ley de Mediación, Conciliación y Arbitraje No. 914, art. 51. As to Costa Rica, *see* Artavia, *supra* n. 77 at pp. 170–171; Chile, Law 19971 on International Commercial Arbitration, art. 16(1).

[80] The case of Perú deserves special mention. The Peruvian Ley General de Arbitraje (art. 126), modelled in this respect after the Swiss Arbitration Act, permits the parties to an international arbitration taking place in Perú to waive the means to set aside the award provided in the Peruvian legislation, although the award will be considered a foreign one for the purposes of its enforcement or recognition in Perú.

facilitating arbitration or ensuring its efficacy, or advanced results notoriously incompatible with the policies favourable to arbitration underlying the new and updated legal arbitration framework. On the other hand, the ratification of the New York and Panama Conventions by Latin American countries has not been accompanied by rules clarifying their reciprocal scope of application or in respect of a myriad of Inter-American and regional or sub-regional conventions also claiming application to the recognition and enforcement of arbitral awards. If in part the lack of sufficient understanding and knowledge of the new laws and conventions, as well as of the operation of commercial arbitration at large, is accountable for these problems, their profound reasons are often rooted in exogenous political and socio-economic factors, not always unprecedented. An overview of these different problems ensues.

A. The 'Compromiso' or Specific Submission

19-57 There are national legal provisions – such as the Argentine National Code of Civil and Comercial Procedure – that require the execution of a 'compromiso',[81] or special submission, to render the arbitration agreement fully effective and enforceable. Although doctrinal opinions and some isolated decisions would indicate that the special submission is not applicable to international arbitrations, there is not always a firm and established string of court decisions permitting to reach such conclusion in countries that, like Argentina, still require the execution of a specific submission as a precondition to the actual initiation of the arbitral proceedings before the arbitrators. One of the main consequences under Argentine law derived from such requirement is that any dispute relating to the incorporation in the special submission of matters to be resolved by the arbitrators – which include the designation of the arbitrators and the determination and demarcation of the disputed issues – is to be resolved by a court of law vested with exclusive jurisdiction to do so, and that so long as the latter's decision is pending, the arbitral proceedings may not be commenced or continued.[82]

19-58 For example, should a party to the reference raise an objection to the arbitrability of a matter or matters submitted to arbitration, the decision on whether such matter may be incorporated into the specific submission – and thus be heard and decided by the arbitrators – is exclusively entrusted to a court of

---

[81] Argentine National Code of Civil and Comercial Procedure (Arg. Pr. Code), arts 739–741.
[82] Arg. Pr. Code, art. 742.

law. This is exactly what happened in an ICC domestic arbitration case – the Ecofisa case – involving Argentine parties and venued in Buenos Aires, Argentina, despite the fact that the ICC International Court of Arbitration had approved terms of reference incorporating the alleged non-arbitrable matter among those prima facie submitted to the decision of the arbitrators.[83]

19-59 By vesting local courts with such exclusive powers to determine the contents of the compromiso, the arbitrators are denied authority to decide on their own jurisdiction. In addition, the exercise of such powers constitutes an unwarranted interference in the normal course of the arbitral proceedings by the courts of law, which may give rise to considerable delay in the conduct of the arbitration, since the decision of the first instance judge on the contents of the specific submission is subject to a chain of successive appeals which, in the case of Argentina, might only end in the Argentine Supreme Court.

19-60 The Brazilian Arbitration Act (Law 9307 of 1996) also incorporates the compromiso requirement among its provisions.[84] This requirement has given rise to different problems, respectively regarding the recognition of effects to the arbitration agreement, and the recognition and enforcement of foreign arbitral awards, that have been fortunately resolved by the Brazilian courts in a way favourable to the development of international arbitration.

19-61 In one of those instances, the issue was whether a Brazilian court would take jurisdiction to impose the execution of a specific submission in connection with an ICC arbitration having Paris, France, as its seat; the other case concerned the enforcement in Brazil of an award rendered in Spain. In this latter case, what was at issue was whether an award rendered in arbitral proceedings that took place outside Brazil without the prior execution of a compromiso could be enforced in Brazil. In accordance with article 5 of the Brazilian Arbitration Act, the Superior Court of the State of São Paulo (Tribunal de Justiça)[85] (in the first case) and the Brazilian Supreme Court (in the second case) came to the

---

[83] See *Pérez Companc SA and Bridas SA* v. *Ecofisa SA and Petrofisa SA*, National Commercial Court of Appeals; English version in (1991) 6 International Arbitration Reports No.2 (February 1991) and H. Grigera Naón, 'Argentine Law and the ICC Rules: A Comment on the ECOFISA Case' (1992) 3 World Arbitration and Mediation Reports 100.

[84] Articles 6–7.

[85] Tribunal de Justiça do Estado de São Paulo, Agravo de Instrumento No.124.217.4, votos 8580–8581, 16 September 1999, published in (2000) 3 *Revista de Direito Bancário, do Mercado de Capitais e da Arbitragem* 336.

conclusion that the execution of a compromiso or specific submission is not necessary when the arbitration rules selected by the parties to govern their arbitration do not require it.[86] In this latter case, the Brazilian Supreme Court also dismissed arguments challenging the constitutionality of the provisions of the Brazilian Arbitration Act that would permit a Brazilian judge to allow the specific performance of the arbitration agreement by approving a compromiso over the objections of a recalcitrant party.[87]

19-62 Unlike in Argentina, where so long as the legislation on arbitration in that country is not changed the compromiso requirement remains in full force and effect with the only possible exception of international arbitrations, in Brazil, a compromiso will only be required both in domestic and international arbitrations if not explicitly or implicitly contracted out of by the parties, and thus, its real practical relevance has been substantially reduced.

19-63 That such level of analysis has not been reached in Argentina has been eloquently confirmed by a recent decision of a Federal Judge sitting in Buenos Aires who has taken jurisdiction to decide on the contents of a compromiso in connection with an ICC arbitration involving a binational entity formed by the governments of Paraguay and Argentina, the Entidad Binacional Yaciretá, as respondent and a private consortium controlled by French and Italian interests as claimant having Buenos Aires as its seat. The arbitration arose out of disputes between the owner and the contractor originated in the construction of a dam in fluvial waters shared by Argentina and Paraguay. As in the Ecofisa case – albeit this time in connection with an international arbitration – the Argentine judge assimilated the terms of reference approved by the ICC International Court of Arbitration to a compromiso under Argentine procedural law. The respondent had refused to sign the terms of reference because the arbitral tribunal refused to incorporate certain modifications proposed by the respondent. The judge based her exclusive jurisdiction to determine the contents of the terms of reference held to be a compromiso not only on national Code on Civil and Commercial Procedure provisions regarding the compromiso, but also on the Argentine public interests involved by virtue of the participation of the Argentine state in the

---

[86] Opinion (*Voto Vista*) of Justice Nelson Jobim *Agravo Reg. em Sentença Estrangeira N.5206-7 Reino da Espanha.*

[87] J. Bosco Lee, 'Brazil' in N. Blackaby, D. Lindsey and A. Spinillo (eds), *International Arbitration in Latin America* (2002), pp. 61, 63–66. In general, *see* H. Grigera Naón, 'ICC Arbitration and Courts of Law: Practical Experiences in Latin America' in *Liber Amicorum Karl-Heinz Böckstiegel* (2001), pp. 231, 236–242.

binational entity. Because of the public interests involved, and also by taking into account that the ICC International Court of Arbitration rejected the respondent's challenge of the three members of the arbitral tribunal and approved the terms of reference, the judge issued an interim order suspending the arbitral proceedings until the issuance of a final decision on the merits regarding the contents of the terms of reference by the Federal Court.[88]

19-64 Decisions such as this raise the vexed question of the often uneasy relationship between courts of law and arbitral tribunals that even today is not uncommon in Latin America, as we will consider next.

B. Arbitration as an Exception to the Jurisdiction of the 'Natural Judge'

19-65 In many Latin American countries the principle still prevails that arbitration constitutes an exception to the jurisdiction of courts of law. As a result, arbitration agreements are narrowly interpreted when it comes to determining their validity, scope, effects and enforcement. Argentina[89] and Venezuela are examples of countries upholding this principle, that is contrary to the prevailing idea – at least in connection with international transactions – that arbitration has become the normal means of resolving business and economic disputes.

19-66 The case of Venezuela deserves particular attention, since on the basis of such principle this country has departed from a former attitude much more favourable to international arbitration. In the late 1990s, the Venezuelan Supreme Court recognised the validity and enforceability of an arbitration clause referring to arbitration in the USA a dispute alleged by one of the parties, on the basis of provisions of the Venezuelan Code of Procedure, to fall under the exclusive jurisdiction of Venezuelan courts. By jointly referring to the converging provisions of the Panama Convention and the New York Convention, both ratified by the USA and Venezuela, the Venezuelan Supreme Court upheld the

---

[88] Juzgado de 1a. Instancia en lo Contencioso Administrativo Federal No.3, Secretaría No.5, causa 26.444/04: *Entidad Binacional Yaciretá c/Eriday y otros s/proceso de conocimiento*, decision of 27 September 2004.

[89] For example, National Commercial Court of Appeals, 'D', decision of 5 May 2000 in *La Ley*, vol. 2000-E, pp. 489–490; same tribunal, 'E', decision of 28 April 2000 in *El Derecho*, vol. 194, pp. 151–155; National Civil Court of Appeals, 'F', decision of 27 August 1999, in *Jurisprudencia Argentina*, vol. 2000-III, at 40–41. *See*, in general, M.A.N. Cuomo, 'En Torno a la Imposibilidad de Cumplir un Acuerdo Arbitral y Sus Efectos' in *El Derecho*, vol. 189, p. 576.

validity and enforceability of the arbitration agreement and decided, accordingly, that the Venezuelan courts lacked exclusive jurisdiction to decide the dispute.[90]

19-67 However, more recently, the highest court of Venezuela seems to have embarked on a path much less favourable to international arbitration, essentially based on the idea that arbitral jurisdiction is exceptional, and that any perceived lack of clarity in the arbitration agreement should be resolved by referring the dispute to the decision of the courts of law rather than resorting to an exercise of construction and interpretation of the arbitration clause aimed at rescuing the underlying parties' will to have the dispute arbitrated instead of adjudicated by a court of law.[91]

19-68 Such a vision, notoriously circumscribing the role and scope of arbitration, is combined with the acceptance of the extraordinary recourse of amparo as a means of safeguarding the constitutional rights of citizens to access the Venezuelan court system to oppose enforcement of arbitration agreements within or without Venezuela on the basis, for example, of the presumed lack of clarity of the clause referring to arbitration. As a result, and despite the letter of the recent Venezuelan Arbitration Act, the right of the arbitral tribunal to decide on its own jurisdiction is trumped by the self-assumed powers of the Venezuelan judiciary to decide first on the validity, meaning, scope and effects of the arbitration agreement. Additionally, the Venezuelan Supreme Court now permits directly introducing the amparo means of recourse – destined to protect the citizenry's constitutional rights – against or in connection with arbitral awards. Therefore, the Supreme Court has abandoned its so far continuous and firm practice of permitting the introduction of such recourse only against court decisions dealing with challenges to arbitral awards that could be considered as infringing constitutional rights. In consonance with this new approach, the Venezuelan Supreme Court has decided, in a recent case concerning the introduction of amparos regarding arbitral proceedings taking place in Miami, Florida, that the existence of a pending arbitration outside of Venezuela does not foreclose the right of any of the parties, having challenged the validity or application of the arbitration agreement giving rise to the arbitral proceedings, to

---

[90] Corte Suprema de Justicia de Venezuela – Sala Político-Administrativa, Expte 13.354, decision of 9 October 1997 in the *Pepsi Cola Panamericana* case.

[91] Tribunal Supremo de Justicia de Venezuela – Sala Político-Administrativa, Expte. 0775, decision of 20 June 2001, *Hoteles Doral C.A. c/Corporación L'Hoteles CA en demanda por resolución de contrato*. See also B. Weininger and D. Lindsey, 'Venezuela' in N. Blackaby, D. Lindsey and A. Spinillo, *supra* n. 87 at pp. 231–232.

resort to the Venezuelan courts in connection with disputes within the purview of such proceedings despite the fact that the arbitral tribunal had rejected such challenge introduced by the Venezuelan respondent in connection with such disputes; and that, by analogical application of article 53(6) of the Venezuelan Private International Law Act on the recognition and enforcement of foreign court decisions, arbitral awards rendered outside of Venezuela cannot be enforced in Venezuela if there are pending legal actions before the Venezuelan courts on the same subject matter and involving the same parties covered by the arbitral proceedings, when such actions have been initiated before the rendition of the arbitral award at stake.[92] This latter determination of the Venezuelan Supreme Court apparently means that the enforcement of foreign arbitral awards in Venezuela may be postponed sine die so long as pending court proceedings in Venezuela on the case subject to arbitration remain extant, irrespective of whether such proceedings are frivolous or not, and also irrespective of Venezuelan treaty obligations under the Panama and New York Conventions.

C. Arbitral Tribunals: a Component of the Judiciary, or a Non-Judicial, Independent, Dispute Resolution Mechanism?

19-69 The reasoning advanced by the Venezuelan Supreme Court to circumscribe the area of influence of arbitration described above is in part premised on the idea that since arbitral tribunals do not belong to the judiciary, their ability to exercise the jurisdictional function – considered essentially as a sovereign attribute primarily entrusted to the national judicial system – should be limited whenever possible. Inherent in it is the principle that the authority of national courts should be advanced as soon as there are elements in the arbitration clause permitting the inference that it does not constitute a full, irrevocable, unequivocal and unconditional referral to arbitration of all covered disputes. The practical conclusion of this way of looking at things is to limit – on the basis of a pro-judicial adjudication bias – the effectiveness of arbitration agreements, particularly in connection with international cases.

---

[92] In general, J.E. Anzola and F. Zumbiehl, 'El Tribunal Supremo de Venezuela Riñe con el Arbitraje' (unpublished). The reference is to the AAA arbitration (Commercial Arbitration Rules) between Four Seasons Hotels and Resorts BV, Four Seasons Hotels Limited, Four Seasons Caracas CA, as claimants, and Consorcio Barr SA, as respondent, further discussed *infra*. The last Venezuelan Supreme Court (*Tribunal Supremo de Justicia*) decision on this case was issued by its Constitutional Chamber (*Sala Constitucional*) on 19 November 2004, *Consorcio Barr, CA* v. *Four Seasons* (expe. No. 04-0163) (www.tsj.gov.ve).

19-70 However, the opposite reasoning may also lead to the same undesirable consequences, as proven by certain Argentine court decisions. Under the Argentine court system, when different judges assert their competence to decide the same case, the ensuing conflict is resolved in the following manner. The judge asserting its competence sends a rogatory communication, or *inhibitoria*, to the other judge inviting the latter to decline hearing the case. If the invitee declines asserting its jurisdiction, the matter ends there, and the inviting judge will decide the case. If not, a court exercising overarching jurisdiction over both judges (e.g., a Court of Appeals, or the Argentine Supreme Court of Justice) will decide on the one whose competence is to prevail for hearing and adjudicating the case in question.

19-71 In a relatively recent case,[93] the Argentine Supreme Court interpreted that this provision also applies to arbitral tribunals. According to the Court, an arbitral tribunal's claim of jurisdiction on a matter in respect of which a court of law asserts exclusive jurisdiction, is to be dealt with as if only courts of law were involved. Thus, a judge claiming jurisdiction to hear a case on which an arbitral tribunal equally asserts jurisdiction should send an *inhibitoria* to the arbitral tribunal as explained above. Should the arbitral tribunal reject the rogatory request to decline jurisdiction, it is for the superior court – in this case, the Supreme Court of Justice – to finally decide the issue. The arbitrators are impeded from continuing hearing the case so long as the superior court shall not have decided on the 'jurisdictional' conflict.

19-72 Such an approach clearly implies denying the arbitral tribunal the faculty to decide, without court interference, on its own jurisdiction or, should the arbitral tribunal affirm its jurisdiction, to hear and decide the case on the merits so long as the jurisdictional conflict will not have been resolved by the superior court. It provides a party wishing to sabotage arbitration proceedings with a powerful tool as soon as it finds a court of law willing to assert jurisdiction on the case subject to arbitration. In fact, the Kompetenz-Kompetenz principle is effectively neutralised, since the arbitrators have to await the final determination of the so-called jurisdictional conflict by a court of law before they can proceed. The end result of this approach is thus notoriously contrary to the opposite trend also present in other decisions of the Argentine judiciary in favour of recognising

---

[93] Argentine Supreme Court of Justice, *Nidera Argentina SA.* v. *Alvarez de Canale, Elena G.*, in *La Ley*, no. 24, advanced sheet of 2 February 1990.

authority to arbitrators to decide on their own jurisdiction, despite existing doubts on this topic resulting from older decisions.

19-73 The right approach would be, of course, not to view the problem as a conflict of jurisdictions or competencies between courts of law leading to an exchange of rogatory requests between the court of law and the arbitral tribunal vying for jurisdiction, but simply as a determination on the validity and effects of the arbitration agreement at stake. Such approach also necessitates making a policy decision (by the judge or the legislator) on who will be the first called to make this determination – the judge or the arbitrator – and its ensuing effects. Rather than a matter of conflict of competencies or jurisdiction, it is a question, first, of the degree of deference to be paid to the determinations of an arbitral tribunal on jurisdictional matters in light of the Kompetenz-Kompetenz principle, and secondly, of the validity and effects of the arbitration agreement from the perspective of the national court called to decide on the issue, which is totally alien to a notion of jurisdictional or competencies conflict within the judicial organisation of a state. Clearly, an arbitral tribunal is not a component of the judicial structure of a state and thus should not be subject to rules destined to resolve competence or jurisdictional problems involving courts of law.

19-74 Such right approach would require postponing any court decision regarding the jurisdiction of the arbitrators to hear the case until a foreign arbitral award is presented for recognition or enforcement, or when an award rendered in the forum is attacked through a means to set it aside. In the meantime, the arbitrators should be entitled to continue hearing the case. In fact, this approach is the one that seems prevailingly followed by Argentine courts when arbitration agreements or the initiation of arbitral proceedings are judicially challenged but where no Argentine court of law has asserted its exclusive jurisdiction in parallel court proceedings initiated in disregard of the arbitration clause. Perhaps, an appropriate compromise could be struck, in this latter case, by allowing – along lines similar to the French model – the court proceedings to trump the arbitral ones whenever the invalidity of the arbitral agreement is manifest and the arbitral tribunal has not yet been constituted. However, in such case the stay of the arbitral proceedings should be the exclusive outcome of a final court decision on the validity of the arbitration agreement taken without addressing an inhibitoria to the arbitral tribunal at issue.[94]

---

[94] This solution is in fact the one endorsed (athough with some variations) by a significant number of Latin American countries: Perú, Ley General de Arbitraje No. 26572 (arts 16, 99); Bolivia,

19-75 The theoretical and practical insuperable nature of the problems raised by following a different course of action in this respect have been eloquently evidenced by a recent decision of the Commercial Court of Appeals of Buenos Aires, which allowed the issuance of an *inhibitoria* addressed to an arbitral tribunal sitting in Dallas, Texas, under the American Arbitration Association (AAA) Arbitration Rules, to the purpose of asserting the jurisdiction of an Argentine court on the dispute submitted to the arbitrators.[95] The *inhibitoria* was issued as a result of proceedings initiated before an Argentine court, based on a joint venture and a farm-in agreement – the first one referring disputes to ICC arbitration in Buenos Aires, Argentina, and the second having a choice-of-forum clause designating the Federal Courts of Buenos Aires, Argentina for resolving any ensuing disputes. On the basis of these contracts, without hearing the foreign party to the arbitration proceedings (who was not a party to such contracts), the Commercial Court of Appeals concluded on the existence of exclusive international jurisdiction of the Argentine courts to hear the dispute. However, the AAA Arbitration was based on a related, although different, contract – a stock purchase agreement – whose parties were different from the parties to the farm-in and joint venture agreements. The discrete question submitted to the arbitrators was whether the claimant had been induced to buy shares from the respondents through untrue statements. The arbitral tribunal found that it had jurisdiction to decide on this matter, did not accept the jurisdictional claims of the Argentine court, denied extra-territorial effects to the *inhibitoria*, and declined not to continue hearing the case.

19-76 The surrealistic facets of the situation are underlined by the obvious fact that there is no superior, overarching, Argentine, national or international court with authority to resolve a supposed conflict of jurisdictions between an Argentine court of law and an international arbitral tribunal sitting in a different country. The fiction that the arbitral tribunal is a part of the Argentine judiciary or of some other all-encompassing judicial structure was thus exposed in all its hollowness. By virtue of the inevitable realities today characterising the international plane where international transactions and arbitrations are situated, it was clearly impossible for any Argentine court, let alone the Argentine

---

Ley de Arbitraje y Conciliación (art. 12) (*see also*, F. Montilla Zavalía, 'La Excepción de Arbitraje en el Procedimiento Jurisdiccional Boliviano' in *La Ley*, vol. 2001-E, pp. 1270–1273, on the confirmation by the Bolivian Constitutional Court of the constitutional validity of this provision); El Salvador (closely following the Bolivian model), Ley de Mediación, Conciliación y Arbitraje, Decree No. 914, art. 31.

[95] National Commercial Court of Appeals 'B', decision of 23 September 1999, *Compañía General de Combustibles SA*, Jurisprudencia Argentina, vol. 2002-III, at 53 *et seq.*

Supreme Court, to resolve the supposed 'jurisdictional' or 'competencies' conflict, or to curtail the powers of an arbitral tribunal sitting abroad to decide on its own jurisdiction pursuant to its authority to do so under the American Arbitration Association arbitral rules and the lex arbitrii (US federal law).

19-77 Actually, the fiction could not be maintained any longer when the ensuing arbitral award on the merits was brought for enforcement in Argentina. Another decision of the same National Commercial Court of Appeals (but by different judges) authorised such enforcement, both because of the absence, in an international scenario, of a superior, overarching court of law permitting to decide the jurisdictional conflict according to the Argentine procedural law rules, and because the court acknowledged that the arbitral tribunal had properly asserted its jurisdiction under the AAA rules and its lex arbitrii. In fact, the court recognised that the assertion of jurisdiction by an Argentine judge by way of a rogatory letter addressed to the arbitrators constituted an infringement of the agreement to arbitrate and an invalid attempt to interfere in the arbitral proceedings.[96] Consequently, the decision of the arbitrators in favour of their own jurisdiction remained untouched, although an extraordinary means of recourse before the Argentine Supreme Court introduced against the National Commercial Court of Appeals decision is presently still pending. It is surprising to see, however, that in its decision enforcing the award, the National Commercial Court of Appeals did not refer either to the Panama or the New York Convention – both ratified by Argentina and the USA – and relied exclusively on the provisions in this respect existing in the Argentine procedural legislation. This is another sign of the parochial attitude not infrequently adopted by Latin American judges even when rendering decisions favouring the effectiveness of international arbitration agreements and awards.[97]

19-78 At least one relatively recent decision of the Argentine Supreme Court seems to abandon the idea that an arbitral tribunal – domestic or international – is a component of the national judiciary.[98] Let us hope that by following this new

---

[96] Commercial Court of Appeals, 'D', decision of 5 November 2002, *Reef Exploration Inc.* v. *Compañía General de Combustibles SA* in *El Derecho*, vol. 203, p. 32. *See* comment by R. Caivano and R. Bianchi, 'El Exequatur de un Laudo Extranjero y la Inhbitoria en Relación con un Arbitraje Internacional' in *Jurisprudencia Argentina*, advanced sheet of 16 July 2003, pp. 38–46.

[97] *See* Comment by M. Noodt Taquela in *Derecho del Comercio Internacional (DeCita)* (2004), vol. 1, pp. 344–345.

[98] Argentine Supreme Court of Justice, decision of 11 November 1997, *Yacimientos Carboníferos Fiscales y Otros s/Constitución del Tribunal Arbitral*, in *El Derecho*, advanced sheet of 29 June

orientation, the rights of arbitrators to decide on their own jurisdiction will remain free of the negative consequences derived from a misunderstanding of the interaction between arbitral and court proceedings and the respective roles of arbitrators and courts of law, and that any departure from such orientation will remain merely anecdotal.

D. National Courts and Arbitrators: Partners or Rivals?

19-79 In fact, the different situations considered in (a) to (c) above are examples of a more general problem that may be characterised as the sometimes difficult interaction between courts of law and arbitral tribunals in connection with Latin American or Latin American-related arbitration cases.

19-80 The Four Seasons case, briefly described above,[99] is nothing less than a crossfire of opposing orders involving the Venezuelan courts of law, the arbitral tribunal having its seat in Miami, Florida and, indirectly, the Florida US Federal Court called to determine if the partial award on jurisdiction rendered in this case should be confirmed or not. On the one hand, the order of the arbitral tribunal to have the Venezuelan respondent discontinue existing legal actions in Venezuela or the initiation of new ones, contained in a partial arbitral award issued in Miami where the arbitral tribunal also asserted its jurisdiction to hear the case after dismissing the Venezuelan respondent's objections, was counteracted by decisions of the Venezuelan Supreme Court that denied practical effects to the arbitral tribunal's Kompetenz-Kompetenz powers or determinations and any extra-territorial effects to foreign arbitral awards so long as legal actions initiated in Venezuela before the rendition of the arbitral award in connection with the same case subject to arbitration remained pending. On the other hand, there are pending court proceedings before the US Federal Court in Florida regarding the confirmation of the partial award granting the order mentioned above.[100] An additional and relevant aspect of the situation is that, some time after the issuance of the partial arbitral award in question, a Venezuelan court issued an order addressed to the members of the arbitral tribunal mandating the suspension of the

---

1998; *see* commentary by H. Grigera Naón in (1999) *Revue de l'Arbitrage, Chronique de Jurisprudence Etrangère* 655, nos. 15–19, at pp. 660–663.

[99] *Supra* n. 92 and corresponding text.

[100] The partial award in the *Four Seasons/Consorcio Barr* case was initially confirmed by the US District Court for the Southern District of Florida, Case No.02-23249-CIV-Moore, by order issued on 4 June 2003. Nevertheless, it has been vacated and remanded for further consideration of an argument raised by Consorcio Barr SA by a decision of the US Court of Appeals for the Eleventh Circuit dated 20 July 2004 DC Docket No.01-04572-CV-KMM.

arbitral proceedings. As a consequence of this order, the Venezuelan member of the arbitral tribunal decided to resign in order to avoid being held in contempt of court, and was replaced by the American Arbitration Association. In its new composition, the arbitral tribunal rendered a final award on the merits in favour of the claimants.

19-81 The Merck case, which involved parallel arbitral proceedings in Colombia under the Rules of the Bogotá Chamber of Commerce, and in the USA under the ICC Arbitration Rules, is another example of both the situation just described, and of the contradictory – often confusing and confused – attitude of certain Latin American courts, some of them highly placed in the judicial hierarchy, in respect of arbitration. Although at the end of a string of decisions that culminated in the Colombian Constitutional Court, arbitral proceedings commenced in Colombia in disregard of a clear and unequivocal ICC arbitration clause referring to arbitration in the USA were put to an end, the Colombian Supreme Court first denied recognition to the arbitral tribunal's partial award dismissing the Colombian respondent's jurisdictional objections. The Supreme Court considered that although both Colombia and the USA had ratified the New York Convention, the Convention only covers 'final' and not 'partial awards'.[101] When the final award on the merits rendered in the same case against the Colombian party was taken to the Colombian Surpreme Court for enforcement, the Court decided to allow the respondent Tecnoquímicas SA to review the claimant's files in search of evidence 'that would counter the parties' explicit understandings and stipulations in the agreement between them'. The ultimate result was that the claimant Merck accepted to settle the case.[102]

19-82 The Colombian Council of State is not free from fluctuating attitudes regarding arbitration. If in the recent Termorío case it annulled the arbitral award rendered by an arbitral tribunal sitting in Colombia in a dispute involving a Colombian state respondent on the basis of a legal technicality,[103] in the

---

[101] A general description of the case may be found in Grigera Naón, *supra* n. 87 at pp. 232–236. Specifically on the Colombian Constitutional Court decision, *see* E. Zuleta, 'Special Constitutional Action to Preserve International Arbitration' in (2001) 18 *Journal of International Arbitration* 475.

[102] *See* interview of Merck's counsel Kay Boulware-Miller (by Jonty Rushforth) in (2003/2004) 2 *Latin Lawyer* (December–January) 28.

[103] *See* F. Mantilla Serrano, 'Termorío: Un Duro Golpe al Arbitraje' in (2004) 1 *Revista Internacional de Arbitraje* 191.

Drummond[104] case it adopted a position that is exactly the reverse of the one observed by the Venezuelan Supreme Court of Justice in the Four Seasons case as far as the recognition of the Kompetenz-Kompetenz powers of arbitrators is concerned.

19-83 The Termorío case concerned an ICC arbitration having its seat in Colombia concerning a state contract between a private company and a state party that was characterised as a domestic arbitration by the Council of State in light of the legislation applicable to the arbitration agreement when modified to refer contractual disputes to ICC arbitration, but which would have been considered an international one at the moment of initiation of the arbitral proceedings. It is in the light of such legislation that the Council of State considered the validity of the arbitral agreement as modified, that had been challenged by the state party. Since the provisions of Colombian Decree-law 2279 (the arbitration law in force at that moment) required that all domestic arbitrations be conducted according to its provisions, that could not, in the view of the Council of State, be contracted out of by the parties, the Council of State held that the arbitral agreement referring to the ICC Arbitration Rules was null and void, as well as the award rendered under such Rules.[105]

19-84 In the Drummond case, an arbitral tribunal sitting in Paris, France, issued a partial award deciding, inter alia, to dismiss a Colombian state party co-respondent's jurisdictional objections. This party sought the annulment of the partial award in Colombia before the Council of State, which declined to take jurisdiction because of the international nature of the arbitration – which excluded the application of Colombian law, including its provisions on the setting aside of arbitral awards – and the provisions of the New York Convention (ratified by both Colombia and France), particularly its Article II, which requires granting effects to an arbitration agreement unless rendered null and void by the competent court which, it is implied from the Council of State decision, in the instant case would be the French courts of the seat of the arbitration. The Council of State later rejected a means of recourse introduced thereafter to have it review its decision not to take jurisdiction.

---

[104] Consejo de Estado de Colombia, Sala de lo Contencioso Administrativo, Sección Tercera, expte.: 11001032600020030003401 (25261), decision of 24 October 2003.

[105] Consejo de Estado de Colombia, Sala de lo Contencioso Administrativo, Sección Tercera, *Electrificadora del Atlántico S.A. E.S.P.* v. *Termorío S.A. E.S.P* expte. 11001-03-25-000-2001-004601 (21041), 1 August 2002.

19-85 In a proximate – but different – scenario, contradictions and inconsistencies result from the clash of governmental policies favouring arbitration and expressed through modern arbitral legislation and the ratification of leading arbitration treaties enjoying wide international acceptance, and opposing judicial policies regarding arbitration developed by national Latin American judiciaries, and particularly their Supreme Courts. One recent example is the long debate, alluded to above, at the Brazilian Supreme Court on the constitutionality of provisions of the 1996 Brazilian Arbitration Act precisely permitting the exclusion, through the parties' express or implicit agreement, of the requirement of a specific submission. An even more recent one is the decision of the Panamanian Supreme Court regarding a domestic arbitration case. The Supreme Court concluded (despite the provision in the Panamanian Arbitration Act vesting arbitrators with Kompetenz-Kompetenz powers and contrary amicus briefs filed by the Panama Chamber of Commerce and the Panama Arbitration Center) that objections to the jurisdiction of arbitrators are to be decided by a court of law and not by the arbitrators themselves. The Supreme Court based its decision on constitutional provisions according to which nobody may be denied access to the jurisdiction of national courts of law in defence of his, her or its rights; and that determinations on whether arbitral tribunals may assert or not their jurisdiction with the possible effect of removing the case from the decision of national courts must be exclusively made by the national courts themselves.[106] The latest piece of news on this matter – which illustrates the contrast sometimes existing between general governmental and judicial policies regarding arbitration – is that Panama seems to be presently considering a modification of its Constitution to overcome this problem.

19-86 Contradictory attitudes regarding arbitration in Latin America may be also detected when comparing lower court and Supreme Court decisions on arbitral matters made within the same country. During the long period of almost four years in which the decision on the constitutionality of vital provisions of the Brazilian Arbitration Act remained pending, the Brazilian lower courts showed a positive attitude towards the application of the new law, including the very provisions whose constitutionality had been questioned before the Brazilian Supreme Court. It would seem, indeed, that the lower courts were less hesitant – and more penetrating – in understanding and advancing arbitration and its effects on the adjudication of commercial and economic disputes.

---

[106] Supreme Court of Justice of Panama, decision of 13 December 2001, *Pycsa Panamá SA.*

19-87   This contrast has perhaps become more notorious in Argentina. Despite certain setbacks, the Argentine lower and appeal courts have gradually attempted to reverse a history of misunderstanding about the operation of commercial arbitration, by, inter alia, upholding the right of arbitrators to decide on their own jurisdiction and concomitantly staying competing court proceedings,[107] granting interim measures of protection,[108] reducing the realm of non-arbitrable disputes, to the extent of allowing arbitrators to pronounce themselves on the unconstitutionality of laws or regulations,[109] and attempting – albeit in isolated cases – to differentiate domestic from international arbitration to circumscribe the scope of application of national or local mandatory legal rules not adapted to international arbitral dispute resolution.

19-88   However, the Argentine Supreme Court, in its recent Cartellone decision regarding a domestic arbitration involving a private party and an Argentine state-controlled corporation, seems to raise some doubts as to whether this trend will enjoy the undivided support of the highest court of the land. A careful evaluation of the true meaning and significance of this Supreme Court decision is then in

---

[107] National Commercial Court of Appeals, 'A', decision of 27 August 1999, *Camuzzi Argentina, SA* v. *Sodigas Sur, S.A.s/sumario*, in *El Derecho*, vol. 185, pp. 128–131 (an ICC arbitration clause in a shareholders agreement was at stake). Also, National Commercial Court of Appeals 'E', decision of 11 June 2003, in ElDial.com., 25 August 2003, no. 1358; National Commercial Court of Appeals, *Softrón SA* v. *Telecom Argentina Stet France Telecom SA y Otro s/Ordinario* (expte. 799840, decision of 28 March 2003).

[108] Civil Court of Appeals of Mar del Plata, 2 December 1999 in *El Derecho*, vol. 187, p. 338, with commentary by Roque Caivano.

[109] National Commercial Court of Appeals 'E', 11 June 2003, *supra* n. 106, also published in (2003) IV *Jurisprudencia Argentina*, advanced sheet of 5 November 2003, pp. 19–21. This decision is not deprived of a certain daring: compare with the cautious general attitude of international arbitrators when confronted with unconstitutionality issues:

> 'As an initial matter, the Tribunal will not decide on Defendant's contention of the alleged unconstitutionality of the RICO statute … As to the unconstitutionality of a national statute, an international Arbitral Tribunal might first doubt whether it is empowered to decide upon it, notwithstanding the jurisdiction it has to decide upon the application of the statute. Indeed, to decide that a statute enacted in a sovereign state is unconstitutional and to refuse to apply it for that reason, would mean that a Tribunal rejects the validity and effects of an element of the law of that state, which is still in force inside the territory of such state, and has not been declared unconstitutional by its competent courts. In the view of this Tribunal, it is highly probable that it does not possess and cannot exercise such an extraordinary power, in any case where the statute in question does not infringe upon transnational public policy, as indeed the RICO statute does not'.

(ICC Case No.6320, 6/No.1 in (1995) *ICC International Court of Arbitration Bulletin* 59 at pp. 60–61.

order, not the least because some of the opinions issued both by those who defend and criticise this decision seem to be somewhat ideologically charged.

19-89 In the first place, the Supreme Court decided to annul an arbitral award rendered ultra petita on matters not included in the compromiso for not having observed the date provided in the compromiso as from which sums payable were to be calculated. This conclusion of the Supreme Court – without passing judgment on its inherent correctness – is of course perfectly in accordance, from a strictly theoretical standpoint, with well accepted legal principles that permit setting aside an award when rendered beyond the authority vested in the arbitrators.[110] However, the Supreme Court proceeded next to look into other aspects of the award regarding the criteria observed by the arbitrators, acting within the margins of the compromiso, to calculate interest on the principal amounts to be paid by the respondent. When doing so, the Supreme Court expressly indicated that it was carrying out a review of the merits of the award in disregard of the waiver to introduce means of appeals on the merits validly made by the parties when entering into the compromiso as permitted by the applicable law,[111] and even though the party challenging the award had not filed an appeal on the merits but sought the annulment of the award. The Supreme Court was of the view that when public policy principles are affected, such waiver is not valid. Finally, the Supreme Court decided to strike down also this aspect of the award after finding that the interest calculation was contrary to public policy principles of morality and justice because it led to the capitalisation of interest or interest compounding.

19-90 Indeed, a comparative law survey will probably show that arbitral awards may be at least partially annulled when granting interest judged excessive according to the mandatory laws of the forum – the lex arbitrii – although applicable statutes do not expressly provide for a public policy means to set aside an arbitral award rendered in the forum. This may be the case of state courts in the USA or Federal Court applying the law of a US state irrespective of whether the merits of an arbitral award may be reviewed or not.[112] Had the Argentine

---

[110] Arg.Pr.Code, art. 760.

[111] Arg.Pr. Code, art. 758.

[112] On public policy limitation on interest compounding, *see* J. Gotanda, 'Compound Interest in International Disputes' (2003) 34 *Law and Policy in International Business* 419. For an example of a statutory limitation on the rate of interest to be observed by arbitrators sitting in the forum enacting it, *see* New York Consolidated Service Civil Practice Law and Rules (NY CLS CPLR)

Supreme Court followed a similarly pretorian approach and characterised its decision not as one reviewing the merits of, but as partially annulling, the award, it would have avoided making the troubling choice of disregarding a waiver of appeals on the merits perfectly valid under the applicable law, but not extending, under such law, to the grounds for annulling or setting aside an arbitral award. On the other hand, it is not unusual either to see national statutes applicable to international arbitration incorporate a doctrine, often first developed through case law, permitting the annulment of an award rendered in the forum if judged contrary to public policy principles or ordre public international, without further defining the meaning of such expression.[113] Since the Cartellone case concerned a domestic dispute, it is not yet possible to determine whether interest considered excessive under national mandatory rules will also be considered a part of Argentine general public policy principles to justify the setting aside of an arbitral award rendered in Argentina in an international case.

19-91   On the other hand, the Argentine Supreme Court held in broad terms that an arbitral award may be subject to court review if contrary to public policy, unconstitutional, illegal or 'irrational', without however giving much indication as to the meaning and scope of those terms.[114] A proper interpretation would possibly lead to concluding that most of such terms actually refer to grounds of annulment of an award rather than for reviewing it on the merits; and also, that an arbitral tribunal would incur a public policy violation when deciding on matters not subject to compromise or settlement, i.e., non-arbitrable matters, which of course are not covered by a waiver of means of recourse on the merits.[115] If excluded from arbitration by constitutional provisions, it would be both unconstitutional and contrary to public policy to arbitrate on such matters. Also, an award based on arbitral proceedings in violation of the essential constitutional right of due process would be both unconstitutional, contrary to public policy, undoubtedly the outcome of an essential defect in the arbitral proceedings leading to it, and thus clearly covered by one of the grounds of annulment set

---

§ 5004 (2003): 'Interest shall be at the rate of nine percentum per annum, except where otherwise provided by Statute'.

[113] Arbitration Act 1996 (UK), s. 68(2)(g) (that is a mandatory provision under Sch. 1 to the Act) and the commentary by R. Merkin in his *Arbitration Act 1996* (2000), p. 142: 'Section 68(2)(g) states a series of obvious principles relating to fraud and public policy, although there are few modern authorities on these possibilities'; France, Code of Civil Procedure, arts 1502, 1504.

[114] Corte Suprema de la República Argentina, *José Cartellone Construcciones Civiles SA* v. *Hidroeléctrica Norpatagónica SA o Hidronor SA s/proceso de conocimiento*, 1 June 2004, J.87 XXXVII.

[115] Arg.Pr.Code, arts 737, 752; Civil Code, arts 21, 872.

forth in the procedural law that cannot be waived.[116] Finally, if arbitral tribunals sitting in Argentina may decide on the constitutionality of Argentine laws and regulations,[117] it is only logical to consider that an arbitral award determinative of such matter may be subject to an ordinary means for setting it aside before an Argentine court of law concerning the constitutionality issue. This would still be a means seeking the annulment of the award rather than its review on the merits, and thus excluded from the waiver of the parties.

19-92 If read with all the above caveats, the Cartellone decision does not appear to strike a dissonant note, except for one thing: its broad holding – most likely an obiter dictum – that an award may be set aside because considered 'irrational' is clearly unacceptable, does not find any legal basis or justification, and opens the doors to judicial arbitrariness, except in the extreme case in which the award or one of the decisions contained by it would be totally deprived of reasons, in which case the arbitral proceedings would have been vitiated by an essential defect permitting the annulment of the ensuing arbitral award under applicable Argentine procedural law.[118] Beyond such narrow limits, there is no firm line of precedent in Argentina that an arbitral award may be set aside for 'irrationality' grounds or systematically reviewed on the merits by a court of law on 'irrationality' grounds.

19-93 However, because of the loose way in which the Argentine Supreme Court refers to 'irrationality' as a possible ground for reviewing an arbitral award, it suggests that a court of law may look into the merits of an arbitral award – even if reasons have been given for the decisions contained by it – to decide on whether it should be upheld or not on the basis of its 'irrationality'. The strong emphasis laid by this decision on the powers of the judiciary to review arbitral awards on constitutionality grounds or on grounds of 'irrationality' may also indicate that the Argentine Supreme Court will persevere in following a course favourable to directly subjecting arbitral awards to an extraordinary means of recourse before the Argentine Supreme Court on the basis of alleged arbitrariness or violation of constitutional guarantees, which implies reversing a traditional string of precedent on this matter.[119] According to

---

[116] Arg.Pr.Cod, art. 760.

[117] *See supra* n. 109 and corresponding text.

[118] Arg.Pr. Code, art. 760.

[119] Such change is already present in a previous and recent decision of the Argentine Supreme Court of Justice: *Meller Comunicaciones SAUTE* v. *ENTel*, decision of 5 November 2002, *La Ley*, vol. 2003-B, pp. 905–923; G. Bidart Campos, 'El Control Constitucional y el Arbitraje' in

the Supreme Court's traditional position, only court decisions upholding or denying the annulment of arbitral awards are subject to this extraordinary means of recourse. Abandoning such position would bring about the unfortunate consequence of introducing an additional procedural hurdle unduly conspiring against the prompt effectiveness of arbitral awards. If such were the case, it would be impossible not to see an obvious parallel between the new positions assumed by the Argentine Supreme Court regarding commercial arbitration, and the similar evolution in the case law of the Venezuelan Supreme Court already described.[120] However, the Cartellone decision was issued in connection with a domestic arbitration involving a state-controlled entity, the presence of which presumes the existence of some degree of public interest involved. This decision does not necessarily govern an international arbitration venued in Argentina, nor indicate that in such case the Argentine Supreme Court would advance the application of domestic public policy or mandatory rules and principles.

19-94   Nevertheless, the Cartellone decision – irrespective of whether properly or improperly understood – is already influencing Argentine lower courts also in connection with international arbitrations. The Argentine Federal Judge who granted an interim measure suspending the ICC arbitral proceedings in the Entidad Binacional Yaciretá[121] case mentioned before – an international arbitration having its seat in Argentina – also based her decision on the broad powers recognised by the Cartellone decision to the Argentine judiciary to control and review arbitral awards for public policy or constitutionality reasons. The Entidad Binacional Yaciretá case is not isolated in Latin America. In the recent Copel case[122] (involving as parties a Brazilian state entity of the state of Paraná and a Brazilian private company) a Brazilian judge has issued an interim measure of protection to suspend ICC arbitral proceedings taking place in Brazil. The measure – expressly notified by order of the judge to the ICC International Court of Arbitration – was granted within the context of court proceedings challenging the validity of the arbitral agreement based on the fact that the dispute concerned the public interest since as a result of its outcome the state party involved could be forced to acquire a plant independently of whether so doing would be convenient or not. The judge also fixed a daily fine equal to 0.5

La Ley (suplemento constitucional), advanced sheet of 17 August 2004; J. Bosch, 'Apuntes Sobre el Control Judicial del Arbitraje (A Propósito de la Sentencia "Cartellone c/. Hidronor")' in *El Derecho*, advanced sheet of 24 August 2004.

[120] See *supra* n. 92 and corresponding text.

[121] See *supra* n. 88 and corresponding text.

[122] *Companhia Paranaense de Energia (Copel)* v. *UEG Aráucaria Ltda*, decision of 3 June 2003, Juiz de Direito da Vara das Fazendas Públicas do Estado do Paraná, on file with the author.

per cent of the disputed amounts should the suspension of the arbitration not take place. Although, unlike the Yaciretá case, the Copel case concerned a domestic arbitration, both cases denote an unmistakable trend towards asserting the exclusive jurisdiction of national courts in connection with arbitrations where the existence of a public interest is perceived irrespective of whether the state entity involved is or not acting iure gestionis or whether applicable national legal provisions and freely contracted for arbitral rules on the authority of the arbitrators to decide on their own jurisdiction are disregarded or not.

19-95 To a certain extent, the unfavourable attitude regarding arbitration evidenced by some of the recent Supreme Court or other court decisions referred to above seem to be a throwback to the anti-arbitration trends prevailing between the early 1930s and the late 1970s. A clarification is however in order in respect of these trends. The Calvo Doctrine and Clause essentially sought to assert the exclusive jurisdiction of the courts of the host state in connection with specific matters, namely the treatment of foreign aliens, foreign investment, and diplomatic protection. The ideas of Nicolás Matienzo, also described above, only attempted to exclude the arbitrability of public law and constitutional matters concerning the exercise of state sovereign rights. None of these ideas or doctrines sought to extend their influence – at least on any principled basis – to commercial or economic matters normally falling within the ambit of international commercial arbitration at large. It seems, then, that some of such decisions, covering the broader spectrum of commercial cases subject to arbitration, are really closer to the anti-liberal traditions that exerted their influence on the procedural law of many Latin American countries particularly between the 1930s and 1940s as a result of then prevailing nationalistic ideas aimed at strengthening the powers and authority of the state and each of its expressions, including its judiciary, to the detriment of individual autonomy and methods of dispute resolution not controlled by the state.

19-96 Notwithstanding this clarification, more general political motives – not entirely detached from central governmental policies – may still be present behind some of these decisions. For example, rightly or wrongly, some observers suggest that the Cartellone decision is not unrelated to the more general stance recently adopted by the Argentine government adverse to acknowledging the validity or granting recognition or enforcement of awards rendered against Argentina within the context of international arbitrations under BITs ratified by that country, most of which are being conducted within the context of ICSID and the Washington Convention.[123] In the aggregate, the economic value of the BIT cases filed against Argentina is approximately equivalent to the exposure of Argentina vis-à-vis the International Monetary Fund, a circumstance underlining the macro-economic and political significance of these claims from the Argentine perspective.

19-97 Be that as it may, some arguments have been advanced on the Argentine side – in part on the basis of ideas that may be traced back to the Matienzo Doctrine – to argue that such treaties are unconstitutional[124] and that any adverse arbitral awards against Argentina would be subject to review and eventually annulment by the Argentine Supreme Court. A possible reason explaining why such arguments are now being brought to bear by counsel representing Argentina in connection with BITs to which Argentina is a party is the adverse reaction of the present Argentine authorities to the insufficiently meditated decision-making process on the Argentine side that led previous Argentine authorities to endorse the massive ratification of BITs by Argentina.

19-98 However, from an international law perspective, one fails to see on what legal basis the Argentine Supreme Court would be able to extend its authority to review or annul – in any case with international effects – awards rendered outside of Argentina, in a Washington Convention country, and within a public international law procedural context isolated from any national procedural law, including Argentine law. On the other hand, there seems to be general consensus that every signatory of the Washington Convention – including Argentina – is obligated to recognise and enforce Washington Convention pecuniary obligations imposed through Washington Convention arbitral awards and recognise their binding nature without going through exequatur proceedings or the possibility of raising public policy reservations against such awards.[125] If, when rendering the Cartellone decision, the Argentine Supreme Court was envisioning a possible future extension of its jurisdiction or the jurisdiction of Argentine courts in ways

---

[123] *See e.g.*, J. Martínez de Hoz(h) and V. Macchia, 'La Doctrina del fallo Cartellone: Resulta Aplicable a los Laudos del CIADI?' in G. González Campaña, 'Desnaturalización del Arbitraje Administrativo' in *La Ley* (suplemento administrativo), advanced sheet of 8 August 2004; A. Corti and L.Constante, 'La Nueva Corte Impone La Ley por Encima de los Arbitrajes' in *Ambito Financiero*, 18 June 2004.

[124] H. Rosatti, 'Los Tratados Bilaterales de Inversión, El Arbitraje Internacional Obligatorio y el Sistema Constitucional Argentino' in *La Ley*, advanced sheet of 15 October 2003.

[125] 1965 Washington Convention, Art. 54(1). Ch. Schreuer, *The ICSID Convention: A Commentary* (2001), p. 1129.

incompatible with such premises,[126] it would appear to be prompted more by extra-juridical concerns than firm legal grounds from the international law perspective. Undoubtedly, such a course of action would have regrettable legal repercussions likely not to be limited to arbitrations involving state interests, but extending – as illustrated by historical precedent described in this lecture – its adverse effects to the broader spectrum of commercial arbitration in or in connection with Argentina.

19-99 Both from a practical and theoretical standpoint, it seems more appropriate to search in the modern evolution of international law elements to advance the Argentine position, in consonance with the traditions of Carlos Calvo and Luis María Drago, oriented towards the defence and the fashioning of the rule of public international law.[127] As a distinguished Argentine public international law expert, close to Luis María Drago, wrote several decades ago when referring to the international responsibility of states, 'experience shows that internal law provisions are normally of little effect', it is a matter that 'cannot be abandoned to measures of internal law and much less to political fluctuations, as it is the case even now', and the state may not seek to avoid its responsibility by 'invoking contrary provisions found in its own law or raising as an argument that the illicit conduct at stake is attributable to its internal subdivisions: Federal states, municipalities, colonies, protectorates, etc'.[128] It is submitted that the Cartellone decision should not be interpreted or followed in ways incompatible with such persuasive wisdom.

E. Latin America and the Ratification of International Treaties on Commercial Arbitration

19-100 It is not my purpose here to refer in any detail to the massive ratification by Latin American countries of two leading international conventions, the Panama Convention or the New York Convention, nor to analyse the undeniably positive impact that this relatively recent circumstance has had and continues to have on the development of international commercial arbitration in the region.

---

[126] Such interpretation has been vigorously and publicly denied by the Legal Undersecretary of the Argentine Ministry of Economy and Production: O. Siseles, 'Ratifican Una Añeja Doctrina Sobre Laudos' in *La Nación*, 7 July 2004.

[127] *See e.g.*, B. Pallarés, 'Los Tratados de Promoción y Protección de Inversiones en el Derecho Argentino: Un Esquema de Trabajo' in (2004) 15 *Revista Mexicana de Derecho Internacional Privado y Comparado* 179.

[128] Podestá Costa, *supra* n. 46 at pp. 193, 196, 220 (author's free translation from the Spanish original).

Much has been already exhaustively written on these topics, and no more need be said.

19-101 My intention is to cover a less felicitous aspect of this phenomenon, namely, the disorderly proliferation in the region of overlapping and not infrequently conflicting conventions regarding commercial arbitration, without clear rules accepted by all ratifying countries permitting the establishment of an order of precedence in the application of such conventions. Such situation is all the more regrettable, not only because of the ensuing lack of clarity as to the applicable rule of law in any specific case, but also because any such case may end up governed by treaty provisions not always adapted to the modern trends in international commercial arbitration. Since, of course, international treaties on the recognition and enforcement of arbitral awards or concerning international arbitration agreements have played and continue to play a vital role in ensuring that agreements to arbitrate are fully effective and enforceable, particularly in respect of their ultimate emanation, the arbitral award, it should be no wonder that the elucidation of this matter is of paramount importance to evaluate the level of efficacy of arbitral stipulations in Latin American countries.

19-102 It is well known that except for the USA, no other country ratifying the Panama Convention has passed legislation permitting the determination of the conditions of application of this convention by the local courts. Although the Panama Convention indicates that it applies to international commercial arbitrations, it nowhere defines such terms or its conditions of application. In addition, all countries having ratified the Panama Convention have also ratified the New York Convention. Except for the USA, no such countries have provided clear rules to establish when the application of one such Convention should prevail over the other on the matters where their provisions overlap.[129] Excluding the USA, the determination of these matters is left to the courts of law of the member countries, with the ensuing risk of contradictory decisions on the application of these conventions. It is to be expected that both conventions will be interpreted and applied harmoniously together according to their common spirit favourable to the development of international arbitration and in line with Article 30(3) of the Vienna Convention on the Law of Treaties (the 'Vienna Convention'),[130] as has already been the case.[131]

---

[129] An obvious area where such overlap does not exist is Art. 3 of the Panama Convention governing the arbitral procedure, unless the parties to the reference otherwise agree, by the Arbitration Rules of the Inter-American Arbitration Commission.

[130] UN Publication E.70.V.5; A/Conf.39/11/Add.2, art. 30(3):

19-103 There is also a certain level of doubt about the order of precedence to be observed when considering the application of the 1979 Montevideo Inter-American Convention on the Recognition and Enforcement of Court Decisions and Arbitral Awards (the 'Montevideo Convention'), and the Panama Convention. Both Inter-American Conventions overlap to the extent that they both cover the recognition and enforcement of arbitral awards. Although the majority of opinions privilege the application of the Panama Convention to the recognition and enforcement of arbitral awards, as prevailing lex specialis on the matter, there is no well-settled case law in this respect in the member countries. This is not a minor question, since the Montevideo Convention still maintains the obsolete double exequatur requirement for the recognition and enforcement of foreign arbitral awards. It is to be expected that the same lex specialis principle will prevail in case of conflict between the New York and Montevideo Conventions.[132]

19-104 Treaty-making activity within the context of the Mercosur and associated countries has rendered an already complicated situation still murkier. The Mercosur countries have adopted in 1992 a Las Leñas Protocol (the 'Las Leñas Protocol') on the recognition and enforcement of court decisions and arbitral awards in civil, commercial and labour law matters that re-introduces the double exequatur requirement in respect of foreign arbitral awards despite the fact that three of the Mercosur member countries – Argentina, Uruguay and Paraguay – had already ratified the Panama and New York Conventions that banished it. The problem is that the Las Leñas Protocol (Article 35) establishes that its provisions will prevail over those of any treaty signed before the Protocol if incompatible with the Protocol's provisions. If one would strictly abide by this inter-temporal rule, the Protocol's provisions should be deemed as superseding the more favourable provisions found in the New York Convention – already ratified by Argentina, Paraguay and Uruguay when the Protocol came into existence – that do not require, for example, the double exequatur of arbitral awards.[133]

'When all the parties to the earlier treaty are parties also to the later treaty but the earlier treaty is not terminated or suspended in operation under article 59, the earlier treaty applies only to the extent that its provisions are compatible with those of the later treaty'

(In general, Latin American countries ratified first the Panama Convention and then the New York Convention, which would render the New York Convention the 'later' treaty).

[131] *Pepsi Cola* case decided by the Venezuelan Supreme Court, *supra* n. 90 and corresponding text.

[132] *See in general*, J. Kleinheisterkamp, 'Conflict of Treaties and International Arbitration in the Southern Cone' in *Liber Amicorum Jürgen Samtleben* (2002), pp. 680–687.

[133] H. Grigera Naón, 'Recent Trends Regarding Commercial Arbitration in Latin America' in B. Cremades (ed.), *Enforcement of Arbitration Agreements in Latin America* (1999), pp. 103–106.

19-105 However, since then Brazil – the other Mercosur country – has ratified the New York Convention. Accordingly, the New York Convention has become lex posterioris to the Las Leñas Protocol in all Mercosur member countries because the ratification of the convention by all such countries was completed after their ratification of the said Protocol. Consequently, in light of Articles 30(3) and 59[134] of the Vienna Convention, the member countries may either consider the Las Leñas Protocol terminated as far as the conditions for recognition and enforcement of arbitral awards is concerned because of the blatant incompatibility of the provisions of both treaties on this matter, or only applicable in that respect to the extent not incompatible with the provisions of the New York Convention, including its Article VII that permits the preferential application of legislation or treaty provisions more favourable to the recognition and enforcement of arbitral awards in effect in the country where the award is sought to be relied upon.

19-106 One would hope that a similar approach is followed in connection with the 1998 Buenos Aires Mercosur Agreement (the 'Buenos Aires Agreement'), which contains substantive and conflict of laws provisions on different procedural and applicable law aspects regarding the conduct of international commercial arbitrations and the setting aside of arbitral awards, the decision of the dispute on the merits and the recognition and enforcement of arbitral awards. In this latter respect, the Buenos Aires Agreement lists the Montevideo, Panama Conventions and the Las Leñas Protocol as those governing the recognition and enforcement of arbitral awards falling within the scope of application of the Buenos Aires Agreement (albeit without giving any clue as to the order in which they are to apply). Even more surprisingly, the Buenos Aires Agreement omits any reference to the New York Convention. In view of such omission, one may infer that the New York Convention does not apply to the recognition and enforcement of arbitral awards when the conditions of application of this Agreement are met. Nevertheless, now that after the recent incorporation of Brazil, the New York Convention has been ratified by all the Mercosur countries, it is to be hoped that the absence of any reference to the New York Convention in

---

[134] Vienna Convention, Art. 59(1):

'A treaty shall be considered as terminated if all the parties to it conclude a later treaty relating to the same subject matter and: (a) it appears from the later treaty or is otherwise established that the parties intended that the matter should be governed by that treaty; or (b) the provisions of the later treaty are so far incompatible with those of the earlier one that the two treaties are not capable of being applied at the same time'.

the Buenos Aires Agreement will be piously forgotten, and that by resorting to Articles 30(3) and 59 of the Vienna Convention and Article VII of the New York Convention as indicated above, this latter Convention will prevail in fully exercising its healthy influence when it comes to recognising or enforcing arbitration awards.

19-107 The Buenos Aires Agreement, which does not apply to contracts with state parties, presents other features that seriously compromise its real contribution to the development of international commercial arbitration in the region or its ability to attract third country economic operators to arbitration in the Mercosur. Its scope of application is determined by exorbitant and overreaching provisions, which if literally observed, would govern any arbitration – even if not venued in a Member Country – dealing with disputes originated in a transaction having significant contacts with such country.[135] As indicated above, the Buenos Aires Agreement also introduces a number of substantive and conflict of laws provisions – not all of them adequate or adapted to modern trends[136] – governing procedural and other aspects of international arbitrations, including the setting aside of arbitral awards. Since the Buenos Aires Agreement has the effect of introducing uniform legislation in the ratifying countries on the arbitral matters it covers, it risks forestalling the unilateral introduction of more progressive and meditated legislation on such matters by the member countries, or superseding existing and more appropriate legislation already found in those countries. Brazil has for that reason introduced a reservation regarding Article 20 of the Agreement on the selection of the applicable law because it is contrary to the broad autonomy of the parties granted in that respect by article 2 of the Brazilian Arbitration Act.[137]

19-108 In part, the confusing and unsatisfactory Latin American situation regarding the interaction of international treaties on international arbitral matters inter se or with national laws is also the consequence of exogenous political

---

[135] See commentary on Art. 3 of the Agreement providing for its conditions of application in H. Grigera Naón, 'El Acuerdo Sobre Arbitraje Comercial Internacional del Mercosur: Un Análisis Crítico' in (2003) *Revista Brasileira de Arbitragem* (Ediçao Especial do Lançamento) 16 at pp. 17–19. *See also*, J. Bosco Lee, 'L'Arbitrage commercial international dans le Mercosur: l'Accord de Buenos Aires de 1998' in (2004) 3 *Revue de l'arbitrage* 565.

[136] Grigera Naón, *supra* n. 135 at pp. 19–26.

[137] N. de Araujo, 'A Arbitragem Internacional-O Papel da Codificaçao Interamericana e Os Laudos Arbitrais Estrangeiros No Brasil' in (2004) 15 *Revista Mexicana de Derecho Internacional, Privado y Comparado* 109 at p. 124, who refers to Decree 4719 of 4 June 2003, gazetted on 5 June 2003, enacting this Agreement in Brazil.

factors, the uneven perception of the importance of commercial arbitration by the different countries of the region, the dissimilar pace of liberalisation of their economies or international trade, and their concomitant different pace in overcoming anti-arbitration prejudices. There seems to be little doubt that the less progressive provisions found in the Panama Convention regarding the enforcement of arbitral agreements, or the double exequatur provisions regarding the recognition and enforcement of arbitral awards present in the Las Leñas Protocol and the Montevideo Convention, or the absence of any reference to the New York Convention in the Buenos Aires Agreement, respond to peculiarities of arbitral legislation in Brazil predating its 1996 Arbitration Act, or to the fact that Brazil had not yet ratified the Panama or New York Conventions when those treaties were negotiated and ratified. In the case of the Mercosur agreements, another political factor should also be mentioned.

19-109 The pace of the political agendas of the different Mercosur countries regarding their economic integration often required advancing in other relatively secondary aspects of the organisation of Mercosur, such as the implementation of certain complementary legal instruments to facilitate intra-Mercosur economic cooperation (like the Las Leñas Protocol) without always properly analysing or understanding the legal technicalities involved or the ulterior repercussions of the texts finally adopted on the desirable future evolution of the covered legal field. This circumstance was aggravated by the absence of extended consultation on such legal matters with the different social, economic and specialised sectors whose activities are directly affected by those texts. The final result was the lack of a sufficiently planned and educated approach by the Mercosur countries to the shaping and ratification of international treaties aimed at fostering and facilitating the utilisation of international commercial arbitration and the ensuing multiplication of overlapping treaties with conflicting, backward or unclear provisions. Such an unsatisfactory outcome could have been obviated had the European Union example of ratifying the New York Convention and avoiding the adoption of uniform common rules on arbitral matters been followed.

VII. CONCLUSION

19-110 Although having points in common, general commercial arbitration differs from semi-public arbitrations within the context of BITs or involving foreign investment or foreign alien treatment issues, in that the latter are closely related to matters of sovereign national interest falling, in the domestic context, within the purview of public and constitutional law although largely governed, from the international perspective, by public international law. These circumstances render the submission of such questions to international arbitration a matter of high political sensitivity and public visibility. The outcome of these arbitral cases also has, almost invariably, a political impact. In Latin America, as mentioned above, the political fluctuations of Latin American governments regarding the arbitration of these kinds of disputes has affected and continues to affect the official attitude in respect of such arbitrations that, however, extend, often with a multiplying effect, to the treatment of commercial arbitration at large even when it does not concern vital public interests or foreign investment. If in some cases such fluctuations are beneficial for the growth of arbitration when there is a positive attitude towards the submission to arbitration of semi-public disputes, they have an excessively expansive adverse effect when the trend goes the contrary way. In any case, a pronounced dependence of the growth of arbitration in Latin America on political fluctuations in one sense or another conspires against the lasting effects of any progress attained and weakens the efficacy and reliability of the rule of law.

19-111 Recent developments confirm the damaging effects of these pendulum fluctuations. Reference has been made to the widespread acceptance in Latin America during the last two decades of international commercial arbitration in connection with both foreign investment and general commercial arbitration that is the consequence of political and socio-economic factors described above. One of the characteristics of this trend is that it was essentially the consequence of governmental decisions prompted by a specific vision of the world economy and the ways and means of inserting Latin American national economies into the world scenario.

19-112 Unlike the early expansion of arbitration in certain regions of Latin America in the 1915–1930 period, this more recent and much more general movement favourable to arbitration was triggered at governmental level, i.e., from top to bottom, rather than from bottom to top, and as a part of a more general policy aimed at creating what was supposed to be a general atmosphere favourable to free trade and the attraction of foreign investment. For this reason, this movement was too closely allied to – and dependent on – the political circumstances prompting it and was often launched before the courts, the legal profession and local business circles became familiarised with the role and advantages of international commercial arbitration. This accounts for the fragility of the pro-arbitration movement of the recent decades and the possibility of a relapse into prior history should the political and economic ideas underlying it disappear.[138]

19-113 However, on the other hand, this pendulum oscillation favouring arbitration had an unprecedented characteristic by Latin American standards. It found expression through massive governmental action radically changing the legal framework – both through the introduction of new legislation and the ratification of treaties on the recognition and enforcement of arbitration agreements and foreign arbitral awards and BITs – regarding arbitration, in ways that often compromised the international obligations of Latin American states. For these reasons, it gained an unparalleled level of institutional crystallisation and permanence never before attained by previous efforts favouring arbitration in Latin America, as well as recognition by a substantial number of court decisions in different countries of the region.

19-114 Notwithstanding such circumstance, some of the examples given above – particularly those concerning Argentina or Venezuela – may indicate that some Latin American countries are embarked on a backswing of the political pendulum, with an adverse impact on the growth of arbitration in these countries. It is possibly too early to predict whether this is an anecdotal regressive movement prompted by momentary political strategies, just rhetoric for internal political consumption, or is more firmly rooted in deeper conviction and determination. However, such backswing is a confirmation of the fragile bases on which the pro-arbitration movement in Latin America really stands. It is clear that even today, in many Latin American countries two different schools of thought uneasily coexist: one adverse to commercial arbitration and the other favouring it. Both schools have adherents in the judiciary and in academia, and in some countries, like Argentina and Venezuela, the first school seems to enjoy the approval of government circles and is heavily influenced by political considerations. Other countries, like Brazil, have adopted a more mature attitude towards international arbitration. With the exception of the possibly anecdotal

---

[138] Frutos Peterson, *supra* n. 49 at p. 449; esp. at p. 450:

'Malheureusement, ce processus de reconnaissance, qui va "de l'extérieur à l'intérieur", risque de réduire l'efficacité de l'arbitrage commercial latinoaméricain, puisqu'une grande majorité de ces pays ont décidé d' adopter de manière inconditionnelle ce réglement des différends dans le seul but d'attirer plus d'investissements étrangers sans se soucier véritablement de l'importance ou des conséquences qu'implique l'apport de cette méthode de règlement des litiges au niveau du cadre juridique national'.

Copel case referred to above,[139] the Brazilian courts seem to have distanced themselves from a general adverse attitude regarding commercial arbitration confirmed by the final dismissal by the Brazilian Supreme Court of objections regarding the constitutionality of the Brazilian Arbitration Act.[140] The Mexican courts seem to be oriented in the same direction.

19-115 In any case, if the anti-arbitration trend noticeable in some countries of the region persists, it will soon negatively affect, not only the growth of arbitration in those countries, but also the respect for and advancement of the rule of law, domestic or international. Court or governmental action responsive to such a regressive trend – either because the courts of law had not evolved their attitude towards arbitration in parallel with the pro-arbitral stance evidenced by modern legislation or treaties, or because the political pendulum swung back to historical positions less favourable or adverse to arbitration – is necessarily incompatible with the legal framework favourable to international arbitration largely adopted by Latin American countries, including Argentina and Venezuela, that has already taken the form of legislation and the assumption of international treaty obligations. The main effect of such an unsympathetic attitude towards arbitration, which implies ignoring existing legal realities, is confusion and uncertainty, and the frustration of legitimate expectations created by such realities; briefly said, it leads to undermining the rule of law, with all the adverse social and economic consequences thereby entailed; and certainly conspires against the growth of arbitration in the region.

19-116 It is true that the adverse impact of political factors on the growth of arbitration is far from being an exclusively Latin American phenomenon. It is no secret that governmental sectors and interest groups in the USA have carried frontal attacks against NAFTA and particularly its Chapter 11, and that allegations as to the unconstitutionality of NAFTA dispute resolution provisions are from time to time revived. Thus it has been recently written that:

> when the United States is on the receiving end of a request of arbitration, protests are heard about 'American laws being overridden' by NAFTA tribunals. American legislators warn 'against sacrificing state and local laws at the altar of ill-defined investor rights' … Opposition to NAFTA by special interests groups within the United States has resulted in a retreat from the traditional level of American governmental support for binding

---

[139] *See supra* n. 122 and corresponding text.
[140] *See supra* n. 86 and corresponding text.

arbitration as a means to protect foreign investment. This policy shift is highly problematic, and ultimately will cause significant harm to American interests abroad.[141]

19-117 This is undoubtedly a troubling development apparently premised on a double standard approach to the treatment of foreign investment and international relations. Ironically, such unsympathetic US reactions to international arbitral adjudication of foreign investment claims are almost a replica of similar homeward attitudes registered in Latin American countries mentioned above, that also seek justification in domestic public and constitutional law considerations. If the USA ends up endorsing this trend, it will thereby help legitimise similar positions held by anti-arbitration sectors in the Latin American states and contribute to the expanded adoption of similar anti-arbitration policies by Latin American governments, with inevitably profound adverse consequences for advancing and upholding the rule of law through international arbitration.

19-118 However, it was precisely to combat double standards in international relations that Sarmiento, Calvo and Drago developed ideas aimed at fashioning the international rule of law and resorting to international arbitration in its support. In view of the existing international undertakings and obligations already assumed by many Latin American states, particularly in the area of foreign investment protection, relying upon and defending the international rule of law and the international dispute resolution mechanisms putting it into effect are of paramount importance for Latin American countries in their efforts to protect and advance their rights and interests. Because of that circumstance, failure to observe a line of action consistent with such strategy, i.e., one responsive to the existing legal situation, by seeking an illusory refuge within the confined limits of national boundaries and courts, is a course of action without a future. The most damaging effects of such an autistic approach – which cannot legitimately claim the support of the Doctrine of either Carlos Calvo or Luis María Drago – would certainly be felt at the international level, in part because of its vast global irradiations and the difficulty to reverse later the ensuing negative impact.

19-119 Within the context of the present and already assumed international obligations of many of the Latin American states, the only proper and sound course of action is then to assert their rights by upholding and relying upon the

---

[141] G. Aguilar Alvarez and W. Park, 'The New Face of Investment Arbitration: NAFTA Chapter 11' in (2003) 28 *Yale Journal of International Law* 365 at p. 395 (footnotes omitted).

international rule of law before the international arbitration tribunals, the decisions of which they freely committed to accept. In such context, it is only the international rule of law that can guarantee such states a treatment permitting them 'to attain their full measure of freedom through sustainable development'.[142] Such a course of action would be, at the end of the day, nothing more than following the profound teachings of Calvo and Drago, whose efforts were always oriented towards the fashioning and defence of the rule of law in the international context through peaceful means of dispute resolution, and particularly, through international arbitration, i.e., a rule of law conceived, not 'for the passing hour' but as the expression of 'principles for an expanding future'.[143]

19-120 As we said at the beginning, it is only within a historic context that present realities can be properly assessed and a proper future course of action adopted: 'Today we study the day before yesterday, in order that yesterday may not paralyze today, and today may not paralyze tomorrow'.[144] It is to be hoped that enlightened Latin American political leaders, jurists and judges will look back to the profound Latin American law traditions based on respect of the international rule of law to prevent a distorted and short-sighted understanding of such traditions from paralysing the present and future growth of arbitration in or in connection with Latin America.

---

[142] 'Groping Towards Grotius: The WTO and the International Rule of Law', unpublished version of the address by James Bacchus, Chairman, Appellate Body, World Trade Organisation, delivered at Harvard Law School, Cambridge, MA, on 1 October 2002, p. 14.

[143] B. Cardozo, *The Nature of the Legal Process* (Yale University Press, 1921), p. 83.

[144] Maitland, as quoted by Cardozo, *supra* n. 143 at p. 51.

*Julian D.M. Lew QC**

CHAPTER 20

ACHIEVING THE DREAM: AUTONOMOUS ARBITRATION?

I. INTRODUCTION: DREAMS AND NIGHTMARES

20-1 Do you dream? When do you dream? What do you dream about? Do you dream about international arbitration? Is there a dream for international arbitration? Is the concept of delocalised arbitration, or arbitration not controlled by national law, a dream or nightmare? Is autonomous arbitration a reality, or is 'every arbitration necessarily … a national arbitration, that is to say, subject to a specific system of national law'?[1]

20-2 As long ago as the mid-1950s, when participating in the drafting of the New York Convention, Frédéric Eisemann, then Secretary-General of the ICC International Court of Arbitration, lobbied for a denationalised, international arbitration award.[2] It was then too early for international arbitration to be detached from national law. Nonetheless, in many ways the New York Convention laid the seeds for autonomous international arbitration.

20-3 The ideal and expectation is for international arbitration to be established and conducted according to internationally accepted practices, free from the controls of parochial national laws, and without the interference or review of

---

* Professor Julian D.M. Lew QC, Barrister/Arbitrator, Head of School of International Arbitration. The author acknowledges the assistance of Angie Raymond, Lecturer in Commercial Law at the School of International Arbitration.
[1] F.A. Mann, 'Lex Facit Arbitrum' in P. Sanders (ed.), *International Arbitration: Liber Amicorum for Martin Domke* (1967), p. 157 at p. 159. Also at (1986) 2 *Arb. Int'l* 241 at p. 244.
[2] 'Enforcing Arbitration Awards under the New York Convention: Experience and Prospects', prepared text of speech in honour of the New York Convention. Day Speech, delivered in 1998, contained in the speech by Ottoarndt Glossner, delegate to the 1958 Conference.

Julian D.M.Lew and Loukas A. Mistelis (eds), Arbitration Insights, 455-486
© 2007 Kluwer Law International. Printed in the Netherlands

national courts. Arbitration agreements and awards should be recognised and given effect, with little or no complication or review, by national courts.

20-4 By corollary, the nightmare scenario exists in situations where national laws control a narrow right of access and the subject matters capable of being resolved in international arbitration. These nightmare scenarios undermine the international arbitration process. There can be no justification for national courts to intercede in the arbitration process or second-guess the determinations and analyses of an international arbitration tribunal. Courts which do so for parochial local law reasons, or because the court thinks its procedures and analyses are preferable and more reliable than those that exist in arbitration, ignore the intention and expectation of the parties and the autonomy of international arbitration.

20-5 Nightmare scenarios include anti-arbitration injunctions. These can be directed against a party to the arbitration agreement, the arbitrators or the institution.[3] These have been made for the intended purpose of protecting nationals of the issuing court[4] and to intimidate the tribunal.[5] Such orders have also been made where the national court thinks itself more appropriate to determine the validity of the agreement to arbitrate, despite the acceptance of the doctrines of separability and competence-competence.[6]

20-6 It is essential to remember that, in every international arbitration, parties and arbitrators are invariably from different jurisdictions. The place of arbitration is frequently selected as a neutral country. The parties have rejected the normal jurisdiction offered by national courts. They have intentionally placed themselves and their dispute settlement mechanism in a neutral, non-national domain. For this reason, national laws have no interest in controlling the arbitration process.

---

[3] E. Gaillard (ed.), *Anti-suit Injunctions in International Arbitration* (Institute of International Arbitration (IAI), 2005).

[4] Examples given by S.M. Schwebel, 'Anti-suit Injunctions in International Arbitration' in Gaillard, *supra* n. 3 at 5; Baum, 'Anti-suit Injunctions Issued by National Courts to Permit Arbitration Proceedings' in Gaillard, *supra* n. 3 at 19; and J.D.M. Lew, 'Anti-suit Injunctions Issued by National Courts to Prevent Arbitration Proceedings' in Gaillard, *supra* n. 3 at 25.

[5] E.g., *Himpurna California Energy* v. *Indonesia* (2000) XXV YBCA 11; *Hub Power Co. (Hubco)* v. *Pakistan WAPDA* in (2000) 16 *Arb Int'l* 1439. *See also* P. Cornell and A. Handley, 'Himpurna and Hub: International Arbitration in Developing Countries' in (2000) 15(9) *Mealey's International Arbitration Report* 39.

[6] *See* e.g., UNICTRAL Model Law, art. 16; UNCITRAL Arbitration Rules, art. 21.

II. Practical and Theoretic Development of Arbitration

20-7 Since the beginning of recorded time, arbitration has existed in some form as a dispute resolution mechanism.[7] As a private mechanism, commercial parties have fashioned and varied its form and structure to their needs with increasing refinement and success. National laws have variously sought to control, organise, administer, support or even interfere with the process.

20-8 Why has arbitration survived the test of time? Simply because it has served the users well. It has met the needs of those business entities which have considered national courts to be unsuited to their needs or even rejected the courts as inappropriate for the particular relationship.[8] It should never be ignored that the arbitration agreement is itself a definitive contract, often commercially driven (such as price, payment and delivery terms, and warranties), the specific purpose of which is to exclude national courts being involved in disputes between the parties.

20-9 Throughout the years there have been tensions between state control of arbitration and the authority of parties to determine the jurisdiction and finality of the arbitration process. This has been the battle for supremacy between national law, on the one hand, and the independence or autonomy of the arbitration process system, on the other hand. For much of the time party autonomy was the driving force in international arbitration, even if not the ultimate power. The parties' agreement that their disputes be resolved by arbitration was the basis of the arbitrators' jurisdiction and authority and of the form of the arbitration. However, national law prescribed party autonomy, limited the powers of arbitrators and the extent of the arbitrators' jurisdiction, and in some form reviewed arbitrators' determinations.

20-10 Today, there is increasingly, I suggest, a new regime. International arbitration is a *sui juris* or autonomous dispute resolution process, governed primarily by non-national rules and accepted international commercial rules and practices. Party autonomy is still today the principal basis for arbitration.[9] As

---

[7] For a further discussion, *see* 'A Brief History of Arbitration' in *Domke on Commercial Arbitration*, Part I, *The Nature of Arbitration*, ch. 2.

[8] Parties to arbitration 'usually seek an independent decision-maker, detached from the courts, governmental institutions, and cultural biases of either party': G.A. Born, *International Commercial Arbitration* (2nd edn, 2001), p. 2.

[9] Though, admittedly, there are an increasing number of arbitrations without privity of contract based on BITs.

such, the relevance and influence of national arbitration laws and of national court supervision and revision is greatly reduced.

20-11   It is my theme that international arbitration is, and should be recognised to be, an autonomous process for the determination of all types of international business disputes. It exists in its own space – a non-national or transnational or, if you prefer, an international domain. It has its own space independent of all national jurisdictions. This has implications for the approach of national courts and law when their involvement with a particular arbitration is sought. At the very least, the existence, structure, procedure and effect of international commercial arbitration are, or at least should be, above the direct controls of national laws and courts.

20-12   It is essential to recognise the reality of when, how and why arbitration is chosen. The courts and law should be wary of interjecting where they have been intentionally and expressly excluded. The courts are only involved when one party seeks to involve the court despite it having been rejected as a suitable body for the parties' differences. The court should therefore become involved only to assist and on very limited grounds of support, within defined limits, and should not exercise its powers to review issues of substance.

20-13   Admittedly, international arbitration must coexist with national laws.[10] It needs the recognition and support of national laws – the users of or parties in international arbitration expect that national laws will recognise and support the arbitration process. However, the users of international arbitration, and the system itself, expect that national courts will not interfere in the arbitration process, will not review the parties' decision to submit their disputes to arbitration, and will not seek to review or know better than the arbitrators in any particular case.

20-14   There are rules of private international law that regulate the interaction of different or conflicting national laws. There are also rules to regulate the relations between national laws and international arbitration. These rules have their origin in public international law, private international law and intergovernmental and

---

[10] 'An inevitable conflict results from the mixture of private consent and public power in arbitration. Aspirations toward delocalised dispute resolution collide with the national norms that must be invoked if an arbitration clause is to be more than a piece of paper': W.W. Park, 'The Lex Loci Arbitri and International Commercial Arbitration' in 32 *Int'l and Comp. LQ* 21 (1983) at p. 55 n. 30.

non-government instruments which have developed procedures and practices that have wide international acceptance. Inevitably there are tentacles that float down from the international arbitration domain to the national jurisdiction, to assure recognition of the agreement to arbitrate, to give effect to awards of international tribunals and to obtain assistance for the international arbitration process when needed.

20-15 I propose to explore the development of this autonomous international arbitration system. In doing so I will look at: (i) the history of international arbitration; (ii) developments in recent times; (iii) changing factors which have affected the international business environment; (iv) international and national instruments relating to international arbitration, and (v) some national court decisions which reflect acceptance of the autonomous character of international arbitration.

III. HISTORICAL DEVELOPMENT OF INTERNATIONAL ARBITRATION

20-16 There are three distinct time frames in the development of international arbitration: the Middle Ages to about the eighteenth century; the eighteenth century to soon after the Second World War, and the 1950s to the present day.[11] In each time frame there was a different attitude towards international arbitration.

20-17 In the first time period, the regulation of arbitration by national law was non-existent or minimal. The business community was left free to structure and use an arbitration system it considered suitable for its needs. The early forms of arbitration often existed without the blessings of, and perhaps oblivious to, the judicial mechanisms and national laws of the sovereign states in which they operated and which may have been relevant. In fact, at that time arbitration was crafted specifically to facilitate the dispute resolution needs of a particular industry or a community.[12] There was no need or desire to imitate the procedures of any judiciary; that was often precisely what the industries sought to avoid.

20-18 To determine these disputes, arbitrators applied relevant established custom, created out of the merchants' own needs and views, as the legal rules and standards according to which rights and obligations of the parties were determined, often shunning the legal technicalities and substance of local law.

---

[11] *See* Domke, *supra* n. 7.
[12] For a brief discussion, *see* A. Redfern and M. Hunter, *The Law and Practice of International Commercial Arbitration* (4th edn, Sweet & Maxwell, 2004), paras 1–03 and 1–04.

This was an international commercial law applicable to these international transactions – the *lex mercatoria*[13] of those times.

20-19   During the second time period, the eighteenth century to the 1950s, the sovereign state sought to control many aspects of arbitration through its national laws and judicial intervention. It was during this time that arbitration became more formalised with the development and adoption of specific arbitration legislation, for example, the English Arbitration Act 1698,[14] the French arbitration law in the Code of Civil Procedure of 1806 and the German Code of Civil Procedure of 1879.[15]

20-20   Despite the emerging national arbitration laws and the widespread use of business arbitration, the state courts of many jurisdictions were unwilling to accept arbitration as an appropriate dispute resolution mechanism. In fact, states established tight controls over arbitration in both domestic and international matters. For example, German and English courts would refuse to hear a dispute that had been previously submitted to arbitration and even imposed penalties for such a submission.[16] By the end of the second time period, it was clear that states felt the need to control activity that occurred within its jurisdiction and especially the dispute resolution mechanisms of the international commercial community of the particular country.

20-21   The judicial basis of control was threefold. First, the attitude was that every activity which occurred within a jurisdiction should be within the purview of the state law and court. Many courts and judges took the approach, and still do today, that they have been created by the state, through its constitutional means, for the specific purpose of determining disputes of parties within the jurisdiction and in accordance with the law of the court. Secondly, there emerged the realistic possibility and concern that an alternative mechanism would erode the authority of and respect for the national courts' jurisdiction. Thirdly, there has been and

---

[13]   *See* J.D.M. Lew, L.A. Mistelis and S.M. Kroll, *Comparative International Commercial Arbitration* (Kluwer, 2003), p. 453. *See also* C.M. Schmitthoff, 'The Law of International Trade, its Growth, Formulation and Operation' in C.M. Schmitthoff (ed.), *The Sources of the Law of International Trade* (London, 1964); Goldman, 'Lex Mercatoria' in (1983) 3 *Forum Internationale* 194.

[14]   Note: there was earlier legislation giving recognition to arbitration agreements and awards.

[15]   *See* Lew, Mistelis and Kroll, *supra* n. 13 at p. 71. *See also Fouchard, Gaillard, Goldman on International Commercial Arbitration* (Kluwer, 1999), p. 75 at para. 160.

[16]   *See* Domke, *supra* n. 7.

still is 'judicial jealousy' of the alternative mechanism which resolves disputes in a more efficient and effective manner.[17]

20-22 This judicial scepticism towards the arbitration process was expressed in many court decisions and in legislation. Arbitration was allowed as an exception rather than as a right. Courts were jealous that their authority, indeed obligation, to determine disputes between parties within the jurisdiction was not to be eroded. Accordingly, where arbitration was allowed it was rather a toleration leaving limited areas for final determination of the arbitrators and the right of judges to review and revise many aspects of the arbitrators' conclusions. This attitude is well illustrated by the refusal of the US Supreme Court in 1845 in *Tobey* v. *County of Briston*[18] to recognise an arbitration agreement. Joseph Story J[19] said: 'It is certainly the policy of the common law, not to compel men to submit their rights and interests to arbitration, or to enforce agreements for such a purpose'.

20-23 Similarly, in England, Lord Campbell in *Scott* v. *Avery*[20] held that parties by contract may not oust the jurisdiction of the courts.[21] The long-standing pattern of judiciaries having to struggle with the tension of sovereign control and party autonomy over dispute resolution remains today.[22]

20-24 The last time period, the 1950s to date, has spanned some 50 years of rapid change. There has been an increased internationalisation founded upon the arbitration community's ability to address the needs of both the commercial world and the sovereign's desire to ensure basic fairness – hence the wish to control the freedom of arbitration decisions. An examination of each of these, in

---

[17] In *Scott* v. *Avery* (1856) 5 HL Cas. 811, Lord Campbell stated that the doctrine of hostility to arbitration 'probably originated in the contests of the different courts in ancient times for extent of jurisdiction all of them being opposed to anything that would deprive one of them of jurisdiction'.

[18] *Tobey* v. *County of Briston* 23 F. Cass. 1313 (C.C. Mass. 1845).

[19] Supreme Court Justice Joseph Story is best known for the case of *United States* v. *Amistad*. He also wrote numerous commentaries, including *Commentaries on the Conflict of Laws* (1834), p. 1321.

[20] (1856) 5 HL Cas. 811.

[21] E.S. Wolaver, 'The Historical Background of Commercial Arbitration' in (1934) 83 *U Pa. L Rev.* 132, cited in Domke, *supra* n. 7.

[22] This struggle is not absolute. For example, in the well-known case of *Parsons and Whittmore* v. *Société Générale de l'Industrie du Papier (RAKTA)* 508 F. 2d 969 (2d. Cir. 1974), the court expressed a hands off approach, as evidenced by the statement: '[a] court has no general power of review or to enter into the arbitral chambers'.

turn, will demonstrate that the evolution of international arbitration has been a slow process of assimilation and convergence of the two overarching entities, i.e., the commercial community and the state which have together provided the bedrock of ideas and beliefs upon which international arbitration is based.

20-25   In particular, this period has seen major changes to the political and legal environment generally. In the aftermath of the Second World War, the economic power moved from Europe to the USA and the 'Cold War' stand off between the Soviet Union and the West influenced attitudes towards dispute settlement by arbitration.[23] The colonial era drew to a rapid close and the countries of Asia and Africa became independent from colonial powers such as Britain, France, Germany, Holland and Spain. The effect of decolonisation was the emergence of many independent and developing countries.[24] It was no longer possible for the European business world to impose their will in respect of applicable law and national court jurisdictions.

20-26   The former colonies took time to develop their own laws and systems. However, from the outset parties from those countries had a large measure of scepticism about the equality of their commercial arrangements with parties from the developed countries, and the possibility of a fair and impartial hearing in a dispute settlement forum, court or arbitration in the country of the old colonial powers.

20-27   In the late 1980s, the communist system collapsed and those countries needed enormous foreign investment. The 'tiger economies' in Asia offered new opportunities for the developed business world, in markets that were not mature and were growing. In addition to the normal trading arrangements there was enormous developed world investment in these countries. This was on the back of the now almost 2,500 bilateral investment treaties (BITs); there were only 700 in 1990, 15 years ago.

20-28   Finally, modern technology, air travel, instant communication and globalisation generally have changed the whole face of international business. Almost all past certainties have gone. The regimes and environment are new and

---

[23] For further discussion, *see* Y. Dezalay and B. Garth, *Dealing in Virtue: International Commercial Arbitration and the Construction of a Transnational Legal Order* (Chicago, University of Chicago Press, 1996).

[24] In 1947 the United Nations had 57 members. Currently, there are 191 member states. Information available at www.un.org/Overview/growth.htm

constantly changing. The applicable law, and English law in particular, can no longer be imposed to govern the substance of contractual arrangements. It must be selected for its real merits not for presumed neutrality. National courts are unacceptable and routinely and intentionally avoided in the greatest number of international situations. International arbitration, before neutral arbitrators, in a third country, with non-national or international procedures being followed, has become the essential mechanism for the settlement of all kinds of international business disputes. Increasingly too, it would appear, arbitrations are taking place under all systems in many non-European or US venues.

20-29   All these events necessitated changes to the regimes of international arbitration. This began with the New York Convention on the Recognition and Enforcement of Foreign Awards 1958, and the Washington Convention on the Settlement of Investment Disputes between States and Foreign Investors 1966. There then followed the efforts of UNCITRAL with its Arbitration Rules in 1976 and the Model Law in 1985. Many national laws were updated and radically changed; the emphasis, direction and structure were changed to reflect modern thinking of the business world. Existing arbitration institutions revised and updated their rules, and innumerable new arbitration institutions have been established.[25]

20-30   These changes all recognised and reflected the move from national to international factors. This movement was essential if arbitration was to remain an acceptable international dispute resolution system. The control of national courts and national laws became subordinate to the intentions of the parties and the arbitrators' authority. The law is and can be no longer a control factor in arbitration; rather it is a facilitator if and when necessary and if invoked by one of the parties.

IV. THE LEGAL NATURE OF ARBITRATION

20-31   No discussion of this topic would be complete without a reference to the doctrinal discussions of the legal nature of arbitration.[26]

---

[25] For a brief discussion, *see* Redfern and Hunter, *supra* n. 12 at paras 1–05 and 1–06.
[26] The written arguments on this issue were largely among civil lawyers, especially in France. *See in particular*, G.A. Born, *International Commercial Arbitration* (2nd edn, 2001), p. 4; Fouchard, Gaillard and Goldman, *supra* p. 15 at pp. 140–142.

20-32   Initially, arbitration was considered to have a 'jurisdictional' character.[27] This was to reflect that arbitration could only take place within the jurisdiction of any country if allowed by the law; the arbitration was subservient to and controlled by the legal system. Party autonomy was considered to have little or only limited relevance, but for the choice of arbitration as the dispute settlement mechanism for international business. That choice was only effective because the law recognised and gave it effect.[28]

20-33   On the other hand, because it existed solely because of the doctrine of party autonomy, others considered arbitration to have a 'contractual' character. This required recognition that the parties' agreement should be given primary importance, as it controls all aspects of the arbitral process.[29] In the absence of agreement there could be no arbitration. Furthermore, party autonomy could influence most aspects of the arbitration, including in particular the form of arbitration, the issues to be resolved, the number and persons of the arbitrators, the law or rules to be applied to determine the substantive rights and obligations of the parties, and the procedure to be followed.

20-34   The problem in theoretical terms is that neither the jurisdictional nor the contractual theories of arbitration encapsulate the fundamental and real nature of arbitration. Accordingly, it was suggested that arbitration had a mixed or hybrid nature; it recognised the attributes of both the jurisdictional and contractual influences on international arbitration as well as the specific characteristics themselves. Essentially, arbitration was made up of two elements: the authority of the local law and party agreement. However, the mixed theory also did not reflect the practical aspects of arbitration: it ignored the various other factors that are inherent in arbitration, such as the arbitrator.

20-35   The fourth and most recent theory looked at arbitration for its specific characteristics and structure. It considered arbitration to have an autonomous nature, recognising that arbitration is a stand-alone mechanism. Notwithstanding the overwhelming importance of party autonomy, it is not in itself a defining

---

[27]   *See* e.g. Mann, *supra* n. 1; A. Jan Van Den Berg, *The New York Convention of 1958* (1981), pp. 28–51; William W. Park, 'The Lex Loci Arbitri and International Commercial Arbitration' in (1983) 32 *ICLQ* 2; F.A. Mann, 'England Rejects "Delocalised" Contracts and Arbitration' in (1984) 33 *ICLQ* 193.

[28]   *See* e.g., *Amin Rasheed Shipping Corp.* v. *Kuwait Insurance Co.* [1984] 1 App. Cas. 50 at 60.

[29]   Statutory or compulsory forms of arbitration are of a totally different nature to the arbitration with which we are concerned.

factor.[30] National laws, non-national arbitration rules, international instruments, the mixed nationalities of the parties and the arbitrators, the neutral place of the arbitration and the special purpose procedure all support the independent and unique nature of the international arbitration process. This does not deny or detract from the circumstances in which national law allows state courts to intervene in the arbitral process. Under all the major rules, in the absence of contrary agreement of the parties, arbitrators have the power and authority to decide how the arbitration should be organised, and the procedure to be used. This autonomous theory recognises arbitration as a stand-alone mechanism for dispute settlement in international business transactions.

20-36 Just as many commercial transactions have momentum and natures of their own, so too does the agreement to arbitrate. For example, finance transactions, bank guarantees, agreement for the sale and purchase of shares, intellectual property licences, agency and distribution contracts, and, frankly, all kind of contracts have their own momentum. For these contracts, the law is there to support, recognise and if necessary give effect to those forms of specialised contractual relationships. However, the law is not there to validate the parties' agreement, or to second-guess the parties' agreement and the obligations which they have created. Furthermore, the exceptions to the enforcement of the parties' agreement exist in limited circumstances and only in those situations where there is mandatory law or a public policy element. Similarly, in the case of international arbitration, the agreement to arbitrate should be recognised by the law and given effect to by the courts. The awards of tribunals should be recognised and enforced and the exceptions to the general rule of finality should be precisely exceptions, i.e. applied in limited circumstances, within specific and well-defined parameters.

V. DEVELOPMENTS IN RECENT TIMES

20-37 Prior to and during the times of great change, arbitrations were considered to be national or domestic. Even though the parties may have come

---

[30] 'In the field of international arbitration, the principle of the autonomy of the arbitration agreement is of general application, as an international substantive rule upholding the legality of the arbitration agreement, quite apart from any reference to a system of choice of law, because the validity of the agreement must be judged solely in the light of the requirements of international public policy': *Gatoil International Inc.* v. *National Iranian Oil Co.*, 17 December 1991, in (1992) *Rev. Arb.* 281 (for an English translation, *see* (1992) 7(7) Mealeys Int'l Arb. Rep. B1, B3).

from different jurisdictions, and be 'foreign' to the country of the place of arbitration, the arbitration remained a domestic arbitration, subject to the law and the control of the local courts in accordance with the law of the place of arbitration. There was no distinction between domestic and international arbitration. Most national laws had one arbitration regime to recognise and determine the effects to be given to arbitration agreements and awards, and to regulate arbitration in the jurisdiction.

20-38 If arbitration was not domestic, it was foreign. That meant it had taken place outside the jurisdiction and subject to some other national law. In this case the national law had to determine, in accordance with the prevailing conflict of laws rules, whether to recognise the arbitration agreement and/or the arbitration award. As stated by Dr F.A. Mann in 1967:

> every arbitration is necessarily subject to the law of a given State. No private person has the right or power to act on any other level other than that of a municipal law. Every right or power a private person enjoys is inexorably conferred by or derived from a system of municipal law.[31]

20-39 The late Professor Philippe Fouchard, in his seminal work L'arbitrage commercial international in 1965[32] sought to distinguish between national/domestic arbitrations and international arbitrations. This necessitated a recognition that different legal regimes applied to different arbitrations. If the parties were of different nationality and subject to different laws, then a different approach was needed to determine the procedure, issues and applicable law.

20-40 Nonetheless, there remained at this time much support for the Sauser-Hall Institute of International Law[33] and F.A. Mann views that the law of the place regulated all aspects of arbitration. This was manifest in England by the way shipping, insurance, and commodity arbitrations mirrored the procedures of the English courts. There was a presumption that the choice of England as the

---

[31] Mann, *supra* n. 1; Mann, *supra* n. 27; Lew, Mistelis and Kroll, *supra* n. 13 at pp. 74–76; *Dallal v. Bank Mellat* [1986] 1 QB 441; *Naviera Amazonica Peruana SA* v. *Compania Internacional de Seguros del Peru* [1988] 1 Lloyd's Rep. 116; *Coppee Lavalin SA NV* v. *Ken-Ren Chemicals and Fertilisers Ltd* [1994] 2 All ER 449.

[32] Dalloz, Paris. Professsor Fouchard, who died so tragically two years ago, should be recognised as one of the fathers of modern international commercial arbitration.

[33] *See* Sauser-Hall and Reports of Institut de Droit International, (1952) 44-I *Ann IDI* 469; developed further in (1957) 47-II *Ann IDI* 394. For a further discussion, *see* Lew, Mistelis and Kroll, *supra* n. 13 at pp. 79–80.

place of arbitration meant a choice of English law to govern not only the arbitration but also the substantive issues to be determined in the arbitration.[34]

20-41 However, the internationalism following the end of the Second World War resulted in the recognition that national laws had to show a greater degree of respect and therefore recognition of concepts and institutions which were inherently international. The changes were slow but continuous and are well known. They occurred on various levels: through international conventions and instruments; the establishment of new international arbitration institutions or the revision of their arbitration rules; the adoption of new national arbitration laws; the increasing reference to international arbitration as the dispute resolution mechanism between states or state entities and foreign investors or trading parties.[35]

20-42 Many of these developments are pertinent as direct precursors to international arbitration becoming an international regime, and providing the basis for the autonomous nature of arbitration.

20-43 The New York Convention 1958[36] was the beginning of internationalism in arbitration.[37] It recognised that arbitration agreements, proceedings and awards would have their origin and seek to be effective in different jurisdictions. The Convention fundamentally changed the regime for the recognition and enforcement of arbitration agreements and awards that existed in many countries and as reflected in the Geneva Protocol 1923[38] and Convention 1927.[39] Now it was recognised that arbitration agreements were to be recognised worldwide except in the narrow confines where they are 'null and void, inoperative or

---

[34] This presumption was denied only in 1971 in *Compagnie d'Armement Maritime SA* v. *Compagnie Tunisienne de Navigation* [1971] AC 572 (HL). The courts now look to the circumstances of the contractual arrangement to decide what national or other rules govern an international contract, notwithstanding an English court or arbitration choice. *See* D. McClean and K. Beevers, *Morris: The Conflict of Laws* (6th edn, Sweet and Maxwell, 2005), pp. 334–336 and 346–348.

[35] International arbitration is the dispute resolution system of choice in some 2,500 BITs.

[36] The early parties to the Convention were France, Russia, Morocco, India, Israel, Egypt, Czechoslovakia and the Federal Republic of Germany. The USA ratified the Convention in 1970, the United Kingdom in 1975. Today, 137 countries have ratified the Convention.

[37] For a brief discussion, *see* Redfern and Hunter, *supra* n. 12 at pp. 1–18. *See also*, Lew, Mistelis and Kroll, *supra* n. 13 at pp. 20–22.

[38] The 1923 Geneva Protocol on Arbitration Clauses.

[39] The 1927 Geneva Convention, (1929–30) 92 LNTS 302.

incapable of being performed'.[40] And arbitration awards are to be enforced if the successful party shows the existence of an arbitration agreement and the ensuing award.[41] National courts were granted the discretion to refuse enforcement only on the limited grounds in Article V of the Convention.[42]

20-44   This was appositely described by Professor Pieter Sanders, one of the original architects of the New York Convention, and a delegate to the United Nations when the Convention was adopted in 1958:

> The main [aims] ... were, first of all, the elimination of the double exequatur, one in the country where the award was made and another one in the country of enforcement of the award. Under the 1927 Geneva Convention we always requested both. It is logical to require an exequatur only in the country where enforcement of the award is sought and not also in the country where the award was made, but no enforcement is sought. Another element of the proposal was to restrict the grounds for refusal of recognition and enforcement as much as possible and to switch the burden of proof of the existence of one or more of these grounds to the party against whom the enforcement was sought. This again stands to reason.[43]

20-45   Essentially, the New York Convention established just three fundamental standards for international arbitration: the arbitration must conform with or come within the terms of the arbitration agreement; the parties must be treated fairly and with equality (i.e. international due process); and the award must respect international public policy both with respect to its content and its subject matter. These are, of course, the grounds which may allow a national court to refuse to enforce an award made outside its jurisdiction. More importantly, these three simple principles are the cornerstone of modern international arbitration. These rules have been incorporated into most national arbitration laws and are fundamental to autonomous international arbitration.

20-46   What is unfortunate is how national laws, especially in some so-called arbitration-friendly countries, have placed narrow and parochial interpretations

---

[40]   New York Convention, Art. II.3.
[41]   *Ibid.* Art. III.
[42]   *Ibid.* Art. V.1.
[43]   Pieter Sanders, 'Enforcing Arbitral Awards under the New York Convention: Experience and Prospects' (UN No. 92-1-133609-0, 1998), 3, available at www.uncitral.org/pdf/english/texts/arbitration/NY-conv/NYCDay-e.pdf.

on these rules. The effect has been invariably to limit their application and make them subordinate to national law, which in turn gives national courts increased opportunity to intervene in the international arbitration process.

20-47 Then followed the European Convention on International Commercial Arbitration 1961,[44] the first time the international epitaph was used in a modern arbitration instrument. Again, it sought to establish a regime at a level separate from but recognised by national laws.

20-48 Following on the work of the United Nations Economic Commissions for Europe and Africa and the Far East in the mid-1960s,[45] UNCITRAL's work on international arbitration began in the 1970s. This culminated in the UNCITRAL Arbitration Rules adopted in 1976[46] and the Model Law on International Commercial Arbitration of 1986.

20-49 The UNCITRAL Model Law had two principal aims:[47] first, to provide a model based on internationally or at least widely accepted principles that could be adopted directly into national law by countries that do not have arbitration legislation or which want to modernise their arbitration laws; secondly, it sought to provide a harmonised arbitration law to avoid the then existing patchwork of domestic legislation based on an out-of-date attitude to arbitration, which was inappropriate for international arbitration and which often hindered arbitration operating as a viable international dispute resolution mechanism, autonomous from domestic judicial systems.[48]

---

[44] The European Convention on International Commercial Arbitration (1961) 484 *UNTS* 364, No. 7041 (1963–1964).

[45] For a discussion, *see* P. Benjamin, 'New Arbitration Rules for Use in International Trade' in Sanders, *supra* n. 1, vol. III at p. 361.

[46] Of course, some of the work on these Rules had been done in the context of the United Nations Economic Commissions for Europe (ECE) and for Africa and the Far East (ECAFE). *See* Lew, Mistelis and Kroll, *supra* n. 13 at paras 2-33-2-41.

[47] The Model Law was developed by a working group from 36 countries, and observers from international organisations with specific arbitration expertise, such as the International Chamber of Commerce and the Chartered Institute of Arbitrators. *See* H. Holtzmann and J. Neuhaus, *A Guide to the UNCITRAL Model Law on International Commercial Arbitration: Legislative History and Commentary* (1989), pp. 1230–1232.

[48] United Nations, UNCITRAL: The United Nations Commission on International Trade Law (U.N. No. E.86.V.8, 1986), p. 30 (speaking specifically to the domestic laws as outdated and containing arbitration procedures better suited for court litigation).

20-50 The Model Law provided a reduced role for local court supervision over international arbitrations and allowed a wide berth to the parties to choose and fashion the arbitration system they wanted. The Model Law Explanatory Notes confirm the first aim:

> As evidenced by recent amendments to arbitration laws, there exists a trend in favour of limiting court involvement in international commercial arbitration. This seems justified in view of the fact that *the parties to an arbitration agreement make a conscious decision to exclude court jurisdiction and, in particular in commercial cases, prefer expediency and finality to protracted battles in court.*[49]

20-51 Accordingly, to limit court interference, Article 5 of the Model Law specified that '[i]n matters governed by this Law, no court shall intervene except where so provided in this Law'.[50]

20-52 The intent of the drafters not to regulate the arbitration process but rather allow the parties to craft a dispute resolution mechanism suitable to their needs[51] is expressed as follows:

> Autonomy of the parties to determine the rules of procedure is of special importance in international cases since it allows the parties to select or tailor the rules according to their specific wishes and needs, unimpeded by traditional domestic concepts and without the earlier mentioned risk of frustration. The supplementary discretion of the arbitral tribunal is equally important in that it allows the tribunal to tailor the conduct of the proceedings to the specific features of the case without restraints of the traditional local law, including any domestic rules on evidence. Moreover, it provides a means for solving any procedural questions not regulated in the arbitration agreement or the Model Law.[52]

20-53 The Model Law has to date been adopted in 47 countries and in four states in the USA. It is unfortunate that none of the so-called major arbitration

---

[49] Explanatory Note by the UNCITRAL Secretariat on the Model Law on International Commercial Arbitration, UNCITRAL Model Arbitration Law (1994), p. 18, para. 14 ('Model Law, Explanatory Note') (emphasis added).

[50] Model Law, art. 5.

[51] *Ibid.* art. 19.

[52] Model Law, Explanatory Note, *supra* n. 49 at para. 31.

jurisdictions[53] have adopted the Model Law, especially seeing that they all actively participated in developing its philosophy and drafting, and are participating in (and even seeking to lead) the ongoing discussions of UNCITRAL to further develop the Model Law. Nonetheless, with the Model Law having been adopted in all these jurisdictions, other countries have espoused many of its principles. This has given the Model Law and its rules a greater significance than an ordinary national law. At the very least, the Model Law rules are now generally accepted rules for international arbitration, akin to international trade usages or even a part of the lex mercatoria. The Model Law could also be used to interpret and apply national legal rules. These rules have become a transnational law of international arbitration that further supports the autonomous nature of arbitration.

VI. EMERGENCE OF THE INTERNATIONAL ARBITRATION MECHANISM

20-54 All this led to a changing attitude to international arbitration in the business world and the national laws had to follow. Whatever the interest the state may have in a domestic arbitration involving its citizens, there was little or no interest in international arbitration. The need was to support and give effect to the system.

A. National Legislative Changes in the Major Arbitration Centres

20-55 The national laws which have not adopted the Model Law have moved on to adopt similar provisions. The focus has changed from control and supervision by national law and courts, to freedom to arbitrate and non-intervention. It is illustrative to look briefly at the legislation adopted in a few countries.

20-56 Probably the most liberal reformed arbitration law exists in Switzerland under Private International Law Act 1990 ('Swiss PILA'). This contains liberal substantive rules,[54] gives clear power to the arbitrators to control the arbitration as they consider appropriate, except in those specified cases where the parties agree otherwise.[55] The court's role is to provide 'judicial assistance' especially for the

---

[53] For example, England, France, USA, Sweden, Switzerland.
[54] Particularly with respect to the arbitration agreement, *see* Swiss PILA, art. 178.
[55] *See* e.g., Swiss PILA, arts 183, 184 and 187 with respect to interim relief, taking of evidence and determining the applicable law, respectively.

taking of evidence or interim relief,[56] and only limited court intervention is allowed.[57] Where neither party is domiciled or has a place of business in Switzerland, the parties can expressly agree to exclude all judicial recourse, subject to few restrictions.[58]

20-57 Sweden adopted a new Arbitration Act in 1999 in a similarly liberal vein. Court involvement is largely directed to supporting the arbitration process[59] and arbitrator authority applies to most aspects of the arbitration;[60] challenges to the award are on limited grounds which include dealing with issues outside the scope of the arbitration agreement, or an irregularity in the procedure followed.[61] However, one should note that the Swedish courts have for many years prior to the new law applied a liberal arbitration regime.[62]

20-58 The French New Code of Civil Procedure (NCPC) adopted in 1981 adopted a moderate, yet modern, arbitration system. Parties were given almost unlimited freedom to provide for their own arbitration procedure, either by specific agreement or by incorporating a set of rules, without requiring them to refer to a national law of procedure.[63] Moreover, in a situation where the parties have not made a selection, the arbitrators are given the power to make the determinations. Furthermore, the NCPC does not allow any grounds to appeal against an award (which is allowed in domestic arbitration) but does allow for international awards made in France to be set aside if the award exceeds the authority of the arbitration agreement, if there has been a breach of due process or the award is contrary to international public policy.[64]

---

[56] *Ibid.* arts 183–185.

[57] *Ibid.* arts 179–180.

[58] *Ibid.* art. 192.

[59] *See* e.g. ss. 4, 14–17 and 20 with respect to constituting the tribunal, and s. 26 with respect to summoning witnesses.

[60] E.g. ss. 21–25 subject in limited circumstances to party autonomy.

[61] *See* the decision in *Titan Corp.* v. *Alcan CIT SA* in 2005, where the SVEA Court declined to consider a challenge to an award where, depite the express agreement that Sweden was the place of arbitration, the parties and tribunal agreed to hold hearings of the arbitration outside Sweden for convenience of the parties.

[62] *See* Fouchard, Goldman and Gaillard, *supra* n. 15 at para. 164, *citing* J. Paulsson, 'Arbitrage international et voies de recours: La Cour supreme de Suede dans le sillage des solutions belge et helvetique' in (1990) 117 *JDI* 589.

[63] NCPC art. 1494.

[64] NCPC arts 1502 and 1504.

20-59 Despite the radical changes to English arbitration under the Arbitration Act 1996, it has still a more conservative approach than Switzerland, Sweden, France or the Model Law. Notwithstanding the acceptance of party autonomy and the powers given expressly to arbitrators, the English courts have retained substantial powers of intervention,[65] arbitrations are subject to numerous mandatory provisions,[66] and there are lengthy lists proscribing 'serious irregularities affecting the tribunal, the proceeding, or the award' which all allow a party to challenge an award.[67] Where the courts consider that there has been a serious irregularity, the English courts will rehear the issues in the arbitration, despite the arbitration agreement.[68]

20-60 One significant change, reflected in almost all national laws, has been the lessening of importance of arbitrability. There are ever fewer restrictions on subjects and contract types that can be submitted to arbitration. Most jurisdictions now accept that where parties have agreed that their disputes should be resolved by arbitration there is no good legal or policy reason to reserve any of these issues for the courts. Even the 'holy cow' of EU competition law can now be considered by an arbitration tribunal.[69] The European Commission has accepted this factor under the EC Merger Regulation[70] where it has allowed arbitration to be the determinative procedure in the event of a challenge to observance of the conditions on which the merger was approved. Furthermore, under Council Regulation 1/2004 an arbitration tribunal can now decide whether exemption under Article 81(3) is appropriate in particular circumstances.

20-61 Most national laws now recognise that the arbitration tribunal has the primary responsibility for determining its own jurisdiction. This is through the doctrine of separability, first recognised in the USA by the US Supreme Court decision in Prima Paints v. Flood and Conklin in 1967.[71] This doctrine is now enshrined in Article 16.1 of the UNCITRAL Model Law which states:

---

[65] E.g. Arbitration Act 1996, ss. 45 and 69 which allow the courts to determine preliminary points of law when English law is applicable.

[66] Arbitration Act 1996, Sch. 1.

[67] Arbitration Act 1996, s. 68.

[68] *See Gulf Azov* v. *Baltic Shipping* [1999] 1 Lloyd's Rep. 68.

[69] For a further discussion, *see* A. Mourre, 'Réflexions critiques sur la suppression du contrôle de la motivation des sentences arbitrales en droit français' in (2001) 19(4) *ASA Bulletin* 634.

[70] Merger Directive: EC Regulation 139/2004 of 20 January 2004 ('ECMR').

[71] 388 U.S. 395 (1967).

The arbitral tribunal may rule on its own jurisdiction, including any objections with respect to the existence or validity of the arbitration agreement. For that purpose, an arbitration clause which forms part of a contract shall be treated as an agreement independent of the other terms of the contract. A decision by the arbitral tribunal that the contract is null and void shall not entail ipso jure the invalidity of the arbitration clause.[72]

20-62 This is also allowed in all the main international arbitration rules. Article 21 of the UNCITRAL Arbitration Rules provides:

(1) The arbitral tribunal shall have the power to rule on objections that it has no jurisdiction, including any objections with respect to the existence or validity of the arbitration clause or of the separate arbitration agreement.

(2) The arbitral tribunal shall have the power to determine the existence or the validity of the contract of which an arbitration clause forms a part. For the purposes of article 21, an arbitration clause which forms part of a contract and which provides for arbitration under these Rules shall be treated as an agreement independent of the other terms of the contract. A decision by the arbitral tribunal that the contract is null and void shall not entail ipso jure the invalidity of the arbitration clause.[73]

20-63 Backed by the Model Law, the reformed or modern arbitration laws which now exist, in most major arbitration countries and in the developing countries, all seem now to (1) recognise the doctrine of party autonomy; (2) acknowledge that the tribunal is the sole authority for all aspects of the arbitration, including jurisdiction and procedure, subject to the safeguards of the validity and ambit of the arbitration agreement and due process; (3) establish and reinforce the hands off approach of the courts, subject to narrow exceptions; and (4) ensure the enforcement of arbitration awards and agreements – with limited exceptions.

B. Institutional Rules

20-64 This autonomy is now reflected in all the major arbitration rules. One thing is clear: there is no reference to any national procedural law in any of the rules: not that of the parties, the arbitrators or even the place of arbitration. The

---

[72] There are similar provisions in Swiss PILA, art. 186 and English Arbitration Act 1996, s. 7.
[73] *See also* art. 23 of the LCIA Rules in very similar terms to art. 16 of the Model Law.

power is given to the tribunal to fix a procedure suitable for the case. Typically, Article 15 of the UNCITRAL Arbitration Rules provides:

(1) Subject to these Rules, the arbitral tribunal may conduct the arbitration in such manner as it considers appropriate, provided that the parties are treated with equality and that at any stage of the proceedings each party is given a full opportunity of presenting his case.

(2) If either party so requests at any stage of the proceedings, the arbitral tribunal shall hold hearings for the presentation of evidence by witnesses, including expert witnesses, or for oral argument. In the absence of such a request, the arbitral tribunal shall decide whether to hold such hearings or whether the proceedings shall be conducted on the basis of documents and other materials.

20-65 The key conditions are to treat the parties equally, and to allow them the opportunity to present their case.

20-66 An important question in every arbitration is the form of presenting claims, defences, evidence and argument in international arbitration. The national laws and arbitration rules are silent on detailed procedure. The ICC Rules leave it to the tribunal to determine the facts by whatever means it considers most appropriate, but makes no provision for written submissions.[74] The UNCITRAL, LCIA and Swiss Rules by contrast do provide for written statements of case and defence.[75] The Rules also are silent in respect of the form and procedure at any oral hearing. However, all the rules provide that the specifics of the form, content and number of submissions from the parties and the timetable for these submissions, as well as procedure generally, are ultimately a matter for the tribunal except in some circumstances where the parties agree the procedure.

20-67 Subject to these Rules, the arbitral tribunal may conduct the arbitration in such a manner as it considers appropriate, provided that it ensures equal treatment of the parties and their right to be heard. National procedural rules, including that of place of arbitration, should not be presumed to be applied in the absence of the parties' agreement.

20-68 At any stage of the proceedings, the arbitral tribunal may hold hearings for the presentation of evidence by witnesses, including expert witnesses, or for

---

[74] *See* Rules of Arbitration of the ICC, art. 20.
[75] UNCITRAL Model Law, arts 18 and 19; LCIA, arts 1 and 2; Swiss Rules, arts 18 and 19.

oral argument. After consulting with the parties, the arbitral tribunal may also decide to conduct the proceedings on the basis of documents and other material.[76]

VII. IMPLICATIONS OF THE AUTONOMY OF INTERNATIONAL ARBITRATION

20-69 As already indicated, the effect of the autonomy of international arbitration is to remove the process from the control of national law and courts. The arbitration exists in a different domain, a non-national or international sphere. The parties have chosen to remove their contractual disputes and place them on a non-national or transnational level, and the New York Convention, international instruments, international laws and arbitration rules all support this factor. The implications of this autonomy are two-fold:

    (a)   the conduct of the arbitration process is not subject to the procedures of national law, and

    (b)   national courts should only interfere with the arbitration process in exceptional circumstances.

A. International Arbitration Procedure

20-70 There is no definitive procedure for international arbitration; there is no international arbitration procedural code. Rather, a suitable procedure is fixed by the tribunal for each arbitration, to reflect the needs of the case and without reference to any national law, including the law of the place of performance. There are two limitations to this very general rule. First, the procedure must conform to any mandatory rules of the place of arbitration. This is not really an issue as most national arbitration laws are permissive as regards the conduct of arbitration. Secondly, the parties must be treated fairly and equally, and each party given the opportunity to present its case and respond to that presented against it.

20-71 The procedure adopted for international arbitration varies from case to case. However, it invariably involves sequential submissions, which involve all testamentary and documentary evidence, expert reports, legal argument and materials on which the party relies. It also generally involves a hearing with the parties, primarily to question the witnesses presented by the parties.

---

[76] *See similarly*, ICC Rules, art. 20(6); Swiss Arbitration Rules, art. 15. *See also*, Arbitration Act 1996, s. 34 and UNCITRAL Model Law, art. 19, where the power and authority of arbitrators is made subject to the will of the parties.

B. Approach of National Courts

20-72 As already seen, the New York Convention, the international arbitration rules, the Model Law and national laws, all provide the framework for little or no interference with the international arbitration process. Effectively, this reflects the autonomous nature of arbitration, or at least allows for autonomy provided the law is not applied or interpreted by the courts in a narrow, parochial or controlling fashion. In principle, national courts should aim always to give effect to the agreement to arbitrate and the resultant award, as well as the effects of this approach. This means that when matters come to a national court, it should consider such applications with an international approach, looking to the overriding intent of the parties in their arbitration agreement, which is for their dispute to be settled by arbitration in whatever form specified. National standards and preferences should not influence the decisions of national courts whose assistance is sought in connection with an international arbitration. National judges should not seek to impose their parochial or narrow national viewpoint and approach in place of the non-national and international process and approach sought and expected by the parties' choice of arbitration as their dispute resolution mechanism.

20-73 The problem in today's litigious world is that parties often, when a dispute has arisen, seek to obtain tactical advantage by challenging the arbitration agreement or the award. Within the confines discussed earlier, courts should enforce the arbitration agreement and final award as a fundamental rule of international trade. If this agreement to arbitrate is not honoured, what chance is there of other aspects of the commercial agreement being respected? It was for that reason that the US Supreme Court in *Scherk v. Alberto-Culver Co.*[77] states that the failure to do so would 'damage the fabric of international commerce and trade, and imperil the willingness and ability of businessmen to enter into international commercial agreements'.[78]

20-74 The USA has for long had one of the most positive pro-arbitration attitudes to international arbitration. As long ago as 1968, in the *Prima Paint*[79] decision, the US Supreme Court held that an arbitration tribunal could properly determine its own jurisdiction even where the claim was for fraudulent inducement of contract. The arbitration clause provided for the reference of any controversy or claim arising out of the agreement to be referred to arbitration.

---

[77] 417 U.S. 506 (1974).
[78] *Ibid.* at 517.
[79] 388 U.S. 395 (1967).

The doctrine of separability has since become one of the most widely accepted principles, and as mentioned above is now part of most national laws. Jurisdiction questions have been ceded to the arbitration tribunal.

20-75 Whatever the past level of judicial scepticism, there is now a definitive pro-arbitration attitude in the USA, especially in international arbitration. Accordingly, in 1974 in *Scherk*, the US Supreme Court upheld an arbitration clause even though the dispute concerned securities' claims and allegations of fraud on the grounds that:

> An agreement to arbitrate before a specified tribunal is, in effect, a specialised kind of forum-selection clause that posits not only the situs of suit but also the procedure to be used in resolving the dispute and the invalidation of the arbitration clause in the case before us would not only allow the respondent to repudiate its solemn promise but would, as well, reflect a parochial concept that all disputes must be resolved under our laws and in our courts ... We cannot have trade and commerce in world markets and international waters exclusively on our terms, governed by our laws, and resolved in our courts.[80]

20-76 Relying on this pro-international arbitration attitude, the US Supreme Court went further in *Mitsubishi Motors Corp. v. Soler Chrysler-Plymouth, Inc.*[81] It stated that US courts should 'subordinate domestic notions of arbitrability to the international policy favoring commercial arbitration' and held that issues of antitrust violations could be determined by arbitration. The Court stated:

> We are well past the time when judicial suspicion of the desirability of arbitration and of the competence of arbitral tribunals inhibited the development of arbitration as an alternative means of dispute resolution.[82]

20-77 There have been several decisions in recent years where national courts have enforced an international arbitration award even though the award has been set aside in the place where it was made, i.e. the seat of the arbitration.

20-78 Probably the best known case in relation to this 'hands off' approach is that of *Chromalloy Aeroservices v. Arab Republic of Egypt.*[83] The US District

---

[80] *Scherk*, *supra* n. 77, looking to the decision in *The Bremen* v. *Zapata Off-Shore Co.*, 407 U.S. 1, 519 (1972).
[81] 473 U.S. 614, 105 S. Ct. 3346, 87 l.Ed. 2d 444, 455 (1985).
[82] *Ibid.*
[83] 939 F. Supp. 907 (D.D.C. 1996).

Court for the District of Columbia allowed the enforcement of an arbitral award within the USA despite the award being rendered null by the Egyptian courts.[84] In coming to this determination, the court was cautious to note that the arbitration agreement provided that the decision of the arbitrator could not 'be made subject to any appeal or other recourse'.[85] As such, the court determined that the enforcement of the award was in line with the expressed language of the parties' arbitration agreement.

20-79 The position of the US Supreme Court in *Chromalloy* has long been the standard approach in France. In *General National Maritime Transport Co. v. Gotaverken,*[86] the Paris Court of Appeal enumerated the principle that 'parties to international arbitral proceedings are free to select the legal order to which they wish to attach the proceedings, and this freedom extends to the exclusion of any national system of law'.[87] The award in *Hilmarton* also was enforced in France[88] despite the fact that the award has been set aside in Switzerland,[89] the place where the arbitration had been held.

20-80 Most recently, the Cour d'Appel de Paris in *Department of Civil Aviation of the Government of Dubai v. International Bechtel Co.*[90] determined that an award annulled in Dubai could be enforced in France even though it had been annulled even before the enforcement application was filed in France. The Dubai court had annulled the award because of an alleged procedural flaw.

20-81 There have been two recent English decisions where the question of review of an arbitration award was raised. These decisions have important implications for international arbitration in England.

---

[84] Reported in (1996) 11(8) *Mealey's International Arb. Rep.* C1..
[85] *Chromalloy*, 939 F. Supp. at 912.
[86] (1980) D.S. Jur. 568 (Cour d'appel Paris), excerpts translated in English, (1981) 30 *ICLQ* 385, as discussed in J. Paulsson, 'Arbitration Unbound: Award Detached from the Law of its Country of Origin', 30 ICLQ 358, at 385 (1981); and J. Paulsson, 'Delocalisation of International Commercial Arbitration: When and Why It Matters', 32 ICLQ 53 (1983). For excerpts from the arbitration decision, *see* (1983) VI *YB Com. Arb.* 133.
[87] (1981) 30 *ICLQ* 366.
[88] *Hilmarton v. Omnium de Traitement et de Valorisation (OTV)*, Cour de cassation, 23 March 1994, (1995) XX *YB Com. Arb.* 663.
[89] *Hilmarton v. Omnium de Traitement et de Valorisation (OTV)*, Tribunal Federal, 17 April 1990, (1993) *Rev. Arb.* 315.
[90] Interestingly, the US District Court in the District of Columbia determined to stay the award pending a second appeal in Dubai: 300 F. Supp 2d 112 (2004).

20-82 English law does allow for the revision of arbitration awards by the courts. This is provided for in sections 67–69 of the Arbitration Act 1996, relating to challenges based on the absence of jurisdiction of the tribunal, there having been some irregularity in the conduct of the arbitration, and appeals on a point of law respectively. In dealing with these challenges, the English courts have the power to confirm, vary or set aside the award, and in some circumstances to remit the award to the tribunal for reconsideration. This provides the opportunity for the courts to review the decisions of arbitrators.

20-83 It was not the intent of the 1996 Act to regularly review the decisions of arbitrators. Regrettably, there have been an increasing number of cases that have been going to the courts under these heads and the courts have taken the opportunity to review awards with increasing regularity. We should not forget that during the 1970s, as modern international arbitration began to expand, England lost favour as a venue for international arbitrations. This was due to the case stated system, one of the major factors behind the Arbitration Act 1979. Regrettably, in respect of reducing the involvement of the English courts in reviewing arbitration awards, the 1979 Act was a failure. The 1996 Act was intended to resolve this problem and has, successfully, won back much confidence for arbitration in England. This is something that should be carefully guarded as confidence in the system can easily be lost again.

20-84 The first case is *Lesotho Highlands Development Authority v. Impregilo SpA*.[91] It arose out of an ICC arbitration with its seat in London. It concerned payments claimed in respect of work undertaken for the construction of a dam in Lesotho. The applicable law was Lesotho law. The arbitrators decided that additional payments were due and that the tribunal was entitled to decide the currencies in which the additional costs should be reimbursed and how interest rates should be applied. The award was challenged under section 68 of the 1996 Act on the basis that there had been a serious irregularity by the tribunal which had 'exceeded its powers' in that it made an error of law by awarding payment in several European currencies rather than in Lesotha currency and by granting pre-award interest.

---

[91] [2005] UKHL 43.

20-85 This challenge was upheld in both the High Court[92] and the Court of Appeal.[93] The House of Lords overturned this decision. It held that there had been no 'excess of power by arbitrators' and that even if there had been an error of law it was not a ground to review the award. Any error of law by the tribunal was an error within its power.

20-86 Most international arbitrations take place under different laws in different countries, with arbitrators from different jurisdictions. Parties are aware of the risks they are taking with respect to arbitration awards with the law being applied correctly. There are few allegations that arbitrators have got it wrong, but even where they do, this is a risk that the parties undertake. It is not for the courts in England to intervene to review the arbitrators' powers or decisions on questions of law – whatever the national law applicable.

20-87 This is an important decision. One distinguished commentator, who was also the counsel for the successful party in this arbitration, expressed the view that in the event that the House of Lords would not have upheld the award this could have had serious implications for England as a venue for arbitrations because of the reputation of the English courts for reviewing decisions of arbitrators.[94]

20-88 The second decision is the Court of Appeal decision in *Occidental Exploration Production Co. v. Republic of Ecuador*.[95] It concerned whether an English court can determine a challenge to the substantive jurisdiction of an arbitration tribunal under section 67 of the Arbitration Act 1996. The arbitration had its source in a BIT between the USA and the Republic of Ecuador. The arbitration had been commenced by the claimant selecting the mechanism of arbitration provided for in the BIT. As the parties were unable to agree on the place of arbitration, the tribunal chose London, on the basis of its 'perception as being neutral'.

---

[92] The judge remitted the decisions on currency and interest to the tribunal with directions as to how they ought to carry out their task afresh: *Lesotho Highlands Development Authority* v. *Impregilo SpA* [2003] 1 All ER (Comm) 22.

[93] [2004] 1 All ER (Comm) 97.

[94] A. Crivellaro, 'Note: Award of 7 December 2001 in Case No. 10623 Summary of the Arbitral Proceedings: International Arbitrators and Courts of the Seat – Who Defers to Whom?' in (2003) 21(1) *ASA Bulletin* 60.

[95] [2005] EWCA Civ 1116.

20-89   The Court of Appeal decided that the question of jurisdiction could be considered by the English courts. It did not look at any of the specifics. Mance LJ (as he then was) stated:

> we see no incongruity in a conclusion that the consensual arbitration intended under the Treaty carries with it the usual procedural supervisory remedies provided under English law as the relevant procedural law. That being so, we do not see any sensible basis for suggesting that there is or should be any difficulty about an English court, in the context of an English award, determining the scope of arbitrator's jurisdiction under section 67 or (in the case of an application to enforce) under section 66.

20-90   It is also noted that under section 66, the English court is given no option at all but to refuse enforcement, if 'the person against whom it is sought to be enforced shows that the tribunal lacked jurisdiction to make the award'.[96]

20-91   The case reverted to the High Court for a review whether the tribunal had substantive jurisdiction (section 67) and whether there had been a procedural irregularity by the tribunal exceeding its authority (section 68). On the first matter the English Court held, having construed the meaning of the USA-Ecuador BIT, that the tribunal had jurisdiction to consider whether Ecuador was in breach of its duties under the Treaty[97]. The section 68 applications were also rejected, the court confirming that the tribunal had the authority to decide and make declarations as to breaches of international law[98].

20-92   Two issues arise from this decision. First – and it is this issue with which the English courts were specifically concerned – is whether the fact that the arbitration had its seat in England justified the application of the English Arbitration Act and the supervisory jurisdiction of the English courts. Much of this discussion related to the effect of public international law and the Treaty background to this case. That is a discussion for another place.

20-93   The second issue was the extent to which the award is reviewable by the court. English courts should take a narrow approach when considering whether

---

[96] *Ibid.* para. 55 (emphasis added).
[97] *The Republic of Ecuador* v. *Occidental Exploration & Production Co* [2006] EWHC 345 (Comm), para. 110.
[98] Even though the English court reviewed both issues from an international law perspective the appropriateness of the English court reviewing an award of this kind under sections 67 and 68 remains.

there is a valid arbitration agreement and whether the arbitration agreement extends to the matters before the arbitrators. This is particularly so when the tribunal has already decided the scope of its jurisdiction. This was the intention of the parties by selecting arbitration through the mechanism of the BIT. For an English court to review that decision, applying English criteria in the interpretation of a BIT, ignores the intentions and expectations of the parties and the autonomy of the arbitration process. It can only result in the application of English law interpretation to an international matter, on the flimsy basis of the selection of London as a neutral and convenient place of arbitration.

20-94 The Court of Appeal decision in *Occidental Overseas* ignores certain fundamentals of international arbitration. The Court's reference to the 'usual procedural supervisory remedies provided under English law' ignores that in the context of arbitration like this, English court supervision is inappropriate and undesirable. Equally, the fact that the award was made in England does not make it an English award. It is an international award, between non-English parties, made by international arbitrators of different national origins, and the seat of the arbitration was a mere coincidence. In the absence of an express agreement, there is no basis for a national court to assume that a US multinational and the government of Ecuador intended English law to govern these issues.

20-95 In contrast, it is to avoid this type of national court interference with arbitration that courts in France and the USA and elsewhere will enforce awards even if they are being challenged or have been set aside in the country where made.

20-96 Another area where the autonomy of arbitration can be seen is through the discretion exercised by the courts when asked to refuse to enforce an arbitration award because it is contrary to international public policy. This is provided in Article V(2)(b) of the New York Convention. The doctrine of international public policy could provide national courts with the opportunity to avoid and refuse enforcement on grounds that reflect parochial and national interests. However, increasingly, international public policy is interpreted from a non-national, a-national or transnational standard, reflecting the autonomous character of arbitration.

20-97   This is well illustrated by the recent decision of Cour d'appel de Paris in the case of *Thales v. Euromissiles*.[99]

20-98   This case concerned the application of EU competition law which is accepted to have a public policy character. An arbitration award had awarded damages for wrongful termination of a contract. The party against whom the award was made sought to have the award set aside because the underlying contract was anti-competitive and therefore void under EU law. This point was not argued in the arbitration itself. The Cour d'appel de Paris held that the French court could not review the merits of the award and the decision of the tribunal. Accordingly, the court held that in the absence of fraud or of a 'flagrant, real and concrete' violation of French international public policy, the reviewing judge may not examine the complex issue of conformity of a particular contract with EU competition law. The court concluded that the arguments exchanged by the parties and the evidence produced did not reveal a manifest violation of EU competition law.

20-99   In this instance, in accordance with the French law position not to review the merits of an award, the appeal court adopted a minimalist approach to the extent of control over conformity of arbitral awards with EC competition law.[100]

VIII. AUTONOMY OF INTERNATIONAL ARBITRATION

20-100 In conclusion, my contention, which I leave you to ponder, is this:
  (1) Every international arbitration exists to determine disputes arising from a contract between parties from two or more jurisdictions. The arbitrators may also be from different jurisdictions. Invariably, the arbitration has its seat in a third jurisdiction, frequently selected because of geographical location or neutrality, and not for its specific arbitration laws (or its substantive commercial laws). These arbitrations are often subject to some agreed international arbitration rules.
  (2) In the conduct of an international arbitration, the laws of the parties and the place of arbitration have only peripheral relevance. It is

---

[99] 18 November 2004, (2005) 8(2) *Int'l ALR* 55; (2005) *Juris Classeur* 357, note Alexis Mourre.
[100] It is unclear whether the approach of the Cour d'appel de Paris complied with the ECJ judgment in C-126/97 *Eco Swiss* v. *Beneton* [1999] ECR I-3055. The court said that the ECJ judgment required only that the review of the award at the enforcement stage should be limited.

expected that if the laws are arbitration friendly; they will respect and recognise the process.

(3)   International arbitration exists in a sphere or domain independent of and separate from national laws and jurisdictions.

(4)   International arbitration exists due to the agreement of the parties, or through an international convention, which intentionally removes the dispute from the jurisdiction of national courts because national courts are unacceptable, unsuitable or inappropriate for the case. This is so even though a national law applies to the substantive issues between the parties.

(5)   International arbitration is subject to the agreement of the parties, international law, non-national regulations and extensive and well-established international arbitration practice.

(6)   International arbitration coexists with national laws and jurisdictions to the extent only that it is expected, and international law and comity require, that national laws will recognise and support the international arbitration process.

(7)   There are tentacles that descend from the domain of international arbitration to the national legal arena. Which national arena varies from case to case. These tentacles require the recognition and enforcement of the agreement to arbitrate, that the award be recognised and enforced, and that the arbitration process itself be given the effective support it may require.

(8)   International arbitration has itself established certain fundamental standards to which it is subject. These standards are policed at the national jurisdiction level. They are that the award is in accordance with and within the terms of the arbitration agreement; due process has been respected and the subject matter of the award does not offend international public policy.

20-101 These are the reasons why international arbitration is today an autonomous, largely self-regulating dispute resolution mechanism.

SUBJECT INDEX

A

AAA (American Arbitration Association)
- arbitrators' broad powers in granting relief, 5-2, 5-3, 5-7, 5-37
- activism of arbitrators, article 16, 9-9
- ADR by arbitral institutions, 10-48
- AAA construction mediation rules, 10-51
- revisions of AAA rules, 13-51
- issuance of an inhibitoria, 19-75

AAA (American Arbitration Association) ICDR
- Code of Ethics, 17-4

American College of Commercial Arbitrators
- professional guidelines, 17-4
- "Best Practices" for business arbitration, 17-4

Anti-suit injunctions,
- anti-arbitration injunctions, 20-5

Applicable Law *see also Arbitration Agreement, Individual countries, Individual Institutional Rules, Lex Arbitri, New York Convention, Lex Mercatoria, mandatory rules, Seat*
- applicable law provision and the private law aspect of the arbitration, 2-40
- undertaking of the State to arbitrate and State consent, 2-61 conclusion 4
- punitive damages, 5-10, 5-11
- arbitrator's power, 5-16, 5-27
- vacate an award, 5-19, 5-27
- conflict rules, 6-40
- arbitrator's determination, 6-40
- *lex mercatoria* principles, 6-40
- arbitrator's wide discretion, 9-9, 9-10, 9-39, 20-52
- applicable rules, 3-22, 15-39, 15-51, 19-101
- national rule of conflict of laws, 15-22
- non-national rules, 20-10
- choice of law, 2-40, 5-7, 5-37, 5-41, 15-23, 15-24
- conflict of laws, 2-51, 6-10, 6-18, 6-36, 6-40, 15-1, 15-18 *et seq*, 19-106 *et seq*, 20-38

Julian D.M. Lew and Loukas A. Mistelis (eds), Arbitration Insights, 487-505
© *2007 Kluwer Law International. Printed in the Netherlands*

H

I

IBA (International Bar Association)
- IBA/UNCITRAL Joint Project Monitoring the Implementation of the New York Convention, 13-87
- 'objectivisation' of arbitration, 17-43
- Rules of Ethics for International Arbitrators, 13-60
- rules of evidence, 9-29, 17-43

ICC (International Chamber of Commerce) Arbitration Rules
- arbitrators' terms of reference, ICC Rules (Art. 13), 3-40
- 'Compromiso' or Specific Submission, 19-58 *et seq,*
- control delay, 4-23
- creation of the ICC Court of International Arbitration in 1922, 14-09
- dissenting opinions, 18-46 *et seq,*
- fast-track arbitration, 9-4
- forms of submissions, 2-66,
- seat of arbitration, 12-16
- sole conciliator, 10-52
- Supplementary 'Opt-In' Rules, 17-45
- Two meanings of 'rules' in arbitration, 17-13 *et seq,*

ICSID (International Centre for Settlement of Investment Disputes) Rules
- generally, 2-3, 2-8, 16-11,
- Additional Facility Rules, 16-12
- applicable law, 16-37,
- deliberations, Rule 15,18-64
- free to choose the seat, 16-65
- jurisdiction of tribunal 16-15 *et seq*
- law, applicable, 16-37 *et seq.*
- plea of State immunity in relation to execution of awards, 16-73
- political motives behind decisions, 19-96

ICSID Convention, *see Washington Convention*

International Court of Justice (ICJ)
- appeal of arbitral awards from mixed arbitral tribunals, 11-3
- Encourage settlement, between states, 2-14
- Inter-state arbitration, 11-4
- Judgement, majority vote, 11-16 *et seq*
- Jurisdiction, 2-9
- Validity, 11-1,

International public policy
- 5-29 *et seq*, 7-40, 13-99, 20-45, 20-58, 20-96, 20-98

International rule of immunity
- 2-28,

International rule of law
- 19-118 *et seq,*

M

- 3-12,

S
Seat of arbitration:
- Arbitration Act 1996, 12-9,
- arbitrariness and artificiality, 16-64
- applicable law, 13-35, 13-77, 13-80, 20-94
- fixing of dates and places, 14-38
- free to choose the seat, parties or the tribunal, 16-65
- ICC, London as the seat of arbitration, 12-16, 20-84
- ICSID system, and, 16-12
- interim measures and, 13-78 *et seq*, 16-61
- neutral, 15-59
- power to review the validity of awards, 16-59, 20-77
- rule of conflict of laws, 15-19
Separability
- 6-18 *et seq*, 8-14 *et seq*, 20-5, 20-61, 20-74,
Settlement
- ADR, Ch 10
- Settlement agreement, 2-16, 13-73 *et seq*, 14-45 *et seq*,
Singapore
- Delay in arbitration, 4-17
- foreign counsel, 13-61
- State immunity, Singapore State Immunity Act 1979, 2-20
State Immunity
- 2-19 *et seq*,
- Arbitral proceedings or/and court proceedings assisting or controlling those proceedings, 13-31
- Article 12 of the European Convention on State Immunity 1972, 2-25,
- Australian Act, and, 2-27
- exclusion (or waiver) of, 13-97, 16-45
- Section 9 of the State Immunity Act 1978, 2-21 *et seq*,
- States' co-operation, and, 2-30
- State immunity from execution, 13-97, 16-11, 16-45, 16-73
Stockholm Chamber of Commerce Arbitration Institute (rules)
- Article 23 of the Stockholm Rules, 4-18,
Stay of proceedings
- -6-11
Sweden
- Arbitration Act in 1999, 20-57
- award, challenge, 7-31, 18-26
- country of origin, exclusion of the action for setting aside in, 7-57 *et seq*,
- delay in arbitration, 4-27
- equality amongst the arbitrators, 18-65

1. Moshe Hirsch, *The Arbitration Mechanism of the International Center for the Settlement of Investment Disputes* (ISBN 0792319931)
2. Aida B. Avanessian, *Iran-United States Claims Tribunal in Action* (ISBN 1853339024)
3. Isaak I. Dore, *The UNCITRAL Framework for Arbitration in Contemporary Perspective* (ISBN 1853335738)
4. Christian Bühring-Uhle, *Arbitration and Mediation in International Business: Designing Procedures for Effective Conflict Management* (ISBN 9041102426)
5. Vesna Laziæ, *Insolvency Proceedings and Commercial Arbitration* (ISBN 9041111158)
6. Joachim Frick, *Arbitration in Complex International Contracts* (ISBN 9041116621)
7. Katherine Lynch, *The Forces of Economic Globalization: Challenges to the Regime of International Commercial Arbitration* (ISBN 9041119949)
8. Christoph Liebscher, *The Healthy Award: Challenge in International Commercial Arbitration* (ISBN 9041120114)
9. Hamid G. Gharavi, *The International Effectiveness of the Annulment of an Arbitral Award* (ISBN 9041117172)
10. Abdullah Sayed, *Corruption in International Trade and Commercial Arbitration* (ISBN 9041122362)
11. Gabrielle Kaufmann-Kohler and Thomas Schultz, *Online Dispute Resolution. Challenges for Contemporary Justice* (ISBN 9041123180)
12. Christopher R. Drahozal and Richard W. Naimark (eds), *Towards a Science of International Arbitration: Collected Empirical Research* (ISBN 9041123229)
13. Ali Yeşilırmak, *Provisional Measures in International Commercial Arbitration* (ISBN 9041123539)
14. Bernard Hanotiau, *Complex Arbitrations: Multiparty, Multicontract, Multi-issue and Class Actions* (ISBN 904112442X)
15. Loukas A. Mistelis and Julian D.M. Lew (eds), *Pervasive Problems in International Arbitration* (ISBN 9041124500)
16. Julian D.M. Lew and Loukas A. Mistelis (eds), *Arbitration Insights – Twenty Years of the Annual Lecture of the School of International Arbitration, Sponsored by Freshfields Bruckhaus Deringer* (ISBN 9041126066)